# 스포츠法學의 새로운 地平
# New Prospects of Sports Law

연기영 엮음
*Edited by Kee-Young YEUN*

역락
YR Publishing co.

# 스포츠法學의 새로운 地平

초판 인쇄 2013년 10월 14일
초판 발행 2013년 10월 21일

엮은이 연기영
펴낸이 이대현
편  집 이소희

펴낸곳 도서출판 역락
주  소 서울 서초구 반포4동 577-25 문창빌딩 2층
전  화 02-3409-2058, 2060
팩  스 02-3409-2059
등  록 1999년 4월 19일 제303-2002-000014호
이메일 youkrack@hanmail.net

ISBN 978-89-5556-097-8 93360
정 가 60,000원

* 파본은 교환해 드립니다.

## New Prospects of Sports Law

ISBN 978-89-5556-097-8 93360
U.S. $100(Order to YOUKRACK PUBLISHING CO.(2nd floor, Moonchang Bldg, 557-25, Banpo 4-dong, Seocho-gu, Seoul, Korea, TEL 82-2-3409-2058, FAX 82-2-3409-2059, E-mail youkrack@hanmail.net))

Prined in Seoul, Korea.

# 머리말

　오늘날 우리사회에 스포츠가 차지하는 중요성과 비중이 날로 증가하고 있다. 인간은 경제가 성장함에 따라 스포츠에 대한 관심과 참여가 크게 늘어나고 더욱 건강하고 행복한 삶을 추구하게 되었다. 우리는 올림픽이나 월드컵축구 경기 대회가 열리면 경기장에 가서 직접 관람하거나 또는 세계 도처에서 TV 등 매체를 통해 선수들의 경기 모습을 화면으로 보면서 찬사를 보내고 함께 즐거움을 느낀다.

　국제적인 스포츠대회는 지구촌이 온통 하나가 되어 세계 평화와 인류 공동번영을 기원하는 화합과 축제의 마당이 되기도 한다. 또한 이를 기반으로 한 스포츠 산업의 발전은 국가경제나 세계경제에도 커다란 영향을 미치고 있다.

　이렇듯, 스포츠 활동이 국내뿐 아니라 국제적으로 활발히 이루어지고 있음에도 불구하고 이를 제도적으로 뒷받침해줄 수 있는 스포츠법제에 관한 연구와 논의는 그에 상응하지 못한 것이 사실이다. 예를 들면, 스포츠 기본권의 보장, 스포츠선수 관련 계약, 스포츠사고와 선수의 보호, 스포츠 관련 분쟁의 해결, 스포츠 관련 규범위반과 처벌, 스포츠산업 관련 법제, 학교체육의 진흥 등 스포츠를 둘러싼 다양한 법률문제에 관한 입법론적인 대응과 학문적 연구는 아직 만족할 만한 성과를 거두지 못하고 있는 실정이다.

　또한 스포츠계의 고질적인 폐습으로 지적되어 온 선수들의 승부조작과 선수들의 약물복용, 폭행과 폭력, 대학입학이나 선수스카우트에 있어서 부정행위 등을 막을 수 있는 법제도의 정비도 시급하다고 본다. 이 책에 실린 글들은 바로 이러한 스포츠법제의 쟁점사항을 파악하고 해답을 얻는 데 중요한 정보를 제공할 것으로 믿는다.

　이 책은 세계 스포츠법학의 현황과 과제를 짚어보고 미래 스포츠 법의 새로운 지평을 열어 가기 위해 기획편집 되었다. 이에 미국과 유럽, 아시아 등 12개국에서 스포츠법 분야의 연구와 교육에 매진하면서 탁월한 업적을 쌓고 있는 저명한 스포츠법학자들의 주옥같은 논문 37편을 엮어 펴낸 것으로 스포츠법학의 이론과 최근 동향을 파악하고 스포츠법의 발전 방향을 탐색하는 데 소중한 지침서가 될 것으로 기대한다.

끝으로 연구와 강의 및 국제적 학문 활동에 쫓기면서도 엮은이의 편집기획에 동의하여 주옥같은 논문을 보내주신 국내외 스포츠법학자 여러분께 깊은 감사를 드린다. 그리고 이 책의 출판을 맡아준 역락출판사 이대현 사장님과 편집팀 여러분께도 진심으로 감사드린다.

2013년 10월
가을 단풍 고운 남산을 바라보며
大東研究室에서 엮은이 延基榮

# Editorial Foreword

Today, the importance of sports is constantly increasing. Interest and involvement in sports have grown significantly. People are seeking happier and healthier lives as the economy strengthens. During the Olympics and World Cup, fans enjoyed the games and praised the fine play of the teams. International sports games play a role in bringing and uniting communities of the world. As such, the sports industry is greatly influencing national as well as the international economic growth.

Although sports events and their importance are increasing at both the domestic and international levels, it is apparent that research and development of sports law has fallen behind the changing times. For example, academic research on sports law underperforms in terms of protecting sports rights, such as player-related contracts, protecting players from injury, school sports promotion, dispute mediation, violation and sanctions against sports related rules, legalization of sports related industries etc. Moreover, there is an urgent need of adopting a legal system against sports games manipulation, as evidenced by drug use, violence and vandalisme, malpractice in entering university and scouting.

This book will provide answers and important information for controversial regarding the normalization of sports law. It was planned and edited to provoke the discussion of the future of sports law by analyzing and scrutinizing the world's sports laws as it exists today. This book provides 37 theses from pre- eminent sports law experts from 12 different countries from America, Europe and Asia who are dedicated to the pursuit of researching, teaching and producing excellent performance in sports law. This book is expected to be a guide, directing sports law developments by scrutinizing recent trends in sports law theory. I would like express my sincerest gratitude to the efforts of domestic and foreign sports law experts who have sent me their invaluable theses and who have participated in the editing of this book in spite of busy schedules. Finally, I would like to thank

CEO Daehyun Lee and the supportive staff of YOUKRACK Publishing Co. for all of their hard work and effort in publishing this book.

Professor Dr. Kee-Young YEUN
October 2013
Daedong Research Center
In the heart of the Republic of Korea
Gazing at the autumn leaves covering Mt. Namsan

# Table of Contents

# American and Korean Law and Sport: Then and Now

ANNIE CLEMENT*

*The article begins with a tribute to Korean sport professionals whose outstanding students the author has had the privilege of advising. Sport law, its foundation and position in international law, is the topic. An overview of the history and evolution of American law and the aspects of American law that have influenced sport are addressed. Current international agreements including NAFTA, WTO, GATT, WIPO and the Madrid Protocol are described. Changes in Korean law, particularly in the area of intellectual property, as observed by the author, are outlined. Predictions of the future of international sport law completes the discussion.*

**Key word:** United States Sport Law; Future of International Sport Law; Change in Sport Law

$F$irst, Congratulations Professor Yeun on your 60th birthday. May there be many years ahead!

I wish to thank the Country of South Korea and your professionals for the outstanding students whose doctoral dissertations I have had the pleasure of advising.

Joo, Jongmi (Fall, 2003). *The identification of collective bargaining issu es in the Korean Baseball Organization.* Doctorate, Florida State University.

Park, Chanmin (Fall, 2012). *Implementation of automatic external defibrillators in South Korean health/fitness facilities.* Doctorate, University

---

* Retired Cape Canaveral, Florida, USA

of New Mexico.

Choi, Eui-Yul (Spring, 2013). *Investigating the factors influencing game piracy in the E-sport setting in South Korea.* Doctorate, University of New Mexico.

There are a number of other South Korean students who have been members of my classes at Florida State University and the University of New Mexico. It has been a pleasure to work with each and every one of them. My visits to South Korea and work with these students have been wonderful experiences.

In 2001, in my first visit to speak in South Korea, I choose the topics of intellectual property and change. At that time the United States patent applications and certification in sport had nearly doubled in the past ten years (U. S. Patent Office). Golf was the sport most often patented. Among South Korean patents in the United States at that time, Samsung Electronics Corporation ranked fourth behind the American companies, IBM, NEC and Cannon, Inc. (Rhodes, 2000). Today, South Korean products are seen in every department store in the U.S. My new phone is a fantastic Samsung product.

Among the international agreements influencing United States intellectual property are the North American Free Trade Agreement (NAFTA), the World Trade Organization (WTO), the General Agreement on Tariffs and Trade (GATT), the World Intellectual Property Organization (WIPO), and the Madrid Protocol. NAFTA, a working agreement among the North American countries, has improved trade and created the opportunity for employment exchanges across borders.

The World Intellectual Property Organization is a 160 member group, established by the United Nations in 1989 in Geneva, to oversee the Berne Convention for the protection of literary and artistic works. It was the first international effort to cover copyright and concentrates on online communication.

To become a member of the World Trade Organization (WTO), a country must be willing to open their domestic markets and participate in global economy. Also, membership is conditioned on compliance with the intellectual property components of the General Agreement on Tariffs and Trade (GATT) that was recently integrated into the Trade-Related Aspect of Intellectual Property (TRIP) Agreement. GATT is an agreement among countries to adhere to minimum standards in copyright.

In 1989, nineteen countries agreed to unify trademark practices worldwide under the Madrid Protocol. As a member of Madrid a nation was required to extend protection to a mark after its filing date no matter what the home country rule was for the mark. Madrid has a fee schedule and is independent of the rights provided by the home country. The language of the agreement is French and English. Applications are processed through the World Intellectual Property Organization; WIPO assigns the registration date (Koch, Riley, & Gibbon, 1996). Japan and China joined the agreement early. America was slow in joining the agreement and had not joined when this presentation was made in 2001. Since that time they have joined the agreement. Prior to Madrid, filings had to occur in each country.

Under the Madrid Protocol, written notice has to be provided to the infringer prior to attempting to seek claims. Only actual damage awards are permitted. "Cancellation of an international registration does not affect the right of the owner to seek domestic protection" (Fukada & Patermo, 1999).

In 2010, major changes had occurred in the South Korean education of lawyers and the country's interest in law as a career (Wilson, 2010; Kim, 2009). Law schools in South Korea had become three year graduate schools. Their education model had moved from "memorization to questioning ... about facts and issues relating to specific situations and creating legal solutions" (Young-Cheal, 2010). These changes suggested to the writer that the door was open to a viable study and practice of law as it applied to sport.

Another change observed by the author was the level of legal research coming from South Korea and published in the East Asian Law Review, the Asian-Pacific Law and Policy Journal, and the many United States Law School Law Reviews (San Diego, Cardozo, Penn. State, and New York University). Many articles published in U. S. journals were written by Korean students and faculty. These articles have served as comprehensive teaching aids for American students. As a result of these changes I choose, in 2010, to write about American law, how it evolved, and what it stood for. The following is taken from that presentation.

Sport Law in the United States is, in most cases, U. S. law adapted to the sport environment. U.S. law is largely derived from the British common law.

It is the foundation for our federal government and for the majority of our state government laws. U.S. law consists of four major sources: constitutional, statutory, administrative regulatory, and common law, including the results of court decisions. The Constitution is the primary law of the land; no U.S. law can conflict with the U.S. Constitution. Each state in the United States has also accepted British law with the following exceptions. The state of Louisiana law is based, in part, on French and Spanish law. Many of our western states that were originally Mexican Territory, including California, Arizona, and New Mexico retain property and water rights laws unique to the Spanish.

The state of Iowa, for example, treats the inheritance of property different from states with limited farming land. Contract, tort, criminal, and family law are considered state law. Today, contract law is also a significant element of federal law. Each of our states and the District of Columbia (Washington, DC) are separate sovereignties with their own constitution, government, courts, and schools. Yes, U. S. schools are run by state law. (This is probably the reason why the United States has failed to establish a national play-off in high school football).

Efforts have been made in the United States to codify law and make it as general as possible. The American Law Institute published Restatement of the Law of Torts- Negligence in 1965, in 1976, and 2011; Product Liability, published in 1998, assisted those publishing and teaching law in sport to remain up to date.

Law in sport had its early beginnings in law schools and in sport management programs. American athletes have sustained severe injuries since the beginning of sport. The National Collegiate Athletic Association (NCAA) was created at the turn of the 19th Century in an effort to control the injuries associated with football, one of our most dangerous sports. In the United States, the injured party is responsible for the cost of his or her injuries and rehabilitation. Often, the injured party finances these expenses through insurance. Lack of insurance or inadequate insurance will often force the victim to seek legal help in an effort to pay the bills. That was the beginning of the use of tort law.Civil rights law became important to sport as women began to request equal opportunities, a situation that has improved but has never become equal. The business components of law have become important to sport interests the same as they have in every other business.

A statute unique to sport in the United States was the Amateur Sport Act of 1978, renamed the Ted Stevens Amateur Sport Act of 1998. It outlines the Olympic Organization, the role of the national governing bodies, and the U.S. Olympic Committee. It holds the intellectual property rights for all United States Olympic brands. Among the organization's responsibilities are the selection, education, and preparation of athletes representing the U. S. in international competition (Clement, 2010).

Sport in the United States is somewhat unique; while we participate in the Olympics and in international boating regattas, our emphasis is on collegiate and professional sport. As a result, sport law, provided by American Universities Law Schools, concentrates on professional and collegiate sport. Sport law taught in sport management programs address collegiate and amateur sport with limited time spent on professional sport. The areas of law most popular in law school sport law courses are contracts, antitrust, and intellectual property. Law in sport in sport programs place emphasis on tort or accidents; civil rights, primarily Title IX equity issues;

and issues related to intercollegiate and scholastic athletics.

In the second presentation (2010), Globalization and Change, I also mentioned that although business leaders plan for the world we must remember that "all of us identify with many different cultures. Some are highly influenced by religion; others have unique codes of ethics" (Clement, 2010). Hassall and Saunders (2002), in discussing Asian Pacific Constitutional Systems, pointed out that, "law is not an independent discipline, but an integral part of a way of life. Leaders do not 'make' law but give 'wise counsel of what ought to be, or be avoided'" (17). We, in sport, are in an enviable position (and remain so today). Sport management and sport law are new disciplines and as a result we can easily share our thinking.

This theme took me to a discussion of intellectual property as a commonality among numerous countries of the world. The presentation ended with the following words of change or our potential to move to a global economy in sport business.

> Professional sport is growing so fast there is a need for athletes, agents, and representatives to possess common knowledge. We must know sport organizations. We need to create law similar to what is found in intellectual property. Recently, a title found in an American
> Sports Business Journal, gives us the challenge,
> "GOING GLOBAL BRINGS OUT THE BEST IN BUSINESS"
> GOING GLOBAL is where sport management and sport law is GOING!
> GOING GLOBAL WILL BRING OUT THE BEST IN SPORT!
> GOING GLOBAL WILL BRING OUT THE BEST IN ALL OF US!

> An indication of this global direction is the enthusiasm of the American businesses rapidly signing sponsorship agreements for the 2008 Beijing Olympic Games.
> Another indication is the NFL's significant push to bring football to China. And I find it interesting that the U. S. teams, L. A. Clippers and N. Y. Knicks, are signing sponsorships with Chinese beer companies. American sport marketing firms operate in nearly every country of the world. They

are working with brands for many international teams.

And, now for the future! I predict that sport in the United States will become varied with a far higher interest in international and individual events. Today, participants seem to be highly interested in avoiding injuries and members of our society are beginning to favor fitness over competition. Those who look to sport only as a means of entertainment continue to want high level, intense, accident type sports on televisions and in the arena.

Parents are beginning to question the value of their young sons facing a concussion just to play a team sport, particularly football. When the masses of young men and their parents no longer aspire for them to become professional or collegiate football players and when institutions of higher education face the legal and medical damages significant to supporting an event that is believed to harm participants, our desire, as a nation, for football will no longer be fulfilled. Last night our local television witnessed a young injured football player helicptered from the middle of a playing field during a high school game. And, the game went on! These fans want to be served with sport events that are high paced and dangerous. They want to sit on the edge of their seats before a television or in an arena waiting for the next car crash, athlete injury, or spectacular pile up.

I recently visited the Americas Cup venue in San Francisco (USA) where promoters were open about the change in the equipment to dangerous, fast, high powered crafts, in response to what society wants, at least it was perceived that it was what American's want. When one of the Americas Cup very talented crew members was killed in practice, safety became an issue. As a person who raced foredeck, on a competitive boat for nearly twenty years and attended previous Americas Cup events, I realized that this event had been taken over by the emphasis on entertainment.

At the same time that Americans focus on dangerous spectator attractions, the masses are turning to fitness and looking for reasonable competition and friendly interaction. As our public become participants in tennis, volleyball, golf, and boating for leisure and competition their requests for entertainment may change. In fact, we see many more United States cities sponsoring professional, as well as amateur tennis tournaments and golf matches.

Just how will sport law become global? The internet and skype allow today's professionals to interact across boundaries and continents. It permits ideas to be shared as they are conceived. It enables professionals, interested in a particular topic, to find persons around the world fascinated by the same idea. Each of us will find it easy to communicate with those around the globe who share common concerns and research. These interactions will be a force to achieve professional and personal goals. Previously, we attended professional meetings and symposiums to meet those whose ideas were similar; today, we know those persons, and will attend the same meetings to begin to build personal relationships with our identified colleagues. The professional relationship has been established.

Our research will be broad and will be shared across oceans as well as continents. When language becomes a barrier, the printed page will easily be translated into the language of the reader. Also, Americans will begin to acquire cultural knowledge and language skills earlier than they have in the past and will strive to be better equipped to interact with others.

Another change is that the traditional lecture/listening way of acquiring knowledge is rapidly being replaced across the world with interaction. Interaction by questioning, by debating, and, by challenging, the ideas of those with whom you visit. This will enable each of us to profit from the views of those whose environment is different. Prior to now, we have consumed considerable time merely with what was considered important for today. The world is moving so fast, our focus needs to shift to the identification of problems and opportunities far in advance of their happening in order to be ready for the inevitable changes that will occur. For example, the issue of concussion in sport should have been identified long before it became an epidemic. A red flag should have been raised when someone first referred to a retired professional athlete as a "dumb jock". Were they describing a failed identification of a concussion?

Recently, The Futurist (2012) noted that "a better future doesn't happen on its own. We create it with our ideas, plans, and action. Group thinking is the digital age. Dialogue across nations and cultures will enhance the creativity of those who participate" (Docksai, 2012). Also, it will enable people to seek out those who enjoy dreaming about similar events.

You may have noted, in the literature, that change is accelerating far faster than before! This requires that people become alert and more creative than what was required for success in the past. Creative and futuristic thinking must be developed by all. Also, data will become the fuel to stimulate creativity. For example, most of sports marketing today is based on purchasing statistics rather than psychological behavior.

Law, in sport, may not be treated as a separate subject but be embedded in all areas of sport affected by law. For example, intellectual property may become instant knowledge when one copies a product intentionally or by accident on an I phone or computer. The I phone or computer will remind the offender that they have violated the intellectual property of another. Sport equipment, placed on the gymnasium floor in an unsafe manner, will result in a flash message reporting the probability of an accident. It will not be long before a professional trainer goes to the equipment room to prepare for a session, presses a button for an athlete or an obese participant, and the proper equipment lights up. These are only models of what we, as inventors, will create in the next few years. Persons, in all fields, will be expected, not only to understand what exists but to be ready to use that knowledge to extend the product or its use or to create a new product or use. Merely, surviving in the environment will no longer be required; the ability to transform the situation in new and difference ways will be essential for success.

Each of us professionals will identify a human pool of colleagues across all nations who enjoy positive feelings about similar ideas and those who feel negatively about our ideas. Then, when one experiences a high risk of success they will run the idea past persons holding negative views regarding the idea. When one is fragile about an idea they will consult with those supportive people for help. Only, by interacting and sharing across all borders, will we achieve the ultimate in research and philosophy. And, most important in this element of sharing we will eventually find peace across nations.

Thank you for an opportunity to share my dreams!

## References

Amateur Sports Act of 1978; Ted Stevens Olympic and Amateur Sports Act, 36 U. S. C. 220501.

Clement, A. (2010). Law in Sport in the United States. XXVI IASL World Congress.

Docksai, R. (November/December, 2012). Dream, design, develop, deliver: From great ideas to better outcomes, TheFuturist, 48-50.

Fakadea, H. & Palermo, C. J. (July 12, 1999). To compete globally, Japan amends trademarks abroad. The National Law Journal.

Hassall, G. & Saunders, C. (2002). Asia-Pacific Constitution Systems. Cambridge University Press.

Kim, J. (2009). 10 Asian-Pacific L. & Pol'y J. 322.

Koch, R., Riley, S. A. & Gibbon, R. L. (May 20, 1996). Madrid agreements protect trademarks abroad. The National Law Journal, C23.

Restatement of the Law of Torts, St. Paul, NM: The American Law Institute.

Rhodes, G. W. (September 18, 2000). In Taiwan and Korea, patent laws begin to progress.

The National Law Journal, B 12-14.

United States Patent Office, Patent Act, 35 USC 101.

Wilson, M. J. (Spring, 2010). 18 Cardozo J. Inter'l & Comp. L. 295.

Young-Cheal (2010). 5 E. Asian L. Rev. 155.

# Controlled Clinical Trials with Doping-substances in German Sports Law

ERWIN DEUTSCH*

*The article begins with the interpretation of both norms, i.e. Art. 6a AMG and Art. 40 AMG. § 6a AMG prohibits the distribution and the possession of no small amount of doping substances. In § 40 Sec.1, Subsec. 2 AMG the predicable risks and disadvantages as compared with the usefulness for the person which is a member of the controlled clinical trial and the expected impact of the drug is for medicine in general. Moreover the test must be allowed by medical standards. Doping is the non-physiological augmentation of the corporal abilities of the person taking part in sports.*

*The sports clubs and parliament have set up a list naming the doping substances It is t be found in the annex to the statute. There are a lot of legal questions starting with the problem whether it is allowed to test the substances for safety and efficacy in general or under the special circumstances of the test. If there is a duty to inform a certain group, its violation allows just the members of the protected group (f.i.) gives them a claim to damages to bring a suit because of misinformation.*

**Key word:** doping, Informed consent, Controlled clinical trials, non–physiological augmentation, the doping substances, Applying the teleological reduction

## Introduction

The research ethics committee of a German Medical University recently faced a totally new problem. The members of the department for medical sports had to decide what to do with a controlled clinical trial about the

---

* Professor of law, Göttingen University

safety and efficacy of doping substances in cycling.

Doping is the non-physiological augmentation of the corporal abilities of the person taking part in sports. The sports clubs and parliament have set up a list naming the doping substances It is t be found in the annex to the statute. There are a lot of legal questions starting with the problem whether it is allowed to test the substances for safety and efficacy in general or under the special circumstances of the test.

Article 6a of the German medicinal drug statute (AMG) says clearly that it is not allowed to have in possession a medicinal substance that is prescribed as doping substance in the annex of a special statute.

Since these substances are drugs in the sense of the §§ 3 et seq. AMG they have to undergo clinical trials before they can be certified. Here Art. 40 AMG sets exact rules for the testing of the substance. To do this the substance has to be given in possession of the people who do the testing.

Both norms, i.e. Art. 6a AMG and Art. 40 AMG, are set against each other. According to German methodology we have first to ask whether one of the usual rules can be applied, for instance the special rule precedes the general one or the later rule does the same with the former. Both do not help: both rules are special and since both rules are to be found in the same statute, there is no former or later rule. Therefore we have to decide what to do with plain contradictory rules. The prevailing opinion is that both rules cancel each other out so that in this regard there is no rule at all. It means that doping-substances can be freely tested and to certify these substances clinically controlled trials are not necessary. We have now to decide how to fill the gap created by the contradictory rules. According to the prevailing opinion one has to create a new rule that fits the circumstances and follows the intention of the statute. Here it is clear that the doping substances should be tested by clinical trials to know whether they are effective or dangerous. The gap is filled by the rules about clinical trials. These should take into consideration that doping substances are no ordinary drugs; therefore the catalogue of Art. 40AMG has to fit the circumstances and the information has to be given to other persons taking part in the sport, especially if there are sport events.

For the purpose of establishing the safety and efficacy of the substances used for doping, it is necessary to allow clinical trials. There are rules concerning the general and the special medical trials. If one does not follow the problem of the norm collision there are other ways to help us out of the prohibition of Art. 6a AMG.

Firstly there are the general rules in § 6a Sec.1 & 2 AMG among which we have to establish an exemption for controlled clinical trials. Secondly we would have to apply § 40 AMG which states general rules of clinical trials. The second step could only be gone if we would have allowed clinical trials of doping substances in general. As has been suggested you cannot refer to the time when both provisions, i.e. § 40 and § 6a AMG, were enacted. In the meantime there have been many general revisions of the statute and both rules are now regarded as published at the same time.

According to German criminal law we have either to role back the general rule or to find a justification for the clinical trial. Both ways are equally useful because all the people concerned with a clinical trial are not subject to the general criminal rule of § 6a AMG anymore. As a measure of justification § 34 German Criminal Statute (StGB) could be applied, if the value of the clinical trial would be superior to the statutory provision.

## Distribution and Possession of Doping Substances, § 6a AMG

§ 6a AMG prohibits the distribution and the possession of no small amount of doping substances. It is useful to keep in mind that the rule about possession was introduced into the statute in 2007. Up to that time the sportsperson was not criminally liable for using the substance because that statutory provision was treated as a highly personal one.

### Limitation of § 6a AMG

There are two ways to limit the impact of § 6a AMG, generally not allowing distributing or possessing substances for doping in sports. We could read an exception into the text of the statute itself or we could apply the methodical rule of reducing the text of a statute according to the intention of the law giver. This rule has been established in German methodical writing especially in the publications of *Larenz*. It is called the *"teleological reduction"*. Particularly if the written law has been too large it could be reduced according to the purposes of the statute.

### The first way of reducing § 6a Sec. 1 & 2 AMG

The general rule of § 6a Section 1 & 2 AMG would be to write an exemption into the statute. There are already provisions for all treatments of illnesses by using the substance.

This exception establishes the justification of using the substance for the treatment of patients. There is no provision for controlled clinical trials but it is obvious that clinical trials should be read into the text of § 6a AMG. This has to be done by an interpretation, correcting the text of the statute. There has to be compelling reasons to use the form of correcting interpretation.

### The second way of reducing § 6a Sec. 1 & 2 AMG

Taking up the *teleological reduction*, it is necessary to have a written rule that is too large for its purpose. Here it is the prohibition of distributing or possessing no small amount of the doping substance behind its purpose. The clinical research into the safety and efficacy of the substance is necessary to establish the substance as useful for doping and not harmful to the sportsperson. If the clinical trial comes to the result that there is no augmentation of the physical abilities the substance should not be named in the annex of the statute. If the result of the trial is moreover that the substance is dangerous to the sportsperson it should not be allowed because of the danger. Now it is necessary to limit the general rule and allowing clinical trials. That would fit exactly in the category of *teleological reduction*.

Therefore an exemption could be read into the statute allowing clinical trials with those substances.

### Court cases in criminal law

There are a few criminal cases concerning the "small amount". The most recent one is a decision by the Federal Supreme Court of Nov. 17th, 2011 (A&R 2012, 34.).

Here the accused was interested in chemistry and for a certain time had a small laboratory at home, where he worked with amphetamine-derivates. Because of a prostata carcinoma he suffered in erectile dysfunction. While building up his laboratory he found a crystalline substance, which he used treating his illness. For the further consumption he put the substance into small bags which totally contained 915 gr. methamphetamine hydrochloride.

The lower court held the substance for no small amount of the proscribed medication. The Federal Supreme Court partially agreed with the lower criminal court, but held the small amount established as up to 10 gr. of the substance as you look at effective (wirkungsbestimmende) base.

The court relied heavily on the chemical results of the substance. The court followed the former cases which established the no small amount by the concrete effect and intensity of the substance.

## Corrective Interpretation

### Introduction

Both ways, the corrective interpretation and the teleological reduction, have their advantages and disadvantages. The first one is limited to reducing a norm. The second one is all-encompassing, i.e. it embraces not only reducing but helping with correcting obvious failures. Finally the corrective interpretation might lead to adding another piece to the norm which obviously hadn't covered the whole field. The whole field was intended to be regulated, but somehow the ministry of health and the federal parliament did not see that the regulation fell to short.

## Advantages of teleological reduction

### Advantages in general

The teleological reduction can lead only to the limiting of the text of a statute. Therefore we have to have a statute which is written in a big way and has to be limited so that it fits the intention of the law-giver.

### Applying the teleological reduction in this field

If we look at the text of the AMG we find in § 40 allowing clinical trials in a very limited ways. In § 40 Sec.1, Subsec. 2 AMG the predicable risks and disadvantages as compared with the usefulness for the person which is a member of the controlled clinical trial and the expected impact of the drug is for medicine in general. Moreover the test must be allowed by medical standards. Here routinely we have to substitute the text according the intention of the law-giver. He wanted to allow clinical trials with a possible use for the proband itself on the one hand and on the other purely scientific trials with no possible use for the patient but with limited risks for him for the medical science in general. To do this we have to substitute the small word "and" by "or" which today is routinely done. The statute was from the beginning intended to allow purely scientific trials as well. That way we can do a purely scientific test which does not hurt the patient but allows solving real need of the medical science.

There are more places where the teleological reduction has to be used. The main form is by the general text of § 40 AMG. It looks like all clinical trials should be under the certain conditions allowed, which is not quite obvious according to the text. An example could be the controlled clinical trial of a new substance instituting one substance instead of more, which are used now. That trial would not have of any use for the patients concerned but is effective for medicine in general.

### Overall text and reality of clinical trials

According to § 40 AMG the clinical trial should just concern one patient.

This is rarely the case. Therefore other criteria are used for clinical trials. In clinical trials there are at least two groups are compared with each other. One consists of ill persons and the other are comparisons. We talk about the test group and the control group. The letter consists of healthy persons or patients with another illness.

There are all kinds of comparisons: they might be in exchange of the members of the patients group and of the control group; there might be a time-gap before the starting of the test; the controlled clinical trial could be split up into under-groups, sometimes a bewildering number of sub-groups; these are named after the roman military formations: for instance cohort-studies etc.

In the text of the statute no word tells us that there will be comparisons in a broad sense. In a new edition of the text it should take into account the modern ways of clinical trials and use the most recent expressions of it.

## Advantages of corrective interpretation

### History of corrective interpretation

The corrective interpretation at a long time ago started with the necessity to alter a word or substituting a new one into the text. Usually the final work on the text of the statute led to an obvious failure. Therefore sometimes the word "no" should be struck out of the text or put into it. Later on the more distant future the law-giver might be subject to corrective interpretation.

### Advantages and limits of Analogy

Here one could work with analogies, but they have their own drawbacks which should be taken into account. Analogy needs a place in the statute where regulation was expected but had been forgotten. Sometimes the necessity of an analogy turned up in the time after the statute was published. Then we have to look at comparable regulations and can take over one regulation. This is not easy, but sometimes possible. There has to be a compelling reason to allow an analogy. This was the case with the so called *"positive violation of the contract"*. We are not so sure whether the statute preparing committee left that piece intentionally unregulated or one had not even noticed the necessity of regulation. Today it is even more important because two thirds of the gross national product is created by the "service sector". In medical law it is the same normally the violation of the contract by the doctor is some kind of "positive violation". Therefore the violation of the contract is the first and general case of the cases against the doctor because of ill-treatment of the patient.

Moreover, as far as criminal law is concerned, the analogy is limited. *Analogies in malam partem* are not allowed, Art. 103 Abs. 2 GG. Therefore in this field we have to treat carefully, not to violate Art. 103 Abs. 2 GG

Other advantages of corrective interpretation

The corrective interpretation is all in-compassing. This shows at the same time the big limits of this field. To use corrective interpretation one has to have really compelling reasons to do so.

One of the really compelling reasons for a corrective interpretation came out of the complex of the equality of sexes. In former times a good many clinical trials were expressly limited to males. This happened not only in the research protocol, but sometimes in the legal text, be it a statute, be it a lower form of legally binding code. The real reason behind this limitation is to be found in the problem Contergan / Thalidomid. In 1961 it became apparent that the malformations in the babies was due to the mother having taken Thalidomid in a certain period of pregnancy. The possibility that pregnant women might take part in a controlled clinical trial forced regulations, excluding pregnant women from participating in the trial. In recent times it has become evident that today one is able to exclude pregnant women from participating, in the trial. Therefore females should participate in a controlled clinical trial as well as males. The problem was what to do with the old regulation. At that time it was not customary to go back to the federal constitution because of which both sexes are to be equally treated. Instead the rule limiting the trial to males was changed at the next possible moment. But before this was possible there was the necessity of corrective interpretation. In the meantime the majority of doctors working in a controlled clinical trial saw no reason to exclude females from participating in the trial. One had to be able to exclude pregnant women from the process of selecting the patients or probands it should not only be possible but because of compelling reasons to include women at the process of selecting participants of the trial. Here there were compelling reasons not to exclude half of the population from participating in the trial. The outcome of the trial might even be more representative because not only males but also females were members of the trial population.

Finally as far as trials on children and their parents are concerned, males should be treated alike as the females. This is the other side of the coin of treating both sexes equally. The compelling reasons here are the same as including females into the controlled clinical trial.

### Parallel problems in customary law

Customary law has nearly almost vanished in modern law, be it in the system of the codification or the case-law, that has become nearly encompassing new problems of law. It is still worthwhile considering the corrective interpretation to look at the prerequisites of customary law.

To begin with the customary law requires *longa consuetude.* This means that due to the circumstances of the case a considerable time must have run out. The *longa consuetudo* is typical for customary law. To adopt customary law there has to be a custom that once established is followed and followed and followed. A custom has to be developed over a long time, in so far the parallel to corrective interpretation does not help establishing the reason for a correction.

The second point of customary law is the *opinio nececitatis.* With the *opinio nececitatis* there is a direct link to corrective interpretation. The *opinio nececitatis* needs likewise a compelling reason that has been recognized, at least at the last time before the question came up in court.

Recently there was the question whether the limitation of the obligatory insurance for trials can be limited to material damage or has to include immaterial damage as well. The insurance companies relied on their general terms that just material damage had to be compensated. The majority of writers held otherwise and felt that there should be at least some compensation for physical and mental discomfort. Recently it has been said that the long practice of the insurance companies to limit their payments to material damage amounted to customary law[1]. This opinion fell short of the *opinio nececitatis* that has to be shared. There have been no court cases in this field. In the commentaries to § 40 I AMG and the textbooks a considerable minority is of the other opinion. They felt that the reason for introducing obligatory insurance involved not only material damage but immaterial as well. Therefore customary law does not come to help the insurance companies. Recently one has pointed out to article 253 Civil Code, which includes immaterial damages within the meaning of damage does only cover legal obligations, be it out of a contract or out of delict.[2] It does not cover obligations out of an insurance contract. It is a custom by the insurance companies, nothing else.

## Special Problems of Sports Law

General provisions of the German allowances to market a certain drug

Since 1976 Germany has a codification of the drugs trade. To give the allowance for a drug to be marketed, there has to be a controlled clinical trial establishing that the new drug is not dangerous and promised better results in treating an illness.

Controlled clinical trials

In § 40 section 1 AMG there are the general prerequisites of the trial

---

1) Taupitz, VersR 2008, 158.
2) Laufs/Katzenmaier, 6th ed, p. 486.

named. To begin with this statute does not go into the modern controlled clinical trials i.e. control with a control group, double-blind trials, trials with lots of subsequent studies (mostly named after Roman military formations). The statute does not take any of them into account. This makes it not easy to adapt the modern forms of controlled clinical trials to the old text of § 40 section 1 AMG. Then there is an obstacle no one has thought of. In the first versions of § 40 section 1 subsection 1 AMG it formally read: "The risks, which are involved for the person with whom the trial is to be carried out are medically just justifiably, when compared with the anticipated significance of the drug for medical science". Now it reads that Art. 40 AMG requires that the clinical trial resulted that the risk is compared with the advantage for the propend and the impact of the drug for the treatment of illnesses is medically acceptable. If one looks at this section closely one has the feeling that just clinical trials were allowed which bring the patient an immediate advantage for his health. This would mean that controlled clinical trials are just allowed for measures that are of immediate advantage to the patient.

This leaves a big part of medical trials open and it looks like they were not allowed. This would be a pity and certainly not intended by the lawgiver, who changed the text from the first version to the new one. At the time of the changed wording nobody thought of excluding purely scientific experimentation. Purely scientific experimentation should also be allowed if the danger and advantages for science are controlled and the probands do not suffer an unacceptable risk. As far as this miscarriage of the text has been recognized there is reason for a corrective interpretation. Ethics committees and the BfArM all allow purely scientific trials.

Here in testing doping substances it is a purely scientific enterprise. Since the obvious dangers of this trial can be contained the trial should proceed as planned. To the contained dangers belong all problems that the proband could face participating in the trial.

## Informed consent of competitors and others

### Informed consent

Among the most important prerequisites is the informed consent. Firstly the proband has to give his consent to be given the medication knowing the contents of it. Secondly the consent has to find its basis in the information. There is no consent without information and all the necessary knowledge is contained in the information. The proband has to be informed about the alleged doping drug, its expected results and its dangers. On this knowledge his consent is built.

### Inforationm of others

The testing of the doped cyclists can be a singular event. In this case there is no need to inform someone. The test run with the doping substance is than a single race. Moreover the cyclists can be put among others and they might race aginst each other maybe to win some kind of trophy. If this is the case, the other competitors have to be informed about their colleague cycling under the influence of an alleged doping substance. Especially the organiser of the event should be informed. If it is an event where betting is allowed maybe then it has to be publicly announced. Otherwise the public might be misinformed which under any circumstances must be out of the question. It amounts to fraud.

### Damages for misinformation

If the necessary information is not given to the public or it contains obvious mistakes there can be a delict according to § 823 section 1 BGB. The next norm, § 823 section 2 BGB, does not come into play because the obligation to inform is not due to a legally binding information obligation. Therefore we have to look for special obligations to inform if there is no negligence. The obligation to inform forms part of the normally information to the public but it is necessary to give the public notice of the doping. Otherwise it would be amount to foul play if the information were not given.

### Protection of certain groups

If there is a duty to inform a certain group, its violation allows just the members of the protected group (f.i.) gives them a claim to damages to bring a suit because of misinformation.

## Conclusion

1. Controlled clinical trials on cyclists with alleged doping substances are not prohibited. Moreover they are allowed. The reason for that is that the prohibition in § 6a AMG now carries a teleological reduction or a corrective interpretation for controlled clinical trials.

2. The controlled clinical trials with doping substances require the informed consent by the cyclists.

3. According to the circumstances others have to be informed too. These are competitors and the organisers of the event and finally the public. If that duty is violated, you can sue for negligence out of § 823 section 1 BGB because of negligence.

4. If the ethics committee has to regard a controlled clinical trial with doping substances it should in general give its approval.

## References

Hans-Jürgen Ahrens, Christian Bar, Gerfried Fischer und Andreas Spickhoff, *Medical and Liability: Festschrift for Erwin German 80th Birthday* (German and English Edition), Springer, Germany, 2009.
Erwin Deutsch, Hans-Ludwig Schreiber, Andreas Spickhoff and Jochen Taupitz,

*Die klinische Prüfung in der Medizin / Clinical Trials in Medicine: Europäische Regelungswerke auf dem Prüfstand...* , Springer, Germany, 2004.

Erwin Deutsch, Hans-Dieter Lippert, R. Ratzel and K. Anker, *Kommentar zum Arzneimittelgesetz (AMG)* (German Edition), Springer, Germany, 2001.

Erwin Deutsch, Gunnar Duttge, Hans-Ludwig Schreiber and Andreas Spickhoff, *Die Implementierung der GCP-Richtlinie und ihre Ausstrahlungswirkungen*, Springer, Germany, 2011.

Erwin Deutsch and Andreas Spickhoff, *Medizinrecht: Arztrecht, Arzneimittelrecht, Medizinprodukterecht und Transfusionsrecht* (German Edition), Springer, Germany, 2008.

Erwin Deutsch, Hans-Dieter Lippert, Rudolf Ratzel and Brigitte Tag, *Kommentar zum Medizinproduktegesetz (MPG)* (German Edition), Springer, Germany, 2010.

# Advancing Players' Rights: An Examination of the Unique History and Structure of Player's Rights in Korean Professional Baseball League Compared with the History and Players' Rights in Major League Baseball

DANIEL GANDERT* · JOON-WOO KIM**

*While baseball has become popular in both the United States and Korea, the leagues in the two countries have developed different financial models and rules relating to free agency and contract negotiation, with the rules in the U.S. being more favorable to players. One of the reasons for this difference is that U.S. baseball teams are generally profitable on their own while Korean teams are generally unable to survive without financial assistance from their parent companies. An unprofitable league makes it difficult to justify paying players higher amounts, so the Korean Baseball Organization (KBO) needs to become more profitable in order for the situation to become more favorable to players.*

*Major League Baseball (MLB) has been around much longer than the KBO. MLB players went through many years of struggles, strikes, and legal battles before receiving their current level of players' rights and compensation. As the KBO is still young, it is understandable that it may take some time for changes to come about.MLB's history demonstrates that forming a union is one of th most important steps that can bring upon changes in a league that are favorable for players. Unionization is likely needed in order for KBO players to receive better players' rights and compensation.*

**Key word:** baseball, players' rights, labor, salary, history, draft, union

---

\* Clinical Assistant Professor at Northwestern University School of Law

\*\* Joonwoo Peter Kim, Seoul, South Korea, Studies in Economics and Operations Research at Columbia University in the City of New York (BA, cum laude), Studies in Law at Northwestern University School of Law in Chicago (JD).

## Introduction

While baseball has been described as America's pastime since the creation of the sport, people have been playing the sport in Asia for almost as long as in the United States.[1] The sport spread across the United States around the same time that it was introduced to Korea.[2] While the sport has become popular in both countries, their leagues have developed different financial models and rules relating to free agency and contract negotiation, with the U.S. rules being more favorable to players.[3]

## Differences in the History of the Leagues

Differences between the two leagues start with differences in their history. Professional Baseball in the United States has early origins with the amateur National Association of Base Ball Players, which was founded in 1858.[4] Clubs started to pay players "under the table," pay them with revenue from admissions, and supply them with meals and clothing.[5] The Cincinnati Red Stockings became the first team consisting of all professionals in 1869.[6] The first U.S. professional baseball league was started in 1871 and the National League, which is one of the two leagues that makes up Major League Baseball, was founded in 1876.[7] Organizers were quick to embrace

---

1) Jules Tygiel, Past Time: Baseball as History 8 (Oxford Univ. Press 2000); William W. Kelly, *Is Baseball a Global Sport? America's 'National Pastime' as Global Field and International Sport*, 7 Global Networks 187, 200 (2007).
2) Kelly, *supra* note 1, at 191. Baseball spread across the United States during the 1960s and was introduced to Korea in the 1970s.
3) Major League Baseball, the professional baseball league in the United States, also includes Canadian teams.
4) Stephen D. Guschov, The Red Stockings of Cincinnati: Base Ball's First All-Professional Team 3 (1995).
5) *Id.* at 5–6.
6) Steven A. Riess, *Historical Perspectives on Sport and Public Policy*, 15 Review of Policy Research 3, 4 (1998).
7) *Id.*; John M. Milan, *National Pastime: How Americans Play Baseball and the Rest of the World Plays Soccer*, 5 Esporte e Sociedade 1, 2 (2007). For a description of how the American League and National League came together, see *The Commissionership;*

and exploit the sport's commercial value.[8]

The Korean Baseball Organization (KBO) was not created until 1981, when the dictatorial military president Chun Doo-Hwan ordered top conglomerates to organize professional baseball teams.[9] The sport was used to divert the public's anger away from his regime during the period of political turmoil that occurred shortly after his election.[10] Teams were created without a thorough economic evaluation and have reported losses of millions of dollars every year, unable to survive on its own without financial assistance from parent companies.[11] This contrasts heavily with teams in MLB which are generally profitable on their own.[12] Because KBO teams do not make profits, players' rights are seriously compromised as teams scoff at efforts to create more sensible, fairer rules with the stance that players need to wait until teams make money.[13]

## Unionization Struggles

MLB players also had an unfavorable situation related to player rights and salaries prior to their unionization. Attempts to unionize professional baseball players started during the early days of professional baseball, although early attempts were not very successful.[14] Players initially had

---

*A Historical Perspective*, MLB.com,

http://mlb.mlb.com/mlb/history/mlb_history_people.jsp?story=com(last visited July 30, 2013).

8) *Id.*

9) Myoung-Gwoun Kim, *Political Backgrounds Involved in the Foundation of Korea Professional Baseball*, 7 J. Korean Soc'y for Sport Anthropology 168, 171–72 (2012 ).

10) *Id.* at 179.

11) Ju-Han Park & Yeon-Suk Chu, Current Status and the Future of Professional Sport in Korea, 3 J. Korean Soc'y of Sport Pol'y. 47, 49–51 (2005).

12) *See* Mike Ozanian, *The Business of Baseball 2012*, Forbes.com (Mar. 21, 2012), http://www.forbes.com/sites/mikeozanian/2012/03/21/the-business-of-baseball-2012/.

13) *See* Jae-won Kim, *Forming Union Meets With KBO Wrath*, The Korea Times (Apr. 29, 2004), http://koreatimes.co.kr/www/news/sports/2009/04/600_44081.html.

14) Jordan I. Kobritz & Jeffrey F. Levine, Trying His Luck at Puck: Examining the MLBPA's History to Determine Don Fehr's Motivation for Agreeing to Lead the NHLPA and Predicting How He will Fare, 12 U. Denv. Sports & Ent. Law J. 3, 6 (2011).

"grim working conditions," low salaries, and a reserve clause in contracts which players organized to oppose.[15] The reserve clause prevented players "from negotiating with any team other than the one with which the player had originally signed."[16]

In 1954, the Major League Baseball Players Association (MLBPA) was formed, with the initial interest being to represent the pension interests of players.[17] "[P]layers insisted that their organization was not, nor would it ever be, a 'union'" and were concerned about being on good terms with their teams.[18] In 1965, Marvin Miller, who had prior experience with the United Steelworkers of America, was elected as the MLBPA executive director.[19] Miller led the MLBPA toward its first collective bargaining agreement by convincing players that teams were prosperous enough to provide players with better compensation and that they could get this compensation as well as better working conditions as long as everyone stayed unified in their demands.[20] The first collective bargaining agreement came about in 1968.[21] The Uniform Player's Contract was incorporated into the agreement which ended management from being able to unilaterally change the terms of player contracts as the requirement came about for amendments to come through collective bargaining.[22] In 1970, players gained the right to use grievance arbitration, "an achievement Miller considers the most significant of the union's early years because the process paved the way for future gains."[23] The MLBPA continued to develop, helping players achieve better salaries, rights such as free agency, and has

---

15) *Id.*
16) Glenn M. Wong, Essentials of Sports Law 463 (3rd ed. 2002).
17) Marc Edelman, *Moving Past Collusion in Major League Baseball: Healing Old Wounds, and Preventing New Ones*, 54 Wayne L. Rev. 601, 605 (2008).
18) Kobritz & Levine, *supra* note 14, at 13.
19) History of the Major League Baseball Players Association, MLBplayers.com, http://mlb.mlb.com/pa/info/history.jsp (last visited July 30, 2012) [hereinafter History]; Marvin Miller, A Whole Different Ball Game: The Inside Story of the Baseball Revolution 4-5 (2004).
20) Daniel C. Glazer, Can't Anybody Here Run This Game? The Past, Present and Future of Major League Baseball, 9 seton Hall J. Sports L. 339, 344-45 (1999).
21) *Id.*
22) *Id.* at 345-46.
23) *History, supra* note 19.

become "the most powerful union in sports."[24]

In Korea, players are also trying to empower themselves by forming a legally recognized labor union.[25] The Korean Professional Baseball Player's Association (KPBPA) was created with the purpose of focus of forming a labor union to benefit the entire field of players, ranging from stars to those playing in the minors leagues.[26] It is a community of players that voted to become a union at its 2009 general assembly meeting.[27] However, creating a labor union seems to be a long shot as teams are threatening to quit if a union is formed.[28] Moreover, unlike when superstar players worked to create a KBO-recognized labor community, it becomes increasingly more difficult to involve players making top salaries well over a million dollars in labor matters as they really do not have incentives to do so.[29] In addition, the Samsung Lions are adamant that its parent company, the biggest company in Korea, has a no labor union policy and would not make an exception for its baseball team.[30]

Parallels can be drawn between the current situation of players in Korea and the situation of MLB players prior to the MLBPA becoming a strong union. At the period of the league's history for which KBO is currently at, MLB players also had weak players' rights and in most cases, lower pay.[31] Just as the KPBPA has found it difficult to unionize, the MLBPA went through a lot of struggles during its early years. Owners targeted Miller

24) Kenneth Quinnell, *Once MLBPA Head Marvin Miller Changed the Landscape of Professional Sports*, AFL-CIO NOW (Nov. 28, 2012), http://www.aflcio.org/Blog/Organizing-Bargaining/Once-MLBPA-Head-Marvin-Miller-Changed-the-Landscape-of-Professional-Sports.
25) Ji-Seon Kim & Lee Keun-Mo, *Marxian Approach to Korea Professional Baseball Players Association Activities*, 24 Korean J. Sociology of Sport, 199, 200 (2011).
26) Interview with Sun-Woong Kim, Director of KPBPA (May 6, 2013).
27) *Id.*
28) Ji-Heon Bae, *Baseball Fans need to support KPBPA* (Dec. 8, 2013), http://sports.news.nate.com/view/20091208n03268.
29) Hyuk Kwon, *Berufssport und Arbeitsrecht*, 53 L. Rev. Inst. of L. Studies, Pusan National Univ. 250.
30) Cho, Donmoon, *Labor Control with Panopticon in the Samsung Conglomerate*, 13 Industrial Labor Study 249, 250 (2007).
31) See Miller, *supra* note 19, for a description of how Marvin Miller brought about change to Major League Baseball.

himself, spreading rumors that he would bring racketeering and other problems sometimes associated with unions to baseball.[32] Owners also cited the Taft-Hartley Act to withdraw money from the MLBPA, hoping that the organization would fail for the lack of support.[33] The MLBPA ended up using player dues to fund the union, which helped the union continue. In these ways, the KPBPA's struggles are analogous to those faced by the MLBPA during the organization's early times.

One could make the argument that over time, it would work for KBO players to form a union and that their rights and salaries may increase. However, in strengthening the MLBPA, Marvin Miller convinced players that their teams were strong enough financially that they could afford to pay their players more.[34] The KBO does not seem to be strong enough financially for this type of thing to occur. As described earlier, the biggest underlying problem in KBO is the financial health of teams as they report losses every year and cannot survive on their own without help from parent companies.[35] Teams are in the business mainly for marketing and cannot survive on baseball related income alone,[36] acting as a primary stumbling block for any KPBPA agenda as the hteams' "wait till we make money" stance can be a very effective affirmative defense.[37] Because of this, KBO executives would likely need to create a healthier, more economically sound industry prior to changes coming about for players.

## The Draft

The draft rules is one of the major areas for which MLB rules are more favorable to players than KBO rules. Both leagues use a draft system to

---

32) Susan H. Seabury, The Development and Role of Free Agency in Major League Baseball, 15 Ga. St. U.L. Rev. 335, 346 (1998).
33) *Id.*
34) Glazer, *supra* note 20.
35) How to Solve Deficit Operation of Baseball Teams, Naver Blog (Sep. 25, 2008), http://blog.naver.com/ktjgh1200?Redirect=Log&logNo=40055357706.
36) Id.
37) Id.

assign players to teams. The Amateur Draft (Rule 4 Draft) is for first-year players from high school and college.[38] The Rule 5 Draft is for professional players, which for the KBO, are mainstays in Korean baseball.[39] Unlike in MLB where the Rule 5 draft happens every year, the KBO Rule 5 draft occurs every two years starting in 2011 with an expansion of the league to 9 teams for the first time in KBO's 32 year old history.[40] The KBO draft system was created to level the playing field and to prevent more deep-pocketed teams from running away with many top prospects.[41] On a similar note, it also has the potential to suppress excessive competition among teams for top talents and any ill-effects stemming from shelling out extraordinary signing bonuses to unproven commodities.[42] The primary problem with the current KBO's amateur Rule 4 draft is the length of negotiating rights to draftees. KBO Rule 108 stipulates that a team possesses exclusive negotiating rights to a drafted player for almost 2 years (1 year and 328 days to be exact).[43] This period is only about 5 weeks for MLB,[44] and 5 months for Nippon Professional Baseball (NPB), the professional baseball league in Japan.[45]

This odd structure presented by a very long exclusive negotiating rights held by a drafting team leads to a debate about whether the rule violates a

---

38) KBO, Rule 105 (Amateur Draft).

39) Hyun-Cheol Park, *Loopholes and Remedies of Korean Rule 5 Draft*, Osen (Feb. 12, 2013), http://osen.mt.co.kr/article/G1109540829.

40) Id.

41) Yu-Won Kang, The Problems and Reform Measures of Korean Professional Baseball Draft System, 9 The Korean J. Sports Sci. 111, 117 (2000).

42) Sam-In Han & Jung Doo-Jin, Study on the Problems of Professional Baseball Player Contract in Korea and Direction for Improvement, 15 Korean Ass'n of Sport and Ent. Law 127, 136 (2012).

43) KBO, Rule 108.

44) *See Official Rules*, MLB.com, http://mlb.mlb.com/mlb/draftday/rules.jsp (last visited July 30, 2013); *Draft FAQ*, MLB.com, http://mlb.mlb.com/mlb/draftday/faq.jsp, (last visited July 30, 2013). The rules state that teams hold the draft rights from June, with the exact date varying based upon the year, until August 15.

45) Kozo Ota, *2010 Draft Preview: How Does the NPB Draft Work?*, Tokyo Swallows (Oct. 22, 2010), http://tokyoswallows.com/2010/10/22/2010-npb-draft-preview-how-does-the-npb-draft-work. *See* Rick J. Lopez, *Signing Bonus Skimming and a Premature Call for a Global Draft in Major League Baseball*, 41 Ariz. St. L.J. 349 at 367 for a description of how the Nippon League is the professional baseball league in Japan.

player's freedom of occupation.[46] Albeit without legal authority, the Fair Trade Commission (FTC) in 2002 ruled that a 2-year window for exclusive negotiation is unnecessarily too long.[47]

Moreover, fees that teams must pay for players drafted under KBO Rule 5 Draft need to be lowered substantially to uphold the spirit of such draft. The very purpose of freeing able players stuck in a team is defeated with extremely high costs of $261,000, $174,000, $87,000 for rounds 1, 2, and 3 respectively.[48] The MLB Rule 5 Draft fee is only $50,000 for any draftee.[49] KBO's current rule unfairly discriminates against small market teams and the lack of activity in the Rule 5 draft due to such high costs does no service to either players or teams.

## Free Agency

Free agency is another area for which the MLB is more favorable to players than the KBO. However, MLB players went through many legal struggles to get to the current system of free agency. As described earlier, MLB players started out with the reserve system which perpetually bound players to their teams.[50] Players initially sued under contract law, but contracts were amended to shield owners from these challenges.[51] In 1914, players challenged the reserve clause under antitrust law.[52] The judge determined that baseball did not involve interstate commerce and that because of this, the Sherman Act, which regulates antitrust law, did not apply.[53] In 1922, the U.S. Supreme Court determined that the Sherman Act

---

46) *See* Constitution of the Republic of Korea, art. 15 (Oct. 29, 1987) ("All citizens shall enjoy freedom of occupation."); Seungjae Jeong, *Sports Player's Right for Occupation*, 13 Korean Ass'n of Sport and Ent. Law 84-85 (2010).

47) Fair Trade Commission, Ruling 2002-164, (Aug. 3, 2002).

48) 2011 Rule 5 Draft Results, Naver Blog (Nov. 22, 2011),
http://blog.naver.com/cyberokuk?Redirect=Log&logNo=50127180068.

49) *About the Rule 5 Draft*, MLB.com, http://mlb.mlb.com/mlb/minorleagues/rule_5.jsp?mc=faq (last visited July 30, 2013).

50) Wong, *supra* note 16.

51) *Id.*

52) *Id.*

does not apply to baseball, which gave the sport an antitrust exemption.[54]) In 1953, the court affirmed baseball's antitrust exemption, reasoning that "baseball had been allowed to develop for more than 30 years without being subject to antitrust laws. The Court also observed that Congress did not eliminate baseball's antitrust exemption, thereby evidencing its intention that organized baseball not be covered by antitrust laws."[55])

More momentum for challenging the reserve clause came about during the era of Marvin Miller. The baseball player Kurt Flood was not happy about his team trading him, through which he only learned about through a media interview, and decided to challenge it on antitrust grounds.[56]) This case went to the Supreme Court, and following cases stating that other sports were not entitled to antitrust immunity, determined that while *Federal Baseball* Club and *Toolson* (Supreme court cases that established baseball's antitrust exemption) were decided incorrectly, Congress would need to act in order for these decisions to be overturned.[57]) This was followed by the MLBPA going on strike in 1972, which was followed shortly by the introduction of final-offer salary arbitration.[58])

Free agency finally came about in 1974 for the player Jim "Catfish" Hunter, whose contract allowed him to choose the way for which half of his salary was to be paid.[59]) Hunter chose an annuity, and the team refused to pay with this method once it realized that this would not be tax deductible.[60]) The grievance arbitrator hearing the case determined Hunter to be a free agent.[61]) The same arbitrator, Peter Seitz, found the pitchers Andy Messersmith

---

53) Id.; American League Baseball Club v. Chase, 149 N.Y.S. 6 (N.Y. Sup. Ct. 1914).

54) *Federal Baseball Club v. National League*, 259 U.S. 200 (1922); Seabury, *supra* note 32, at 341.

55) Matthew J. Mitten et. al, Sports Law and Regulation: Cases, Materials, and Problems 406 (2013) (citing Toolson v. New York Yankees, 346 U.S. 356 (1953)).

56) Miller, *supra* note 19, at 172–88.

57) *Flood v. Kuhn*, 407 U.S. 258, 282–85 (1972). *See also* Seabury, *supra* note 32. Congress Amended the Sherman Antitrust Act in 1998 to give the same remedies under antitrust law to baseball players as athletes competing in other professional sports. Mitten, *supra* note 55, at 410–11.

58) Seabury, *supra* note 32 at 350.

59) *Id.*

60) *Id.* There was an attempt to pay Hunter the amount in cash.

61) *Id.*

and Dave McNally to be eligible for free agency in another case and upon being challenged in court, was determined that the arbitration decision could not be excluded.[62] This was followed by a lockout, however, the Basic Agreement of 1976, which followed the lockout, included free agency.[63] The rules related to free agency have since evolved and have led to the rise of player salaries.[64]

Unlike MLB and NPB, a free agent system in KBO was spurred by teams rather than players. In the eyes of many, it was introduced in an effort to deter star players from leaving the league in favor of much bigger foreign markets such as MLB and NPB.[65] Furthermore, financial assistance available from parent companies unburdened most teams from possible salary hikes from free agency.[66] In fact, free agency was introduced in 1999, even before KPBPA came into existence in 2000.[67] This somewhat odd birth story of the KBO free agent system that is supposed to favor players may have instilled a belief in teams that free agency is somewhat of a free gift handed to players and the criteria governing such rule should be dictated by the teams. Possibly reflecting such conviction, there are many distinct flaws with the current KBO free agent rules.

When first implemented, free agency required 10 years of full-time service, but after objections from players for well over a decade, it has been curtailed to 9 and 8 years for players who were drafted out of high school and college respectively.[68] As an exception, a player who has served 7 full years in KBO can be posted in MLB or sign with a Japanese team when granted permission by his team.[69] In MLB, free agency can come about after

---

62) *Id.*
63) *Id.*
64) *Id.*; Andreas Joklik, The Legal Status of Professional Athletes: Differences Between the United States and European Union Concerning Free Agency, 11 Sports Law. J. 223, 235 (2004).
65) Seungheum Baek, *Problems on the Contracts in Professional Sports and Sports Agency*, 11 Korean Ass'n of Sport and Ent. Law 209, 230 (2008).
66) Jinsu Chang, *Various Issues Concerning the Professional Baseball Players' Contracts*, 12 Korean Ass'n of Sport and Ent. Law 219, 232-33 (2009).
67) Han, *supra* note 42, at 144.
68) *Id.*; KBO, Rule 156 (Requirements for Free Agent).
69) *Ryu Hyun-Jin heads for MLB and Posting System*, Naver Blog (Nov. 2, 2012), http://blog.naver.com/kbomarketer?Redirect=Log&logNo=100170694048.

six years of service.[70] Compared to this, the KBO standard is excessive, especially since mandatory military service is required of all Korean males.[71] Taking into account the military service, players are expected to wait about 12 to 13 years before obtaining a free agent status, barring any major injuries throughout such a very long period.[72] Since the average career length for Korean baseball players is seven years, this means that most players can only become free agents past their prime.[73] In addition, KBO limits a number of free agent signings per team based on a number of free agents available in a given year. A team cannot sign more than an average number of free agents available on the market in a particular year.[74]

## Free Agency Compensation

Another major issue related to free agency is the compensation clause. KBO Rule 163 requires teams to compensate the former teams of free agents that they sign by either paying 200% of the past year's salary for the free agent along with one player who is not a part of the protected list of players on the team's roster or three times the amount of the past salary of

---

70) *MLBPA Info*, MLBPlayers.com, http://mlbplayers.mlb.com/pa/info/faq.jsp (last visited July 30, 2013).

71) *Banned South Korean Earns Military Exemption*, The Star Online (Aug. 24, 2012), http://www.thestar.com.my/story.aspx?file=%2f2012%2f8%2f25%2fsports%2f2012-08-24T11 2349Z_1_BRE87N0FS_RTROPTT_0_UK-OLYMPICS-SOCCER-KOREA-MILITARY&sec=spor ts&utm_source=dlvr.it&utm_medium=twitter ("South Korean men between 18 and 35 are required to complete two years of military service. On rare occasions, Korean players can be exempted from military service by winning a gold medal in the Asian Games. There used to be another option of winning a gold medal in the Olympics, but that is no longer a possibility since baseball was removed from the Olympics after 2008."); Korean Military Service Act, art. 47 (2003); *Olympics to Drop Baseball and Softball in 2012*, The New York Times (July 9, 2005), www.nytimes.com/2005/07/08/sports/08iht-oly.html?_r=0.

72) Seung Hyeon Kim, Dept. of Physical Education, Graduate School of Dong-eui University, The Current Programs and Improvement Measures on Free Agent in Korea Professional Baseball League 25 (2007).

73) Jae-Duk Park, Manager Kim Eung-Yong Vows to Never Coach Again, Joynews24 (June 9, 2005).

74) KBO, Rule 164.

the free agent.[75] Unlike in MLB, there are no devices such as a salary tax or a luxury tax in place to curb excessive spending by large market teams.[76] KBO could consider adopting a NPB rule that has a different compensation scheme for different classes of players based on their salaries.[77] Under this type of system, the lowest ranked players would not incur any cost to teams that sign them as free agents and afford them a better chance of signing a free agent contract.[78]

In MLB, compensation is related to the draft. Teams are compensated for the loss of a free agent by receiving a "special draft choice" in the amateur draft.[79] Teams that sign free agents forfeit their highest selection in the upcoming Rule 4 Draft.[80] The rules specifically prohibit other compensation being paid to teams for the loss of a free agent.[81] This system is more favorable to players than that used by the KBO.

## Contract Negotiation

Another issue for KBO players is the manner in which contract negotiations are conducted. Players of all ranks, including those in the majors, minors, and on the practice squad, have expressed that they do not really engage in a contract *negotiation* with teams.[82] The whole process is more of a formality where a player and a team representative sit across the

---

75) KBO, Rule 163.
76) Kim, *supra* note 72, at 42. *See* David Waldstein, *Penny-Pinching in Pinstripes? Yes, the Yanks are Reining in Pay*, The New York Times (Mar. 11, 2013),
   http://www.nytimes.com/2013/03/12/sports/baseball/yankees-baseballs-big-spenders-are-reining-it-in.html?pagewanted=all (describing how Major League Baseball's new financial guidelines have started to cause the New York Yankees, a team known for spending excessively, has started to lower its spending).
77) NPB Free Agency System Explained, Yakyubaka.com (Nov. 18, 2009),
   http://yakyubaka.com/2009/11/18/npb-free-agency-system-explained/.
78) *Id.*
79) 2012–2016 Basic Agreement, http://mlbplayers.mlb.com/pa/pdf/cba_english.pdf (last visited July 30, 2013).
80) *Id.*
81) *Id.*
82) Interview of 6 KBO Players (Kim, Sung, Kim, Lee, Chung, Hong) (June 7, 2013).

table, merely exchange some greetings, briefly review the stats, and simply sign the standardized paper.[83] According to the survey conducted by Korea Society Opinion Institute in 2009, 84 of 103 players (about 82%) claimed that the negotiation process for them lasted less than an hour, while 57% stated that their negotiations lasted less than thirty minutes.[84]

A baseball journalist reported that the Lotte Giants threatened its players that they would be left out from spring training if they did not agree to the salary figures initially presented by the team.[85] This type of coercion is widespread in the KBO and players are often not provided with information regarding the calculation of their salaries.[86] Of the players who reported being strongly displeased with the way the contract negotiation practice currently works, 76% of them found the primary source of their dissatisfaction to be the bullying tactics of their teams as well as their not making any effort to listen to the players.[87]

One contributing factor to negotiations being more player friendly in the MLB is the fact that players in the league use agents for their negotiations.[88] Until March of 2001, KBO Rule 30 only allowed face-to-face contract negotiation and signing between a player and a team.[89] The FTC found such rule to be unfair[90] and KBO subsequently amended the rule to allow lawyers to act as agents for players.[91] However, an agent system is still not in place 12 years after the FTC ruling because KBO Rule 171 states that the agent system will take place only upon further study and agreement by all parties including teams, KPBPA, and the KBO Commissioner at a later date.[92] Teams have

---

83) *Id.*
84) Korea Society Opinion Institute, Empirical Study on the Rights of Professional Baseball Players 6 (2009) [hereinafter Empirical Study].
85) Dong-Hee Park, *Study on NPBPA and Japanese Agent System*, Symposium to Improve Rights of Professional Baseball Players 71 (May 6, 2013).
86) *Id.*
87) Empirical Study, *supra* note 84.
88) *See MLBPA Info*, *supra* note 70. There are currently more than 300 agents certified by the MLB Players. Association.
89) Chang Jae-Ok & Gui Ryon Park, *Unfairness Issues on the Contract for Professional Baseball Players,* 10 Korean Ass'n of Sport and Ent. Law 381, 406 (2007).
90) Fair Trade Commission Ruling 2001-30 (Mar. 9, 2001).
91) KBO, Rule 30.
92) KBO, Rule 171.

been vehemently against the agent system, citing player salary hikes and claiming that the resulting cost increase would drive them out of business in the small baseball market of Korea.[93] However, a face-to-face negotiation between a player and a team pits David against Goliath as the player lacks knowledge of specific baseball rules and contract terms. Furthermore, a player cannot be on equal footing with his team as a worker is not on equal footing when he or she negotiates with a boss.[94]

## Conclusion

While there are many areas for which the MLB is more favorable to its players than the KBO, the MLB players attained many of their benefits through years of dissatisfaction, legal battles, and even strikes. As the KBO is still young, it is understandable that it may take some time for changes to come about; at the same time in the MLB's history, its players did not have favorable labor conditions. As the MLB's history demonstrates, forming a union is one of the most important steps that can help bring about other changes. Additionally, the KBO needs to become profitable in order for the players to see results. An unprofitable league makes it difficult to justify paying anyone, including players, higher amounts. Expanding the revenue pie brings about more money that can be divided up which can help make everyone's share increase in size, including that of the players. Because of this, any attempts to bring about the level of players' rights present in the MLB to the KBO should focus on unionization and making the league profitable.

---

93) Kang-Woong Lee et. al, *State of Sports Agent System and Practical Constraints*, 10 The Korean J. Sport. 117, 125.
94) Baek, *supra* note 65, at 212.

# References

*2011 Rule 5 Draft Results*, Naver Blog (Nov. 22, 2011),
        http://blog.naver.com/cyberokuk?Redirect=Log&logNo=50127180068.

2012-2016 Basic Agreement, http://mlbplayers.mlb.com/pa/pdf/cba_english.pdf
        (last visited July 30, 2013).

*About the Rule 5 Draft*, MLB.com, http://mlb.mlb.com/mlb/minorleagues/
        rule_5.jsp?mc=faq (last visited July 30, 2013).

American League Baseball Club v. Chase, 149 N.Y.S. 6 (N.Y. Sup. Ct. 1914).

*Banned South Korean Earns Military Exemption*, The Star Online (Aug. 24,
        2012), http://www.thestar.com.my/story.aspx?file=%2f2012%2f8%2f25%
        2fsports%2f2012-08-24T112349Z_1_BRE87N0FS_RTROPTT_0_UK-OLY
        MPICS-SOCCER-KOREA-MILITARY&sec=sports&utm_source=dlvr.it&ut
        m_medium=twitter.

Ji-Heon Bae, *Baseball Fans need to support KPBPA* (Dec. 8, 2013),
        http://sports.news.nate.com/view/20091208n03268.

Seungheum Baek, *Problems on the Contracts in Professional Sports and Sports
        Agency*, 11 Korean Ass'n of Sport and Ent. Law 209, 230 (2008).

Jinsu Chang, *Various Issues Concerning the Professional Baseball Players'
        Contracts*, 12 Korean Ass'n of Sport and Ent. Law 219, 232-33 (2009).

Cho, Donmoon, *Labor Control with Panopticon in the Samsung Conglomerate*,
        13 Industrial Labor Study 249, 250 (2007).

*The Commissionership; A Historical Perspective*, MLB.com,
        http://mlb.mlb.com/mlb/history/mlb_history_people.jsp?story=com
        (last visited July 30, 2013).

Constitution of the Republic of Korea, art. 15 (Oct. 29, 1987).

        Marc Edelman, *Moving Past Collusion in Major League Baseball:
        Healing Old Wounds, and Preventing New Ones*, 54 Wayne L.
        Rev. 601, 605 (2008).

Fair Trade Commission Ruling 2001-30 (Mar. 9, 2001).

Fair Trade Commission, Ruling 2002-164, (Aug. 3, 2002).

*Federal Baseball Club v. National League*, 259 U.S. 200 (1922).

*Flood v. Kuhn*, 407 U.S. 258, 282-85 (1972).

        Daniel C. Glazer, *Can't Anybody Here Run This Game? The Past,
        Present and Future of Major League Baseball*, 9 seton Hall J. Sports
        L. 339, 344-45 (1999).

Stephen D. Guschov, The Red Stockings of Cincinnati: Base Ball's First All-Professional Team 3 (1995).

Sam-In Han & Jung Doo-Jin, *Study on the Problems of Professional Baseball Player Contract in Korea and Direction for Improvement*, 15 Korean Ass'n of Sport and Ent. Law 127, 136 (2012).

*History of the Major League Baseball Players Association*, MLB players.com, http://mlb.mlb.com/pa/info/history.jsp (last visited July 30, 2012).

*How to Solve Deficit Operation of Baseball Teams*, Naver Blog (Sep. 25, 2008), http://blog.naver.com/ktjgh1200?Redirect=Log&logNo=40055357706.

Seungjae Jeong, *Sports Player's Right for Occupation*, 13 Korean Ass'n of Sport and Ent. Law 84–85 (2010).

Andreas Joklik, *The Legal Status of Professional Athletes: Differences Between the United States and European Union Concerning Free Agency*, 11 Sports Law. J. 223, 235 (2004).

Yu-Won Kang, *The Problems and Reform Measures of Korean Professional Baseball Draft System*, 9 The Korean J. Sports Sci. 111, 117 (2000).

KBO, Rule 30.

KBO, Rule 105 (Amateur Draft).

KBO, Rule 108.

KBO, Rule 156 (Requirements for Free Agent).

KBO, Rule 163.

KBO, Rule 164.

KBO, Rule 171.

William W. Kelly, *Is Baseball a Global Sport? America's 'National Pastime' as Global Field and International Sport*, 7 Global Networks 187, 200 (2007).

Jae-won Kim, *Forming Union Meets With KBO Wrath*, The Korea Times (Apr. 29, 2004), http://koreatimes.co.kr/www/news/sports/2009/04/600_44081.html.

Ji-Seon Kim & Lee Keun-Mo, *Marxian Approach to Korea Professional Baseball Players Association Activities*, 24 Korean J. Sociology of Sport, 199, 200 (2011).

Interview of 6 KBO Players (Kim, Sung, Kim, Lee, Chung, Hong) (June 7, 2013).

Myoung-Gwoun Kim, *Political Backgrounds Involved in the Foundation of Korea Professional Baseball*, 7 J. Korean Soc'y for Sport Anthropology

168, 171–72 (2012 ).

Seung Hyeon Kim, Dept. of Physical Education, Graduate School of Dong-eui University, *The Current Programs and Improvement Measures on Free Agent in Korea Professional Baseball League* 25 (2007).

Interview with Sun-Woong Kim, Director of KPBPA (May 6, 2013).

Jordan I. Kobritz & Jeffrey F. Levine, *Trying His Luck at Puck: Examining the MLBPA's History to Determine Don Fehr's Motivation for Agreeing to Lead the NHLPA and Predicting How He will Fare*, 12 U. Denv. Sports & Ent. Law J. 3, 6 (2011).

Korea Society Opinion Institute, Empirical Study on the Rights of Professional Baseball Players 6 (2009).

Korean Military Service Act, art. 47 (2003).

Hyuk Kwon, *Berufssport und Arbeitsrecht*, 53 L. Rev. Inst. of L. Studies, Pusan National Univ. 250.

Kang-Woong Lee et. al, *State of Sports Agent System and Practical Constraints*, 10 The Korean J. Sport. 117, 125.

Rick J. Lopez, Signing Bonus Skimming and a Premature Call for a Global Draft in *Major League Baseball*, 41 Ariz. St. L.J. 349.

John M. Milan, *National Pastime: How Americans Play Baseball and the Rest of the World Plays Soccer*, 5 Esporte e Sociedade 1, 2 (2007).

Marvin Miller, A Whole Different Ball Game: The Inside Story of the Baseball Revolution 4–5 (2004).

Matthew J. Mitten et. al, Sports Law and Regulation: Cases, Materials, and Problems 406 (2013) (citing Toolson v. New York Yankees, 346 U.S. 356 (1953)).

*MLBPA Info*, MLBPlayers.com, http://mlbplayers.mlb.com/pa/info/faq.jsp (last visited July 30, 2013).

*NPB Free Agency System Explained*, Yakyubaka.com (Nov. 18, 2009), http://yakyubaka.com/2009/11/18/npb-free-agency-system-explained/. *Official Rules*, MLB.com, http://mlb.mlb.com/mlb/draftday/rules.jsp (last visited July 30, 2013); *Draft FAQ*, MLB.com, http://mlb.mlb.com/mlb/draftday/faq.jsp, (last visited July 30, 2013).

*Olympics to Drop Baseball and Softball in 2012*, The New York Times (July 9, 2005), www.nytimes.com/2005/07/08/sports/08iht-oly.html?_r=0.

Kozo Ota, *2010 Draft Preview: How Does the NPB Draft Work?*, Tokyo Swallows (Oct. 22, 2010), http://tokyoswallows.com/2010/10/22/2010-npb-draft-preview-how-does-the-npb-draft-work.

Mike Ozanian, *The Business of Baseball 2012,* Forbes.com (Mar. 21, 2012), http://www.forbes.com/sites/mikeozanian/2012/03/21/the-business-of-baseball-2012/.

Ju-Han Park & Yeon-Suk Chu, *Current Status and the Future of Professional Sport in Korea,* 3 J. Korean Soc'y of Sport Pol'y. 47, 49–51 (2005). Chang Jae-Ok & Gui Ryon Park, *Unfairness Issues on the Contract for Professional Baseball Players,* 10 Korean Ass'n of Sport and Ent. Law 381, 406 (2007).

Dong-Hee Park, *Study on NPBPA and Japanese Agent System,* Symposium to Improve Rights of Professional Baseball Players 71 (May 6, 2013). Hyun-Cheol Park, *Loopholes and Remedies of Korean Rule 5 Draft,* Osen (Feb. 12, 2013), http://osen.mt.co.kr/article/G1109540829.

Jae-Duk Park, *Manager Kim Eung-Yong Vows to Never Coach Again,* Joynews 24 (June 9, 2005).

Kenneth Quinnell, *Once MLBPA Head Marvin Miller Changed the Landscape of Professional Sports,* AFL-CIO NOW (Nov. 28, 2012), http://www.aflcio.org/Blog/Organizing-Bargaining/Once-MLBPA-Head-Marvin-Miller-Changed-the-Landscape-of-Professional-Sports.

Steven A. Riess, *Historical Perspectives on Sport and Public Policy,* 15 Review of Policy Research 3, 4 (1998).

*Ryu Hyun-Jin heads for MLB and Posting System,* Naver Blog (Nov. 2, 2012), http://blog.naver.com/kbomarketer?Redirect=Log&logNo=100170694048.

Susan H. Seabury, *The Development and Role of Free Agency in Major League Baseball,* 15 Ga. St. U.L. Rev. 335, 346 (1998).

Jules Tygiel, Past Time: Baseball as History 8 (Oxford Univ. Press 2000).

David Waldstein, *Penny-PInching in Pinstripes? Yes, the Yanks are Reining in Pay,* The New York Times (Mar. 11, 2013), Glenn M. Wong, Essentials of Sports Law 463 (3rd ed. 2002).

# Sports Violence in the Italian Legal System

ANNA DI GIANDOMENICO[*]

*Violence is a typical sports offence: in fact, it's sanctioned in a precise manner by technical rules of every sports discipline (and in a more specific manner in those sports that can be defined as "ontologically" violent). In this contribution, I'll wonder about juridical relevance of sports violence, focusing on Italian legal system.*

*First of all, the examination of the case reveals a definitory difficulty, that has consequences on its juridical regulation. Given this difficulty, I'll continue with the analysis of the case considering the involved subjectivities: but even this analysis doesn't solve every difficulties of definition, reaffirming rather the specificity of sport, where sportsmen seem to be exempted from the ordinary regimen of liability, at least in those sports disciplines which are characterized by the possibility of contact among the athletes, or in those sports that are focused on the physical contrast among competitors.*

*This regimen of exemption could be fully justified if it's considered from the point of view of the s. c. "active subjects" but, if it's considered from the perspective of those who suffer that violence, various grey areas emerge, where are highlighted unsolved criticalities to which Italian jurisprudence gave various solutions, often very differentiated among them.*

**Key word:** Sports violence, Italian legal system, Legal theory

## Difficulties of definition

As told above, although this case emerges immediately in the field of

---

[*] Ph.D - Assistant professor at University of Teramo - Faculty of Political Science

sport, it isn't a case easy to circumscribe and, then, to define: a difficulty that arises for at least two sets of reasons, one of a general nature and the other due to the specificity of sport.

## Difficulties of a general nature.

The first order of reasons, then, is of a general nature and arises from the consideration of how this concept, even if so widespread, is marked by an equally uncertain and problematic determination.

### Plurality of meanings in the various disciplines.

This is a difficulty that comes from the observation how this concept belongs to the common language, before to the legal one, assuming a variety of forms, depending on the context where it's used.

So, for a scholar of politics violence may indicate the physical intervention of an individual or a group of persons against another individual or group[1].

For a philosopher, instead, violence could mean an act that is contrary to a moral, or natural, or legal or political order[2].

For a sociologist, more, violence may constitute the extreme form of assault which is concretized in an attack, intentionally destructive, against individuals or things, that represent a value for the victim or the society; or it could be concretized in an imposition, realized using (or threatening the use of) strength and/or weapon in order to achieve the fulfillment of acts contrary to his own will[3].

### Plurality of meaning, because of the evolution of legal doctrine.

Not only, it is possible also encounter a plurality of meanings of the term within the legal doctrine, as consequence of an evolution of its definition,

---

1) In this sense see M. Stoppino, *Violenza*, in N. Bobbio - N. Matteucci - G. Pasquino (eds.), *Dizionario di politica*, UTET, Turin, 1983, p. 1241.
2) So N. Abbagnano, *Dizionario di filosofia*, UTET, Turin, 1968, p. 897.
3) See L. Gallino, *Dizionario di sociologia*, UTET, Turin, 1978, p. 743.

because of which we have gone from a restricted notion toward a conception more and more extensive.

In fact, we started from a traditional conception, which believed that there was violence only when occurred the externalization of physical force: the body had to be involved both as regards the active subject and as regards the passive subject, so that it was believed that violence occurred when there was an action exerted by the body on another body (*vis corpore corpori afflicta*)[4].

A conception that has gradually extended: if initially to detect violence it was considered essential that there was the deployment of physical force[5], then attention has been given to the suitability of the act of force to produce a personnel compulsion and/or win the resistance of the passive subject[6]; finally, it has been affirmed that all means, acted by an active

---

4) In this sense go F. C. Schroeder, *Schreien als Gewalt und Schuldspruchberichtigung durch Beschluss*, in Juristische Schulung", 1982, p. 492, and F. Schneider, *Umfang, Entwicklung und Erscheinungsformen der Gewalt*, in "Juristische Zeitung", 1992, p. 386.

5) In this regard it's emblematic the opinion of Pisapia, who affirmed that, in order to detect violence, was necessary the manifestation of a force "dominating and predominant, such that to win the people's resistance and limiting, thus, the freedom of others" (D. Pisapia, *Violenza minaccia e inganno nel diritto penale*, Jovene, Naples, 1940, p. 32); an approach that was endorsed by Manzini, who described violence as "the explication of an overwhelming physical energy (inherent or not to the persons that acts it) on a person or a thing, in a manner that results in a personal physics compulsion, absolute or relative, positive or negative, or the modification of one thing in conflict with the rights of others on the same thing or producing an impediment to the exercise of the enjoyment of other individuals rights" (V. Manzini, *Trattato di diritto penale italiano*, IV,UTET, Turin, 1981, pp. 625-626). In this sense, see also some pronouncements of the Supreme Court, as Cass. October 24th, 1951; Cass. November 14th, 1961; as well as Cass. March 28th, 1969.

6) See in this sense G. Maggiore, *Diritto penale*, II, t. 2, Zanichelli, Bologna, 1948, especially at p. 859; E. Viaro, *Violenza e minaccia*, in *Novissimo Digesto italiano*, XX, UTET, Turin, 1975, p. 969. In the same direction the Supreme Court, when argued that "in order to detect the existence of violence against the person, as a material element of the improper robbery, is sufficient the explication by the offender of any physical energy, provided that it is capable of producing a personal compulsion aimed at ensuring the stolen good or impunity to the agent"(Court of Cassation, June 13th, 1960, in "Cassazione penale. Massimario", 1960, p. 92, m. 175). An tendency, moreover, not isolated, but confirmed by subsequent pronouncements, such as Cass. June 21st, 1968; Cass. July 4th ,

subject, able to remove capacity of determination and/or autonomy to the passive subject may fall within the concept of violence[7].

From a consideration of violence as mere manifestation of physical force, there was, therefore, a progressive dematerialization of the meaning, probably because it has been believed that a narrow sense can't do justice to all those cases in which violence occurs: from here the shift of focus on the outcome of violent action, a consideration that allows to broaden the configurability of violence, with the consequent possibility of covering some unacceptable voids of justiciability, left by the traditionally narrow conception of violence.

This is a tendency that isn't unanimously shared by doctrine that still fluctuates between the two meanings, without untying the knots about the definition[8].

Different meaning according to an objectual perspective.

Beside the distinction above mentioned, it is possible to identify a further distinction, and thus different definition, looking at the case from the object of violence, which may qualify as *violentia in rem* (when the object of violence is anything, a *res*) or *personal violence* (when the object of violence

---

1977; Cass. June 17th, 1983; and Cass. November 13th, 1985: an approach that focuses on the effect of the action rather than on the concrete manifestation of physical force.

7) This is the opinion of Antolisei, that distinguished between violence in the proper sense and improper violence, including the first "all physical energy practiced by the subject on the sufferer to cancel or restrict its own self-determination capacity", while the second would include any other residual means (except the threat) aimed to achieve the same purpose (F. Antolisei, *Manuale di diritto penale. Parte speciale*, I, Giuffrè , Milan, 1982, p. 130). An opinion also shared by Fiandaca and Musco that define violence as "all that (different from the threat) is suitable for coercion and deprives assaulted of the capacity of constituting or fulfillment of will" (G. Fiandaca - E. Musco, *Diritto penale. Parte speciale*, I, Zanichelli, Bologna, 1988, p.213).

8) It should be stressed how it's a tendency that doesn't however find unanimity in doctrine, since it has been observed that in this way "doesn't define the concept, but it mixes up once again cause and effect, the violence with the state of constriction. [...] Which, among other things, would make impossible to distinguish violence from deception. On a practical level, such an approach would lead - and in fact has led sometimes into applicative practice - in the name of a misunderstanding teleologism, to extend the range of several incriminations beyond any reasonable limit" (G. De Simone, *Violenza*, in *Enciclopedia del diritto*, XLVI, Giuffrè, Milan, 1993, p. 896).

is a person)[9].

If the Italian legal system provides a clear definition of *violentia in rem*, pursuant to art. 392 of criminal code, according to which violence is practiced on things when the *res* is damaged and/or transformed, or when it is changed the end use, not so happens for the definition of personal violence: in fact, our criminal code regulates the personal violence, using more articles, sanctioning from time to time violence to the person (art. 628 penal code[10]), to people (articles 393[11] and 614[12]) as well as in the Chapter I of Title XIII of penal code[13]), and towards people (article 385 of penal code[14])[15].

To make more complex the picture, there is the observation that, sometimes, there could be violence on a person even if the violence is practiced on a third party, in order to bend the will of the subject that is the true object of violence (so there is a double personal violence, exercised

---

9) This is a distinction that is accepted by F. Mantovani (see his *Diritto penale. Parte speciale*, I, *Delitti contro la persona*, CEDAM, Padua, 1995, p. 330).

10) "Anyone, to procure for himself or others an unjust profit, through violence or threat to the person, takes possession of the property of others, depriving its holder, shall be punished with imprisonment from three to ten years and a fine from ITL one million to four million" (art. 628 - Robbery, par. 1)

11) "Anyone, for the purpose indicated in the previous article, and being able to appeal to court, takes the law into his own hands, using violence or threats to persons, shall be punished with imprisonment up to one year" (art. 393 - Arbitrary exercise of his own reasons with violence on people, par. 1)

12) "1) Any person who is introduced in the home of others, or in another private house, or in their belongings, against the express or tacit will of those who have the right to exclude it, or there is introduces himself clandestinely or with deception, it is punished with imprisonment up to three years. [...] 4) The punishment is from one up to five years, and it's automatically prosecuted, if the offence is committed with violence against property or persons, or if the offender is clearly armed" (art. 614 - Housebreaking)

13) Entitled "Crimes against property through violence to things or people."

14) "Whoever, being lawfully arrested or detained for an offence, escapes shall be punished with imprisonment from six months up to a year. The penalty shall be imprisonment from one up to three years if the offender commits the act using violence or threats against individuals or through forced entry, and it is from three up to five years if the offence is committed with violence or threats or weapons or several persons acting together"(art. 385 - Evasion, par. 1).

15) It is interesting to note how this differentiation hasn't significant effect on the meaning: in this sense see the considerations of B. Petrocelli in his *Violenza e frode* (1928), in *Saggi di diritto penale*, CEDAM, Padua, 1952, pp. 184 et seq.

over those "materially" suffers the violent act and over the individual that is the final recipient of violence), as well as there could be a violence on things, as the means to coerce the will of a person.

*Different meanings according to a teleological perspective.*

Not only, there is a further distinction, if violence is considered from a teleological perspective.

Thus there is a *violence as an end* when the purpose of the act is precisely to cause harm and/or injury to the passive subject; as there is *violence as a mean*, when violence is used to bend the will of others, forcing the passive subject to make, or tolerate or, finally, omit something that otherwise would not have done, tolerated or omitted[16].

It has been observed that, like the previous ones, this isn't a diriment distinction: just think how, in its configuration as a means to bend the will of others, violence-means doesn't seem distinguish itself significantly from the violence-end, especially if it's seen from a perspective that accepts an extensive meaning of violence[17].

## Difficulties of definition due to the specific nature of sport.

The intrinsic polysemy of the word, that makes it hard to define and circumscribe, reveals further critical profiles when violence occurs within the sport, also due to specific nature of sport.

In a word, the question is whether it's more correct to assume a narrow sense or it's more appropriate and/or admissible to accept a broad meaning. Not only, given the semantic fluctuations, I wonder what could be an appropriate definition of sports violence.

---

16) This is a distinction identified by Antolisei (in his *Manuale di diritto penale. Parte speciale*, II, cit., p. 135), as much as Mantovani (in his *Diritto penale. Parte speciale*, I, *Delitti contro la persona*, cit., p. 325).

17) In this sense see Giuliano Vassalli, *Il diritto alla libertà morale (Contributo alla teoria dei diritti della personalità)*, in *Studi giuridici in memoria di Filippo Vassalli*, II, Turin, 1960, especially p. 1686).

Narrow meaning vs. dematerialized sense.

These are questions of simple and, at the same time, complex solution.

On the one hand, in fact, it appears rather simple to agree about the opportunity of not joining a perspective that accepts a dematerialized conception of violence, if we don't want incur in an indefinite extension of the case, that may result in the impossibility to resort to an adequate justiciability[18].

As an example, think of the possibility of identifying the extremes of violence in the behaviours of physicians and/or the galaxy of legal persons, when they induce and force sportsmen to doping: obviously, these are suggestive hypotheses, to which, however, could hardly follow a positive feedback in courts, in the first case due to the prevalence of principle of self-determination, and in the second due to the nature of legal persons, that precludes a criminal prosecution.

Not only, adhering to an extensive meaning of violence a series of exegetical difficulties emerges: until, in fact, the induction of young athletes to a practice characterized by an intense and systematized training (a practice, that influences decisively the existence of those young people) may be seen as the result of their own self-determination? And what's the limen, gone beyond this, we get into a case of coercion of the will and, therefore, can be considered that there is violence?

Adhering to a dematerialized meaning of violence there would be, therefore, endless spaces of conflicts, that would result in a substantial impunity, with little chances to get justice because of the uncertain boundaries of the cited case.


Sports exemptions.

Hence, given the opportunity to take a narrower definition of violence, as

---

18) In this regard, Petrocelli argued against an extension of the margins of the case in a dematerializing sense, pointing out the inappropriateness of proposing "a concept so vague and expanded, based on a classification, not useful in a code, above all because of confusions that it will inevitably produce" (B. Petrocelli, *Violenza e frode*, cit., p. 187).

*vis corpore corpori afflicta,* emerges a further difficulty of definition (and this is the second order of specific reasons related to sport), a difficulty which originates in the definition of sport as an activity inherently dangerous[19]: in fact, sport is marked by an essential riskiness, so that this characterization was used often to deny foundation to damage claims, arising from participant to competitions, during which they had suffered injury[20].

To make further complex the exegesis of this category is the consideration that sport isn't only an intrinsically risky activity, but this has been freely chosen: all this makes it rather difficult to understand how far the voluntary nature of the practice can constitute a justification for the consequences of this activity.

In this regard it might help a classification drawn up by the Italian legal doctrine, that has identified a tripartite division which distinguished among non-violent sports, sport characterized as contingently violent, and s. c. necessarily violent sports: thus, it's distinguished "among non-violent sports, where it's prohibited from any contact with the opponent (motor racing, athletics, swimming, tennis), combat sports, whose characteristic element is aggression and knockdown of the opponent (boxing, Greco-Roman wrestling, freestyle wrestling), and finally sports that contemplate the possibility of occurrence during the match of violent contact with the opponents (rugby, football, basketball)"[21].

---

19) This is a characterization of the sport, better described by the term "sports risk", with which it's wanted "to emphasize the feature of danger inherent in any sporting activity. In a more technical sense it is worth to indicate, in the field of civil law, the normal dose of dangerousness of certain games"(F. Albeggiani, *Sport (dir.pen.),* in *Enciclopedia del diritto,* XLIII, Giuffrè, Milan, 1990, p. 539, footnote 4). On sports risks, see *amplius* E. Bonasi Benucci, *Il rischio sportivo,* in "Rivista di diritto sportivo", 1955, pp. 422 et seq.; M. Pascasio, *Il rischio sportivo,* in "Rivista di diritto sportivo", 1961, pp. 73 et seq. In this sense Dini said that "all sports activities may present a risk" (P. Dini, *L'atleta e i limiti del rischio,* in "Rivista di diritto sportivo", 1977, p. 62).

20) In Italy, *leading case* was the pronouncement of the Supreme Court, sentence November 13th, 1958, n. 3702.

21) G. Vidiri, *Violenza sportiva e responsabilità penale dell'atleta,* in "Cassazione Penale", 1992, p. 3157. It's important to highlight how that threefold division is shared by the Italian legal doctrine: in this sense agree, in fact, T. Delogu (see his *La teoria del delitto sportivo,* in "Annali di diritto e procedura penale", 1932, pp. 1301-1302), G. Vassalli (in *Agonismo sportivo e norme penali,* in "Rivista di diritto sportivo", 1958,

According to this classificatory hypothesis, for sports that fall in the first category there aren't problems of interpretation, because they exclude completely the physical contact among athletes and, therefore, there is an ordinary regime of responsibility; for the others, instead, some questions about the profiles of legality of these practices raise, wondering first the underlying *rationale* for the eligibility of such activities, otherwise punished by state legal system, and secondly what is the limit that marks the transition from lawfulness to punishability, namely the limit of permitted risk.

**Lawfulness of injuries caused within sports practice.**

For the first order of questions there are two opposing tendencies.

The first of these is placed on rigorist positions: in this perspective, there is no specificity of sport, so that any damage or injury resulting from sports activities are to be considered and judged as other human activities by subjecting them, therefore, to the ordinary rules of civil and criminal liability.

It is an approach that, even in the moment of greatest diffusion, has always been in the minority and now appears to be completely recessive. A

---

p.181), and G. De Francesco (see his *La violenza sportiva e i suoi limiti scriminanti*, in "Rivista italiana di diritto e procedura penale, 1983, p. 589). Alessandro Traversi accepts the tripartite distinction, but introduced in the classification the risk assessment for the spectators, noting, in particular, that "the sports activities can be divided into three categories: those that don't involve any physical contact among athletes and risks to spectators (such as tennis and athletics); those that, though excluding the use of violence, allow physical contact with the consequent risk to the safety of the athletes (such as, for example, football, hockey and rugby), as well as the activities that are dangerous in itself (for example motor racing); and finally those ontologically violent (so-called "necessarily violent"), where the use of physical violence on the persons doesn't give rise, as in other sports, in violation of rules of the game, but, on the contrary, is the essence the discipline (as in the case of boxing and freestyle wrestling)" (A. Traversi, *Diritto penale dello sport*, Giuffrè, Milan, 2001, pp. 39-40). There is who identify, instead, a quadripartite distinction, as Rampioni, who states that "some [sports] consist in a direct and necessary violence on the person, tending to knock out the opponent, such as boxing and wrestling; others are practiced exercising violence on a person and on a thing at once, such as rugby; there are still others where violence on the persons is only occasional, that is, theoretically, they exclude it, as football; finally, the fourth category includes sports that exercise violence only on things, like tennis" (R. Rampioni, *Delitto sportivo*, in *Enciclopedia giuridica*, X, Treccani, Rome, 1989, p. 1).

tendency that wasn't at all uniform, because within it a plurality of opinions may be identified: there's, in fact, who argued that violent sports adduced raised certain questions that are similar to those found in all dangerous activities, not identifying particular disciplinary regimes[22]; just as there were those who argued, however, that is not relevant to distinguish whether the injury is the result of a behaviour acted in compliance with the rules of the game and/or sports, or less[23].

The second tendency, opposite to the previous one, believes that sports activities, characterized by a potential harmfulness, may be regarded as ordinarily lawful, provided that they don't exceed a level that's functional to their practice[24].

---

[22] In this sense see A. Bernaschi, *Limiti della illiceità penale nella violenza sportiva*, in "Rivista di diritto sportivo", 1976, pp. 4-5; L. Crugnola, *La violenza sportiva*, in "Rivista di diritto sportivo", 1960, p. 55; G. Noccioli, *Le lesioni sportive nell'ordinamento giuridico*, in "Rivista di diritto sportivo", 1953, p. 252; A. Tomaselli, *La violenza sportiva e il diritto penale*, in "Rivista di diritto sportivo", 1970, pp. 319 et seq.

[23] In this sense, Giuseppe Del Vecchio claimed that there was a responsibility for all cases of injury and death of an athlete, which had occurred in a sporting event, even in the event that had been recognized compliance with the rules, unless it could not detect the possibility of unforeseeable circumstances or force majeure (see to that effect his *La criminalità negli "sports"*, F.lli Bocca, Turin, 1927, pp. 83 et seq.; *La colpa con previsione nel nuovo Codice Penale*, in "Nuovo Diritto - La Pretura",1929, pp. 4 et seq.; *La responsabilità penale nell'evento dannoso sportivo*, in "Archivio di antropologia criminale, psichiatria e medicina legale"1937, pp. 611 et seq.). Petrocelli argued that sports injuries are treated in the same way as ordinary injury; not only, he affirmed that the observance of the rules can't expunge the criminal relevance (in this way go his *La illiceità della violenza sportiva*, in "Rivista critica di diritto e giurisprudenza", 1929, pp. 262 et seq.; *I limiti della questione circa la illiceità della violenza sportiva*, in "Il nuovo diritto", 1930, pp. 15 et seq.). Similarly, Penso argued that the injuries inflicted voluntarily and as a direct result of a violent sport and exercise, even in the case of compliance with the rules, must be considered as a common crime against the person (G. Penso, *Studi sul progetto preliminare di un nuovo codice penale italiano*, IES, Milan, 1929, pp. 113 et seq.).

[24] *Ex pluribus* see F. Antolisei, *Manuale di diritto penale. Parte generale*, Giuffrè, Milan, 1997, p. 311; G. Bettiol, *Diritto penale*, CEDAM, Padua, 1982, pp. 370-371; F. Chiarotti, *La responsabilità penale nell'esercizio dello sport*, in "Rivista di diritto sportivo", 1959, pp. 237 et seq.; F. Cordero, *Appunti in tema di violenza sportiva*, in "Giurisprudenza italiana", 1950, II, cc. 313 et seq.; T. Delogu, *La teoria del delitto sportivo*, in "Annali di diritto e procedura penale", 1932, pp.1297 et seq.;V. Manzini, *Trattato di diritto penale italiano*, VIII, UTET, Turin, 1985, pp. 218 et seq.; P.

Even this approach doesn't be uniform in choosing arguments that supported the opinion.

In fact, there are those who supported the lawfulness, but always conditioned, of sports practices characterized by violence and/or dangerousness, arguing that these activities are recognized by the State: the provision of punishment for injury caused to bodily integrity by such activities would be in contradiction with authorization granted to them[25].

Others, instead, have argued that the legality is founded on the justification of the consent the person entitled: participating in the competition, the athlete agrees to the aggressions which are necessarily connected to competitive practice[26].

The Italian jurisprudence, however, seems to have reached an almost unanimous position, arguing that "the player, who's author of the damaging event, but that was respectful of the rules of game, of the duty of loyalty towards the opponent and his bodily integrity, commits a sports illicit, but it isn't criminally prosecutable, since in such a case can't be said to be exceeded the threshold of permitted risk, as it is an element of common

---

Nuvolone, *I limiti taciti della norma penale* (1945), CEDAM, Padua, 1972, p. 181.

25) See in this sense L. Granata, *Presupposti giuridici della colpa punibile nei giochi sportivi*, in "Rivista di diritto sportivo", 1955, pp. 1 et seq. Vidiri said that the enactment of law 23 March 1981, n. 91, *establishing rules on the relationship between society and sports professionals*, has led to the emergence of the sport structure, giving "general range also to rules, dictated by sports federations, which, in addition to fulfilling the technical function of ensuring the regularity of competitions placing the contenders an equal footing, unquestionably fulfill the function of limiting the risks that may arise from basic violence characterizing the specific discipline practiced"(G. Vidiri, *Violenza sportiva e responsabilità penale dell'atleta*, cit., p. 3159).

26) It's an exempting circumstance, invoked by many authors, who, however, attribute to it a diversified extension: in fact, for some such exculpation would act within the limits of the availability of personal integrity sanctioned by art.5 of the Civil Code (in this sense see F. Chiarotti, *La responsabilità penale nell'esercizio dello sport*, cit., p. 261; G. Marini, *Violenza sportiva*, in *Novissimo Digesto italiano*, XX, UTET, Turin, 1975, pp. 982 et seq.; A. Pagliaro, *Principi di diritto penale. Parte generale*, Giuffrè, Milan, p. 428); for others, instead, the exemption would have a wider range, establishing the limits on the basis of rules of customary type (so T. Delogu, *La teoria del delitto sportivo*, cit., p. 1304; R. Rampioni, *Sul c.d. "delitto sportivo": limiti di applicazione*, in "Rivista italiana di diritto e procedura penale", 1975, p. 661 et seq.; R. Riz, *Il consenso dell'avente diritto*, CEDAM, Padua, 1979, p. 276).

experience that, during a competition, the anxiety of outcome, physical tiredness and the competitive spirit, sometimes excessive, can lead to not-voluntary violations of competition rules. Vice versa, when the harmful act occurs because the player violates the rules of the game voluntarily, disregarding the duties of loyalty to the opponent, that, however, should be the essential feature of any sports, then the fact will not fall into the cause of justification, but will be considered a criminal offence"[27].

### The limit of permitted risk.

For the second group of questions, namely those dealing with the search for the limen gone beyond this we pass from the lawfulness of certain conduct to their punishability, it has come to the conclusion that the limit of the permitted risk must be found in the specificity of matter, especially taking into account the voluntariness of the practice, and the playful and agonistic intent of sports activity[28].

---

27) Cass. pen., section V, sentence December 2$^{nd}$, 1999, n. 1951, available online at the link http://www.altalex.com/index.php?idnot=174. This is a well-established jurisprudential trend, confirmed by several judgments of the Supreme Court, that recently affirmed that "in the participation to a competition is inherent acceptance (and thus the giving of consent) of the risk that, from certain actions mainly connoted by the force or the agonistic agitation (think in particular to the "actions" of the game of football "violently" hindered by opposing players, in order to avoid it being scored the goal), adverse events may arise for your personal safety. As also found by the case law of the Court of Cassation (see *Cass.* pen. *, sectionV, sentence May 23rd, 2005, n. 19473*, set out above), you do not exit - nonetheless - from the perimeter of s. c. permitted risk (and consented) if you go beyond the written rules, prearranged to govern the use of violence in football, for example, (and then it is concretized the sports offence) in the case where the conduct "is not voluntary, but constitutes rather physiological development of an action which, in the excitement or in agonistic trance (anxiety of the result) can lead to unintended circumvention of the above rules", well being able, on the contrary, occurring the hypothesis of intentional personal injury, in case of ascertained voluntary or prior acceptance of the risk of affecting the safety of others, or for simply negligent personal injury, when the deliberate violation of the precautionary rule appears aimed "to achieve - in unlawful forms, and therefore, unsporting - a specific agonistic objective" (Cass. pen., section IV, sent. February 28$^{th}$ 2012, n. 7768, available online to the al link http://www.neldiritto.it/appgiurisprudenza. asp?id=7617).

28) It has been observed, in fact, that "the athlete knows *a priori* to undergo a physical risk, because it is aware that the agonistic supremacy is established, depending on the sport, only or with the use of violent means and, therefore, with the endangerment of

It should be stressed how the exemption from liability has ancient origins. Already in the Hellenic civilization was ruled that, if in the course of sports games someone killed another, he was not found guilty of murder: in the Attic Law was provided for the possibility of justified homicide ($\varphi \acute{o} \nu o \varsigma$ $\delta \acute{\iota} \chi \alpha o \varsigma$), occurring in the case of an unintentional homicide of the adversary during a competition[29].

A system of exemption which has been established also in the far more articulate Roman legal culture, where are several provisions governing such cases: among them, the two most significant are constituted by two fragments of Ulpian, such as D.XLVII, 10, 3.3[30], by which it has been provided that the beating suffered during a *certamen* could not give rise to bring an *action iniuriarum*, and D.IX, 2, 7, 4[31], where it was sanctioned immunity from aquilian liability for the athlete who caused the death or injury to the opponent.

Having said this, in an almost unanimous manner a justification, the s. c. "permitted risk", has been identified: a justification which refers to "the risk, that is closely related and consequential to that particular type of sport practiced"[32].

---

their personal integrity and the contender [...]. Those who practice a sport can't ignore that feature and practicing it agree to accept the adverse consequences in view of victory. Those damages, therefore, that occur to the athlete during the competition and that can be considered "normal" compared to it, fall within the risk that, by accepting the dangerous practice, they have voluntarily assumed" (R. Rampioni, *Delitto sportivo*, cit., p. 4).

29) More widely in this regard, see U. E. Paoli, *Omicidio* (Diritto attico), in *Novissimo Digesto italiano*, XI, UTET, Turin, 1965, p. 837. It's interesting to underline how Plato, in outlining its legislative model for an ideal State, dictated a rule similar to that existing in historical reality, so that "if a man has killed a friend in a contest or in public games—whether his death has been immediate or as the after-effect of wounds, —or similarly if he has killed him in war or in some action of training for war, either when practicing javelin-work without armor or when engaged in some warlike maneuver in heavy armor,—then, when he has been purified as the Delphic rule on this matter directs, he shall be accounted pure" (Plato, *Laws*, IX, 865a-b).

30) "*Si quis per iocum percutiat aut dum certat, iniuriarum non tenetur*".

31) "*Sui quis in colluctatione vel in pancratio, vel pugiles dum inter se exercentur alius alium occiderit, si quidem in publico certamine alius alium occiderit, cessat Aquilia, quia gloria causa et voirtutis, non iniur gratia videtur damnum datum*".

32) A. Traversi, *Diritto penale dello sport*, cit., p. 49. In a word, "the sports-related risk is

A justification that includes the generic risk of the foul: a justification, however, which doesn't act when the conduct, because of which sports rules are broken, in addition to being voluntary, "is of a hardness such to result in the predictability of a serious danger of lesions of the opponent, so that he is exposed to a higher risk than acceptable by the average participant "[33].

A justification that does not act in the case of violent conduct, that is separated from the context of the sports competition, occurring far from the action of the game and, especially, with no relation with the same[34].

A justification whose extent is radically limited when it comes out from an agonistic context: during training and/or demonstrative exhibition need to be adopted behaviors marked by prudence and caution, in order to circumscribe to the utmost he possibility of causing physical harm to the opponent[35].

---

substantiated in an increase of danger, in a higher probability of damage that can't be eliminated *a priori*, but it can only be limited by the adoption of appropriate precautions"(E. Bonasi Benucci, *Il rischio sportivo*, cit., p. 423).

33) A. Traversi, *Diritto penale dello sport*, cit.,p. 50.

34) In this regard, it was specified that "there is intent every time when there is no connection between the behaviour of the sportsman and the course of sports activity: in this case, a wrongful conduct must be judged and punished in a criminal court, like if it had occurred outside the sport ambit"(G. Capilli, *La responsabilità derivante dall'esercizio di attività sportive agonistica*, in G. Capilli - P. M. Putti (eds.), *Casi e questioni di diritto privato - XX -La responsabilità nello sport*, Giuffrè, Milan, 2002, p.130). Not only, it is well-established a jurisprudential tendency, aimed at identifying the extremes of the crime of bodily injury, when "the development of competition is just the occasion, the occasional seat of time and location, of acts producing personal injuries, that are out from the needs of development of competition and only given by the will to commit an act of physical violence, damaging another's physical safety" (Cass. pen., section V, sentence May 6th, 1992).

35) In this sense, *ex pluribus*, see the pronouncement of the Supreme Court, where it is argued that "sports activity in the case of exhibition-training requires in the behavior of the contenders greater prudence and caution in order to avoid unnecessary physical prejudices to the opponent and, therefore, greater control of agonistic ardor and of intensity and speed of blows""(Cass. pen., section IV, November 12th, 1999, n. 2286).

## Subjectivities

Taken note of the difficulty of definition, I'll proceed to the consideration of the subjectivities involved, also to verify if looking at the violence according to this perspective angle can help to dissolve problematic knots just highlighted.

In the examination of subjectivities, taking into account the distinction between active and passive subjectivities, in the first instance athletes emerge noting that they can fulfill both roles.

If we adhere to a narrow sense of violence, doesn't seem to glimpse the possibility of a further extension of the subjectivities involved. Instead, if one accepts a dematerialized meaning, being understood the uniqueness of passive subjects, it's profiled the eligibility of other active subjectivities, such as referees and/or officials, technicians and the clubs and/or sports associations as well as sports Federations. To endorse such an extension would be the observation that violence may considered occurred when there are particular behaviors(of commission or of omission) put in place by these entities, because both productive of harmful effects of physical integrity, both of coercion of the will.

This would be an extension not at all groundless, but not free of problems, if we consider the consequent extension of the case, whose gradual enlargement would have only repercussions of substantial impunity: therefore, without wishing to underestimate the severity of the responsibilities attributable to such subjectivities, it would probably be more fruitful sanctioning their behaviors without necessarily connecting them with violence.


Athletes as active subjects.

According to the above, in the first instance emerges the category of athletes as agents that can inflict physical harm to competitors, up to cause sometimes even death.

What are the legally relevant profiles?

The exegetical analysis is rather complex, because sport is characterized by being a controlled exercise of force, better an activity aimed specifically at disciplining the use of force, directing it to the fulfillment of acts that require skill and particularly refined dexterity; a difficulty that is extremely amplified when are considered those sports that are ontologically characterized by the use of force.

To make even more complex the work of exegesis remember how the sport is characterized by a voluntary practice that could constitute a justification of the responsibility of very wide range.

Given this, the decisive interpretative key could be found in the meaning of sport as a practice characterized by a controlled use of force: controlled use, not indiscriminate. From here a distinction quite simple, according to which it could be considered that occurred violence when we encounter a violation of the rules, so that any injuries suffered, when these conditions occurred, might be deemed punishable as outcomes of acts of violence.

However, the question that arises is if it's sufficient that there is the awareness of violation of the rules so that may be considered occurred violence: a question that also arises considering the multiplicity of injuries that could acquire legal relevance.

In this case remember the other feature, mentioned above, namely the peculiar voluntary nature of sport, to which must be added the consideration of the connotation of sport as a risky activity, to conclude that violence could be considered occurred not only when injuries derive from the violation of the rules, but also when is realized another condition, namely that it's found the will to produce such injuries.

This could certainly make easier the work of exegesis, but it still doesn't seem fully satisfactory: may those injuries, that are result of an involuntary violation of the rules, dictated perhaps by mere tiredness, be considered really irrelevant? So, what are the profiles of legal significance of such conduct? If such profiles are not attributable directly to athletes, could responsibilities be traced elsewhere?

Considering, therefore, that even the definition of sport as a controlled use of force fails to provide a criterion to unravel the complex interlacement of responsibilities, perhaps the identification and examination of the assets affected by the acts of violence may provide more stringent suggestions.

For this case emerges the injury of at least three categories of assets, that is, the fairness of sports competition, physical integrity and the constellation of interests of a patrimonial nature.

### Fairness of sports competition.

The lesion of this first order of assets it is easy to detect, as soon as it's observed that violence is a violation of the rules of agonistic contest.

In this sense, it is equally clear the peculiar competence of sports legal system, that is constituted to regulate the agonistic contest: a violation of its rules, as evidently occurs in violence, implies denial of its *raison d'être*[36].

Systems of a public nature, instead, seem to be substantially indifferent to safeguarding this interest, unless the *vulnus* to assets and interests related in various ways to the fairness of the competition is present.

### Physical integrity

The injury to the physical integrity, as outcome of an act deemed violent, seems to be pertaining to the legal systems of a public nature, which ordinarily recognize the relevance of this case, identifying a diversification of the imputation of liability[37], depending on the degree of voluntariness of

---

36) It's interesting underline how it's a recognition of the importance of the behavior that leaves out of consideration the occurrence of the physical injury: the athlete who should be considered responsible is sanctioned with the imputation a foul and the subsequent action for damages that may materialize itself in the assignment of a point to the injured party, or in the grant to be able to restart the game in favorable terms (through the assignment of punishment, penalty, throw-in, and/or free throws). This is the recognition of the relevance that in some team sports can lead to sanction the athlete that acts such behavior, until the expulsion order (temporary or permanent, depending on the specialty sports) and the subsequent disqualification, or by assigning points to the opposing team or the opponent (in the case of individual sports). More, it is to be noted how sports law generally applies a system of strict liability, considering relevant in itself, a violation of the rules, regardless of the voluntariness of the act, which, however, in the assessment of the penalty constitutes rather an aggravating circumstance.

37) If for the safeguard of health can be found a diversification in the attitudes of the various legal systems, it's worth underlining that all state legal systems recognize the legal relevance of injuries caused to physical integrity up to the extreme outcome of

the productive act of the lesion.

But the question regarding the relevance of the lesion occurred in the context of sport remains unsolved, since it appears well-established a doctrinal and jurisprudential tendency, according to which the sport constitutes the reason for an exemption from liability of a rather extensive range: a justification based on two exonerating exemption causes, that of the exercise of a right (pursuant ex art. 51 Italian criminal code[38]), for those injuries as outcome of a behavior that complies with the rules[39], and that of

death.

38) "The exercise of a right or the fulfillment of a duty imposed by a rule of law or by a lawful order of a public authority, excludes punishability. If an act that constitutes an offence is committed pursuant an order of an authority, liable for the offence always the public official who gave the order. Liable for the offense is also who carried out the order, unless, because of an error of fact, he has considered to obey a lawful order. It is not punishable who executes the illegal order, when the law does not allow him any critic about the legality of the order"(art. 51-Exercise of a right or performance of a duty).

39) In this sense see F. Bricola, *Aspetti problematici del c.d. rischio consentito nei reati colposi,* in "Bollettino dell'Istituto di diritto e procedura penale dell' Università di Pavia - a.a. 1960-1961", 1962, p. 123; C. Caianello, *L'attività sportiva nel diritto penale,* in "Rivista di diritto sportivo", 1975, p. 273; L. Crugnola, *La violenza sportiva,* cit., p. 53; G. De Francesco, *La violenza sportiva ed i suoi limiti scriminanti,* in "Rivista italiana di diritto e procedura penale", 1983, p. 597. L. Granata, *Presupposti giuridici della colpa punibile nei giochi sportivi,* cit., p. 1; F. Mantovani, *Esercizio del diritto (dir. pen.),* in *Enciclopedia del Diritto,* Giuffrè, Milan, 1966, p. 647; P. Nuvolone, *I limiti taciti della norma penale,* cit., p. 181; A. Pannain, *Violazione delle regole del gioco e delitto sportivo,* in "Archivio penale", 1962, II, p. 98; G. Vidiri, *Violenza sportiva e responsabilità penale dell'atleta,* cit., p. 3158; S. Zaganelli, *L'illecito penale nella attività sportiva,* in "Rivista di diritto sportivo", 1963, p.222. In this regard, appear interesting the comments of L.M. Flamini, who argues that such exculpation was further supported by Article1 of Law October 17th, 2003, n. 280, where it's stated that the autonomy of the national sports legal system, to which is attributed a disciplinary competence as regards "the observance and enforcement of regulatory, organizational and statutory rules of the national sports law system and its articulations in order to ensure the fairness of sports activities and competitions"(art.2, par. 1 letter a) of Law280/2003). From here it derives that "the national legislation that recognizes the autonomy of sport leads, implicitly but unmistakably, to the reception into the legal system, with a function of exemption pursuing art.51 of criminal code, those technical rules that allow athlete, in the course of official sports activities, violent behaviors against opponents" (L. M. Flamini, *Violenza sportiva,* in *Digesto delle discipline penalistiche. Aggiornamento,* t. 2, UTET, Turin, 2005, p. 1783).

permitted risk (pursuant ex art.50 Italian criminal code[40]), in the case of injuries as result of conduct not in compliance to the rules[41].

I wonder about the extent of such exemption from liability: how far are extended? May the will be an additional diriment criterion?

For the first order of question, an attempt to circumscribe its extension was operated using the concept of "basic-violence", that is violence "as allowed by the technical rules of the single sport"[42]: each sport allows violence in a different measure, so that everything doesn't exceed this level would fall within the exculpation invoked[43].

For the second set of questions, the use of will, as diriment criterion for identifying the extent of the exemption, doesn't seem to be a satisfactory foundation, as soon as it's considered the voluntariness of the access to sport, that has in itself a trait of irrepressible "dangerousness", because of which the acceptance of a general risk of foul is detected, so that "sports guiltiness shouldn't be commensurate on the basis of strict criteria of ordinary

---

40) "It is not punishable who violates or endangers a right, with the consent of the person who may validly dispose about it" (article 50 - Consent of entitled person)

41) There are several authors that accept an exemption pursuant art. 50 of Italian criminal code. *Ex pluribus* remember F. Albeggiani, , *Sport (dir.pen.)*, cit., pp. 538 et seq.;F. Chiarotti, *La responsabilità penale nell'esercizio dello sport*, cit., pp. 259 et seq.; G. De Francesco, *La violenza sportiva ed i suoi limiti scriminanti*, in "Rivista italiana di diritto e procedura penale", 1983, p. 599; T. Delogu, *La teoria del delitto sportivo*, cit., p. 1304; G. De Marzo, *Violazione delle regole del gioco e responsabilità dell'atleta*, in "Rivista di diritto sportivo", 1997, p. 282; G. Marini, *Violenza sportiva*, cit., pp. 982 et seq.; G. Noccioli, *Le lesioni sportive nell'ordinamento giuridico*, cit., p. 251; R. Rampioni, *Sul c.d. "delitto sportivo": limiti di applicazione*, cit., pp. 661 et seq.; R. Riz, *Il consenso dell'avente diritto*, CEDAM, Padua, 1979, p. 276. Among them, Albeggiani, De Francesco and Riz believe that this exemption acts even if there is an infringement of the sports rules.

42) L. M. Flamini, *Violenza sportiva*, cit., p. 1789.

43) In this sense see P. Nuvolone, *I limiti taciti della norma penale*, cit., p. 182. Not only, it was emphasized that "in the concept of lawful activity [...] generally fall also hypothesis, more and more frequent, of sports irregularities (typical example, in the football field, pushing, violent jerks, haphazard entrances, etc.), considered by the technical scheme of the sport as not separated from the purposes of the sport in question, given the proximity to the agonistic spirit that characterizes today's competition and, therefore, their attribution to the area of risk present in every sport" (M. Sferrazza, *La scriminante sportive nel gioco del calcio*, in "Rivista di diritto ed economiadello sport", 2008, 3, p. 54).

prudence, but in view of the peculiar nature of the activity, in itself dangerous and yet allowed, so that fortuitousness finds a wider field of action"[44].

It has been detected thus the possibility of ascribing guiltiness when the behavior, non-compliant with the rules, as well as being voluntary, is of such harshness as to entail the predictability of causing injury to the opponent: a tendency that is copiously detectable even in the jurisprudence of the Court of Cassation[45].

Assets and interests of a patrimonial nature.

Finally, the commitment of acts of violence within the sports practice outlines the lesion of interest and/or assets of a patrimonial nature, therein recognizable: on the one hand it's recalled that the agonistic confrontation is characterized by an intrinsic patrimonial feature, because of its requirement of the necessary identification of a winner, whose recognition passes through the awarding of a prize, consisting of a medal and/or a cup, that are often accompanied by an award assessed in strictly economic terms[46]; on the

---

44) F. Mantovani, *Esercizio del diritto (dir. pen.)*, cit., p. 648.

45) It has been recognized by Court of Florence that "in the exercise of sports, such as karate, to whose essence and regulation violence is extraneous, considering it only in its pathological and extra-regulatory impact, as an expression of lack of self-control and adequate training by the athlete and, as such, sanctioned, the harmful event resulting in hard physical contact with opponent constitutes culpable offence" (Court of Florence, December 17th, 1984). As well as the Court of Udine stated that "is criminally responsible the football player who, in the course of match and in the occasion of an impact with an opponent aimed at countering him, even without possession of the ball, hit him voluntarily with a punch to the body causing serious personal injury: in fact, it isn't, in this case, a blow disciplined by the rules of this manly and violent sport" (Court of Udine, June 6th, 1990). On this point the Supreme Court has intervened repeatedly noting in particular that "the conduct of a player who, in the course of a game at the amateur level, causes serious injuries to an opponent, constitutes a criminal offence, committing against him a voluntary act of such harshness to expose him to a higher risk than acceptable by the participant in that kind of competition, not being able to operate in such a case the exemption of the consent of entitled" (Cass. pen., section V, judgment of April 30th, 1992).

46) On this point see *amplius* A. Di Giandomenico, *Doping: Legal Theory*, Edizioni Nuova Cultura, Rome, 2011, especially pp. 47-48 and 67-69.

other hand, it's observed how the inflicted injuries could affect, in part or in whole, the future ability to compete of the athlete who suffered such acts, so that it's possible to outline the attribution to the agent of a liability not only for the caused physical damage, but also for loss of profit[47].

The protection of these interests, for the first profile doesn't appear alien to a competence of the sports legal system: a competence which, however, doesn't find an appropriate regulation, because, beyond a more or less rigorous sanction of behavior deemed unfair, isn't provided specific forms of reinstatement, as it's expressly provided for the case of doping[48].

For the second aspect, instead, it doesn't seem possible to recognize any kind of competence by the sports legal system: but this is a safeguard that doesn't find adequate compensation even in the legal systems of a public nature, despite their intrinsic competence for safeguarding of such assets.

Probably the reason lies in the special liability regime that characterizes the sport *in re ipsa*: a liability regime (better a particular exemption from liability) that could be considered acquired and founded when the involved parties are adults.

However, when subjects are minors, *quid ius*? In this case, may voluntariness still constitute a valid criterion of exemption? If the response is

---

47) Without claiming to be exhaustive, it's sufficient to remember how the loss of profit represents one of the two prejudices of an economic nature (the other is the s. c. consequential damage), occurring as result of an irregularity. According to the definition stated in art. 1223 of the Italian civil code ("Damages for non-performance or delay must include the loss suffered by the creditor as well as loss of profits, if they are its immediate and direct consequence"), the damage to be refunded is composed by of the emergent damages (the direct consequence of unlawful act/not-fulfillment) and by the loss of profit (loss of income resulting from tort/non-compliance). In particular, "if the object of damage is a present interest, namely the interest concerning an asset already due to a person in the time when the same is caused, there is an emerging damage; if, vice versa, the object of the damage is a future interest, i. e. the interest related to an asset not yet payable to a person, you have loss of earnings" (A. De Cupis, *Il danno*, Giuffrè, Milan, 1954, p. 150).

48) Remember how, in the case of doping, the WADA Code states that "an anti-doping rule violation in *Individual Sports* in connection with an *in-Competition* test automatically leads to *Disqualification* of the result obtained in that *Competition* with all resulting *Consequences*, including forfeiture of any medals, points and prizes" (art. 9 - Automatic *Disqualification* of Individual Results).

affirmative, may the extension of its range be the same as that recognized for the adults?

Not only, can the exemption be considered valid in every moment of the practice, or does it act in a differentiated manner, depending on the situation? Is the comparison in the agonistic or in training mode subject to same evaluation parameters and, therefore, ascription of responsibility?

Whatever is the type of injured interests and/or assets, however, it seems possible to recognize a gradation of responsibility, that erodes the extent of exemption as we move away from the agonistic mode: in fact, it is identified the need to put in place criteria of prudence and caution when we are in training mode and, therefore, away the sports contest in the strict sense[49].

## Athletes as passive subjects.

Until now, the analysis of the category of athletes in the specific role of individuals acting behavior of a violent nature: but, in the case of athletes who suffer these acts, *quid ius?*

The general reflections regarding the legal significance of violence, particularly in sports, just set out in the examination of athletes as active subjects, are still convincing: considerations that give rise to a substantial dissatisfaction about the evaluation criteria developed until now.

Proceeding similarly to the previous section, I'll begin the reflection watching violence from a perspective dictated by the evaluation of categories of assets, that are affected by the violence.

### Fairness of sports competition.

With regard to the injury of the fairness of sports competition, remember how the sports system seems to recognize the relevance of violent behavior, inscribing it within the unsportsmanlike conduct, so as to make it subject to a regime of strict liability, punishing anyway this conduct and trying to restore the competitive balance by giving a chance to those that were

---

49) In this sense see the above mentioned pronouncement of Supreme Court (Cass. pen., section IV, November 12th, 1999, n. 2286).

adversely affected by violence: but it's a reinstatement that can't be considered fully satisfactory[50].

Not fully satisfactory, but this is the only recognition acknowledged too, if we consider the absolute lack of competence of the legal systems of a public nature on this matter.


Physical integrity.

With regard to the injury of physics, it's confirmed the substantial indifference of sports legal system, that has no special provisions to give relevance to the condition of passivity: the physical impairment, temporary or permanent, of athletes doesn't give rise to any particular forms of protection, if not the punishment of those found guilty, without providing ordinarily special aggravating circumstances in the case where there has been a violation of the rules of comparison[51].

Moreover, neither going to consider public legal systems, particular forms of acknowledgement of the relevance of the condition of passivity can be found.

One reason could be traced in the specific exemption from liability because of which the access to agonistic sports practice implies a sort of acceptance of the risk of "foul" and its consequences, although it was noted

---

50) If it's considered that, in the case where the outcome of violence materializes in lesion of physical integrity, this determines for those, who have suffered such injury, the impossibility of continuing in sports competition, and, often, the access to the agonistic contest for a rather long time too. The punishment and any attribution of score or the possibility of restarting the sports contest in favorable condition don't appear, therefore, a measure that fully compensates, as regard fairness of competition, the damage suffered by athletes.

51) Quite exceptional appears, therefore, what's ruled by the *Refereeing Regulation for Karate Contests* (available online on the website of the FIJKALM), which gives particular importance to the occurrence of injuries during competition, establishing a penalty for those that has inflicted the injury. In fact, given that "the competitor assumes full responsibility for any injury, caused by him" (art. 2, sect. Athletes, paragraph 7), in the article 8 (*prohibited Behaviors*) are identified such prohibited behaviors during the contest, giving a significant importance to those actions that cause damage and injury to the opponent. A reinstatement that has a very bitter taste, considering that often these injuries impede to proceed further in the competition.

that "feature of the organized sports activities is the arrangement of a dense plot of rules of conduct which don't always have a preventive function, being aimed exclusively at ensuring equality among competitors during the course of the contest [...]. Nevertheless, a large part of the rules has undoubtedly also the function of restraining the risk related to the sports practice"[52]. Therefore, "it's certainly an essential contribution, that one offered by that part of the technical regulations, resulting in prescription, to which may be recognized the function of limiting the risks of sport within tolerable limits"[53].

In this sense, also goes the Italian jurisprudence that identifies a clear distinction between injuries occurred during competition, achieved as a result of an inappropriate or violent actions, where is detected a substantial impunity (unless that the competition is just the place and the opportunity to realize the desire to cause harm to others), and injuries occurred during training and/or demonstrative exhibitions, that are subject to a civil and criminal regime very close to the ordinary, being required an attenuated competitive ardor, according to it follows the reactivation of a duty of care and caution, otherwise overshadowed[54].

### Assets and interests of a patrimonial nature.

The consideration of the assets and/or interests of a patrimonial nature, potentially involved, results in a denial of the condition of passivity, like that one concerning injuries caused to the asset of fairness of competition as much as to the physical integrity.

To confirm this, it suffices to note how it isn't found any trace of consideration within sports legal system (a consideration that may be realized by a reinstatement, through automatically assignment of victory to

---

52) F. Albeggiani, *Sport (dir. pen.)*, cit., pp. 545-546, footnote 32.
53) *Ibidem*, pp. 545-546
54) In this sense go several judgments of Italian Court, as Court of Appeal of Milan, II penal section, sentence October 14th 1960, and Court of Rome, sentence April 4th 1996, as well as of the Supreme Court, like Cass. pen., section IV, judgment of February 12th 1993; Cass. pen., section IV, November 12th, 1999, sentence n. 2286, (already cited), and Cass. pen., section IV, February 25th 2000, sentence n. 2286.

those that has suffered the injury).

Legal systems of a public nature seem to be oriented in the same direction: they ordinarily abstain from intervening and, when they deem to withdraw from such an attitude, show a particular care in the work of interpretation in order to discern the boundaries of admissibility of petitions aimed at obtaining any compensation. In this way doctrine and jurisprudence have done a meaning work aimed at defining the area within which the invoked justifications could act, identifying from time to time as criterion for the evaluation, firstly, the concept of basic violence; then, the distinction between a conduct acted in a competitive contest and those acted in training and/or demonstrative exhibitions; finally, arriving to consider the utility of the criterion of compliance or less of technical rules, a criterion to which, however, the psychological element of the voluntariness or less of such an infringement must be added.

A very accurate work of delimitation, that doesn't seem to recognize maneuvering space, unless it is detected violent intent, having an autonomous consistency, an intent that is completely extraneous to the agonistic essence.


## Final Considerations

This brief and certainly not exhaustive examination of sports violence showed unsolved critical issues, particularly if the case is considered within Italian legal systems.

To be of greater concern is not so much the rules put in place for the active subjects, but rather the condition of the passive subjects, consequent the aforementioned discipline.

Aside the sports legal system, in fact, would appear a lack of consideration of consideration by Italian legal system: what are the reasons for this apparently unreasonable approach?

Probably the origin lies in the voluntary nature of access to sport, which makes it a sort of "free zone", so that involved subjects would have freely chosen to practice the sport and, likewise freely, accept the consequences: an emphasis on the undertaking of responsibility, that focuses specially on the acting moment to the detriment of the consideration the state of passiveness.

All this doesn't appear exempt from inconsistencies, as soon as it's considered that doesn't seem possible to ignore the gap between an ideal conception and reality: a reality, that is characterized, not in a so pronounced manner, by a full awareness of responsible acceptance, thus leading to undoubted voids of justiciability, which seem to ignore in an almost systematic manner the claim for justice that rises by those who suffer violence. *Quid ius* for them?

# References

## About Violence in general

Antolisei F., *Manuale di diritto penale. Parte speciale*, I, Giuffrè , Milan, 1982, pp. 130 et seq.

De Simone G., *Violenza*, in *Enciclopedia del diritto*, XLVI, Giuffrè, Milan, 1993

Gallo P., *Violenza*, in *Digesto delle Discipline Civilistiche*, XIX, UTET, Turin, 1999, pp. 731 et seq.

Manzini V., *Trattato di diritto penale*, IV, UTET, Turin, 1981, pp. 584 et seq.

Mezzetti E., *La nozione di violenza*, in "Studium iuris", 2000, pp. 197 et seq.

Mezzetti E., *Violenza privata e minaccia*, in *Digesto delle Discipline Penalistiche*, XV, UTET, Turin, 1998, pp. 264 et seq.

Neppi Modona G., *Sulla posizione della "violenza" e della "minaccia" nella struttura della fattispecie criminale*, in "Rivista italiana di diritto e procedura penale", 1964, pp. 522 et seq.

Pecoraro Albani A., *Il concetto di violenza nel diritto*, Giuffrè, Milan, 1962

Petrocelli B., *Violenza e frode* (1928), in *Saggi di diritto penale*, CEDAM, Padua, 1952, pp. 184 et seq.

Pisapia D., *Violenza minaccia e inganno nel diritto penale*, Jovene, Naples, 1940

Velotti G., *Violenza minaccia ed inganno nel diritto penale*, in "Archivio penale", 1976, I, pp. 193 et seq.

Viaro E., *Violenza e minaccia*, in *Novissimo Digesto italiano*, XX, UTET, Turin, 1975

## About Sports Violence

Albeggiani F., *Sport (dir. pen.)*, in *Enciclopedia del diritto*, XLIII, Giuffrè, Milan, 1990, pp. 538 et seq.

Covassi G., *L'attività sportiva come causa di esclusione del reato*, CEDAM, Padua, 1984

De Francesco G., *La violenza sportiva ed i suoi limiti scriminanti*, in "Rivista italiana di diritto e procedura penale", 1983, pp. 593 et seq.

Delogu T., *La teoria del delitto sportivo*, in "Annali di diritto e procedura penale", 1932, pp. 1297 et seq.

Flamini L. M., *Violenza sportiva*, in *Digesto delle discipline penalistiche. Aggiornamento*, t. 2, UTET, Turin, 2005, pp. 1787 et seq.

Marini G., *Violenza sportiva*, in *Novissimo Digesto italiano*, XX, UTET, Turin, 1975, pp. 982 et seq.

Rampioni R., *Delitto sportivo*, in *Enciclopedia giuridica*, X, Treccani, Rome, 1989, pp. 1 et seq.

Rigitano R., *Responsabilità penale degli atleti, dei medici sportivi, degli istruttori e degli spettatori*, in Guardamagna A. (ed.), *Diritto dello sport. Profili penali*, UTET. Turin, pp. 23 et seq.

Sciancalepore G., *L'illecito sportivo*, in Cantamessa L. - Riccio G. M. - Sciancalepore G. (eds), *Lineamenti di diritto sportivo*, Giuffrè, Milan, 2008, pp. 245 et seq.

Traversi A., *Diritto penale dello sport*, Giuffrè, Milan, 2001, pp. 39 et seq.

Vidiri G., *Violenza sportiva e responsabilità penale dell'atleta*, in "Cassazione Penale", 1992, pp. 3157 et seq.

# The Malaysian Sports Law: Governance and Direction

ZAIDI BIN HASSIM*

*This chapterdiscusses the function of sports law (lexsportiva) from the Malaysian perspective. It focuses on the role of the Malaysian government in developing and regulating sports at national level. This chapter is divided into three parts. The first part discusses all federal legislations related to sport matters; the second part explains the realities of Malaysian sports law, legal application and the role of national sports institutions while the third part analyses positive government intervention and the harmonization of public-private sports governance. The finding shows that the Malaysian concept of lexsportiva has significant impact on the relationship between government-sports associations especially for the interest of sportspersons and sports industry.*

**Key word:** Malaysia, Sports Governance, Federal Sports Acts, Regulations, Harmonization

## Introduction

This chapter discusses the role of the Malaysian government in developing and regulating national sports. Malaysia is comprised of 11 states in the peninsula of Malaysia and two states on the northern part of Borneo. Malaysian law is based on the English Common law system. Parliament enacts federal laws that apply throughout the country while state legislative assemblies enact state laws, which apply in the respective states. Sport is part of culture and regulated by state law. The intervention of the federal government in state affairs for sports matters has a considerable impact on the development of Malaysian sports.

---

* Faculty of Law, Universiti Kebangsaan Malaysia

## Background

Legal research into the history of Malaysian sports shows virtually no direct government involvement in the internal administration of sports associations, which are fully controlled by the executive committees, appointed by general members and form private associations. The associations' founders enjoyed close connections with political figures and the royal families and thus decided the direction their associations take. The relationship was formed on a contractual basis, and the members of the association were bound by its constitution and self-regulation. This was evidenced in 1963 with the creation of a national private association of the Olympic Council of Malaysia (OCM) that functioned as an umbrella body and was responsible for ensuring the participation of athletes from national sports bodies (NSB) in both national and international competitions. Later, in February 1972, the federal government created the National Sports Council (NSC) via the Ministry of Youth and Sports (KBS) to act as a coordinating body for all NSB with the objective to promote sports participation, competition and the general development of sports in Malaysia. This situation illustrated the conflict of interest existing between OCM and KBS and also raised concern over sports falling under the legal jurisdiction of the federal law affecting the private affairs of NSB.

In the 1980s, sports governing bodies established themselves more firmly at the national level. Modern sports began drawing more attention to the federal government as sports could promote good values among the Malaysian public. Malaysian sports were seen as a form of public service, and in 1988, the government decided to promote and further develop it by drafting the National Sports Policy. In order to implement this policy, the federal government passed a number of federal jurisdictions on matters related to sports. This was possible because 'sports' was listed under the Ninth Schedule, List III, Section 9B of the Concurrent List of the Federal Constitution, the Supreme Act of Malaysia. If a subject matter is listed in the Concurrent List, the federal as well as the state government has the jurisdiction to make laws. At the federal level, sports are exclusively controlled by Ministry of Youth and Sports (KBS).

As part of its good sports governance practise, KBS adopted a general sports policy based on the four federal legislations. However, the NSB continued to view itself as a separate autonomous private entity. The NSB formed a hierarchically structured pyramid so as to provide itself with its own internal government at a national level and join the assembly of international federations (IFs) and the International Olympic Committee (IOC). The constitution and by-law constituted the essential elements of organisation and regulation. Its authority did not originate from an external body, it did not sub-serve any political ideology, and it was not subject of the government.

This study focuses on the function of sports law (*lex sportive)* from the Malaysian perspective and is divided into three parts. The first part discusses all federal legislations related to sport matters; the second part explains the realities of Malaysian sports law, legal application and the role of sports institutions while the third part analyses positive government intervention and the harmonisation of public-private sports governance.

## Malaysian Sports Legislations

The first part discusses the federal legislations relevant to sports. The government intervenes in Malaysian sports by regulating and administering sports through four federal legislations. The first federal Act is known as the *Merdeka Corporation Act 1957* which established a corporate body to manage the administration of generally utilized sports facilities. The second act consisted of the *National Sports Council of Malaysia Act, 1971* which created a body to manage the administration of sports in terms of development, research, professionalism and management at all levels. The third *Sports Development Act 1997* introduced the Sports Commissioner Office to ensure the smooth administration and registration of all national sports governing bodies and monitor and supervise sports events and activities. The *National Sports Institute Act 2011* was passed in order to enhance the role of the National Sports Institute in directing scientific research and allocating resources for the advanced performance of Malaysian athletes. The main aspects of these four legislations are summarized as follows.

### The Merdeka Corporation Act 1957 (Act 433)

The aim of this Act was to establish the corporate body of *'Merdeka Stadium Corporation'* with the purpose of managing and maintaining the *Merdeka Stadium,* one of the first sports facilities available at that time.

The Corporation had the power to establish and maintain a stadium or other facility for use in connection with sports, games, athletics, recreational activities, exhibitions and parades[1] or to erect any building on any immovable property of the Corporation and lay out and prepare such property for any sports, games, athletics or any recreational activities which may suitably be held, for example, to provide stands, pavilions, gymnasiums, refreshment rooms or other such amenities and conveniences.

The Corporation was also responsible to hold and promote any sports, games, athletics and recreational activities. In addition, it also granted or contributed towards prizes, awards and distinctions for the development of sports and recreational facilities in Malaysia.

### The National Sports Council of Malaysia Act, 1971 (Act 29).

The Act is divided into preliminary, council, board of management, state sports councils, administration, finance and general. Gazetted on 29 April 1971, it was the first Act to coordinate sports governance in Malaysia. It successfully promoted and formulated the policy to facilitate the development of sports in Malaysia. For example, it formulated the National Sports Policy 1988 which emphasized on the participation of local / amateur (mass sports) and international / high performance (elite) sports.

---

1) *Merdeka Corporation Act 1957*, Section 4 (2) (a).

The primary aim of the Act was to establish the National Sports Council of Malaysia (Council)[2] with the function of advising the Minister of Youth and Sports on matters pertaining to sports in general and to the proper and more effective implementation of sports in Malaysia.[3] The Council coordinated the activities in respect to sports events conducted by government departments or governmental or non-governmental agencies. Furthermore, it was to offer recommendations to the Malaysian Government as to the methods, measures and policies to be adopted to facilitate the development of sports. Where approved by the Government, it was asked to assist in the implementation of sports in Malaysia. The Langkawi Sports Convention, for example, came forth with successful resolutions to improve Malaysian sports. Lastly, the Council was to promote Malaysian sports locally as well as internationally and to participate in all world-class competitions for the development of sports in Malaysia.[4] Rule 8 of the Second Schedule states the duties and responsibilities of the State Sports Council which include the establishment of District Sports Councils to provide adequate facilities for the promotion of amateur sports and recreation at the district level, and to have power over any sports association, club, institution or other body of amateur sports within the State.[5]

In order to ensure the smooth running of the Act at federal level, a Federal Territory Sports Council was established, added by a State Sports Council in every state.[6] The functions of the 14 State Sports Councils were to (a) promote the general interest of sports in the state and in particular to provide adequate facilities for the advancement of all branches of sports at the state and district level; (b) to undertake the coordination of all state sports associations and other sports agency within the state; and (c) to raise and administer any fund for the furtherance of its objectives with the National Sports Council of Malaysia.[7]

---

2) National Sports Council of Malaysia Act 1971, Section 3.
3) *Ibid.*, section 4 (1)(a).
4) *Ibid.*, section 4(1)(b) – (d).
5) Zaidi, H. *An Introduction to Sports Law in Malaysia, Legal Guidelines for Sports Administrators and Sportspersons*, Malayan Law Journal, Malaysia: Lexis Nexis, p. 39.
6) National Sports Council of Malaysia Act, 1971, section 7 (1).
7) *Ibid.*, section 7 (1) Second Schedule.

The Sports Development Act 1997 (the SDA 1997)

The SDA 1997 was passed by the Malaysian Parliament for the development of sports under the ministry of *Tan Sri Dato' Muhyiddin bin Haji Mohd Yassin* in 1997. The seven parts of the Act in the preliminary spelled out the three basic components of sports, namely 'Sports Bearer' (Sports Administrators), 'Sports Body' and 'Sportspersons' and 'Sporting Activity'. The Act was gazetted on 25 September 1997 and constituted the extended control of the government to regulate sports administration in Malaysia. Part II provided the guidelines of sports development in coordination with the Minister of Youth and Sports and other ministries and the development of sports sciences courses in institutions of higher learning in Malaysia. The National Sports Council serves as the overall coordinating body for all sports bodies to promote and develop sports.[8] Part III deals with the responsibility of the National Olympic Committee of Malaysia (OCM) to ensure that Malaysia participates in international events.[9]

Part IV and V of the Act give a Commissioner of Sports the power to register sports bodies and the process of registration.[10] Section 16 of the Act urges any sports body registered under the Societies Act 1966 to apply for registration with the Sports Commissioner under this Act to carry out any sporting activity within five months. A company shall not involve itself in any sporting activity or in any other activity related to sports, as may be prescribed by the Minister in the regulations, unless it is licensed to do so by the sports Commissioner.[11] The commissioner may refuse to register any association, club, society or company as a sports body or impose any conditions on the registration or revoke or suspend the registration. A certificate of registration shall be issued upon the registration of the sports bodies. The ground for refusal of registration is spelled out in section 19, and the Commissioner may revoke the registration if he is satisfied that such

---

8) Section 7 of the SDA 1997, this section is pursuant to the National Sports Council of 1971.
9) Zaidi, H., *An Introduction to Sports Law in Malaysia*, Malaysia, p. 37.
10) Sports Development Act 1997, section 15.
11) *Ibid.*, section 36.

sports body has been registered as a result of fraud or a mistake or misrepresentation in any material particular[12] or has failed to comply with any conditions imposed or has contravened any provision of the Act.[13] The consequences of refusal of registration or revocation are stated in section 25(1)(a)-(e). Among others are that such sports body shall not organise, conduct, sanction or participate in any sporting activities, events or forums whether within or outside Malaysia and shall not receive funding from the Government, the National Sports Council or any statutory body.[14]

The Sports Commissioner can annul or suspend the registration of a sports body if he is satisfied that an organisation is inactive or no longer a proper entity to represent sports in any State or in Malaysia. The issue of inactive organisations arose in connection with voting rights as all registered affiliates should enjoy basic rights and should not be respected if they become inactive and unproductive in choosing the new president and its office bearers.[15] The SDA 1997 decided the structure and hierarchy that needs to be adhered to in order to be registered under this Act, namely club, district, state and national level. Club and associated members can only consist of individual members who cannot be accepted as full members. All sports clubs, especially individual sports clubs and sports academies must be affiliated to the respective state association to enhance grassroots development and ensure the direct funding of active clubs.

Before making any decision to revoke or suspend sports bodies, the Sports Commissioner evaluates the arguments submitted against their proposed revocation and suspension.[16] A sports body aggrieved by a decision of the Sports Commissioner who refuses to register or imposes conditions on the registration can appeal to the Ministry of Youth and Sports within thirty days from the date of the notification.[17] The Ministry refers to the Sports

---

12) *Ibid.*, section 20 (1) (a).
13) *Ibid.*, section 20 (1) and (2).
14) Zaidi, H., *An Introduction to Sports Law in Malaysia*, p. 38.
15) Shenton Gomez, *No Votes for Inactive Bodies*, NST, Thursday, 25 November 2004, p. 53.
16) *Ibid.*, Section 20(2).
17) *Ibid.*, Section 21(1).

Advisory Panel for advice[18] and can allow the sports body to continue its operations and appoint an *ad hoc* committee to manage its affairs for a period not more than one year.[19] The Sports Advisory Panel constitutes the final avenue to check all irregularities without fear and favour.[20]

### National Sports Institute Act 2011 (Act 729)

The Act defines a potential athlete as a sportsperson with excellent physical capacity according to age capable of mastering locomotors skills and emotional intelligence learning processes. He or she also needs to possess a strong competitive spirit.[21] To achieve this level of sportsmanship, the role of the National Sports Institute (ISN) is to formulate, recommend and review scientific methods and measures that enhance the performance of athletes; consultancy services in sports science and sports medicine; record information of the performance of athletes, and conduct development and innovation activities in the field of sports science and sports medicine.[22] The research to enhance athletic performance is conducted jointly with government entities, public or private higher educational institutions, sports bodies or organisations.[23]

ISN is the service provider to the NSC and other government sports agencies, especially in school and university sports.[24] The institute provides sports science and sports medicine services in athletic training programmes, recommends the application of relevant skills and techniques pertaining to sports science in any athletic field, event or competition; carries out examinations, tests and performance assessments and supervises medical treatment in the case of medical conditions or injuries suffered by the athletes and referred by other sports institutions.[25]

---

18) *Ibid.*, Section 21(2).
19) *Ibid.*, Section 22.
20) Arnaz M. Khairul, *Advisory Panel Takes Over*, NST, 24 December 2004, p. 54.
21) National Sports Institute Act 2011, Section 2.
22) *ibid.*. Section 5.
23) *ibid.*, Section 6.
24) *Ibid.*, Section 21.
25) *ibid.*, Section 21 (2)(a)-(d).

The process of identifying new talents is carried out by ISN with the assistance of NSB, schools and universities. ISN may also request for any additional information relating to the athletes or potential athletes with the purpose of enrolling them into talent identification programmes.

## Malaysian Model of *lex sportiva*

This part explores the realities surrounding government intervention and good governance. It explores the realities of Malaysian sports law, legal application and the role of sports institutions. Legitimate governmental intervention in sports ranges from a minimum to a maximum degree. The Malaysian government's intervention in the administration of NSB reaches a maximum degree when all supervisory levels are government institutes, such as reflected in the supervisory powers of the Sports Commissioner and the role of the National Sports Council and the National Sports Institute. Such extensive intervention would certainly lead to the decline of the autonomous power of the sports organisations, especially in respect to their exclusive right to sport management.

Minimum intervention occurs when there exist no specific government norms affecting the internal affairs of the sports sector or when NSB administers its function on an entirely 'private' basis. The Malaysian government intervening in sports to a maximum degree would very likely cause irreparable damage to sports governance and the self-regulatory power of NSB. This assumption is based on the following reasons.

### The Ministry of Sports as Sports Controller.

The creation of a sports ministry leads to jurisdictional conflicts between the internal autonomous powers of self-regulated sports associations. Their selected democratic executive members regulate NSB while the sports institution established under the general statutory power is controlled by the government. The issue arises since Malaysian sports are going through a globalization process as a consequence of increased mobility, information networks and mass media.[26] This conflict is worsened if the external governance (the regional and international sports federations) overrides domestic sporting regulators and government authorities, which hinders them from effectively regulating the activities falling within their jurisdiction.[27] Domestic law (state and federal) may be considerably affected by a variety of forces outside of the control of the local decision makers.[28] However, through its court system and statutory legislation the government plays an important role in influencing the direction as well as the internal affairs of Malaysian NSB.

It is necessary for sports justice to remain autonomous. The intrusion into the independence of sports and the fact that ordinary courts are not equipped to adequately decide on sports issues prove this point. Decisions in sports must not be left to ordinary courts.[29] It is the responsibility of the IOC, International Federations and OCM to develop a legal system, which allows quick factual decisions and thus guarantees fair play in the field of law.

Supervisory jurisdiction over decisions made by administrative bodies in Malaysia is exercised ultimately by the ordinary courts of law. However, our courts have frequently proven to be reluctant to intervene in sporting disputes. In this respect, Abdool Cader SCJ in *Datuk TP Murugasu v Wong Hung Nung* [1988] 1 MLJ 291 held that only the Disciplinary Committee is empowered to exercise the jurisdiction of the Council of the Football Association of Malaysia (FAM) in all cases of misconduct and infringement of Constitution. Disciplinary proceedings occupy an important place in sports law and it is essential that misconduct should be visited with appropriate

---

26) Read De knop, P., *Globalisation, Americanisation and Localisation in Sports*, 2000, 2 International Sports Journal, p. 20.
27) Simon Gardiner, Sports Law, London: Cavendish Publishing Limited, 1998, p. 191.
28) Nafziger, JAR., *International Sports Law*, New York: Transnational, 1988, p. 3.
29) Thomas, B., *Decisions of Sports Organisations in Ordinary Courts, International Symposium on Sport and Law.* Official Proceedings. Monte Carlo, Menaco. Thursday, 31 January 1991, p. 98.

punishment.[30] Section 23 of the SDA 1997 gives NSB the power to resolve disputes arising among its members, or with its committee in accordance with its internal procedure as prescribed in the regulations and constitution. It is perceived that the sports body can adjudicate a dispute better than a court of law, principally owing to the expert knowledge it possesses of sporting events.[31]

Let us consider the nature and scope of the punitive jurisdiction exercised by NSB over a sportsperson. Such sportsperson must necessarily have a prior legal relation of some sort with the body exercising disciplinary jurisdiction.[32] Judge *Zakaria Yatim* in *Dollah bin Salleh v Muhyiddin Bin Hj. Mohd Yassin & Anor* [1989] 1 MLJ 311 held that the plaintiff had not exhausted all remedies available to him since there was no direct contractual relationship or privity with FAM. However, on appeal, it was in the discretion of the court to grant or not to grant the respondent the declaration of denied access to the court.[33] Such may occur by virtue of the indirect contractual relationship between NSB and the sportsperson where the latter may submit to the jurisdiction and the disciplinary regime established from time to time by the governing body.[34]

The court does not entertain a challenge founded on the contention that the governing body has come to an erroneous conclusion in point of facts, unless such conclusion was based on no evidence or is considered as irrational. A plaintiff seeking to impugn a decision is required to prove that it was wrong in point of law or tainted by other vitiating factors rendering it legally objectionable.[35]

---

30) Michael, J. B., *Sports Law*, Oxford and Portland: Hart Publishing, 1999, p. 171.
31) Zaidi, H. *An Introduction to Sports Law in Malaysia*, p. 40.
32) Read Parker, *Disciplinary Proceedings from the Governing Bodies' Point of View*, Sports and the Law Journal, 1995, Vol. 3, Issue 3.
33) *per* Hashim Yeop A Sani CJ (Malaya), [1989] 3 MLJ 484, at p. 485.
34) See Singaporean case of *Haron bin Mundir v Singapore Amateur Athletics Association* [1994] 1 SLR 47, CA where the Singapore Court of Appeal had no difficulty in entertaining a private law action brought by an athlete.
35) Micheal, J.B., *Sports Law*, p. 222.

In the case of Chin Mee Keong & Ors v Sports Commissioner [2007] 6 MLJ 193, the High Court dismissed the application of the office bearers of the Malaysian Taekwondo Association (MTA) principally on the ground that the judicial review application was premature as the appellants had an alternative remedy under s 21(1)(c) of SDA 1997 to appeal to the Minister of Youth and Sports. The same issue of whether the court should go into the merits of the case at the leave stage or not was discussed earlier in *Tang Kwor Ham & Ors v Pengurusan Danaharta Nasional Bhd & Ors* [2006] 5 MLJ 60. The Federal Court in the judgment delivered by *YA Alauddin FCJ*, reversed the majority judgment of the Court of Appeal and upheld the High Court's leave refusal *in limine.*

Since the applicants failed to establish any of the above-cited exceptional circumstances against the Sports Commissioner, the court was unable to determine any fact falling within the compass of exceptional circumstances.[36] This decision made legal history although the MTA did have a significant public standing but it affected more than 300,000 Taekwondo sportspeople.[37] However, in the Court of Appeal, the court allowed the appeal and decided in favour of the MTA. The court not only recognised the representation by exco-members of the sports associations but, most importantly, the right of appeal to the open court, thus denying authoritative control of the Ministry of Sports. Sports associations succeeded in creating their own mechanism, jurisdictions, rules and regulations for controlling its administration.

## The Role of the Mediation and Arbitration Board, OCM and the Kuala Lumpur Regional Centre of Arbitration (KLRCA)

Nafziger identified the normative trends influencing the process of solving disputes.[38] NSB resolve disputes occurring within their borders. International federations review the decision made by the NSB in respect to

---

36) *Per Low Hop Bing JCA*, para 80, p. 217.
37) Paras 93-94; per Suriyadi JCA.
38) Nafziger, *International Sports Law as a Process for Resolving Disputes* [1996] Vol. 45 ICLQ 130, at p. 133.

a particular sport. The National Olympic Committees operate across different sports and intervene in disputes at a national level. International federations may review the decision of a National Olympic Committee while independent arbitration panels deal with ad hoc disputes. The courts of various countries recognize and enforce arbitration awards (foreign arbitration awards) or court judgments as provided in their national law and in accordance with international agreements and principles of comity, reciprocity and judicial cooperation.

In Malaysia, it is common practice that courts not to intervene in sports disputes as such matters are expected to be settled privately by the sports bodies or the sports commissioner. Intervention is considered appropriate only in the most extraordinary circumstances whereby there is irreparable harm to the aggrieved party, and the aggrieved party has exhausted all internal remedies. However, injunctive relief is limited to correcting the breach (natural justice) and not the merits of the underlying disputes. The NSB and the sports commissioner who hear the appeals are experienced and knowledgeable in sports and the nature of the problems.

Generally, courts do not object to sports disputes being resolved by Arbitration (ADR). In the case of *Lennox Lewis v The World Boxing Council and Frank Bruno*,[39] the High Court ordered Lewis to settle the dispute with Bruno and the WBC over a fight with Mike Tyson by compulsory mediation (as required by the WBC Rules). The judge considered this move as 'a perfectly proper independent process of mediation'. Paulsson argues that international sports federations, which seek 'maximal control', may find themselves in courts if the aggrieved party possesses sufficient funds and determination. If, however, litigation is wished to be avoided, arbitration provides the best prospect. Although arbitral awards may under the law of most countries be challenged collaterally, the designated decision makers have the authority to make definite rulings on the merits of the controversy.[40]

---

39) (1995) *unreported*, Gardiner, S., p. 253.
40) Paulsson, *Arbitration of International Sports Disputes*, Arbitration International, Vol.

As suggested by OCM in 2005, an arbitration clause may be written into the rules of NSB and plays an important part in SDA 1997. It requires aggrieved members to proceed in accordance with the procedure established by the rule and not by court proceedings. In *Colchester United FC Ltd v Burley*,[41] the attempt to resort to the courts without regard to an arbitration clause failed. The High Court generated a stay of proceedings at the behest of the defendant. An arbitration clause is unlikely to displace the right of access to court in a case where the claim is for membership of a body rather than a claim by an existing member against the body. A non-member is not bound by an arbitration clause in the rules of the body of which it seeks to become a member. However, such a claim may nevertheless proceed by arbitration, either through an ad hoc agreement or through the medium of an arbitration clause in the rule of an umbrella body of which both parties are members.[42]

Section 8 of the SDA 1997 provides that the International Olympic Committee (IOC) as the National Olympic Committee for Malaysia recognizes the OCM. The Constitution of the OCM gives it the power to control any dispute arising in sports, including the affairs of the GSB. Article 5.13 of the constitution allows the OCM to settle disputes between it and its members (athletes) or between members. The GSB are considered members of the OCM and are bound to comply with its constitution. The OCM as an umbrella sports body has the power to intervene in any dispute if deemed necessary. Not all disputes arising in a GSB may be resolved by its board whose power is limited. This is for example the case where the dispute involves an athlete from another GSB which is not related with the games.[43]

Article 5(14) of the OCM constitution states that it has the power to resolve disputes involving athletes and OCM officials and also OCM

---

9, No. 4, p. 359.

41) *Unreported*, transcript 30 October 1995 in Beloff, M., p. 254.

42) See *Stevenage Borough FC Limited v The Football League Limited* [1997] 9 Admin.LR 109, CA.

43) Jady@Zaidi Hashim, *ADR and Sports*, Paper presented n National Conference on Dispute Resolution 2011 20 October 2011, Puri Pujangga UKM.

members (GSBs) through mediation or arbitration. Article 5(15) asserts that the settlement reached through mediation or arbitration is final and cannot be appealed to the court for further adjudication. Article 6(14) gives the OCM the power to resolve any dispute that may arise between members and other OCM members and between OCM and its own members. Members who fail to attend after receiving the notice to settle the dispute referred to in this section, are deemed to have waived their right to settle the dispute which may be settled without their presence according to Article 6(15). The OCM also has the power to take action against any member or athlete or OCM official who contravenes any provisions of the constitution.[44]

Article 22.1 states that any dispute involving a GSB and the OCM or another GSB or between a GSB and its member (state, club or individual) shall be settled amicably for the first time through the process of mediation. Mediation shall be carried out by the process of appointing mediators by the parties concerned from the panel members of the Mediation Committee. The mediators' role is to act independently and facilitate the mediation process. They decide the mediation procedure agreed to by the parties concerned. If the mediation is successful, the parties sign an agreement testifying to the amicable settlement of the dispute, which is considered as final, conclusive and binding upon the parties.

The Malaysian Arbitration Act 2010 (Act 646) enhances the use of ADR in Malaysia. It recognises domestic and international arbitrations without local court intervention.[45] This Act adopts most of the broad principles outlined in the UNCITRAL Model Law, which forms a sound basis for the desired harmonisation and improvement of national law.[46] Section 10 of the Act makes it mandatory for a court to refer to arbitration disputes brought before the Court where the disputes are the subject of an arbitration

---

44) *Ibid.*
45) Section 8 of the Act 2010 reads *'unless otherwise provided, no court shall intervene in any matters governed by this Act'.*
46) Holtzmann, H., & Neuhaus, J., *A Guide to the UNCITRAL Model Laaw in International Commercial Arbitration*, Kluwer, 1994, p. 11.

agreement. Subsection (2) states that the court in granting a stay of proceeding pursuant to subsection (1) may impose any conditions as it deems fit. The court power to impose conditions can be useful provided it is used as appropriate steps to proceed with the arbitration.[47]

The emphasis given to arbitration under Malaysian law is that of finality and ready enforceability of the arbitral award. However, for an award to be recognized and substituted to a judgment, an arbitral tribunal is generally required to follow the forms and procedures set forth by a national law.[48] Section 11 contains a saving clause empowering the High Court to appoint an arbitrator in case the concerned parties have not agreed to an appointing body. Three conditions must be fulfilled: first, there has to exist a dispute within the terms of the arbitration agreement; second, the applicant must apply to the court for a stay of proceedings before taking any other step; third, he or she is ready and willing to do all things necessary to ensure the proper conduct of the arbitration. The applicant must satisfy the court that he or she is ready and willing to proceed in accordance with the arbitration agreement, and the court must also be satisfied that there is no sufficient reason why the matter should not be referred according to the agreement.[49]

## The Harmonisation of Sports Intervention in Malaysia: an analysis

The harmonisation of Malaysian sports institutions serves the purpose of ensuring appropriate government intervention and integration of public-private sports governance. However, the task is shouldered by independent sporting bodies, which can represent the government and NSB on the basis of impartiality.

Ken Foster looked at *lex sportiva* as a global sports regulation.[50] He

---

47) See Davidson, W.S.W., & Sundra, R., *The New Malaysian Arbitration Regime 2005* [2006] 4 MLJ cxxx.
48) Samuel, A, *Jurisdictional problems in international commercial arbitrations*, Swiss Institute of Comparative Law, 1989. Zurich, p. 31.
49) Sundra, R., *The Process of Arbitration in Resolving Sports Disputes* [2003] 4 MLJ cxlviii.

found the new regulations and legislative systems drafted by sports organisations to be too exclusive and autonomous in nature while controlling sports on the international stage. The main character of the organisation is to build contractual relationships on a global scale. Through agreements and contracts, all sports bodies in the world can place authoritative powers under the auspices of that global organisation. Thus, national legislation systems and governments cannot interfere in disputes. The Court of Arbitration for Sports (CAS) is one of these institutions, which settle sports disputes. CAS is also known as *Tribunal Arbitral du Sport* (TAS),[51] an institution that has autonomous powers in managing high profile sports disputes. All national and world sports bodies under the auspices of the Olympic Council and the International Olympic Council are subject to the arbitration process by CAS.[52] CAS is a legal entity body administered by the *International Council of Arbitration for Sport* (ICAS).[53]

CAS occupies a unique position as it can determine new norms that have legislative and social powers. Its constitution has a global outlook and has legislative power over all sports bodies under its auspice. The regulations drafted contain standard social obligations that need to be adhered to. Comprehensive and general traditions and practices need to be harmonised legally and be brought in tune with all sports associations under its jurisdiction around the world. The IOC status has been recognised by U.S. courts as an international personality in the Defrantz *v USOC* case'.[54] In that case, the United States Olympic Council (USOC) objected to participating in the 1980 Moscow Olympics as a sign of protest to Russia's invasion of Afghanistan. The USOC was established through the passing of the Amateur

---

50) K. Foster, 'Is there a global sports law?' (2003) 2 (1) *Entertainment and Sports Law Journal* 8-10.

51) http: www.tas-cas.org (22 Januari 2009).

52) S. Gearhart, 'Sporting arbitration and the International Olympic Committee Court of Arbitration for Sport' (1989) 6 (4) *Journal of International Arbitration* 40.

53) J. Nafziger, 'International sports law as a process for resolving disputes' (1996) 45 (1) *ICLQ* 143. See Morris, P. & Spink, P., Court of Arbitration for Sport, in Steward W (Ed.), *Sports Law: The Scots Perspective*, T & T Clark, Edinburgh, 2000, p. 61.

54) [1980] 492 F. Supp 1181.

Sports Act 1978 to enable it to send a team representing the U.S. in the Olympics. In fact, the Act was argued as not awarding or establishing legislative powers to the USOC but only recognising the existence of autonomous powers of the USOC as part of the IOC's auspices. With that, the court decided:

> *Congress was necessarily aware that a National Olympic Committee (NOC) is a creation and a creature of the International Olympic Committee, to those rules it must conform. The NOC gets its power and its authority from the IOC, the sole proprietor and owner of the Olympic Games.*

The legislative framework created by the IOC is immune and free from the interference of national courts. It is not a domestic and locally focused institution and it declines honourably the recognition and validation from the national judiciary system. The global sports and judiciary system is what described by Teubner as 'global law without a state'.[55]

### The Olympic Council of Malaysia

The same role must be carried out by IOC's representative in Malaysia, namely the Olympic Council of Malaysia (OCM) as determined under Part III of the SDA 1997. This non-governmental and non-profit multi-sports organisation was registered under the Societies Act 1966 (Rev. 1987) and re-registered under SDA 1997 with the Commissioner of Sports Office in the Ministry of Youth and Sports. Its original objectives were to promote and encourage sporting activities, to act as the coordinating body for the governing association for the various sports, to promote competitions and to arrange for representative teams to take part in international sporting functions. The OCM was not designed to control or dominate any sports organisation in Malaysia but functioned as a sports caretaker at the national and international level.

---

55) G. Teubner (Ed.), *Global Law without a State*, Andover, Dartmouth, 1997, p. 56.

The fundamental principle concerns the certainty of rights and the clarity of the relationship between the OCM and the national government (Ministry of Youth and Sports). This relationship needs to be founded upon the respect of democratic liberties and on the recognition of the general interest, which a just and healthy development of sport has for society as a whole.

The SDA 1997 had to first define the sports policy of the government (Malaysian National Sports Policy 1988) which aimed at developing a healthy, disciplined and united society through greater participation and better opportunities in sports enjoyed at all levels of society.[56] Parliament and Government were responsible for the overall direction of the sports policy, programmes and of the quantitative increase and qualitative progress of sports. The SDA 1997 also had to recognise the creation of the OCM as the official National Olympic Committee of Malaysia and its function of administering, spreading and promoting the overall progress of the organisation of sports, of primary participation and of top-level sports. Unfortunately, Part III of SDA 1997 only recognised the status of the OCM as a 'sports body'[57], which acts as the governing or representative body of sport in Malaysia.[58]

The OCM was expected to be fully responsible for its technical internal regulations and sports orientation within the framework of the International Olympic Council in which the NSB participate. International experience suggests that the government needs to have an exclusive and direct relationship with the Olympic Committee (OCM) as the sole representative of all the existing associations and not only with individual national organisations. It was reported previously that ex-Sports Minister Datuk Hishammuddin Hussein (1999-2004) gave priority to the OCM as arbitrator over the Sports Commissioner in dealing with NSB disputes. Only if its arbitration failed, the Sports Commissioner would settle the disputes and

---

56) Zaidi, H., p. 16.
57) Sports Development Act 1997, section 9.
58) Ibid., section 2.

look into the NSB's affairs.[59]


### Malaysian Sports Advisory Panel

Section 27 of the SDA 1997 provides for the establishment of a panel known as the 'Sports Advisory Panel' to advise the Minister on all sports matters. The Sports Advisory Panel (SAP) consists of a chairman and not more than eight other members, two of whom should be candidates nominated by the Olympic Council of Malaysia.[60] Subject to section 32 of SDA 1997, the Minister may make regulations prescribing the procedures to be adopted by the panel in dealing with any matter referred to it, the manner in which the panel shall be convened and the place where it shall hold its sittings for the better carrying out of their duties and functions.[61]

Today, the SAP is expected to determine an appropriate framework on modern effective alternative dispute resolution in general and to deal with key areas such as deregistration of NSB, anti-doping cases, corruption and match fixing. The non-binding advisory opinion of the SAP is a very useful tool in clarifying legal issues in a manner that is time saving, low in cost and safeguarding relationships. However, the SAP must first of all be wholly independent and conduct arbitration proceedings in such manner as it considers fit – irrespective of the interests and opinions of third parties. It ought to create regulations prescribing the procedures to be adopted and not subject itself to the power of the Minister.


## Conclusion

Malaysia lacks independent sports institutions, which can effectively avoid unnecessary government intervention and the court system. Sports disputes involve complicated arrangements and are often about personal and

---

59) Jugjet, S. and Boopathy, K.M., *OCM requested to arbitrate*, NST: 30 August 1999.
60) Sports Development Act 1997, section 28 (1)(a)(b).
61) *Ibid.*, Section 32 (a)(b)(c).

organizational power. The Malaysian statute of SDA 1997 lacks notable cohesion and uniformity in redressing sports disputes. Being more than a decade old, it should start to consider accepting the amendment of the Act by adding the provision on sports dispute resolution and establishing a Malaysian form of the *lex sportiva* forum. The interests of national sports are better served if litigation cases would not interfere with running sports activities initiated again and again by individuals seeking to challenge the decisions of the regulating bodies.[62] It is recommended that the Malaysian SDA 1997 is completed by an obligatory internationally coordinated arbitration system. This system should allow it to exercise real arbitrary functions. A court of arbitration needs to possess an independent organisation and independent arbitrators and must guarantee regular procedures in conformity with the existing law. Other than the Sports Advisory Panel, the OCM is deemed the most suitable institution for the resolution of sports disputes in Malaysia. In 2005, the OCM approved the *Mediation Handbook*, which lists six mediators and six arbitrators registered in its forum. In conclusion, sport is protected by a specific law known as *lex sportiva*. The concept of *lex sportiva* has impact on the private sphere by placing the political rules of sports bodies outside the sphere of national legislation politics. Its purpose is to protect and provide justice to the sports industry and to professional sportsmen.

## References

Holtzmann, H., &Neuhaus, J. 1994. *A Guide to the UNCITRAL Model Law in International Commercial Arbitration*, Deventer: Kluwer Law.

Michael, J. B. 1999. *Sports Law*, Oxford and Portland: Hart Publishing.

Nafziger, JAR.1988. *International Sports Law*, New York: Transnational.

Simon Gardiner. 1998. *Sports Law*. London: Cavendish Publishing Limited.

Hassim, J.Z. 2005. *An Introduction to Sports Law in Malaysia, Legal Guidelines for Sports Administrators and Sportspersons*. Malaysia: Malayan Law Journal, Lexis Nexis,

---

62) See *Reel v Holder* [1981] 3 All ER 321.

# Discourage the Courage?
# A Comment on the Mu-Yen Chu Case of CAS

CHEN-HUANG LIN*

*A Taiwanese Taekwondo gold medal winner of Athens 2004 Summer Olympics, Mu-Yen Chu, was nominated by the IOC as one of the candidates of its Athletes' Commission in 2011. After the voting, the IOC disqualified his candidacy for allegedly breaching the 'Rules of Conduct applicable to campaigns for election to the IOC athlete's commission' governing the election. The Chinese Taipei Olympic Committee and Mr Chu jointly filed an appeal against the IOC's decision to CAS. CAS released the 2012/A/2913 award (hereinafter referred to as "the Award" and dismissed this appeal on 15 March 2013.*

*This article analyzes the reasoning of the award from the semantic perspective and the theory of legal reasoning developed by Alexy. We find if the presumption of the award has been made clear, the conclusion may become skeptical. We also argue that the reasonings of the award unstained through a strict methodological scrutiny. Finally, we suggest that the applying of argumentative forms as a framework of legal discourses in analyzing the awards of CAS would create a reasonable condition in international sports law.*

**Key word:** CAS, international sports law, legal reasoning, methodology, interpretation

---

* Adjunct Assistant Professor of Graduate Institute of International Sport Affairs at National Taiwan Sport University, President of the Committee of Sports and Entertainment Law of Taipei Bar Association.

## Introduction

A Taiwanese Taekwondo gold medal winner of Athens 2004 Summer Olympics, Mu-Yen Chu, was nominated by the IOC as one of the candidates of its Athletes' Commission in 2011. After the voting during 2012 London Summer Olympics, it was believed that Mr Chu had secured one of the four places on the Athletes' Commission, the IOC disqualified his candidacy, along with another Japanese candidate, for allegedly breaching the "Rules of Conduct applicable to campaigns for election to the IOC athlete's commission" (hereinafter referred to as "Rules of Conduct") governing the election. The Chinese Taipei Olympic Committee and Mr Chu jointly filed an appeal against the IOC's decision to CAS. CAS released the 2012/A/2913 award (hereinafter referred to as "the Award") and dismissed this appeal on 15 March 2013.[1]

This article examines the Mu-Yen Chu case of CAS from an interpretative point of view and the theory of legal reasoning developed by Alexy to see if the the legal reasoning of CAS meet the purpose of the "Rules of Conduct Applicable to Campaigns for Election to the IOC Athletes' Commission" issued by the IOC. We will first summarize the assertions of both parties and the reasons of the award, then subject the premise and reasonings of the award to a methodological critique to explore the fundamental defects of the award.

## The Facts Ascertained by CAS

### The reasons of IOC's decision

The decision of IOC Executive Board asserted that: (1)Mr Mu-Yen Chu, first breached the Rules of Conduct by distributing gifts, contrary to such Rules of Conduct. The Committee sanctioned this breach by giving him a confidential written warning on 26 July 2012, (2) The Committee subsequently

---

1) Aavilable online at website of CAS www.tas-cas.org.

noted that, despite this warning, the Athlete, Mr Mu-Yen Chu, further breached the Rules of Conduct by subsequently campaigning in an area, and by using methods of campaigning, that were prohibited by such Rules of Conduct.

The decision stated that the accusations of Mr Chu's breach of the Rules of Conduct were proven, after considering the nature of seriousness, decided to withdraw his candidacy for the IOC Athletes' Commission election.

In its answer to the CAS panel, the IOC further noted that Mr Chu violated the Rules of Conduct by (1)handling out unapproved name cards, displaying extracts of the Election Manual in his iPad to athletes, (2) distributing lollipops in the residential area of the Olympic village, informing athletes that they would be given a complimentary umbrella provided by the Election Committee, as financial inducements to vote.

### The statement of Mr Chu

The appellant Mr Chu admitted following facts as the award writes: (1)he never accompanied anybody to the voting station, (2)he simply informed the other athletes that they would receive an umbrella, courtesy of the IOC, if they voted, (3)the distribution of business cards is the normal way in Asia by which a person introduces him/herself, the cards he distributed bore the indication of his name and of his sporting achievements and profession, without any reference to his candidature, and were the normal cards he still currently uses, he stopped distributing name cards after being warned by Ms Genoud-Cabessa on 19 July 2012, (4)the iPad he used contained only material coming from the election manual prepared by the IOC, and (5)he never distributed lollipops to anybody as immediately confirmed to Mr Genoud-Cabessa upon receipt of the letter of 26 July 2012

### The disputes between the parties

After deliberating the submissions of the parties, the panel ascertained the following main disputes: (1)whether Mr Chu is responsible for any violation of the rules governing the campaigning activity for the election to the IOC Athletes' Commission taking place at the London OG; and (2) in the event any violation is found, whether the decision to withdraw the candidature of Mr Chu is appropriate.

The panel also noted the facts which were not disputed and in dispute. The partied agreed that (1) distributed name cards, (2)displayed the election manual to athletes, (3)used iPad to display extracts of the Election Manual, and/or of the IOC website, (4)informed the athletes that they would be given a complimentary umbrella if they voted. The disputed issues were that whether Mr Chu (1)took such action in order to promote his candidature, (2)distributed lollipops, (3)promoted his candidature in the restricted area, (3)undertook any campaigning activity in a way inconsistent with the Rules of Conduct after receiving warning from the IOC.

In determining the burden of proof, the panel decides by applying the Article 8 of the Swiss Civil Code which was manifested in the precedents of CAS that the IOC shall bear the burden to provide evidence of the facts on which its decision to find Mr Chu's violations of its Rules of Conduct and to impose sanctions thereof was based.

## The Reasons of the Award

First, the panel found that the distribution of name cards, the display of the Election Manual to the athletes and the use of an iPad to display extracts of the Election Manual, and/or of the IOC website, by Mr Chu in order to promote his candidature, constitutes a violation of Article 3, sixth paragraph of the Rules of Conduct.

Second, the panel also found that the indication to the athletes that they would be given a complimentary umbrella if they voted, constitutes an inducement to cause athletes to take part in the vote, and thus was contrary to Article 3, seventh paragraph of the Rules of Conduct.

Third, the panel accepted the testimony of a witness who would be elected after Mr Chu's withdrawal, and found that Mr Chu presented in a restricted area to promote his candidature that violated Article 3, second paragraph of the Rules of Conduct.

In applying the IOC's Rules of Conduct, the panel especially emphasized the plain meaning of the text: 'On the contrary, their meaning was clear; no contentious issues of interpretation could be identified by the Panel. Nor could it fairly be said that the Rules could not be fully understood by the candidates, given the information provided to them and the cooperative attitude shown by the IOC representatives in their application.'

## The Questions of the Interpretation of Rules of Conduct

### Implication of the Premise of the Award

As mentioned above, the Award asserted that the meanings of the Rules of Conduct are so manifest as not to be further interpreted. But in fact this assertion of a 'self-evident' meaning of words appears to be skeptical even they are seemed so prima facsi. The claim that there need not to explore the meaning of words may veil the orientation or teleological character of interpretation and blur the real process of reasoning.

In practical legal discussion, those who involved has his/her own point of view towards the instant fact situation that in fact includes such as the legal meaning of the facts, the finding of legal rules applicable to it, the understanding of legal categories constitute the rules and so on, all which are interlocked in the process of legal reasoning. Many works of legal methodology have endeavored to make explicit the logic and nature of legal reasoning to validate interpretation of legal rules. It is rare for a modern jurist or lawyer to insist that legal reasoning is just a pure logical subsumption from which a right conclusion can be automatically derived. Even applying pre-existing legal rules to a specific case, there are rooms for judicial creativeness.[2]

It is doubtful that if a so-called 'clear case' does exist. As Alexy pointed out that:' Whoever claims that a decision is uncontroversial is to be understood as asserting that there are no arguments which might give rise to serious doubts.'[3] From a more comprehensive perspective of the logic of language, a word could signify two or more different meaning, and conversely is true two or more words could have the same meaning.[4] This linguistic reality naturally leads to Hermeneutics which concerns the interpretation of text, such as religious, aesthetic, philosophical, and legal one, and finally developed into a contemplation on the being of humanity as a whole.[5] It is especially interesting that legal interpretation had played a role in the development of modern hermeneutics.[6]

According to Gadamer, the operation of language is motivated and teleological,[7] this assertion is also true in the realm of legal science. Any legal argument has to articulate the purposes of specific rules that can be derived form the semantic meaning, or even beyond the scope of text if the factual instance demands so. Without these, the possibility of a reasonable legal discourse will be deprived.

Such different lines of thinking shed light on the very nature of legal interpretation without referring to the controversies between legal positivism and natural theory, even if an interpretation is motivated by a moral end.[8]

---

2) Stone, J,. 'Legal System and Lawyers' Reasonings', 1968, at 304.
3) Alexy, R., 'A Theory of Legal Argumentation', translated by Adler, R., and MacCormick, N., 1989, at 8.
4) Wittgenstein, L., 'Tractatus Lofico-philosophicus', translated by Ogden, 2003, at.31.
5) A general introduction of hermeneutics, see Bleicher, J., 'Contemporary Hermeneutics', 1980.
6) Ibid, at 13.
7) Gadamer, Hans-Georg, 'The Universality of Hermeneutic Problems', translated by David E. Linge, 'Language and Understanding', translated by Richard E. Palmer, in 'The Gadamer Reader', edited by Richard E. Palmer, 2007, at 86, 103-104.

Although any account of legal reasoning presupposes the nature of law,[9] the teleological character is a transcendental frame common to both legal theories from a hermeneutic point of view.

Alexy has correctly put: 'Presuppositions which might otherwise have remained hidden must be explicitly formulated. This increases the possibility of recognizing mistakes and criticizing them.'[10] The methodological assertion of the Award to presuppose a self-manifest meaning of legal rules stands to lose under the scrutinies of the theory of legal reasoning and hermeneutics. It would be a fundamental flaw when the Award did not explore the purpose of the Rules of Conduct to see if the interpretation accord to it.

## The Model of Legal Discourses

Before we proceed to examine the concrete justification of the Award given in the case, a theory of legal argumentation will be introduced in advance to serve a basis for discussion. We will first sketch some parts of Alexy's legal discourse theory, then reflect on the justification of the Award.

Alexy makes distinction between internal and external justification, the former deals with the logical subsumption of so-called 'legal syllogism', and the latter concerns the correctness of the premises used in the process of internal justification.[11] The external justification can in turn be classified into six groups: statute, dogmatics, precedent, reason, facts and special legal arguments.[12]

Alexy further elucidates six different forms of argument which constitute the canons of interpretation and their role in legal discourse. Semantic argument justifies an interpretation from a linguistic perspective if an assertion can be validate semantically,[13] i.e. a justification can be defined

---

8) Alexy, *ibid*, at 8-9.
9) MacCormick, N., *'Legal Reasoning and Legal Theory'*, 1978, at 229.
10) Alexy, *ibid*, at 230.
11) Alexy, *ibid*, at 221, 230.
12) *Ibid*, at 232.

within the denotation and connotation of a word.

Genetic argument give rise to a fictitious legislator, as Kelsen argued,[14] whose intention can be deduced to justify an interpretation.[15]

Historical argument resorts to facts concerning the history of a particular solution of the legal problem to sustain or oppose some interpretative outcomes.[16] Comparative argument refers to the legal state of affairs of another society and can be changed into a historical one.[17]

Systematic argument refers to a contradiction between norms. If an interpretation which can not be validated by any other norms contradicts a norm, it must be abandoned as a valid one.[18] Teleological argument or objective-teleological include systematic-teleological argument justifies interpretation by way of rational ends, means, aims and goals prescribed in the legal order. These ends are not a matter of empirical findings but a normative determinations, and thus differs from the genetic argument where an intention of historical legislator can be traced.[19] But the teleological argument can turn into a reasoning from universal principles, such as 'The dignity of man should be respected', while a borderline case arises from competing legitimate goods.[20]

Alexy claims that a full analysis of argument forms would produced something analogus to the grammar of language in legal discourses. But these forms are not strict logical rules which give the conditions to be followed up, but more than mere guidelines for raising questions.[21]

---

13) Ibid, at 235.
14) Kelsen, H., 'The Pure Theory of Law', translated by Max Knight, 1967, at 285.
15) Alexy, ibid, at 236.
16) Ibid, at 239.
17) Ibid, at 239.
18) Ibid, at 240.
19) Ibid, at 240-241.
20) Ibid, at 243.
21) Ibid, at 245.

## Critique on the Reasoning of the Award

### The Act of Displaying Election Manual

The Award held that the candidate displayed the Election Manual to the athletes violated Article 3, sixth paragraph of the Rules of Conduct.

The heading of Article 3 of the Rules of Conduct 'PROMOTION OF THE CANDIDATURE DURING THE OLYMPIC GAMES' sets the confinement of interpretation, while interpreting any words prescribed in the paragraphs should conform to this limit, that is, any behaviour that is helpful to promote the candidature would fall into the meaning of the text. Let's suppose a fictitious factual situation, a candidate shows Article 61 of the Olympic Charter and tells the athlete: 'You can appeal to the CAS if you dispute on the your score of competition during the Olympic Games.' Does this behaviour constitute a violation of the Rules of Conduct? Apparently, this behaviour just iterates a matter of status quo and is irrelevant to the promotion of candidature.

Moreover, Article 3, fourth paragraph of the Rules of Conduct allows the candidate produces a document at his own expense, so any document that can be construe to be a promotion of candidature shall not those that produced or provided by IOC. This observation can be ascertained by referring to Article 4, second paragraph of the Rules of Conduct which stated: 'The IOC... will also publish and distribute the IOC Athletes' Commission Election Manual...'. What is the difference between showing a copy of Election Manual distributed by IOC and an electric one installed in a digital apparatus by a candidate? Is there any difference if a candidate substitute the electric Election Manual for a written one? To interpret an act of showing the document of IOC violated the the Rules of Conduct will constitute a systematic-contradiction to the rule both mentioned above.

It is evidently that the reasoning of the Award can not be sustained either semantically or systematically. In addition, at least to the extend of the interaction between different rules, what kind of behaviour would fall into the category of 'promotion of candidature' has not been so self-evident even for a native English speaker, nor of course for a non-native one.

### Informing of a Complimentary Umbrella

The Award found that the indication to the athletes that they would be given a complimentary umbrella if they voted, constitutes an inducement to cause athletes to take part in the vote, and thus was contrary to Article 3, seventh paragraph of the Rules of Conduct: 'No form of material (such as t-shirt, caps, pictures, etc.) or financial inducement to vote for a candidate or take part in the vote is permitted.'

The semantic meaning and purpose of this regulation evidently prohibits those material or financial inducement provided by the candidate or his/her supporters. Suppose a state-run political election, the government announced it will give any citizen a notebook to encourage taking part in the vote, does a candidate who notifies the voter this information be guilty of bribe? It will be absurd to attain such a conclusion.

This reasoning of the Award is also apparently committed an mistake semantically and teleologically.

### The Credibility of a Competing Candidate

The reasoning of the third dispute primarily concerned the credibility of witness, then turn out to be a question about the form of argument. The panel accepted the testimony of two Zimbabwe witnesses, one of them would be elected after Mr Chu's withdrawal, another is Chef de Mission at the London OG of the National Olympic Committee of Zimbabwe, and found that Mr Chu presented in a restricted area to promote his candidature that violated Article 3, second paragraph of the Rules of Conduct.

An officer of IOC Sports Department who was summoned to testify stated that she had met the candidate in the restricted area but only before the map defining it had been circulated; but after that, she had never seen him campaigning in that restricted area. Except the two witnesses at stake, there had no evidence to prove the facts accused.

Section 1, Article 26 of Swiss Rules of International Arbitration stated: 'The arbitral trubunal shall determine the admissibility, relevance, materiality and weigh of the evidence offered.' It is a common evidential principle that evidence should be excluded if its probative value was outweighed by its prejudicial effect, as Rule 403 of U.S. Federal Rules Of Evidence of 2013 stated: 'The court may exclude relevant evidence if its probative value is substantially outweighed by a danger of one or more of the following: unfair prejudice...'. Even though the panel has full power to review the fact and the law,[22] it should adhere to such evidential principle.

The credibility problem of evidence was well known by a philosopher like Gadamer: 'In the administration of justice, it is the case of the witness, at least in certain case, is ask questions of which the witness does not know the purpose. In some cases, the evidential value of an assertion that a witness make rests solely on the fact that it cannot be desired by the witness to be either defending or incriminating the person charged, because the witness does not comprehend the context that has to be clarified.'[23] The evidential principle of non-prejudice seems to be true for a non-legal expert and laymen.

Although the evidential rules did not be promulgated expressly in the Code of Sports-Related *Arbitration*, but a reasoning against a universally accepted legal rule would still constitute an error of systematic argument.

It is ironic when the Award concluded with a praise of the appellant's character of integrity : 'The Panel would add that, in its view, Mr Chu was guilty of excessive zeal rather than of a desire to cheat. His actions were

---

22) R.57 of the Code of Sports-Related Arbitration.
23) Gadamer, Hans-Georg, "*Language and Understanding*', translated by Richard E. Palmer, in '*The Gadamer Reader*', edited by Richard E. Palmer, 2007, at 103-104.

overt, not covert. His breach of election rules should not be equated to dishonesty. His reputation and integrity as a sportsman remains untarnished.' But should the purpose of Rules of Conduct is to punish an honest person with eagerness to service the athletic community rather than one who has intentionally tried to take advantage from violating the campaigning rules? If so, the rules encouraging people to compete will unfortunately lead to the opposite side.


## Conclusion

CAS has won the high prestige through arbitrating disputes arising from sporting arena since its establishment in 1984. A lot of awards have accumulated for further research. In this respect, the rules of legal methodology should be used as a helpful tool to examine the plausibility of the reasoning of CAS's awards. To merge legal reasoning into a context of rational discourses is a routine task for any jurist or lawyer. It is the same in the realm of sports law. The forms of legal argument server as criteria for meaningful legal discourses would refrain legal reasoning from arbitrary and unilateral casuistry, unveil the implicit unreasonable presumption, and thus keep a sound procedural guarantee for mutual discussion and understanding,

The award of Mu-Yen Chu Case posed many methodological problems which deserves to detailed discussion. It tacitly enlarged the denotation of the concepts of the Rules of Conduct, and left the purpose and accurate semantic meaning of them unexplained. If the purpose and meaning of the Rules of Conduct had made clear, the contradiction of the reasoning would emerge in evident.

This article surveys the reasons of the Award from an interpretative point of view which based upon the theory of legal reasoning and methodology. The analysis and critique of the courts' decisions has long been a flourishing academic tradition both in civil law and common law system, it would be so by a critical investigating into the international sports law which has been embodied through the awards of CAS.

## References

Alexy, R., 'A Theory of Legal Argumentation: The Theory of Rational Discourse as Theory of Legal Justification', translated by Ruth Adler and Neil MacCormick (Oxford, 1989).

Bleicher, J., 'Contemporary Hermeneutics: Hermeneutics as Method, Philosophy and Critique' (Routledeg & Kegan Paul, 1980).

Gadamer, Hans-Georg, 'The Gadamer Reader: The Bouquet of Later Writings', edited by Richard E. Palmer (Northwestern, 2007).

Kelsen, H., 'The Pure Theory of Law', translated by Max Knight (California, 1967).

MacCormick, N., 'Legal Reasoning and Legal Theory' (Oxford, 1978).

Stone, J., 'Legal System and Lawyer's Reasonings' (Stanford, 1964).

Wittgenstein, L., 'Tractatus Lofico-philosophicus', translated by Ogden (Barnes & Nobel, 2003).

# The Sports Broadcasting Act of 1961 and its Effects on Competitive Balance in the National Football League*

MATTHEW J. MITTEN** · AARON HERNANDEZ***

*The Sports Broadcasting Act of 1961 ("SBA") exempts a professional sports league's collective sale of its member clubs' television rights to free "over-the-air" national and regional broadcasters from antitrust challenges. By providing limited antitrust immunity, the SBA facilitated the centralized sale of television rights by professional sports leagues during a critical period in which network television rights fees were increasing significantly and resulting revenue disparities threatened league-wide competitive balance if clubs individually sold these rights and retained the revenues. Since the SBA was enacted, the NFL has collectively and exclusively sold all of its clubs' television rights and distributed the net revenues on a pro rata basis to each club, an important form of horizontal revenue sharing among league clubs. Empirical analysis shows a positive correlation between NFL clubs' pro rata sharing of collectively sold television rights and competitive balance within the NFL from 1962-2012.*

Key word: Sports Broadcasting Act of 1961, collective sale of television rights, horizontal revenue sharing, competitive balance

---

\* This article is based on a prior article by the same authors titled "The Sports Broadcasting Act of 1961: A Comparative Analysis of its Effects on Competitive Balance in the NFL and NCAA Division I FBS Football," which will be published in Volume 39, Issue 3 of the Ohio Northern University Law Review. We are pleased to contribute this article as part of the series of sports law papers celebrating Professor Kee Young Yeun's 60th birthday, and wish him good health and much happiness.

\*\* Professor of Law and Director, National Sports Law Institute and LL.M. in Sports Law Program for Foreign Lawyers, Marquette University Law School.

## Introduction***

$O$ne of the relatively few United States sports-specific statutes[1] enacted by Congress or a state legislature is the Sports Broadcasting Act of 1961 ("SBA"),[2] which exempts a professional sports league's collective sale of its member clubs' television rights to free "over-the-air" national and regional broadcasters[3] from antitrust challenges. This federal legislation was enacted in response to a 1953 United States Department of Justice antitrust suit challenging National Football League (NFL) bylaws prohibiting league clubs from televising games in other clubs' home territories,[4] which resulted in a 1961 federal district court ruling that prohibited the NFL from collectively selling its clubs' television rights.[5] Since the SBA statute was enacted, the NFL has collectively and exclusively sold all of its clubs' television rights and distributed the net revenues on a pro rata basis to each club. This form of horizontal revenue sharing among league clubs is positively correlated to a significant degree of on-field competitive balance among NFL clubs from 1962-2012. In addition, the NFL's successful pro rata revenue sharing model, which was significantly facilitated by the SBA, is the genesis of the currently common practice of other North American major professional sports leagues (e.g., Major League Baseball ("MLB"), the National Basketball Association ("NBA"), and the National Hockey League ("NHL")) to centrally

---

*** B.BA, University of Notre Dame 2010; J.D., Marquette University Law School 2013.

1) There are relatively few sport-specific federal statutes; for example, the Ted Stevens Olympic and Amateur Sports Act, 36 U.S.C. §220501, et seq; Sports Agent Responsibility Trust Act, 15 U.S.C. §§7801 et seq.; Sports Broadcasting Act of 1961, 15 U.S.C. §§1291 et seq.; Equity in Athletics Disclosure Act, 20 U.S.C. §1092; Professional and Amateur Sports Protection Act (PASPA), 28 U.S.C. §3701, et seq; the Bribery in Sporting Contests Act, 18 U.S.C §224; Professional Boxing Safety Act of 1996, 15 U.S.C. §§6301 et seq.; Muhammad Ali Boxing Reform Act, 15 U.S.C. §6307a-h ; and the Curt Flood Act of 1998, 15 U.S.C. §26b. Similarly, there are only a few sport-specific state statutes, which include athlete agent statutes (e.g., ORC 4771.01), youth sports concussion statutes (e.g., ORC 3707.511)and some laws limiting or establishing tort liability standards (e.g., Illinois Baseball Facility Liability Act, 745 ILCS §38/10).

2) 15 USC §1291 et seq.

3) See supra notes 25-27 and accompanying text.

4) US v NFL, 116 F. Supp. 319 (E.D. Pa. 1953).

5) US v NFL, 196 F. Supp. 445 (E.D. Pa. 1961).

sell or license all or part of their respective member clubs' television, trademark, and Internet rights and to distribute the revenues pro rata as means of promoting competitive balance.[6]

Section II of this Article briefly describes the federal government's antitrust litigation against the NFL arising out of its restrictions on the telecasting of its clubs' games and summarizes the scope of the SBA's antitrust exemption, legislative history, and objectives, which provides a limited antitrust exemption for collective sale of television rights by a professional sports league.[7] Section III surveys recent economic literature concerning the effects of revenue sharing on competitive balance within a professional sports league and evaluates the SBA's impact on competitive balance among NFL clubs. Initially, we compare NFL clubs' respective playoff appearances and league championships from 1953-1961 (eight years prior to enactment of the SBA when league clubs sold television rights independently and retained the individual revenues) with 1962-1970 (a corresponding period during which the league sold all television rights collectively and distributed their revenues pro rata). Next, we take a broader look at the overall degree of competitive balance in the NFL from 1962-2012, a fifty-year period during which the league's collective sale of television rights has been its largest single source of revenue sharing among its clubs.

---

6) Financial stability of their respective clubs and competitive balance within major professional sports leagues outside of the U.S. also may be enhanced by collectively selling league clubs' television rights and sharing the revenues. For example, Miguel Cardenal, Spain's Secretary for Sport, has stated that a new Spanish law will require La Liga soccer clubs "to negotiate the sale of television rights collectively as in other major European leagues." Currently, individual clubs individually sell their television rights, with Real Madrid and Barcelona, the two most popular clubs, splitting approximately half of the annual television revenues. Cardenal said the clubs would have the freedom to decide how the revenues are distributed, but he indicated "it would be natural to expect the gap between those who get the most and those who get the least to narrow." *Spain Planning New Law To Force Collective Bargaining For TV Revenue*, SportsBusiness Daily Global, April 19, 2013.

7) 15 USC §1291. The Act also immunizes the collective sale of television rights by the National Basketball League, National Hockey League, and Major League Baseball from antitrust liability. *Id.*

## Government Antitrust Litigation Leading to Passage of Sports Broadcasting Act of 1961

Prior to the enactment of the SBA, NFL clubs individually sold television broadcast rights to their respective home games and retained the revenues. To protect against reduction of a club's home game ticket sales and reduction of local viewership of its televised home or away games, Article X of the NFL bylaws prohibited each club from permitting its games to be telecast into another club's home territory (which encompasses a 75 mile radius from the city where it was located) without that club's consent (which generally was not given).[8] Thus, Article X effectively permitted only the local NFL club's games to be telecast within its home territory, thereby preventing local viewers from watching televised NFL games in which the local team was not playing.

In *United States v. National Football League*("*NFL I*"),[9] a 1953 case that is the only sports industry antitrust suit ever filed by the federal government, the Department of Justice alleged that Article X is an agreement that unreasonably restrains trade in the market for televised NFL games in violation of §1 of the Sherman Act[10] and sought injunctive relief against the NFL's enforcement of this rule. The federal district court initially determined that this bylaw constitutes an agreement among NFL clubs that affects interstate trade, which is subject to judicial scrutiny under §1. It characterized the NFL's telecasting restrictions as "a clear case of allocating marketing territories among competitors, which is a practice generally held illegal under the anti-trust laws,"[11] but recognized that "[p]rofessional football is a unique type of business."[12]

The court explained:

---

8) The NFL also prohibited a club's home game from being broadcast within its home market unless it was sold out.
9) 116 F. Supp. 319 (E.D. Pa. 1953).
10) 15 U.S.C. §1.
11) 116 F. Supp. at 322.
12) *Id.* at 323.

Professional teams in a league, however, must not compete too well with each other, in a business way. On the playing field, of course, they must compete as hard as they can all the time. But it is not necessary and indeed it is unwise for all the teams to compete as hard as they can against each other in a business way. If all the teams should compete as hard as they can in a business way, the stronger teams would be likely to drive the weaker ones into financial failure. If this should happen not only would the weaker teams fail, but eventually the whole league, both the weaker and the stronger teams, would fail, because without a league no team can operate profitably....

The winning teams usually are the wealthier ones and unless restricted by artificial rules the rich get richer and the poor get poorer ... Thus, the net effects of allowing unrestricted business competition among the clubs are likely to be, first, the creation of greater and greater, inequalities in the strength of the teams; second the weaker teams being driven out of business; and, third, the destruction of the entire League.[13]

Because ticket sales constituted the largest component of NFL clubs' revenues in the early 1950s, the court concluded that "[r]easonable protection of home game attendance is essential to the very existence of the individual clubs, without which there can be no League and no professional football as we know it today."[14] It ruled that Article X's prohibition against the telecasting of outside games into the home territories of other NFL clubs when they are playing at home is a reasonable restriction that it necessary to maintain the financial viability of the clubs and has the procompetitive effect of preserving the NFL's existence. However, the court held that the bylaw's prohibition against the simultaneous telecasting of an outside game

---

13) *Id.* at 323-324.
14) *Id.* at 325.

into a local NFL club's home territory when its away game is telecast would not adversely affect attendance at NFL games and, therefore, was an unreasonable restraint.[15] It enjoined the NFL and its clubs from restricting the sale of television rights, although restricting the telecast of outside games into a club's home territory during a home game is permissible.

In 1961, the NFL entered into a contract with the Columbia Broadcasting System (CBS) that granted CBS the exclusive right to televise all league games for two years for a $4,650,000 annual license fee, which would be distributed pro rata to its member clubs. This agreement gave CBS the sole discretion to determine which NFL games to televise and their respective broadcast areas. This was the first time the NFL collectively sold its clubs' television rights to their home games, which previously had been individually sold by each NFL club. The NFL petitioned the court for an interpretation of the final judgment resolving the 1953 antitrust litigation that would validate its television contract with CBS, which was opposed by the Department of Justice.

On July 20, 1961, in *United States v. National Football League* ("*NFL II*"),[16] the court ruled that the contract between the NFL and CBS is the product of an agreement between NFL clubs to eliminate economic competition among themselves for the sale of television rights to their home games and violated its 1953 injunction prohibiting them from agreeing to restrict the geographical areas into which NFL games will be telecast except within a club's home territory when it is playing a home game. Finding that the contract gave CBS the right and discretion to determine which games will be telecast and where, the same court concluded:

> Clearly this provision restricts the individual clubs from determining 'the areas within which * * * telecasts of games

---

15) *Id.* at 326-327. For the same reason, the court ruled that Article X's prohibition against radio broadcasts of outside games into a club's home territories during its home games or telecast away games also unreasonably restrained trade. *Id.* at 327.

16) 196 F. Supp. 445 (E.D. 1961).

> \* \* \* may be made \* \* \*,' since defendants have by their contract given to CBS the power to determine which games shall be telecast and where the games shall be televised. I am therefore obliged to construe the Final Judgment as prohibiting the execution and performance of [this] contract . . .[17]

*NFL II* prohibited the NFL from collectively selling its clubs' television rights, an important and increasing source of league gross revenues that had risen from $1,239,000 in 1953 to $3,510,000 in 1961,[18] and distributing the net proceeds on a pro rata basis to each club, a form of revenue sharing to equalize the widely disparate value of each club's television contract. This judicial ruling had the potential to diminish league-wide competitive balance and to weaken the financial stability of some NFL clubs (particularly those in very small markets such as Green Bay, Wisconsin), adverse effects that threatened the NFL's long-term survival and were recognized by the court in *NFL I*. Moreover, although the American Football League, a competing professional football league, and the NBA collectively sold their member clubs' television rights without antitrust challenge by the Department of Justice, *NFL II* precluded the NFL from doing so.

Congress swiftly overruled *NFL II* by enacting the SBA in September of 1961.[19] It is ironic that is the federal government's only sports industry antitrust suit led to Congressional enactment of one of the relatively few sports-specific federal laws in existence. The SBA immunizes from antitrust challenge a professional football, baseball, basketball, or hockey league's collective sale or transfer of "all or any part of the rights of such league's

---

17) *Id.* at 447.
18) ABA Section of Antitrust Law, *Federal Statutory Exemptions From Antitrust Law* at 219 (2007).
19) 15 U.S.C. § 1291, et seq. Congress amended the SBA in 1966 to permit the NFL and AFL to merge. 15 U.S.C. § 1291 (antitrust law "shall not apply to a joint agreement by which the member clubs of two or more professional football leagues ... combine their operations in [an] expanded single league ... if such agreement increases rather than decreases the number of professional football clubs so operating, and the provisions of which are directly relevant thereto.").

member clubs in the sponsored telecasting of [their] games."[20] The SBA's purpose is to "enable the member clubs . . . to pool their separate rights in the sponsored broadcasting of their games and to permit the league to sell the resulting package of pooled rights to a purchaser, such as a television network, without violating the antitrust laws."[21] However, the SBA does not require these revenues to be shared among league clubs on a pro rata or any other basis.

The SBA's legislative history evidences Congressional recognition that "a league needs the power to make 'package' sales of the television rights of its member clubs to assure the weaker clubs of the league continuing television income and television coverage on a basis of substantial equality with the stronger clubs. Such income and coverage … often mark the difference between profitable and losing operations."[22] During hearings before the Antitrust Subcommittee concerning this legislation, Joe Foss, the American Football League commissioner, testified that "television revenues are such a significant part of the overall financial success of a professional football team that it is necessary to prevent too great disparity in the television income of the various clubs," which "requires the pooling of revenues and a package contract."[23] Because "the structure of the league would become impaired and its continued operation imperiled" if weaker clubs floundered financially, the Antitrust Subcommittee concluded that "the public interest in viewing professional league sports warrants some accommodation of antitrust principles to avoid these consequences."[24]

---

20) 15 U.S.C. § 1291.

21) S. Rep. No. 1087, 87th Cong., 1$^{st}$ Sess., at 1 (1961).

22) H. R. Rep. No. 1178, 87th Cong., 1$^{st}$ Sess., at 1 (1961) ("H. R. Rep."). For an argument that the SBA lacks any current procompetitive economic justifications from the perspective of consumers, see Federal Statutory Exemptions From Antitrust Law, supra note 19, at 238-240.

23) H. R. Rep., supra note 23, at 3.

24) *Id.* As one court observed, "The purpose of the SBA, as opposed to the purpose of the Sherman Act itself, was not to promote competition. It was to establish the legality of a practice which tends to restrain competition, package sales to the networks." *Chicago Prof 'l Sports Limited Partnership v. NBA(Bulls I)*, 754 F. Supp. 1336, 1352 (N.D. Ill. 1991), *aff 'd*, 961 F.2d 667 (7$^{th}$Cir. 1992).

Therefore, Congress provided professional football, baseball, basketball, and hockey leagues with an antitrust exemption to enable the sharing of television broadcast revenues among league clubs, which has contributed to each league's financial viability and competitive balance. In recognition of the unique nature of a professional sports league and the economic interdependence of its clubs, MLB, NBA, NFL, and NHL pooled rights telecasting contracts are immunized from antitrust scrutiny, which in turn has facilitated the prevailing practice of pro rata revenue sharing to enable all clubs to receive an equal share of these collectively generated revenues.[25]

However, the SBA's antitrust exemption provides immunity only for a professional sports league's collective sale of "sponsored telecasting" rights,[26] which has been narrowly interpreted by courts as not including subscription television provided via cable networks or satellite distributors[27] in order to ensure the continuing availability of free national and local over-the-air telecasting of league games.[28] Consistent with *NFL I*, it does not provide

---

25) "National TV contracts in all sports uniformly involve equal sharing of such revenues by all league teams (with some negotiated, temporary exclusions for expansion franchises). In a one-team-one vote environment, equal sharing is more or less guaranteed because the national contract can be approved only if there is a virtual consensus among league teams. Weak-drawing teams can block unequal sharing proposals by refusing to permit televising of them involving them and the strong-drawing teams." Rodney Fort and James Quirk, *Cross-subsidization, Incentives, and Outcomes in Professional Team Sports Leagues*, 32 J. Econ. Literature 1265, 1291 (Sept. 1995). "Strong-drawing teams, which contribute more audience than weak-drawing teams, certainly are subsidizing weak-drawing teams because each is receiving an equal share of national TV revenues." *Id.*

26) The legislative history states that the SBA's antitrust exemption "does not apply to closed circuit or subscription television." H. R. Rep., *supra* note 23, at 5.

27) See, e.g., *Shaw v. Dallas Cowboys Football Club, Inc.*, 172 F.3d 299, 300 (3d Cir. 1999) (package sale of television broadcast rights to satellite distributor not "sponsored telecasting" immune from antitrust scrutiny); *Chicago Prof 'l Sports Ltd. Partnership v. NBA (Bulls III)*, 808 F. Supp. 646, 650 (N.D. Ill. 1992) ("sponsored telecasting" encompasses only "free television," such as "national network and local over-the-air broadcasting provided at no direct cost to viewers," not league's pooled television rights contract with cable television programming service).

28) However, an increasing number of professional sports league game packages are collectively sold to cable television networks such as ESPN or to satellite television providers. See, e.g., Matthew Futterman, *NFL, DirecTV Extend Pact in $4 Billion Deal*

antitrust immunity for any joint agreement that prohibits a purchaser of a league's pooled television rights from telecasting the games in a particular area "except within the home territory of a member club of the league on a day when such club is playing a game at home."[29] Thus, prohibiting telecasts of other league games into a club's home territory when it has a home game does not violate the antitrust laws; whereas, any other collective limits on the geographical scope of broadcasts of league games are subject to antitrust challenge.

## The Relationship Between Competitive Balance, Revenue Sharing, and the SBA

Professional sports leagues such as the NFL produce a unique product (i.e., games with an uncertain outcome) that necessarily requires competitive balance among the opposing teams, which is distinct from other forms of entertainment such as movies and theater that always have the same outcome or ending. Rodney Fort and James Quirk, two prominent sports economists, have noted that "[s]ports leagues are in the business of selling competition on the playing field" and "need to establish a degree of competitive balance on the field that is acceptable to fans."[30] Another sports economist, Allen Sanderson, observes that "producing and maintaining competitive balance is of paramount importance."[31] "Although there are some disagreements and ongoing debates about the extent of the problem and the efficacy of alternative correctives," he states "there is an arguable consensus about the desirability of [competitive] balance and the role that the distribution of financial resources plays in creating and maintaining it."[32]

---

at http://online.wsj.com/article/SB123786503490122053.html (last visited May 13, 2013).

29) 15 U.S.C. § 1292.

30) Fort and Quirk, supra note 26, at 1265.

31) Allen R. Sanderson, *The Many Dimensions of Competitive Balance*, 3 J. Sports Economics 204, 205 (May 2002) See also Stephan Kesenne, *Revenue Sharing and Competitive Balance in Professional Team Sports*, 1 J. Sports Economics 56, 56 (Feb. 2000) (Competitive balance "is an important element affecting public interest and the financial health of the industry of professional team sports.").

Sports law professor Gary Roberts points out that "competitive balance" has the dual meaning of "parity" (i.e., the extent to which all teams playing at the same level are able to play close and exciting games during a season of competition) and "potential to change" (i.e., teams' ability to improve their relative performance in terms of on-field success vis-a-vis other teams over time).[33] Focusing on the second part of this definition, we consider "what has happened to competitive balance over time or as a result of changes in the business practices of pro sports leagues."[34] In particular, we examine the correlation between the NFL's collective sale of television rights and pro rata distribution of the revenues to its clubs, a business practice the NFL adopted soon after Congressional enactment of the SBA and continues to utilize, and league-wide competitive balance.[35] As a rough means of determining the existence of such a correlation,[36] we have compiled and compared information

---

32) Sanderson, supra note 32, at 205.

33) Gary R. Roberts, *The NCAA, Antitrust, and Consumer Welfare*, 79 Tul. L. Rev. 2631, 2664-2665 (1996).

34) Rodney Fort and Joel Maxcy, *"Competitive Balance in Sports Leagues: An Introduction,"* 4 J. Sports Economics 154, 155 (May 2003).

35) We recognize that the NFL has derived very substantial revenues in recent years from the collective sale of its clubs' television rights to cable networks such as ESPN, which are not immunized from antitrust challenge by the SBA, and that the "SBA appears to have been rendered largely obsolete by changing economic circumstances and changing judicial application of antitrust law." Federal Statutory Exemptions From Antitrust Law, supra note 19, at 217. Nevertheless, "The act did facilitate the introduction of comprehensive sharing of broadcast revenue among all the teams in professional football. That, in turn, may have facilitated greater sales of programming by reducing the transaction costs of revenue sharing. The sharing of this revenue as it has grown in importance has made it possible for teams such as those in Pittsburgh, Green Bay, and Buffalo, with relatively small home markets to survive and achieve parity with teams based in the largest markets." Id. at 234.

36) Sanderson, supra note 32, at 223. ("Commonly employed yardsticks" to measure competitive balance within a professional sports league include "the distribution of championships, the correlation between pay and performance or winning percentage and market size, and the variance of won-lost percentages."). We have included teams making the playoffs because the NFL's league champion (i.e., the winner of the Super Bowl) is determined by a playoff system rather than by the team achieving the most regular season victories. See Fort and Quirk, supra note 26, at 1269 (observing that a championship playoff system increases the number of "'successful' teams from a single champion to all teams qualifying for the playoffs").

regarding NFL clubs' respective playoff appearances and league championships from 1953-1961 (when NFL clubs individually sold television rights and retained the revenues) and 1962-1970 (a corresponding period during which the NFL collectively sold its clubs' television rights and distributed their revenues pro rata) along with corresponding data from 1962-2012. Admittedly, this is an imprecise measure because proving the existence of a causal relationship between the NFL's collective sale of television rights and pro rata revenue distribution, which could not lawfully be done prior to passage of the SBA, and competitive balance with mathematical precision would require sophisticated economic analysis that considers and quantifies the effects of other relevant variables.[37] Nevertheless, we believe it is sufficiently accurate to show this correlation and supports an inference that the SBA has been a significant contributing factor.

Sports economist Stephan Kesenne observes that the degree of competitive balance in a professional sports league "depends primarily on the distribution of playing talent among teams"[38] and explains how revenue sharing among clubs can improve competitive balance. In general, an individual club's revenues are positively correlated with the success of its on-field performance (i.e., number or percentage of games won), which largely depends on the quality of its players relative to those of other clubs (i.e., teams with better players usually win more games during the season than those with inferior players).[39] In a competitive labor market, a profit- maximizing club will equate its aggregate player salaries with the marginal revenue of its players'

---

37) For example, our analysis does not consider the effects of other current forms of revenue sharing (e.g., gate receipts, trademarked merchandise royalties), labor market restraints (e.g., draft, hard salary cap, free agency restrictions, and a ban on the cash sale of players), and other relevant variables (e.g., unbalanced scheduling pursuant to which clubs with more wins and playoff success are given a more difficult schedule for the next season) on the degree of competitive balance in the NFL. The NFL formed NFL Properties in 1963 to collectively license third parties to sell merchandise such as clothing and headwear bearing the trademarks of its clubs. The NFL draft began in 1936, cash sales of players have been banned since the early 1960s, free agency restrictions have existed since 1963, and there has been a "hard" salary cap since 1994.
38) Kesenne, supra note 32, at 56.
39) *Id.* at 57-59.

talent.[40] Because a club's market size is the primary factor that determines its revenue-generating potential,[41] "the level of the demand for playing talent by the big clubs is higher because of their larger market size."[42] Absent any revenue sharing, large market clubs will have a larger amount of aggregate player talent because they can afford higher player salaries, which will have corresponding adverse effects on competitive balance among league clubs, particularly those in the smallest markets.

Kesenne observes that a club's "incentive to buy extra playing talent is less if the marginal revenue of the playing talent has to be shared with other clubs in the league," and it has been "generally accepted that revenue sharing does not affect the competitive balance in a league if clubs are profit maximizers," which is based on the assumption that each club's falling demand curve for the best players remains the same.[43] However, he notes that "the downward shifts of the demand curves will leave the distribution of playing talent among clubs unaffected only if the size of these shifts at the market equilibrium point are the same for all clubs."[44] In reality, the marginal revenue of aggregate player talent differs for each league club because its respective market size varies; therefore, "the downward shift of the labor demand function, due to revenue sharing, is different for each club" and "is larger for the big clubs [which] will reduce their demand for playing talent more than the small clubs."[45] In other words, because revenue sharing reduces large market clubs' demand for high quality player talent and simultaneously increases small market clubs' demand (by providing increased revenues to attract better, higher-paid players in an effort to increase their quality of play, number of wins, and total revenues), it results in "a more equal distribution of playing talent among the big and small clubs."[46]

---

40) *Id.* at 59.
41) A club's on-field success, closeness of its games, and quality of its opponent (all of which are preferred by its fans) also affect its revenue-generating potential. *Id.* at 57-58.
42) *Id.* at 60.
43) *Id.* at 60.
44) *Id.* at 60.
45) *Id.* at 61.
46) *Id.*

Relying on empirical evidence indicating that North American major professional sports league clubs seek to win games rather than merely maximizing profits (i.e., at least to some degree, clubs are willing to forego profits for wins), other more recent economic research also demonstrates that revenue sharing among league clubs may increase competitive balance.[47] Sports economists Helmut Dietl, Martin Grossman, and Markus Lang identify a new effect of revenue sharing they call the "sharpening effect," which creates an incentive for weaker clubs to invest in player talent and "proves to be an efficient instrument for improving competitive balance in an unbalanced league."[48] Consistent with Kenesse, they show that revenue sharing has the potential to enhance competitive balance within a professional sports league, but caution that the actual effects of revenue sharing will vary based on league clubs' respective preferences for winning and profitability as well as the impact that an increase in player talent will have on a particular club's marginal revenue.

Observing that "in reality, most [club] owners operate as win-maximizers as long as their budget constraints dictate that it is profitable to do so,"[49] sports economists Evan Totty and Mark Owens analyzed the degree of competitive balance in the NFL (measured by the variation in wins between the best and worst teams each year) based on data from the 1978-2010 seasons.[50] Their research found "no evidence that salary caps improve competitive balance and consistent evidence that revenue sharing does improve competitive balance."[51] They explain:

> This is consistent with economic theory which suggests that
> talent will move to the location for which it generates the

---

47) Helmut M. Dietl, Martin Grossmann, and Markus Lang, *Competitive Balance and Revenue Sharing in Sports Leagues With Utility Maximizing Teams*, 12 J. Sports Economics 284 (2011); Evan S. Totty and Mark F. Owens, *Salary Caps and Competitive Balance in Professional Sports Leagues*, 11 J. For Economic Educators 46 (Fall 2011).
48) Dietl, et. al, supra note 48, at 294.
49) Totty and Owens, supra note 48, at 48.
50) *Id.* at 50. They also analyzed and compared similar data for the NBA and NHL for the same time period.
51) *Id.* at 54.

greatest revenue. This movement is independent of the salary cap, but does depend on the nature of revenue sharing in the league. Thus, revenue sharing plans are more effective at addressing the primary cause for the disparities in competition across teams, the disparities in revenue generation across teams.[52]

By immunizing the collective sale of NFL clubs' television rights from antitrust challenge, the SBA enabled increased revenue sharing among NFL clubs, which contributed to a slight initial increase in league-wide competitive balance in the 8-year period immediately after its 1962 implementation and maintenance during the past 50 years. An analysis of empirical data comparing NFL clubs' respective playoff appearances and league championships from 1953-1961 with 1962-1970 along with an evaluation of the same data from 1962-2012 reflects a positive correlation between NFL clubs' pro rata sharing of television revenues (which currently is the NFL's largest single form of revenue sharing)[53] and league-wide competitive balance.

From 1953-1961, 75% of NFL teams made the playoffs at least once. By comparison, during 1962-1970, the percentage of NFL teams qualifying for the playoffs increased slightly to 77.27%. Moreover, it is remarkable that several NFL expansion teams in smaller markets (e.g., Kansas City, Minneapolis, Oakland) made the playoffs at least once from 1962-1970, while more established teams in larger markets such as the Washington Redskins and Philadelphia Eagles did not make the playoffs during this time. This data shows that the SBA contributed to increased competitive balance among NFL teams soon after its Congressional enactment, thereby furthering its primary objective.

---

52) *Id.*
53) It is estimated that the aggregate value of the NFL's television contracts for the 2012 season was approximately $4.1 billion. WR Hambrecht + Co., The U.S. Professional Sports Market & Franchise Value Report 2012 at 49. [Note to ONU Law Review editors- you can find this publication online by typing in its name, but I'm not sure how to cite it.]

More importantly, the SBA also appears to have facilitated competitive balance within the NFL from 1962-2012 based on an analysis of the number of clubs qualifying for the playoffs. From 1963-1993 (a 30-year period after enactment of the SBA, but prior to the 1994 establishment of the NFL's "hard" salary cap), 95% of NFL clubs (all of them except the St. Louis Cardinals) made the playoffs at least once. By comparison, 100% of current NFL clubs made the playoffs at least once from 1994-2012 and 1962-2012. Thus, pro rata sharing of television revenue sharing among NFL clubs, which began in 1962 and has been occurring continuously since then, seems to be a major impetus for league-wide competitive balance.

The long-term impact of the SBA's incentive for NFL clubs to pool and share television to enhance competitive balance also is evident based on the relative percentages of playoff participation by NFL clubs. From 1962-2012, only four teams, the Dallas Cowboys (60%), Minnesota Vikings (54%), Pittsburgh Steelers (52%), and Baltimore Ravens/former Cleveland Browns (50%) have participated in the NFL playoffs 50% or more of the time. Although the Cowboys made the playoffs 30 times, the club failed to do so 20 times (40%) since 1962. Since 1962 twenty different NFL teams, including several small and mid-market clubs (Buffalo Bills, Green Bay Packers, Indianapolis/Baltimore Colts, Jacksonville Jaguars, Kansas City Chiefs, Miami Dolphins, Minnesota Vikings, Pittsburgh Steelers, San Diego Chargers, and Seattle Seahawks) have appeared in the playoffs at least 30% of the time they have been NFL member clubs. Since 1962 or the time of their existence, all NFL clubs (except the current Cleveland Browns, an expansion team in existence since 1999) have made the playoffs at least 11.3% of the time. Notably, small market clubs such as the Pittsburgh Steelers (49.1%) and the Green Bay Packers (43.4%) made the playoffs more frequently than large market clubs such as the New York Giants (34%), Chicago Bears (28.3%), and New York Jets (26.4%).

The Indianapolis Colts and the Green Bay Packers each made the playoffs twelve times from 1990-2009, which exceeded the total number of playoff appearances by clubs in large markets such as the New England

Patriots (11), New York Giants (9), New York Jets (7), and Chicago Bears (6). With twelve appearances, the Pittsburgh Steelers made the playoffs as many times as the Philadelphia Eagles, whose metropolitan area is much larger. From 2000-2009, the Indianapolis Colts made nine appearances, which equaled the number of times the Dallas Cowboys, Chicago Bears, and Washington Redskins combined in the same time period. In the 1990s the Buffalo Bills's(eight playoff appearances) equaled the combined total of the Chicago Bears (3), New York Giants (3) and New York Jets (7). It is interesting to note that not only has there been a significant degree of overall competitive balance in the NFL since the SBA was enacted, but also that relatively few NFL teams have maintained their dominance by consistently qualifying for the playoffs during the 1990s and 2000s. Some of the most successful teams from the 1990s (e.g., Buffalo Bills, Dallas Cowboys, San Francisco 49ers, Detroit Lions) in terms of playoff appearances did not experience similar success in the next decade; whereas, the reverse was true for teams like the Baltimore Ravens/former Cleveland Browns and Seattle Seahawks, which had considerably more playoff appearances in the 2000s compared to the 1990s. Only two teams, the small-market Pittsburgh Steelers and Green Bay Packers, qualified for the NFL playoffs 60% of the time during both decades.

Eighteen of the current thirty-two NFL clubs (56%) have won the Super Bowl since its inception in 1967 (six years after the SBA was enacted). A small market club, the Pittsburgh Steelers, has won the most Super Bowls with six victories. Despite being in the NFL's smallest market, the Green Bay Packers' four wins ties the New York Giants for the fourth most Super Bowl championships. By comparison, the New York Jets and Chicago Bears, which are located in the leagues' two largest markets respectively, each has won only one Super Bowl.

In summary, the foregoing analysis demonstrates the existence of a significant degree of competitive balance in the NFL from 1962-2012 (including during 1963-1993, before a "hard" salary cap was implemented), as measured by playoff participation and the distribution of Super Bowl championships, which is positively correlated with its clubs' initial pooling and pro rata sharing of television revenues immediately after enactment of the SBA. This statute's antitrust exemption was the catalyst for collective licensing and sale of league clubs' intellectual property rights, which has enabled teams in small television markets to be financially viable and have competitive success on the playing field. As the value of NFL clubs' television rights have skyrocketed, pro rata revenue sharing among league clubs becomes an even more important means of achieving these objectives and enables the NFL to produce a very popular product attractive to consumers, although non-exempted collective sales of television rights to cable networks such as ESPN and satellite distributors such as DirecTV constitute multi-billion dollar components of the overall value of NFL television contracts.[54]

## Conclusion

By providing limited antitrust immunity, the SBA facilitated the centralized sale of television rights by professional sports leagues during a critical period in which network television rights fees were increasing significantly and resulting revenue disparities threatened league-wide competitive balance if clubs individually sold these rights and retained the revenues. This federal statute enabled professional sports league clubs to share national television broadcasting revenues pro rata, a substantial current form of revenue sharing designed to achieve and preserve competitive balance, which is essential to a professional sports league's long term financial viability and survival as a form of entertainment attractive to consumers. The foregoing empirical analysis shows a positive correlation between NFL clubs' pro rata sharing of collectively sold television rights and competitive balance within the NFL, a result that Congress intended the SBA to achieve.

---

54) The NFL Signs TV Deals Worth $27 Million, Forbes, available at
   http://www.forbes.com/sites/kurtbadenhausen/2011/12/14/the-nfl-signs-tv-deals-worth-
   26-billion/ (December 14, 2011). Beginning in 2014, it is estimated that each NFL club
   will receive an annual pro rata share of more than $200 million from the sale of media
   rights, primarily television broadcasting rights.

# References

Statutes and Legislative Materials

H. R. Rep. No. 1178, 87th Cong., 1st Sess., at 1 (1961).

S. Rep. No. 1087, 87th Cong., 1st Sess., at 1 (1961).

Sports Broadcasting Act of 1961, 15 USC §1291 et seq.


Cases

*Chicago Prof 'l Sports Limited Partnership v. NBA (Bulls I)*, 754 F. Supp. 1336, 1352 (N.D. Ill. 1991), *aff 'd*, 961 F.2d 667 (7th Cir. 1992).

*Chicago Prof 'l Sports Ltd. Partnership v. NBA (Bulls III)*, 808 F. Supp. 646, 650 (N.D. Ill. 1992).

*Shaw v. Dallas Cowboys Football Club, Inc.*, 172 F.3d 299, 300 (3d Cir. 1999).

*United States v. Nat'l Football League*, 116 F. Supp. 319 (E.D. Pa. 1953).

*United States v. Nat'l Football League*, 196 F. Supp. 445 (E.D. Pa. 1961).


Secondary Sources

*Spain Planning New Law To Force Collective Bargaining For TV Revenue*, SportsBusiness Daily Global, April 19, 2013.

Allen R. Sanderson, *The Many Dimensions of Competitive Balance*, 3 J. Sports Economics 204, 205 (May 2002).

Evan S. Totty and Mark F. Owens, *Salary Caps and Competitive Balance in Professional Sports Leagues*, 11 J. For Economic Educators 46 (Fall 2011).

Gary R. Roberts, *The NCAA, Antitrust, and Consumer Welfare*, 79 Tul. L. Rev. 2631, 2664-2665 (1996).

Helmut M. Dietl, Martin Grossmann, and Markus Lang, *Competitive Balance and Revenue Sharing in Sports Leagues With Utility Maximizing Teams*, 12 J. Sports Economics 284 (2011).

Kurt Badenhausen, *The NFL Signs TV Deals Worth $27 Million*, Forbes (Dec. 14, 2011), http://www.forbes.com/sites/kurtbadenhausen/2011/12/14/the-nfl-signs-tv-deals-worth-26-billion/.

# The Legal Regime against Doping
# in Major League Baseball

JAMES A.R. NAFZIGER*

*Until 2002 Major League Baseball (MLB) in the United States had taken almost no action to deter or combat the doping of players despite clear evidence of a serious problem of doping, involving even the top players. A series of further revelations by players themselves about the extent of the problem, however, led to congressional hearings and resulting pressures on MLB to take immediate and effective action consistent with the World Anti-Doping Code and in furtherance of the mission of the World Anti-Doping Agency (WADA). The MLB finally seems to have moved in that direction by implementing a Joint Drug Prevention and Treatment Program, but the underlying problem of doping continues. In 2013 the MLB's suspensions of 14 players for doping violations, including superstar Alex Rodriguez, demonstrated the MLB's recognition of the limitations of even rigorous physical testing of players and its need therefore to rely on athlete profiling over time and extrinsic, circumstantial evidence of the use of prohibited substances. This development conforms to trends at the international level, as reflected in decisions of the Court of Arbitration for Sport (CAS). It is difficult for the legal imagination to keep up with scientific ingenuity in devising new performance- enhancing and masking agents. Experience has shown, however, that the rules of a forward-looking, vigorous anti-doping program, if they are fair, can protect the rules of the game.*

**Key word:** Doping, international Olympic Comittee, International Sports Law, Major League Baseball

---

* Thomas B. Stoel Professor of Law and Director of International Programs, Willamette University College of Law (U.S.A.). Professor Nafziger is the Honorary President of the International Association of Sports Law

## Introduction

In honor of Kee-Young Yuen's extraordinary contributions to the growth of sports law, it is fitting to address a core topic with dimensions of domestic, comparative and international law. Baseball, the focus of this essay, is part of the shared culture of Professor Yuen's Korea and this author's United States. But just as Professor Yuen's achievements are broad, so is the global scope and visibility of baseball.

The first World Baseball Classic confirmed that baseball is no longer simply the national pastime of a single country, the United States, where the sport began.[1] It is now thoroughly international. The sport has become a national pastime in several other countries, including Cuba, the Dominican Republic,Japan, Mexico, Nicaragua, Panama, Taiwan, South Korea, and Venezuela. (It is clear from this list that international politics is irrelevant.) Major League Baseball (MLB) rosters in North America are replete with foreign nationals. Foreign teams regularly win the Little League World Series for young people, as in 2013 when Japan's team won. Latin Americans make up 37% of all players under contracts with MLB clubs. In 2006, for example, Venezuela won a Caribbean World Series and Japan won the first World Baseball Classic.

To be sure, the globalization of baseball has been uneven. Sometimes the process has been two steps forward and one step backward. For example, the demise of the Montreal Expos in 2004[2] left MLB with only one

---

1) The first World Baseball Classic, which was intended to be a sort of World Cup in the sport, took place in March 2006. See Tom Verducci, Global Warming, SPORTS ILLUS., Mar. 6, 2006, at 56. Having begun as a triennial event, the Classic is now held every four years. Sixteen national teams compete in the event. In three Classics (2006, 2009, 2013), the following teams have won gold, silver or bronze medals: Cuba, Dominican Republic, Japan, Puerto Rico (with its own team separate from that of the United States), South Korea and Venezuela. A United States team has never placed among the top three teams. It is debatable whether baseball is the national pastime of the United States, but there is no doubt that it is a national pastime. For example, when John Roberts appeared before the Judiciary Committee of the United States Senate for a hearing on his (eventually successful) nomination to become Chief Justice, his opening statement was couched in a baseball metaphor (—Judges are like umpires. Umpires don't make the rules; they apply them.". N.Y. TIMES, Sept. 13, 2005, at A16.

2) See George Vecsey, Take the Renewal, Leave the Memories, N.Y. TIMES, Jan. 13, 2005, at

Canadian franchise, the Toronto Blue Jays, and in 2005 the International Olympic Committee (IOC) dropped baseball as an Olympic sport beginning after the 2008 Games.[3] The process of globalization nevertheless continues apace, as the MLB's anti-doping program demonstrates. Of particular interest was the period of 2002-05, the genesis of the program and the focus of this study.[4]

## Baseball's Doping Crisis

The most significant issue confronting professional baseball has been the use by players of performance-enhancing drugs.[5] During the summer of 2013, Major League Baseball took its most drastic anti-doping action ever by imposing lengthy suspensions of players, ranging from 50 to 211 games. The suspensions have extraterritorial consequences insofar as they are honored by foreign professional leagues, particularly in Japan, South Korea and Taiwan. The longest suspension was imposed against the one of the best-known, and arguably best, player in the MLB, Alex Rodriguez.

All of the suspended players were linked to Biogenetics, an anti-aging clinic in South Florida, which was unquestionably the players' source of performance-enhancing drugs (PEDs) banned by the MLB, mostly testosterone and human growth hormone. None of the suspended players had failed drug testing. Instead, all of the suspensions were based on nonanalytic positive evidence, including documentation and eyewitness accounts related to transactions involving Biogenetics. In the case of Alex Rodriguez, part of the severe suspensions was attributable to his attempt to purchase the evidence against him from Biogenetics and otherwise impede the MLB's investigation

---

D2.

3) See Lynne Zinser, I.O.C. Drops Baseball and Softball, N.Y. TIMES, July 9, 2005, at D1. Softball also was dropped from the Olympic roster, quite likely because of its association with baseball despite their gender-related and other differences. The modern pentathlon was also subject to removal but was retained because of European support for it. The last previous sport to be removed from the IOC list was polo in 1936.

4) This study draws substantially on the author's earlier article, Baseball" Doping Crisis and New Anti-Doping Program, 2006/ 1-2 INT'L SPORTS L.J. 10

5) *See generally* James A.R. Nafziger, International Sports Law 147-64 (2d ed. 2004).

of him.[6]

This dramatic development highlights the MLB's decade-long campaign against doping. This campaign is noteworthy at least in three respects. First, in only a decade it has evolved from baseball's notorious inaction against the use of PEDs to one of the most rigorous anti-doping programs in professional sports. The MLB clearly takes its Joint Drug Prevention and Treatment Program seriously. Second, the substantial evidence against the suspended players dramatized the persistence of the doping problem despite the anti-doping program and the challenge of trying to stay ahead of advancements in the science, technology and business of PEDs. Third, the evidence against the suspended players took the form, not of failed drug tests but of nonanalytic positive evidence indicating the players' involvement in questionable transactions of PEDs.

As early as the late 1980's, the widespread use of steroids, in particular, led to a doping crisis in the sport and irresistible pressures for reform emanating from congressional hearings in the United States on the crisis. As a result, MLB first accepted minimum testing procedures and sanctions against doping in 2002 and then, under continuing public and congressional pressures, rapidly instituted a respectable program of testing and sanctions in 2005. Frontier issues involving difficult-to-detect and undetectable drugs remain to be resolved in the future.[7] What may be particularly significant about baseball's anti-doping program in 2013, known as the Joint Drug Prevention and Treatment Program, is not simply its rapid development under pressure but its growing conformity with the standards and procedures of international sports law—a significant development, given the independent role of player contracts and collective bargaining in professional baseball. This study first summarizes baseball's doping crisis, then discusses

---

6) *See, e.g.,* Tyler Kepner, *A Big Name in the Lineup, but Crossed Off Baseball's List,* N.Y. Times, Aug. 6, 2013, at 1 (summarizing the MLB sanctions—a 65-game suspension in July followed by thirteen 50-game suspensions and the 211-game suspension of Alex Rodriguez in August—and highlighting the specific investigation and suspension of Rodriguez). *See also* Tom Verducci, *Pain Delay,* Sports Illus., Aug. 12, 2013, at 15 (noting the support of players for the MLB's Joint Drug Prevention and Treatment Program and, in the end, a clean, even playing field).

7) *See* James A.R. Nafziger, *Circumstantial Evidence of Doping: BALCO and Beyond,* 16 Marq. Sports L. Rev. 45 (2005).

MLB's response to it and the significance of the response in the context of international sports law and the globalizing process.

It is not entirely clear why the IOC decided to drop baseball as an Olympic sport so soon after it had been added in 1992. The sport's lack of a popular following in many countries may have been a factor.[8] Many other Olympic sports, however, also would fail that test—for example, curling, skeleton, the pentathlon, synchronized swimming, the biathlon, and Greco-Roman wrestling. Moreover, in reducing the breadth and complexity of international competition, the International Olympic Committee (IOC) and international federations (IFs) are divided over the issue of whether to eliminate entire sports or, rather, excessive or redundant events within a particular sport.

Instead, it is likely that baseball's demise as an Olympic sport was attributable to two other factors: the unwillingness of the players, especially the superstars, to participate in the Olympics and other sanctioned competition; and baseball's reputation in the past for turning a blind eye to its doping problem, which involves a widespread use of performance-enhancing steroids. It is true, of course, that other sports such as cycling, swimming, and track and field have been seriously tainted by doping, but their respective sports federations have taken substantial measures to respond to the problem—generally in conformity with international sports law. Unfortunately, the International Baseball Federation, headquartered in Switzerland, has been ineffective in establishing MLB anti-doping measures. In any event it is reasonable to infer from the IOC decision a direct link between MLB noncompliance in the past with international anti-doping standards and baseball's demise in Olympic and related competitions.

Professional baseball's doping crisis came to a head only in the late 1990s. Although the first claims of steroid use date back to the late 1980s,[9] MLB's

---

8) *See* Zinser, *supra* note 3.
9) José Canseco claimed that steroids made their appearance in MLB on September 2, 1985, the day he debuted for the Oakland Athletics. *See* José Canseco, Juiced: Wild Times, Rampant 'Roids, Smash Hits, and How Baseball Got Big 53 (2005). In any case, Canseco was the first prominent baseball player to be publicly accused of using steroids—an accusation leveled in 1988 by Thomas Boswell, the distinguished *Washington Post* sportswriter. *E.g., Baseball Insider*, St. Petersburg Times, Sept. 30,

concerns about substance abuse in that decade centered on criminally prohibited (so-called recreational) drugs, especially cocaine.[10]

In 1983, after four Kansas City Royals players had received jail sentences on cocaine convictions, MLB first proposed comprehensive drug testing. The following year players and franchise owners reached agreement on for-cause testing whereby a player could be tested if a club claimed to have reasonable cause to believe the player was using drugs. Unfortunately the agreement died in 1985 because the Major League Baseball Players Association, the players union, refused to cooperate in implementing it. During the same year, however, MLB Commissioner Peter Ueberroth announced his intention to establish a mandatory testing program for all minor league players and major league officials.

In 1986 a second scandal resulted from the conviction of a Pittsburgh cocaine dealer who had found a market among players on the Pittsburgh Pirates, the local MLB franchise team. The bad publicity generated by this scandal led Commissioner Ueberroth to suspend eleven team members conditionally for cocaine use. The incident also prompted the Commissioner to propose a program under which major league players would be tested up to four times a year for cocaine, heroin, marijuana, and morphine, without a penalty for a first-time positive test. Implementation was stalled, however, when an arbitrator struck down clauses in players' contracts that provided for random drug testing because they had not been negotiated in the process of collective bargaining between MLB and the players union. It had again delayed efforts to respond to baseball's growing drug problem. The scourge of drug abuse continued unabated.

During the next decade the use of anabolic steroids, which had barely been apparent in baseball, began to grow. Some of these synthetic agents, which mimic testosterone and other hormones, have the metabolic effect of boosting the production of muscle mass and thereby the strength of batters.[11]

---

1998, at 4C.

10) Lee Jenkins et al., *Another Chance for Baseball to Settle Its Score With Drugs*, N.Y. Times, Dec. 12, 2004, § 8, at 1 (from which the history of doping in baseball, as follows in this text, is primarily drawn).

11) *See generally* Steven Shapin, *Hitters*, New Yorker, Apr. 18, 2005, at 191. Other types of steroids accelerate recovery between activities, increase aggressiveness, and perform

As the problem emerged full-blown in the mid-1990s, MLB took no action to test players for the use of steroids or to impose sanctions against their use. By contrast, the IOC and several professional sports organizations not directly governed by IOC rules have prohibited their use, based on five principles. These principles are the "unnaturalness" of steroids, their unfairness to competing athletes who do not choose to use them, the consequential unevenness of the playing field or competitive balance on it, the uncertain long-term effects of steroids on the health of athletes, and their questionable effect on the role of athletes as models for youth.

In the mid-1990s the Federal Bureau of Investigation (FBI) of the United States Department of Justice notified MLB of the growing use of steroids among players.[12] In 1998 home-run king Mark McGuire admitting using a testosterone-boosting supplement, androstenidione (andro).[13] Although the IOC, IFs, and several professional sports organizations such as the National Football League (NFL) had banned the agent, MLB did not. MLB Commissioner Bud Selig responded to the controversy, however, by initiating a study of andro that was later published, undertaking to educate players with a pamphlet on the known dangers of performance-enhancing agents and hiring medical expertise to advise MLB on doping.[14] In 2004 Congress amended the Anabolic Steroid Control Act of 1990 so as to ban the sale of andro.[15] As of the new millennium, however, MLB still had no testing program or mandatory sanctions against doping.

Further reports of rampant doping among players contributed to a crisis in baseball, but there was still no effective response to the problem. In 2002 the players union and owners finally agreed to a steroid-testing program after Ken Caminiti, MLB's Most Valuable Player in 1996, admitted that he had used steroids, claiming that the majority of players did so, too.[16]

In summary, "[f]rom 1986 until 2002, about the only way a team could

---

various other functions. Regarding the five principles, *see id.*, at 191-92, 194.

12) *See* Andrew Zimbalist, *Stamping Out Steroids Takes Time*, N.Y. Times, Mar. 6, 2005, at SP 7.

13) *See*, e.g., William C. Rhoden, *Baseball's Pandora's Box Cracks Open*, N.Y. Times, Aug. 25, 1998, at C1.

14) *See* Zimbalist, *supra* note 12.

15) *See* Jenkins et al., *supra* note 10, at 6.

16) *See* Tom Verducci, *Caminiti Comes Clean*, Sports Illus., May 28, 2002.

take recourse [against doping] was if a player was arrested on drug charges."[17] In retrospect, what explains MLB sluggishness in responding to a serious and growing problem of which it was clearly aware? Several likely explanations include the concerns of the players union about breaches of personal privacy, the confidentiality of physician-player relationships, and MLB's confidence in the ability of the owners to control doping without outside intervention.[18] Perhaps the most likely explanation, at least until recently, was public tolerance, if not encouragement, of steroids whenever their use might help the superstars set new records on the baseball diamond. The public loves big hitters. By 2002, however, public tolerance had waned, putting new pressure on Congress to conduct investigations, on the MLB to take effective action, and on the players union to cooperate in efforts to address the doping problem.

## Major League Baseball's Response to the Crisis and Its Significance

### MLB's Response

#### The 2002 Program

MLB's first step in 2002 toward an effective anti-doping program initiated a year of anonymous, random testing. According to the program, if more than five percent of the tests proved to be positive, mandatory testing and sanctions would follow. The sanctions included suspension of players and disclosure of their names, along a scale calibrated according to the number of offenses. First-time offenders would remain anonymous and be subjected only to mandatory treatment. In late 2003 the stricter program went into effect after a determination that the five-percent threshold of use had been reached.[19]

Despite growing skepticism about the efficacy of MLB's minimal 2002

---

17) Jenkins et al., *supra* note 10.
18) *See* Zimbalist, *supra* note 12.
19) Jenkins et al., *supra* note 10, at 6. Subsequently, within a year, the incidence of doping dropped dramatically to about 1.7%. *See* Curry, *infra* note 37.

program, it was at least a first step. On the other hand, it might not have led very soon to more effective measures had it not been for the BALCO controversy.[20) In 2003 a police raid on the Bay Area Laboratory Cooperative (BALCO) in Burlingame, California, brought to light documents that indicated BALCO's widespread distribution of performance-enhancing drugs to leading athletes. As the ensuing cause célèbre developed in the Olympic year of 2004, much of the public attention was focused on track-and-field superstars. Several baseball stars, notably Barry Bonds, Jason Giambi, and Gary Sheffield,[21) however, were also linked to BALCO and testified before grand juries. Barry Bonds' stature as a home-run king brought him sharply into the public limelight following media reports of his admission before a grand jury that he had used two kinds of steroids: "the clear" (taken orally) and "the cream" (rubbed on the skin).[22) He attracted further attention when his trainer was indicted on BALCO-derived evidence in early 2004.[23) Bonds, however, publicly denied using steroids.

Suffice it to say here that the BALCO controversy led to an expression of concern by President Bush in his 2004 State of the Union address,[24) to an investigation by Congress the same year,[25) and eventually, in 2005, to another congressional inquiry into the reportedly widespread use of performance-enhancing agents in baseball.[26)

---

20) *See generally* Jere Longman & Liz Robbins, *Top U.S. Sprinter Barred as Drug Scandal Grows*, N.Y. Times, May 20, 2004, at 1.

21) See Jenkins et al., supra note 10, at 6.

22) See Mark Sappenfield, Yield *on Bonds and Baseball: Dropping?*, Christ. Sci. Monitor, Dec. 6, 2004, at 2. *See generally* Mark Fainaru-Wada & Lance Williams, Game of Shadows (2006).

23) *Id.*

24) *See State of the Union: The President's Address,* N.Y. Times, Jan. 21, 2004, at A14, A15.

25) The congressional inquiry centered on a hearing before the United States Senate Commerce, Science and Transportation committee featuring baseball Commissioner Bud Selig and Donald Behr, Executive Director of the MLB Players Association. SeeStatesman-Journal (Salem, Or.), Mar. 28, 2004, at 6B.

26) *See* Anne E. Kornblut, *Now Batting: Hearings in Congress on Steroids*, N.Y. Times, Mar. 13, 2005, § 8, at 8.

### Public Opinion

The 2005 congressional inquiry took place against a background of public disenchantment concerning baseball's sorry record in combating doping. Opinion polls showed that 86% of the public agreed that steroid use was at least a serious problem, if not a threat to the future of the sport. Some 69% doubted that MLB had done enough to prevent steroid use, and 59% agreed that the records of players who had used performance-enhancing agents should not remain in the record books.[27]

In interpreting these statistics, however, a few notes of caution are in order. First, at bottom, the public has become used to performance-enhancement and the use of dietary supplements, some of which are at the margins of prohibited performance-enhancing drugs. The growing use of prescription drugs and the general acceptance of chemically enhanced activity have desensitized people to the use of steroids and other so-called enhancers. Moreover, the public perceives that the social impact of such products pales by comparison to that of street drugs such as cocaine and heroin. Second, it must be noted that younger people—some 41% of all people under the age of 30—expressed no concern at all about the problem of doping.[28] One can reasonably conclude from this finding that the younger generation, which is more inured to the use of street drugs and doping of athletes, may be less inclined to adopt strict programs of control in the future.

Third, despite the statistics, sports that rely on the use of steroids for effect, such as televised professional wrestling in the United States, are more popular than ever. It may be, of course, that such sports attract only a distinct minority of the population, whereas baseball is still more of a national pastime, thereby generating higher public expectations about the ethical behavior of the players. In other words, the sport may still symbolize the best in American sports to a substantial majority of the population, even persons who do not participate in it or watch it. On the other hand, to

---

27) *See* Harry Bruinius, *Will steroids alter baseball records, too?*, Christ. Sci. Monitor, Mar. 24, 2005, at 11.

28) *See* Jere Longman, *Revelations Only Confirm Suspicions About Drugs*, N.Y. Times, Dec. 5, 2004, § 8, at 1.

sound a fourth cautionary note about the public's intolerance of doping, one poll revealed that, whatever the sport, 48.7% of the Americans acknowledged that they themselves would take steroids if doing so would boost their income into the millions of dollars.[29] One should be cautious, therefore in reaching conclusions derived from anything as volatile as the aggregate opinion of a spectator public easily excited by brute strength and record-setting.

Despite this evidence of cynicism, public opinion strongly favored some kind of response in Washington to the doping crisis. The congressional inquiry in 2005 was also conducted against the background of a published exposé by superstar José Canseco, naming many names, about the rampant steroid juicing of players in the MLB.[30] Although Congress was criticized for yet another self-indulgence in its own pastime of investigating baseball,[31] the inquiry appears to have prompted MLB's replacement of its initial 2002 program with a tougher regime of drug testing and sanctions. The Canseco book, for its part, appears to have prompted additional testing, leading quickly to the revelation that yet another superstar, first baseman Rafael Palmeiro, had tested positive.[32]

### The 2005 Program

Whatever may have been the pressures on MLB, the industry took a

---

29) *See* Sappenfield, *supra* note 22.

30) Canseco, *supra* note 9.

31) Historically, hearings about baseball's conduct has been a popular congressional pastime. Since the early 1990s there have been as many as two dozen inquiries into various baseball topics in at least six committees and subcommittees. Kornblut, *supra* note 26.

32) *See* Hal Bodley, *Palmeiro, baseball won't fight Congress*, USA Today, Aug. 4, 2005, at 1C; Mike Todd, *Experts: Stanozolol Tough to Mask*, USA Today, Aug. 4, 2005, at 6C; Mike Todd & Dick Patrick, *Critics: Palmeiro case exposes flawed policy*, Aug. 3, 2005, at 6C. Palmeiro had denied using steroids in his testimony at a March 2005 congressional hearing, but after being confronted with evidence to the contrary, he admitted using them, but denied using them knowingly. Instead, he speculated that the presence of stanozolol in his body resulted from his taking a contaminated nutritive supplement. *See also* a later sensational exposé about super-slugger Barry Bonds. Fainaru-Wada & Williams, *supra* note 22.

second step, effective during spring training 2005. For the first time, the players union agreed to reopen an agreement with MLB in order to strengthen its anti-doping clause. Under the new program,[33] each player had to undergo at least one random test between the beginning of spring training and the end of the regular season. Players also had to submit to additional testing based on reasonable cause to believe prohibited activity may have occurred, as well as random testing initiated by the Commissioner. The program was extended to the off-season and could be conducted outside the United States. It also established elaborate provisions for protecting the confidentiality of tests and the identity of tested players, as well as a procedure for appealing administrative decisions. Only when a player is actually suspended, however, may his identity be disclosed.

"Positive" test results, with clinical and administrative consequences, included not only meeting biological levels set forth in annexed testing protocols but also refusals by players to cooperate in the program and attempts by players to alter tests. All players on entry into the program were to be put on a clinical track, which might involve treatment for some of them. Players might be moved from the clinical to the administrative track, involving the possibility of sanctions, after testing positive for other violations of the law (for example, the use or sale of a prohibited substance) or for failure to cooperate in initial evaluations or in the course of required treatment.

This second step in the development of an effective anti-doping program defined "prohibited substances" as both drugs of abuse (cocaine, LSD, marijuana, opiates, and so on) and performance-enhancing agents. The program broadened the list of banned substances to include not only steroids but also steroid precursors, designer steroids, ephedra, human growth hormone, masking agents, and diuretics (but not stimulants), but imposed specific penalties only against the use of steroids. The penalties fell short of stiffer ones proposed by MLB but nevertheless moved professional

---

33) For commentary on the summary of this 2005 agreement (the first of two) that follows in the text, *see* Major League Baseball, Major League Baseball's Joint Drug Prevention and Treatment Program 11-12 (2005). For a comparison of suspensions, as between the 2002 and the first 2005 MLB testing programs, *see* Bruinius, *supra* note 27, at 12.

baseball another step closer to compliance with the established standards of international sports law and practice.[34]

Then, in November 2005, continuing pressure from Congress and MLB Commissioner Selig's invigorated leadership led MLB to take a third step. It reopened the existing collective-bargaining agreements for the second time in ten months, resulting in tougher penalties, increased frequency of testing, and a first-ever prohibition of the use of amphetamines.[35]

The revised sanctions substantially lengthened penalties for steroid offenses, as follows: a 50-day suspension for a first offense, a 100-day suspension for a second offense, and a lifetime suspension for a third offense with a right to seek reinstatement after two years. This third set of reforms also eliminated alternative fines as well as tolerance of a positive test after a third one. The new program increased the frequency of testing from once during the training and regular season, with additional random testing, to once each during spring training physicals and the regular season, with additional random testing. Players continue to be subject to off-season testing as well. The new penalties for presence of amphetamines are as follows: mandatory follow-up testing for a first positive test, a 25-game suspension for a second positive test, an 80-game suspension for a third positive test, and, for a fourth positive test, a penalty at the Baseball Commissioner's discretion, including the possibility of a lifetime ban from MLB.

Besides MLB's stricter program, the congressional inquiries generated several bills that called for more frequent, random drug testing, made reference to international standards, and largely adopted World Anti-Doping Code sanctions against violations, as implemented by the World Anti-Doping Agency (WADA). Although the players union raised broad objections to the bills, baseball Commissioner Selig raised little objection to their substance and embraced the idea of stricter penalties.[36] The globalization of the MLB

---

34) *See* George Vecsey, *Baseball Union Comes a Long Way*, N.Y. Times, Sept. 28, 2005, at C22.

35) *See* Jack Curry, *Baseball Backs Stiffer Penalties for Steroid Use*, N.Y. Times, Nov. 16, 2005, at A1.

36) *See* letter from Bud Selig to Donald Fehr, Apr. 25, 2005, *available at* www.businessofbaseball.com/seligletter_2005JDA.htm.

was apparent from the influence, if only indirect, of the World Anti-Doping
Code.


### The Significance of MLB's Response in the Process of Globalization

It is too early to judge the effectiveness of MLB's initiatives in the revised
2005 program to control doping. A reported 8% drop in home runs during
the 2005 season may indicate that the more modest initial program in 2005
deterred would-be violators because of either the lost protection of their
anonymity or longer suspensions,[37] but it would be foolish to jump to
conclusions based on that statistic alone.

What is clear is that 2002 MLB moved extraordinarily slowly in response
to the huge problem of doping among players until several important
developments put it in high gear. MLB's first step in 2002, when the players
union finally agreed to a threshold program, was a milestone. Between 2002
and 2005, Congress put continued pressure on the MLB to take further steps.[38]
The MLB's program still fell short of longer-established programs in
professional sports such as that of professional football, as well as the
standards set by the World Anti-Doping Code within the framework of
international sports law.[39] The current program, established in November
2005, was influenced by the Code and approximates it, even though it still
falls short of full compliance with the Code's requirements.

It is ironic that the IOC decided to drop baseball after the 2008 Games
just as the MLB, under public and congressional pressure, was substantially
strengthening the sport's anti-doping program. Very likely, MLB's failure
until November 2005 to impose strong penalties for doping helped explain

---

37) Jack Curry, *Fall in Home Runs Raises Some Doubts*, Int'l Herald Trib., Aug. 18, 2005, at
    18.
38) *See, e.g.*, Richard Pound, *The New Testing Policy Does Not Begin to Solve the Drug
    Problem*, N.Y. Times, Mar. 20, 2005, at 10. Mr. Pound, a former Vice President of the
    IOC, is Chairman of the World Anti-Doping Agency (WADA), headquartered in
    Montreal, Canada.
39) *See* Nafziger, *supra* note 5, at 161-64. *See also* Klaus Vieweg, *The Definition of Doping
    and The Proof of a Doping Offense (an Anti-Doping Rule Violation) Under Special
    Consideration of the German Legal Position*, 15 Marq. Sports L. Rev. 37 (2004).

why baseball's appeal as an Olympic sport faded, and why baseball became the first castoff by the IOC in nearly seventy years. Another plausible explanation for the IOC decision was that the IOC concluded that many of the best players were not competing in the Olympic Games. Baseball has never fielded anything resembling professional basketball's Dream Team in the Games. To the contrary, many of the best MLB players have largely avoided the kind of international competition that would enhance the visibility and global stature of the sport. That may be due to the scheduling of the Olympic Games during the peak season of baseball. In any event, MLB has provided little encouragement to players who may wish to take time off from prescribed league schedules to join national teams in open international competition at the Games or elsewhere.

In other sports, however, the effect of open competition in the Olympics and other sanctioned international events has been profound. The tough requirements of international sports law and the *lex sportiva*,[40] including the globalizing World Anti-Doping Code, have governed many professional athletes preparing for and participating in open competition, if only sporadically and temporarily. One effect of those requirements has been to discourage professional players from doping even long after such competition. Another effect has been to encourage professional sports bodies—for example, the European football (soccer) leagues—to move toward the tougher international standards and procedures of international sports law.[41]

Professional sports bodies therefore have been gradually adopting standards, procedures, and sanctions consonant with international sports law. Baseball, too, finally seems to have moved in that direction. The extent of doping in 2013, and therefore the continuing challenges facing the MLB's Joint Drug Prevention and Treatment Program, became clear when MLB imposed lengthy suspensions of 14 players.[42] But the 2013 doping crisis also demonstrated MLB's determination since the seminal period of 2002-05 to take doping seriously. The 2013 crackdown on performance-enhancing drugs also demonstrated a recognition of the limitations of even rigorous physical

---

40) *"Lex sportiva"* refers to a growing jurisprudence of the Court of Arbitration for Sport. *See* James Nafziger, *Lex Sportiva*, Int'l Sports L.J., 2004-1/2, at 3.
41) *See generally* Nafziger, *supra* note 5, at 132-35, 163.
42) *See* text at note 6, *supra*.

testing of players and thus the need to rely on profiling and extrinsic evidence of transactions in prohibited substances. Non-analytic positive evidence has become as important, if not more important, in the MLB's anti-doping program as physical testing. Moreover, this development conforms to trends in enforcement at the international level, as reflected in decisions of the Court of Arbitration for Sport, for example.

The international framework has great merit to players and sports bodies alike. It is both effective and uniform, thereby overcoming the unfairness to players of radically different standards, procedures, and sanctions from one sort to another. Baseball and other professional sports may continue to be governed by player contracts and collective bargaining, but that need not affect the adoption by players and owners of adequate, uniform procedures and sanctions, as major league baseball in North America has finally been pressured to do.

## References

Tom Verducci, Global Warming, Sports Illus., Mar. 6, 2006.

James A.R. Nafziger, International Sports Law 147-64 (2d ed. 2004).

James A.R. Nafziger, Circumstantial Evidence of Doping: BALCO and Beyond, 16 Marq. Sports L. Rev. 45 (2005).

José Canseco, Juiced: Wild Times, Rampant 'Roids, Smash Hits, and How Baseball Got Big 53 (2005).

James Nafziger, Lex Sportiva, Int'l Sports L.J., 2004-1/2.

# The Greek Constitution Concerning Sport and Sports Federation

DIMITRIOS P. PANAGIOTOPOULOS*

*The Sport, as a physical activity taking place out of school environment, is consecrated in a formal way as an institution within the Constitution in force, through which citizens' participation in sports action as well as in sport.*

*In this work field of research is, the institutional existence of Sport and the people's participation in sports activities. as a social activity forms, which achieved, under state supervision and protection.*

*The sports reality of the existence of a federation contributes to the determination of its particular nature, as the only supreme authority of a sport, governing all relevant clubs and developing that specific sport.*

*In Greece, the administration controls, according to the law which regulates the operation of sports federations, if their operation is in accordance with the Constitution, that constitutes the fundamental state rule on sport.*

*The Greek sports federation presents a particular legal status, since it is not only an administrative body but also a legislative and a disciplinary one.*

**Key word:** Physical Education, Greek Constitution, physical activity, Lex Sportiva, sports law, institutional autonomy, Sports Legal Order, sports federation, regulations, Sports Disputes, Sports Jurisdiction

---

* Professor at the University of Athens, Advocate, Attorney-at-law, President of International Association of Sports Law (IASL)

## Introduction

The Greek constitutional legislator, influenced by the Greek sports tradition, has included very early in the Greek Constitution (article 16) some provisions which refer to the participation in a physical activity, under the form of Physical Education, as well as in the sports action. Paragraph two (2) of the article 16 deals with Physical Education, as a form of physical activity involved in the educational process; its content is the following: *"Education is one of the State main tasks. It is focused on the moral, spiritual and physical education of the Greeks, on the development of their national and religious conscience and on their shaping as free and responsible citizens".* In paragraph nine (9) the sports system is regulated as follows: *"...Sport is placed under the protection and the highest supervision of the State. The State funds, by means of subventions, and controls all forms of sports clubs, as stipulated by law. It is a Law that also determines the allocation of the funds distributed to the sports associations in accordance with their purpose...".*

We shall, therefore, presently examine the attitude of the Greek legislator towards the Physical Education and Sport issue, taking into consideration their distinction, as well as the institutional existence of Sport and of people's participation in sports activities.

## Institutional Guarantee of Sport

The Greek Constitution article 16 par. 9 provisions constitute the institutional guarantee of the right to the free development of sports activities; it indicates to the Greek legislator that he must proceed to establishing the necessary regulations so as to create a well organized and competitive sports reality. These regulations establish a context for the exercise of the constitutional right to the free individual and collective sports action under state supervision and protection.

In this sense, Sport, as a physical activity taking place out of school environment, is consecrated in a formal way as an institution[1] within the

Constitution in force, through which citizens' participation in sports action as well as in sport, as a social activity form, is achieved, under state supervision and protection.

In this context, under the terms and conditions established by the constitution, the following questions need to be answered:

(1) Under the constitutional rules and Sports Law, in which way is determined Sport, physical exercise and workout for the citizens?

(2) Which is the internationally accepted way in which the right to participate in sports practice, in the physical exercise and workout is met? How is the right to physical wellbeing as well as to sports workout and activity guaranteed? And which are the indicated spaces and bodies which allow the exercise of these rights?

(3) Should this right be satisfied by schools, sports clubs or by local authorities and especially Municipalities, since they are the most vibrant molecules of society's democratic structure?

(4) Which can be nowadays the structure and the organization of sports and physical activity in general, as well as of the physical activity taking place in special facilities destined to sports practice aiming to high results and high physical education?

---

1) Greek Constitution 75/75, Article 16, paragraph 2 and Article 16, paragraph 9, compare with Venizelos El. (1993), «Η Συνταγματική υποδοχή του Αθλητισμού» ("The Constitutional Reception of Sport"), in: Proceedings of the International Congress, The Olympic Games Institution - interdisciplinary approach, Olympia, 3-7 September 1991 and Pandektis ISLR, 1:2, 1992, p. 212-214, by the same author (1993), «Αθλητισμός και κράτος δι καίου - τα όρια της νομικής απορύθμισης και επιστροφή στο Σύνταγμα» ("Sport and State of Law - the limits of the legal deregulation and the return to the Constitution"), in: Proceedings of the 1st International Congress of Sports Law, Athens of 11-13 December 1992, ΕΚΕΑΔ (Hellenic Center of Research on Sports Law): Athens, p. 125-130. Compare with D. Panagiotopoulos (1993), "Le Droit du Sport Selon la Constitution" in: Revue Juridique et Economique du Sport, No 25:2, p. 109-116, Loberdos A. (1993), ), «Η προστασί α του αθλητισμού ως ατομικό και κοινωνικό δικαίωμα» ("The protection of sport as an individual and a social right") in: Proceedings of the 1st International Congress on Sports Law, December 11-13, Athens 1992, ΕΚΕΑΔ: Athens 1992, p. 171-175, as also: Dimitropoulos A. (1996), Ζητήματα Συνταγματικού Δικαίου ("Issues of Constitutional Law"), Athens, by the same author (1998), Συνταγματικό Δίκαιο (Syntagmatiko Dikaio, Constitutional Law), Athens p. 594 as well as the bibliography and the case-law mentioned.

These are only a few of the questions that need to be answered in the context of this research, which are examined in the relevant chapter.

## Institutional Autonomy and Administrative Control

The establishment of sports clubs, associations and federations, as a special expression of people's right to associate themselves[2], indicates that Sport has an institutional autonomy[3]. This autonomy is also manifested in the Constitution, where the freedom of the private initiative to lead to the creation of sports clubs is mentioned. In German Law, sports clubs' and associations' autonomy exists within the framework of state laws establishing limits on doping and prohibitions[4]. Sports federations are controlled by the State, as provided by law, on the basis of the principle

---

2) D. Panagiotopoulos (1993), "Ζητήματα επιστημολογικής οριοθέτησης και εφαρμογής του Αθλητικού Δικαίου" ("Questions of epistemological delimitation and application of Sports Law"), 1st International Congress on Sports Law, in: ΕΚΕΑΔ (H.C.R.L.S): Athens, p. 63-88 and Yearbook of Sports Law, I.1994, p. 37, compare with E. Venizelos, "Αθλητισμός και κράτος Δικαίου – τα όρια της νομικής απορρύθμισης και επιστροφή στο Σύνταγμα" ("Sports and the State governed by Law –the limits of legal deregulation and return to the Constitution) op. cit., p. 125-130, compare with A. Loberdos, "Η προστασία του Αθλητισμού ως ατομικό και κοινωνικό δικαίωμα" ("The protection of Sports as a personal right") op. cit., p. 171-175, compare with Dimitrios P. Panagiotopoulos (2011). Sports Law: Lex Sportiva –Lex Olympica: theory and praxis N. Sakkoulas: Athens., pp. 18-105.

3) Dimitrios P. Panagiotopoulos (2004), "Theoretical foundation of sports law" (1st Part: Sports Law: A Special Scientific Branch, Sports Legal Order in Sports Activities, Sports Regulation and Law Limits, Institutional Autonomy and Economic Freedom in Sports Activities), in: Sports Law [Lex Sportiva] in the World (D. Panagiotopoulos Ed.), Ant. N. Sakkoulas: Athens, p. 19-80.

4) The legal base of this autonomy of German associations is the Article 9, I of the German Constitution (Grundgesetz - GG), according to which the all Germans have the right to form associations and companies that operate and enjoy protection. The article 25 of the German Civil Code stipulates that a sports association is not only governed by the previous provisions, but also by its own statutes' provisions, Vieweg Kl. (1999), "Basic liberties and autonomy in sports - from the perspective of German and European law", in: The Sports Law in the 21st Century: Professional Sports Activity D. P. Panagiotopoulos H.C.S.L.R., Trikala, 4-6 June 1999, Ion: Athens p. 166-187, compare with: same author (1990),"Normsetzung und - anwendung deutscher und internationaler Verbende", Berlin, p. 154 and following.

that they are the unique high sports authorities in every sport, giving them a monopoly and dominant position[5]. The undisputable domination of sports federations and especially the one of international federations, such as the FIFA or the UEFA, have been contested for the first time in the Bosman case[6]. The International Sports Federations are generally associations of a non-profitable purpose, governed by national laws[7].

The domestic associations are considered to be "businesses" by Article 102 TFEU (ex Article 82 TEC) since it is stipulated by the international federations' statutes that they are bound to participate in events organized by them[8]. These domestic federations contribute a percentage of the gross earnings of every international event to the international ones and they are acknowledged to be, in accordance with the international federations' statutes, the owners of the exclusive broadcasting rights of the events in question; all these elements indicate that a genuine financial activity, involving sports events, has developed[9].

In the same way, the international federation, as an entity uniting all

---

5) On this issue, as far as European Law is concerned, Articles 104 and 106 TFEU (ex Articles 84 and 86 TEC)

6) D. P. Panagiotopoulos (1997), "Ελεύθερη Κυκλοφορία Εργαζόμενων- Επαγγελματίες Ποδοσφαιριστές ς, Υπόθεση C-415/1993 (Bosman)" ("Freedom of movement for workers - Professional Footballers, Affair C- 415/1993 (Bosman)"), in: Νομικό Βήμα (Nomiko Vima, Legal Podium), vol. 45/97 (ECJ Case law), p. 681-683.

7) Basketball Federation is a German association, having its seat in Munich. The International Federation of Football (F.I.F.A.) is a Swiss association, having its seat in Geneva. The first sports federations were created in England. Thus, the "Football Association" was founded in 1863 and the "Football-Rugby Association" in 1871 (when the first international rugby games took place). In Germany, a "Confederation of German Sports" (Deutscher Sportbund) was founded and it assembles nowadays more from 65.000 Clubs and Associations. In Switzerland, having a population of 6.000.000 residents, are established 30.000 Clubs and Associations approximately, K. Chrisostomidi 1997, op. cit, p. 237.

8) Moreover, as it was previously stressed, the unilateral characterization, operated by an association or a sports federation, of athletes or groups, as being "amateur" ones, is not sufficient so as to consider them as amateur athletes and clubs and not professional ones, if they have financial activities, in the sense of the article 2 of the European Community Treaty. Compare with relevant decisions of the ECJ of April the 11th 2000: C-51/96 and C-191/97, Deliège, Collection 2000, p. I-2549, paragraph 46.

9) Also, First Instance Court decision of 9 November 1994, T-46/92, Scottish Football vs Committee, Collection 1994, p. II-1039

domestic federations[10]), constitutes an *"association of undertakings"* in the sense of Article 101 TFEU (ex Article 81 TEC)[11]). This provision also applies to the domestic federations, since their activity and the one of the businesses that they join aims to the goals described in this specific article[12]).

On the basis of the unique representation principle, all domestic and international federations have monopoly characteristics[13]), just like the Domestic Olympic Committees. The character of the domestic sports federation, in the legal context in force, is, therefore, a dual one: On a basis level, a sports club substantially contributes to Sport's development, in the framework of the private initiative development. On a higher level, this initiative is particularly limited and operates under the supervision of the State, by means of the control of one and exclusive federation. The existence of one and only sports federation, situated in a dominant position[14]), serves the

---

10) As the International Federation of Football (F.I.F.A.), The international Federation of Basketball (FIBA), the Marine Ski, the Classic Sports of Volleyball and others, Decision in Piau affair CJEC T-193/02, op. cit., relevant chapter. Lex Sportiva and European Community Law.

11) Decision of Court of Justice of 30th January 1985, 123/83, BNIC, Collection 1985, p. 391, thought 17.

12) Decision of Court of Justice of 15th May 1975, 71/74, Frubo vs Committee, Collection vol. 1975, p. 181, thought 30.

13) The article 1 of the F.I.F.A. statutes, the article 4 of the I.A.A.F statutes and the article 42 of the F.I.B.A statutes declare that only one member can be acknowledged by them for each country or geographic region and this member will be recognized by the International Federation to be the only body having the right to manage football or amateur sports or basketball in this country or region. According to K. Chrysostomidi "This rule however has some noticeable exceptions: In the United Kingdom's football exist more than one operating bodies: the Football Association for England, the Football Association of Wales for Wales, the Scottish Football Association for Scotland and the Irish Football Association for Ireland. Rugby is also traditionally represented by two international bodies: the International Federation of Amateur Rugby (Federation Internationale Du Rugby Amateur), having its seat in France and the Rugby Association (Rugby Union) assembling all four British Associations and the Associations of Australia, New Zealand and South Africa. In some sports pure financial interests break the sports monopoly; Formula 1 has left the International Federation of Cars Sports (Federation Inernationale Du Sport Automobile). Boxing, golf and professional tennis are other such examples. Despite these exceptions, however, monopoly remains the rule in sports", K. Chrissostomidis, op. cit., p. 238.

14) Relevant decisions of the ΕφΑθ (Athen's Court of Appeal) 5722/1996 and 10383/96, according to which recognition of only one overlying association on each branch of

following purposes:

a) Maintaining control and a uniform operation at the basis level of sports activity, namely all sports clubs, and
b) Maintaining a united form of operation of the sports action at the top level, leading to the determination of the total sports and competitive action as being a national and domestic issue.

The uniform operation at the basis level of sports action is the result of the relevant constitutional provisions, which consider Sport to be part of a nation's culture and find it necessary, given this specific belief, for sports to take place through society's participation and through the accumulation of specific cultural characteristics and particularities of social groups, which are related to their own perception of Sport.

Furthermore, the organized structure of the private law sports entities, such as the sports Club, the Sports Association and the Sports Federation, which all form a pyramidal hierarchy, serves and guarantees -amongst others- *"the use of the funds made available to associations, through subventions, in accordance with their purposes of constitution"*[15], as allowed by the Constitution and by special law, in accordance with the relevant Constitutional approval[16].


## Sports Federations

### The nature of the Sports Federation

The sports federation, in accordance with the law, is the highest form of organization of the sports clubs practicing the same sports or being active in the same sector of sports activity. It serves the purpose of the development of a sport or of a sports sector in a specific country[17], on a national level. It

---

exercising is not contrary to the Constitution.
15) Greek Constitution article 16, paragraph 9, 2. The use of state's financial support provided to the federations should take place in accordance to their purposes.
16) Ibid, article 16, paragraph 9 and Law 2725/99, in ΑθλΚ (Sports Code, 2009).
17) Id, paragraph 1 of article 19 Law 2725/99, in ΑθλΚ (Sports Code, 2009), p. 22 and

operates in accordance with the sports law and with the Civil Code's provisions on unions in general[18]. So as to determine, in an absolute manner, the nature of the sports federation, as a legal entity, there is more than the private law governing it that need to be examined[19].

The nature of a sports federation, as a private law entity, is determined by the fact that:

a) It results from an association of private entities and persons and has private powers,

b) It manages the financial issues of private entities, namely the clubs which have joined it, and

c) It serves, as a sports federation, the private interest that its members share, which is sports oriented, namely the development of the free physical culture of people and entities which have joined it.

In its inner administration, its relations with the clubs and with third parties, a sports federation is a private law entity, governed by the special provisions of the Sports Law in force[20]. Furthermore, a federation manages, as the unique authority for each sport, in accordance with the law[21] and on the basis of this monopoly situation; the clubs sport activity on a domestic level. It also internationally represents the sport that it develops, in accordance with the regulations of the relevant international bodies (International Federation - IOC)[22]. It constitutes national teams, composed by athletes who are its members. These national teams, although their member come from sports clubs, operate on a different level than theirs, so as to promote the

---

following.

18) Id, paragraph 1 of article 19 and AK (Astikos Kodikas, Civil Code), articles 78 and following.

19) AK (Civil Code) articles 78 and following, as well as its own statutes.

20) P. Dionissatos, D. Panagiotopoulos (1994), "The nature of the athletic federation's decisions'", in: Yearbook of Sports Law I, Anl. N. Sakkoulas: Athens, p. 96-100. The void, that is created, is supplemented with the Civil Codes's provisions with an adaptation to the athletic associations' special nature and aim. ΕιρΑθ (Peace Court of Athens) relevant decision 3154/1976, EEN (Greek Law Practitioners Journal), 43, p. 642, Ειρλαμ (Peace Court of Lamia) decision 13/1981, ΕλΔ/νη (Greek Justice Journal) 1981, p. 274 and ΕιρΑθ (Peace Court of Athens) decision 3154/1976, EEN 43, p. 642.

21) Article 19, op. cit., paragraph 2 Law 2725/1999, also article 14 and Law 75/75 article 13.

22) Ibid paragraph 2, section 2.

national participation in events. They are considered to serve the national interest and the satisfaction of a nation's national pride, through wining in sports games and competitions. An athlete belonging to a national team does not belong to his club anymore, during international sports events; although he comes from it, by participating in the national team, he is considered to act in favour of the Sport and of the presence of his country on the international sports competitive level.

The legislative provisions referring to a federation's constitution, may seem opposed to the individual right of people to associate themselves with others, stipulated in article 12, par.1 of the Constitution. Still, if many federations were created for each sport, they would lead to a chaos; they would be dysfunctional and make difficult the control of sports by the competent bodies of the state administration. It is, therefore, for public interest as well as for this reason, that this legislative regime has been established for sports federations. This regime results in a prohibition, whenever a sports federation of clubs already exists in a sports sector, to create a second one, even if it has been constituted by other clubs, which have not already joined the existing one[23].

The sports reality of the existence of a federation contributes to the determination of its particular nature, as the only supreme authority of a sport, governing all relevant clubs and developing that specific sport. A domestic sports federation constitutes the only entity representing a country's domestic sports activity at the international level and communicating with the international federations. These international sports federations impose the observation of the rules that they establish to the domestic ones[24], thus creating a Law that does not belong to any country, the Lex Sportiva[25],

---

23) ΠολΠρωτΑθ (Athens Multimember First Instance Court) decision 3068/1996, according to which if a second (new) sports Federation is founded, the already existing and functioning Federation is provided with the possibility of asking the cancellation of the judicial decision that recognized the second federation as operating in the same sports sector, by means of a third-party opposition, according to the articles 583,586 and 773 of ΚΠολΔ (Civil Procedure Code).

24) L. Silance (1977), The Sports Law, op. cit., p. 79 and following. J. Schroeder (1976), Symbolik der Olympischen Schunzes, Doctoral thesis, Mainz, , p. 81, G. Fleuridas (1974), Ladministration et l' Organisation des Jeux, Doctoral thesis, Un. De Paris VII, p. 85.

25) D. .P. Panagiotopoulos (2003),"Sports Legal Order in national and international sporting

which is introduced in the domestic law and many times imposed by the domestic federation, on the basis of the transformation and the incorporation theory[26]. A federation is responsible for all the technical adjustments, which shall take place in its own country whenever international or "Olympic" games[27] take place in it, according to the IOC rules and to the International Sports Federation.

The Greek sports law, in accordance with a constitutional approval[28], situated in the Lex Sportiva context, as previously mentioned, acknowledges that a sports federation is the sports supreme authority in the domestic sports clubs hierarchy, fulfilling an administrative, disciplinary and regulating role; it also manages the subventions received for the development of a sport and for the organization of sports events at a domestic and at an international level. The powers of the federation distinguish it as a particular sports club of the highest rank. The general sports reality is not just a clubs issue but also a wider sport order that is situated at the circle of sports activity. This activity presents characteristics of a public interest and some of its elements should, therefore, be governed by public law. Indeed, when a sports activity takes place in an organized state, it provides a service to the public and satisfies a social need, to which the public interest is related.

All the above mentioned, resulting into conferring to this body, namely the sports federation. As far as it's operating administration is concerned,

---

life" in: International Sports Law Review Pandektis (ISLR/Pandektis), Vol.5: 2, p. 227-242, (2004) " Lex Sportiva: Sport institutions and rules of law, in: ISLR/Pandektis, p. 316-327.

26) Greek Constitution, article 28 paragraph 1-2.

27) Olympic Charter, I.O.C. 2010, Rule 47. Also, on the participation to the Olympic Games, article 45 of the Participation Code and explanatory provision of the article 45 in the Chart, p. 29-30 and p. 44. Compare with D. Panagiotopoulos, (1991), Δίκαιο των Ολυμπιακ ών Αγώνων (Olympic Games Law), Ant. N. Sakkoulas Editions. Athens, p. 205 and following, same author, (2005), "Ερασιτεχνική και επαγγελματική ιδιότητα των αθλητών κ αι η συμμετοχή τους στους ολυμπιακούς αγώνες"("Amateur and professional attribute of athletes and their participation to the Olympic Games"), in: Ολυμπιακοί Αγώνες και Δίκα ιο( Olympic Games and Law), Proceedings of the International Congress of Athens University Faculty of Law (N. Klamaris and others), Ant. N. Sakkoulas Editions: Athens, p. 227 and following.

28) Article 19, paragraph 9 Law N 2725/99 as it is in force. (Sports Code, 2009), p. 23.

some characteristics that can be met in legal entities of the wider public sector. Still, the theory of the "award of a public duty" should not apply to sports federations, as it is wrongly suggested by some sports law theoreticians, since the nature of the sports federation is different to the one of public bodies, which is are recipients of duties, the powers of which are determined by a public authority or by the state by virtue of a special agreement concluded for this purpose[29]. In the case of federations, which have a similar way of functioning, whether they exist at the European or at the international level[30], they are entitled to assume tasks of a public interest, such as sports events' organization; still they maintain a private law body status[31].

The legal status of sports federations in France is the one of relative autonomy. Under their guidance, a special body is created so as to monitor professional activities. Sport is considered to be an activity of public interest and the federations are entrusted with the task of serving it[32]. In the Italian law, where special and general legal provisions on federations coexist, the jurisdictional control is always operated by court decisions controlling the observation of the general provisions and combining them with the regulations established by the CONI, the Italian Olympic Committee, which establishes rules for the sports activity[33]. The English sports clubs have a substantial autonomy, as long as they do not offend fundamental public interests and they do not jeopardize, for no important reason, the funds allowing athletes to subsist; they maintain a status of private law entities[34].

The administrative, disciplinary and regulating powers of the sports

---

29) Ep. Spiliotopoulos (2000), Εγχειρίδιο Διοικητικού Δικαίου (Handbook of Administrative Law), Ant. N. Sakkoulas, Athens, p. 388 paragraph 380.

30) On the international sports federation, D. Panagiotopoulos (2005), Διεθνείς Αθλητικοί κα ι Ολυμπιακοί Θεσμοί...(International Sports and Olympic Institutions...), op. cit., p. 307-321.

31) On the significance of public interest, Ep. P. Spiliotopoulos (2000), Εγχειρίδιο Διοικητικού Δικαίου (Handbook of Administrative Law), op. cit., p. 95 paragraph 2.

32) French Presidential Decree 236/23-2-1985; compare with R. Dondoux, The Sports Law, op. cit., p. 162 and following, who reports that the French Law assigns the federations with a real mission of prevention, control and sanctioning (for example, it can decide a temporary or permanent license withdrawal), Ibid p. 162.

33) IASL Bulletin Information (1997), "4ᵗ International Congress on Sports Law...", op. cit., p.48.

34) Andrew C. Evans (1989), «English Law of Sport», op. cit., p. 91, 95.

federation, which serve the public interest purpose of Sport, do not cease to manifest themselves exclusively in the Lex Sportiva context, ending up in satisfying the public interest purpose in the same way that Sport does[35]. All other powers, which are related to Sport but are situated out of the Lex Sportiva, are exercised by public authority bodies to which they are entrusted by law or by regulating administrative acts, following a legislative approval. In this case, there can be no reference to the theory of "awarding a public duty" to private entities[36] since the public duty is entrusted to public bodies.

The management of the financial means by a sports federation, whenever these are legally provided by the State, can be characterized as a sponsorship destined to the achievement of the organization of a sports event. This sponsorship, in this context, contributes to the satisfaction of the public aims served by Sport, on the basis of which takes place the legality control of all management acts of the sports federation, operated by bodies exercising public authority. This control aims to establish if the financial means used by the sports federation, in the context of its disciplinary, agential and administrative power as well as of the Lex Sportiva, have been used for the purpose for which they were given to the federation and not for other purposes, that may also exist in the context of the federation's operation. This financial control on federations, wherever it takes place, is considered to constitute a loose supervision of the State on Sport. It is the case of Greece. In other countries there is even no control of the state administration, which does not interfere with the world regulated by Lex Sportiva[37].

---

35) R. Dondoux, The Sports Law, op. cit., p. 162 and following, who reports that the French Law assigns the federations with a real mission of prevention, control and sanctioning (for example, it can decide a temporary or permanent license withdrawal).

36) Ep. P. Spiliotopoulos, (2000), Εγχειρίδιο ... (Handbook...), op. cit., p. 387 paragraph 379.

37) Liberal system: Complete autonomy, Germany, Free and Independent Sport, Law 1949, Sechster Sportbericht der Bundesregierung, Bonn 1987. Base of the associations' autonomy, according to Cl.Vieweg, is the article 25 of German Civil Code, according to the article 91 of the German Constitution, according to which the Germans have the right to found associations, Cl. Vieweg (1999), "Basic Freedom and Autonomyin Sports-from the Perspective of German and European Law", in: Proceedings of 1st Pan-Hellenic Congress of Sports Law with International attendance, Trikala 4-6 June 1999, Ion: Athens p. 166-168. In France, Organization of sports through private initiative

In Greece, the administration controls, according to the law which regulates the operation of sports federations, if their operation is in accordance with the Constitution, that constitutes the fundamental state rule on sport. Given this supervision, the positions of the personnel to be employed by a sports administration are determined by the competent ministry following a proposal of the Board of Administration (BoA) of the federation in question, which assumes the amount of the fees of the specific personnel[38].

In all cases, it cannot be considered that a sports federation exercises powers of public authority that have been transferred to it by the State. A law defines the framework of the domestic Lex Sportiva[39], which is manifested by the domestic sports federation. Whenever stipulated by law, the administration exercises a legality control on various aspects of a federation's operation, such as the financial management and the regulating role. This control takes place due to the social function of Sport[40], in accordance with the constitution, and to the protection of the public purpose of Sport. It is, therefore, very accurately considered that a sports federation is a potential vector of public authority[41]. The opinion according to which the legislative regulation of the Greek sports field could be based on the public duties award to federations at both a domestic and a federal state level[42] is contradicted by the Lex Sportiva theory, on which, relies the

---

1975, no report to the Constitution, Italy (AK (Civil Code), CONI).

38) Article 30 Law 2725/1999, ΑθλΚ (Sports Code, 2009), p. 37.

39) Dimitrios P. Panagiotopoulos (2013) "Lex Sportiva- Lex Olympica and International Sports law", in: *SPORTS LAW: Structures, Practice, and Justice - Sports Science and Studies* [ Dimitrios P. Panagiotopoulos, Wang Xiaoping (Eds)], EKEAD: Beijing-Athens, pp 20-31. Dimitrios P. Panagiotopoulos (2005), "Lex Sportiva: Sport Institutions and Rules of Law", in: Sports Law Implementation and the Olympic Games [Dimitrios Panagiotopoulos Ed.], Ant. Sakkoulas: Athens, pp. 33-45 and in: International Sports law Review Pandektis (ISLR/Pandektis),Vol. 5:3, pp. 315-327.

40) Article 27 Law 2725/1999, ΑθλΚ (Sports Code, 2009), p. 30, article 52 Law 2725/1999, Αθ λΚ (Sports Code, 2009), p. 115, article 16 paragraph 9 of Greek Constitution, (Sports Code, 2009), p. 3.

41) R. Dondoux, The Sports Law, op. cit., p. 157-158, compare with D. Panagiotopoulos (2001), Αθλητικό Δίκαιο …(Sports Law…), op. cit., p. 277 and following and p. 148.

42) A. Malatos (2005), Παραδόσεις Αθλητικού Δικαίου (Sports Law Courses), Ant. N. Sakkoulas Editions, Athens, p. 245.

whole sports edifice, Sport at the domestic and the international level. According to this theory, the federation represents a sport at the international level, in accordance with the rules of the relevant International Sports Federation and of the IOC[43] in force. Their members, the athletes take place in international meetings through the federation's participation, since it is the sole supreme body for each sport in and out of a country's territory, following its approval or –in special cases- after a minister's decision[44]. Through this system a country's sport[45], and not the sport practiced by individuals, is presented, via the domestic federations, to the international level. A national team's athlete expresses the common national interest and not his own interest or the one of his club.

*Since a sports domestic federation is the one managing the sport at the national level,* it bears the responsibility of the domestic sport practiced under state supervision and control. This federation needs to operate in the context of the Lex Sportiva, but also in accordance with the public interest. Given all this, a State must provide, in accordance with the Constitution, whenever allowed by law, its protection to Sport, by funding a sports federation, so as for it to fulfil its purpose of constitution. In this manner, the domestic sports federation, for the circle of its activities, namely the domestic sports action and competition and the problems arising from it, is considered to be a vector of public authority for the management of sports issues, of the activities taking place out of clubs and for the so-called "sports order". The federation exercises a power in the public interest and in favour of the domestic sports and competitive activity. It is to this activity that state funding is provided and only for this one a control takes place so as to ensure that this funding is used for the satisfaction of the public interest. And of the public purpose that sport serves. In this context, any state interventionism over the autonomous institutional operation of the sports federation, as a body which is issue of the clubs, which are governed by

---

43) Law 2725/1999, article 19, paragraph 2, section 2 and article 33, paragraph 7 and 8.
44) Ibid, article 33, paragraph 7. According to these provisions, in the Greek inter-club championships and the cup games, foreign athletes of Greek origin or other foreign athletes are allowed to participate following a relevant sports federation's proposal and a competent minister's decision.
45) Ibid, article 7, paragraph 6, op. cit., in Sports Code (2005), p. 49.

private law, and is regulated by means of special legal provisions, is justified in the sense that this sports supreme union does not manage only the competitive sport practiced by these clubs but also the sport based on an accumulation of national characteristics, which serves the satisfaction of a public interest. All above mentioned attribute to the sports federation the particular form of a public function service[46].

## Constitution and Composition

Sports clubs or their associations constitute the core of the sports federation of a specific sport. Moreover, any sports club can join a sports association or a federation by the submission of a formal declaration, along with the name list of its athlete-members and the request for the issuance of an athlete's identification document for these members (athlete's identification card)[47]. The federation which develops a sport, to which this sport belongs in exclusivity, following a central administration decision, being this sport's unique and supreme authority, is the only body entitled to issue athletes' cards for this sport. A basic requirement for this card issuance is that the relevant club observes the statutes and the regulation of this federation[48]. No distinction is allowed to take place between the members of a sports federation, such as regular, novice or presiding ones[49].

For the constitution of a sports federation to take place, some requirements need to be fulfilled such as:

 - a decision of the Boards of Administration and of the General Assemblies of the sports clubs or of the associations involved
 - these clubs and associations develop the same sport or operate in the same sports sector.

---

46) R. Dondoux, The Sports Law, op. cit., p. 157-158 and D. Panagiotopoulos (2001), Αθλητικό Δίκαιο... (Sports Law...), op. cit., p. 277 and following, as also p. 148 and following.
47) Article 33, paragraph 9 Law 2725/1999 Health Bulletin, in ΑΘλΚ (Sports Code, 2009), p. 48, compare also with previous Law 75/1975, article 13, paragraph 4 and ΑΘλΚ (Sports Code 2005), p. 63.
48) Article 20 op. cit.
49) In older regulations the members that were registered in a sports club, for the first time, were rendered for one year obligatory as novice or assistants, Law 75/75, Article 1, paragraph 9.

If these requirements are fulfilled, the sports clubs participating in the federation's constitution need to be at least twenty and the sports associations at least five. This minimal number of clubs and associations needs to have already developed a competitive activity[50]. Neither is this activity strictly defined in the law nor the conditions and the mode on the basis of which this activity is established and certified. This is why the opinion that such an activity can even be a virtual one has been expressed. According to the case-law, the number of clubs having founded the federation needs to be established as well as the number of the founding club members that have attended the initial General Assembly of the federation[51].

In case where the number of the acknowledged clubs that practice the same sport or are active in the same sports sector decreases to less than fifteen and as long as no other sport is also incorporated in the same federation, this sport and the clubs practicing it need to be placed under the authority of another, legally operating federation, following a decision of the competent authority on sports matters[52].

A member's registration in a sports federation takes place after a federation's board of administration decision. The radiation of a member ca only take place by means of a decision of the federation's General Assembly[53]. There can be no distinction or discrimination between the members of a federation, such as distinguishing them to regular members, novice members, presiding ones etc[54]. The sports law stipulates that the provisions

---

50) Law 2725/1999, article 20, paragraph 1.
51) Pre-judgment decision 5014/2005 of the ΜΠρωτΑθ (Athens' One-Member First Instance Court) (not published).
52) Ibid, Article 28, paragraph 4, "Specifically for the sports federations of golf and cricket, the provision of the previous section applies provided that the number of the club members is limited to five (5)", the paragraphs 4 and 5 of article 28 Law 2725/1999 were unified as above-mentioned with the paragraph 5 of article 74 Law 3057/2002. Also: The sport of basketball in wheelchairs, practiced by disabled athletes, is placed under the authority of the already existing Ομοσπονδία Σωματείων Ελλήνων Καλαθοσφαι ριστών με Καρότσι (Ο.Σ.Ε.Κ.Κ.) (Federation of Greek Wheelchairs Basketball Players Clubs), which is also member to the International Wheelchair Basketball Federation (I.W.B.F.)", paragraph 4 of article 29 Law 2725/1999, as it was amended and completed by the article 18 paragraph 3 and 4 of Law 2947/2001, the way the last sub-paragraph of paragraph 4 was completed by paragraph 3 of the Law 3262/2004 Article 28.
53) Ibid, article 20, paragraph 2.

of clubs' statutes establishing a maximum number of members as well as establishing financial or other discriminations between their members are null[55]. The possibility and the conditions for sports clubs and associations participating in a federation, to exercise a voting right even before receiving their special sports acknowledgement, are determined by the statutes of the relevant federation[56].

A sports club, by providing to its members more than ones sports and allowing them to practice them, can join more than one federation, which develop a specific sport or, in exceptional cases, more than one special categories sports. This rule is justified by the fact that clubs exist so as to allow their members to practice a sports, while federations exist so as to develop a sport through the clubs' activity, which have joined them and through the athletes' achievements in every sport.

A sports federation has the possibility, in special cases, to incorporate not only its basic sports but also some other sports, under condition that they are not already the object of another federation or union[57]. The law does

---

54) In previous regulations the members that had registered for the first time in a sports club were considered to be novice members for one whole year: Law 75/75, Article 1, paragraph 9.

55) The clubs are compelled to modify their statutes according to the provisions of sports law, Law 2725/1999, Article 136, paragraph 2, as 135 paragraph 8, as it was replaced in the above-mentioned way by paragraph 3 of Law 3262/2004 Article 28.

56) Ibid, article 20, paragraph 2, on sports clubs' ability to take part in the General Assemblies.

57) Law 2725/1999, article 19, paragraph 2, and roughly similar provisions in article 13, paragraph 1, section 2 of the Law 75/1975. An example of such a sports association, covering more sports, is the Σύνδεσμος Ελληνικών Γυμναστικών Αθλητικών Σωματείων (Federation of Greek Gymnastics Associations), which, apart from the classic gymnastics sports, had also incorporated some other sports such as the modern gymnastics. Still, after court litigation, this specific sport has been acknowledged to constitute the object of a separate Federation: ΜΠρωτΑθ (Athens One-Member First Instance Court) decision 6458/1996, conditions of constitution of a separate Federation for a sport that is placed under the authority of an existing federation. ΜΠρωτΑθ (Athens First Instance Court) decision 28228, annulment of an interim order (requested due to reasons of direct and irreparable harm that could be sustained), which was awarded until the judgment of a demand for the suspension of the execution of a decision, following a third-party opposition. The ομοσπονδία Κωπηλασίας (Rowing Federation) is another example where a federation had incorporated more than one sports: It had indeed incorporated Rowing as well as Canoe Kayak, which was not the

not clearly indicate when a sport cannot be the object of a separate federation as well as which is the process for its incorporation in an already existing federation of another sport. For a sport or for a sports sector which are not the object of an acknowledged sports federation or the incorporation of which to another federation is contested, the competent minister for sports matters can place it under the authority of an already existing acknowledged by means of a decision of his[58].

A sports sector which gets differentiated from the federation in which it was initially incorporated, so as to be acknowledged as an independent sports federation, needs to meet the conditions set by sports law, such as the following:

a) the sport or the sports sector developed by the new federation has to be included in the Olympic Games official program,

b) an international federation needs to already exist for this sport or sports sector,

c) this federation has to be acknowledged by the International Olympic Committee (IOC),

d) all the conditions for the participation of a representative of this new federation to the plenary session of the Greek Olympic Committee

---

object of any other Federation until the Ministerial Decision 43775/20- 3-1987 officially placed the sport of Canoe Kayak under the authority of the ΕΚΟΦΝΣ (Greek Rowing Federation of Naval Sports Associations). Compare with D. Panagiotopoulos (1991), Ίδρυσ η νέας Ομοσπονδίας Αθλήματος που υπάγεται σε άλλη" ("Foundation of a new Federation in a Sport already governed by another"), Διοικητική Δίκη (Diikitike Dike, Administrative Trial Journal), 3, p. 25-28, with regard to the issuance of an athlete's card. Consultation, D. Panagiotopoulos (1990) "Έκδοση δελτίου αθλητή αθλήματος νέου, ο τα πλαίσια ομοσπονδίας άλλου αθλήματος" ("Issuance of a new athlete's card in the context of a federation which develops a different sport"), ΣΤΑΔΙΟΝ (STADION, Stadium), 1:1, p. 95-97.

58) Paragraph 6 of article 28 Law 2725/1999 as it was again numbered later as being paragraph 5, by paragraph 6 of the article 74 Law 3057/2002. The legislator did the same previously, in a similar case. Article 23 paragraph 4 Law 423/1976 by mans of which the paragraph 6 section 1 of the Law 75/1975 and the paragraph 6 section 2 of the article 13 of Law 75/1975 were added; also ΑΘλΚ (Sports Code), p. 30. More by D. Panagiotopoulos (1991), Διοικητική Δίκη (Diikitike dike, Administrative Trial Journal), op. cit., 26 and following and draft of the Ministerial Decision 43775/20.3.1987 on the subordination of the sport of Canoe Kayak to the ΕΚΟΦΝΣ (Greek Rowing Federation of Naval Sports Associations).

have to be met, as well as all the rules of the Constitutive Chart of the IOC have to be observed, and

e) relevant decisions of the Boards of Administration and of the General Assemblies of more than fifty percent (50%) of the sports clubs practicing this sport and having received the special sports acknowledgment stipulated by law need to have been taken and their total number must be at least twenty[59].

All clubs which practice the same sport or operate in the same sports sector, that did not take a decision to leave the previous federation and join the new one, are ipso jure radiated from the previous federation and incorporated in the new one, when it is constituted, unless they decide not to join it, in which case they are only radiated from the previous one upon the new one's constitution[60].

## Powers

According to a theoretic opinion, sports federations, as legal entities, have operated a major contribution to positive law during the 20$^{th}$ century[61].

---

59) Law 2725/1999, Article 28, paragraph 3, compare with ΜΠρωτΑθ (One-Member Athens First Instance Court) decision 6458/1996. Third-party opposition of an association that had incorporated more than one sport, against a decision acknowledging the foundation of a federation for one of the sports it had already incorporated. Also compare with 28228/1996: Annulment of an interim suspension order, which was awarded following a third-party's opposition, until the time of the suspension application judgment. Direct and irreparable harm sustained and substantial harm caused to the general operation of organized sports.

60) Ibid, article 28, paragraph 3 section c, in ΑθλΚ (Sports Code) (2005) p. 70.

61) R. Dondoux (1979), Law and Sports, op. cit., p. 159. The type of the overlying conjunction of legal persons in sports reveals another situation and an old perception, P.d. Coubertin, "The Olympic Games, in Athens 1896", B' Part., p. 6, compare with N. Muller (1975): "Die Olympische Idee Pierre de Coubertins und Carl Diems", In: Ihrer Auswirkung ouf die internationale Olympische Akademie (I. O. A.). Fine guellenge Schichtliche Untersuchung, Doctoral Thesis, Graz, p. 33, I. Chrisafis (1930), Σύγχρονοι Δι εθνείς Ολυμπιακοί Αγώνες ("Modern International Olympic Games"), Athens, p. 177. P. Manitakis (1962), 100 χρόνια Νεολληνικού Αθλητισμού ("100 years of Neo-Hellenic Sports"), Athens, p. 33.

Amongst the powers of sports federations mainly figure the organization of a sport as well as ensuring its competitive presence at the top level.

The Greek sports federation presents a particular legal status, since it is not only an administrative body but also a legislative and a disciplinary one[62]. It therefore has powers which concern the sport itself and its competition, such as the organization and the supervision of all sports events and competitions[63]. It also shapes the principles of a sport and of the clubs operation governing the relations of their members, the sport development and the people implicated in a sport's life. Last but not least, it has controlling powers and a disciplinary authority over all the sport's aspects previously mentioned.

The powers of a sports federation need to be classified as follows:

a) *Organizational powers,* such as the power to constitute and to establish special bodies of a technical, disciplinary, jurisdictional nature and others necessary for the purpose of the federation's existence. Many of the decisions of these bodies require ratification by the federation's Board of

---

62) D. Panagiotopoulos (1990), Θεωρία (Theory), p. 19, same author 1991 in: Διοικητική Δίκη (Administrative Trial Journal), p. 20, K. Remelis (1993), "Concept and nature of disciplinary sport", ΕΚΕΑΔ (H.C.R.L.S): Athens 1993, p. 325-336, compare with D. Panagiotopoulos (1995), "The Institutional Problem of the Greek Sport Federation", In: Marquette Sports Law Journal, vol. 5:2, p.247-249. The imposition of disciplinary sanctions creates private disputes, which, according to the case law, come under the jurisdiction of political courts. Private disputes springs up for example from the imposition of a sentence of prohibition of entry in the gaming space by the Federation as responsible for the particular sport, ΣτΕ (State Council) decisions 619/1983, 3402/1984, 623/1987 and 2359/1987, because these precise relations have as source the rules of internal order of this organization and the free will of its members in the frame of institutional autonomy, compare with Delligiannis-Skouris, Αρμενόπουλος (Armenopoulos Journal) 1986, p. 587, as also D. Panagiotopoulos (1993), "Ζητήματα επιστη μολογικής οριοθέτησης και εφαρμογής του Αθλητικού Δικαίου" ("Questions of epistemological delimitation and application of Sports Law") in: Διοικητική Δίκη (Administrative Trial Journal), 3, p. 973, D. Panagiotopoulos (1995), "The Institutional Problem of the Greek Sports Federation", op. cit., p. 243-250 and Yearbook of Sports Law III, Ant. Sakkoulas: Athens.

63) The Board of Administration's decision for the proclamation of games must be based on approved games' organization regulations, ΑΣΕΑΔ (Ανώτατο Συμβούλιο Επίλυσης Αθ λητικών Διαφορών, High Council for the Resolution of Sports Disputes) decision 109/2002.

Administration, like the decisions of the competent committee on transfers within a specific sport[64].

b) Powers of a regulatory nature.

The sports federation has the power to issue special rules – regulations for its internal operation, which apply to the people involved in the club and in the sport's life circle as well as to the people practicing a specific sport. Any issue that is relevant to the sport is regulated by means of specific rules that are adopted by the federation members' general assembly, by the association or by the union (in the case of a sports sector). The sports federation rules and regulations need to observe the international sports regulations of the relevant international federation and all clubs and associations which are bound by the authority of the domestic federation of a specific sport[65] need to abide by these international sports regulations too.

The regulations also need to be in accordance with the sports law provisions. All decisions of the IOC on Doping[66] and drugs use also need to be incorporated to the regulations in question. In this regime, sports federations assume the institutional duty, as supreme sports authorities, to fight against Doping, while a unified regulatory effort to face this problem is attempted on the basis of the international practice[67], by incorporating the

---

64) It is constituted following a Board of Administration's decision, which is notified to the ΓΓΑ (General Secretariat for Sports) and to every federation; paragraph 3 of article 33 combined with the article 27 of Law 2725/99, ΑθλΚ (Sports Code) p. 87 and 68; compare with relevant Ministerial Decision 21451, article 9, paragraph 1 and 2(o) in 475/1-7-1991 vol. B). Relevant decision 128/1990 of the ΑΣΕΑΔ (Ανώτατο Συμβούλιο Επίλ υσης Αθλητικών Διαφορών, High Council for the Resolution of Sports Disputes). In this decision the virtual registration of a Track athlete was accepted after the expiration of the relevant deadline available for its ratification by the Federation's Board of Administration.

65) Ibid, article 27. Ilia's One-Member First Instance Court decision 1250/2004 on a club's demand for interim measures against a Federation, in order for its athletes to be included in a summer skiing international competition.

66) Id, article 26, paragraph 4, compare with article 27 Law 2725/1999, also Code of International Olympic Committee (I.O.C.), Olympic Chart 1999 -2002, as it is adopted since 1989, compare with European Convention Anti-Doping, ratified by the Law 2371/1996 with an indicative list of substances and doping methods, Sports Code (1997), 370-394, compare also with Anti-Doping Code (WADA) [2003].

67) Article 26 paragraph 4 in combination with the article 27 Law 2725/99, Sports Code,

unified relevant regulation in the operating regulations of the sports federations. The sports federation is not only a sport's administrative body but also the legislative body for a sports sector, especially on all issues related to the relations established in the sports activity. The federation's legislative work is controlled, as far as its legality is concerned, by the central administration[68].

c) Disciplinary powers.

The sports federation has also a disciplinary power over the actions and omissions of the people and the bodies implicated in sports life, in the field of the sport that it develops; it also has the right to implement sanctions through decisions of its bodies. It therefore has the power to appoint controlling, disciplinary and technical bodies, so as for the disciplinary authority to be exercised from the federation to its members, to the clubs and to the sports life in general. This disciplinary power has to respect the federation's regulations, which are in accordance with the rules of international Sport, of the IOC and with the principles of fair play[69]. A federation has the right to impose sanctions[70]on sports discipline issues, on Doping as well as on fair play, honest competition or on games and on physical and moral health issues in general. Its power on these issues results

---

I., p. 67-69, compare with ΑΣΕΑΔ (Ανώτατο Συμβούλιο Επίλυσης Αθλητικών Διαφορών, High Council for the Resolution of Sports Disputes) decision 53/2002, with which the sentence of exclusion that was imposed by a sports federation to an athlete in a doping affair in international games was cancelled.

68) After the expiration of two months since its notification for approval to the ΓΓΑ (General Sports Secretariat) it is tacitly considered as having been approved, ΑΣΕΑΔ (High Council of Resolution of Sports Disputes) decision 109/2004 with regard to the disciplinary regulation of Federation of Modern Pentathlon.

69) Olympic Chart, I.O.C., articles 2 and 50, compare with L. Silance, "Sports Law", op. cit., p. 79, and following, D. Panagiotopoulos, Sports Fan Attribute, Ant. N. Sakkoulas, Athens, p. 15-24, same author, Olympia's Moral Horizon and the Branch of the Victory, op. cit., p. 29-33.

70) No 104/1-3-2000 Objections ΕΕ/ΕΠΟ (Appeals Committee /Greek Football Federation) with which an amateur footballer's Objection on an imposed sentence of retraction of the athletic attribute's bulletin and three years exclusion from each game was rejected, because he used factitious justifying for its publication; compare also with ΑΣΕΑΔ (High Council of Resolution of Sports Disputes) decision 124/2002, with which a sentence of suspension of the gaming bulletin and exclusion from the games to an athlete because of infringement of regulations of the sports Federation is decreased.

from law provisions[71], from its statutes and from the games operational regulation[72], which all form a domestic Lex Sportiva.

In order to take decisions on disciplinary matters, a sports federation does not only need to observe the substance of its statutes or of its regulation[73]. It also needs to observe the required legal procedure and the proper operation of its own disciplinary bodies.

It indeed has to ensure the following:

a) the lawful invitation of the Board of Administration (BoA) members, as required by law or by the federation's statutes or by its regulation, since the BoA members need to receive a written invitation, to attend the BoA disciplinary meeting, in which the specific issues to be examined must be mentioned and

b) the secrecy of the Board of Administration members' votes during the decisional process, since the voting process is a secret one[74].

In the context of the exercise of the powers above mentioned, it has often been observed that their exercise by the same authority results in a confusion of powers and in a lack of objectivity[75] as well as in the

---

71) Article 128 b paragraph 3 in ΑθλΚ (Sports Code) (2005), p. 308.
72) ΑΣΕΑΔ (High Council of Resolution of Sports Disputes) decision 99/1997 according to which, the federation of each sport is the only responsible for the conduct of championships in its sport, for the publication of familiar proclamations of games, as well as for the change, the suppression or their replacement in the legal deadlines.
73) ΑΣΕΑΔ (High Council of Resolution of Sports Disputes) decision 85/2002, with which a sentence imposed by a sports federation, after the decision of the familiar jurisdictional committee, because of violation of the principle of prohibition of proportion of the disciplinarily punishable character of the particular behaviour of the persecuted one, is cancelled.
74) Relevant ΑΣΕΑΔ (High Council of Resolution of Sports Disputes) decision 159/1990, with which a federation's decision is cancelled, just because the legal convocation of the Board of Administration and the secrecy of voting were not ensured, as it was necessary. The case-law constantly accepts that the Civil Code's provisions apply on of sports associations' issues that are not explicitly regulated by law: comment of G. Dionisatos in Pandektis/ISLR, op. cit., p. 117 and relevant case-law: ΕιρΑθ (Peace Court of Athens) decision 3154/1976, ΕΕΝ (Greek Law Practitioners Review).
75) ΕφΑθ (Court of Appeal of Athens) decision 4243/1997, Ελληνική Δικαιοσύνη (Hellinike Dikaiossyne, Hellenic Justice Journal), 39:1998,p. 410, according to which, in accordance with the dominant law theoreticians' opinion, the disciplinary power of an association is exercised as a manifestation of its autonomy and its self-government; still, it is not

satisfaction of objectives that are not in total accordance with the nature and the morals of Sport. This confusion creates new, more complicated problems[76], resulting from the infringement of the laws and of the regulations by the bodies constituted by the sports federation.

## Regulating Power

In order to ensure the good operation of the sports federation the general assembly of the federation's members adopts general and special regulations, by means of which are established some rules applying to all issues related to the organization of a Sport or of sports incorporated in it as well as every other relevant detail[77]. All international relevant regulations are taken into consideration upon the establishment or a domestic federation's regulations; sports clubs that have joined such a federation are bound to observe its regulations[78].

The regulations, the rules resulting from them and their amendments, adopted by a federation's General Assembly, in their present or future form, are the object of a legality control operated by the minister within a two-month period[79]. The force of the rules established by the federation

arbitrary and is governed by the general principles applicable to all forms of sanctions, in the framework of the democratically constituted society. Such a principle is the principle "ne bis in idem"; therefore, imposing two separate disciplinary sanctions for the same disciplinary fault is not allowed, compare with D. Panagiotopoulos (1990), Θεω ρία (Theory), op. cit., p. 49-56.

76) ΣτΕ (State Council) decision 2426/1986, ΑΣΕΑΔ (High Council for the Resolution of Sports Disputes) decisions 212/1984,200/1988,188/1991, compare with D. Panagiotopoulos (1993), "Sports law aspects in Implementation", in: Proceedings 1ˢᵗ IASL Congress, Athens, p. 77-78, D. Panagiotopoulos (1997) Αθλητική Δικαιοδοσία (Sports Jurisdiction), Ant. Sakkoulas Editions, Athens, p. 18 and following.

77) The regulations applying to private legal entities, such as sports clubs and federations, are mandatory and applicable to everyone who participates in sports competitions, exception made of all private law entities that have been constituted by means of a private agreement; all disputes related to these entities, regardless the legal rules which apply to them and the purpose these rules serve, are judged by the court in the geographical district of which the agreement has been concluded, ΣτΕ (State Council) decision 1738/1986.

78) Article 27 in ΑθλΚ (Sports Code) p. 68-69.

79) Article 27, as it was modified by the paragraph 3 of the Law 3057/2002 article 74.

depends on this legality control operated by the central administration and on having observed the legality control procedure. This specific rule, which figures in the sports law, is a mandatory one.

When the legality control takes place[80], if some provisions of the regulation are found to require an amendment, a completion or a harmonization, the federation is invited to operate these modifications within a ten-day period[81]. If the legal deadline for the legality control of specific regulations ends without their having been controlled, the relevant regulations are considered to have been legally issued[82].

All matters concerning the organization, the administration and the operation of a sports federation and of its associations as well as the status of their employees, are dealt with by means of a special regulation adopted by the federation's BoA and approved by the competent sports minister. The obligation for a federation to submit this regulation to the central administration for approval does not apply in case where this federation is partially funded by the General Secretariat for Sports (G.S.S.) or by another body that is supervised by the ΓΓΑ (G.S.S.), to a percentage smaller than fifty per cent (50%) of its total income[83]. In such a case, the use of this amount, although smaller than 50% of the federation's income, remains uncontrolled by the central administration. Still the funding depends on the way that the funds will be used, regardless the approval of the federation's regulation by the central administration. The control should, therefore, even in such a case, be mandatory, sine it is constitutionally necessary; the administration should be forced to exercise its legality control for all funds provided to

---

Following their approval, the federations' regulations are published in the Hellenic Official Journal; published regulations and relevant Ministerial Decisions of the Minister of Culture in: Κώδικας Νομικού Βήματος (Kodikas Nomikou Vimatos, Legal Podium Code Journal) 2000, Vol. 48, p. 3066-3068.

80) Issued by the competent Minister: Law 2725/1999, article 27. According to the ΠολΠρΑθ (Multi-member Athens First Instance Court) decision 488/1985, the provisions related to sanctions imposed by the ΓΓΑ (Secretary-General for Sports) and applicable to basketball coaches or clubs, are private law ones.

81) The Board of Administration has that power: article 27 Law 2725/99, amended as above mentioned by paragraph 3 of the article 74 of Law 3057/2002, in ΑθλΚ (Sports Code) (2005), p. 68-69.

82) Ibid, article 27.

83) Id, article 30, paragraph 1, section 3.

federations regardless their amount.

In such a regulation are determined:

a) All organic posts and the federation's inner structure,

b) the positions' number per object and specialization,

c) the required typical skills and

d) the duties related to every position[84].

All posts described in the regulation and approved by the administration are organic ones to every federation and unique for the whole of the associations incorporated in it. The employment of personnel without the existence of corresponding structural positions is strictly and explicitly forbidden by sports law. Any form of personnel employment needs to take place by means of a procedure similar to the one for the employment of people in the public sector[85], exception made of all special associates, coaches and trainers, technical consultants, physiotherapists, doctors of all specialties, lawyers, scientific associates, care takers, journalists and public relations consultants. It becomes evident that this state intervention in the affairs of a federation, which is a private law entity, especially the one related to federation's personnel, places the federation under the immediate control of the central administration. This control is also focused on the issues that arise with regard to the remuneration of sports federations' personnel. The implementation of the employment's contract of a sports federation employee, who is included in the federation's regular personnel that follows a General Secretary's for Sport approval, is a particular procedure, since his salaries are subjected to the application of the rules on the uniform remuneration of public servants[86].

---

84) Id, article 30, paragraph 1, section 1.

85) Id, article 30, paragraph 3; compare with the last sections of paragraph 3 of article 30, as they were adopted by means of paragraph 20 of the Law 3207/2003 article 8; according to this provision, all federations' personnel working by virtue of a private law employment contract of an undetermined duration, that proves to be redundant, can be transferred, under the same employment regime, to another federation or to the Greek Olympic Committee, in accordance with the provisions of the sports law.

86) On the uniform wages regime of Law 1505/1984: decision 1137/1991 and article 361 of the AK (Civil Code), as well as AΠ (Greek High Court's) decision 854/1986, Νομικό Βήμα (Nomiko Vima, Legal Podium Journal) 35, p. 1197, Athens; ΕφΑθ (Athens Court of Appeal) decision 5117/1989, Νομικό Βήμα (Nomiko Vima, Legal Podium Journal) 38, p.

## Conclusion

The Greek Constitution provisions constitute the institutional guarantee of the right to the free development of sports activities;

These regulations establish a context for the exercise of the constitutional right to the free individual and collective sports action under state supervision and protection.

The establishment of sports clubs, associations and federations, as a special expression of people's right to associate themselves, indicates that Sport has an institutional autonomy.

Sports federations are controlled by the State, as provided by law, on the basis of the principle that they are the unique high sports authorities in every sport, giving them a monopoly and dominant position.

The sports reality of the existence of a federation contributes to the determination of its particular nature, as the only supreme authority of a sport, governing all relevant clubs and developing that specific sport. A domestic sports federation constitutes the only entity representing a country's domestic sports activity at the international level and communicating with the international federations. These international sports federations impose the observation of the rules that they establish to the domestic ones, thus creating a Law that does not belong to any country, the Lex Sportiva, which is introduced in the domestic law and many times imposed by the domestic federation, on the basis of the transformation and the incorporation theory.

Since a sports domestic federation is the one managing the sport at the national level, it bears the responsibility of the domestic sport to be practiced under state supervision and control. This federation needs to operate in the context of the Lex Sportiva, but also in accordance with the public interest. Given all this, a State must provide, in accordance with the Constitution, whenever allowed by law, its protection to Sport, by funding a sports federation, so as for it to fulfil its purpose of constitution.

The federation exercises a power in the public interest and in favour of

---

825; compare with D. Panagiotopoulos, (1997), ΑθλΚ (Sports Code), p. 91, footnote 28, Ant. N. Sakkoulas Editions, Athens.

the domestic sports and competitive activity. It is to this activity that state funding is provided and only for this one a control takes place so as to ensure that this funding is used for the satisfaction of the public interest. And of the public purpose that sport serves.

All above mentioned, attribute to the sports federation the particular form of a mandate public function service.

## References

Alexandrakis Vagelis (2009), "The Employee Status for Sportspersons in English and Greek Law", in: Sports Law: an Emerging Legal Order - Human Rights of Athletes [Dimitrios Panagiotopoulos Ed] Nom. Bibliothiki: Athens, pp.225- 236.

Anagnostopoulos Ioannis C. (2009), "Labour Rights of Minor Athletes", in: Sports Law: an Emerging Legal Order - Human Rights of Athletes [Dimitrios Panagiotopoulos Ed] Nom. Bibliothiki: Athens, pp. 260- 275.

Auneau Gerard (2009), "Le traitement des Contentieux Sportifs par le Mouvement Sportif international et Francais", in: Sports Law: an Emerging Legal Order - Human Rights of Athletes [Dimitrios Panagiotopoulos Ed] Nom. Bibliothiki: Athens, pp. 323- 330.

Auneau Gérard (2008), "The Treatment of Exceptional Sports Cases in Common, National and European Law: Moving Towards an International Customary Law of Sport", In: I.S.L.R. Pandektis, Vol. 8:3-4, pp. 415-423.

Auneau G, (1992), "L' Application de la Legislation Sociale du Secteur Sportif et du Loisir Sportif dans l' Europe Communataire de 1993'", in: International Sports Law Review Pandektis, pp. 231-247, and in: Proceedings 1st International Congress on Sports Law, pp. 89-107

Bredimas Antonis (2005) "Multilateral diplomacy for sport: The Case of Unesco", in: Sports Law: Implementation and the Olympic Games [D. Panagiotopoulos ed.], Ant. N. Sakkoulas: Athens, pp 327-334.

Boundoux R (1978), «The law and the sports», In: Proceedings of the 18th I.O.A. Conf. Athens.

Carretero Lestón José Luis, Morte Ferrer Ricardo(2009), "Taxation of Sports Sponsorship in Spain", International Sports Law Review Pandektis,

(ISLR Pandektis) Vol 8:1-2, p.p. 11-15.

Gardiner Simon (2004),"The Emergence of a Lex Sportiva: The Regulation of English Football", in: Sports Law [Lex Sportiva] in the World (D. Panagiotopoulos Ed.), Ant. N. Sakkoulas: Athens, pp. 258-284.

Giandomenico Anna Di (2009), "Doping and patrimonial interests", in: Sports Law: an Emerging Legal Order - Human Rights of Athletes [Dimitrios Panagiotopoulos Ed] Nom. Bibliothiki: Athens, pp. 291- 303.

Dimitropoulos A. (1998), "Issues of Constitutional Law"), Athens.

Jacq P (1993), "L' Intervention du Juge dan les Etats-Membres de la Communaute Europeene", in : Proceedings 1st International Congress on Sports Law, Athens, pp. 401-407.

Karaquilo P. J. (1997), Le droit du sport, connaissance du droit (2e edition, Dalloz: Paris.

Mavromatis Achilleas (2009), "The prohibition of suspension award for violence crimes in sport fields in Greece", in: Sports Law: an Emerging Legal Order - Human Rights of Athletes [Dimitrios Panagiotopoulos Ed] Nom. Bibliothiki: Athens, pp. 308- 313.

Meirim José Manuel (2004), "The legal framework of the Portuguese sportive system", in: Sports Law [Lex Sportiva] in the World (D. Panagiotopoulos Ed.), Ant. N. Sakkoulas: Athens, pp.310-336.

Mournianakis Ioannis (2009), "Sport and EC Competition Law: application and exemption", in: Sports Law: an Emerging Legal Order - Human Rights of Athletes [Dimitrios Panagiotopoulos Ed] Nom. Bibliothiki: Athens, pp. 196- 215.

Mournianakis Ioannis (2008), "EU sport policy: the new approach in the treaty of Lisbon", In: I.S.L.R. Pandektis, Vol. 8:3-4, pp. 663-664.

Nafziger James A.R. (2005) "Circumstantial evidence of doping: Balco and beyond", in: Sports Law: Implementation and the Olympic Games [D. Panagiotopoulos ed.], Ant. N. Sakkoulas: Athens, pp.267-275.

Nafziger James A.R. (2004), "Lex Sportiva", in: The International Sports Law Journal, ½, pp. 37-44.

Nafziger James A.R. (2004), *International Sports Law*, Transnational Publishers: N. York.

Nemes Andras (2009), "The Potential Correlations between the Legal rules related to Sport and the Efficiency", in: Sports Law: an Emerging Legal Order - Human Rights of Athletes [Dimitrios Panagiotopoulos Ed],

Nom. Bibliothiki: Athens, pp. 29-35.

Loberdos A. (1993), ("The protection of sport as an individual and a social right") in: Proceedings of the 1st International Congress on Sports Law, December 11-13, Athens 1992, ΕΚΕΑΔ: Athens 1992, p. 171-175.

Muller N. (1975): "Die Olympische Idee Pierre de Coubertins und Carl Diems", In: Ihrer Auswirkung ouf die internationale Olympische Akademie (I. O. A.). Fine guellenge Schichtliche Untersuchung, Doctoral Thesis, Graz.

Panagiotopoulos Dimitrios (2013) "Lex Sportiva- Lex Olympica and International Sports law", in: SPORTS LAW: Structures, Practice, and Justice - Sports Science and Studies [Dimitrios P. Panagiotopoulos, Wang Xiaoping (Eds)], EKEAD: Beijing-Athens, pp 20-31.

Panagiotopoulos Dimitrios (2012), "Sports Law, a Primitive Theory", in: *International Sports Law Review Pandektis* (ISLR/Pand), Vol. 9: 3-4, pp. 256-258.

Panagiotopoulos Dimitrios. (2012), "Lex Sportiva: International or sui Generis – 'Unethnic' Law?", in: "SPORTS LAW: PROSPECTS OF DEVELOPMENT", sixth International scientific practical conference, Moscow State Law Academy et all, Russia. 30 May 2012 MoskBa, pp. 25-31.

Panagiotopoulos Dimitrios (2011). Sports Law: Lex Sportiva –Lex Olympica: theory and praxis N. Sakkoulas: Athens.

Panagiotopoulos Dimitrios (2010), "Institutional Foundation of Physical Education and Sports Games, International Journal of Physical Education (IJPE) 1: 2010 ,pp 25-35.

Panagiotopoulos Dimitrios (2010 "Lex Sportiva and International Legitimacy Governing the Protection of Professional Players" In: Journal of US-China Law Review", No. 8, Vol. 1.

Panagiotopoulos Dimitrios (2009 ed), Sports Law: *An* Emerging Legal Order - Human Rights of Athletes, Nomiki Vivliothiki: Athens, Athens .

Panagiotopoulos Dimitrios (2009), "Lex Sportiva and Lex Olympica, in: XIII Olympic Congress, Copenhagen 2009, [part, Olympic Family Contributions: The structure of the Olympic Movement], IOC: Lausanne, pp. 368-369.

Panagiotopoulos Dimitrios (2008), "Legal Policy for Sports Law in the European Union", in: Protection of Sports Rights and Legal Challenge for the National Sport Promotion [Kee-Young Yeun (ed)], Korean Association of Sports & Entertainment Law (KASEL), Supporter: Seoul- Korea, pp.141-152.

Panagiotopoulos P. Dimitrios (2004), Sports Law [Lex Sportiva] in the World, Ant.

N. Sakkoulas: Athens.

Panagiotopoulos Dimitrios (2005), "Lex Sportiva: Sport Institutions and Rules of Law", in: Sports Law Implementation and the Olympic Games [Dimitrios Panagiotopoulos Ed.], Ant. Sakkoulas: Athens, pp. 33-45 and in: International Sports law Review Pandektis (ISLR/Pandektis), Vol. 5:3, pp. 315-327.

Panagiotopoulos Dimitrios (2004), "Theoretical foundation of sports law" (1st Part: Sports Law: A Special Scientific Branch, Sports Legal Order in Sports Activities, Sports Regulation and Law Limits, Institutional Autonomy and Economic Freedom in Sports Activities), in: Sports Law [Lex Sportiva] in the World (D. Panagiotopoulos Ed.), Ant. N. Sakkoulas: Athens, p. 19-80.

Panagiotopoulos Dimitrios. (1995), "The Institutional Problem of the Greek Sport Federation", In: Marquette Sports Law Journal, vol. 5:2, p.247-249.

Panagiotopoulos Dimitrios (1993), "Le Droit du Sport Selon la Constitution" in: Revue Juridique et Economique du Sport, No 25:2, p. 109-116.

Panagiotopoulos Dimitrios (1993), "Questions of epistemological delimitation and application of Sports Law"), 1st International Congress on Sports Law, in: ΕΚΕΑΔ (H.C.R.L.S): Athens, pp. 63-88.

Panagiotopoulos Dimitrios (2003),"Sports Legal Order in national and international sporting life" in: International Sports Law Review Pandektis (ISLR/Pandektis), Vol.5: 2, p. 227-242.

Panagiotopoulos Dimitrios (1991), "Foundation of a new Federation in a Sport already governed by another", Diikitike Dike, (Administrative Trial Journal), 3, pp. 25-28.

Panagiotopoulos D. (1990) "Issuance of a new athlete's card in the context of a federation which develops a different sport", STADION, Stadium , 1:1, p. 95-97.

Panagiotopoulos Dimitrios P., Xiaoping Wang (Eds) (2013) SPORTS LAW: Structures, Practice, and Justice - Sports Science and Studies, EKEAD: Beijing-Athens.

Panagiotopoulos Dimitrios., Ioannis Mournianakis, Vaggelis Alexandrakis, Sergios Manarakis (2010), "Prospects for EU Action in the Field of Sport after the Lisbon Treaty", in: *International Sports law Review Pandektis*, Vol. 8:3-4, pp. 301-310.

Remelis K. (1993) "Restrictions to the conventional freedom of professional athletes", in: *I.S.L.R. Pandektis,* Vol. 1:4, pp. 547-560.

Saito Kenji (2005) "Sports Law In Japan", in: Sports Law: Implementation and the Olympic Games [D. Panagiotopoulos ed], Ant. N. Sakkoulas: Athens

Silance Luc (2005) "Les ordres juridiques du sport et les arrets Bosman et Kolpak", in: Sports Law: Implementation and the Olympic Games [D. Panagiotopoulos ed.], Ant. N. Sakkoulas: Athens.

Silance Luc (1998), Les sports et le droit, Droit actuel, De Boeck Université, De Boeck et Larcier, Paris-Bruxelles.

Silance Luc (1976) "Problems de Droit International en Sport", in: Proceeding International Congress on Physical Activity Sciences, Vol.9, pp. 391-340.

Silance Luc (1971), "The Rules of the International Olympic Committee and the Law' in Proceedings of the 11th Conference, IOC: Olympia, p.142.

Souri Kh. W., Panagiotopoulos D., Vagenas G., (2001), "Awareness of Sports Legislation and Reaction of Team Sport Athletes towards the Infliction of Penalty", in: International Sports Law Review Pandektis, Vol. IV: 1/2, pp. 53-61.

Sugranes M. Teresa Franquet (2005) "The right of publicity of professional sportsmen", in: Sports Law: Implementation and the Olympic Games [D. Panagiotopoulos ed.], Ant. N. Sakkoulas: Athens

Staveren v.H.T (1988), "The rules of the Sport Community and the law of the State", In: Sports and the Law, Proceedings of the 18th Congress of the Eighteenth Colloquy on European Law, 12-14 October, Maastricht.

Strurzebecker Russel L. (1994), "The role of Law", in: *I.S.L.R. Pandektis*, Vol. 2:1, pp. 24-28

Yeun KeeYoung (2010), Sports Law : Lex sportiva, National Sports Law and International Sports Law, !6th IASL Congress Proceedings, Hanyahng University, Seoul, Korea.

Yeun KeeYoung (2009), "The Unification and Harmonizing of the Asian Sports Law", in: Sports Law: an Emerging Legal Order - Human Rights of Athletes [Dimitrios Panagiotopoulos Ed], Nom. Bibliothiki: Athens, pp. 73- 83, and in: International Sports Law Review Pandektis, (ISLR Pandektis) , Vol 8:1-2, p.p. 46-58.

Xiaoping Wang (2009), "The construction and the future of Arbitration for Sport in China", in: Sports Law: an Emerging Legal Order - Human Rights of Athletes [Dimitrios Panagiotopoulos Ed] Nom. Bibliothiki: Athens, pp. 437- 442, and International Sports Law Review Pandektis, (ISLR Pandektis), Vol 8:1-2, p.p. 84-90.

Venizelos El. (1993), "The Constitutional Reception of Sport", in: Proceedings of the International Congress, The Olympic Games Institution - interdisciplinary approach, Olympia, 3-7 September 1991 and Pandektis ISLR, 1:2, 1992, p. 212-214.

Venizelos El. (1993), "Sport and State of Law - the limits of the legal deregulation and the return to the Constitution"), in: Proceedings of the 1st International Congress of Sports Law, Athens of 11-13 December 1992, ΕΚΕΑΔ (Hellenic Center of Research on Sports Law): Athens, p. 125-130

Vieweg Klaus (2004), "Basic freedoms and autonomy in sport – from the perspective of German and European Law", in: Sports Law [Lex Sportiva] in the World (D. Panagiotopoulos Ed.), Ant. N. Sakkoulas: Athens, pp.285-305.

Wolohan John (2010), "Sports Image Rights in the United States", in: International Symposium on Scientized Sports Law, Research Center of Sports Law of China, Univ. of Political Science and Law School, China

Zagklis Andreas (2004), "Strike and Lock - out in Greek Professional Sport", in: Sports Law [Lex Sportiva] in the World (D. Panagiotopoulos Ed.), Ant. N. Sakkoulas: Athens, pp.422-440

# Challenges to the Authority of CAS

MARIOS PAPALOUKAS*

*The grounds for a successful appeal before the Swiss Federal Tribunal against an award issued by the CAS are very restrictive. Nevertheless, there are some landmark cases of the Swiss Federal Tribunal setting aside CAS awards. The purpose of this paper is to present these cases as well as the arguments used when these awards were challenged.*

**Key word:** Sports Law, Arbitration, Swiss Law, Private International Law, The Court of Arbitration for Sport (CAS), Swiss Federal Tribunal, Public Order

## Introduction

The Swiss Private International Law Act (PILA)

According to the Swiss Private International Law Act on international arbitration (henceforth PILA) all pecuniary claims may be submitted to arbitration. The provisions of the PILA apply to arbitrations if the seat of the arbitral tribunal is in Switzerland and if at least one of the parties at the time the arbitration agreement was concluded was neither domiciled nor habitually resident in Switzerland. Even if this is the case the parties can exclude themselves from the application of the PILA if they have done so in writing and agreed to the exclusive application of the cantonal rules of procedures concerning arbitration.[1]

Any party may challenge an arbitrator if he does not possess the

---

* Associate professor of sports law at the University of Peloponnese, Sparta, Greece, Dept. of Sports Management
1) See art. 176 of the PILA.

qualifications agreed upon by the parties; if there exist grounds for challenge in the rules of arbitration adopted by the parties; or if the circumstances permit legitimate doubt about his independence.[2] An arbitration award may be challenged only before the Swiss Federal Tribunal (henceforth SFT). If neither party has a domicile, a place of habitual residence, or a place of business in Switzerland, they may, by an express declaration in the arbitration agreement or in a subsequent written agreement, exclude all appeals against the award of the arbitral tribunal.[3] This however does not mean that there is no appeal against these awards whatsoever. Even if the parties exclude all appeals against the award, when a party seeks enforcement of the award it may be appealed according to articles IV and V of the New York Convention.

According to Art. 190 para. 2 of the Switzerland's Federal Code on Private International Law (PILA) an arbitration award can be can be attacked only:

(1) if a sole arbitrator was designated irregularly or the arbitral tribunal was constituted irregularly,
(2) if the arbitral tribunal erroneously held that it had or did not have jurisdiction,
(3) if the arbitral tribunal ruled on matters beyond the claims submitted to it or if it failed to rule on one of the claims,
(4) if the equality of the parties or their right to be heard in an adversarial proceeding was not respected, or
(5) if the award is incompatible with Swiss public policy.

## The Swiss Federal Supreme Court

It seems that the Swiss Federal Tribunal adopts a non-interventionist approach to what arbitration awards are concerned.[4] The grounds for annulment of arbitration awards under the PILA are very restrictive. Furthermore, the Court seems very reluctant to set aside arbitration awards.

---

2) See art. 180 of the PILA.
3) See art 192 of the PILA.
4) See Hurni, C, «How Arbitration Friendly is the Swiss Federal Supreme Court?», http://papers.ssrn.com/sol3/papers.cfm?abstract_id=2191715

The appeal procedure is very quick. The appeal against the award must be filed within 30 days after the award was serviced. In most case the final decision of the Swiss Federal Tribunal is issued no later than three to six months after the appeal was filed. The fact that an award is arbitrary does not qualify as a reason for annulment. The Swiss Federal Tribunal will replace the award only in case the arbitral tribunal erroneously held that it had or did not have jurisdiction. In all other cases it will remit the matter to the arbitration court for reconsideration.[5]

## The CAS's Independence Recognition

### The Gundel Case

Before the formation of the ICAS, CAS was financed entirely by the IOC which could also modify the CAS statutes and possessed considerable power to appoint the president as well as its members. Elmar Gundel was a horse rider who appealed to the CAS in February 1992 an international Equestrian horse-doping decision disqualifying him and imposing a suspension and fine upon him.[6]

The CAS panel did not rule entirely in favour of the rider[7] and so he filed a public law appeal with the Swiss Federal Tribunal contesting the validity of the award, which he claimed was rendered by a court which did not meet the conditions of impartiality and independence needed in order to be considered as a proper arbitration court. The Swiss Federal Tribunal in its judgement of 15 March 1993,[8] rejected Gundel's appeal and recognised the

---

5) See Dickenmann, Ph., «Arbitration in Switzerland», pp. 898-890.
   http://eguides.cmslegal.com/pdf/arbitration_volume_I/CMS%20GtA_Vol%20I_SWITZER
   LAND.pdf
6) See McLaren, R., «Twenty Five Years of the Court of Arbitration for Sport: A Look in
   the Rear-view Mirror», Marquette Sports Law Review, Vo. 20, Issue 2, p.304-333.
7) See CAS 92/63 G. v/ FEI in Digest of CAS Awards 1986-1998.
8) See published in the Recueil Officiel des Arrêts du Tribunal Fédéral [Official Digest of
   Federal Tribunal Judgements] 119 II 271.

CAS as a true court of arbitration. It noted that the CAS was not an organ of the FEI, that it did not receive instructions from this federation and retained sufficient personal autonomy with regard to it, in that it placed at the disposal of the CAS only three arbitrators out of the maximum of 60 members of which the CAS was composed. However, the most important part of the judgment was the obiter statement of the SFT in which it drew attention to the numerous links which existed between the CAS and the IOC. In the event of the IOC's being a party to proceedings before CAS, the fact that the CAS was financed almost exclusively by the IOC, that the IOC was competent to modify the CAS Statute and the considerable power given to the IOC and its President to appoint the members of the CAS, could call into question the independence of the CAS. The SFT therefore sent a clear message to the CAS, that it should be made more independent of the IOC both organisationally and financially.[9]

### The Lazutina Case

The reform that followed the SFT's judgment on the Gundel case could have been put to the test in 2000, when a Romanian gymnast, Andrea Raducan, appealed to the SFT against a CAS award. Unfortunately, the Federal Tribunal decided to dismiss the appeal without tackling the question of the independence of the restructured CAS[10] and so the effectiveness of the reforms implemented after the Gundel judgment by the SFT were put under scrutiny three years later in May 2003 when the SFT re-examined the Court's independence in detail, having heard an appeal by two Russian cross-country skiers, Larissa Lazutina and Olga Danilova, against a CAS award disqualifying them from an event at the Olympic Winter Games in Salt Lake City.[11] The SFT seized the opportunity to decide whether the CAS would be considered a truly independent international arbitration tribunal even if the IOC was a party to the dispute.[12] In a remarkably detailed and

---

9) See The Court of Arbitration for Sport Site: http://www.tas-cas.org/history
10) See The Court of Arbitration for Sport Site: http://www.tas-cas.org/history
11) See SFT decision 4P.267/2002 of 27 May 2003
12) See McLaren, R., «Twenty Five Years of the Court of Arbitration for Sport: A Look in the Rear-view Mirror», Marquette Sports Law Review, Vo. 20, Issue 2, p.304-333.

exhaustive judgement, the Federal Tribunal found that the CAS was not "the vassal of the IOC" and was sufficiently independent of it, as it was of all other parties that called upon its services, for decisions it made in cases involving the IOC to be considered as true awards, comparable to the judgements of a State tribunal. The SFT also noted the widespread recognition of the CAS amongst the international sporting community and the necessity of its existence: *"There appears to be no viable alternative to this institution, which can resolve international sports-related disputes quickly and inexpensively. (...) The CAS, with its current structure, can undoubtedly be improved. (...) Having gradually built up the trust of the sporting world, this institution which is now widely recognised and which will soon celebrate its twentieth birthday remains one of the principal mainstays of organised sport".[13]*

## Landmark SFT Cases Appealing CAS Decisions

### Obligatory Arbitration

The Canas v. ATP Tour case[14] concerned a professional tennis player who committed a doping offence and sentenced with a 2 years suspension. The athlete stated that he accidentally absorbed the banned substance and therefore there was no fault. The CAS decision reduced his sentence to 14 months suspension. The federation's rules (signed obligatorily in advance by the athlete) contained a player's consent clause according to which the player had agreed to comply with and be bound by all of the provisions of the 2005 ATP Official Rulebook, including, but not limited to, all amendments to the ATP Rules and all the provisions of the Anti-Doping Program incorporated in the ATP Rules. He also acknowledged that he had received and had an opportunity to review the ATP Rules. Also he consented and agreed that any dispute arising out of any decision made by the Anti-Doping Tribunal, or any dispute arising under or in connection with the

13) See The Court of Arbitration for Sport Site: http://www.tas-cas.org/history
14) See SFT decision 4P.172/2006 of 22 March 2007

Anti-Doping Program, after exhaustion of the Anti-Doping Program's Anti-Doping Tribunal process and any other proceedings expressly provided for in the Program, shall be submitted exclusively to the Appeals Arbitration Division of the CAS for final and binding arbitration in accordance with the Code of Sports-Related Arbitration. The decisions of CAS shall be final, non-reviewable, non-appealable and enforceable. Finally he agreed not to bring any claim, arbitration, lawsuit or litigation in any other court or tribunal.

The SFT examining the athlete's appeal against the CAS decision stated that «*a Sports competition is characterized by a highly hierarchical structure, as much on the international as on the national level. Vertically integrated, the relationships between athletes and organizations in charge of the various sports disciplines are distinct from the horizontal relationship represented by a contractual relationship between two parties (...) This structural difference between the two types of relationships is not without influence on the volitional process driving the formation of every agreement (...) Experience has shown that, by and large athletes will often not have the bargaining power required and would therefore have to submit to the federation's requirements, whether they like it or not. Accordingly, any athlete wishing to participate in organised competition under the control of a sports federation whose rules provide for recourse to arbitration will not have any choice but to accept the arbitral clause, in particular by subscribing to the articles of association of the sports federation in question in which the arbitration clause was inserted (...)*».[15] Having as alternative either to submit to the jurisdiction of a specific arbitration or to practice sport in his back yard and watch the sports events in his television the athlete who wishes to be a part of serious competitions or whose only source or revenue comes from these competitions is forced (nolens volens) to submit to this jurisdiction.[16] As a

---

15) See Mitten, M., «Judicial Review of Olympic and International Sports Arbitration Awards: Trends and Observations», Peperdine Dispute Resolution Law Journal, 2009, Vol. 10:1, p. 51-67.

16) See SFT decision 4P.172/2006 which states in french language: «*Le sport de compétition se caractérise par une structure très hiérarchisée, aussi bien au niveau international qu'au niveau national. Etablies sur un axe vertical, les relations*

counterbalance of a serious restriction or breach of the athlete's fundamental rights and procedural guarantees possibly committed by the arbitrators, the CAS award was reviewed by the SFT.[17]

## Correct Application of a Rule

After 2005 the principle of independence of CAS was already well established. Subsequent appeals to the SFT have not succeeded to challenge it. In 2008 in case of Azerbaijan Field Hockey Federation v. Federation Internationale de Hockey,[18] the Azerbaijan federation team appealed a decision of the International Hockey federation seeking to replace the

---

*entre les athlètes et les organisations qui s'occupent des diverses disciplines sportives se distinguent en cela des relations horizontales que nouent les parties à un rapport contractuel). Cette différence structurelle entre les deux types de relations n'est pas sans influence sur le processus volitif conduisant à la formation de tout accord. En principe, lorsque deux parties traitent sur un pied d'égalité, chacune d'elles exprime sa volonté sans être assujettie au bon vouloir de l'autre. Il en va généralement ainsi dans le cadre des relations commerciales internationales. La situation est bien différente dans le domaine du sport. Si l'on excepte le cas - assez théorique - où un athlète renommé, du fait de sa notoriété, serait en mesure de dicter ses conditions à la fédération internationale régissant le sport qu'il pratique, l'expérience enseigne que, la plupart du temps, un sportif n'aura pas les coudées franches à l'égard de sa fédération et qu'il devra se plier, bon gré mal gré, aux desiderata de celle-ci. Ainsi l'athlète qui souhaite participer à une compétition organisée sous le contrôle d'une fédération sportive dont la réglementation prévoit le recours à l'arbitrage n'aura-t-il d'autre choix que d'accepter la clause arbitrale, notamment en adhérant aux statuts de la fédération sportive en question dans lesquels ladite clause a été insérée, à plus forte raison s'il s'agit d'un sportif professionnel. Il sera confronté au dilemme suivant: consentir à l'arbitrage ou pratiquer son sport en dilettante. Mis dans l'alternative de se soumettre à une juridiction arbitrale ou de pratiquer son sport "dans son jardin" en regardant les compétitions "à la télévision", l'athlète qui souhaite affronter de véritables concurrents ou qui doit le faire parce que c'est là son unique source de revenus (prix en argent ou en nature, recettes publicitaires, etc.) sera contraint, dans les faits, d'opter, nolens volens, pour le premier terme de cette alternative.»*

17) See Mitten, M., «Judicial Review of Olympic and International Sports Arbitration Awards: Trends and Observations», Peperdine Dispute Resolution Law Journal, 2009, Vol. 10:1, p. 51-67.

18) See SFT Decision 4A_424/2008

Spanish team by the team of Azerbaijan because the Spanish team was burdened with doping violations. The SFT dismissed the appeal stating that it does not review whether the CAS applied correctly the law upon which it based its decision.[19]

### CAS Panel Impartiality and Bias

An essential procedural guarantee of every arbitration tribunal is that the dispute should be adjudicated by an independent, impartial not biased panel. In the Lazutina case[20] the SFT ruled that «*it should be assumed that the members of a tribunal are capable of rising above the eventualities linked to their appointment when they are required to render concrete decisions in the discharge of their duties*». The mere fact that a CAS arbitrator has ruled against a party or has served as a counsel in a previous arbitration case is not enough to question his impartiality.[21] [22]

In 2008 the SFT issued a decision in the Biolley Case. In this case the appellant contested the impartiality of the CAS panel based on the fact that the panel included two arbitrators who were members of the same association which formed a closed world-wide group of eight CAS arbitrators in total. The SFT refferred to the IBA Guidelines on Conflicts of Interest in International Arbitration concluding that the mere fact that a party which is

---

19) See McLaren, R., «Twenty Five Years of the Court of Arbitration for Sport: A Look in the Rear-view Mirror», Marquette Sports Law Review, Vo. 20, Issue 2, p.304-333.

20) See SFT decision Lazutina, 4P.267/2002 of 27 May 2003.

21) See Mitten, M., «Judicial Review of Olympic and International Sports Arbitration Awards: Trends and Observations», Peperdine Dispute Resolution Law Journal, 2009, Vol. 10:1, p. 51-67.

22) See SFT decision Lazutina, 4P.267/2002 of 27 May 2003, stating in french language: «*Seules des circonstances additionnelles pourraient justifier la récusation de tels arbitres. Celles qu'invoquent les recourantes - les arbitres auraient partagé des repas, auraient vraisemblablement logé dans le même hôtel et se seraient déplacés ensemble - ne sont en tout cas pas de cette nature. La qualité des personnes concernées permet de penser que ces contacts ne sont pas propres à altérer leur indépendance d'esprit et d'opinion. De fait, selon la jurisprudence du Tribunal fédéral, on doit présumer la capacité des membres d'un tribunal de s'élever au-dessus des contingences liées à leur désignation lorsqu'ils sont appelés à rendre des décisions concrètes dans l'exercice de leur charge.*»

a member of a certain association systematically selects one of its members as a CAS arbitrator is not enough to establish objectively that an arbitrator is biased. To the contrary the fact that an arbitrator systematically rules in favour of a counsel who is affiliated with a certain association would be an indication for a possible bias.[23] [24]

In 2010 the SFT issued a decision in the Valverde Case.[25] In 2009 the Spanish cyclist Alejandro Valverde was sentenced with a two year ban by the Anti-Doping tribunal of the Italian Olympic Committee (CONI). The athlete appealed the decision before CAS. The arbitrator designated by CONI had been involved in the revision of the World Anti-Doping Code in 2006-2007 and had also acted as Chairman of the WADA Independent Observer Team during the Athens 2004 Olympics. The athlete challenged

---

23) See SFT decision, Biolley, 4A_506/2007 of 20 March 2008, stating in french language: «*Des associations telles que E. sont d'ailleurs nombreuses en matière de droit du sport, comme le relève l'intimée avec références à l'appui. Les données statistiques fournies par le recourant à l'effet de démontrer que les représentants d'une partie affiliés à E. choisiraient systématiquement pour arbitre une personne membre de cette association ne sont pas suffisantes quantitativement pour établir ce fait. Au reste, comme le TAS le fait remarquer à juste titre dans sa réponse, l'intimée a désigné son arbitre - S. - avant même d'avoir mandaté C. pour défendre ses intérêts devant cette juridiction arbitrale. En outre, la démonstration esquissée par le recourant porte sur une circonstance qui n'est pas nécessairement pertinente, s'agissant d'apprécier l'impartialité et l'indépendance des arbitres. Comme on l'a déjà souligné de longue date, il y a lieu de présumer la capacité des membres d'un tribunal de s'élever au-dessus des contingences liées à leur désignation lorsqu'ils sont appelés à rendre des décisions concrètes dans l'exercice de leur charge. En d'autres termes, même si les éléments statistiques fournis par le recourant correspondaient à la réalité, cela ne signifierait pas encore que la circonstance ainsi établie soit susceptible d'éveiller objectivement un doute légitime au sujet de l'indépendance de l'arbitre membre de E désigné par le représentant d'une partie affilié à la même association. La conclusion inverse ne pourrait être tirée que s'il était statistiquement avéré que, dans un tel cas de figure, la Formation comprenant un arbitre désigné de cette façon donne systématiquement raison à la partie représentée par un mandataire affilié à E., démonstration qui n'a même pas été tentée en l'espèce.*»

24) See Mitten, M., «Judicial Review of Olympic and International Sports Arbitration Awards: Trends and Observations», Peperdine Dispute Resolution Law Journal, 2009, Vol. 10:1, p. 51-67.

25) See SFT decision Valverde, 4A_234/2010 of 19 November 2010.

the arbitrator's impartiality and the ICAS dismissed it. The CAS unanimously upheld CONI's two year ban and the athlete challenged the award before the SFTon the grounds provided for in Art. 190(2)(a) on the alleged irregular constitution of the panel and Art. 190(2)(d) on the alleged breach of the principles of equality of the parties and their right to be heard.

The first question the SFT had to answer is whether all arbitrators of the panel even those designated by the parties, should be bound by the same (high) standard of independence and impartiality. The Court absolutely rejected the idea of arbitrators that act as advocates for the parties since this would jeopardize the whole fundamental concept of arbitration. Therefore the standard of independence and impartiality should be applied equally to all members of the CAS panel even those designated by the parties. The Court further recognized that there are some inherent specific factors in the sports-related arbitration that should be taken into account. Since arbitrators are required to have full legal training and a recognized competence with regard to sport, the list of possibilities is shorter than in other cases. During their career's course CAS arbitrators are therefore expected (if not required) to have contacts sports entities, organizations and authorities.[26] [27]

---

26) See SFT decision Valverde, 4A_234/2010 of 19 November 2010 stating in french language: «*En outre et surtout, cette jurisprudence ne fait plus de différence entre la situation d'un membre du tribunal arbitral et celle du président du tribunal arbitral, rejetant implicitement l'idée d'une telle distinction. Il convient de le faire ici de manière expresse. Force est, dès lors, d'admettre que l'indépendance et l'impartialité requises des membres d'un tribunal arbitral s'imposent aussi bien aux arbitres désignés par les parties qu'au président du tribunal arbitral. En énonçant ce principe, le Tribunal fédéral est certes conscient qu'une indépendance absolue de tous les arbitres constitue un idéal qui ne correspondra que rarement à la réalité. Aussi bien, le mode de désignation des membres du tribunal arbitral crée, qu'on le veuille ou non, un lien objectif, si ténu soit-il, entre l'arbitre et la partie qui l'a désigné, puisque celui-là, à l'inverse du juge étatique, ne tient son pouvoir et sa place que de la volonté de celle-ci. Il s'agit là toutefois d'une conséquence inhérente à la procédure arbitrale, dont il faut s'accommoder. Elle implique qu'un arbitre ne puisse pas être récusé du seul fait qu'il a été choisi par l'une des parties en litige. Doit être exclu, en revanche, le système dit de l'arbitre-partie dans lequel l'arbitre désigné par chacune des parties ne serait pas astreint à la même indépendance et à la même impartialité que l'arbitre appelé à présider le tribunal arbitral. L'idée que l'arbitre puisse n'être que l'avocat de "sa"*

Fair Hearing

In the Canas v. ATP Tour case[28] the SFT ruled that case law does not provide for a strict reasoning in the arbitral award. The CAS award must discuss all of a party's arguments so as to establish that the arbitrators have considered all the arguments proposed even if in the end they are dismissed.[29]

The Meaning of Public Policy

---

*partie au sein du tribunal arbitral doit être résolument écartée sous peine de mettre en péril l'institution de l'arbitrage comme telle. En ce sens, le Tribunal fédéral peut faire sienne la conclusion suivante, tirée voilà bientôt quinze ans déjà par des professeurs de droit français faisant autorité dans le domaine de l'arbitrage international: "compte tenu de la dégradation des moeurs parfois constatée dans l'arbitrage international et des manoeuvres auxquelles se livre parfois l'arbitre désigné par une partie, il n'est pas suffisant d'exiger de lui un comportement de bonne foi: il est préférable de s'en tenir aux principes, en espérant qu'ils permettront, en pratique, de tempérer les dérives des arbitres-partisans"»*

27) See Von Segesser, G., Shellenberg, W., «Swiss Federal Tribunal Rejects Multiple Standards of Independence and Impartiality among Arbitrators», 25 January 2011, http://kluwerarbitrationblog.com/blog/2011/01/25/swiss-federal-tribunal-rejects-multiple-standards-of-independence-and-impartiality-among-arbitrators/

28) See SFT decision Canas, 4P.172/2006 of 22 March 2007

29) See SFT decision Canas, 4P.172/2006 of 22 March 2007 stating in french language: *«De jurisprudence constante, le droit d'être entendu en procédure contradictoire, consacré par les art. 182 al. 3 et 190 al. 2 let. d LDIP, n'exige pas qu'une sentence arbitrale internationale soit motivée. Toutefois, la jurisprudence a également déduit du droit d'être entendu un devoir minimum pour l'autorité d'examiner et de traiter les problèmes pertinents. Ce devoir a été étendu par la jurisprudence au domaine de l'arbitrage international et, partant, à l'arbitrage international en matière de sport (arrêt 4P.26/2005 du 23 mars 2005, relatif au TAS, consid. 3.2). Il est violé lorsque, par inadvertance ou malentendu, le tribunal arbitral ne prend pas en considération des allégués, arguments, preuves et offres de preuve présentés par l'une des parties et importants pour la décision à rendre. En effet, la partie concernée est alors lésée dans son droit de faire valoir son point de vue auprès des arbitres; elle est placée dans la même situation que si elle n'avait pas eu la possibilité de leur présenter ses arguments. Il incombe à la partie soi-disant lésée de démontrer, dans son recours dirigé contre la sentence, en quoi une inadvertance des arbitres l'a empêchée de se faire entendre sur un point important. C'est à elle d'établir, d'une part, que le tribunal arbitral n'a pas examiné certains des éléments de fait, de preuve ou de droit qu'elle avait régulièrement avancés à l'appui de ses conclusions et, d'autre part, que ces éléments étaient de nature à influer sur le sort du litige.»*

It seems that it is very difficult for an appellant before the SFT to be successful invoking a claim that a CAS award violates principles so fundamental that the award is incompatible with public policy. The SFT has ruled that the public policy argument in order to be upheld should lead to a shocking violation of the most fundamental principles of the legal order.[30][31]

Even manifestly wrong application of a rule or the obviously incorrect finding of a point of fact will not suffice for a revocation of an arbitral award on grounds of public policy.[32] In the N.J.Y.W v. FINA case[33] as well as in the Biolley case[34] before the SFT one may find evidence of the

---

30) See SFT decision 4p_54/2006 of 11 May 2006 stating in german language: «*Ein Schiedsurteil verstösst gegen den materiellen Ordre public, wenn es grundlegende Rechtsprinzipien derart verletzt, dass es mit der massgebenden Rechts- und Werteordnung schlechterdings nicht mehr vereinbar ist. Derart schwerwiegende Verstösse sind immerhin so selten, dass sie in der Praxis kaum je bejaht worden sind. Zu den grundlegenden Rechtsprinzipien gehören insbesondere die Vertragstreue (pacta sunt servanda), der Grundsatz von Treu und Glauben, das Verbot des Rechtsmissbrauchs sowie das Verbot diskriminierender oder entschädigungsloser Enteignungen. Eine offensichtlich falsche oder aktenwidrige Feststellung reicht dagegen für sich allein nicht aus, um einen internationalen Schiedsentscheid aufzuheben; denn der Begriff der Willkür stimmt nicht mit dem Ordre public gemäss Art. 190 Abs. 2 lit. e IPRG überein. Insbesondere kann ein Verstoss gegen den Ordre public nicht daraus gefolgert werden, dass ein Schiedsentscheid im Ergebnis unhaltbar ist.*»

31) See Hurni, C., «How Arbitration-Friendly is the Swiss Federal Supreme Court?», http://papers.ssrn.com/sol3/papers.cfm?abstract_id=2191715

32) See Mitten, M., «Judicial Review of Olympic and International Sports Arbitration Awards: Trends and Observations», Peperdine Dispute Resolution Law Journal, 2009, Vol. 10:1, p. 51-67.

33) See SFT decision 5P.83/1999 of 31 March 1999 stating in french language: «*Les juges cantonaux ont estimé que les considérants de cet arrêt étaient aussi pertinents lorsqu'il s'agissait d'examiner la durée d'une suspension sous l'angle de l'arbitraire. Pour eux, il n'était pas manifestement insoutenable d'infliger une suspension de deux ans à un coureur cycliste reconnu coupable de dopage et une telle sanction, en dépit de sa sévérité, ne heurtait pas de manière choquante le sentiment de la justice et de l'équité, d'autant qu'elle était expressément prévue par la réglementation applicable. L'autorité intimée a encore indiqué qu'une certaine retenue était de mise dans un domaine où la juridiction arbitrale spécialisée est mieux à même que le juge étatique d'apprécier la gravité du comportement contraire aux règles antidopage.*»

34) See SFT decision, Biolley, 4A_506/2007 of 20 March 2008, stating in french language:

difficulties an appellant has to overcome in order to support the public order argument.

In a 2010 case[35] the SFT ruled on an appeal against a CAS award imposing a lifelong ban on an athlete due to a doping rule infringement. The appellant invoked Art. 190 (2) (e) of the Swiss Private International Law Act (PILA) according to which an award can be set aside when it is found to be incompatible with public policy. In order to establish the breach of the aforementioned article of the PILA, the appellant invoked three arguments. The reformatio in peius, the non retroactivity and the lex mitior argument. The SFT first stated that there were no grounds that supported the reformatio in peius argument. The SFT did not answer the question whether a violation of the reformatio in peius principle falls under the scope of public policy. But to what the non-retroactivity arguments and the lex mitior arguments are concerned the SFT entered into the merits of the claims. If this implies that these two principles fall under the scope of public policy then this case should be considered a landmark case.[36]

## Fundamental Procedural Principles (The Carvalho Case)[37]

In 2000 Carvalho concluded a 4 year contract with football team Benfica. Three months after joining the club he terminated his contract for cause and joined the club Atletico Madrid. FIFA's Special Committee awarded a

---

«Une sentence est incompatible avec l'ordre public si elle méconnaît les valeurs essentielles et largement reconnues qui, selon les conceptions prévalant en Suisse, devraient constituer le fondement de tout ordre juridique. Est contraire à l'ordre public matériel la sentence qui viole des principes fondamentaux du droit de fond au point de ne plus être conciliable avec l'ordre juridique et le système de valeurs déterminants; au nombre de ces principes figurent, notamment, la fidélité contractuelle, le respect des règles de la bonne foi, l'interdiction de l'abus de droit, la prohibition des mesures discriminatoires ou spoliatrices, ainsi que la protection des personnes civilement incapables.»

35) See SFT decision, 4A_624/2009 of 12 April 2010.
36) See Voser, N., «Three Decisions of the Swiss Federal Tribunal on Sports Arbitration Matters», 2-6-2010, http://arbitration.practicallaw.com/6-502-4347
37) See SFT decision Benfica v. Atletico Madrid, 4A_490/2009 of 13. April 2010.

sum to Benfica for its investments in the player. Atletico Madrid challenged the decision before the Commercial Court of Zurich which voided FIFA's decision on the grounds that FIFA's 1997 Transfer Regulation was breaching Swiss as well as European Community's competition law. Benfica did not challenge this decision but brought a new claim before the FIFA Special Committee over its investment in the player and when the claim was rejected Benfica appealed the decision to CAS.

The CAS decision awarded a sum to Benfica for training and promotion and stated that as Benfica was not a party in the proceedings before the Commercial Court of Zurich, it was not bound by its decision and the res judicata principle could not be invoked.[38]

Atletico brought the case before the SFT and in 2010 the Court reviewed CAS's award stating that public policy within the meaning of Art. 190(2)(e) covers both procedural as well as substantive matters and also that an arbitral award violating fundamental procedural principles such as the res judicata breaches procedural public policy.[39]

---

38) See Berger, J., and Sun, C., «Swiss Federal Tribunal Overturns Arbitration Award on Public Policy Grounds», August 2010, http://www.paulhastings.com/assets/publications /1712.pdf

39) See SFT decision Benfica v. Atletico Madrid, 4A_490/2009 stating in german language: *«Der Ordre public (Art. 190 Abs. 2 lit. e IPRG) hat sowohl einen materiellen als auch einen verfahrensrechtlichen Gehalt.Ein Verstoss gegen den verfahrensrechtlichen Ordre public liegt vor bei einer Verletzung von fundamentalen und allgemein anerkannten Verfahrensgrundsätzen, deren Nichtbeachtung zum Rechtsempfinden in einem unerträglichen Widerspruch steht, so dass die Entscheidung als mit der in einem Rechtsstaat geltenden Rechts- und Wertordnung schlechterdings unvereinbar erscheint.Das Schiedsgericht verletzt den verfahrensrechtlichen Ordre public, wenn es bei seinem Entscheid die materielle Rechtskraft eines früheren Entscheids unbeachtet lässt oder wenn es in seinem Endentscheid von der Auffassung abweicht, die es in einem Vorentscheid hinsichtlich einer materiellen Vorfrage geäussert hat. Die Rechtskraftwirkung beschränkt sich auf das Urteilsdispositiv. Die Urteilsbegründung wird davon nicht erfasst. Die Urteilserwägungen haben in einer anderen Streitsache keine bindende Wirkung, sind aber gegebenenfalls zur Klärung der Tragweite des Urteilsdispositivs. Die Tragweite des konkreten Urteilsdispositivs ist demnach im Einzelfall anhand der gesamten Urteilserwägungen zu beurteilen.»*

Economic Freedom (The Matuzalem Case)[40]

In 2007 Brazilian football player Francelini Da Silva Matuzalem broke his contract with Ukrainian Club Shaktar Donetsk without cause, in order to join Real Zaragosa club. The case was brought before the CAS which ruled that Real Zaragosa and Matuzalem should jointly or severaly pay Shaktar the amount of 12 million euro plus interest. Neither Zaragosa nor Matuzalem were capable of paying this amount so Shaktar applied to the FIFA Disciplinary Committee which ruled that Matuzalem would be banned from taking part to any football-related activity until the fine was paid. Matuzalem (as well as Zaragoza) appealed the decision to CAS which confirmed FIFA's decision issuing an award in 2011. Matuzalem petitioned the SFT in an effort to have the award set aside claiming that the award breached the public policy rule of Art. 190(2)(3) of PILA.

The SFT held that according to Article 27(2) of the Swiss Civil Code, an individual is allowed to restrict its own rights by entering into a contract or by acceding to statutes of a sporting association. However a contractual limitation of an individual's economic freedom is considered excessive in cases where it submits the fate of one contracting party to the absolute discretion of another party or if it eliminates economic freedom entirely or to such an extent that the individual's financial existence is threatened. The economic freedom can therefore be restricted but not eliminated and this should be considered as a fundamental principle forming a part of any legal order. The SFT concluded that such an open-ended ban to play imposed on an athlete, which could take effect at the sole discretion of a former employer, constitutes a severe infringement on the player's individual rights.[41] [42]

---

40) See SFT decision Matuzalem, 4A_558/2011, of 27 March 2012.

41) See Voser, N., George, A., Wittmer, S., «Landmark Ruling of Swiss Supreme Court Setting Aside CAS Award for violation of Substantive Public Policy», 2-5-2012, http://arbitration.practicallaw.com/1-519-2649

42) See SFT decision Matuzalem, 4A_558/2011, stating in german language: «*Die auf Art. 64 Abs. 4 des FIFA-Disziplinarreglements gestützte Androhung eines unbegrenzten Berufsverbots stellt einen offensichtlichen und schwerwiegenden Eingriff in die Persönlichkeitsrechte des Beschwerdeführers dar und missachtet die in Art. 27 Abs. 2 ZGB verankerten grundlegenden Schranken rechtsgeschäftlicher Bindung. Der*

## Conclusions

Due to the fact that grounds for annulment of arbitration awards under the PILA are very restrictive as well as the fact that the Swiss Federal Tribunal adopts a non-interventionist view towards arbitration awards, the SFT is very reluctant to set aside arbitration awards and appeals against awards issued by the CAS are very rarely successful. This is why Switzerland could be characterized as an arbitration-friendly country.[43]

Up until 2003 the major issue that concerned the SFT was the independence of the CAS due to its relation to the IOC. Even after that issue was resolved some very important cases have been brought before the SFT that challenged CAS awards on various grounds such as public policy (fundamental rights), obligatory arbitration, panel impartiality and fair hearing.

## References

Berger, J., and Sun, C., «Swiss Federal Tribunal Overturns Arbitration Award on Public Policy Grounds», August 2010

Dickenmann, Ph., «Arbitration in Switzerland», pp. 898-890.

http://eguides.cmslegal.com/pdf/arbitration_volume_I/CMS%20GtA_Vol%20I_S WITZERLAND.pdf

Hurni, C., «How Arbitration-Friendly is the Swiss Federal Supreme Court?»,

---

*angefochtene Schiedsentscheid führt bei Ausbleiben der auferlegten Zahlung nicht nur dazu, dass der Beschwerdeführer der Willkür seines ehemaligen Arbeitgebers ausgesetzt, sondern insbesondere seine wirtschaftliche Freiheit in einem Masse eingeschränkt wird, dass die Grundlagen seiner wirtschaftlichen Existenz gefährdet sind, ohne dass dies durch ein überwiegendes Interesse des Weltfussballverbands bzw. seiner Mitglieder gerechtfertigt wäre. Aufgrund der entsprechenden Androhung stellt der Schiedsentscheid des TAS vom 29. Juni 2011 eine offensichtliche und schwerwiegende Persönlichkeitsverletzung dar und ist mit dem Ordre public (Art. 190 Abs. 2 lit. e IPRG) unvereinbar.»*

43) See Papaloukas, M., «CAS: The Court of Arbitration for Sport», 2013, Papaloukas Editions.

http://papers.ssrn.com/sol3/papers.cfm?abstract_id=2191715

McLaren, R., «Twenty Five Years of the Court of Arbitration for Sport: A Look in the Rear-view Mirror», Marquette Sports Law Review, Vo. 20, Issue 2, p.304-333

Mitten, M., «Judicial Review of Olympic and International Sports Arbitration Awards: Trends and Observations», Peperdine Dispute Resolution Law Journal, 2009, Vol. 10:1, p. 51-67

Papaloukas, M., «CAS: The Court of Arbitration for Sport», 2013, Papaloukas Editions.

The Court of Arbitration for Sport Site: http://www.tas-cas.org/history

Von Segesser, G., Shellenberg, W., «Swiss Federal Tribunal Rejects Multiple Standards of Independence and Impartiality among Arbitrators», 25 January 2011,

http://kluwerarbitrationblog.com/blog/2011/01/25/swiss-federal-tribunal-rejects-multiple-standards-of-independence-and-impartiality-among-arbitrators/

Voser, N., George, A., Wittmer, S., «Landmark Ruling of Swiss Supreme Court Setting Aside CAS Award for violation of Substantive Public Policy», 2-5-2012

CAS decision 92/63 G. v/ FEI in Digest of CAS Awards 1986-1998

SFT decision 5P.83/1999 of 31 March 1999

SFT decision Lazutina, 4P.267/2002 of 27 May 2003

SFT decision 4p_54/2006 of 11 May 2006

SFT decision Canas, 4P.172/2006 of 22 March 2007

SFT Decision 4A_424/2008

SFT decision, Biolley, 4A_506/2007 of 20 March 2008

SFT decision, 4A_624/2009 of 12 April 2010

SFT decision Valverde, 4A_234/2010 of 19 November 2010

SFT decision Benfica v. Atletico Madrid, 4A_490/2009 of 13. April 2010.

SFT decision Matuzalem, 4A_558/2011, of 27 March 2012.

# "De Novo" Hearing and Appealability before the CAS

MARIOS PAPALOUKAS*

*By refusing appealability to decisions related to the so called «rules of the game», by defining the exact meaning of an appealable decision and by hearing cases de novo, the CAS addresses all issues relating to the fairness of the hearing before the Tribunal of First instance and therefore safeguards the integrity and legal certainty of the global sports system. The purpose of the present paper is to present these basic procedural rules as they are identified in CAS's jurisprudence.*

**Key word:** Sports Law, Arbitration, Swiss Law, Private International Law, The Court of Arbitration for Sport (CAS), Swiss Federal Tribunal, De Novo Hearing, Appealability, Rules of the Game

## De Novo Hearing of the Case

The concept of «in order to do justice» means that the Panel is a fortiori allowed to review the appealed decision if it is arbitrary, i.e. if it severely fails to consider fixed rules, a clear and undisputed legal principle or breaches a fundamental principle. A decision may be considered arbitrary also if it harms in a deplorable way a feeling of justice or of fairness or if it is based on improper considerations or lacks a plausible explanation of the connection between the facts found and the decision issued. In order to exercise such a review, the CAS must be able to examine the formal aspects of the appealed decisions but also, above all, to evaluate – sometimes even de novo – all facts and legal issues involved in the dispute.[1]

---

* Associate professor of sports law at the University of Peloponnese, Sparta, Greece, Dept. of Sports Management

According to Art. R57 of the Code of Arbitration the CAS panels have the power to consider the subject matter of the dispute de novo. This means that the panel has full power to review the facts and the law. It may issue a new decision which replaces the decision challenged or annul the decision and refer the case back to the previous instance.

Even if there was a procedural defect in the first instance the CAS case law is quite clear that the de novo rule is intended to address and cure any procedural defect that occurs at the initial stage, after all relevant parties have been heard.[2] [3] If the hearing in a given case was insufficient in the first instance, as long as there is a possibility of full appeal to the CAS, the deficiency may be cured.[4] The virtue of an appeal system which allows for a rehearing before an appeal body is that issues relating to the fairness of the hearing before the Tribunal of First instance fade to the periphery.[5] Based on the Swiss Federal Tribunal's jurisprudence,[6] CAS jurisprudence states that any infringement of the right to be heard can be cured when the procedurally flawed decision is followed by a new decision, rendered by an appeal body which had the same power to review the facts and the law as the tribunal of first instance and in front of which the right to be heard had been properly exercised.[7] This CAS jurisprudence is actually in line with European Court of Human Rights decisions,[8] according to which even where an adjudicatory body determining disputes over civil rights and

---

1) See award CAS 2009/A/1926 & 1930 ITF v. Richard Gasquet & WADA v. ITF & Richard Gasquet of 17 December 2009, paras. 2 and 17.
2) See award CAS 2009/A/1920, para. 87.
3) See awards CAS 2008/A/1594 para. 109, CAS 2006/A/1175 paras. 61 and 62, CAS 2006/A/1153, para. 53, CAS 2003/O/486, para. 50.
4) See award CAS 94/129 USA Shooting & Q. / UIT, of 23 May 1995, para. 59.
5) See award CAS 98/211 B. / FINA, award of 7 June 1999, para. 8 and also SFT decisions ATF 114 Ia 307, ATF 110 Ia 81.
6) See SFT decisions ATF 124 II 132, ATF 118 Ib 111 and ATF 116 I a 94.
7) See award CAS 2006/A/1177 Aston Villa FC v. B.93 Copenhagen, award of 28 May 2007, para. 7.3.
8) See para. 41 of the famous ECHR decision Wickramsinghe v. the United Kingdom, 9 December 1997 no. 31503/96 and X. v. the United Kingdom, no. 28530/95, 19 January 1998 as well as other ECHR decisions Eur. Court HR, Albert and Le Compte v. Belgium judgment of 10 February 1983, Series A no. 58, p. 16, para. 29, referred to in Eur. Court HR, Bryan v. the United Kingdom judgment of 22 November 1995, Series A no. 335-A, p. 16, para. 40.

obligations does not comply with Article 6 (1) ECHR in some respect, no violation of the Convention will be found if the proceedings before that body are subject to subsequent control by a judicial body that has full jurisdiction and does provide the guarantees of Article 6 (1).

Based on CAS jurisprudence[9] when hearing a case de novo a panel cannot go beyond the scope of the previous litigation. It is limited to the issues arising from the challenged decision.[10] Also,[11] when a CAS panel is acting following an appeal against a decision of a sports-related body, the power of such a panel to rule is also determined by the relevant statutory legal basis and, therefore, is limited with regard to the appeal against and the review of the appealed decisions, both from an objective and a subjective point of view. When the appellant includes in its appeal also a subsidiary motion which was neither object of the first instance proceedings nor in any way dealt with in the appealed decision, the panel does not have the power to decide on it.[12]

## Appealable Decisions

A sport entity's final decision is appealable before the CAS. However, the exact meaning of a final decision is a matter that needs clarification.

According to Swiss legal scholars, an appealable decision of a sport association is normally a communication of the association directed to a party based on an "animus decidendi", i.e. an intention to decide on a matter, even if this is only a decision on its competence (or non- competence).[13]

The existence of a decision does not depend on the form in which it is issued and thus a communication made in the form of a letter may also

---

9) See awards CAS 2008/A/1478, CAS 2007/A/1294, TAS 2007/A/1433, TAS 2002/A/415 & 426.
10) See award CAS 2007/A/1396 & 1402 WADA & UCI v. Alejandro Valverde & RFEC, of 31 May 2010, para. 46.
11) See award CAS 2007/A/1426.
12) See award CAS 2009/A/1974 N. v. S.C.F.C. Univ. Craiova & RFF, of 16 July 2010, para. 8.
13) See award CAS 2007/A/1396 & 1402 WADA & UCI v. Alejandro Valverde & RFEC, of 31 May 2010, para. 2.

constitute a decision subject to appeal before CAS. A communication intending to be considered a decision shall contain a unilateral ruling sent to one or more recipients and tending to affect the legal situation of its appellant or other parties.[14)]

If a sports entity body refuses without reasons to issue a decision or delays the issuance of a decision beyond a reasonable period of time, there can be a denial of justice, opening the way for an appeal against the absence of a decision. A sport entity's decision not to open a disciplinary procedure – or the mere lack of action – must therefore be considered as a final decision and therefore subject to an appeal with CAS.[15)] The same applies also when there is a decision where the sports body issues a ruling as to the admissibility or inadmissibility of a request, without addressing the merits of such request.[16)]

However, it is not considered as a decision appealable before CAS a letter which does not contain any formal decision of a sports body, but only an opinion of the administration of the latter, so long as it has a purely informative character and does not prejudice any decision which could be taken in the future by any deciding sports body in the matter in question or in a similar matter: so long as a sports entity is stating in its letters that it is not in a position to intervene in the matter submitted by the Club in the way it has been submitted, but leaves the door open to deal with the case if appropriately filed before its bodies, this does not constitute a situation of strict and final denial of justice eventually challengeable before CAS.[17)]

The general principles that can be extracted from CAS jurisprudence in this respect are mainly the following:[18)]

1. The existence of a decision does not depend on the form in which it is issued. CAS jurisprudence[19)] states that the form of a communication has no

---

14) See award CAS 2008/A/1634 Hertha BSC GmbH & Co KgaA v. Football Association of Serbia, of 17 December 2008, para. 1.
15) See award CAS 2005/A/899.
16) See award CAS 2008/A/1634 Hertha BSC GmbH & Co KgaA v. Football Association of Serbia, of 17 December 2008, para. 1.
17) See award CAS 2008/A/1634 Hertha BSC GmbH & Co KgaA v. Football Association of Serbia, of 17 December 2008, para. 2.
18) See award CAS 2008/A/1634 Hertha BSC GmbH & Co KgaA v. Football Association of Serbia, of 17 December 2008, paras. 10-11.

relevance to determine whether there exists a decision or not. In particular, the fact that the communication is made in the form of a letter does not rule out the possibility that it constitutes a decision subject to appeal.

2. A communication intending to be considered a decision shall contain a ruling tending to affect the legal situation of its appellant or other parties. CAS jurisprudence states that in principle, for a communication to be a decision, this communication must contain ruling, whereby the body issuing the decision intends to affect the legal situation of the appellant or other parties.

Also in another CAS award[20] the Panel considering if a letter constitutes a decision in the sense of the code, susceptible to an appeal to the CAS, which is a necessary condition to the jurisdiction of the CAS to rule in the present matter, referred to a Swiss Federal Tribunal's Decision[21] stating that the decision is an act of individual sovereignty addressed to an individual, by which a relation of concrete administrative law, forming or stating a legal situation, is resolved in an obligatory and constraining manner. The effects must be directly binding both with respect to the authority as to the party who receives the decision. A decision is thus an unilateral act, sent to one or more determined recipients and is intended to produce legal effects.

In a 2004 CAS award[22] it is stated that if a letter contains in fact a clear statement of the resolution of a sports entity which had the additional effect of resolving the matter in respect of all interested parties, in other words, the legal situations of the appellant and of the other concerned parties are materially affected, then the letter should be considered an appealable decision. A letter could also be considered an appealable decision when the entity issuing it, intended such communication to be a decision issued on behalf of the sports entity.

3. A ruling issued by a sports-related body refusing to deal with a request can be considered a decision under certain circumstances.

Thus in the above mentioned 2007 CAS award[23] the court ruled that by

---

19) See awards CAS 2005/A/899 and also CAS 2007/A/1251.
20) See award CAS 2004/A/659, paras. 35-36.
21) See SFT decision ATF 101 Ia 73.
22) See award CAS 2004/A/748.
23) See award CAS 2007/A/1251.

responding in such manner to the appellant's request for relief, the sports body clearly manifested it would not entertain the request, thereby making a ruling on the admissibility of the request and directly affecting the appellant's legal situation. Thus, despite being formulated in a letter, the sports body's refusal to entertain the request was, in substance, a decision.

In a 2005 CAS award[24] it is stated that if a sports body refuses without reasons to issue a decision or the issuance of a decision is delayed beyond a reasonable period of time, there is a case of a denial of justice, allowing for an appeal against the absence of a decision[25] [26] Thus as already explained the mere lack of action is considered as a final appealable before the CAS decision. According to Swiss case law, there can be a denial of justice (so-called "substantive" denial of justice - déni de justice matériel") even after a decision has been issued, if such decision is arbitrary, i.e. constitutes a very serious breach of a statutory provision or of a clear and undisputable legal principle, or when it seriously offends the sense of justice and equity.

In another 2005 CAS award[27] the court ruled that in principle, for a communication to be a decision, this communication must contain ruling, whereby the body issuing the decision intends to affect the legal situation of the appellant of the decision or other parties. However, there can also be a decision where the body issues a ruling as to the admissibility or inadmissibility of a request, without addressing the merits of such request. Based on the above, an appealable decision of a sport association or federation «*is normally a communication of the association directed to a party and based on an «animus decidendi», i.e. an intention of a body of the association to decide on a matter [...]. A simple information, which does not contain any «ruling», cannot be considered a decision*».

---

24) See award CAS 2005/A/994.
25) See award CAS 2005/A/899.
26) See Paulsson, J., «Denial of Justice in International Law», Cambridge University Press, New York 2005, p. 176-178.
27) See award CAS 2005/A/899, paras. 10-11.

## Appealability of the Rules of the Game

The "Game Rules" are the rules intended to ensure the correct course of the game and competition respectively. The application of such rules cannot, save in very exceptional circumstances, lead to any judicial review. On the contrary, the "Rules of Law" are proper statutory sanctions that can affect the judicial interests of the person upon whom a sanction has been imposed other than in the course of the game or competition. For this reason, they have to be subject to judicial review.[28] [29]

In principle, the CAS has jurisdiction to try and review decisions concerning rules of the game. Where there is a relevant procedure in place to resolve such issues, however, the CAS accepts the decision reached as final except where it can be demonstrated that there has been arbitrariness or bad faith in arriving at this decision.[30] This position is consistent with traditional doctrine and judicial practice which have always stated that rules of the game, in the strict sense of the term, should not be subject to the control of judges, based on the idea that "the game must not be constantly interrupted by appeals to the judge".[31] In some legal systems, particularly in the United States and France, the rules of the game are not shielded from the control of judges, but their power of review is limited to that which is arbitrary or illegal.[32] Before a CAS Panel will review a field of play decision, there must be evidence of bad faith or arbitrariness. In other words the appellant must demonstrate evidence of preference for, or prejudice against, a particular team or individual.[33]

Award CAS OG 02/007, clarifies the situation: "The jurisprudence of CAS in regard to the issue raised by the application is clear, although the language used to explain that jurisprudence is not always consistent and can be confusing. Thus, different phrases such as "arbitrary", "bad faith", "breach

---

28) See decisions of the Swiss Federal Tribunal ATF 118 II 271 and also ATF 120 II 369.
29) See award CAS 2003/A/461 & 471 & 473 WCM-GP Limited v/ FIM, award of 19 August 2003
30) See awards CAS OG 96/006 also CAS OG 00/013 and also CAS OG 04/007.
31) See decision from the Swiss Federal Tribunal, ATF 118 II 12/19.
32) See CAS OG 96/006.
33) See CAS 2004/A/727 Vanderlei De Lima & BOC v. IAAF, award of 8 September 2005, paras. 9-10.

of duty", "malicious intent", "committed a wrong" and "other actionable wrongs" are used apparently interchangeably, to express the same test.[34] In the Panel's view, each of those phrases means more than the decision is wrong or that no sensible person could have reached this decision. If it were otherwise, every field of play decision would be open to review on its merits. Before a CAS Panel will review a field of play decision, there must be evidence, which generally must be direct evidence, of bad faith. If viewed in this light, each, of those phrases mean there must be some evidence of preference for, or prejudice against, a particular team or individual. The best example of such preference or prejudice was referred to by the Panel in the Segura Case,[35] where they stated that one circumstance where the CAS Panel could review a field of play decision would be if a decision were made in bad faith, e.g. as a consequence of corruption. The Panel accepted that this places a high hurdle that must be cleared by any applicant seeking to review a field of play decision. However, if the hurdle were to be lower, the flood-gates would be opened and any dissatisfied participant would be able to seek the review of a field of play decision".[36]

## Conclusions

The CAS has imposed its authority on the sports world not because of the power of the IOC that created it. The CAS was established mainly because of its recognised integrity and high legal standards. In order to achieve these standards it had to adopt some basic procedural principles. The most important procedural rules in order to appeal a decision to the CAS, include one definition and two basic principles; the definition of a sport entity's decision, the principle of de novo hearing and the principle of non appealability of the rules of the game.

There are thousands of different sport entities introduced by national

---

34) See CAS OG 96/006 and CAS OG 00/013.
35) See CAS ad hoc Division OG 00/013, Bernardo Segura / IAAF, award of 30 September 2000, para. 17.
36) See CAS 2004/A/727 Vanderlei De Lima & BOC v. IAAF, award of 8 September 2005, para. 10.

federations that issue decisions of first instance worldwide. The legal status of some of these entities and their decisions is very questionnable in terms of integrity and followed procedure. They come by different names such as courts, judges, tribunals, committees but sometimes they fail to provide even the basic standards of procedural fairness. It is often hard to discover when there is actually a final decision affecting the interests of an appellant. The CAS by refusing appealability to decisions related to the so called «rules of the game», by defining the exact meaning of an appealable decision and by hearing cases de novo, addresses all issues relating to the fairness of the hearing before the Tribunal of First instance and therefore safeguards the integrity and legal certainty of the global sports system.[37]

## References

Papaloukas, M., «CAS: The Court of Arbitration for Sport», 2013, Papaloukas Editions.

Paulsson, J., «Denial of Justice in International Law», Cambridge University Press, New York 2005, p. 176-178.

CAS 94/129 USA Shooting & Q. / UIT

CAS 98/211 B. / FINA

CAS ad hoc Division OG 00/013, Bernardo Segura/IAAF

TAS 2002/A/415 & 426

CAS 2003/A/461 & 471 & 473 WCM-GP Limited v/ FIM

CAS 2003/O/486

CAS 2004/A/659

CAS 2004/A/727 Vanderlei De Lima & BOC v. IAAF

CAS 2004/A/748

CAS 2005/A/899

CAS 2005/A/994

CAS 2006/A/1153

CAS 2006/A/1175

CAS 2006/A/1177 Aston Villa FC v. B.93 Copenhagen

TAS 2007/A/1433

37) See Papaloukas, M., «CAS: The Court of Arbitration for Sport», 2013, Papaloukas Editions.

CAS 2007/A/1251

CAS 2007/A/1294

CAS 2007/A/1396 & 1402 WADA & UCI v. Alejandro Valverde & RFEC

CAS 2007/A/1426

CAS 2008/A/1478

CAS 2008/A/1594

CAS 2008/A/1634 Hertha BSC GmbH & Co KgaA v. Football Association of Serbia

CAS 2009/A/1920

CAS 2009/A/1926 & 1930 ITF v. Richard Gasquet & WADA v. ITF & Richard
       Gasquet

CAS 2009/A/1974 N. v. S.C.F.C. Univ. Craiova & RFF

CAS OG 96/006

CAS OG 02/007

CAS OG 04/007

CAS OG 00/013

SFT decision ATF 101 Ia 73

SFT decision ATF 110 Ia 81

SFT decision ATF 114 Ia 307

SFT decision ATF 116 I a 94

SFT decision ATF 118 Ib 111

SFT decision ATF 118 II 12/19

SFT decision ATF 118 II 271

SFT decision ATF 120 II 369

SFT decision ATF 124 II 132

ECHR decision Wickramsinghe v. the United Kingdom, 9 December 1997 no.
       31503/96

ECHR decision X. v. the United Kingdom, no. 28530/95, 19 January 1998

ECHR decision, Albert and Le Compte v. Belgium judgment of 10 February 1983

ECHR decision, Bryan v. the United Kingdom judgment of 22 November 1995

# Sports as a Sphere of Show-business

IGOR PONKIN* · ALENA I. PONKINA**

*The article is dedicated to the peculiarities of sports as a sphere of show-business. The concept and structure of the sports industry, its main segments and its core –the segment of sports entertainment show business were considered. The article studies the meaning and origins of the show- entertaining aspect of sports, segments of the sports industry as a sphere of public relations and business activities. It is concluded that modern sports industry has already overstepped the limits of sports in its classic sense, far beyond original purposes, and the sports industry has more similarities with the industry of cinema, theater, circus, than with any other segments of business. But sport significantly differs from any other show business segments. First of all, it is determined by the autonomy of sport including some autonomy from business structures. The article studies the concept of the "sports entertainment product".*

Key word: sports entertainment show business, sports industry, sports, recreation function of sports, sports law, sports marketing, sports management, "sports entertainment product", autonomy of sport

As it develops, the sphere of sports is more and more being interlinked with business. Originally, sport has been mainly non-commercial by force of

---

* Lawyer, doctor of science (Law), full professor of chair of the legal support of the state and municipal services of the faculty "International Institute of Public Administration and Management" of the Russian Presidential Academy of National Economy and Public Administration (Moscow, Russia), State Professor, expert of Consortium of Sports Law Specialists (Moscow, Russia).
** Lawyer, PhD (Law), expert of Consortium of Sports Law Specialists(Moscow, Russia), lecturer of Sports Law Chair of the Kutafin Moscow State Law Academy.

its nature. However, the sports industry, on the one hand, had become an integral part of sports by the present day, but on the other hand, with a broader view, it has considerably extended its limits, has overstepped the limits of sports and now includes sports as a part of itself. We can and probably shall discuss the challenges and threats of sports commercialization. But the fact is that a large part of modern sports is closely linked to business when offering sports entertainment events, when transferring rights to broadcast sports events, when attracting sponsorship and funds through advertising in sports.

## The Meaning and Origins of the Show-entertaining Aspect of Sports

«If sports and its personalities can be packaged and sold, then why not do it?» – the rhetorical question is asked in the book "The Marketing of Sport" edited by John G. Beach and Simon Chadwick[1].

The sports industry is a sphere of public relations and business activities, focused on deriving revenues from exploitation of individual human and public interest to any forms of competitiveness and to competitiveness in sports in particular, as well as interest to entertainment and leisure activities (with an element of uncertainty), which includes the following segments (activities):
  - business activities related to ticketing sports entertainment events (ticket business, ticket issue and distribution);
  - commercial exploitation of brands and trademarks in the field of sports;
  - business activities related to the organization and holding of mass sports entertainment events (sports and close to sports show business);
  - business activities related to broadcasting sports entertainment product and transferring rights to such broadcasting, with other

---

1) *The Marketing of Sport* / Edited by J. Beech and S. Chadwick. – Harlow (England): Pearson Education, 2007 – xxxv; 555 p. – P. 4.

production and supply of sports entertainment product on the media markets;

- business activities related to sports merchandise and symbols, to the production and circulation of sports goods;
- business activities related to the issue of print and web-based media in the field of sports;
- the implementation execution of advertising activities in sports;
- business activities related to sports fashion and fitness;
- business activities related to the training of athletes and their "selling" to sports clubs;
- business activities related to the commercial exploitation of sports facilities.

And these are just the largest courses (segments) of the sports industry in general.

Today the whole sphere of sports relations is closely and fully connected to the sports goods industry, because it is impossible to go in for sport or even just athletic activities without sportswear and athletic shoes, sports equipment.

Business activities related to sports merchandise and symbols are (except for souvenir products) business anyway based on the production and circulation of sports product. Often just a slightly wider range of offers is used to be interpreted as such a product than it would have been reasonable.

Then, today premium cars are positioned in many cases and are presented as "sport cars", although hardly anyone would make up their mind to participate in professional car racing (except for street racing) by using these high-priced cars. The same now goes for stylish sports small vessels, which are more related to the confirmation of their owner's status rather than actually to sports activities.

The study of business activities related to sports merchandise and symbols, requires an analysis of common business bases in the sphere of sports merchandise and symbols, features of legal regulation and implementation of business activities related to sports merchandise and symbols, with the production and circulation of sports goods: athletic shoes and sportswear, sports accessories, sports outfit, sports equipment, sports facilities, sports mascots and sports tattoos. An important place is given to business marketing strategies in the sphere of sports merchandise and symbols, sports goods, sports facilities and equipment, sports outfit.

In many cases, it is reasonable to talk about the full and integrated business cycle of major international sports events: the Olympic business cycle, the business cycle of the FIFA World Cup, the business cycle of the UEFA European Championship, the business cycle of the Ice Hockey World Championship, the business cycle of the Tennis World Championship, etc.

The research objective of such cycles is divided into the research objectives of the following questions, for example, concerning the FIFA World Cup:

- concept and peculiarities of the business cycle of the FIFA World Cup;
- structural elements and stages of the business cycle of the FIFA World Cup;
- FIFA marketing activities and financial management;
- sources of FIFA funding; sources of funds that make up the budget of the next FIFA World Cup;
- FIFA revenues from selling rights to broadcast matches;
- FIFA revenues from sponsors;
- FIFA revenues from advertising;
- revenues from business activities related to FIFA merchandise and symbols and the particular FIFA World Cup;
- FIFA costs.

The modern sports industry has already overstepped the limits of sports in its classic sense, far beyond original purposes. The sports industry has more similarities with the industry of cinema, theater, circus, than with any other segments of business.

The main element (core) of the sports industry is sports entertainment show-business.

The range of entertainment activities can include not only major sports entertainment events, but can also integrate music, business projects related to economic exploitation of brands, sales of souvenirs, etc.

The modern form of sports has begun to form and actively develop since the middle – the second half of the 19th century. And the convergence of sports and show business is a tendency of not earlier than the beginning of the 20th century, and mostly of the second half of the 20th century and the current period of the 21st century.

Though ancient Greek sports games, tournaments in medieval Europe had elements of a spectacular show, their nature and objectives were not associated with it. In some measure gladiatorial combats in ancient Rome, demonstration of fights and actions of masters of combat sports in China, Korea and Japan in the ancient and middle ages can be considered as "sports" show business, because the objectives of entertainment nature played an important role among the objectives of their holding.

The industrialization at the 19th and 20th centuries, social changes in the sphere of employment, resulting in the emergence of free time among broad sectors of population, the emergence of financial possibilities for entertainment – all these facts led to the development of sports as a sphere of sports entertainment show-business. So far, the sphere of sports has undergone considerable changes and now a significant place in it belongs to spectacular events organized for the sake of profit.

Kenneth Cortsen notes, «the influx of commercialization in the sports industry has created a melting pot in which the junction between sport and entertainment is a key ingredient. In the contemporary sports industry, serious and leading actors are competitively and continuously trying to find innovative ways to capitalize on this junction. Brand building and brand management are at the heart of this capitalization process and strong sports brands»[2].

Professionalism has existed in certain sports since the nineteenth century, – Jean Gadrey shows, – but has only recently become widespread. Money really began to enter sport from the 1970s onwards, and the principles of amateurism were gradually 'deregulated' during the 1980. Thus we are dealing with a threefold transformation: (1) the transformation of sport into show business; (2) the televised broadcast of sports events; (3) the intervention

---

[2] Cortsen K. *Sport as show business* // <http://kennethcortsen.com/sport- economy/sport-as-show-business/>.

of advertisers, who are prepared to spend vast sums to purchase airtime on this most favoured of media, making them the main sources of finance for the networks that carry the broadcasts[3].

That is, in addition to the development of sports in its classic sense (pursuit of sports records, competitiveness, emergence and recognition of new sports, etc.), sport also develops to meet commercial interests of those who carry out organizational activities in sports.

Significant revenues of famous athletes, owners of sports clubs, sports reporters are determined not by traditional economic criteria of their labor capacity, but by the fact that professional sport is increasingly becoming a sphere of show business, and so it lives according to the laws of show business, on the basis of the law of supply and demand on sports entertainment product.

Today the situation in professional boxing with famous athletes most clearly reflects the fact that at the present day the sphere of sports has really acquired signs of show business.

As Rafael Tenorio points, one way in which boxing promoters are able to mitigate the risks they face is by signing the top fighters to multi-year or multi-fight contracts. Since the boxing promoter now has a vested interest in certain fighters, it may be to his advantage not to match his fighters against the best opponents so as to minimise the probability that they will lose and thus have their market value reduced[4].

On the other hand, sport significantly differs from any other show business segments.

First of all, it is determined by the autonomy of sport including some autonomy from business structures[5].

---

3) Gadrey J. *New Economy, New Myth.* – London: Routledge, 2003. – 163 p. – P. 70.
4) Tenorio R. On the competitive structure in professional boxing, or why the best boxers very seldom fight each other // *Handbook on the Economics of Sport / Ed. by W. Andreff, S. Szymanski.* – Cheltenham: Edward Elgar Publishing Limited, 2006. – 830 p. – P. 364–368. – P. 366.
5) For more details, see: Ponkina A.I. Autonomy of sport: legal aspects // *International Sports Law Review Pandektis.* – 2013. – Vol. 10. – № 1–2. – P. 204–215; Ponkina A.I. *Governance and autonomous institutionalization in sport.* – Moscow: Sports Law Commission of the Russian Association of Lawyers, 2013; Ponkina A.I. *Autonomy of sport. Legal study.* – Moscow: Sports Law Commission of the Russian Association of

According to Resolution of Parliamentary Assembly of the Council of Europe № 1602 (2008) of 24 January 2008 "The need to preserve the European Sport Model», «european sports model... is underpinned by the twin principles of financial solidarity and openness of competition. Sport undoubtedly has a specific nature that sets it apart from any other field of economic activity. It has important social, educational and cultural functions. Solidarity between different levels in sport is a fundamental aspect of the European sports model... We have witnessed the internationalisation of sport and, above all, the unprecedented development of the economic dimension of sport, driven in particular by the value of television rights" (paragraphs 3, 4 and 8)[6].

## Sports Entertainment Product

In addition to the consumption of sports and goods and services related to sports, it is reasonable to allocate the consumption of sports events.

The relations in the sphere of the sports industry include 3 main elements:
- consumers of sports entertainment product,
- sports entertainment product in essence,
- suppliers of sports entertainment product.

A distinctive characteristic of sports entertainment product (in most cases) is that it is a nonmaterial product.

Individual sports events might be offered as sports entertainment product, but more often it is a series of sports events (championships, season games, etc.). Mixed forms of sports entertainment events might also be offered, where sport is more or less integrated with show product (a spectacular event), for example, the show "ice dancing", entertainment programs with participation of athletes. The criterion is the same –

---

Lawyers, 2013.

6) Resolution of Parliamentary Assembly of the Council of Europe № 1602 (2008) of 24 January 2008 «The need to preserve the European Sport Model» // <http://assembly.coe.int/ASP/XRef/X2H-DW-XSL.asp?fileid=17628&lang=EN>.

possibility of selling this product to a consumer either directly (via ticketing or selling opportunities to watch events on television) or indirectly (via sponsorship, advertising, transferring rights to broadcast). Basically, a combination of several forms is realized.

It might be offered not only sports entertainment product produced and consumed at the same time, simultaneously (mainly), but also (less often) product, which might not be consumed by consumers in real time, but it is expected to be broadcasted in recorded form.

A sport event should be considered in all its diversity.

Jeff Borland considers sports events in 3 aspects: a sport event as a phenomenon in the product market, the labour market and the capital market[7].

To provide competitive advantages, organizers of sports events should make full use of its lucrative potential, but this is difficult because the balance of supply and demand in the sphere of sports show business is constantly changing, being exposed to a variety of factors. Some of these factors might be political events and perils (Olympic boycott, riots in the streets), lack of rent at a particular region or excessive expensiveness of rent of necessary sport infrastructure, financial crisis phenomena and many other factors.

The problem of uncertainty is also aggravated by the following fact.

According to Daniel Funk, "selling the benefits received and needs fulfilled from watching or participating in a sport event are hard to pinpoint"[8].

That is one of the key members in sports, considering it as a sphere of show business, is a consumer who can have a significant impact on the organization of sports events in view of its preferences and features.

A payment made by consumers of sports entertainment product (directly – for tickets to sports events, for a right to watch broadcasting on television and others, as well as indirectly – via sports sponsorship and sports

7) Borland J. The production of professional team sports // *Handbook on the Economics of Sport* / Ed. by W. Andreff, S. Szymanski. – Cheltenham: Edward Elgar Publishing Limited, 2006. – 830 p. – P. 22–26. – P. 23.
8) Funk D.C. *Consumer Behaviour in Sport and Events. Marketing Action.* – Oxford: Butterworth-Heinemann, 2008. – 247 p. – P. 10.

advertising) allows maintaining and developing sports.

The nature of a sport competition as sports entertainment product is significantly unpredictable, which actually attracts a consumer of the product, providing not only entertainment, but also a certain intrigue, uncertainty.

Consumers of sports entertainment product in the form of a sport competition are not only spectators but also participants of the sports competition (players of a sport team or participating athletes, athletic trainers, sports judges, arbitrators), as well as indirectly sports sponsors and those who place advertising at sports events.

The powerful entertainment potential of sports as a sphere of show business is determined by the fact that, according to John Beech and Simon Chadwick, a key feature of sports product is its uncertainty, the uncertainty of results, which is one of the main reasons why so many people are motivated to consume it. One of the most important challenges that sports marketers face is the sale of excitement, stress and emotional tension provoked by the uncertainty of outcome of sports events[9].

According to Neil Simon, "sport is the only entertainment where, no matter how many times you go back, you never know the ending"[10].

Not by accident a consumer's behavior is studied by organizers of sports events and sports marketers, and those issues are one of the key courses of sports marketing, because they allow to adjust an offer of sports entertainment product quickly and to communicate with persistent groups of consumers of the product.

"The aim must be to deliver a quality product in a form that is attractive to everyone involved even to participants, sports must be well presented and offered in a way that is attractive. - David Watt writes. - An obvious example of how the product can be substantially changed is in the case of the many games who have introduced mini versions in order to please, suit and attract potential participants, especially young people, and tailor the

---

9) Chadwick S., Beech J. Introduction: the marketing of sport // *The Marketing of Sport / Edited by J. Beech and S. Chadwick.* – Harlow (England): Pearson Education, 2007 – xxxv; 555 p. – P. 3–22. – P. 9.

10) Cited by: The Marketing of Sport / Edited by J. Beech and S. Chadwick. - Harlow (England): Pearson Education, 2007 - xxxv; 555 p. - P. 3.

product to the demands of these groups. Indoor bowls also fundamentally changed the whole format and rules of their game in order to make it more attractive to television, sponsors and participants"[11].

Enhancing this entertainment value [of sport], usually by changing aspects of the basic game, has been prevalent in most professional sports. Shortening matches, widening goalmouths, changing (shortening) boundaries and allowing technological improvements in equipment are all examples of trying to enhance entertainment value[12].

Aaron Smith notes that there are various motivations to attend sports entertainment events. Sport watching offers aesthetic (or visual) pleasure to fans, sport fans are often prepared to pay to witness excellence, such as skilful play or memorable moments; in some sports focus may be done on appearance of the participants as in the case of beach volleyball or athletics, for example[13].

Any sports event aims at attracting spectators, in particular, at least the following categories: fervent admirers and passionate sports fans who entirely keen on sports and are followers of certain sports teams; unreliable fans of sports teams, whose commitment is determined by the achievements of teams; as well as spectators who get pleasure from observing an event. The policy of marketers of sports events for different categories of spectators is different. So, the place of holding an event, music and other trappings are more important for the last category of spectators than for the rest[14].

The specific character of sports as a sphere of show business also imposes certain imprints on the employment relationships in sports.

More famous athletes, as Mark Conrad writes, bring considerable publicity to the sports event they participate in, and, respectively, revenues from

11) Watt D.C. *Sports Management and Administration.* - London: E&FN Spon, 1998. - 255 p. - P. 160.

12) Trenberth L., Garland R. Sport and consumer buying behaviour // *The Marketing of Sport / Edited by J. Beech and S. Chadwick.* - Harlow (England): Pearson Education Limited, 2007. - 555 p. - P. 83–101. - P. 92.

13) Smith A.C.T. *Introduction to Sport Marketing. A Practical Approach.* - Oxford: Butterworth-Heinemann, 2008. - 326 p. - P. 37.

14) Trenberth L., Garland R. Sport and consumer buying behaviour // *The Marketing of Sport / Edited by J. Beech and S. Chadwick.* - Harlow (England): Pearson Education Limited, 2007. - 555 p. - P. 83–101. - P. 93.

ticket sales for such events are increasing. An athlete's career, as well as a theatre and film actor's career, is fickle. If an athlete does not make certain progress in the sports for a period of his/her career, he/she might incur fans' displeasure and might be dismissed[15].

Another important fact is that, unlike other spheres of show business, in the sports entertainment show business consumers are foremost (and it is not uncommon) or at least strongly sure of being qualified experts, connoisseurs of the sport, for the opportunity to see the sports entertainment product of which they are ready to spend their money, spend their time, express their support, etc. This means that organizers and participants of the sports entertainment product guide it to extremely demanding, you might even say, biased spectators. For example, consumers always notice new players in a sport team or changes of sports rules, moreover, consumers have an impact on many important management issues made by sports organizations.

In addition, an important role belongs to channels of communication of audio-visual information about a sports entertainment event, which is being held or has been held, to a consumer (most consumers), which defines a whole segment of the sports industry and sport financial market that is related to transferring rights to broadcast sports events (one of the largest sources of sport funding).

## A little about Russia...

In the run-up to the 2014 Winter Olympics in Sochi and the 2018 FIFA World Cup the impressive preparation of sports infrastructure has been carried out in Russia. Russian laws have also undergone substantial changes in order to create more favourable conditions for the sports in its classic sense.

But today you cannot name the Russian legislation sufficiently effective in creating opportunities and conditions for the development of sports show

---

15) Conrad M. *The Business of Sports – A Primer for Journalists.* – London: Lawrence Erlbaum Associates, publishers, 2006. – 329 p. – P. xxiv, xxii.

business in Russia.

Only recently adopted Federal Law No. 108-FZ of 07.06.2013 "On preparing for and holding the FIFA 2018 Football World Championship and the FIFA 2017 Confederations Cup in the Russian Federation, and amending certain legal acts of the Russian Federation"[16], as well as some of the recent amendments in Federal Law of Russian Federation No.329-FZ of 04.XII.2007 "On Physical Culture and Sports in the Russian Federation"[17] have created some opportunities for the development of the production and circulation of sports entertainment product. But a lot remains to be done.

Meanwhile, the question is not useless. The sports entertainment product called "the Winter Olympics" (in spite of all the moral and political values of the Olympic Games, they are sports entertainment product) must be offered and sold to a consumer, to at least partially restore expired costs to the state and private investors.

## References

Borland J. The production of professional team sports // *Handbook on the Economics of Sport / Ed. by W. Andreff, S. Szymanski.* - Cheltenham: Edward Elgar Publishing Limited, 2006. - 830 p. - P. 22–26.

Chadwick S., Beech J. Introduction: the marketing of sport // *The Marketing of Sport / Edited by J. Beech and S. Chadwick.* - Harlow (England): Pearson Education, 2007 - xxxv; 555 p. - P. 3–22.

Conrad M. *The Business of Sports – A Primer for Journalists.* - London: Lawrence Erlbaum Associates, publishers, 2006. - 329 p.

Cortsen K. *Sport as show business //* <http://kennethcortsen.com/sport-economy/sport-as-show-business/>

Funk D.C. *Consumer Behaviour in Sport and Events. Marketing Action.* - Oxford: Butterworth-Heinemann, 2008. - 247 p.

Gadrey J. *New Economy, New Myth.* - London: Routledge, 2003. - 163 p.

Legislation Bulletin of the Russian Federation. - 10.VI.2013. - № 23.

---

16) Legislation Bulletin of the Russian Federation. – 10.VI.2013. – № 23. <http://www.garant.ru>.
17) Legislation Bulletin of the Russian Federation. – 10.XII.2007. – № 50. As in force on – <http://www.garant.ru>.

Legislation Bulletin of the Russian Federation. - 10.XII.2007. - № 50.

Ponkina A.I. Autonomy of sport: legal aspects // *International Sports Law Review Pandektis.* - 2013. - Vol. 10. - № 1-2. - P. 204-215.

Ponkina A.I. *Governance and autonomous institutionalization in sport.* - Moscow: Sports Law Commission of the Russian Association of Lawyers, 2013.

Ponkina A.I. *Autonomy of sport. Legal study.* - Moscow: Sports Law Commission of the Russian Association of Lawyers, 2013.

Resolution of Parliamentary Assembly of the Council of Europe № 1602 (2008) of 24 January 2008 «The need to preserve the European Sport Model» // <http://assembly.coe.int/ASP/XRef/X2H-DW-XSL.asp?fileid=17628&lang=EN>.

Smith A.C.T. *Introduction to Sport Marketing. A Practical Approach.* - Oxford: Butterworth-Heinemann, 2008. - 326 p.

Tenorio R. On the competitive structure in professional boxing, or why the best boxers very seldom fight each other // *Handbook on the Economics of Sport / Ed. by W. Andreff, S. Szymanski.* - Cheltenham: Edward Elgar Publishing Limited, 2006. - 830 p. - P. 364-368.

*The Marketing of Sport /* Edited by J. Beech and S. Chadwick. - Harlow (England): Pearson Education, 2007 - xxxv; 555 p.

Trenberth L., Garland R. Sport and consumer buying behaviour // *The Marketing of Sport / Edited by J. Beech and S. Chadwick.* - Harlow (England): Pearson Education Limited, 2007. - 555 p. - P. 83-101.

Watt D.C. *Sports Management and Administration.* - London: E&FN Spon, 1998. - 255 p.

# Current Aspects of International and European Sports Policy and European Sports Law*

KARL-HEINZ SCHNEIDER**

*The article looks at the main tasks of European and international Sports policy as well as European sports law.*

*The prepararatory work undertaken to include sport in Community law, i.e. the incorporation of sport in the Lisbon Treaty, is specifically highlighted. The tasks and competences of the European Union are explained in detail. Furthermore, sports policy cooperation with international organizations -. in addition to supranational cooperation with the EU -. is illustrated. In this context the focus is on the Council of Europe and UNESCO.With regard to UNESCO, the Conference of Ministers and Senior Officials Responsible for Physical Education and Sport (MINEPS V/ World Conference of Ministers of Sport) to be hosted in Berlin in May 2013 by Germany is mentioned and the conference's topics are presented (e.g. match fixing).*

*The third part of the article deals with the question of what sports law actually is. The answer focuses on both the national and the European perspective.*

*This followed by the thesis that national and European sports law should develop into international sports law to ensure the necessary equality of all athletes before the law.*

*Given increasing globalization and closer international cooperation, it is certainly necessary to create in future an international sports law.*

Key words: International and European Sports Policy, Sports law, International Sports law, Lisbon Treaty, UNESCO, EU, Council of Europe, Globalization

---

* Head of Division at the Federal Ministry of the Interior and Lecturer at the Johannes Gutenberg University, Mainz at the 18th IASL (International Association of Sports Law) Conference in Beijing from 9 to 12 October 2012
** Bundesministerium des Innern, Ministerialrat, Head of section SP2, EU und international sport affairs

$I$ would like to thank you for the invitation to this major congress and I am looking forward to the interesting and stimulating discussion in the wonderful atmosphere here in Beijing. The title of my talk is: "Current Aspects of International and European Sports Policy and European Sports Law". Today, I would like to present a number of aspects illustrating how the Federal Government – in this case, the Federal Ministry of the Interior, since this falls within its remit – participates in the formative process of shaping European and international sport policies and how new and current developments are viewed.

I would like to divide my talk into three short sections:

I.   (Firstly) A brief review of European sport polices over the last years and a definition of the term "European sport policies" .The preparatory work undertaken to include sport in Community law, i.e. the incorporation of sport in the Lisbon Treaty, is specially highlighted. The tasks and competences of the European Union are explained in detail.

II.  (Secondly) some aspects of the status quo and the current sport policies, and the aims of the EU White Paper, furthermore , sports policy cooperation with international organizations – in addition to supranational cooperation with the EU – is illustraded . With regard to UNESCO, the Conference of Ministers and Senior Officials Responsible for Physical Education and Sport (MINEPS V) to be hosted in Berlin in May 2013 by Germany is mentioned and the three main conference's topics are presented :Access to Sport as a Fundamental Right for All (Inclusion in sport – Implementing the UN Convention on the Rights of Persons with Disabilities- Access of women and girls), Promoting Investment in Sport and Physical Education Programmes (Promoting quality physical education, Awarding of sport mega events and their sustainability), Preserving the Integrity of Sport (Commitment to the values of sport and the fight against match fixing, doping and corruption in sport);

III. (Thirdly) I would like to offer a brief look ahead, addressing the issues that I consider will be of concern to Member States, associations and the EU Commission in the near future and the coming years, and where a solution needs to be found. In my opinion we have to come in the future to an international sports law. We need a harmonised international legal order governing sport. A lot of EU- and UNESCO Member States has specific sport laws. Globalisation requires us to put in place an international legal order governing sport (international sports law). Since there is no uniform global sports law, this leads to: Inequality, Fragmentation of legal provisions and Legal uncertainty.

# I

By way of introduction, let me start by saying something about the term of "European sport policies". Due to the complex and diverse culture of sport in Europe, every kind of definition is always difficult. Nevertheless, as I see it, "European sport policies" refers to policies building on the so-called "European model of sport" and which, naturally, also include all actors in the sports sector represented on the European level, including social partners and international organisations such as, for example, the Council of Europe and UNESCO. In the context of my contribution today, however, I would like to place the emphasis more on the European Commission's sport policies and less on bilateral cooperation with other European Union Member States or cooperation with the Council of Europe. Naturally, the Council of Europe also plays a key role – here, one only has to recall the area of the European Convention Against Doping – although one needs to bear in mind that the work on sport policies has, as I see it, been newly established and re-organised within the Council of Europe; the Federal Government will be observing this closely and considering how it can contribute here in future.

Although I mentioned in my introduction that I intended to offer a brief review of "European sport policies", I would like to reassure you that I am not planning to present the last 10 years of European sport policies in the context of a historical retrospective. Nonetheless, in my view, it does seem important to realise that we have indeed made significant progress in this area over the last 13 years. In 1999, when Germany held the EU Presidency, I can remember voluminous debates not only with numerous Member States but also with the EU Commission over the sense of incorporating a European Article on Sport into Community law and, at that time, there was considerable resistance from many States to declaring a readiness to openly support the incorporation of such an Article. Ten years ago, there was merely the so-called "Joint Declaration on Sport" agreed within the framework of the Amsterdam Treaty. However, this merely dealt with a political declaration of intent that had no import and binding force in Community law. Consequently, this "Joint Declaration" did not give the Commission the adequate competence to establish a requisite budget line, i.e., an independent "budget" in the sport sector or for the pertinent studies and actions. For the necessary expenditure, the European Court of Auditors required a clear legal basis in Community law. For this reason, the situation at that time did not offer a satisfactory basis for the Commission to pursue a correspondingly active sport policy.


## II

I would now like to move on to the second part in which I intend to look at the status quo in somewhat more detail. As an introduction, I would like to say one or two sentences about how the Federal Government is at present contributing or can contribute to participating in forming European sport polices within the EU framework.

The 1957 Treaties of Rome failed to mention sport explicitly. Therefore, sport did not at first present an integral part of the European integration movement. It was not before 1985 that the EU recognised sport as an instrument of international understanding (Adonnino-Report 1985, Walrave and Koch case 1975, Bosman case 1995). Nowadays, sport is generally a subject matter of Community law (indirect EU sports policy) and the "specific characteristics" of sport are taken into account by the ECJ (European Court of Justice). The ECJ is "sport-friendly".

Finally, Lisbon Treaty was adopted (entry into force on 1 December 2009). The procedures of changing the EU Presidency every six months are still in place, and meetings of EU Directors-General and Ministers Responsible for Sport respectively are held twice a year. Hence, essentially, as yet there have been four major meetings annually where the particular Director-Generals or Ministers can exchange views. In addition, there are also special meetings between the IOC and Ministers, and a range of Working Groups on the EU level that are primarily organised by the EU Commission in Brussels and deal with, for example, volunteer work, the EU White Paper, or the doping problem. I do not intend to give you any exhaustive list of these here. All in all, as things stand, adequate opportunities do exist for communication.

From today's perspective, the last years were truly successful years for European sport policies in a number of ways.

On the one hand, for the first time since the treaties establishing the European Economic Community, sport has now been successfully anchored in Community law and, on the other, following the German Presidency of the EU, the EU Commission has succeeded in presenting, from our perspective, a White Paper truly oriented to the future. In the White Paper put forward, the EU Commission addresses the topic of sport comprehensively for the first time, and naturally the German Federal Government has very much welcomed the inclusion in the EU White Paper of all the topics we also dealt with in the course of the EU Presidency, for example, sport and the economy, combating doping, dual career, and sport and integration. In the Federal Government's view, the 'Pierre de Coubertin' Action Plan similarly proposes crucial sport-related measures on the EU level for the coming years, and in principle they receive our support.

In this connection, I would like to emphasise that the German Bundestag's Sports Committee has also expressly welcomed the presentation of the Commission's White Paper on sport, and the White Paper was an object of related discussions and consultations on a number of occasions. In September 2007, the Bundesrat too expressed views indicating that it welcomes the Commission's White Paper as a contribution to promoting an important social and economic sector. Nevertheless, the Bundesrat also contained critical voices that noted with concern the one or other of the White Paper's goals, since they were regarded as tending to expand non-existent EU competences.

As far as the enactment of the White Paper is concerned and, naturally, also after the Lisbon Treaty has been ratified and Article 165 TFEU (Treaty on the Functioning of the European Union) with its provisions on sport is in force , the Federal Government will certainly be keeping a watchful eye on EU organs and bodies to ensure that neither the autonomy of sport is encroached on nor the so-called principle of subsidiarity is violated.

Article 165 TFEU merely provides for a "supporting and supplementing competence". It does not empower the EU Commission to adopt legislative acts, neither in primary nor in secondary law. Nor does the Commission have the right to adopt legal measures seeking to harmonise the situation among Member states. This means that Art. 165 TFEU is mor or less a "toothless tiger". Main competences continues to rest with the EU Member States.

III

As regards European sport policies and international sport law, what do we need to work on especially in the coming years? What will be the main objectives and which problems will we have to try and solve?

Here, I would only like to mention a few key points, singling out some areas where, in my view, we will need to address these topics in particular:

- The question of greater legal certainty in the area of sport and antitrust law;
- The composition of national teams, youth training, the status of

players' agents, safeguarding sports funding;
- Issues concerning the central marketing of media rights and its compatibility with antitrust law;
- Concerns about a dual career and controlling the management of professional clubs;
- Measures against match fixing and illegal on line betting and
- Implementation of an international Convention who protect the integrity of sport.

To achieve greater legal certainty within the States many of these points need to be settled in a comprehensive and in-depth way, and it is understandable that sport functionaries and associations are calling here for more legal certainty for their daily work.

There is no uniform "Sports Law". Legal conflicts tend to concern a great number of legal fields. With a view to globalisation in sport we should look at how to bring about a harmonised international legal sport order. In view of globalization and closer international cooperation the international community should make an effort to develop international sports law and recognise access and participation in sport as a human right.

# References

Fritzweiler, Jochen, Pfister, Bernhard, Summerer, Thomas: Praxishandbuch Sportrecht, Verlag C.H.Beck, München 2007;

Nolte, Martin: Sport und Recht, Ein Lehrbuch zum internationalen, europäischen und deutschen Sportrecht, Verlag Karl Hofmann, Schorndorf 2004;

Nolte, Martin und Horst,Johannes (Hrsg.): Handbuch Sportrecht, Verlag Hofmann, Schondorf 2009;

Schimke, Martin: Sportrecht, Fischer Taschenbuchverlag, Frankfurt 1996;

Haas, Ulrich und Martens, Dirk-Reiner: Sport, Deutscher Taschenbuch Verlag, München 2004;

Schleiter, Pieter: Globalisierung im Sport, Realisierungswege einer harmonisierten internationalen Sportrechtsordnung, Boorberg Verlag, Stuttgart 2009;

Wax, Andreas: Internationales Sportrecht, Unter besonderer Berücksichtigung des Sportvölkerrechts, Verlag Duncker & Humblot, Berlin 2009:

Scherrer, Urs und Ludwig, Kai: Sportrecht, Eine Begriffserläuterung, Verlag Orell Fuessli, Mai 2010;

Schneider, Karl-Heinz: Die Verankerung des Sports im Gemeinschaftsrecht, in: SpuRt 4/2002, S. 137-140:

Schneider, Karl-Heinz:" Der Traum der roten Kammer" – Aspekte zum chinesischen Sportrecht und zur bilateralen Zusammenarbeit zwischen der Bundesrepublik Deutschland und der Volksrepublik China – in: Causa Sport, Heft 4/2009, Seite 297 – 305;

Schneider, Karl-Heinz u.a.(Hrsg.): Der Sport verbindet unsere Staaten, Chinesisch-Deutscher Sportwissenschaftlicher Kongress vom 16.- 18. November 2009, Bejing, China, Tagungsband, publiziert von ICSSPE/CIEPSS, Berlin 2010, British Library Cataloguing in Publication Data, ISBN 978-3-9811179-3-6;

Schneider, Karl-Heinz u. Song Luzeng (Hrsg.): Deutsch-Chinesischer Sportrechtskongress, 15. bis 20. Oktober 2010, Bonn, Deutschland, Tagungsband, publiziert von ICSSPE/CIEPSS, Berlin 2011, British Library Cataloguing in Publication Data, ISBN 978 - 3 -9811179-3-6;

Schneider, Karl-Heinz u. Zhang, Jian (Hrsg.): Current Perspectives in Modern Sport Sciences and Sport Policies in China and Germany: Sport Management, Sport Psychology and Sport Legacies, 3rd Chinese-German Symposium, 1-3 November 2011, Hangzhou, China, Proceedings publiziert von ICSSPE/CIEPSS, Berlin 2012, British Library Cataloguing in Publication Data, ISBN 978 - 3 - 9811179 - 3 - 6;

Schneider, Karl-Heinz u.a. (Hrsg.): Sport as a Mediator between Cultures, International Conference on Sport for Development and Peace, September 15th - 17th, 2011, Wingate Institute for Physical Education and Sport, Israel, Proceedings publiziert von ICSSPE/CIEPSS, Berlin 2012, British Library Cataloguing in Publication Data, ISBN 978 - 3 - 9811179 - 4 - 3;

Muresan, Remus: Die neue Zuständigkeit der Europäischen Union im Bereich des Sports, in: Causa Sport Heft 2/2010, S. 99 – 105

Adolphsen/Nolte/Lehner/Gerlinger (Hrsg.): Sportrecht in der Praxis, Kohlhammer Verlag, Stuttgart 2012;

Eßig, Natalie: Nachhaltigkeit von Olympischen Sportbauten – Analyse der Umsetzbarkeit und Messbarkeit von Nachhaltigkeitsaspekten bei Wettkampfstätten von Olympischen Spielen, Fraunhofer-Verlag, Stuttgart 2010;

Kistner, Thomas: Fifa-Mafia – Die schmutzigen Geschäfte mit dem Weltfußball, Droemer Knaur, München 2012;

Weinrich, Jens: Korruption im Sport, Forum Verlag, Leipzig 2006;

Hill, Declan: „Sichere Siege", Kiepenheuer & Witsch, 2008;

EU-Kommission (Hrsg.): Studie zu „Match-fixing in sport", A mapping of criminal law provisions in EU 27, March 2012.

# Russian Legal Policy of Intellectual Property in Sports Competition

OLGA SHEVCHENKO*

*In the article considered the questions of intellectual property in sports competition. We prove that the production of creative product as the copyright object takes place in the competition. However, in Russian Federation the complication does not provide a definition of the term "creative product", though it is necessity to study this concept and elaborate a unified approach to its definition.*

**Key word:** intellectual property in sports, sport competition, creative product

The regulatory framework of the Russian Federation in the field of physical fitness and sports is dynamically evolving and improving, especially on the threshold of the large and prestigious sports events that are of great significance for Russia. In the literature, one can even find the opinion about the necessity of codification of the sports legislation of Russia[1].

At the same time, the issues of the legal regulation of the intellectual rights remain outside the field of the scientific interest and legal regulation.

Pursuant to part 1 of article 34 of the Russian Constitution, everyone is entitled to freely use their capabilities and property for entrepreneurship and other business activities not prohibited by law, and pursuant to part 1 of article 37 of the Russian Constitution, everyone is entitled to freely

* Ph.D., Assistant Professor, Department of Labor Law and Social Security Law, Moscow State Law University

1) A.A. Solov'yov. *Russian and foreign experience of systematization of the sports legislation*: Monography / Sports Law Committee of the Lawyers Association of Russia. M., 2011

dispose of their capacity for labor, select the occupation and profession. Part 1 of article 44 of the Russian Constitution guarantees the freedom of literary, artistic, scientific, technical and other kinds of creative work and teaching to everyone. Law protects the intellectual property.

Article 1226 of the Civil Code of the Russian Federation uses the term "intellectual rights" including the exclusive right that is the property right, and in cases prescribed by the Code, also the personal non-proprietary and other rights (the artist's resale royalty, privilege, and other). A citizen due to whose efforts the result of intellectual activity was created is acknowledged as the author pursuant to cl. 1 art. 1228 of the Civil Code of the Russian Federation.

The author of the result of intellectual activity owns the authorship right, the right on name, the right of integrity and the right to publish the artwork that are inalienable and untransferable. The alienable right is the exclusive right that the author, as its initial holder, may transfer to third parties under an agreement. Cl. 2 art. 1270 of the Civil Code of the Russian Federation includes, in particular, the right to distribution, reproduction, public demonstration, translation and publication in this category. The author's rights are called copyright and are a type of the intellectual right.

A complicated issue is referring a sports event to the copyright objects.

Thus, some kinds of sports imply the mandatory existence of a sports and creative compound when the sports result is achieved by a sportsperson's performance of an original sports work at a competition. Therefore, a relationship emerges between a sportsperson and the authors of the performance in regard to the results of their intellectual activity.

For example, from the sports point of view, at the sports dancing competitions, the sportsmen perform the same technical elements, but the way these elements are tied together, what music they are performed to, what image the sportsmen perform in, individualizes then and adds a creative nature to their activity. The sportsperson's image and acting skills, etc., also have an impact on the results of the competition.

It is possible to say that production of creative product as the copyright object takes place. However, the complication lies, first of all, in the fact that the law of the Russian Federation does not provide a definition of the term "creative product", though the scientists have raised the issue of the necessity to study this concept and elaborate a unified approach to its definition many times.

I believe, one should distinguish the kinds of sports having a creative compound. In the Russian Federation, the sports register maintained by the Ministry of Sports provides the segregation of the kinds of sports only by whether they are or are not included into the program of the winter Olympic Games, summer Olympic Games.

In our opinion, in order to ensure the due copyright protection in the field of sports the so-called creative kinds of sports (e.g. figure skating, synchronous swimming, rhythmic gymnastics, sports aerobics, sports dancing, etc.) must be distinguished on the legislative level. In these kinds of sports, the sportsperson's activity has a certain specificity: at the competitions he/she performs a sports work that is a result of the intellectual labor. The peculiarity also lies in the fact that the judges assess the performance by two grades: for technical skills and the artistic impression, and the second grade has the priority, as in the event of an equal performance of the sportsmen from the point of view of technical skills, the preference is given to the one who has made a brighter aesthetic impression.

In legal practice, there are many issued related to the determination of the copyright object. Pursuant to the Russian Law, the copyright objects are the works of science, literature and art that are the result of creative activity regardless of the designation and the merit of the works, as well as the ways of their expression. Herewith, the creative contribution must be established with the account of the specificity of the created work. The list of the copyright objects contained in the law is not comprehensive. A creative work expressed in an objective form is subject to legal protection as a copyright object, but not its content. Thus, ideas, teaching methods, chess games, scientific discoveries, etc., are not protected by the copyright.

In one of the district courts of Moscow, a case of a chess player against the company K was contemplated. As the ground of action, the complainant specified the fact that in 2000 the defendant released a compact disk with a computer database of chess games that included the games played by the complainant. The chess player had not granted the exclusive right to use their chess games to the company K. In connection to the above said, the complainant requested that his co-authorship be recognized and the losses for the illegal use of his chess games be compensated for. The court dismissed the claim, specifying that a chess game represents an aggregate of moves made in turns by both competitors. The record of the moves is made with the help of the generally accepted chess notation. A move in a chess game made by a player from a certain game position represents an idea through which a player intends to achieve the desired result. The idea is not protected by the copyright.

The similar approach is contained in the decision of the European Court. Thus, pursuant to the decision of the EC dated 04.10.2011 on the cases N C-403/08, C-429/08 "Premier League Football Association and others vs. QC Leisure and others (case C-403/08) and Caren Murphy vs. Media Protection Services (case C-429/08"[2]), sports events cannot be contemplated as a result of intellectual creation and classified as a result of activity according to the meaning of the Decree on the Copyright. This, in particular, refers to football games embraced by the rules of game that leave no space for creative freedom for the copyright purposes.

Considering a creative work as a copyright object subject to legal protection requires a number of factors that are generally called criteria or the signs of protectability.

Usually, the following signs and conditions of protectability of the creative works are distinguished in the scientific literature:

- Acknowledgement of a creative work as a result of creative activity;
- The existence of an objective (material, "real-valued" form);
- The possibility of reproduction of the given work in any way.

Therefore, a sports work must be contemplated as a copyright object on the grounds that it meets the conditions of protectability – is expressed in an objective form and is the result of creative activity.

Special attention should be paid to the justification of the use of the

---

2) Judgment of the Court (Grand Chamber) of 4 October 2011. Football Association Premier League Ltd and Others v QC Leisure and Others (C-403/08) and Karen Murphy v Media Protection Services Ltd (C-429/08) // European Court reports 2011.

copyright objects at a sports competition. Such a necessity is clearly seen on the example of the situation that involved the Russian figure skaters Oksana Domnina and Maxim Shabalin. They were accused of the violation of a copyright to a musical piece used as the accompaniment for their performance at the Olympics in Vancouver in 2010. The British singer Sheila Chandra stated that in their performance "Aboriginal Dance" Domnina and Shabalin illegally used her work "Speaking in Tongues II". This statement was made shortly before the start of the Olympics. The figure skaters were considered as the main candidates for the gold medals[3]. Such legal flaws endanger the success of the performance at the competitions.

## Conclusions

It is proposed to distinguish and legislate the so-called creative kinds of sports including the sports and creative compound in the Russian Federation. As a result, a sports work is created that is expressed in an objective form and has a creative nature, which allows referring it to the objects of copyright and apply it to the creation, performance and use of the exclusive property regulation.

Such legislation will allow ensuring the observance of the rights and legal interests of the sports subjects and, as a consequence, should have a positive impact on the professional results of the sportsmen.

## References

Gusov K.N., Shevchenko O.A. Sports law. The legal status of athletes, coaches, judges and other professionals in the field of physical culture and sports: Manual. M., 2011

Ponkin I.V., Solov'yov A.A., Ponkina A.I. Educational-methods complex of "Sport Law". M., 2011.

---

3) Kamenkova V.Y. Issues of legal regulation of intellectual property in the sphere of sports in Belarus // *Sports: economics, law, management.*, 2012. N 2. Pp. 26 - 28.

S.V.Alekseev. Sports Law: Text book / Ed. P.V. Krashennikov. M.:, 2013

Yu.V. Zaitsev, D.I. Rogachev. Everyday work in the world of sports: Specifics of the sportsmen's and coaches' labor regulation. M., 2012.

A.A. Solov'yov.
Russian and foreign experience of systematization of the sports legislation: Monography / Sports Law Committee of the Lawyers Association of Russia. M., 2011.

N.V. Kashapov. Regulation of intellectual rights in the field of sports: autoabstract of the thesis in candidacy for a scientific degree of the candidate of legal science. M., 2010.

V.Y. Kamenkova Issues of legal regulation of intellectual property in the sphere of sports in Belarus // Sports: economics, law, management. , 2012. N 2. Pp. 26 - 28.

# Korean Product Liability Law

JAE-SEON SO* · JUNG-EUN SONG**

*In most legal systems producers are now subject to special liability regimes which appear much stricter than the fault-based liability regime applying in general: producers are liable irrespective of fault for damage caused by defective products they put into circulation. These stricter rules on product liability originate in the USA. But the concept spread rather quickly worldwide. It inspired, for example, the European Union to design its Product Liability Directive, which is not only influential in the EU, but has also provided the conceptual basis for new laws elsewhere.*

*The almost worldwide tendency to provide for strict product liability raises quite a few interesting questions, which should – as far as possible- be discussed in the analyses to be extant the questions can be subdivided into those which can be characterised as justification, and those focussing upon the concepts employed. I will start with the fundamental questions and then go on the conceptual issues.*

Key word: Product liability, Strict product liability, Tort law, Contract law, Hypothetical cases, Analyses

## Purpose

The Korean Product Liability Law ("KPL") is the law in which manufacturers, distributors, and others who make products available to the public are held responsible for death, injuries, or damage to any item of

* Professor of Law School of KyungHee University of Korea.
** Ph.D Candidate of Law School of Renmin University of China, researcher of Research Center for Civil and Commercial Jurisprudence and Professor of Law School of Renmin University of China.

property (other than the defective product itself) due to a defect of the product. The KPL, which defines the liability of manufacturers as absolute liability, was enacted on January 1, 2001 and has been effective since July 1, 2002. The purpose of the KPL is to rectify the inadequate remedy of victims for damages caused by defective products through tort law or contract law (Article 1 of the KPL). The KPL is applied to products supplied by a manufacturer on and after its enforcement date of (Section 1, 2). Before the enactment of the KPL, a party injured by a defective product would generally bring a tort claim under Article 750 of the Korean Civil Law ("Civil Law"). In the process, the manufacturer's negligence would be assumed, and the victim's burden to prove a causal relationship lightened. Even when the manufacturer of the product is also the vendor of the product, tort law under Article 750 of the Civil Law had been applied. The manufacturer of the product is usually not the vendor of the product, and the subject of product liability is generally secondary losses due to a defect in the safety of the products (Article 3(1) of the KPL).

## Subjects

Product Liability is liability for damage caused by manufacturers, distributors, and others who make products available to the public when the product is defective and thereby caused death, injuries, or damage to properties besides the defective product itself. Any damage to the defective product itself shall not be the subject of the KPL.[1]

## Scope of Application

The term "Products" means all movables, industrially manufactured or processed, even though incorporated into another movable or into an immovable. The term "Process" means adding new attributes or values to a movable, while maintaining its original nature, and the term "Manufacture" means a series of actions including designing, assembling, and inspection. It

---

1) Dapan 2000.7.28.,98 35525.

is a narrower notion than production and does not include services.

KPL is not be applied to intangible services, real properties, unprocessed agricultural products and any losses due to flaws in software and information.

There have been arguments in Korea over whether human body components such as blood are products that are manufactured or processed. Although blood and organs are parts of the human body, it is apparent that they are movables once detached from the body. The problem is that the standard for such body parts to be viewed as a product that is processed or manufactured is unclear. For example, a medicine that has blood as one of its base materials is considered a product, and so are blood derivatives.[2] Even the blood packs for transfusion can be thought as products[3] because blood packs include anticoagulant and conservative solution for preservation.

KPL is applied to products supplied by a manufacturer on and after the enforcement date of this Act (Section 1, 2).


## Defects

The term "defect" means a defect of any product in manufacturing, design or expression falling under any of the following items, or a lack of safety that the product ordinarily should provide: and

(a) The term "defect in manufacturing" means the lack of safety caused by manufacturing or processing of any product deviating from the originally intended design, regardless of whether the manufacturer faithfully exercises his/her duty of care and due diligence with respect to the manufacturing or processing;

(b) The term "defect in design" means the lack of safety caused by the failure of the manufacturer to adopt a reasonable alternative design in a situation in which any damage or risk caused by the product would otherwise be reduced or prevented; and

(c) The term "defect in expression" means that a manufacturer fails to give reasonable explanations, instructions, warnings or other indications on the product, and there occurs any such damage or risk caused by

2) Seoul of Justice, 2008.1.10. 2005 na 69245.
3) Kim chunsoo, Product Liability Law: Notion of Prodect, No.16-1, 2004, p.54-55.

the product that would otherwise be reduced or prevented;

(d) When determining the existence of a defect, i) the frequency and magnitude of the danger and the utility of the product, ii) causality and seriousness of the damage, iii) the date of supply, iv) the rationally-to-be expected usage of the product, and v) other safety concerns shall be thoroughly considered.

### Negligence and Causation

Under the KPL, negligence is not a requirement for establishment of product liability, and product liability is strict. Therefore, a victim shall not carry the burden to prove that the defects in the product arose from the negligence of the manufacturer.

Although the KPL does not have any regulations regarding the burden to prove the causal relationship, it specifies that matters concerning any liability for damages caused by defective products shall be governed by the Civil Law except as otherwise provided for in the act (Article 8). Thus, it can be assumed that the victim carries the burden to prove that there is a defect in the product and the defect has caused damage, but precedents in Korea generally have eased consumers' burden of proof by presuming the existence of a causal relationship.[4]

### Exemptions

Where a person who is liable for damage in accordance with the provisions of Article 3 proves the fact falling under any of the following subparagraphs, he shall be exempted from such liability:

1) that the manufacturer did not supply the product;

2) that the state of scientific or technical knowledge at the time when the manufacturer supplied the product was not such as to enable the existence of the defect to be discovered;

3) that the defect is due to compliance of the product with any act or

---

4) Dapan 2004.3.12, 2003 da 16771. And Dapan 2011.9.29, 2008 da 16776.

subordinate statute at the time when the manufacturer supplied it; and

4) that, in case of raw materials or components, the defect is attributable to the design of the product in which any raw materials or components have been fitted or to the instructions concerning manufacturing given by the manufacturer of the product using them.

Where a person, in spite of the fact that he knows or would be able to know the existence of any defect of the product after it has been supplied, is liable for damage under the provisions of Article 3 and fails to take appropriate measures to prevent the damage caused by the defect from occurring, he shall not be given any exemption referred to in paragraph (1) 2 through 4.

## Responsibility

A "manufacturer" shall be liable for death, personal injuries, or damage to any item of property (other than to the defective product itself) due to a defect of the product (Article 3(1) of the KPL). The term "manufacturer" refers to a person who is engaged in a business of manufacturing, processing, or importing any product. Furthermore, a person who presents himself as a manufacturer by putting his name, firm name, trademark, or any other distinguishable feature(hereinafter referred to as "his name, etc,") and a person who puts his name, etc. on the product in a manner mistakable for a manufacturer are also deemed manufacturers (Article 2(3) of the KPL).

If the manufacturer of a defective product cannot be identified, the distributor shall be liable for any damage it causes, unless the distributor informs the victim of the identity of the manufacturer or the supplier within a reasonable period of time (Article 3(2) of the KPL).

Where not less than two persons are liable for the same damage, they shall be jointly and severally liable (Article 5 of the KPL).

## Scope of Compensation of Damages

Manufacturers, suppliers, distributors, and others who make the product available to the public shall be liable for death or personal injuries, or damage to any item of property caused by a defect of the product, except when the damage is to the defective product only.

## Case Analysis

### Case 1: Brake Pad Failure

*X Ltd manufactures bicycles. In 2011, it started to use a new material for its brake pads, which X Ltd believed on the basis of its testing to be a cheaper, longer-lasting and generally more effective alternative to traditional materials. X Ltd was aware of a very small risk that – given a combination of particular circumstances (temperature, surface water, oil, etc) – the new brake-pad material might suddenly be rendered ineffective, but it considered that the risk was likely to eventuate only very rarely and did not outweigh the general advantages of the new material. It included a statement about the possibility of failure in the small print of the product instructions supplied with all of its bicycles incorporating the new brake pads. A, who purchased one of the bicycles, is one of a handful of people injured in accidents attributable to the failure of the new brake pads; A's bicycle is also damaged. B, a passer-by, is injured in the same accident.*

*Analysis*

*What is X Ltd's liability to A and B? Pay particular attention to the various possible bases of liability (a general tortious liability for fault, vicarious liability, contractual liability, or a special strict liability regime?). Would it make any difference to your analysis if Y, who is (i) an employed researcher in X Ltd's laboratory, or alternatively (ii) an independent research contractor, had covered up the risk that the new brake-pad material might fail?*

Remedy under Product Liability Act

A bicycle falls within the range of products of the KPL. Generally, a manufacturer shall manufacture products with appropriate level of safety in use considering modern technology and economy. When the product fails to maintain the level of safety due to a defect and has caused any damage, the manufacturer shall be liable for compensation. If the manufacturer fails to adopt a reasonable alternative design in a situation in which any damage or risk caused by the product could otherwise be reduced or prevented, the defect is called a defect in design. Whether there is such defect in design shall be determined by socially accepted ideas regarding consumers' expectation of the product, seriousness of the risk, consumers' awareness of the risk, possibility of consumers' evasion of the risk, possibility and costs of alternative design, and comparison between the original and alternative design.

The bicycle's X ltd manufacturer carried a risk that the new brake-pad material might suddenly be rendered ineffective when given a combination of particular circumstances (temperature, surface water, oil, etc.), and the risk actually occurred even though consumers' used them properly, thereby causing damage to the bodies and properties of A and B. Since the KPL imposes strict liability if causal relationship between the product and the defect has been proven, whether X ltd was aware of the risk beforehand needs not be considered. That the new brake-pad is cheaper, longer-lasting, and generally more effective than pre-existing brake pad is merely marketing for economic profit and irrelevant for the functional essentials of brake pads, so it need not be considered the existence of the defect either.

Even when a defect in design or defect in manufacturing has not been found, a manufacturer may still be held responsible for a defect in expression if he failed to give reasonable explanations, instructions, warnings and other indications on the product that would have reduced or prevented the damage the product caused, and whether there is such defect shall be determined by socially accepted ideas regarding consumers' expectation for the product, seriousness of the risk, consumers' awareness of the risk, possibility of consumers' evasion of the risk, and the normally expected usage of the product.

However, since the defect in this case is evidently a defect in design, a defect in expression cannot be applied.

Therefore, X Ltd shall be liable to compensate for the damage the product caused to A's body and property (Article 3(1) of the KPL). Since victims in the KPL are not limited to consumers and B is exempt from any liability, X shall compensate for the damage B suffered as well.

The KPL does not provide an express provision regarding the range of compensation, so claims for compensation for loss of life and property need not follow the general principles of compensation regarding tort under Civil Law. Nonetheless, the KPL stipulates that compensation for the damage to the defective product itself shall be in the form of contract liability or tort liability, for the KPL has developed in the direction of holding manufacturers responsible for the lack of safety of their products.

### Tort Law

Before the enactment of the KPL, a party injured by a defective product would generally bring a tort claim under Article 750 of Civil Law.

X ltd was fully aware of the slight risk that the new brake-pad might fail on operation but did not take any action, and therefore is liable for negligence. A brake-pad is an essential component that is directly related to consumers' safety. Since it is apparent that its breakdown would cause a serious risk on consumers' lives, failure to secure sufficient stability of the new brake-pad certainly constitutes negligence. In this case, A may obtain compensation for his loss of life and property.

B may obtain compensation for his loss from A under Article 750 of Civil Law, and then A may exercise the right of indemnity to X Ltd, who was totally negligent.

### Remedy under Sales Contract

Under Article 580 of Civil Law, which defines a seller's liability for warranty against defect, if the subject-matter of a sale lacks the objective quality or functionality that is conventionally expected or that the seller guaranteed, the seller shall bear security liability due to the defect. Since stability of a brake-pad on a bicycle is a conventionally expected quality, X ltd, the seller, bears the security liability due to the defect to A.

B may obtain compensation for his loss from A under Article 70 of Civil Law, and then A may exercise the right of indemnity to X Ltd, who was totally negligent.

## Researchers and Vicarious Liability

If a researcher of X Ltd's laboratory hid the possibility that the new brake-pad material might fail while on operation, then vicarious liability is relevant.

In Korea, vicarious liability is specified in Article 756 of the Civil Law, which is based on strict liability theory. An employer hires an employee in order to widen its area of activity and pursue benefits, so an employer's business activity and an employee's actions are closely interrelated. It is ideally equitable that an employer bearthe others' loss arising from his widened area of activity is, and therefore "in principle" an employer shall bear the liability for his employee's tort related to the execution of operations.. However, vicarious liability is valid only if the employer was strictly liable for not exercising due care when hiring and supervising. Thus, with respect to vicarious liability, an employer is bound to compensate for damage caused by an employee when the employee is strictly liability for negligence. As long as X ltd proves that it has exercised due care when hiring and supervising Y, X ltd carries no vicarious liability.

Vicarious liability is a joint and several liabilities with the share of liability depending on the internal relationship. The burden of an employer is determined considering his internal relationship with the employee.

In this case, since X ltd has not exercised due care when hiring and supervising Y, the internal relationship between X ltd and Y is not considered regarding the outside liabilities of X ltd.

## Liability of Person who ordered Work to be Done

If a contractor conducted research independently and hid the potential risk of the new brake-pad material, the person who ordered the work does not carry the burden of compensation for the damage the contractor caused to consumers under Article 757 of Civil Law, because the contractor handles his work independently and therefore is not an employee of the person who ordered the work. Thus, any Civil Law articles regarding the responsibilities of a person who ordered the work assumes that Article 756 of Civil Law shall not be applied. However, if the person who ordered the work was guilty of gross negligence in placing the order or providing instructions, he shall be responsible to the victim (Article 757 of Civil Law). In such case, the person who ordered the work shall be responsible for compensation for the damage the contractor caused to consumers by himself or with the contractor. Also, if the person who ordered the work gives the contractor specific instructions and supervises, the employer-employee relationship shall be deemed to exist and the person who ordered the work will hold vicarious liability.[5] The employer-employee relationship shall not be deemed if the person who ordered the work simply conducts inspections to check whether the process is following the original design.[6]

However, under Article 3 of the KPL regarding responsibility, a person who presents himself as a manufacturer by putting his name, firm name, trademark, or any other distinguishable feature and a person who puts his name, etc. on the product in a manner mistakable for a manufacturer shall be responsible as well.

## Case 2: Infected Blood

A is infected with Hepatitis N as the result of a blood transfusion conducted in X Hospital in 2005. The source of the infection was blood supplied to X Hospital by Y Ltd, who had collected it from a donor; Z. Unknown to himself, Z was a carrier of the Hepatitis N virus. At the time, the risk of Hepatitis N in donated blood had been identified in a single published paper in a scientific journal, but only a handful of research laboratories in the world had the capacity to test for its presence in specific

---

5) Dapan 1991.3.8., 90 da 18432.
6) Dapan 1983.11.22, 83 daka 1153.

quantities of blood. Furthermore, the majority of the scientific community did not believe that the condition (Hepatitis N) really existed. It was only subsequently that the condition's existence came to be generally accepted and that a test was developed that allowed hospitals and blood suppliers to screen out infected parcels of blood.

*Analysis*

What is the liability to A of X Hospital, Y Ltd and Z? Pay particular attention to the various possible bases of liability (a general tortious liability for fault, vicarious liability, contractual liability, or a special strict liability regime?). Would it make any difference to your analysis if A contracted the virus as the result of a blood transfusion conducted in 2001, but her condition only manifested itself in 2012? (In this context, consider in particular differences in the time limits applied to the various possible bases of liability.)

In this case, the remedy that Plaintiff can recover differs depending upon 2 factors which should be considered first. One of the factors which should be considered first is the time when the Korean Product Liability Law is in force. The other factor is whether the blood product is included in the definition of 'product' by the KPL.

Since the KPL applies to the initial product supply by manufacturer, KPL will only apply to a blood product which had caused Hepatitis N if the date of its first supply is after 2002. 7. 1., the date when KPL came into force.

It also has been controversial issue in Korea whether blood product is product defined by KPL. It is certain that blood or a body part is a chattel but being a chattel itself is not enough to qualify as product. However, blood product is product to which KPL applies since it is categorised as medical supplies made from blood according to Article 2 of the Pharmacist Act and Article 2(6) of the Management of Blood Act.

## Application of tort law based on negligence

Even if the KPL did not apply, blood supplier still has a duty of care to produce blood product meeting the standards in structure and safety feature aspects with technology and cost effectiveness available at the time. He will be held for liability based on torts for damage when there was breach of that duty.[7] In fact, there has been no case concerning blood products in which the Korean court has accepted strict liability under KPL.

For a claim to be accepted in tort, the additional condition of a breach of a duty of care by the manufacturer of blood must be met. The blood manufacturer will be held to a higher degree of care which requires him to do his best to keep the pureness of blood and the proper management of blood. The specific detail of the high degree of care in this case is a duty to 'expect' and 'prevent' foreseeable harmful results using all the medical knowledge available at the time of production. For example, the duty includes keeping infection-suspected groups from donating blood.

In consideration of the breach of duty by blood manufacturer, we have to evaluate the method and the process used in manufacturing blood products at the time, the infection rate resulting from contaminated blood product, seriousness of damage to the patient caused by blood product, and the cost which will be incurred by requiring the duty to evade the risk.[8]

What matters most is the specific standard to be applied to the duty of care.

According to Korean cases, the duty of care should be evaluated by the national level of normative standard exercised by an average doctor in the community, not by the standard exercised by a specific doctor or medical institution.[9] However, it was hard to know the risk of Hepatitis N infection from the blood product which was published in a single paper at the time. X and Y are not held for liability of tort in Korea so as long as X and Y had done the test required by the Blood Safety Act and the Ministry of Health and Welfare Act to make sure of the safety of the blood and the blood product.

---

7) Supreme Court 1977.1.25. 75 da 2092; Supreme Court 1992.11.24. 92 da 18139.
8) Supreme Court 1998.2.13. 96da7854.
9) Dapan 1997.2.11, 96Dapan 5933.

Application of the KPL

### (1) Whether blood product can be a product according to the KPL

Even though blood itself or a body part is not a product under the KPL, blood product made from elements extracted from blood is a product under KPL even if it is for transfusion, since it is combined with the additional substances like anticoagulant and can be tested about foreseeable risk in the process of production. These blood products are frequently used in medicine.

Article 2(6) of the Management of Blood Act defines blood product as 'medicine' produced primarily from blood. There is no reason not to apply KPL to blood product since it comes from a manufacturing process and can be movable like any other chattel.[10]

### (2) Meaning of defect

The elements of the KPL to prove strict liability are manufacturing defect, design defect, and inadequate warning. The manufacturer is held liable when one the elements are present.

( i ) A manufacturing defect is a lack of safety and endurance with respect to the structure, quality, or performance of the product at the time when it left manufacturer's hands.[11] So although the blood had no defect in the design stage, there exists a manufacturing defect when it does not satisfy the feasible safety features at the time of market circulation of that product. What matters here is the feasible safety features at the time of market circulation of that product. In our case, not only the risk of Hepatitis N had been identified but it is possible to test its presence although only a handful of research laboratories in the world were capable of the test. And the patient was getting transfusions in the anticipation of full recovery in health. The blood product manufactured by Y is defective since it does not meet the feasible safety features at the time of market circulation of that product.

The manufacturer of the blood product is held liable in case that the infected blood product due to a manufacturing defect has caused damage to the patient for whom the blood product was used.

---

10) Lee sangjung, Legal Issues Regarding Product Liability Act of Korea, Justice (2002.7), p.12.
11) Seoul Central District Court 2007.1.25., 99 Gahab 104973(tobaco civil litigation).

(ⅱ) Design defect

A defect which is inherent in the process by design means that there is an alternative design which is safer, inexpensive and still useful for primary purpose of the product. Therefore, product liability is applicable to manufacturer of blood product when there exists an alternative design which reduces or removes the risk of infection when using blood product. In deciding whether such an alternative exists, We have to consider all the factors as a whole by the social standards at the time, for example, the nature and usage of blood product, the expected performance from patient, the expected risk and the possibility of risk evasion by patient, and the feasibility and cost-effectiveness of alternative and other pros and cons of those alternatives.[12]

(ⅲ) Inadequate labelling or warning

If the patient who had a transfusion with blood product got infected as a result of inadequate warnings, product liability also applies. In deciding whether inadequate labelling exists, we have to consider the characteristics of blood product, foreseeable usage, and expected performance of the blood product anticipated risk of transfusion, and the possibility of removing the risk, etc. as whole in light of social standard.[13]

**(3) Unavoidably unsafe.**

The KPS recognizes unavoidably unsafe products as an exception to strict liability.

If the manufacture of blood product had no way to discover the unit of blood infected with Hepatitis N by any scientific knowledge level available at the time, then he is not liable. Here scientific knowledge level means established technological and scientific knowledge which is objectively available as whole including the highest level of knowledge at the time.[14] That is, unavoidably unsafe defence will not be accepted on account of difficulty in discovering infected blood product if it is still possible to

---

12) YEUN Kee-Young, Medicine and medical supplies accidents and Product liability, *Medical Jurisprudence*, No.3-2(2002.12), p.33-34.
13) Supreme Court 2004.3.12, 2003 da 16771.
14) An bubyong, Medical and product liability, *Korea Law Review*, No.40(2003.6), p.191.

discover defective one.

### (4) Party held to liability in KPL

According to Article 2(3) of the KPL, manufacturer(A) is still liable to defect that resulted from parts or elements purchased from other manufacturer(B) who is also held liable for the defect as long as that defect existed when it was in the hands of (B).

In Korea, only medical institutions and the Korean Red-cross can do blood collection according to The Management of Blood Act. As a result, manufacturers need to get supplies of blood from blood collection institutions for production. When blood supplied by blood collection institution is contaminated, (A) and (b) will be jointly and severally liable under Article 5 of the KPL.

## Damage claim for the violation of duty to explain.

The duty of explanation required in medical treatment is also required here since the injection of drugs is also a kind of medical treatment.[15] In particular, the duty of explanation cannot be exempted for the reasons that the expected rate of risk or side effects are quite low. Doctors must fulfil the duty of explanation if those risk and side effects are typically related with injection regardless of how small the chances of happening are.[16]

If the doctor didn't inform the patient about the risk of infection from transfusion, it constitute tortuous behaviour which deprives the patient from giving informed consent.[17]

A follow up questions is whether the drug instruction written down on product can substitute for the duty of explanation. It is not enough to put down instructions abstractly on the care patients should take or to state general warning about side effects. Instead detailed instructions that enable patients to recognize the side effect instantly and to stop using the product

---

15) Chen Deayub, Medical duty of explanation, Important Decisions of the Supreme Court, No.54(2005),p.307-327.
16) Supreme Court 1995.1.20, 94 da3421.
17) Supreme Court 2011.3.10, 2010 da72410.

while consulting with a Doctor.[18] So the drug instruction attached with blood product can not serve to fulfil a Doctor's duty of explanation.

### Statute of limitation for damage claim

According to Article 766(2) of the Korean Civil Law, the statute of limitations for a damage claim is 10 years from the date when the damage from tortuous act occurred not the date when tortuous act was committed.[19] A was infected during the transfusion in 2001 and her condition only manifested in 2012. When it is hard to fathom the stage to which the disease had progressed, the statute limitation should starts from the day the disease manifested not from the date it was in dormant condition.

The recovery for damage should be claimed within 10 years from the date when the manufacturer supplied the product under Article 7(2) of the KPL. However, Article 7(2) of the KPL says that for the damage from accumulation of hazardous material in human body or disease which manifest after some period, the statue limitation starts from the date when the damage is realized. That is, although 10 years have passed after manufacturer provided the blood product, the statute of limitation starts when the symptom of disease appears.

## Case 3: Bridge Collapse

A, a pedestrian using a public right of way, is injured by the collapse of a bridge constructed by X Ltd on land belonging to Y, who commissioned the construction, on the basis of a plan drawn up by architect Z, whom Y also commissioned directly. It transpires that Z's plan was defective and caused the collapse. Y incurs the cost of instructing a different architect to redesign the bridge. Under the terms of its initial engagement, X Ltd is obliged to construct the new bridge for no additional remuneration.

---

18) Supreme Court 2005.4.29, 2004da 64067.
19) Supreme Court 1979.12.26., 77da1895.

*Analysis*

What is the liability to A of X Ltd, Y and Z? Is the architectural plan itself a 'product', and so subject to strict product liability, or does it merely represent the performance by Z of a service, to which some alternative liability regime applies? What further liability, if any, does Z have to X Ltd and Y, whether on the basis of a direct claim or a recourse action?

The scope of products for Korean Product Liability Law is limited to movables. Real estate cannot be an object of product liability. A portion of what constitutes real estate can be included within the scope of products. For example, elevators and cooling systems are movables, but they still constitute parts of real estate. Therefore, even though a bridge is a human construction, it is not considered as a product under the KPL. If a third person gets injured from a bridge collapse, he or she can receive relief from the damage in accordance with the liabilities for possessor of structures or with the liabilities of owners, as stipulated in Article 758 of Korean Civil Law.

## A's Means of Remedy

Since real estate is not considered as a product under the KPL, liabilities for structures such as for house wall or a bridge fall under the provisions of liabilities for possessor of structures as stipulated in Article 758 of Korean Civil Law.

Liabilities for structures occur in cases when someone suffers damage from installations of structures or defects of their maintenance. Liabilities for structures are distinguished from torts as they do not require intermediate illegal or harmful acts.. Generally, many people view liabilities for structures as responsibility for risks. In accordance with Article 758 of the Civil Law on liabilities for structure, if a possessor, who holds the primary responsibilities, pays his or her primary responsibilities and proves that they have fulfilled their duty to prevent further damage, the possessor may free themselves from the liabilities. When the possessor is entitled to avoid the liabilities, compensation may be demanded to the owner, who holds the secondary responsibility. There is, however, no possibility for owners of defective structures to be exempt from responsibilities.

If a structure is installed and maintained by a national or local government, Article 5 from the State Tort Liability Act applies.

According to the provisions of the third clause of Article 758 of the Civil Law, a possessor or an owner who paid for damage to a victim can exercise the right of indemnity against those who are responsible for causing the damage, namely a producer of structure or ones who were entrusted for maintenance.

Therefore, Y primarily holds liability for damage to A even when Y is not culpable. After paying for damage to A, Y may exercise the right of indemnity against the final liability holder.


## X's Exemption

If there occurs any damages to the object constructed by contractor X, the contractor bears warranty responsibility for the construction to an independent contractor in accordance with Article 28 of Korea Framework Act on the Construction Industry.

According to Article 28.2.2 of this provision, however, the contractor does not hold warranty responsibility if he or she proceeded the construction in conformity with the contractor's order. Although X constructed the structure with Z's design, there exists no direct contractual relationship in between them; Y is the one who made a direct contract with Z. Z provided Y with the design and Y ordered X to construct the structure by providing X with the design. Consequently, by the Korea Framework Act on the Construction Industry, X is free from the warranty responsibility for the collapse of the bridge. If, however, X knew about the defects from the design, but still did not inform Y of the them, either by intention or by negligence, X has to pay any possible property damage to the contractor in accordance with provisions on a construction project manager's negligence prescribed in the fifth clause of Article 26 of the Framework Act on the Construction Industry. Also, X and Z hold collective liability for damage from the collapse of the bridge if they constructed the bridge under mutual supervision of X and Z.

## Liability of Compensation between Z and Y

Construction designs in themselves are a form of intellectual property which do not include themselves within the scope of products defined by the KPL. There is an opinion that it is not plausible to attach strict liability to information such as intellectual property in general, because intellectual property, including software, do not carry the risks of casualty or fire, they can be redeemed by contractual warranty responsibility, and also because their concepts, contents, and functions are too diverse.

Therefore, under the contractual relationship between Z and Y, Z holds warranty responsibility for a specific thing vendor as stipulated in Article 580 of the Civil Law. If the object's damage is too significant to hinder the accomplishment of the purpose of the contract, Y can not only request for compensation, but also for the cancellation of the contract as a whole. Y may ask the final liability holder Z for the right to indemnity and other compensations for A.

## Liability of Compensation between Z and X

Despite the Z's negligence, it is X who holds the liability to construct a new bridge for Y without any charge in accordance with the initial contract. As it is mentioned above, X does not hold any liability to compensate Y, but X had to construct the new bridge for Y without charge due to the contract. All the costs and labours needed to construct the new bridge wouldn't have been spent if Z had not committed any faults. Consequently, X may request for compensation for the damage caused by Z's defects by citing the provisions on torts in Article 750 of the Civil Law.[20]

Likewise, real estate, information, and other intellectual property do not fall within the KPL. This means relief can only be sought through negligence and breach of contract. Therefore this will necessarily imply multiple law suits in a single case.

---

20) Guan teasung, Software and product liability law, The Information Industy, No.173 (1996.9), p.31.

As the industrialization becomes more intense and scientific technology reaches its full development, the number of quality intellectual products such as technology-intensive skyscrapers will increase. Thus, it is expected that these products which entails high risks will have closer relationships with our lives, and we will have to seek for ways of protecting rights in possible cases in the future.

## References

Kim, Chun-Soo, Product Liability Law, Notion of Prodect, No.16-1(2004).

Lee, Sang-Jung, Legal Issues Regarding Product Liability Act of Korea, Justice (7. 2002).

Yeun, Kee-Young, Medicine and medical supplies accidents and Product liability, Medical Jurisprudence No.3-2(12. 2002).

An, Bub-Yong, Medical and product liability, Korea Law Review No.40(6. 2003).

Chen, Deayub, Medical duty of explanation, Important Decisions of the Supreme Court, No.54(2005).

Guan, easung, Software and product liability law, The Information Industy, No.173(9.1996).

Seoul of Justice, 2008.1.10. 2005 na 69245.

Dapan 2000.7.28.,98 35525.

Dapan 2004.3.12, 2003 da 16771. And Dapan 2011.9.29, 2008 da 16776.

Dapan 1991.3.8., 90 da 18432.

Dapan 1983.11.22, 83 daka 1153.

Dapan 1997.2.11, 96Dapan 5933.

Supreme Court 1977.1.25. 75 da 2092; Supreme Court 1992.11.24. 92 da 18139.

Supreme Court 1998.2.13. 96da7854.

Supreme Court 2004.3.12, 2003 da 16771.

Supreme Court 1995.1.20, 94 da3421.

Supreme Court 2011.3.10, 2010 da72410.

Supreme Court 2005.4.29, 2004da 64067.

Supreme Court 1979.12.26., 77da1895.

Seoul Central District Court 2007.1.25., 99 Gahab 104973(tobaco civil litigation).

# 'Techno-Doping' – Legal Issues Concerning a Nebulous and Controversial Phenomenon*

*'Techno-doping' is a term which is very widely used, but which is perhaps not very suitable or clear. Keeping in mind that sporting performance is the result of various factors which form a complete system, it is suggested, as a first step, to take into account the seven scenarios set out in the article and then, in a second step, to consider the aims of equal opportunities and fairness, the health and bodily integrity of the athletes and the reputation of the sporting discipline. In a third step, it is up to the federations to stipulate what is permitted and what is forbidden. Of course, these decisions can be subject to judicial review. Two famous cases have been ruled on by courts of justice (Casey Martin) and the Court of Arbitration for Sports (Pistorius).*

**Key word:** Techno Doping, Disability, Equal Opportunities and Fairness

## I. Introduction

So-called techno-doping is one of the most exciting and topical subjects in sports law worldwide: 'Techno-doping' was the main topic of the congress of the German Association of Sports Law at the beginning of October 2012.

The discussion which took place there demonstrated that the term 'techno-doping' is not very clearly defined and must be linked to the aims which it seeks to achieve, in particular, those of equal opportunities and

---

\* This article is taken from a paper presented on 13th October 2012 at the 10th KASEL International Conference on Sports Law in Suwon.

\*\* Professor, Institut für Recht und Technik, Erlangen, Germany

fairness in sport. In that discussion, I favoured a broad definition (see Ⅱ), bearing in mind that sporting performance is the result of various different factors which form a complete system. Proceeding from this broad definition, it is then up to the federations to prohibit specific measures, methods and equipment in order to achieve equal opportunities and fairness (see Ⅲ).

With regard to this general approach, I would like to refer to the 'classic cases' of Casey Martin and Oscar Pistorius. These cases highlight the general problems relating to disability in sports (see Ⅳ).

To give an initial introduction to the topic, I refer to the 200-meter final of the Paralympics in London this summer and some photographs showing the 'catapult shoe' used by the Soviet high-jumper, Yuriy Stepanov, Casey Martin with his golf cart and 'jump weights' used by a Spartan competitor (Akmatidas) in the Olympics (ca. 550–525 B.C.).

## Ⅱ. Definition

As already mentioned, a precise definition of 'techno-doping' is very difficult to arrive at, as sporting performance depends on a complete system which encompasses the physical and mental abilities of the athlete, the equipment and apparatus and the training opportunities. In this context, it should be mentioned that athletes with disabilities, whose use of technical apparatus in order to participate in their respective sports is legitimate, are sensitive to being linked to doping, which is clearly forbidden.

In order to provide an impression of the broad scope of the phenomenon of 'techno-doping', I would like to draw attention to the following *scenarios*:

(1) Body enhancement by means of surgery (e.g., breast reduction, the strengthening of sinews and ligaments by means of bodily tissues and artificial tissues, implants and amputations);

(2) The supplementation of missing body parts, or of body parts which do not function well (e.g., Oscar Pistorius' blades; more generally, prosthetics and orthotics, glasses for participants in shooting);

(3) Additional equipment to balance any physical and/or mental deficits (e.g., Casey Martin's golf cart; more generally: wheelchairs);

(4) Equipment (e.g., Stepanov's catapult shoes; full-body swimsuits; suits used in ski-jumping);

(5) Sporting apparatus (e.g., technical developments with regard to bicycles, bobsleighs and rowing boats; software in Formula One cars);

(6) Training methods and possibilities (e.g., wind tunnels, low pressure chamber, training with a new artificial knee);

(7) Competition (e.g., adjudicative technology, such as Hawk Eye and video recordings).

Irrespective of the criticism with which the term 'techno-doping' is generally met, in my view it is helpful to have regard to the classical definition of 'doping' in order to arrive at the decision as to what is permissible, and what is not. In doing so, one must consider the three classic grounds, upon which doping is forbidden: the avoidance of an unfair advantage in competition, the protection of the health and bodily integrity of the athlete and his competitors, and, finally, the reputation of the particular sport.[1]

Regarding the seven scenarios mentioned above, it is instructive to apply these three grounds which lead to the prohibition of doping, however, in order to avoid misunderstandings and regulatory loopholes, I would suggest replacing the term 'techno-doping' with 'forbidden measures and methods'. This definition would include technical measures which are suited to creating unfair advantages in competition, to endangering the health and bodily integrity of the athletes, and/or damaging the reputation of the sporting discipline and the organisations representing it. This definition allows us to comply with the principle of fairness, which requires differentiation without discrimination.[2]

---

1) See e.g. K. *Vieweg*, The Appeal of Sports Law, www.irut.de/Forschung/ Veroeffentlichungen/OnlineVersionFaszinationSportrecht/FaszinationSportrechtEnglisch. pdf, p. 39 (accessed on December 18, 2012).

2) See e.g. K. *Vieweg*, Bans on Discrimination and Duties to Differentiate in the German

## III. Competence to rule on 'techno-doping' cases

The matter of competence to rule on 'techno-doping' cases can be regarded as a new aspect of the well-known problem in sports law of the autonomy of associations and federations and its limits. To this extent, I can confine myself to saying that, primarily, the federations and associations have the right to set and enact norms in order to regulate their sports. Accordingly, they can define 'techno-doping' and can rule on specific cases. However, such decisions may be subject to judicial review by courts of law and courts of arbitration. Consequently, the IAAF (International Association of Athletics Federations) had the right to forbid Stepanov's catapult shoes and the FIS (Federation Internationale de Ski) was entitled to allow the 'skating style' in cross-country skiing.

The matter of the obligation of the sporting associations and federations to regulate and to decide is much more complicated. In an earlier work of mine, I concluded as follows: "Uncertainty, loopholes and, partly, the complete absence of provisions is widespread among sporting associations and federations. This is based on various grounds: apart from the pragmatic considerations of ensuring that charters and by-laws are as brief as possible, two additional aspects are also significant. These are a lack of consciousness of the conflicts, and the aim of the associations and federations not to limit their own ability to act by means of self-binding regulations. The lack and uncertainty of regulations lead to two questions: First, do the associations and federations have a duty to create regulations which are sufficiently clear in order to be applied by the competent organs of the associations and federations, as well as a basis for the decisions of the members? Secondly, is there an obligation on the part of the associations and federations to reach decisions if their rules and regulations do not expressly mention such decisions? What is the legal basis, what are the conditions, and what are the objects of such duties to regulate and to decide?"[3] In my view, there exists a duty of the associations and federations to support their members.

---

Law of Sports Organizations, in: The International Sports Law Journal 2006, p. 96 et seqq.
3) *K. Vieweg*, Normsetzung und -anwendung deutscher und internationaler Verbände, Berlin 1990, S. 143 ff.

Consequently, there is a duty on the part of the associations and federations to make clear rules and regulations, and to apply them consistently.[4] Regarding forbidden measures and methods, I would like to refer to my lecture at the conference of the German Sports Law Association which took place in October 2012.[5]

In addition, a further problem should be mentioned – it is not enough to formulate and apply rules and regulations. It is also necessary to ensure, by means of checks, that athletes comply with these rules and regulations. For example, it is imperative that, in the Paralympics in the sprint competitions, only permitted blades are used.[6] Another example is the control of the thickness of the underwear worn by ski-jumpers, taking into account that the International Ski Federation (FIS) requires a maximum thickness of 3 mm.[7]

## Ⅳ. The Cases of Casey Martin and Oscar Pistorius as Examples of Disability in Sports

Traditionally, the set of problems relating to 'techno-doping' are associated with two well-known cases: that of Casey Martin, and that of Oscar Pistorius. Both cases were of global significance, dealing, as they did, with the problem of discrimination against disabled athletes. At this juncture, I would like to cite the relevant part of the contribution made by Saskia Lettmaier and myself to the Handbook on International Sports Law, edited by James A.R. Nafziger and Stephen F. Ross.[8] There, we wrote:

---

4) *K. Vieweg*, ibid., S. 244 ff.; The Appeal of Sports Law
   http://www.irut.de/Forschung/Veroeffentlichungen/OnlineVersionFaszinationSportrecht
   /FaszinationSportrechtEnglisch.pdf, p. 7 et seqq. (accessed Novemer 28, 2012.
5) *K. Vieweg*, 'Techno-Doping' – Regelungs- und Durchsetzungsmöglichkeiten der Sportverbände,
   in: K. Vieweg (Hrsg.), 'Techno-Doping', Stuttgart 2013 (in print).
6) As to the conflict between H. Popow and W. Czyz, see Frankfurter Allgemeine Zeitung
   (September 8, 2012), S. 28.
7) FIS Changes to the Specifications for Competition Equipment Ski Jumping 2012, No. 4.3.
8) *K. Vieweg/S. Lettmaier*, Anti-discrimination law and policy, in: J. Nafziger/S. Ross (eds.),
   Handbook on International Sports Law, Cheltenham, UK/Northampton, MA, USA, 2011,
   p. 258, 271 et seqq.

The principle of equal opportunities in sports led to a distinction between the able-bodied, on the one hand, and handicapped persons, on the other. In time, the concept of competition gained acceptance in disabled sports and caused the evolution of new types of competition (e.g. wheelchair-basketball) as well as the definition of disability categories. At an international level, certain competitions are pointing the way to the future – in particular, the Paralympics which have been taking place since 1992. Some spectacular cases (Casey Martin, Oscar Pistorius) have drawn the attention of sports law to this difficulty. These cases will be examined in more detail below. In particular, problems relate to the participation of handicapped persons using technological aids in able-bodied competitions (see 1.); the exclusion of athletes because of a risk of self-injury (see 2.); the participation of the able-bodied in contests for the disabled (see 3.); and the classification of disabled sports by type and degree of disability (see 4.).

## 1. Ensuring access through special accommodations

Until relatively recently, there had been little litigation involving persons with disabilities and sports. The most highly publicized case on the issue arose in 2001, when Casey Martin, a professional golfer afflicted with Klippel-Trenaunay-Weber syndrome, a degenerative circulatory disorder that obstructs the flow of blood from Martin's right leg back to his heart, fought all the way to the United States Supreme Court to obtain a reasonable accommodation for his disability in the form of the use of a golf cart in professional golf tournaments.[9] The *Martin* case marked the first stage in a growing controversy surrounding the integration of disabled athletes into mainstream competitive athletics. Most recently, the focus of this debate has been on the South African sprinter Oscar Pistorius, who was aiming to run at the Beijing Olympics in the summer of 2008, either in the 200 meter or the 400 meter or as a member of the South African relay team, despite the fact that – born without fibula bones – he had had both legs amputated below the knee before his first birthday.[10] The question was whether Oscar

---

9) *PGA Tour,* Inc. v. Martin, 532 U.S. 661 (2001). For an in-depthdiscussion, see *S. Zinger,* Diskriminierungsverbote und Sportautonomie, Berlin 2003, S. 192 f.

Pistorius should be allowed to compete in the Olympics using a pair of J-shaped carbon fiber blades known as 'Cheetahs' attached to his legs.[11]

Requests like those by Martin and Pistorius - for special accommodations or a change in the rules of the game on account of their physical shortcomings - present the tension between equality and the competitive ethos of sport in unusually stark relief. Thus, one might argue that the very idea of special accommodations is inappropriate for sports competitions because these competitions, by their very nature, are intended to identify and reward the very best. As Justice Scalia of the United States Supreme Court remarked in his forceful *Martin* dissent:

[T]he very *nature* of competitive sport is the measurement, by uniform rules, of unevenly distributed excellence. This unequal distribution is precisely what determines the winners and losers - and artificially to 'even out' that distribution, by giving one or another player exemption from a rule that emphasizes his particular weakness, is to destroy the game.[12]

However, unlike in the sex discrimination context, where, as we saw above, a separate-but-equal model still seems to represent the dominant approach, one of the key principles of anti-disability discrimination law is the concept of mainstreaming. The policy is that individuals with disabilities should be allowed to participate in programs in the least restrictive environment.[13] Thus, the main anti-disability discrimination statute in the

---

10) Pistorius was the gold medalist in the 200 meter as well as the bronze medalist in the 100 meter at the 2004 Summer Paralympics in Athens. In addition, he is the double amputee world record-holder in the 100-, 200- and 400-meter events. See, e.g., *P. Charlish/S. Riley* (2008), 'Should Oscar Run?', 18 Fordham Intell. Prop., Media and Ent. L.J. 929.

11) *M. Pryor*, 'Oscar Pistorius is Put through his Paces to Justify his Right to Run', The Times (London) (November 20, 2007), available at
www.timesonline.co.uk/tol/sport/more_sport/athletics/article2903673.ece
(last accessed October 24, 2009).

12) *PGA Tour, Inc.* v. *Martin*, 532 U.S. 661, 703-04 (2001) (emphasis in original). Justice Thomas joined in the dissent.

13) See, e.g., the provisions of the Americans with Disabilities Act, 42 U.S.C.A. § 12182(b)(1)(B) ('accommodations shall be afforded to an individual with a disability in the most integrated setting') and (C) ('Notwithstanding the existence of separate … programs … an individual with a disability shall not be denied the opportunity to participate in such programs … that are not separate').

United States – the Americans with Disabilities Act (ADA) of 1990[14] – requires that 'reasonable modifications' be made for a qualified person with a disability.[15] The relevant legislation in England and Wales is similar. Under the Disability Discrimination Act (DDA) 1995, as amended in 2005,[16] a duty exists to make reasonable adjustments to accommodate the disabled individual to whom the act may apply.[17] In fact, a positive duty to make reasonable accommodation for disabled persons exists throughout the European Union: Article 5 of Council Directive 2000/78/EC, which is binding on Member States as to the object to be achieved, provides that in order 'to guarantee ... equal treatment in relation to persons with disabilities, reasonable accommodation shall be provided ... unless such measures would impose a disproportionate burden on the employer.'[18]

Once it has been determined that the relevant anti-disability discrimination provision is in principle applicable – and, as we saw above, there may be some difficulty in enforcing the legislation against private entities[19] – much will depend on the reach of the statute's exempting provisions, i.e. on the recognized limits to integration. Broadly speaking, defenses to a claim of disability discrimination in the sports context can arise in two kinds of case.

---

14) 42 U.S.C.A. §§ 12101-213. The ADA expanded upon the provisions of the Federal Rehabilitation Act (RA) of 1973, 29 U.S.C.A. §§ 701-96, which was limited to the federal government, its contractors and grantees. The ADA prohibits discrimination against people with disabilities by employers (Title I), public entities (Title II), and privately owned businesses and services that provide public accommodations (Title III).

15) 42 U.S.C.A. § 12182(b)(2)(A)(ii) and (iii).

16) Public Acts 1995 c. 50.

17) See, e.g., Part III (Discrimination in Other Areas) sec. 21.

18) Official Journal L 303, 02/12/2000, p. 19.

19) See section II.(a)(3) supra. The Supreme Court expressly considered the reach of the ADA in *PGA Tour, Inc. v. Martin*. The PGA is a private tour that does not employ professional golfers and receives no funds from the state or federal governments. It argued that it was a public accommodation only with respect to the spectators, not the competitors. The Supreme Court agreed with the lower courts that the tournaments held by the PGA were, in fact, public accommodations for the competitors as well as the spectators, making Title III of the Act applicable (532 U.S. 661, 678-80). The case sends the broader message that courts should construe the ADA's coverage liberally. It is likely that only a few events, held at legitimately private clubs that own their own facilities, will avoid ADA coverage.

### a) Fundamental alterations

In *PGA Tour, Inc.* v. *Martin*, a case which continues to define the legal issues surrounding disability and mainstreaming in sports, the PGA Tour did not actually dispute that Martin had a disability for which the use of a golf cart was both a reasonable and a necessary accommodation. Rather, it defended its actions based on the language of § 12182(b)(2)(A)(ii) of the ADA, which provides an exemption from the modification requirement if 'the entity can demonstrate that making such modifications would fundamentally alter the nature of such goods, services, facilities ... or accommodations.' The case was then argued on the basis of whether waiving the PGA Tour rule requiring golfers to walk the course without the use of a cart in Martin's case would fundamentally alter the nature of the PGA Tour event.

The United States Supreme Court held that there were two ways in which a rule change might fundamentally alter the activity in question: by changing 'such an essential aspect of the game of golf that it would be unacceptable even if it affected all competitors equally', or by giving the disabled person not only equal access but 'an advantage' over other competitors.[20] As regards the first part of the inquiry, the Court concluded that allowing the use of a cart would not change an essential aspect of the game of golf because 'the essence of the game has been shot-making.'[21] The court also noted that the ban on carts is not required by golf's general rules and that carts are indeed strongly encouraged in much of golf.[22] By contrast, allowing a wheelchair user to return the ball after its second bounce in racquetball has been held to alter such an essential aspect of the game that it would be unacceptable even if the modification affected all competitors equally. The Supreme Judicial Court of Massachusetts reasoned that the essence of the game of racquetball, as expressly articulated in the official rules, was the hitting of a moving ball before the second bounce and that giving a wheelchair player two bounces and a footed player one bounce in head-to-head competition would create a new game, calling for new strategies, positioning, and movement of players.[23] The second leg of the

---

20) 532 U.S. 661, 682.
21) *Ibid.* 683.
22) *Ibid.* 685–6. Even the PGA does not ban carts in some of its tours.

Supreme Court's inquiry in *Martin* concerned whether the modification in question – the use of a cart – would give Martin a competitive advantage. The court held that the ADA required the PGA to make an individualized assessment of Martin's claim. Relying on the trial court's findings that Martin 'easily endures greater fatigue even with a cart than his able-bodied competitors do by walking'[24], the court found that using a cart did not give Martin an advantage and that it was the PGA's duty under the ADA to provide him with one.

While *Martin* opened the door for suits by athletes seeking accommodations or rule modifications for their disabilities, it does not make every modifications suit a winner. The more recent Pistorius controversy is illustrative in this regard. Pistorius' bid for entry into the 2008 Summer Olympic Games ran up against a March 2007 amendment to its competition rules by the IAAF.[25] The amendment banned the 'use of any technical device that incorporates springs, wheels or any other element that provides the user with an advantage over another athlete not using such a device'[26]. Undoubtedly, the artificial limbs used by Pistorius were technical devices, and, equally undoubtedly, they afforded Pistorius a performance advantage over and above anything he could have achieved without such limbs. The crucial question, however, was whether the artificial limbs overshot their (permissible) aim of compensating for Pistorius' lack of lower legs and instead constituted an (impermissible) enhancement – what some have called 'techno-doping'[27]. A 2007 study conducted by German professor Gert-Peter Brüggemann for the IAAF found that Pistorius' limbs used 25% less energy than able-bodied runners to run at the same speed and that they led to less vertical motion combined with 30% less mechanical work for lifting the body.[28] Brüggemann concluded that Pistorius had considerable advantages

---

23) *Kuketz* v. *Petronelli*, 433 Mass. 355, 821 N.E.2d 473 (2005).

24) *Ibid.* 690 (quoting *Martin* v. *PGA Tour, Inc.*, 994 F.Supp. 1242, 1252 (D. Or. 1998)).

25) Some have suggested that this rule was introduced specifically to deal with the threat posed by Pistorius, an allegation vehemently denied by IAAF council member Robert Hersh. *Charlish/Riley*, note 10 supra, 930.

26) IAAF Competition Rule 144.2(e) (2008).

27) For the term, *J. Longman*, 'An Amputee Sprinter: Is He Disabled or Too-Abled?', The New York Times (May 15, 2007), available at www.nytimes.com/2007/05/15/sports/othersports/15runner.html?_r=1&oref=slogin (last accessed October 24, 2009).

over athletes without prosthetic limbs.[29] Based on these findings, the IAAF ruled Pistorius' prostheses ineligible for use in competitions conducted under the IAAF rules, including the 2008 Summer Olympics.[30]

In May 2008, however, the Court of Arbitration for Sport (CAS) reversed the ban, clearing the way for Pistorius to pursue his dream, although the athlete ultimately failed to qualify for the Olympics. A major component of the court's decision was that there was insufficient evidence that the prosthetics provided an *overall* advantage to Pistorius when their disadvantages were taken into account.[31] In other words, the court held that what mattered was the whole package of benefit and detriment over the entire course of the race – the net status of performance – rather than the impact of the prosthetic limbs in isolation.[32] For instance, while Pistorius' prosthetics may return more impact energy than the human foot, as the Brüggemann study found,[33] this benefit might be offset by their also causing slower starts,[34] being ill adapted to rainy and windy conditions, and

---

28) For further information, G.-P. *Brüggemann/A. Arampatzis/F. Emrich, et al.* (2008), 'Biomechanics of Double Transtibial Amputee Sprinting Using Dedicated Sprinting Prostheses', Sports Technology 1 (2008), No. 4-5, 220, 226 et seq.; 'Blade Runner Handed Olympic Ban', BBC Sport (January 14, 2008), available at http://news.bbc.co.uk/sport2/hi/olympics/athletics/7141302.stm (last accessed October 24, 2009).

29) 'Studie beendet Olympiatraum von Pistorius', Welt Online (December 19, 2007), available at www.welt.de/welt_print/article1475643/Studie_beendet_Olympiatraum_von_Pistorius. html (last accessed October 24, 2009).

30) 'IAAF Call Time on Oscar Pistorius' Dream', The Daily Telegraph (January 10, 2008), available at www.telegraph.co.uk/sport/othersports/athletics/2288489/IAAF-call-time-on-Oscar-Pistorius-dream.html (last accessed October 24, 2009).

31) The evidential burden of proving the 'advantage' in terms of IAAF rule 144.2.(e) is on the sports association which imposed the suspension. The applicable standard the association must apply to prove that the user of the prosthesis has an overall net advantage over other athletes not using such devices is the 'balance of probability'; CAS 2008/A/1480, *Pistorius* v. *IAAF,* para. 92.

32) The IAAF did not ask Professor Brüggemann to determine whether the use of the prosthesis provides an overall net advantage or disadvantage. CAS 2008/A/1480, *Pistorius* v. *IAAF,* paras. 85, 93 = Sp*u*Rt 2008, 152, 154. The only purpose of the determination was the question whether Pistorius' use of the prosthesis provided him with any kind of advantage.

33) 'Studie beendet Olympiatraum von Pistorius', Welt Online (December 19, 2007), available at www.welt.de/welt_print/article1475643/Studie_beendet_Olympiatraum_von_Pistorius.html (last accessed October 24, 2009).

difficult to handle in navigating bends. Similarly, just as Pistorius has the advantage of suffering no fatigue in his legs below his knees, so also is he subject to the disadvantage of only being able to produce propulsive effects via muscles above his knees.[35]

Of course, the net effect of technical aids on a disabled athlete's overall performance must be difficult, if not impossible, to quantify accurately (and any attempt to do so is bound to have significant resource implications[36]). One suspects that one reason why *Martin* has not set off a barrage of suits by disabled athletes seeking an accommodation to participate in mainstream sports[37] is that, because of the ethos of competition, most disabled athletes do not want, or accept, any actual or perceived favors. To receive or to be suspected of receiving special aid devalues the athletic achievement. As Pistorius told reporters, 'If they [the IAAF] ever found evidence that I was gaining an advantage, then I would stop running because I would not want to compete at a top level if I knew I had an unfair advantage.'[38]

---

34) Observing Pistorius' run, one can see that he was slower than other able-bodied runners off the starting blocks and during the acceleration phase, but faster during the second and third 100 meter; CAS 2008/A/1480, *Pistorius* v. *IAAF*, 41 = SpuRt 2008, 152, 153.

35) *Charlish/Riley*, note 10 supra, 936. Another advantage the use of a prosthesis may provide is the mental impact on the other athletes who have to start next to an amputee. It is an open question whether this is the case and whether a possible psychological obstacle of the able-bodied athletes may be considered given the non-discrimination rule.

36) The tests conducted on Pistorius cost in the range of €30 000. See *Charlish/Riley*, note 10 supra, 939. If funding such tests is left to the individual athlete, challenges are unlikely to be brought. If sports governing bodies are left to pick up the tab, on the other hand, the financial burden on these might also be immense. The respective sports association should, however, regulate the process by which a disabled sportsperson who uses a prosthetic can take part in competitions for able-bodied sportspeople in a way that guarantees safety and saves money. Thus, the sports association should compile a list of all institutions to be considered in the necessary studies, enumerate all factors to be investigated, and set out the procedure to be followed in the event that a disabled sportsperson makes an administrative appeal. *A. Chappel* (2008), 'Running Down a Dream: Oscar Pistorius, Prosthetic Devices, and the Unknown Future of Athletes with Disabilities in the Olympic Games', 10 NC JOLT On line Ed. 1, 16, 26.

37) On the limited impact of *Martin* in terms of similar cases brought, *H.T. Greely* (2004), 'Disabilities, Enhancements, and the Meanings of Sports', 15 Stan. L. & Pol'y Rev. 99, 111.

What if the tests carried out on Pistorius had been conclusive that the prosthetic limbs did in fact go further than merely redressing his overall performance balance? Indeed, in some cases, it might not be possible to accommodate a disabled athlete without at the same time improving his situation beyond that of the average competitor. This need not necessarily preclude participation. One solution to the dilemma might be to impose a scoring handicap equivalent to the (illicit) advantage on the athlete concerned.[39] Sports have developed a sophisticated machinery to set various forms of handicaps: occasionally, better competitors are physically hindered;[40] in team sports, weaker teams are sometimes given special advantages;[41] and in a few sports, the actual scoring is adjusted to help inferior competitors.[42] Perhaps we should consider using these various handicapping methods to further the integration of disabled athletes into mainstream sports.

### b) Risk of injury to others

Allowing a disabled individual to compete with the help of an accommodation may present substantial injury problems with other competitors. For instance, if Pistorius had qualified for the Olympics and been allowed to run in the main pack of the race, his running blades might have posed a safety hazard for fellow athletes.[43] Under the ADA, the

---

38) 'Pistorius Is No Novelty Sprinter', The Daily Telegraph (Sport) (July 11, 2007), available at www.telegraph.co.uk/sport/othersports/athletics/2316794/pistorius-is-no-novelty-sprinter.html (last accessed October 24, 2009).
39) For a similar proposal see *Greely*, note 37 supra, 122 et seq.
40) In most thoroughbred horseracing, e.g., weight is added to some of the horses to balance out the different weights of the jockeys.
41) In many professional leagues in the United States, the worst teams get the first choice of players who enter the draft, presumably allowing them to equalize ability in the league over time.
42) Amateur golf and bowling, e.g., give special scoring advantages to weaker competitors based on their previous results.
43) IAAF general secretary Pierre Weiss in fact voiced this concern, expressing a wish that the South African Olympic Committee not select Pistorius for its relay team 'for reasons of safety'. See 'Relay Safety Fears Over Pistorius', BBC Sport (July 15, 2008), available at http://news-bbc.co.uk/sport2/hi/olympics/athletics/7508399.stm (last accessed October 25, 2009). The CAS did not, however, address the question whether the use of prosthetics could lead to an increased risk of stumbling, thereby creating a greater risk

employment qualification standards under Title I may include 'a requirement that an individual shall not pose a direct threat to the health and safety of other individuals in the workplace'[44], while Title III declares that public accommodations are not obliged 'to permit an individual to participate ... where such individual poses a direct threat to the health and safety of others ... that cannot be eliminated by a modification of policies, practices, or procedures or by the provision of auxiliary aids or services'[45]. In *Badgett v. Alabama High School Athletic Ass'n*,[46] Mallerie Badgett, a minor wheelchair-bound track-and-field athlete with cerebral palsy, brought a claim against the Alabama High School Athletic Association (AHSAA) under the ADA because she wished to compete in the able-bodied track-and-field competition. The court denied her claim, finding that the AHSAA had made reasonable modifications by establishing a separate wheelchair division. The court held that in deciding what was reasonable both competitive and safety considerations had to be taken into account and that there were legitimate safety concerns about having able-bodied and wheelchair-bound athletes compete in mixed heats.

## 2. Excluding athletes because of a risk of self-injury

Quite apart from the question of whether there is a duty to ensure access for disabled individuals through special accommodations, there is the issue of whether a disabled athlete can be excluded on the (paternalistic) ground that participation carries a high risk of self-injury.[47] An example is the person who has only one kidney but still wants to participate in a contact sport such as interscholastic wrestling.[48] In the United States, the focus of the inquiry is on whether the disabled athlete is an otherwise 'qualified

---

of injuring other athletes.
44) 42 U.S.C.A. § 12113(b).
45) 42 U.S.C.A. § 12182(b)(3).
46) 2007 WL 2461928 (N.D. Ala. May 3, 2007).
47) For discussion, see *Paul M. Anderson*, Sports Law: A Desktop Handbook, Milwaukee, WI, USA, 1999, p. 52 et seq. and *S. Zinger*, Gleichbehandlung im Sport – Unter besonderer Berücksichtigung US-amerikanischer Rechtsprechung, in: K. Vieweg (Hrsg.), Spektrum des Sportrechts, Berlin 2003, S. 1, 13 f.
48) *Poole v. South Plainfield Bd. of Ed.*, 490 F.Supp. 948 (D.C.N.J. 1980).

individual'[49]), i.e. whether he is able to meet all of the program's requirements in spite of his handicap.[50]

In *Pahulu v. University of Kansas*,[51] the plaintiff was injured during football practice and later diagnosed with a very narrow cervical canal, leading team doctors to believe that he was at very high risk of serious neurological injury. As a result, Pahulu was suspended from football. He sued, claiming the university discriminated against him by disqualifying him only on account of his disability. The court denied Pahulu's injunction, holding that he failed to meet the 'otherwise qualified' standard because he did not fulfill the team's medical requirements. The court found that the team doctors' risk assessment provided a reasonable and rational basis for the disqualification, precluding further judicial scrutiny.[52]

Where a disabled athlete is aware of and willing to incur the dangers involved in continued athletic participation, allowing a third party to interpose its 'benevolent paternalism'[53], as the *Pahulu* court did, requires some strong justification. Citing a sport organization's 'inherent right to protect an athlete's health'[54] – from himself (!) – should not be regarded as sufficient as this amounts to justifying paternalism for paternalism's sake. Whether protecting the organization's reputation, which might be tarnished by a competitor being severely injured or killed in competition,[55] or averting

---

49) Many of the cases predated the ADA and were decided under § 504 of the Rehabilitation Act of 1973 (RA), which prohibits discrimination against 'otherwise qualified' individuals, in federally funded programs, solely because of their handicap (29 U.S.C. § 794).

50) *Southeastern Community College* v. *Davis*, 442 U.S. 397, 398 (1979).

51) 897 F.Supp.1387 (D. Kansas 1995).

52) *Ibid.* 1394. For a similar decision, see *Knapp* v. *Northeastern University*, 101 F.3d 473 (7th Cir. 1996) (holding that requiring medical qualification did not violate the RA, provided the school had significant medical evidence indicating a serious risk of injury). For a decision that went in the opposite direction, see *Poole* v. *South Plain Field Bd. of Ed.*, 490 F.Supp. 948 (D.C.N.J. 1980) (holding school had neither duty nor right under RA to exclude student who knew of dangers and – with parents' consent – still chose to compete).

53) For this term, see *B.P. Tucker* (1996), 'Application of the Americans with Disabilities Act (ADA) and Section 504 to Colleges and Universities: An Overview and Discussion of Special Issues Relating to Students', 23 J.C. & U.L. 1, 33.

54) For this argument, see *M.J. Mitten* (1998), Enhanced Risk of Harm to One's Self as a Justification for Exclusion from Athletics, 8 Marq. Sports L.J. 189, 192.

a liability risk should trump the athlete's right to decide is questionable, especially where the athlete is prepared to sign a waiver that would release the organization from all liability.[56] While paternalism might be appropriate in amateur, in particular in high school and collegiate sports (where the persons protected are usually minors), it seems very hard to justify in the case of *professional* (adult) athletics. Where a competent athlete's livelihood is threatened if made to abstain from sports participation, his right to decide what is in his own best interests should be regarded as paramount.[57]

### 3. Participation of the able-bodied in competitions for the disabled

Another facet to the participation problem presents itself where able-bodied athletes wish to take part in competitions for the disabled. In wheelchair-basketball, for example, up to two non-disabled athletes may be included on a team. Also, an able-bodied athlete could take the view that he has no advantages in sports intended for the disabled, giving him a right to participate. Similarly, an able-bodied person might wish to take part in a marathon for persons using wheelchairs. This particular problem may be approached in the following way: the relevant association rules and their application are subject to judicial scrutiny. The facts of the individual case and the principle of proportionality are the decisive criteria. The question of whether participation may be confined to disabled persons, as intended by the association, has to be addressed by balancing the interests at stake.

### 4. Classifications by type and degree of disability

In disabled sports, there are various classifications to ensure equal opportunities. The need for classification arises from the existence of

---

55) *Knapp* v. *Northwestern University*, 942 F.Supp. 1191, 1199 (N.D. Ill. 1996); *Mitten*, note 54 supra, 192.

56) On the legal validity of waivers, see *T.G. Church/J.R. Neumeister* (1998), 'University Control of Student-Athletes with Disabilities under the Americans with Disabilities Act', 25 J.C. & U.L. 105, 180 et seq.

57) For the argument that a distinction be drawn between professional and amateur sports, *Mitten*, note 54 supra, 221 et seq.

different types of disabilities and their varying severity. There is a distinction, for example, between physical and intellectual disability. Persons who are physically disabled are further categorized into subgroups, such as athletes with a visual impairment or athletes using wheelchairs. These groups are again subdivided according to the severity of the disability, in particular according to the individual's mobility impairment due to the disability. This classification, however, may run into difficulties. On the one hand, the various categories should not be overly strict, given that, otherwise, there would not be a sufficient starting field. On the other hand, they should only cover athletes who have similar physical conditions in order to comply with the principle of equal opportunities. Finding a solution to such a conflict of objectives is difficult and can lead to judicial review if an athlete feels discriminated against by the definition of the categories or by his or her classification. In discus throwing, for example, various grades of disability are united in one competition to provide a sufficient starting field. To offset this, however, a points system based on the grade of the disability is introduced: the more severe the impairment, the less the distance required in order to gain an accordant score. To ensure equal opportunities in discus throwing, it is of the utmost importance that the conversion factor which determines the score be non-discriminatory with regard to the grade of disability[58].

Up until now, these questions have not been subject to judicial review. For this reason, questions of proof which would be much more relevant in this context than in the *Martin* and *Pistorius* cases have not played a role so far.


## V. Conclusion

'Techno-doping' is a term which is very widely used, but which is

---

58) Marianne Bruchhagen, e.g., a paraplegic discus thrower, abandoned her career because she found the points system to be unfair. The system is based exclusively on the respective world record of one grade of disability: see Frankfurter Allgemeine Zeitung (July 7, 2008), S. 31.

perhaps not very suitable or clear. Keeping in mind that sporting performance is the result of various factors which form a complete system, I suggest, as a first step, taking into account the seven scenarios which I have already mentioned and then, in a second step, considering the aims of equal opportunities and fairness, the health and bodily integrity of the athletes and the reputation of the sporting discipline. In the third step, it is up to the federations to stipulate what is permitted and what is forbidden. Of course, these decisions can be subject to judicial review. Two famous cases have been ruled on by courts (Casey Martin) and the Court of Arbitration for Sports (Pistorius).

## References

*K. Vieweg,* The Appeal of Sports Law, www.irut.de/Forschung/Veroeffentlichungen/ OnlineVersionFaszinationSportrecht/FaszinationSportrechtEnglisch.pdf.

*K. Vieweg,* Bans on Discrimination and Duties to Differentiate in the German Law of Sports Organizations, in: The International Sports Law Journal 2006, p. 96.

*K. Vieweg,* Normsetzung und -anwendung deutscher und internationaler Verbände, Berlin 1990.

*K. Vieweg,* 'Techno-Doping' – Regelungs- und Durchsetzungsmöglichkeiten der Sportverbände, in: K. Vieweg (Hrsg.), 'Techno-Doping', Stuttgart 2013 (in print).

*K. Vieweg/S. Lettmaier,* Anti-discrimination law and policy, in: J. Nafziger/S. Ross (eds.), Handbook on International Sports Law, Cheltenham, UK/Northampton, MA, USA, 2011.

*S. Zinger,* Diskriminierungsverbote und Sportautonomie, Berlin 2003.

*P. Charlish/S. Riley* (2008), 'Should Oscar Run?', 18 Fordham Intell. Prop., Media and Ent. L.J. 929.

*G.-P. Brüggemann/A. Arampatzis/F. Emrich, et al.* (2008), 'Biomechanics of Double Transtibial Amputee Sprinting Using Dedicated Sprinting Prostheses', Sports Technology 1 (2008), No. 4–5, 220.

*A. Chappel* (2008), 'Running Down a Dream: Oscar Pistorius, Prosthetic Devices, and the Unknown Future of Athletes with Disabilities in the

Olympic Games', 10 NC JOLT On line Ed. 1, 16.

*H.T. Greely* (2004), 'Disabilities, Enhancements, and the Meanings of Sports', 15 Stan. L. & Pol'y Rev. 99.

# Arguments for Promoting the Right to Practice Sports as a Fundamental Right

ALEXANDRU VIRGIL VOICU*

> „Play is a uniquely adaptive act,
> not subordinate to some other adaptive act,
> but with a special function of its
> own in human experience."
> Johan Huizinga

*The theme of this article covers the benefits of sport for society in general, but also the provisions of Romanian Law no. 69/2000 on Physical Education and Sport, as subsequently amended, as well as all the relevant Romanian legislation arising from the provisions of European Union (EU) law on the subject, in particular The White Paper on Sport and the Charter of Fundamental Rights of the European Union, documents which entered into force pursuant to the Treaty of Lisbon. Last but not least, the article debates the possibility of enhancing the importance of practicing physical education and sport as an inherent human right.[1]*

Key word: sport, Physical education, fundamental rights and liberties, natural law

## The Sporting Phenomenon – a Significant Social Phenomenon

Every individual is keen on developing speculations and debates regarding the causes, consequences and even the content itself of various phenomena and processes that he or she might encounter in daily life. The

---

* Attorney&Mediator, Professor at the Babes-Bolyai University Cluj-Napoca, Faculty of Physical Education and Sports, alexvirgilweisz@yahoo.com

most probable outcome of such an endeavor would most probably be that of referring to these subjects from different perspectives that is, ascertaining different point of views – subjectivity owing, in this case, mainly to conditional experience and common sense. Therefore, one must position himself in a position that claims a prudent attitude – if not total rejection – towards intuition, speculation, horse sense (the fundamentals of common sense), and strive for the rigors of the scientific method.

It is thought that human rights are an ideological projection in order to justify certain social actions, a philosophy, a concept on the world and the existence. Human rights are, foremost, a sociology of contemporary life, inasmuch that they encompass facts, phenomena, social processes and relationships alike, mentalities, states of mind, imagery, representations, interests and perceptions. Max Weber spoke of the design of the world and man's place in it. The topic on human rights is often reduced to a legislative concept, and human rights education bears a technical nature – law articles, pros and cons debates in sustaining a certain idea, case analysis etc. In this particular context, one cannot ignore the existence of a sporting phenomenon, which has developed into an important social phenomenon. Its importance is foremost justifiable by man's dependence on his physiological and social needs to participate in organized or random sporting activities, also used – more recently – with the aim of satisfying a professional avocation (professional sports).

We see it imperative to remind ourselves that man "is not static, he is profoundly dynamic, he is a living reality in a tireless state of wanting, restless until reaching his goal".[2] It is from this psychology-of-the- (dynamic)- person perspective that we will be able to appreciate the three forms of human development: biological, dynamic and psychological, reaching the conclusion that these are the working fundamentals of the motivational theories. Whether one agrees or not – ultimately confident in the social-cultural calling of the human nature – man is concurrently nature and culture. That is why one can argue that the need to exert physical activity – viewed as a means of physical education and sport, whether professional or amateur – is also a biological need that is integrated in man's various organic necessities, as are those "linked to the assimilation and dissimilation process, or anabolism and catabolism, such as hunger, thirst and breathing, on one hand, and the necessity to preserve the species, or sexual instinct, on the other."[3]

Every single need-related work motivation theory drawn up by authors such as Maslow, Clayton Alderfer (ERG theory – Existence, Relatedness, Growth), McClelland[4] (Necessities theory), Faverge J.M[5], states that until elementary necessities, more urgent and pressing, have not been fulfilled, all others remain in the background; as one category of needs is satisfied, another, superior one, is sought after. This justifies our statement that human needs have been reevaluated, in time, as being inherent rights of the human being – transposed in generations of fundamental human rights.

Therefore, taking into consideration that *the need to practice sports is an inherent right of the human being*, the European Sports Minister of the Council of Europe has already ascribed a **legal value** to this need, appreciating it as a *fundamental right* through the European Sport for all Charters in 1975. The first article stated that *every individual shall have the right to participate in sport*. "From that date on, sport policies in Europe were endowed with a common programme based on the conviction that the values of sport would contribute to the fulfilment of the ideals of the Council of Europe"[6] Later, in 1992, inspired by the same charter, the European Sport Charter was adopted with the aim of providing a common set of principles for the European countries. The Charter was completed afterwords with the Code of Sport Ethics, promoting the principle of fair play[7].

On international level, in 1978 the General Conference of the UNESCO adopted the International Charter of Physical Education and Sport, which expressly states in its first article that the practice of sport is a fundamental right for all.

Similarly, a child's right to play has been enshrined in article 31 of the

Convention on the Rights of the Child, which recognizes "the right of the child to rest and leisure, to engage in play and recreational activities appropriate to the age of the child".

"Several other United Nations instruments also acknowledge the importance of access to and participation in sport, such as the Convention on the Elimination of All Forms of Discrimination against Women. Similarly, ILO Conventions Nos. 138 and 182 concerning child labor require Governments to establish policies for the rehabilitation of child laborers. Here, sport is considered an effective policy tool."[8]

In spite of these international instruments, the right to sport and play is often denied or neglected, often gender and ability based discrimination. It is also frequently due to political neglect of the importance of sport in society, exemplified by the decline in spending on physical education and the lack of appropriate spaces and resources necessary for sport.[9]

Human rights are inherent to the human being, "taken individually or as part of a predetermined social group"[10]. Human rights are fundamental to our nature. The deprivation or denial of these rights amount to the inability to exist as humans beings and open the path to political and social disorder. Exercising these rights freely can only be possible in a legal protection system that guarantees and implements human rights. In the preamble of the *Universal Declaration of Human Rights*[11] (par. 1) it is stated that "recognition of the inherent dignity and of the equal and inalienable rights of all members of the human family is the foundation of freedom, justice and peace in the world".

## The Functions and Values of Sports

It seems that the present day finds us witnessing an overturning of all values. We deny everything, even that which not long ago surrounded us with respect. Still, we must not forget that the struggle of values for preeminence is defined by a permanent contradiction. History shows us that the values which are imposed on everyone are only those that "completely satisfy the logical and psychological criteria of the human soul" – the foundation of a value needs to be based on logic and the theory of knowledge. The wideness and validity of value can only be established through logic. Two points of view are to be taken into consideration when discussing the issue of value, as follows: a. *subjective-psychological*, which induces a value-based psychology, and b. *objective-logical*, which determines the most profound and thorough research, *the logic of value.*[12]

The concept of sport is attributed numerous functions, more significantly: *conative function* (satisfaction of the desire to move, to act), *competition function* (stimulation and satisfaction of the desire to compete), *performance maximizing function* (performance capacity development in a biological, psychological and social scheme), *social function* (integration, social assertion, communication, emulation – also comprising the national identity representation, cultural and economic functions).

The sporting culture is an essential element of economic development and social regeneration and stands as an indicator of the quality of life and individual welfare. The law – seen as a normative phenomenon – is also entrusted to create the legal framework in an ample social phenomenon such as sports. It is imperative that all participants to sporting activities are guaranteed a legal reliability, in the sense that individual behavior needs to be influenced in the name of value requirements that encompass both legal values and positive values of sports – more so in the current context, marked by the excessive commercial nature of sports and its transformation into an instrument of political manipulation (which can lead to a legitimization of illicit behavior both in and off "the court").

The sporting phenomenon requires a prior understanding and embracing of meanings attributed to various notions and concept, such as: society and globalization, social system, state, culture, politics, deontology, law, rights and liberties, social values, interest groups etc. If we accept Warren Weaver's definition of communication – mainly relevant through its pragmatism - „Communication is *the totality of processes by which one mind can influence another*"[13] - then we can understand the importance of the functions served by all communicators[14] (medics, priests, pedagogues, psychologists, coaches, athletes, managers, science communicators, actors, artists, lawyers, magistrates etc.) – including mass-media which – not seldom – act as a social control tool, a source of social pressure on the individual.[15]

Communication made by sports communicators has a political dimension, but also a cultural conditionality. It is in this respect that cohabitation between systems of different cultures should be promoted – *cultural cohabitation* – truly a unity in diversity, more effective than multiculturalism seen as a prerequisite of a nation-state.[16] "While sport and play are repeatedly acknowledged as a human right, they are not always seen as a priority and have even been called the "forgotten right". Sports is seen as a by-product of development, not as an engine."[17]

Human rights should not form an enclosed philosophical, political, religious and social system. They should be kept open to diverse ways of thinking, to diverse beliefs, cultures and social practices. Each person is a subject of law. This is a common feature which establishes the link with society. The human being has inalienable rights, irrespective of the will of the authorities. The concept of fundamental rights makes a direct reference to the natural rights philosophy, inspired from the European humanist movement.

Debates over natural rights are open as a result of new situations that arise in human life, of new claims – both on a national and international level. The international human rights law constitutes a summation of natural rights expressed in the present context of globalization, to which states must associate in order to transform them in positive rights – rights that establish common principles and can be applied by a concrete international jurisdiction. Contemporary legal papers on the protection of human rights provide a large number of philosophical notions that can constitute the basis for a consensus. This international law of human rights texts focus on the link between the individual and the authorities, on the legitimacy of the latter's actions and on the conditions under which individuals with equal rights coexist. Owing to the respect of each individual and the equality in rights and dignity, human rights constitute an open system for the peaceful coexistence of a multitude of cultures, beliefs, practices and social organizations.[18]

## Returning to Natural Law – Starting Point for Promoting other Fundamental Rights

Research on human rights has developed a history of concepts related to them, as well as a history regarding the struggle to validate these rights. The philosophy of rights originates from individualist theories.[19] According to these theories, the legitimacy of power centers on human individuality. Power is legitimate only if it acknowledges the rights of the individual as an entity. Starting from here, we can question ourselves regarding the historic origins of individualism.

On a long term, human rights encourage self-interest to the prejudice of community spirit, because they favor individualism without balancing it with the community. It is a well-known fact that individualism is the fundament of human rights, hence the critic upon human rights transforms into a critic upon modernity, which, in turn, is based on individualism. First generation human rights arise from the affirmation of the individual, which has substantially marked the destiny of modernity up to present times.

The term "human rights" remained unknown until the French Revolution of 1789. That is why it has been said that it represents a construct meant to create a new authority, to replace the divine authority. The cause of this authority was found in *man* and his will power. It is extremely difficult now to renounce rights, if not impossible without creating insurmountable difficulties. What can and should be done is to bring individual rights in balance with the community spirit, considering the fact that individual rights cannot exist unless the *relationships* between humans change substantially – that is to say liberty – e.g. – cannot manifest without the background of a well organized society. Only a person with optimal relations with others can benefit from freedom. From here, a come-back to natural law is inherently necessary, more so in order to promote the right to practice sporting activities as a fundamental human right.

## The Actuality, Utility and Definition of the Legal Grounds for the Existence of Acquired Rights

First generation fundamental rights and liberties cannot be extended to all citizens without a proper protection of second generation rights. In this case, the two generations of rights are not only non-contradictive, but complementary. One cannot talk about the right to life, to freedom, if these comprise only a part of society, the rest being eluded through various means. In fact, there is considerable controversy about what should constitute 'human rights' and what rights are most important, including topics such as the excessive promotion of individual rights over collective rights, civil and political rights while neglecting economic and social rights.[20] Another set of debates covers the tension between the rights and the corresponding responsibilities[21]. However, state intervention can assure a certain degree of social equilibrium. Profound social movements have changed the balance between social forces and have required the state to intervene in order to grant first generation rights to everybody.

One of the causes for the decline of human rights is their unjustified multiplication and extension to various fields that, often, seem utterly fanciful. Their multiplication leads to a decrease in their importance, which in turn can provoke an increase in the state's power stance. This ambiguity of human rights derives from the paradoxical nature of the human being, which strives on being free of constraints while concurrently stating the necessity of order. What should be considered is that the two concepts should be balanced and mutually dependable. We agree with the statement that "individual freedom cannot be limitless, but the same forces that determine the necessity for limitations can, if permitted, unbearably restrain the scope of human freedom"[22]. The multiplication of human rights cannot be measured only from a quantitative and qualitative perspective. If in the field of quantity, the essential aspect is measurement, we ask ourselves if the right to life and freedom can be measured.

Considering the social importance of the sporting phenomenon, it is necessary to promote the right to practice sports – as a fundamental right of the human being – because this right identifies itself with many civil, political and economical and social rights (the right to work, the right to health welfare), cultural ones (the right to benefit from education, the right to participate in cultural life, the right to have a protection of the moral and material interests deriving from one's work – with emphasis on sporting creations), a person's right to fulfill their economic, social and cultural rights in order to maintain dignity – laid down as fundamental rights in national and international legislations. Along the history of the last half century it has been held, that along other international conventions, such as, the Convention on the Elimination of All Forms of Racial Discrimination, the Convention on the Elimination of Discrimination Against Women, the Convention on the Rights of the Child, etc, the Charter on Physical Education and Sport proclaimed by UNESCO has "contributed to a much broader commitment to human dignity throughout the world, in both in the abstract and in the concrete."[23]

The updating methods are conceived differently by the theorists that have pondered in this field. A concern for updating the concept of freedom has always been present, and it focuses on the relationship between individual freedom and power, a relationship which leads to a conception on human rights. As latency is updated, history unfolds itself, and human rights tend to impose themselves. We feel that the multitude of acquired rights – comprised of the third generation fundamental human rights - are in decline also because they are not justified form a legal point of view. These have to be defined by bringing together four essential conditions, without which no right can exist, both in the positive and natural law: **1.** a *bearer* who can exert a right; **2.** a *scope* that can give meaning to that right; **3.** *opposability* which allows the bearer to exert his right in court; **4.** an organized *sanction* (as to realize the right)[24].

## The Right to Practice Sports and its Role, as Prescribed by the Law

In Romania, according to Article 2, par. (5) Of Law no. 69/2000 on Physical Education and Sport, "the practice of physical education and sport is a human right, without any discrimination, guaranteed by the state. Exercising this right is free and voluntary and independently undertaken or as part of associated sports structures." Physical education and sport stand for "all forms of physical activities aimed, through an organized or independent participation, to express or improve physical fitness and mental well-being, to establish civilized social relations and lead to results in competitions at any level" – art. 1 par. (2). As prescribed by the law, physical education and sports activities include physical education, school and university sports, sports for all persons, high-level sports performance, exercise carried out for maintenance, physical development or therapeutic purposes – art. 2 par. (3).

By guaranteeing the promotion of this right, its social importance arises from the content of art. 2 and 3 of the law: "Art. 2 - (1) physical education and sports are activities of national interest supported by the state, (2) In accordance to the applicable legislation, the state recognizes and stimulates organizational actions to promote physical education and sports, held by public authorities and, where appropriate, non-governmental organizations focusing on education, the national defense institutions, public order, national security, health, in companies and other sectors of social life, (4) The State guarantees the performance of specific functions in the public and private sector in physical education and sport, in accordance with the principles of collaboration and responsibility of all interested parties, (5) The practice of physical education and sport is a human right, without discrimination and guaranteed by the state. Exercising this right is free and voluntary and undertaken independently or as part of associated sports structures, (6) The State recognizes and guarantees the natural and legal right to free association for the establishment of sports entities. Art. 3 par. (1) The government units and educational institutions, sports institutions and nongovernmental organizations have the obligation to support sports for all persons and high-level sport performance and to ensure organizational and material conditions for practicing physical education and sport in local communities, (2) The public government authorities and institutions referred to in paragraph (1) shall foremost ensure proper conditions for practicing physical exercises with respect to preschool children, young persons and the elderly, for purposes of social integration, (3) The public administration authorities must offer the necessary conditions for practicing physical education and sport to persons with physical, sensory, mental and other handicaps in order to sustain their personal development and integration within society and the resources to allow disabled athletes to participate in national and international competitions organized for such persons".

It is necessary to make a clarification of terminology, to distinguish between the definition provided by the Romanian legislature in year 2000 with respect to "physical education and sport activities", with that established and enshrined in the European Union's White Paper on Sport. For reasons of clarity and simplicity, the White Paper on Sport uses the definition of „sport" which was established by the Council of Europe in its European Sports Charter[25]: „*Sport* means all forms of physical activity, which, through casual or organized participation, aims at expressing or improving physical fitness and mental well-being, forming social relationships or obtaining results in competition at all levels."

In consistency with one of its objectives – the welfare of its citizens, in all forms – the E.U. declared 2004 as the "European Year of Education through Sports"[26]. The aims of this initiative were established as follows: to make educational institutions and sports organizations aware of the need for cooperation in order to develop education through sport and its European dimension, given the great interest that young people take in all kinds of sports; to take advantage of the values conveyed through sport to develop knowledge and skills whereby young people in particular can develop their physical prowess and readiness for personal effort and also social abilities such as teamwork, solidarity, tolerance and fair play in a multicultural framework; to promote the educational value of student mobility and exchanges, particularly in a multicultural environment, through the organization of sporting and cultural contacts as part of school activity; to create a better balance between intellectual and physical activity in school life by encouraging sport in school activities etc.[27]

In 2007, the Lisbon Treaty introduces sports within the categories and fields of competence of the EU. Therefore, according to art. 6 of the Treaty on The Functioning of the European Union[28] (TFUE), the Union shall have competence to carry out actions to support, coordinate or supplement the actions of the Member States. The areas of such action shall, at European level, be:

(a) protection and improvement of human health;
(b) industry;
(c) culture;
(d) tourism;
(e) education, vocational training, youth and **sport**;
(f) civil protection;
(g) administrative cooperation.

Title XII - Education, Vocational Training, Youth and Sport provides, in **article 165 TFUE that the Union shall contribute to the promotion of European sporting issues, while taking account of the specific nature of sport, its structures based on voluntary activity and its social and educational function.** Union action shall be aimed at developing the European dimension in sport, by promoting fairness and openness in sporting competitions and cooperation between bodies responsible for sports, and by protecting the physical and moral integrity of sportsmen and sportswomen, especially the youngest sportsmen and sportswomen.

The importance of sports in achieving the objectives set forth at EU level, among which resides the free movement of persons[29], is obvious, furthermore taking into consideration that, according to the European Court of Justice in Luxemburg[30], professional athletes are considered workers in terms of EU law and are therefore provided with all rights that occur from this quality.

Olympic Charter in force as from 8 July 2011 provides the Fundamental Principles of Olympics:

1. Olympics is a philosophy of life, exalting and combining in a balanced whole the qualities of body, will and mind. Blending sport with culture and education, Olympism seeks to create a way of life based on the joy of effort, the educational value of good example, social responsibility and respect for universal fundamental ethical principles.
2. The goal of Olympics is to place sport at the service of the harmonious development of humankind, with a view to promoting a peaceful society concerned with the preservation of human dignity.
3. The Olympic Movement is the concerted, organized, universal and permanent action, carried out under the supreme authority of the IOC, of all individuals and entities who are inspired by the values of Olympics. It covers the five continents. It reaches its peak with the bringing together of the world's athletes at the great sports festival, the Olympic Games. Its symbol is five interlaced rings.
4. **The practice of sport is a fundamental right**. Every individual must have the possibility of practicing sport, without discrimination of any kind and in the Olympic spirit, which requires mutual understanding with a spirit of friendship, solidarity and fair play.
5. Recognizing that sport occurs within the framework of society,

sports organizations within the Olympic Movement shall have the rights and obligations of autonomy, which include freely establishing and controlling the rules of sport, determining the structure and governance of their organizations, enjoying the right of elections free from any outside influence and the responsibility for ensuring that principles of good governance be applied.

6. Any form of discrimination with regard to a country or a person on grounds of race, religion, politics, gender or otherwise is incompatible with belonging to the Olympic Movement.

7. Belonging to the Olympic Movement requires compliance with the Olympic Charter and recognition by the IOC.

## Closing Statements

The purpose of this article was to describe the importance of the role attributed to sports in contemporary society. Our initiative can contribute to a more concrete and circumstantial legalization of the sporting domain, by using the protection and guarantee instruments that are particular to fundamental rights.

Sport is a growing social and economic phenomenon which makes an important contribution to the European Union's strategic objectives of solidarity and prosperity. The Olympic ideal of developing sport to promote peace and understanding among nations and cultures as well as the education of young people were born in Europe and have been fostered by the International and the European Olympic Committees. Sport attracts European citizens, with a majority of people taking part in sporting activities on a regular basis. It generates important values such as team spirit, solidarity, tolerance and fair play, contributing to personal development and fulfillment. It promotes the active contribution of EU citizens to society and thereby helps to foster active citizenship. The Commission acknowledges the essential role of sport in European society, in particular when it needs to bring itself closer to citizens and to tackle issues that matter directly to them. In addition, the United Nations holds that "sport is about participation. It is about inclusion and citizenship. Sport brings individuals and communities together, highlighting commonalties and bridging cultural and ethnic divide.[31] However, sport is also confronted with new threats and challenges which have emerged in European society, such as commercial pressure, exploitation of young players, doping, racism, violence, corruption and money laundering. (White Paper on Sport, Introduction, par. 1-3).

In this context we find it necessary to underline the following: "*The case law of the European courts and decisions of the European Commission show that the specificity of sport has been recognized and taken into account. They also provide guidance on how EU law applies to sport. In line with established case law, the specificity of sport will continue to be recognized, but it cannot be construed so as to justify a general exemption from the application of EU law.*"[32]

# References

1) *Practicing sports as a fundamental right* by Voicu A.V, Fuerea A, Visoiu D.F, Sustaq Z.D, Bocsa M. I presented at the 17th International Sports Law Congress IASL 2011 in Moscow, 27-30 September 2011.
2), 3) Mărgineanu Nicolae, *Psihologia persoanei* (The Psychology of the Person), Editura Ştiinţifică., Bucureşti, 1999
4) Johns Gary, *Comportamant organizaţional (Organizational Behaviour)*, Editura Economică, Bucureşti. 1996
5) Faverge, J. M., *Introduction a la Psychologie professionnelle*, Presses Univ. de Bruxelles, 1976.
6) History of the European Sport Charter
   http://www.coe.int/t/dg4/sport/sportineurope/charter_en.asp
7) http://www.coe.int/t/dg4/sport/sportineurope/charter_en.asp
8), 9), 17), 31) Report from the United Nations Inter-Agency Task Force of Sport for Development and Peace, 2003,
   http://www.unep.org/sport_env/documents/taskforce_report.pdf
10) Niciu, M. I., *Drept internaţional public*, (International Public Law), Editura

SERVOSAT, Arad, 1997

11) Universal Declaration of Human Rights of December 10th, 1948 – issued by The General Assembly of the United Nations, published in the Brochure of December 10th, 1948.

12) Petre Andrei, *Filosofia valorii* (The Philosophy of Value), Editura Polirom, Iaşi, 1997

13) Prutianu Ştefan, Tratat de comunicare şi negociere îin afaceri (Business Communication and Negotiation Treaty), Editura Polirom, Iaşi, 2008

14) Martine Fournier, (*Coaches and communication – interview with Philippe Meirieu*), in Philippe Cabin, Jean-Francois Dortier (coord.), „Comunicarea" (Communication), Editura Polirom, 20010 (Collegium collection), Iaşi, 2010

15) Elisabeth Noelle-Neumann, „Spirala Tăcerii. Opinia publică – invelişul nostru social" (*The spiral of silence. A theory of public opinion – Our social skin*), Editura Comunicare.ro., Bucuresti, 2004.

16) Sylvain Allemand, *Pentru o coabitare culturală – interviu cu Dominique Wolton (For a cultural ... cohabitation – interview with Dominique Wolton)*, in Philippe Cabin, Jean-Francois Dortier (coord.), „Communication", Editura Polirom, 2010 (Collegium collection), Iaşi, 2010

18) Maria Voinea, Carmen Bulzan, *Sociologia drepturilor omului (Human rights sociology)*, Universitatea din Bucureşti, 2004, ebooks.unibuc.ro/Sociologie/voinea/1.htm

19), 22), 24) Dănişor Gheorghe, Filosofia drepturilor omului (Human rights philosophy), Editura Universul Juridic, Bucureşti, 2011

20), 21), 23) Kidd Bruce, Donnely Peter, Human Rights in Sports, p 5-6, bublished by SAGE, http://www.sagepublications.com/

25), 32) The European Union's White Paper on Sport

26) Augustin Fuerea, „*Manualul Uniunii Europene*"(The European Union Manual), 5th edition, revised and addended, according to the Treaty of Lisbon (2007/2009), Editura Universul Juridic, Bucureşti, 2011 , Annex II.

27) Decision no. 291/2003/EC of the European Parliament and of the Council, of 6 February 2003, establishing the European Year of Education through Sport 2004.

28) Consolidated version (JOUE C 83/120, 30.3.2010).

29) Augustin Fuerea, „*Dreptul comunitar al afacerilor*" (Community Business Law), 2nd edition, revised and addended, Editura Universul Juridic, Bucureşti, 2006, p. 104.

30) Bosman Case (CJE Decision of December 15th 1995, Case no. C-415/1993, Royal Belgian Football Association (ASBL), Royal Club Liéegeois SA and European Football Association Union (UEFA) c. Jean-Marc Bosman).

# Proposals for Improving the Process of Litigation and Mediation of Sports in the "Common Law" and "Lex Sportiva" of the Romanian Law System

ALEXANDRU VIRGIL VOICU*

*It is a well known fact that the legality areas in Sport are the following: the State Order, the Sports Field, and the International Sports Structures, in which of course, we include the Court of Sport Arbitration at Lausanne. The dynamics of Sports development, in all its aspects, including the economics, must also respect the legality which depends on the legal system in which it works, becoming more and more Global. In this paper some aspects of the juridicisation of sports activities in Romania, a member of the European Union, are presented.*

Key word: Romanian legal framework, sports activity, litigation, arbitration, mediation

## General Considerations Regarding the Approached Thematic

It has been a year since we published a work entitled "Issues of the legal framework for sport management in Romania"[1]. We argued then, and we still stand by this statement that the "law of sports" is an integrating part and object of research both of the science of law and of the science of sports. Moreover both sciences aim at what we call today *The Legal Dimension of Ethics and Practices in Sports.*[2]

Traditionally, in the general theory of law, there is a distinction between the norms of *substantial law* and *procedural law*. In the judicial terminology

---

* Attorney, Professor at the Babes-Bolyai University Cluj-Napoca, Faculty of Physical Education and Sports, alexvirgilweisz@yahoo.com

it is considered that the „science of law" only refers to the domain or the category of norms of substantial (material) law. The term „judicial science" includes both the norms of *material law* and of *procedural law,* moreover the activities and institutions from the domain of law, for example, the assembly of the institutions and activities connected to the elaboration and application or enforcement of law. Subsequently, as opposed to the term „*law*", the term „*judicial*" has a larger meaning – „judicial" being a complex phenomenon, objectively functioning on a social canvass (reflecting the social aspects of human existence). In fact on this account the necessity of the judicialization of sport activities is invoked. It is a known fact that sports, in its integrality has become a notable social-economic phenomena.

The nucleus of a human society can consist of nothing but the normative behavioral order – we subject ourselves to certain norms deriving from formal law. In the category of formal law sources we also include certain normative acts issued by organisms or non-governmental organizations which contain sports as their object of activity. The validity of the norms (validity meaning the required quality of the norm in order to satisfy the necessary conditions to produce the legal- effects of their authors), however, their specific way of existence is not exclusively determined by this formal criteria of expressing them in a way accepted as source of law. This validity results from the combination of three elements: formality, effectiveness and legitimacy.

In the modern theory of law it is considered that "the formal validity of judicial norms leads to the presumption of legitimacy and effectiveness, constituting a decisive element for the occurrence of effects desired by the norm in question"[3]. Thus, even acts with generic normative character, issued by organisms or non-governmental organizations –such as associations, foundations, sport clubs, the Romanian Olympic and Sports Committee, companies, cults, etc. are sources of law. The organization and activity of these organisms or non-governmental organizations are performed through their normative acts – articles of incorporation, statutes, regulations etc., issued on the basis and with the obedience of particular laws or other governmental normative acts. When the acts of non-governmental organizations are accepted by governmental authorities – gaining judicial power, they become legal norms.[4)]

We consider, that at least tangentially, we must refer to the rules of social cohabitation in their quality of being the formal source of law. Thus, we must emphasize the importance of moral, ethical, professional technical norms, etc., which constitute the components of deontological norms – also benchmarks of behavioral conduct in sports activities. *Deontological norms* or *professional deontology* is formed in time, these are not the immediate creations of an organization, but are formed gradually. At a given time these can be collected and appropriated by an active manner through a given instruction, registered to a given professional status. The importance of these deontological norms is also revealed by the fact that they can constitute in given situations and limitations, similarly to the norms of customary law, indirect and subsidiary sources of law. This only occurs when the law explicitly refers to such regulations. When we are referring to the practical ethics of deontology of sports, we also have to refer to the aspects of the moral profile of these. In some cases, when professional conscience is in disagreement with the imperatives of professional responsibilities, (as part of social responsibilities) conflicting states can be generated between professional performance and normativity of judicial conscience.

Athletes, who are indisputably opinion leaders – must serve the interests of the city-state (polis)-and be good citizens. Being in conformity with the existence of a "global state" in which we *actually* and *rightfully* live, the accepting of the phrase "good citizen" must cover the quality of interlocutor valid in the material, spiritual and judicial world of the immense –city-state (polis) (global society). It is true that cultural cohabitation with an accent on positive values of sports assumes the latter's connection to judicial culture as part of general culture. Thus, judicial culture differs from community to community, just like in a community there are differences between groups of people and individuals.[5)]

Deontological norms determine a minimum of specific morals when exercising a profession[6)]. In our case we are referring to both sports activities as well as to the nature of the professional aspect (magistracy, arbitration, mediation) which is preoccupied by judiciaization of the social-economic phenomena we are referring to.

Thus, "the law of a state reveals itself not in the form of an arithmetic sum of the totality of judicial norms, but more like the ensemble of these, organized and structured in a system based on certain principles, following a certain finality"[7], giving -certitude to the forms of social control. Therefore, the finality of law becomes consubstantial with the finality of human condition and of society.

## The Reform of the Law System in Romania and its Consequences on the Level of Resolving Sporting Litigations

It is a known fact that until recent, sport was judicialized within three areas: state order, the area of the sports field and the area of sports structures and organizations (international and national).

As of now, the reform of the law system in Romania imposes the reconsideration of the legal areas of sports and the methods of law enforcement within these – in account with established constitutional principles in fundamental law of Romania.[8] [art. 20[9]; art. 21[10]; art. 49, para. (1), (3), (4), (5)[11]; art. 148, para. (2)[12]][13]. Art. 20 of the Constitution must be understood on the level that it was sufficiently argumented that the right to practice sport must be promoted as a fundamental human right.

Regarding what we stated in our paper, footnote 15, in paper no.: „In 2007, the Lisbon Treaty introduces sports within the categories and fields of competence of the EU. Therefore, according to art. 6 of the Treaty on The Functioning of the European Union (TFUE), the Union shall have competence to carry out actions to support, coordinate or supplement the actions of the Member States. The areas of such action shall, at European level, be: (a) protection and improvement of human health; (b) industry; (c) culture; (d) tourism; (e) education, vocational training, youth and **sport**; (f) civil protection; (g) administrative cooperation. Title XII - Education, Vocational Training, Youth and **Sport** provides, in article 165 TFUE that **the Union shall contribute to the promotion of European sporting issues, while taking account of the specific nature of sport, its structures based on**

**voluntary activity and its social and educational function**. Union action shall be aimed at developing the European dimension in sport, by promoting fairness and openness in sporting competitions and cooperation between bodies responsible for sports, and by protecting the physical and moral integrity of sportsmen and sportswomen, especially the youngest sportsmen and sportswomen". Also in this context is justified the White Paper on Sports' judicial power, which came into force on 12.01. 2009 – the date of coming into force of the Lisbon Treaty. The Commission acknowledges the essential role of sport in European society, in particular when it needs to bring itself closer to citizens and to tackle issues that matter directly to them. In addition, the United Nations holds that "sport is about participation. It is about inclusion and citizenship. Sport brings individuals and communities together, highlighting commonalties and bridging cultural and ethnic divide.[15] However, sport is also confronted with new threats and challenges which have emerged in European society, such as commercial pressure, exploitation of young players, doping, racism, violence, corruption and money laundering. (White Paper on Sport, Introduction, par. 1-3). In this context we find it necessary to underline the following: *"The case law of the European courts and decisions of the European Commission show that the specificity of sport has been recognized and taken into account. They also provide guidance on how EU law applies to sport. In line with established case law, the specificity of sport will continue to be recognized, but it cannot be construed so as to justify a general exemption from the application of EU law."*[14]

In this manner we are also guided by the new stipulations of the New Civil Code, and the New Civil Procedural Code of Romania.

Civil Code: **Art. 3 General application of the Civil Code**- the dispositions of the present code are applicable also to the relations between professionals, and to any other relations between them and any other subject of the civil law. (2) All who exploit an enterprise are considered professionals. (3) The exploitation of an enterprise is constituted by the systematic exercise, by one or more individual, of an organized activity which consists in the production, administration or alienation of goods or services, whether having or not having a lucrative purpose. **Art. 4 Prioritized application of international**

**treaties regarding human rights** – (1) in the domains regulated by the present code, the stipulations regarding the rights and freedom of humans will be interpreted and applied in concordance with the Constitution, the Universal Declaration of Human Rights, pacts and other treaties of which Romania is a part of. (2) If there are disagreements between the pacts and treaties regarding fundamental human rights, of which Romania is a part of and the present Code, international regulations have priority, except the case in which the present code has more favorable dispositions. **Art. 5 Prioritized application of European Union law** – In the domains regulated by the present code, the norms of the European Union apply in a prior manner, regardless of the quality or the status of the parties.

Civil procedural code: **Art. 2 The General applicability of the civil procedural code** – (1) The Dispositions of the present procedural code constitute the common law procedure in civil matter. (2) Also, the dispositions of present code apply to other matters as well, to the extent that the laws that govern them do not contain contrary dispositions.**Art.3 Prioritized application of international treaties regarding human rights** - (1) in the domains regulated by the present code, dispositions regarding the rights and freedom of humans will be interpreted and applied in concordance with the Constitution, the Universal Declaration of Human Rights, pacts and other treaties of which Romania is a part of. (2) If there are disagreements between the pacts and treaties regarding fundamental human rights, of which Romania is a part of, and the present Code, international regulations have priority, except the cases in which the present code has more favorable dispositions. **Art. 4 Prioritized application of European Union law** – In the domains regulated by the present code, the norms of the European Union apply in a prior manner, regardless of the quality or the status of the parties.

The new Civil Code has not modernized the provisions of the Civil Code from 1864, but also unified the civil legislation with the commercial one. Thus, at the coming into force of the New Civil Code, the application of the Commercial Code ceases its applicability; the new regulation however contains a series of stipulations regarding professionals and enterprises, notions which include the activities of tradesmen. In the New Civil Code all those are considered professionals who exploit an enterprise. Exploitation of an enterprise means the systematic exercise by one or more individuals of an organized activity which consists in the following: production, administration, or alienation of goods or services, which naturally also include sporting services (n. ns.) it can (the enterprise) have or not have a lucrative purpose [art. 3, paragraph (3) C.civ.].

We also agree with the statement according to which the instrumentalization of law, its transformation into a political instrument can be a real danger towards the state of law- but the dangers threatening in present circumstances (legislative inflation, excess of normativism as a tendency of self-destruction, the possibility of separation and aggravation of the conflict between the values of public order and state values in the process of the application of the law) the existence of the state of law[15], must not alter the normativity of law. Thus, law regarded as a normative phenomenon should represent the activity of realization of law in an ample social phenomenon such as sports. The judicial safety of the participants at such activities should be promoted, also influencing the behavior, in the basis of value requirements which indeed regard the values of law and the positive values of sports – moreover in the actual situation of excessive commercialization of sports and its becoming of an excessive instrument of political manipulation[16] (which can bring to the legitimacy of illicit behavior on the "sport ground" and in connection to it). Also, in this context, the utility of the above argumentation must be specified. Admitting the fact that sports law constituted as a distinct branch of law (also) in the Romanian law system, we will be able to "intensify the task of scientific research both in general theory as well as in departmental knowledge". In conditions of globalization, "jurists cannot afford the luxury of approaching the issue strictly from a local perspective".[17] Both on quantitative and on qualitative levels the economic domain of sports is characterized by dynamicity – this domain transgressed economic crises better than the media. The dynamicity of sports economy is based on the new tendencies of present-day society: reduction of working hours, the use of activities from the spare time in order to create "good spirits" through practicing and watching sports activities, taking care of one's exterior aspect (look), internationalizing of fashion and tastes (trend) etc. Economics has been present in sports for a long time. Sports cannot be protected from financial interference. Sports should be regarded as being part of market economy. Sports is commercialized, sports is transformed into merchandise. A sports economy includes "sports occupations" (in Classification of Occupations in Romania) and "classes of economic sport activities" (in Classification of Economic Activities in Romania), t as well as "sport structures" their object being sports activities. Judicial science has to be in conformity with the other social sciences – it doesn't have an exclusive competence regarding judicial truth, but has to recognize the aspects of "incidental competence". The science of law needs inter- and multidisciplinary approaches, especially with the science of sports. In our case, the enforcement of law, in relation to all aspects regarding judicial security of all the participants in sports activities, claims the consideration of the statute of a branch of law and judicial science as a branch of *sports law*.

By now in Romania too, it is unanimously accepted that sports activities, practice of sports are domains in which we seldom face injuries, mostly caused by accidents. In the lack of special regulations, the judicial consequences of these accidents are resolved through the principles of common law. In damage control, triggered by injuring, the clause of the victim's consent is frequently invoked, as being the cause of exoneration from liability. Thus sport activity is susceptible to a series of risks, which previously are known by the participants and to which the victims-co-participants, supposedly adhered – "the player's consent to the sport risk is manifested through his/her presence in the premises of the stadium"[18]. In this case, the author of an illicit and culpable act, causing physical damage cannot successfully invoke in his defense the consent of the victim, constituted in our case as a clause of un-liability, unless all the compulsory norms for the participants - athletes, coaches,[19] referees, audiences, organizers likewise included – have been respected.,. The risks to which participants of sports activities can be exposed can primarily, have, a number of causes, including an illicit conduct materialized by exceeding the limits of sport regulations; imprudence, negligence, deficiencies in organizing as well as "the more or less dangerous character of the sport competition"[20] etc. Same as the norms of law, the game's regulations (understood as norms which regulate the course of sports activities in the integrity of its forms of organization), should satisfy the requirements of protecting the subjective rights of the participants, and not in the least, to offer the guarantee that these activities won't disrupt the order and the laws of social cohabitation. The race for the result, record, or other satisfaction sports can offer, even on a non-professional level,, can determine illicit conducts with a higher or lower social danger.

Furthermore, criminal liability would prevent and eliminate many illicit conducts from the sports ground. The following was stated in the doctrine: "some restrains of the magistrates of the Public Ministry are not understandable, in cases, quite rare, in which their duty imposes them ex officio to start a criminal investigation when a crime was committed".[21] The athlete should not have immunity from prosecution only because he committed a crime during the exercise of a sport because he/ was already about to be sanctioned by the referee or the competent organisms of the association or federation in question[22]. We must admit that in principle, violence exercised by an athlete over another athlete (active participant in the competition, called opponent) can be by nature the constitutive element of a crime (defined as the ensemble of specific characteristics, typical and essential for the object, the subject, the objective side and the subjective side of the crime, included in the hypotheses of the norms of incrimination), "even though it is hard to differentiate, due to the tension and the stake of the game, between intentional and unintended gestures"[23] – "according to some people, the sanction for violating the game's regulations can only be dictated by the referee. In the present this thesis is unanimously rejected, "because penal judgment is in no way connected to the decisions or the lack of the decisions of the referee".[24] The criminal process' role is to protect public order, the intervention of the referee having a different role, fact which "does not mean that penal justice in the course of exercising its duty cannot or must not consider the referee's decision as being a part of its judgment".[25] In other words the judge who has to apply penal law "in principle will be able to admit the existence of a crime even when all the rules of the game have been followed, in the meantime can deny the existence of illicit behavior even if the rules of the game have been violated". The rules of the game are included both in the proper regulations of the game and in the rules of the organization. These, besides the fact that contain "precaution rules"[26], also aim to assure fairness of sports, equal treatment in the unfolding of the game, evaluation of the game, etc. According to the theory of risk, these cannot contain responsibility, due diligence of the athlete towards the participants in the game". We can and we must admit that the general principle "neminem leadere" is normally integrated in the rule (of security) of the game. But, even though, some courts (we are talking about the courts of the state cited - n.ns - A.V.) have considered that the violation of the game's rules in a manner that it causes serious injuries to an opponent, doesn't mean that the author has committed a felony. Practically, the instance in which it is ascertained that the incriminating behavior is in conformity with the rules of the game, in extremely rare cases, it falls into penal jurisdiction.[27]

After a brief analysis of the problematic of criminal liability in sports activities, from a different angle that of the foreign doctrine and jurisprudence, next we will be making a short analysis to see if the athlete–breaking judicial norms through his actions is liable, and at the same time analyzing his to distinguish the ethical and social value of his actions. Our starting point will be the outstanding psychological state of the athlete in the competition (it is a known fact that before and in the course of the contest his nervous system is subject to changes). The question was raised: to what measure do these changes alter the personality of the athlete in the course of the contest? With the occasion of the Olympic Games, London edition – 1948 researches were initiated on athletes from an anatomic-physiological viewpoint and also their nervous system and endocrine system was analyzed. Amongst other things it was proved that strong emotional states "do not alter bio-psychological moral functions from a judicial viewpoint, the athlete has the perception of ethical and social value of his acts and in the meantime has the possibility to appreciate the motives which stimulate or withhold him from an activity, moreover through the recurrence of these emotions the athlete can adjust these feelings and after a longer period of time can even restrain them– "any behavior is a social behavior before everything else, which has to fit into the formulas or obstacles which characterize the natural background in which it is produced.[28] So it is considered that athletes are in a state of liability, being responsible for their actions on the sports field. In case their actions surpass the limits of (sports) regulations, they become crimes (or civil misdemeanors). If by liability we mean a natural bio-psychological condition of humans in general and considering what we said before that this condition of liability can be assembled in the athlete, we are going to start a short analysis of the second condition of responsibility, precisely the condition of culpability. This time as well, just as with liability, we are able to give an affirmative answer, in the case of the athlete who through his actions which break judicial norms is culpable for these deeds. This viewpoint can certainly be contradicted "with the argument that society doesn't have the right to punish something that is tolerated without any reactions to happen right in front of their eyes", moreover, they encourage sports activities. We line up to the appreciation that this point of view is completely wrong, since the government tolerates boxing, thus permits punching, even though the government through its specialized organisms permits these blows in a restrictive manner, limited by regulations, limitation which certainly excludes any punches of tragic outcome, and does not allow any kind of hits which would have unforeseen consequences, that could end with the death of the victim or the damaging of his physical integrity. Indisputably hitting in sports, where it is permitted, for e.g., boxing, in an objective manner falls under the jurisdiction of criminal law, but the fact that this hitting is admitted by some sports, implicitly governmental, and social regulations (elaborated by the sports community which proved its legality through this legitimacy also), does not represent a social danger, does not violate the norms of law. Thus, the athlete is culpable only when he breaks the rules of the sport in question. It is normal to ask: who is going to establish the athlete's culpability? The referee of the game or the magistrates-? Just as it has already been pointed out, the judge will -determine- the culpability or the lack of culpability, having in mind the referee's notice and opinion, and using his own intimate beliefs. Under no circumstances will the referees be the only competent authority to determine whether the rules of the game have been followed or not. Tackles in rugby, driving a car, hitting in boxing or karate, target shooting, will always be conscious activities; only the operation through which the activity in question is executed, the means of the execution of the activity is automatized. In other words, the athlete, the individual, through automatization of motoric customs of the sports in question (same as the specific accommodations of any profession), does not exclude the process of thinking from the execution of the entire movement, but only removes the special attention he should have over the secondary elements of the entire activity. We consider that this argumentation concludes the same state of culpability each time the athlete finds him/herself outside the regulations of sports.

In conclusion, we can state that the athlete in his activity is responsible, meaning he/ is liable and culpable, each time he breaks sport regulations, action through which determines a series of /damages, causing the opponent personal injury. In such cases the exception of no liability, caused by the alteration of bio-psychological functions, cannot be invoked, because the athlete obligatorily undergoes a complex medical control, which is semestrial and in some sports disciplines happens before each competition. What was shown above has not covered all the hypotheses in which an illicit act on the sports ground can be incriminated as an infraction. Criminal law incriminates other illicit conducts, other than the ones from the group of infractions against personal safety (crimes against life, against physical integrity and of health) as actions with high social danger. This in fact is a natural thing, because sport activities "invaded" society, which on its turn also transmitted its values, some even negative. For example, such conducts can be: bribery, incriminated in art. 254, and 255 Penal code. Active subjects of bribery in the context of our social reality, can be the functionaries of commercial societies with private capital, the administrators and the censors (in conformity with art 254 paragraph 2 of the Penal code "functionary with controlling attributes", "acts committed by other functionaries" incriminated in art. 258 Pen. C., influence trafficking incriminated in art. 257 Pen. C,) just as professional football players hired with individual contracts at football clubs.

The specificity of sport, widely disputed in political documents as well as within sporting structures, is itself object to the actual doctrine of the law of sports. we fully agree with the assumption that "the issue of the specificity of sport is probably the most ambiguous and vague one in the field of the application of EU law on sport".[29] The same author claims that although sport organizations are recognized as autonomous, having their own sports regulation, they also operate in a legal environment and are subject to the rule of law. And although the EU has acknowledged the specificity and autonomy of sport throughout its case-law[30], it is known that unrestricted autonomy cannot exist in a vacuum and the rules adopted by sport organizations need to be compatible with the laws democratically adopted by societies.[31] Therefore, including sport in the competences of EU and developing a regulation of sports – even through soft law-, would surely balance the necessities of respecting the autonomy and specificity of sport, one the one hand and that of accomodating the sporting rules to the laws of societies, on the other. Amongst the future benefits of it, one can list the following: a better control by national governments of the European law, by replacing the informal meetings of the Sport Ministers' meetings with formal ones; a smoother development of the Sports Programs meant to promote the educational and social values of sport Europe-wide and to fight against negative phenomena in sport by the Commission, having a more thorough financial basis for it; the contribution of the European Parliament to the development of the legislative procedure related to Sports; a more interactive communication among Member States and among the interested parties (sport stakeholders); and last but not least, the opportunity of the European Court of Justice to interpret an existing rule of law or terms of great importance for Sport.[32]

In this spirit some courts in Romania – for example, the Supreme Court decided, by a definitive and irrevocable sentence that the FRF (Romanian Football Federation) won't be able to have a judicial competence in sport cases any longer, only if the parties involved require this specifically – moreover, the commissions of the FRF and LPF (Romanian Professional Football League) will not be able to make definitive and irrevocable decisions, and contractual litigations between clubs, players, coaches and agents will be trialed by civil courts. Also, FRF will not be able to issue any regulation articles without the permission of MYS (Ministry of Youth and Sport), and the actual regulation of the federation could be declared void. The decision is in relation with the lawsuit filed by the agent Mircea Moise, related to the case of the transfer of Claudiu Keșeru, from FC Bihor Oradea to FC Nantes, in 2003. Moise, then being the agent of Keșeru, was ignored at the transfer's implementation and he required from FRF one million euro compensation, because it issued out the "green card" without his permission (his commission fee included in the contract with the player being a substantial one). The player's agent lost at the federal commissions, then went to civil court, against FRF regulations. Bucharest Court of Appeal annulled the article from the regulations of FRF, which banned coaches, players, player's agents to address courts of justice and stipulated that decisions made by federal commissions were definitive and irrevocable on a national level! FRF contested the decision at the Supreme Court, where they lost. It should be specified that the sentence doesn't refer to neither disciplinary activities nor competition, bestowed by FRF laws, but only refers to the fact that the federation cannot function, outside legal boundaries, as an extraordinary court, banning individual's right to address justice invoking the specificity of competition activities.

Just as we pointed it out, civil law invaded almost in totality private law. Even an employment contract must respect the principles of the civil code, for example the principle of good-faith when signing a contract. Good-faith is a criteria in the process of appreciation of judicial acts and can be a judicial approach which is in opposition, in a given situation, to excessive formality which refers only to the exterior formality requirements of the act regarding its validity. Thus, the solemnity asked for stipulating a judicial act is not the sole criteria, but its appreciation must take into account the act of will of the parties, namely if these were made of good faith. Therefore in the evaluation of acts regarding their contents, good- or bad-faith is important both for the parties and also for the third parties. Bad-faith of one of the parties can draw its liability to the other party which was of good-faith. But the effects are important for the third parties as well, for example the fraud conveyed by both parties. The presumption of **good-faith** is a general presumption expressively specified in the new Civil Code paragraph (2) of the art. 14 and according to the legal text it is a relative presumption that can be overthrown with a contrary probe of bad-faith (deception, fraud etc.). This general presumption of good-faith in the matter of civil obligations and in the exercise of civil law is in fact the founding of judicial accounts built on good faith as opposed to disbelief or fraud. Through this regulation from the general part of the new Romanian Civil Code, the civil code enters the order of the majority of civil legislations[39] which consecrate the legal presumption of good-faith, until the contrary is proven. The general regulation of good-faith in contractual matters expresses the leading principle of contractual loyalty in conformity with the Principles of European law of contracts.[33]

The role of good-faith has a special regulation in the matter of negotiations, (even though expressing the obligation of good-faith in a negotiation is foreseen in art. 1710 new civ. C.) in art. 1183 par. (2) which shows that "the party who engages itself in the negotiation (of a contract) has the obligation to respect the exigence of good-faith", and the parties cannot limit or exclude this obligation.

The obligation of behaving in good-faith at the negotiation of the contract, or in the pre contractual phase, assumes the obligation of correct and complete informing of contractual clauses; the negotiating parties' interests should be taken into consideration excluding the unjust dominance of one of the parties; the equivalence of the exchange and the request for the promotion of the premises of a collaboration. Such regulations, more or less expressed with the same terms are to be found in German, Italian, French etc. law. In English law there isn't a general provision to state the obligation of good-faith, but in the theories of contracts there is an urgent necessity to respect what is called *"a duty to negotiate with care"*. Paragraphs (3) and (4) of the same article 1183 of NCC regulate the fact that it is contrary to good-faith the conduct of the parties which initiate and continue the negotiation without the intention to close the contract, or break the negotiations contrary to good-faith; for the caused damages the party which didn't respect the exigency of good-faith is accounted for covering the damages caused by the expenses of the negotiations or due to losing other offers. Breaking the negotiation in a brutal way, without cause or the determination of the negotiating partner regarding a clause which afterwards is broken, lead to the responsibility of the part with bad-faith, these solutions pronounced by French jurisprudence. The intention to harm, just like culpable negligence is being sanctioned. Usually, jurisprudence is based on objective data linked to the content of the contract to determine the fulfillment or the good-faith requirement. The general principle of good-faith thus has the tendency to ban any bad-faith in contractual relations.

We made these observations keeping in mind that the regulation of professional contracts (formerly called commercial) is the essence of civil law.

## About the Institution of Private Arbitration

The European institutions' urge to promote alternative means to solution judicial differences is constant and insistent, when considering real, evident advantages which such means procure to the partners in the situation of judicial litigations, but also the undeniably positive consequences coming from their use in the judicial system. Amongst the advantages we would enumerate most of all, the improvement of partnership and of a stable, promising judicial relationship between those who are in a latent or open judicial dispute, finding a proper solution in reference to their interests, avoiding the costs brought by statal law in the justice system, resolving the conflict with maximal celerity, eliminating judicial hazard, the unforeseen which many times is used by courts. We will enumerate from these means, some alternatives which can be benefic in sports litigations.

Recently in Romania, sports litigations can be subject to private arbitration. Private arbitration is regulated by the Procedural civil code (Book IV-a About arbitration) – common law in the matter of arbitration. Arbitration is alternative jurisdiction with a private character, through individuals charged by the litigating parties to form an arbitrary court, in order to put an end to the dispute between them, rights which the parties can have, by a definitive and obligatory decision.

Art. 542 pr. civ. C. specifies that the individuals in their full legal competence can agree to solve their litigations in an arbitrary manner, except those regarding civil status, the capacity of individuals, inheritance disputes, family relations, and the right over something the parties cannot have. The state and public authorities have the ability to close arbitrary conventions only if they are authorized through law or international conventions of which Romania is part of. Legal entities of public law which in their activity, and economic activities are capable of making arbitrary conventions, if it is not the case that law or their establishing or organizing act presumes something else. Individuals in their legal competence can resolve their patrimonial litigations.

According to art. 548 pr. civ. C. arbitrary convention is closed in writing, with the sanction of nullity. The condition of written form is fulfilled when resorting to arbitration was settled by correspondence, no matter the manner, or the change of procedural acts. In the case in which the arbitrary convention refers to a litigation regarding the transfer of the of property rights and/or the construction of any other real right over a tenement, the convention has to be made in an authentic notarial form, under the sanction of absolute nullity. Arbitrary convention can be made or in the form of arbitration clause, written in the principal contract or established in a separate convention, to which the principal contract refers to, or in the form of compromise. The existence of arbitrary convention can result also from a written agreement of the parties stipulated before the arbitrary court.

According to art., by arbitration clause, 550, the parties convene that the litigations stipulated in the contract or relating to it be solved in an arbitrary way, showing themselves, under the sanction of nullity, the modality of naming the judges. In the case of institutionalized arbitration it is sufficient to refer to the institution or the procedural regulations of the institution which organizes the arbitration. The validity of the arbitration clause is independent from the validity of the contract in which it was stipulated. In case of doubt, arbitration clause is interpreted in the sense of all misunderstandings which derive from the contract or from the judicial report to which it refers to. The aim of stipulating the arbitrary convention is to exclude the competence of the judicial court from the process of the litigation in question. In the case when the parties of a lawsuit closed an arbitrary convention, which is invoked by one of them in judicial court, it has to verify its own competence. Through *compromise* (art. 551) the parties convene that a litigation intervened between them and has to be solved by arbitration, showing, under the sanction of nullity, the object of litigation and the judges' names or modality of their designation in case of ad hoc arbitration. In case of institutionalized arbitration, if the parties haven't chosen judges and haven't agreed on the modality of their designation, this will be made according to the procedural rules of the arbitrary institution in question. Compromise can be made even if the litigation between the parties is under the ruling of another court.

The civil procedure's code makes important dispositions regarding the effects of arbitrary decisions, these having definitive judicial nature of court decisions (art. 606). The arbitrary decision vested with an enforcing power, constitutes writ of execution and is enforced same as a court decision (art. 368) pr. civ. C.), according to common law.

Taking in consideration the contractual character of these courts, the law establishes a special plan for the dissolution of these decisions which can only happen through annulment and for serious reasons, described in an explicit and restrictive manner in art. 608 pr. civ. C., at the request of the winning party, arbitrary decision is invested by enforceable formula through closing, being, as shown above, the first step towards writ of execution in case in which it wasn't made in good will.

In Romania there is also *Institutionalized arbitration.* As stated in art. 616 pr. civ. C. this institutionalized arbitration is the form of arbitrary jurisdiction which constitutes, and works in a permanent manner next to internal or international organizations or institutions or like a non-governmental organization with its own public interests, observing the rules, on its own regulations applicable in all litigations stipulated for solutioning with an arbitrary convention. The institutionalized arbitration activity doesn't have an economic character, and doesn't follow profit. In regulating and in the process of jurisdictional activities, institutionalized arbitration is autonomous from the institution which established it. The latter will determine the necessary measures to guarantee its autonomy.

## About the Institution of Mediation

As stated in the Law no. 192/2002 "mediation" was established in our country too. Mediation represents a modality of resolving the conflicts in an amicable manner, with the help of a third party specialized in the quality of mediator, in conditions of neutrality, impartiality, confidentiality and by the free consent of the parties (art. 1 paragraph 1). Methods of Dispute Resolution or Alternative Dispute Resolution are designated in the documents of the institutions of the European Union and are also widely used in the judicial terminology (acronym ADR).

If the law doesn't state any different, the parties - individuals and legal entities - are required to participate in informative sessions about the advantages of mediation, – and if the case, in an ongoing trial in front of a competent court – to find a solution to the conflicts of a civil, familial, penal matter, same as other matters, in the conditions foreseen by the law. Taking part in an informative session about the advantages of mediation is demonstrated by an informing certificate issued by the informing mediator. Should one of the parties refuse in writing to participate in an informative session, would not respond to the invitation described in art. 43 par. (1) or doesn't show up on the informing session, a report is made to be included in the file of court. The court will refute the calling to court as inadmissible in case of not fulfilling the obligation of the petitioner to participate in an informative session about mediation, before the introduction of calling to court, or after the start of the trial, until the deadline given in this scope by the court, for litigations described in art. 60^1 para. (1) lit. a)-f).

The provisions regarding the institution of mediation are applicable also to the conflicts from the domain of consumer affairs, in the case in which the consumer invokes the existence of a damage resulting from buying a faulty product or service; the contractual clauses or the warrants are left out of consideration; the existence of an abusive clause in the contract between consumer and economic agencies, or breaking any other laws in the domain of consumer affairs issued by national legislation or the European union. Strictly personal rights cannot be the object of mediation: such as rights regarding the status of a person, or any other rights which -according to the law- parties cannot have through convention or any other legal manner. In any convention regarding the rights the parties can have, these can introduce a clause of mediation, the validity of which is independent of the validity of the contract of which it is part of. According to art 60^1), in the litigations which can be - according to law - objects to mediation or any other alternative way of resolving conflicts, the parties and/or the interested party, ought to prove that they took part in the informing session regarding the advantages of mediation, in the following matters: a)In the domain of consumer affairs, when the consumer invokes the existence of a damage caused by buying a product or a faulty service, the contractual clauses or the warrants are left out of consideration, the existence of an abusive clause in the contract between consumer and economic agencies, or breaking any other laws in the domain of consumer affairs issued by national legislation or the European union; b) in the matter of family law, in the situations described in art. 64; c) in the domain of litigations regarding possession, delimitation of property boundaries, the displacement of borders, and any other litigations in reference to neighbors; d) in the domain of professional responsibility where it can be applied, also the *causes of malpractice*, if another procedure is not foreseen by special laws; e) in work litigations resulting from closing, executing, and termination of individual work-contracts; f) in civil litigations having the value under 50.000 lei, with the exception of litigations in which an executorial agreement was pronounced an insolvency procedure, the actions regarding the trade register office and the cases in which the parties choose to resort to the procedure described in art. 1.013-1.024 or the one described in art. 1.025-1.032 from the Law no. 134/2010, republished, with ulterior modifications; g) cases when penal responsibility is withdrawn due to the withdrawal of complaints or the parties make up, after the formulation of the complaint if the offender is known or has been identified, and the victim wants to express his/her will to participate in an informing session with the offender; if the victim refuses to take part in this session with the offender, the informing session takes place separately.

It is necessary that the organization of sport activities be formulated by the imperatives of efficiency and legality – in accordance with the social role highlighted in the White Paper on Sports (elaborated by the European Commission on July 11, 2007, which text was adopted by the European Parliament (May 8, 2008, Brussels), also citing art. 165 of the Lisbon Treaty – the reiteration in the Note of the Committee of Regions "The development of the European dimensions of sport" published in the Official Journal of the European Union C 9/74 in January 11 2012.

From the above reasoning we can conclude that it is necessary to elaborate a (new?) ideology of the law of sports and its realization in Romania. What is left is to harmonize the system of judicialization of sports activities and its belongings in concordance to the realization of the law of sports. It is necessary that the special law of physical education and sports be in conformity to what was proposed above and why not the National Commission of sport Discipline[34] to be modified into a true Arbitrary Court of Sports in Romania in the model of CAS in Lausanne. CAS is operating besides the International Olympic Committee. CAS in Romania will operate besides COSR. The promoting of mediation[35] of litigations by lex sportiva is also promoted. In the case of mediating the disputes from the domain of lex sportiva the rules of mediation will be adopted by the International Counsel of Sport Arbitration, both in the cases of national disputes and international ones.[36]

## References

1) Published in the Volume of the Conference „Dreptul sportului în Republica Belarus", Minsk, 2012, ISSN 2304-9626

2), 3) Voicu, A. V., *The Legal Dimension of Ethics in Sports*, The International Sports Law Journal, Volume 3-4, The Hague, 2005, p. 38-42; Márton Tonk, Tünde Nagy-Méhész, Virgil A. Voicu, - „*Autonomy" of Sport Policy and Sport Activities in the European Union: Connections between Human Rights and Sports* - in Acta Universitatis Sapientiae (The International Scientific Journal of Sapientia Hungarian University of Transylvania). Series: European and Regional Studies, ISSN 2066-639X , Vol. I., pp. 34-42, 2009

4) Ceterchi, I., Craiovean, I., „Introducere în teoria generală a dreptului", Editura ALL, București, 1998

5) Mihăilă, A., „Sociologia dreptului", Editura Hamangiu, Bucureș.ti, 2010

6) Craiovan, I., „Tratat de Teoria generală a dreptului", Ediția a II-a . revăzută și adăugită, Ed. S.C. Universul Juridic S.R.L., București, 2009

7) Craiovan, I., „Tratat de teoria generală a dreptului", Ediția a II-a, revăzută și adăugită, Editura Universul juridic, București, 2009

8)-12) Constitution of Romania of October 31st, 2003, issured by The Parliament of Romania, published in: The Official Gazette of Romania no. 767 of October 31st, 2003

13) 1. Voicu, A. V, Kis, R., *Arguments for Promoting the Right to Practice Sports as a Fundamental Right*, in „Efficiency of Legal Norms", Editura Hamangiu, 2012, București, p. 417-427; 2. Voicu, A. V., Fuerea, A., Sustac, Z., D., Bocsa, M. I., *Practicing of Sports - a Fundamental Human Right*, Intute, http://www.intute.ac.uk/, The International Sport Law Jurnal, The Hague, 2011, p.157-162; 3. Márton Tonk, Tünde Nagy-Méhész, Virgil A. Voicu, - *„Autonomy" of Sport Policy and Sport Activities in the European Union: Connections between Human Rights and Sports* - în Acta Universitatis Sapientiae (The International Scientific Journal of Sapientia Hungarian University of Transylvania). Seria: European and Regional Studies, ISSN 2066-639X , Vol. I., p. 34-42, 2009, Cluj-Napoca.

14) White Paper on Sport

15) Craiovan, I., „Tratat de Teoria generală a dreptului", Ediția a II – revăzută și adăugită, Editura Universul Juridic, București

16) Marțian, I., „Structura acțiunii politice", Editura Multimedia, Arad

17) Popa, N., „Teoria generală a dreptului", Ediția a III –a Editura C.H.Beck, București, 2008, p. 11, regarding Twining, W., „Globalization and Comparative Law" (cited from M.F. Popa, „Sistemul juridic englez. Tendințe actuale de evoluție", PHD thesis, 2008

18)-28) Voicu, A.V., „Răspunderea civilă delictuală cu privire la specială la activitatea sportivă", Editura Lumina Lex, București, 1999, p. 158, in reference to Gașpar, C., *Răspunderea civilă și asigurarea în accidentele sportive*, Paper „Legalitatea populară", nr. 6/1957

19) Ripert, G, Boulanger, J., „Traite de droit civil", tome II, Paris, 1957, p. 370: "Coaches are responsible for accidents happening to students during their supervision".

29), 31), 32) Panagiotopoulos, D „Sports Law. Lex Sportiva & Lex Olympica, Ant. N. Sakkoulas Publishers, Athens, 2011

30) Kis, R., *A sportolóok doppingügyekkel kapcsolatos emberi jogai az Európai Bíróság előtt és a sport szelleme: kizárják-e egymást?*, Master diploma paper, presented in February 2012 at the Babes-Bolyai University of Cluj-Napoca, Faculty of Law

33) Les principes contractuelles communes, Societatea de Legislație Comparată, art. 0:301, februarie 2008, Paris

34) 1.Voicu A. V., „A roman nemzeti sport valasztottbirosagarol (Alapitas, kompetenciak, szervezet es mukodes), Kalokagathia - Review of the Faculty of Physical Education and Sport Science - Semmelweis University Budapest, 2007, pp. 34-41; 2. Voicu, A. V., „Romania's Court of Sports Arbitration: Establishment, Competences, Organization and Functioning, Intute, - www.sportslaw.nl, The International Sports Law Journal, 2006, pp. 113-116;

35) Voicu, A.V., Matei, B., "Activitatea de mediere – posibil mijloc de soluționare a litigiilor din activitatea de educație fizică și sport", Universitatea Babeș-Bolyai, FEFS

36) Ian Blackshaw: Mediating Sports Disputes: National and International Perspectives T.M.C. Asser Press, 2002

# Sports Image Rights in the United States

JOHN WOLOHAN*

*The image rights of professional athletes, teams and organizations, if properly managed, can be worth millions of dollars. In fact, for most high profile athletes, endorsing products has become more lucrative then their professional playing contracts. As a result, it is not surprising, that athletes, teams and organizations carefully protect the value of their image. As a way of introducing "image rights," the paper begins by exploring the historical legal developments that lead to the creation of sports image rights, under common law, state statute, and federal legal principles. Next, the paperexplores the development of the modern right of publicity and appropriation and the legal theories behind the modern image rights. Finally, the paper identifies some of the defences available under the First Amendment of the United States Constitution.*

Key Word: Image Rights; First Amendment of United States' Constitution, Rights of Publicity

## Introduction

The image rights of athletes, teams and organizations, if properly managed, can be worth millions of dollars. In fact, for most high profile athletes, endorsing products or lending their name to them has become more lucrative then their professional playing contracts. A good example of the value of an athlete's image is Tiger Woods. In 2009, golfer Tiger Woods earned roughly $100 million more annually in endorsement income, than he did on the golf course. That all changed, however, on November 27, 2009,

---

* Professor of Sports Law in the David B. Falk College of Sport and Human Dynamics at Syracuse University

when Woods crashed his car crash outside his home. Following the crash, a series of news reports linking Woods to numerous extra material affairs came to light. His wife eventually divorced him and his public image as a family man was damaged forever. As a result, several sponsors, including Tag Heuer, Accenture, AT&T, Gatorade, Gillette, and *Golf Digest*, valued at around $35 million either stopped featuring him or dropped him outright.[1]

With so much money at stake, it is not surprising that athletes, teams and organizations carefully protect the value of their image. The only way they are truly able to protect the value of their image or name, however, is by controlling the use of the image. However, as we will see below, theability to control their image is not absolute.

The purpose of this paper is to examine what types of uses of another's image are permitted and which types are would be prohibited. As a way of introducing "image rights," the paper begins by exploring the historical legal developments that lead to the creation of sports image rights, under common law, state statute, and federal legal principles. The section will also look at the modern right of publicity and appropriation. Next, the paper examines the legal theories behind image rights. Finally, the paper identifies some of the defences available under the First Amendment of the United States Constitution.

## Historical Development of Image Rights

"Instantaneous photographs and newspaper enterprise have invaded the sacred precincts of private and domestic life; and numerous mechanical devices threaten to make good the prediction that what is whispered in the closet shall be proclaimed from the roof-tops. For years there has been a feeling that the law must afford some remedy for the unauthorized circulation of portraits of private persons; and the evil of the invasion of privacy by newspapers."[2]

---

1) Ben Spencer, **(April 4, 2011).** Bill for Pounds $82Million Tiger's Sex Romps; Loss of Sponsors hit Earnings. Daily Record, p. 11
2) Samuel Warren & Louis Brandeis, The Right of Privacy, *4 Harvard Law Review* 193

These words are as true today as they were in 1890 when they were first published by Samuel Warren and Louis Brandeis in their article entitled "The Right of Privacy." In the article, Warren and Brandeis outlined a legal theory that would guarantee individuals the right of privacy. The theory, which was unheard of at the time in the American judicial system, held that all private individuals had a basic right to be left alone.

Warren and Brandeis argued that the courts should recognize a right of privacy as a way to protect private individuals against the outrageous and unjustifiable infliction of mental distress caused by the press and advertisers.[3] In developing this new legal theory, Warren and Brandeis pieced together past American and English decisions based on defamation, invasion of property rights, and breach of contract, and argued that there was a broader legal theory entitled to separate recognition by the courts. Warren and Brandeis called the new legal theory "the right to privacy" and argued that it should "extend protection to the personal appearance, sayings, acts, and to personal relations, domestic or otherwise."[4] The general object of the new theory, therefore, was to protect the privacy rights of private citizens, and not prohibit the publication of legitimate news dealing with matters of public or general interest.

After the law review article was published, the New York courts were faced with a case: Mackenzie v. Soden Mineral Springs Co.[5]Morell Mackenzie, a prominent English physician, sought and won an injunction against the American manufacturer of "Soden Mineral Pastilles," which had misappropriated the testimonial and signature of the doctor to sell its product.[6] In issuing the injunction, the court held that using Mackenzie's name without his consent "as a guaranty of the merits of said medicinal preparation ... would produce injury to the plaintiff, in that the plaintiff would thereby suffer damage to his professional standing and income as a physician, and an infringement of his right to the sole use of his own name."[7]

---

(1890).

3) William Prosser, Privacy, *48 California Law Review* 383 (1960).

4) Warren & Brandeis, *Supra Note* 3 at 195.

5) Mackenzie v. Soden Mineral Springs Co., 18 N.Y.S. 240 (1891).

6) *Id.*

7) *Id.*, at 249.

Not every court in New York was willing to accept Warren and Brandeis' new theory however. In 1902, the Court of Appeals in Roberson v. Rochester Folding Box Company[8] held that a young woman, whose picturehad been used on flour advertisement without her consent could not recover damages based on a violation of her right to privacy. In finding that there was no such right recognized at common law, the court concluded that the injury was of a purely mental character, not physical, and that recognizing such a right would potentially flood the courts in lawsuits.[9] Perhaps most importantly, the court feared that due to the difficulty of determining a private from public figure, recognizing a right of privacy would restrict the First Amendment guarantees of freedom of the press.[10] In a strong dissent, one judge concluded that it was "inconceivable ... that ... this young woman must submit to mortifying notoriety" of being pictured in an advertisement without some form of legal protection.[11]

As a result of the public storm that followed the court's decision in Roberson, the New York State Legislature responded by amending the New York State Civil Rights Law to establish a statutory right to privacy. New York Civil Rights Law § 50 provides: "A person ... or corporation that uses for advertising purposes, or for the purposes of trade, the name, portrait or picture of any living person without having first obtained the written consent of such person ... is guilty of a misdemeanor."[12]

As a result, for the first time, the new law made it illegal for a person or corporation to use for advertising purposes, or for the purposes of trade, the name, portrait or picture of any living person without having first obtained the written consent of such person.[13] In addition, New York Civil Rights Law § 51 provides: "Any person whose name, portrait or picture is used within this state for advertising purposes or for the purposes of trade without the written consent first obtained ... may maintain an equitable

---

8) Roberson v Rochester Folding Box Co., 171 N.Y. 538, 64 N.E. 442 (1902).
9) *Id.*
10) *Id.*
11) *Id.*
12) N.Y. Civ. Rights Law, § 50.
13) N.Y. Sess. Laws 1903, ch.132 § 1. Amended in 1921, now cited as N.Y. Civ. Rights Law, § 50.

action ... against the person ... or corporation so using [his/her] name, portrait or picture, to prevent and restrain the use thereof; and may also sue and recover damages for any injuries sustained by reason of such use and if the defendant shall have knowingly used such person's name, portrait or picture in such manner as is ... declared to be unlawful by section fifty of this article, the jury, in its discretion, may award exemplary damages."[14] Thereby allowing individuals to recover civil damages under tort law, including injunctive relief, compensatory damages, and, if the defendant acted knowingly, exemplary damages.[15]

Three years after Roberson, the Supreme Court of Georgia was faced with a similar issue in Pavesich v. New England Life Insurance.[16]In an advertisement for life insurance, New England Life used a photo of Pavesich without his consent. In recognizing that Pavesich had a right of privacy, which the courts should protect against invasion, the Supreme Court of Georgia predicted "that the day will come that the American bar will marvel that a contrary view was ever entertained by judges of eminence and ability."[17]

## Image Rights and Celebrities

After New York codified the right of privacy and the Georgia Supreme Court found such a right in common law, it was not difficult for most courts in the country to concludethat privates citizens had a legally protected right of privacy. The issue, however, was not so clear for people in the sports and entertainment industry. Even after finding a right of privacy, the courts historically refused to recognize a celebrity's right of privacy. In support of this position, the court found that since college and professional athletes and celebrities had dedicated their life to the public, they had thereby waived their right of privacy.[18] The right of privacy, therefore,

---

14) N.Y. Civ. Rights Law, § 51.

15) N.Y. Sess. Laws 1903, ch.132 § 2. Amended in 1921, now cited as N.Y. Civ. Rights Law, § 51.

16) Pavesich v. New England Life Insurance, 122 Ga. 190, 50 S.E. 68 (1905).

17) Id.

18) Melville B. Nimmer, (1954). The Right of Publicity, 19 *Law and Contemporary Problems*

offered them little protection against commercial misappropriation.

A good example of this exclusion was the Fifth Circuit Court of Appeals decision in O'Brien v. Pabst Sales Company.[19] David O'Brien, a famous American college football player, tried to invoke a right of privacy against a brewery after the beer company used his photograph in uniform on calendars. In rejecting O'Brien's right of privacy argument, the court held that because O'Brien was a famous football player and had completely publicized his name and his pictures he had waived his right of privacy.[20]

The courts started recognizing the injustice of allowing others to profit off the image of athletes and other celebrities in commercial ventures in the 1950s andbegan to extend the rights of privacy. In order to protect athletes and other celebrities against commercial misappropriation, and prevent the unjust enrichment of others off a celebrity's reputation, the right of privacy was extended to include a "Right of Publicity" in *Haelan Laboratories, Inc. v. Topps Chewing Gum, Inc.*[21] Haelan, a chewing-gum company, entered into various contracts with professional baseball players, which provided the company the exclusive right to use the player's photograph in connection with the sales of its' chewing-gum. In addition, the contract also stated that the players agreed not to grant any other gum manufacturer a similar right during the terms of the contract. Topps, a rival chewing-gum manufacturer, knowing of Haelan's contracts, deliberately entered into contracts with various players to use the player's photograph in connection with the sales of Topps' gum. Topps claimed that their contracts were valid since the contract between Haelan and the player was no more than a release by the player, which give Haelan the right to use the photographs.

In rejecting Topps argument, Second Circuit Court of Appeals held that "in addition to and independent of that right of privacy, a man has a right in the publicity value of his photograph, i.e., the right to grant the exclusive privilege of publishing his picture,"[22] and that the licensees and assignees of that right could enforce the right against infringing third parties. This right,

---

*203*

19) O'Brien v. Pabst Sales Co., 124 F.2d 167 (1941).
20) *Id.*
21) *Haelan Laboratories, Inc. v. Topps Chewing Gum, Inc.*, 202 F.2d 866 (2nd. Cir. 1953).
22) *Id.*

the court held "might be called a right of publicity."23) It is common knowledge, the court held"that many prominent persons (especially actors and ball-players), far from having their feelings bruised through public exposure of their likenesses, would feel sorely deprived if they no longer received money for authorizing advertisements."24)


## The Modern Right of Publicity

Since the Second Circuit Court's decision in *Haelan Laboratories v. Topps,* the right of publicity has been acknowledged in most states either by common law or statute. Although the right of publicity is not uniformly applied by all the states, most states agree with the three goals behind theright's general purpose. "First, the right to publicity recognizes the economic value of an individual's identity. Second, the publicity right is an incentive for creativity, encouraging the production of entertaining and intellectual works. Finally, the right prevents unjust enrichment of those who usurp the identity of another."25)

Some States have even begun broaden the right of publicity by expanding the "traditional meaning of "name and likeness" to include such things as nicknames, drawings, celebrity look-alikes or by including characteristics such as vocal idiosyncrasies within a more general formulation of identity"26) For example, in Motschenbacher v. R.J. Reynolds Tobacco Co., R.J. Reynolds produced some television ads "utilizing a stock color photograph depicting several racing cars."27) The drivers in the cars were not visible in the photo, the cars had been altered, the numbers were changed and a spoiler was added upon which the company placed their product's name. In finding the ads violatedMotschenbacher's right of publicity, the Ninth Circuit Court of Appeals held that even though Motschenbacher's

---

23) *Id.*
24) *Id.*
25) Cardtoons, L.C. v. Major League Baseball Players Ass'n, 838 F. Supp 1501 (N.D. Okla. 1993).
26) Steven Clay, Starstruck: the overextension of celebrity publicity rights in state and federal courts, *79 Minnesota Law Review 485, 495* (1994).
27) Motschenbacher v. R.J. Reynolds Tobacco Co., 498 F.2d 821 (1974).

personal likeness was unrecognizable; his identity could still be inferred by the distinctive decorations on his car.[28]

Another example is Palmer v. Schonhorn Enterprises,[29] where Arnold Palmer, and other well-known professional golfers, sought an injunction to prevent the use of their names and biographical information in conjunction with and as part of a game. Palmer and the other golfers, who never consented to have their names or statistics used in the game, claimed that the use of their names was an invasion of their privacy and an unfair exploitation and commercialization of their names and reputations.[30] Schonhorn claimed that since the information contained in the profiles was readily obtainable public data and available to all, it should not be denied the privilege of reproducing that which is set forth in newspapers, magazine articles and other periodicals.

After acknowledging that Palmer was a celebrity who derived a substantial portion of his earnings from professional golf and the marketability of his name for endorsement purposes, the Superior Court of New Jersey held that there was little doubt that a person was entitled to relief when his name is used without his consent, either to advertise the defendant's product or to enhance the sale of an article. In particular, the court held that "the basic and underlying theory is that a person has the right to enjoy the fruits of his own industry free from unjustified interference."[31] Therefore even though "the publication of biographical data of a well-known figure does not per se constitute an invasion of privacy, the use of that data for the purpose of capitalizing upon the name by using it in connection with a commercial project other than the dissemination of news or articles or biographies does."[32]

---

28) *Id.*
29) Palmer v. Schonhorn Enterprises, 96 N.J. Super. 72; 232 A.2d 458 (1967).
30) *Id.*
31) *Id.*
32) *Id.*

## Legal Foundations– Rights of Privacy and Publicity

In examining the right of privacy and its' protections the courts have identified four distinct kinds of invasion of privacy. Although tied together by a common name, the four interests have almost nothing in common except that each represents an interference with an individual's right to privacy. The first type of privacy interest "intrusion upon an individual's seclusion or solitude, or into his or her private affairs" protects individuals from both the physical intrusion into their privacy and the unauthorized prying or spying on another. To be protected, the intrusion must be into a matter that was private and must be something that would be objectionable or offensive to a reasonable person. An example of which would include photographers peering into the windows of private homes and yards.[33]

The second type of privacy interest "public disclosure of embarrassing private facts about an individual" protects individuals from the public disclosure of private facts, that when made public would be objectionable or offensive to a reasonable person. The law does not protect the overly sensitive from all public disclosures. An example of this type of tort might be the publication of an athlete's income tax statement. An athlete's arrest record, however, because it is public record, not private, would be allowed.[34]

The third type of privacy interest "publicity which places an individual in a false light in the public eye" protects individuals from others falsely using their name or falsely accrediting statements to them. The law also protects the use of an individual's picture to illustrate a book or an article in which he or she has no reasonable connection. For example, if you used a photo of Tiger Woods for an article on drug use in professional basketball there is an obvious innuendo that the article applies to him, thereby placing him in a false light in the public eye. If however you used Woods' photo in an article on professional athletes who have extra marital affairs that would be fine.[35]

The forth type of privacy interest identified is "appropriation of an individual's name or likeness," protects individuals from the exploitation of

---

33) William Prosser, Privacy, *48 California Law Review 383* (1960).
34) *Id.*
35) *Id.*

their image for the benefit of another. It is this fourth type that the courts refer to as the right of publicity. In order to recover under this theory, an individual must first show that someone has appropriated his or her identity or name for some advantage, usually of a commercial nature.[36]

## Common Law Misappropriation

The courts have generally found that there are two forms of appropriation. The difference between the two is found not in the activity of the defendant, but in "the nature of the plaintiff's right and the nature of the resulting injury."[37] The first type of appropriation is the right of publicity, which is "in essence that the reaction of the public to name and likeness, which may be fortuitous or which may be managed or planned, endows the name and likeness of the person involved with commercially exploitable opportunities."[38] While the other type of appropriation, brings injury to the feelings, that concerns one's own peace of mind, and that is mental and subjective.[39]

The most common form of appropriation involves the use of a person's name or identity in the advertisement of another's products or services. In order to establish a cause of action for common law misappropriation in these situations, the courts have generally held that an individual must demonstrate the following four elements:

1) the defendant used the plaintiff's identity;
2) the appropriation of plaintiff's name or likeness provided the defendant some advantage, commercially or otherwise;
3) lack of consent; and
4) resulting injury.[40]

http://web.lexis-nexis.com/universe/document?_m=48e5ce13d56c8f8087b1d

---

36) *Id.*
37) J. Thomas McCarthy, (1992). *The Rights of Publicity and Privacy.* Clark Boardman Callaghan: Dearfield, IL.
38) Lugosi v. Universal Pictures, 25 Cal. 3d 813; 160 Cal. Rptr. 323; 603 P.2d 425 (1979).
39) Stilson v. Reader's Digest Assn., Inc., 28 Cal.App.3d 270, 273 (1972).
40) Eastwood v. Superior Court, 149 Cal. App. 3d 409, 198 Cal. Rptr. 342 (1983).

115868839a4&_ docnum=11&wchp=dGLbVtb-zSkVb&_md5=aa5d927627d9ad7fe
00dcd0104c6d1a7 - refpt_CA11

In determining whether there is a cause of action for common law misappropriation, one of the hardest questions for the court to answer is whether an individual's identity or likeness was even used. For example, in Newcombe v. Adolf Coors Co.,[41] the Ninth Circuit Court of Appeal was asked to determine whether a beer ad featuring an old time baseball game, showing a pitcher in a windup position misappropriated Newcombe's likeness. Newcombe was a former All Star and the only player in Major League Baseball history to ever win the Most Valuable Player Award, the Cy Young Award, and the Rookie of the Year Award. Even though the player's uniforms did not depict an actual team, and the background did not depict an actual stadium, the Ninth Circuit Court ruled that the player's windup was so distinctive that it made the identity of the player readily identifiable as Newcombe.[42]

Finally, it is important to note that while New York, California and some other states recognize a http://web.lexis-nexis.com/universe/document?_m= 48e5ce13d56c8f8087b1d115868839a4& _docnum=10&wchp=dGLbVtb-zSkVb&_ md5=08be11a0ab720129070cfc3d38447131 - refpt_CA4 common law cause of a ction for the misappropriation of a person's name, photograph, and likeness for commercial purposes, it is not the law in every state. In fact, there are sti ll a number of states that do not recognize a state action for a right of priva cy or common law misappropriation of an individual's name or likeness.

## Statutory Protections

In addition to the common law misappropriation, twenty states have legislatively recognized the right of publicity via statute. Those states include: Arizona, California, Florida, Illinois, Indiana,, Kentucky, Massachusetts, Nebraska, Nevada, New York, Ohio, Oklahoma, Pennsylvania, Rhode Island, Tennessee, Texas, Utah, Virginia, Washington and Wisconsin.[43] Once again,

---

41) Newcombe v. Adolf Coors Co., 157 F.3d 686 (9th Cir. 1998).
42) Id.
43) John Wolohan, (2010). Image Rights. In D. J. Cotton & J. T. Wolohan (Eds.), *Law for*

it must be noted that the protections afforded will vary from state to state, depending on the stature.[44] The two states that have been most active in protecting the right of publicity of individuals are New York and California.

## First Amendment of the United States Constitution

The First Amendment of the United State Constitution states that: "Congress shall make no law ... abridging the freedom of speech, or of the press ... ."[45] Since the intent of the First Amendment is to protect the dual freedoms of speech and the press, the courts will allow the "unauthorized use of an individual's name or likeness" when it is used for the "dissemination of ideas and information," or for other cultural purposes.[46]

The four main First Amendment arguments involving image rights are: transformative use; the newsworthiness doctrine; the incidental use exception; and parody defense.

### Transformative Use Defense

If the challenged work or use contains significant transformative elements or if the value of the work does not derive primarily from the celebrity's fame, the courts will allow the use of under the transformative use defense. The defense "poses what is essentially a balancing test between the First Amendment and the right of publicity."[47] "To determine whether a work is transformative, a court must inquire intowhether the celebrity likeness is one of the "raw materials" from which an original work is synthesized, or whether the depiction or imitation of the celebrity is the very sum and substance of the work in question. We ask, in other words, whether a

---

*recreation and sport managers* (5th Ed.). Dubuque, IA: Kendall/Hunt Publishing Co.
44) *Id.*
45) U.S. CONST. Amend. I.
46) J. Thomas McCarthy, *The Rights of Publicity and Privacy* (2003). Clark Boardman Callaghan: Dearfield, IL.
47) Keller v. Electronic Arts, 2010 U.S. Dist. LEXIS 10719; 38 Media L. Rep. 1353 (N.D. Cal., Feb. 8, 2010).

product containing a celebrity's likeness is so transformed that it has become primarily the defendant's own expression rather than the celebrity's likeness."48) If the court believes that distinctions exist, the First Amendment would bar right of publicity claims based on appropriation of the plaintiff's identity or likeness; if not, the claims are not barred.49)

An example ofthe transformative use defense is Keller v. Electronic Art.50) Sam Keller a former starting quarterback for the Arizona State University and University of Nebraska football teams sued Electronic Arts, Inc. (EA), the National Collegiate Athletics Association (NCAA) and the Collegiate Licensing Company (CLC) over the use of his image in EA's video game "NCAA Football."51) Keller alleges that, to make the games realistic, EA designs the virtual football players to resemble their real-life counterparts: they share the same jersey numbers, have similar physical characteristics and come from the same home state.52) Although EA omits the real-life athletes' names from "NCAA Football," Keller filed suit against EA claiming that its use of his likeness without his consent was in violation of California's statutory and common law rights of publicity.

EA asserts that Keller's right of publicity claim is barred by the First AmendmentTransformative Use Defense. In rejecting EA's defense, the court held that EA's depiction of Keller in "NCAA Football" was not sufficiently transformative to bar his California right of publicity claims as a matter of law.53) In support of this conclusion, the court noted that in the game, the quarterback for Arizona State University shares many of Keller's characteristics. Further, the game's setting is identical to where the public found Keller during his collegiate career: on the football field. As for EA's assertion that the video game, taken as a whole, contains transformative elements. The court held that such a broad view was not supported by precedent.54)

---

48) *Id.*
49) *Id.*
50) *Id.*
51) *Id.*
52) *Id.*
53) *Id.*
54) *Id.*

At the time this chapter was the Keller case was consolidated with a number of other lawsuits involving current and past college athletes in RE: Student-Athlete Name& Likeness Litigation, 763 F. Supp. 2d 1379 (2011).

## Newsworthiness Doctrine

The newsworthiness doctrine permits the media to use the unauthorized likeness of celebrities or anyone of interest in connection with a news item about the person. The definition of "news" has been given a broad reading and includes matters of public concern and interest. One example of how the doctrine relates to athletes and their image rights is Montana v. San Jose Mercury News.[55] Joe Montana a famous professional American football player brought a commercial misappropriation action against the San Jose Mercury News newspaper for reproducing his name, photograph, and likeness in poster form and selling it to the general public without his consent. In ruling that the newspaper had the right to use Montana's image, the California Court of Appeal held that the newspaper accounts of Montana's performance in two Super Bowls and four championships constituted publication of matters in the public interest and was therefore entitled to protection by the First Amendment of the United States Constitution.[56] In particular, the Court of Appeal held that Montana's name and likeness appeared in the posters for the same reason they appeared on the original newspaper pages: because he was a major player in contemporaneous newsworthy sports events and therefore may be republished in another medium, without the person's written consent.[57]

Another example of the interaction between the First Amendment and the right of publicity, and the only right of publicity case to reach the United States Supreme Court, is Zacchini v. Scripps-Howard Broadcasting Co.[58] In Zacchini, the United States Supreme Court was asked to determine whether a news broadcast of Hugo Zacchini's entire 15-second "human

---

55) Montana v. San Jose Mercury News, 40 Cal. Rptr. 2d 639 (1995).
56) *Id.*
57) *Id.*
58) Zacchini v. Scripps-Howard Broadcasting Co., 433 U.S. 562 (1977).

cannonball" act, in which he is shot from a cannon into a net some 200 feet away, was protected under copyright law. Scripps-Howard argued that the broadcast was privileged under the First Amendment, which allows "the press ... to report matters of legitimate public interest even though such reports might intrude on matters otherwise private."59) Zacchini, however, argued that Scripps-Howard appropriated his professional property by filming his entire act and displayed that film on television for the public to see and enjoy.

In overturning the Ohio Supreme Court, the United States Supreme Court held that even though the press "must be accorded broad latitude in its choice of how much it presents of each story or incident, and of the emphasis to be given to such presentation," the broadcast of Zacchini's entire act posed a substantial threat to the economic value of that performance. The First Amendment, the court ruled, does not immunize the media when they broadcast a performer's entire act without his consent, and the Constitution no more prevents a State from requiring respondent to compensate petitioner for broadcasting his act on television than it would privilege respondent to film and broadcast a copyrighted dramatic work without liability to the copyright owner, or to film or broadcast a prize fight or a baseball game.60) The effect of a public broadcast of the performance is similar to preventing Zacchini from charging an admission fee. Moreover, the broadcast of the entire performance, unlike the unauthorized use of another's name for purposes of trade or the incidental use of a name or picture by the press, goes to the heart of petitioner's ability to earn a living as an entertainer. There is no doubt, the Supreme Court, held that entertainment, as well as news enjoys First Amendment protection and that entertainment itself can be important news.61) However, neither the public nor Scripps-Howard would be deprived of the benefit of Zacchini's performance as long as his commercial stake in his act is appropriately recognized.62)

While the court held that Zacchini's right of publicity outweighed the

---

59) *Id.*
60) *Id.*
61) *Id.*
62) *Id.*

First Amendment concerns, it should be noted that the case was based on the unusual facts, the broadcasting of the entire event. Historically, the courts do not believe it is their place to determine which issues may or may not interest the general public and thereforewill usually apply a broad reading to the news media exemption.

### The Incidental Use Exception

The courts have recognized an incidental use exception in cases where a newspaper or magazine has used the image or photo of an athlete or other celebrity previously in a story, for advertisement. The advertisements, the courts have held are simply "incidental" to the original, newsworthy publication. A good example is Joe Namath v. Sports Illustrated.[63] Joe Namath, a famous American football player, sued Sports Illustrated, a weekly sports publication, after it used his photograph, without his consent, in advertisements promoting subscriptions.[64]

In holding that the publication and use of Namath's photo in the advertisements did not violate Namath's right of publicity under New York's Civil Rights Law, the court held that the use of the photograph, originally used in conjunction with a news article, was merely incidental advertising of the magazine. The photograph was originally used in the magazine in conjunction with a news article published by Sports Illustrated the 1969 Super Bowl Game.[65]Therefore, the court noted the reproduction was used to illustrate the quality and content of the magazine in which Namath had earlier been properly and fairly depicted. In addition, the use of the photo in no way indicates Namath's endorsement of the magazine.[66]

### Parody Defense

The First Amendment also allows for the use of parodies under certain

---

63) Joe Namath v. Sports Illustrated, 48 A.D.2d 487; 371 N.Y.S.2d 10 (1975).
64) *Id.*
65) *Id.*
66) *Id.*

circumstances, such as in traditionally non-commercial medium like newspapers, magazines, television programs, books or movies. Parodies, however, used in a commercial context will generally not receive First Amendment protection. For example, in Cardtoons, L.C. v. Major League Baseball Players Association,[67] Cardtoons, a trading card company, designed "parody" trading cards of active major league baseball players. Cardtoons did not obtain either a license or consent from Major League Baseball Players Association (MLBPA).[68] MLBPA learned of Cardtoons plans to market the cards and, as a result, prior to full publication of the cards, the MLBPA sent Cardtoons a cease-and-desist letter.[69]

In ruling for MLBPA, the court stated that while parodies used in a traditionally non-commercial medium such as a newspaper, magazine, television program, book or movie will likely be granted First Amendment protection, the primary purpose behind Cardtoons' parody is commercial.[70] Commercial speech, the court held, does not receive the same type of Constitutional protection. First Amendment rights end when Cardtoons preys on the MLBPA's names and likenesses for purely commercial purposes. Indeed, the court found that the only reason for using the players' likenesses and names was to entice the consumer to purchase the product.[71]

## Conclusion

While it is clear that the legal issues surrounding the image rights of athletes and others is still evolving, it has been clearly established by the courts that an athlete's image, if properly managed, can be valuable then their professional playing contracts. However, in protecting athletes and other celebrities, the courts need to be careful that they do not forget the original intent of "the right to privacy" by broadening the right of publicity

---

67) Cardtoons, L.C. v. Major League Baseball Players Association, 838 F. Supp 1501 (N.D. Okla. 1993).
68) *Id.*
69) *Id.*
70) *Id.*
71) *Id.*

past "traditional meaning of "name and likeness"[72] more than legally necessary.

In the last few years, the courts have been inclined to expand beyond the traditional meaning to include voice, identifying numbers and other characteristics associated with the individual. The question now, however, seems to be how far the courts are willing to expand that right. This important question should in the next few years.

## References

Cardtoons, L.C. v. Major League Baseball Players Association, 838 F. Supp 1501 (N.D. Okla. 1993).

Steven Clay, Starstruck: the overextension of celebrity publicity rights in state and federal courts, *79 Minnesota Law Review 485, 495* (1994).

Eastwood v. Superior Court, 149 Cal. App. 3d 409, 198 Cal. Rptr. 342 (1983).

*Haelan Laboratories, Inc. v. Topps Chewing Gum, Inc.,* 202 F.2d 866 (2nd.Cir. 1953).

Keller v. Electronic Arts, 2010 U.S. Dist. LEXIS 10719; 38 Media L. Rep. 1353 (N.D. Cal., Feb. 8, 2010).

Lugosi v. Universal Pictures, 25 Cal. 3d 813; 160 Cal. Rptr. 323; 603 P.2d 425 (1979).

Mackenzie v. Soden Mineral Springs Co., 18 N.Y.S. 240 (1891).

J. Thomas McCarthy, (1992). *The Rights of Publicity and Privacy.* Clark Boardman Callaghan: Dearfield, IL.

Melville B. Nimmer, (1954). The Right of Publicity, *19 Law and Contemporary Problems 203*

Montana v. San Jose Mercury News, 40 Cal. Rptr. 2d 639 (1995).

Motschenbacher v. R.J. Reynolds Tobacco Co., 498 F.2d 821 (1974).

Joe Namath v. Sports Illustrated, 48 A.D.2d 487; 371 N.Y.S.2d 10 (1975).

Newcombe v. Adolf Coors Co., 157 F.3d 686 (9th Cir. 1998).

O'Brien v. Pabst Sales Co., 124 F.2d 167 (1941).

Palmer v. Schonhorn Enterprises, 96 N.J. Super.72; 232 A.2d 458 (1967).

Pavesich v.New England Life Insurance, 122 Ga. 190, 50 S.E. 68 (1905).

William Prosser, Privacy, *48 California Law Review 383* (1960).

---

72) Steven Clay, Starstruck: the overextension of celebrity publicity rights in state and federal courts, *79 Minnesota Law Review 485, 495* (1994).

Roberson v Rochester Folding Box Co., 171 N.Y. 538, 64 N.E. 442 (1902).

Ben Spencer, (April 4, 2011). Bill for Pounds $82Million Tiger's Sex Romps; Loss of Sponsors hit Earnings. Daily Record, p. 11.

Stilson v. Reader's Digest Assn., Inc., 28 Cal.App.3d 270, 273 (1972).

Samuel Warren & Louis Brandeis, The Right of Privacy, *4 Harvard Law Review 193* (1890).

John Wolohan, (2013). Image Rights.In D. J. Cotton & J. T. Wolohan (Eds.), *Law for recreation and sport managers* (6th Ed.). Dubuque, IA: Kendall/ Hunt Publishing Co.

Zacchini v. Scripps-Howard Broadcasting Co., 433 U.S. 562 (1977).


Legislation:

N.Y. Civ. Rights Law, § 50.

N.Y. Sess. Laws 1903, ch.132 § 1. Amended in 1921, now cited as N.Y. Civ. Rights Law, § 50.

N.Y. Civ. Rights Law, § 51.

N.Y. Sess. Laws 1903, ch.132 § 2. Amended in 1921, now cited as N.Y. Civ. Rights Law, § 51.

U.S. CONST. Amend. I.

# Lex Sportiva from Legal Pluralism Perspective

HUI-YING XIANG*

*legal monism and legal pluralismis the different perspectives for thepeopleunderstandlaw today. Monism concept proposed that lawisenacted orrecognizedby the state, but this concept can not fully explainthe phenomenon of lex sportiva. This paper through analyzing the phenomenonof lex sportiva from legal pluralism perspective, try to explainlex sportivaphenomenon more reasonable.*

*Put forward lex sportiva is supra-nationallevel communityautonomy law from legal pluralism perspective, its scope should within the sport community, its content should include the rules formed by CAS practice and other rules maintain the order of sport community. As non-state law, Lex Sportiva andofficiallaw have antagonistic relationshipin some extent. However, to achieve good governance need lex sportiva and official law more coordination and cooperation.*

**Key word:** Legal Pluralism; Lex Sportiva; Sport Community; Autonomy

## Introduction

Legal pluralism refers to two or more legal or "quasi-legal" co-exist in the same society. Woodman called "deep" legal pluralism, referring to two or more of the legality of their respective owners and the legitimacy of the legal system based on the coexistence state.[1] In the view of Sociology and Anthropology, the legal system of any society is pluralism, rather than monism. The state is not a necessary condition for the legal existence, in

---

* Secretary General of Shanghai University of Political Science and Law Sports Law Center
1) Gordon R. Woodman. Ideological Combat and Social Observation-Recent Debate about Legal Pluralism.J. Legal Pluralism & Unofficial L,1998

addition to state law, there are various forms of non-state law. Austrian sociologist Ehrlich said: "The law is the Commonwealth of internal order, the Consortium include: the commune, national, religious groups, associations, political parties, the agricultural economy of the commonwealth.........". "The internal order of human body is not just primordial law form, and is still the basic form of law."[2] The Japanese scholar Masaji Chiba in the "legal pluralism" proposed law into the official law, non-state law and legal principles of three levels.[3] Therefore, in the view of legal pluralism, whether official law play an important role in the society, it is only a part of the legal order, cannot ignore other forms of various kinds law beside the official law. Also, in some respects, non-state law is more important, more real than the official law.[4]

Lex Sportiva" is proposed by founder the Court of Arbitration for Sport (CAS) at the beginning of CAS was founded. With the development and expansion of CAS, Lex Sportiva has received more and more attention. Attention to the Lex Sportiva is not only the result of Lex Sportiva itself, but also because Lex Sportiva as a new legal phenomenon, influence on the world law concept. However, what is Lex Sportiva? Its nature, connotation have different views, even also contains controversial between legal monism and legal pluralism. This paper from the perspective of legal pluralism analyzes Lex Sportiva, and demonstrated that the interaction of Lex Sportiva with the official law.

## The Legal Nature of Lex Sportiva from Legal Pluralism Perspective

### The controversial of legal nature of Lex Sportiva

The legal nature of Lex Sportiva remains controversial. There are some of

---

2) Eugene Ehrlich. Translation by Ye Mingyi, Yuan zhen. *Fundamental Principles of the Sociology of Law.* China Social Sciences Press,2009
3) [Japan] Chiba Masaji ,Translation by Qiang Shigong et al *Legal Pluralism* [M] Beijing: China University of Political Science and Law press, 1997,148
4) Xu Zhongming. *Reflections and Criticism -- Interpretation of legal culture of China* [M] Beijing: Law Press, 2000, 35

the main ideas:

(1) Lex Sportiva belong to a branch of international sports law, so it is the principles of international law applicable in the field of sports, and this applies is achieved through the CAS.[5] Nafzinger has argued that, 'as an authoritative process of decision-making and legal discipline, international sports law is as much a matter of international law as of sports law'.[6] In fact, this view is based on nationalist (etatist) argued that the state law is only meaningful normative order can be called law.[7] 'anational' law is unthinkable! On this point of view, any legal phenomenon in the world necessarily has to be 'rooted' in a national legal order, it needs at least a 'minimal link' to national law. No non-state authority, be it an international institution, a private business or transnational organization, has the capacity to supplant the State. In fact, they all remain reliant on the State because only the State can provide the complementary resources that non-state actors lack to exercise political authority effectively and legitimately.[8]

(2) Lex Sportiva is global law. In recent years, more and more Chinese scholars have started to pay attention lex sportiva, Jiang Xi, Tan Xiaoyong, also pointed that lex sportiva is a global law.[9] Ken foster argue that lex sportiva should be equated to 'global sports law'. To define it thus as 'global sports law' highlights that it is a cloak for continued self-regulation by international sports federations. It is a claim for non-intervention by both national legal systems and by international sports law. It thus opposes a rule of law in regulating international sport.[10] Lorenzo Casini use the term lex sportiva as a synonym of "global sports law". Global sports law, by contrast, may provisionally be defined as a transnational autonomous legal order

---

5) James A R Nafziger. *International Sports Law*[M]New York :Transational publications, 2004
6) J. Nafziger, 'Globalizing Sports Law' *Marquette Sports Law Journal* 9 (1999), 225, 237.
7) Tamanaha. B Z. The Folly of the Social Scientific Concept of Legal Pluralism[J] *Journal of Law and society.* 1993(20):192-21
8) Genschel, Philipp; Zangl, Bernhard (2008): *Transformations of the state: from monopolist to manager of political authority*, Translate working papers, No. 76
9) TAN Xiaoyong, JIANG Xi. *A Study of Global Sports Law.* China Sports Science,2011,11
10) Ken foster. Is there a global sports law?[J] *Entertainment Law*, Vol.2, No.1, Spring 2003, pp.1-18

created by the private global institutions that govern international sport.

Global law can be adequately explained by a theory of legal pluralism which turned from the law of colonial societies to the laws of diverse ethnic, cultural and religious communities in modern nation-states.

(3) Lex Sportiva is translational private law. Panagiotopoulos think that lex sportive& lex Olympica is different from international law, it is a new kind of law, as "anethnic" law of international practice. Latty used lex sportive as translational sports law.[11] Mitten point out "Through CAS develop a international private sports law, replacing the role of state law in sport, it is appropriate jurisprudence.[12] This point of view emphasis the international and private nature of Lex Sportiva, also affirmed "The center of gravity of legal development therefore from time immemorial has not lain in the activity of the state, but in society itself, and must be sought there at the present time."(Eugen Ehrlich, 1936:390). Acknowledge the existence of private law is the foundation of legal pluralism.

## Lex Sportiva is Supranational Sports Community Autonomy Law

### Lex Sportiva beyond the limits of territory

Sport as a human communication passage "language", which along with economic globalization and the development of commercial, sport has gone beyond the borders to become the world sharing, communication or exchange of cultural products and resources. Lex Sportiva based on worldwide sports, undoubtedly demonstrated transnational and supranational in CAS arbitration practice. "Sports law is not just international; it is nongovernmental as well, and this differentiates it from all other forms of law.[13] When Kaufman-Kohler served as Chairman of CAS Panel, he proposed that a series of rules …… all is cross-national, universal, global, and

---

11) Franck Latty.Transnational Sports Law Lex Sportiva: What is Sports Law? *ASSER International Sports Law Series* 2012, pp 273-286
12) Mitten, Matthew J. Judicial Review of Olympic and International Sports Arbitration Awards: Trends and Observations, [J] *Pepperdine Dispute Resolution Law Journal*: Vol. 10: Iss. 1, (2010)
13) M. Beloff, T. Kerr and M. Demetriou, *Sports Law* .Oxford: Hart, 1999:4-5

they do not rely on the application of regional ties, are not subject to regional restrictions, such global independent law is commensurate with uniform procedural code.14)

## Lex Sportiva is independent of government

Lex Sportiva by the International Olympic Committee, led by the international sports organizations to promote international sports development and the establishment of an autonomous legal system sports community .Lex Sportiva is a sport community autonomy legal system, it is created by international sports organizations led by the International Olympic Committee in order to develop the sport. It is not authorized by the national government, it is not enacted by the national legislature. It is a self-generating creation, nor ensure the implementation by state power, it is not belong to state law. Beloff proposed that Lex sportiva has three main elements: First, it has transnational norms generated by the rules and practices of international sporting federations; Second, It has a unique jurisprudence, with legal principles that are different from those of national courts, and which is declared by the Court of Arbitration for Sport, and Third, it is constitutionally autonomous from national law.[13] 'its normative underpinning derives not from anytreaty entered into between sovereign states but from international agreements between bodies, many of which are constitutionally independent of their national governments'.

## Lex Sportiva acting on global sport community

With the globalization of sports, the world has 205 countries and territories participating National Olympic Committee Olympic Movement and international sporting events. A pyramid structure global sport community headed by the IOC has been formed, which composed by the International Sports Federations and National Olympic Committee. Lex sportiva generated on the ground of legalization of the sport community

---

14) Kaufmann-Kohler.Artbitral Precedent: Dream, necessity or excuse?[J]. Arbitrationa internation, 2007, (3):365.

internal order.[15] "Sports rules are genuine "global law" because they are applied across the entire world, they involve both international and domestic levels, and they directly affect individuals: This happens, for instance, in the case of the Olympic Charter, a private act of a "constitutional nature" with which all States comply".[16] But so far, the scope of Lex Sportiva is still mainly concentrated in the international sports bodies and international sporting events, some national-level sports organizations still follow their own domestic-national law or domestic sport autonomy Law. With the development of sport, found a unified global sport law is a trend.

### The legal resources of Lex Sportiva

Lex Sportiva is special, its legal resources is different from the state law or international law, even different from the most similar Lex Mercateria. Lex Mercateria's legal resources are: international commercial treaties, international commercial conventions, international organizations model law, general principles of law, commercial form contracts, international commercial arbitration awards,etc.[17] While Lex Sportiva resources contains worldwide sports rules of Practice, the international sports regulations and conventions, CAS jurisprudence and so on. Lex Mercateria applicable the private principle, rather Lex Sportiva develop and applicable some public principles. Lex Mercateria adjusted equal parties, when the sports arbitration involving vertical relationship of penalties and contest eligibility, its position of the parties are inequality.

---

15) JIANG Xi, TAN Xiaoyong.A Study of Lex Sportiva[J] *Journal of TUS.* Vol.27 No.4,2012: 314-319
16) JEAN-LOUP CHAPPELET & BRENDA KÜBLER-MABBOTT, *THE INTERNATIONAL OLYMPIC COMMITTEE AND THE OLYMPIC SYSTEM: THE GOVERNANCE OF SPORT* (2008)
17) SHI Jianping. Differentiate between the International Sport Arbitration and International Commercial Arbitration----Centered on the Sport Arbitration of CAS [J] *Sports Science Research.* Vol.33 No.5,2012:33-38

## The Scope and Content of Lex Sportiva

### The scope of Lex Sportiva

What is Lex Sportiva? Its still controversial, even for the existence of Lex Sportiva has been questioned. Polvino defined Lex Sportiva as a dynamic, constantly improve the rules, this rule can avoid sports dispute, also may carry on the management to the athletes, national sports bodies, international organizations and other management agencies, can also solve sports dispute.[18] According to Beloff, "Lex Sportiva" is a loose rule system gradually unified, its main function is to adjust the sports practice and solving sports disputes. It crosses the boundary of traditional law, its core is a unique international principle rules, it provides limited autonomous of non- governmental sports organizations.[19] Siekman believes that sports law exists, and proposed the "Lex Sportiva" is the public part of the sports law, "Lex Ludica" is a private part of the sports law, the hard core of sports law is the "judge-made law".[20] Foster argued elsewhere that the concept 'lex sportiva' is an imprecise term covering several different concepts. Its narrow use is principles that are applicable to sport because they are 'general principles derived from...sports regulations'. It also equate with 'global sports law'.[21] All these views confirm the existence of Lex Sportiva as the law, what is the scope of "Lex Sportiva"? Views are difference. Notably, many views did not distinguish between Sports Law and Lex Sportiva, Sports Law and Lex Sportiva substitute for each other sometimes, it is also easy to cause confusion. Should distinguish these two concepts, or else bring confusion to understanding Lex Sportiva. Sports Law is a larger concept, is legal order of a traditional continuation,

---

18) Polvino. Arbitration as Preventative Medicine for Olympic Ailments: The International Olympic Committee's Court of Arbitration for Sport and the Future for the Settlement of International Sporting Disputes.8 Emory Int'l L. Rev. 347 (1994)
19) MJ.Beloff,T Kerr&M Demetriou. *Sports Law*[M] (Oxford, Hart)1.12(1999).
20) Siekmann What is Sports Law? *Lex Sportiva and Lex Ludica*: A Reassessment of Content and Terminology Introduction to International and European Sports Law *Sports Law ASSER International Sports Law Series* 2012, pp 1-33
21) Ken foster, Lex Sportiva and Lex ludica: the Court of Arbitration for Sport's Jurisprudence. [M] Lex Sportiva : What is Sports Law?, *ASSER International Sports law series*, 2012, 123-148.

legal pluralism and spontaneous evolution.[22] It contains the national and regional levels of state sports law, and the domestic level sports autonomy law, and including international official sports law (such as sports law made by the United Nations) and Lex Sportiva and Lex Sportiva (non-governmental law). That is to say Lex Sportiva is just a part of the Sports Law, the scope of lex sportiva should be within sports community.

### The content of Lex Sportiva from Legal Pluralism

Lex Sportiva is the number of decisions rendered by the CAS has increased to the point that a set of principles and rules have been created specifically to address sport, also has been called "judge-made sport law". Case law in the practice of CAS belongs to the lex Sportiva, which has been widely recognized. So, case law is equal to the lex Sportiva? Lex Sportiva is sporting community autonomy law. According to sociologist Maciver's view," any group in order to carry out normal activities to reach their goal, must have the regulations of its members, this is the group law". In that sense, Lex Sportiva could be extended to all rules and regulations and jurisprudence of sporting community. It should include the constitution of international sports organizations (Such as the Olympic Charter), international sports rules, transnational dispute settlement rules and principles, and so on.

## Lex Sportiva Interact with the Official Law

Official law is recognized by the state legitimate authority, it enacted by state public enforcement. International law as applicable between sovereign states and other entities with international personality, is a continuation of state law, also belong to official law. Lex Sportiva as non-official law interact with the official law in the sports order.

---

22) Möllers, *Transnational Governance Without A Public Law? in Transnational Governance and Constitutionalism*, ed. by C. Joerges, I.-J. Sand, G. Teubner, Oxford (2004), p. 329.

## Lex Sportiva as legal resources

October19, 2005, UNESCO adopted "Against Doping in Sport National Convention", which became effective on December 1, 2007, the Convention has 164 parties until December 7, 2011. The convention has been there are 164 states parties. Lex Sportiva as the resources format the core rules of this convention. Just like Ehrlich considered, there are first-stage norms and second-stage norms in society, the first-stage norms generated from structure and operation of group, which directly regulate and adjust group order. The second-stage norms are outside norms of the group, they do not directly regulate and adjust the group order. It is only to protect, maintain and consolidate groups, do not create groups, state law is a typical representative. The essence of legal pluralism is the first-stage norms "living law" and the second-stage norms "foreign law" co-existence in the same society. The first-stage norms and the second-stage norms can be transformed into each other.[23] Lex Sportiva as resources of an international convention, it also applies to some public law principles, this phenomenon may be interpreted as the first-stage norms and the second-stage norms transformed into each other.

## Judicial Conflict and confrontation

Autonomy unlike rule by others, it has exclusivity. Community autonomy is based on contracts and organization, its effectiveness comes from the members to comply with, the stronger community autonomous by means fewer interventions of the official law. So, there is a certain antagonistic relationship between lex sportiva and the official law, performance conflict and confrontation on the judicial[24]. For example, the conflict between the International Olympic Committee and the Italian government, it took place during the months preceding the opening of the Olympic Games in Turin. The International Olympic Committee according to the World Anti-Doping

---

23) JU Chengwei. Legal Pluralism from Ehrlich Law Sociology perspective. *Tsinghua Journal of Rule of Law*. Vol.22, 2009:234-25

24) XIANG Huiying.The Rationality of "Lex Sportiva" as Law. *Journal of Chengdu Sport University*, 2013, Vol.39 No.6:14-21

Rules for doping cases a two-year suspension, while in accordance with Italian law the case should be criminal sanctions (including up to three years' imprisonment). The final result was Italian anti-doping law temporary "suspension". Thomas considered, the private legal system (the Olympic lex sportiva) over the public legal system (Italian law).[25] Of course, this is also because the government generally does not directly participate in sports disputes.[26]

## Coordination and cooperation

Through years development, CAS gradually got the support of national Olympic Committee, the International Olympic Committee, International Sports Federations and anti-doping organizations and other sports organizations, also received strong support from the Swiss Federal Court. Such as the Gander cases 1998, 2003 A. and B. v. IOC and FIS (Lazutina) , the Swiss Federal Court have publicly declared CAS is impartial and independent. CAS also established a good contact with a number of public authorities. As United Nations, CAS decision in doping cases created "World Anti-Doping Code," which has turn out formed the core rules of the UNESCO convention. "Lex Sportiva" also provides an authoritative framework decision for athlete's eligibility and nationality. CAS also declared that "coexistence of national and international authorities are familiar with the characteristics of......state power can not resist the international regime was recognized".[27] CAS arbitration decision anywhere belong to Lausanne, Switzerland, so the decision outside Switzerland as a foreign arbitration, recognition and enforcement of its decisions has been executed through the "New York Convention". Therefore, it can be said the enforcement of "Lex Sportiva" not only from private authority (the Olympic Movement), but also from some of

---

25) Schultz, Thomas, The Lex Sportiva Turns Up at the Turin Olympics: Supremacy of Non-State Law and Strange Loops. Available at SSRN: http://ssrn.com/abstract =896673, 2006

26) M Mangan. The Court of Arbitration for Sport: Current Practice, Emerging Trends and Future Hurdles[J]Arbitration International.2009,25(4):591-602

27) CAS/A/1149 e CAS/A/1211.WADA vs. FMF and Mr.José Salvador-Carmona Alvarez. Cit,2007,para,2

the public authority.

Although Lex Sportiva as a sports community autonomy has antagonistic relationship with public law, but that does not mean "public law is an obstacle to development of Lex Sportiva", while to achieve good governance in global by interaction Lex Sportiva with the public law sports.Just like Legal pluralism is defined no longer as a set of conflicting social norms but as a multiplicity of diverse communicative processes in a given social field that observe social action under the binary code of legal/illegal.[28]

## Conclusion

Lex sportiva is different from Sports law, it is the part of Sports law.From legal pluralism sports law is the legitimacy pluralism hybrid. It is made of norms enacted not only by states or international governmental organizations, but also by international sporting institutions (such as IOC, IFs and WADA) and by national sporting bodies (such as National Olympic Committees and National Anti-Doping Organizations).

Lex Sportiva is a supra-national level sports community autonomy law, its trends is unified global law. The scope of lex sportiva is within the sport community. The core content of Lex Sportiva is jurisprudence from CAS arbitration practice. Broad Lex Sportiva including all norm system in the global sport community.

There exists antagonistic relationship between Lex Sportiva and official law. However, to achieve good governance need lex sportiva and official law more coordination and cooperation.

---

28) Gunther Teubner .Legal Pluralism in the World Society Gunther Teubner (ed.), *Global Law Without a State.* Brookfield: Dartmouth 1997, 3-28

# References

Gordon R. Woodman. Ideological Combat and Social Observation-Recent Debate about Legal Pluralism.J. Legal Pluralism & Unofficial L,1998

Eugene Ehrlich. Translation by Ye Mingyi, Yuan zhen. *Fundamental Principles of the Sociology of Law*. China Social Sciences Press,2009

[Japan] Chiba Masaji, Translation by Qiang Shigong et al Legal Pluralism [M] Beijing: China University of Political Science and Law press, 1997,148

Xu Zhongming. *Reflections and Criticism -- Interpretation of legal culture of China* [M] Beijing: Law Press, 2000, 35

James A R Nafziger. *International Sports Law* [M] New York :Transational publications,2004

J. Nafziger, 'Globalizing Sports Law' *Marquette Sports Law Journal* 9 (1999), 225, 237.

Tamanaha. B Z. The Folly of the Social Scientific Concept of Legal Pluralism [J] *Journal of Law and society*. 1993(20):192-21

Genschel, Philipp; Zangl, Bernhard (2008): Transformations of the state: from monopolist to manager of political authority, Translate working papers, No. 76

TAN Xiaoyong, JIANG Xi. *A Study of Global Sports Law*. China Sports Science, 2011,11

Ken foster. Is there a global sports law?[J] *Entertainment Law*, Vol.2, No.1, Spring 2003, pp.1–18

Franck Latty. Transnational Sports Law Lex Sportiva: What is Sports Law? *ASSER International Sports Law Series* 2012, pp 273-286

Mitten, Matthew J. Judicial Review of Olympic and International Sports Arbitration Awards: Trends and Observations ,[J] *Pepperdine Dispute Resolution Law Journal*: Vol. 10: Iss. 1, (2010)

M. Beloff, T. Kerr and M. Demetriou, *Sports Law*. Oxford: Hart, 1999:4-5

Kaufmann-Kohler.Artbitral Precedent: Dream, necessity or excuse?[J]. Arbitrationa internation, 2007,(3):365.

JIANG Xi, TAN Xiaoyong. A Study of Lex Sportiva[J] *Journal of TUS*. Vol.27 No.4,2012: 314-319

JEAN-LOUP CHAPPELET & BRENDA KÜBLER-MABBOTT, *THE INTERNATIONAL OLYMPIC COMMITTEE AND THE OLYMPIC SYSTEM: THE GOVERNANCE OF SPORT* (2008)

SHI Jianping. Differentiate between the International Sport Arbitration and International Commercial Arbitration----Centered on the Sport Arbitration of CAS [J] *Sports Science Research.* Vol.33 No.5,2012:33-38

Polvino. Arbitration as Preventative Medicine for Olympic Ailments: The International Olympic Committee's Court of Arbitration for Sport and the Future for the Settlement of International Sporting Disputes. *8 Emory Int'l L. Rev. 347* (1994)

M.J.Beloff,T Kerr&M Demetriou. *Sports Law*[M] (Oxford, Hart)1.12(1999).

Siekmann What is Sports Law? *Lex Sportiva and Lex Ludica*: A Reassessment of Content and Terminology Introduction to International and European Sports Law, *Sports Law ASSER International Sports Law Series* 2012, pp 1-33

Ken foster, Lex Sportiva and Lex ludica: the Court of Arbitration for Sport's Jurisprudence.[M] Lex Sportiva: What is Sports Law?, *ASSER International Sports law series*, 2012,123-148.

Möllers, Transnational Governance Without A Public Law? in *Transnational Governance and Constitutionalism*, ed. by C. Joerges, I.-J. Sand, G. Teubner, Oxford (2004), p. 329.

JU Chengwei. Legal Pluralism from Ehrlich Law Sociology perspective. *Tsinghua Journal of Rule of Law.* Vol.22, 2009:234-25

XIANG Huiying.The Rationality of "Lex Sportiva" as Law. *Journal of Chengdu Sport University*, 2013, Vol.39 No.6: 14-21

Schultz, Thomas, The Lex Sportiva Turns Up at the Turin Olympics: Supremacy of Non-State Law and Strange Loops. Available at SSRN: http://ssrn. com/abstract=896673, 2006

M Mangan. The Court of Arbitration for Sport: Current Practice, Emerging Trends and Future Hurdles[J] Arbitration International. 2009, 25(4): 591-602

CAS/A/1149 e CAS/A/1211.WADA vs. FMF and Mr. José Salvador-Carmona Alvarez. Cit, 2007, para,2

Gunther Teubner .Legal Pluralism in the World Society Gunther Teubner (ed.), *Global Law Without a State.* Brookfield: Dartmouth 1997, 3-28

# A New Trend of Sports Law:
# The Impacts of 2012 Sport Industry Promotion Law on Taiwan

KONG-TING YEH*

*Sport Industry Promotion Law (SIPL) was established in Taiwan since 1 March, 2012. This Law consists of 33 rules to define the key ways of steering the development of sport industry environment in Taiwan, such as the responsibility of government to assist sport related industries, the regulations of subsidizing specific enterprises which meet the criteria of government for funding or promoting their businesses, the supports of providing necessary resources to sport professional individuals or organizations for their empowering of job trainings or organization re-engineering.*

*The impacts generated from SIPL during 2010-2013 are evaluated as follows:*

A. *Costs: totally, there are 17 million USDs for the direct costs (supplied by public sectors or leaked from government incomes), including the subsidized financial grants are 13.2 million USDs; the tax reductions are 2.6 million USDs; administrative expenditures are 1.2 million USDs. Because the above mentioned government expenditures for each year are around 3.3 million USDs, therefore the negative side effect (indirect costs) on other industries is limited from the macro-economic point of view.*

B. *Benefits: for the output values of various sport industry from 2010-2013 are anticipated to 83.8 million USDs, taxes increasing are 16.8 million USDs, reduction from health insurance fees are 28.8 USDs, and the jobs adding are 11,042.*

**Key word:** Sport Industry Promotion Law, impacts, direct costs, indirect costs, benefits

* Professor and Dean, Management College, National Taiwan Sport University, Taiwan

## Introduction

The sport development around the world tends from government domination oriented to market mechanism oriented. However, the government in many nations still plays important roles of handling those sports affairs with the characters of public welfare (Allmen, 2012). Meanwhile, from the sport products consumption point of view, the consumers' preferences are placed to sport spectator products and sport participative products from sporting goods recently. There are more and more people around the world involve both spectator and participative sports. New style of sport facilities tends to be more accessible and low price for their usages in many countries. In order to work in concern with this change, International Association of Assembly Managers (IAAM)" has changed its title to "International Association of Venue Managers (IAVM)" from 2007 to deal with this changing (International Association of Venues Managers, 2012). Therefore, the financial resources which inject to the sport industry market are quite diversity around the world.

Since 2000, started from its establishment, Taiwan Society for Sport Management (TASSM) has promoted the concept of "sport industry" in Taiwan (Yeh, 2000).

During the past 10 years, there are more and more companies involve different kind of sport businesses, the sport management related undergraduate/ graduate programs in the higher education institutions also increased skyrocket to about 160 units to cultivate the sport industry professional human power resources.

Therefore, in order to create an efficient circumstance and encourage the sport industry organizations to have more investment on sport related business in Taiwan, the Sport Affairs Council (it has been merged to Education Ministry titled as Sport Administration since 1 January 2013), Executive Yuan, Taiwanese government launched "Sport Promotion Industry Law (SPIL)" in Taiwan form March 1$^{st}$, 2012 (Sport Affairs Council, 2011).

## The Origin of Sport Promotion Industry Law (SPIL) in Taiwan

In the year of 2013, the economic growth rate were around 3.37%, GDP per capita was 21,059USDs, un-employment rate was 4.44%; however the Price Index is rising constantly (+1.93%). While, sport GDP were about 30 billion USDs (0.7% of GDP), sport employment rate was about 1%, and the average sport consumption per capita was approximately 100 USDs (Sport Affairs Council, 2012; 2013).

The economic performances of sport industry in both demand and supply sides need to be improved when compared them with other sport industry developed countries.

The reasons influenced the above-mentioned situations were as follows:

1. The sport social value in Taiwan is not so high, when compared with other disciplines in this country.
2. The majority of sport industry organizations are either small or middle scale, when compared with other highly developed of sport industry nations, such as Korea and USA.
3. The sport policy related to promote sport industry in Taiwan is inconsistently and limited (Sport Affairs Council, 2009).

On the other hand, there were several positive tendencies in Taiwan related to sport industries with good potentials needed to be aware, such as:

1. The increasing of sport management professional education programs at universities/colleges. These programs may create human power resources and become an important propulsion to stimulate the growth of sport industry in Taiwan.
2. The establishing of sport centers. These 50 local community oriented sport institutes provide ideal places for the general public to take their exercise. The sport populations generated from these sport centers are anticipated about 45 million per year. I
3. The hosting of international sport events are identified by Taiwanese people gradually.
4. The development of Taiwanese brands of cycling companies (such

as Giant and Merida), fitness machines (such as Johnson) with highly international market shares.

5. The water base sport industries are popular by school students gradually during these 5 years.

6. The promotion of sport lottery in Taiwan since 2009. The amount of financial resource injected from lottery revenues is around 2 billion NTDs.

7. Sport tourism is more popular, such as Swimming Cross Sun-Moon Lake, Taroko National Park Marathon Race, and Cycling Taiwan.

8. Even e-sport industry becomes more attracted by Taiwanese young generation.

Therefore, to refer good models from overseas, then legalizing efficient formal system and generate an ideal investing environment of activating the sport industry in Taiwan becomes an important sport policy to Sport Affairs Council.

## The Contents of SIPL

Totally, there are 33 rules within SIPL, containing the responsibility of government to assist sport related industries, the regulations of subsidizing specific enterprises which meet the criteria of government for funding or promoting their business, the supports of providing necessary resources to sport professional individuals or organizations for their empowering of job trainings or organization re-engineering.

The defined of sport industry categories within SIPL include: sporting goods manufacturing, selling/leasing; sport venues architecture and constructing; sport performing; professional sports; sport and recreation education services; sport health care; sport administrative service; sport broadcasting and media; sport lottery; sport information publication; sport tourism; and the other industries which are recognized by government.

There are various acts that government may have supports by consulting or financial allowance/subsidy, according to SIPL.

## The Goal of SIPL

At this stage, the period for implementing SIPL policy is from 2010 to 2013. The government attempts to attend the following goals:

1. The increasing of regular sport population to 0.5% yearly.
2. The increasing of average sport consumption per capita to 5% yearly.

## The Impacts of SIPL on Taiwan Economy

At the first stage (2010-2013), the impacts of SIPL can be described from the costs and benefits sides.

Costs

Direct Costs

    1) The subsidized financial grants to sport industry organizations.
    2) The tax reduction (tax free or discount).
    3) Administrative expenditures.

Table 1 Direct Costs of Promoting SIPL (in million USD)

| Year | Industry Subsidization | Tax Reduction | Administrative expenditures | Total |
|------|------------------------|---------------|-----------------------------|-------|
| 2010 | 3.3 | | 0.3 | |
| 2011 | 3.3 | | 0.3 | |
| 2012 | 3.3 | | 0.3 | |
| 2013 | 3.3 | | 0.3 | |
| Total | 13.2 | 2.6 | 1.2 | 17.0 |

(Source: National Sport Affairs, 2009)

Indirect Cost

Because the above mentioned government expenditures for each year are around 3.3 million USDs, therefore the negative side effect (indirect costs) on other industries is limited from the macro-economic point of view.

### 1) Benefits

According to the concepts of input-output economics, the benefits of promoting SIPL in Taiwan can be referred to direct and indirect benefits.

① Direct benefits
- The increasing of output values.
- The increasing of incomes.
- The increasing of job opportunities.

Table 2 The Direct Benefits of Promoting SIPL

| Year | Output Values increasing (million USD, compared with 2009) | | Health Insurance Savings (million USD, compared with 2009) | Employments increasing (person, compared with last year) | | Incomes Taxes increasing(million USD, compared with 2009) | |
| --- | --- | --- | --- | --- | --- | --- | --- |
| | Revenues | Taxes | | Static Estimating | Dynamic Estimating | Static Estimating | Dynamic Estimating |
| 2010 | 8.2 | 1.60 | 2.11 | 2,562 | 2,484 | 0.77 | 0.76 |
| 2011 | 16.5 | 3.28 | 5.50 | 2,690 | 2,540 | 1.59 | 1.56 |
| 2012 | 25.3 | 5.04 | 8.88 | 2,825 | 2,597 | 2.45 | 2.41 |
| 2013 | 34.8 | 6.89 | 12.26 | 2,966 | 2,656 | 3.34 | 3.30 |
| Total | 84.8 | 16.80 | 28.76 | 11,042 | 10,277 | 8.15 | 8.03 |

(Source: National Sport Affairs, 2009)

② Indirect benefits
- The raising of national reputation.
- The decreasing of health insurance payment.
- The improving of residents' living qualities.
- The decreasing of youth criminal cases.

Therefore, when compared with the positive with the negative impacts of promoting the SIPL in Taiwan, it is obviously to show that the sums of direct and indirect benefits are greater than the sums of direct and indirect costs. Therefore, it is worthy for Sport Affairs Council of Taiwanese government to promote the Sport Industry Promotion Law in Taiwan.

## Challenge and Chances in the Future

This Law is a new legal system to promote sport industry in Taiwan. There are still some challenges need to overcome by Taiwanese government. For example, the using of this Law, because many business persons are not so feminized the contents of SIPL. Moreover, National Sport Council merged to the Education Ministry from 1 January 2013. This situation also causes the uncertainty of the government involvement and support to this Law.

On the other hand, in the end of June, 2013, Education Ministry already established "Sport Policy White Paper" which emphasizes the promotion of sport industry for the coming 10 years (2013-2023) (Education Ministry, 2013). This white paper is anticipated as a strong support to SIPL.

Therefore, there are various challenges as well as chances when promoting and implementing SIPL in the future.

## Conclusions

Sport industry is a newly developing portion within the economic system in many countries. There are many advantages for government to promote sport industry. The main reason is that sport can be referred as a public good which can make great contribution to the public welfare. Starting from the March of 2012, Taiwanese government promotes the Sport Industry Promotion Law in Taiwan based on the above mentioned reasons. It is anticipated that there are various benefits may be caused through the process of promoting this Law. It is important for the Taiwanese government to find ways for reducing the uncertainty due to the government re-engineering process in 2013.

# References

Allmen. P. (2012). *Multiplier effects and local economic impact.* Published in The Oxford hand book of sports economics (Chapter 8). V. 2: Economics through sports. Edited by Shmanske, S., & Kahane, L. UK: Oxford University Press, Inc.

Directorate-General of Budget, Accounting, and Statistic. (2012). The prospect of National incomes and domestic economy situation. October 4th, 2012. Retrieved from:

http://www.dgbas.gov.tw/ct.asp?xItem=31726&ctNode=2858&mp=1.

International Association of Venues Managers (2012). IAVM history: Yesterday, today and tomorrow. October 4th, 2012 retrieved from: http://iavm.org/Governance/hist.asp.

Sport Administration. (2013). The Republic of China Sport Policy White Paper. 24 September 2013 retrieved from http://140.122.64.111/.

Sport Affairs Council. (2009). The Sport Industry Promotion Strategy in Taiwan. Presented in Sport Industry Promotion Law Instruction Will. Hosted at National Taiwan Sport University, Taoyuan, Taiwan,

Sport Affairs Council. (2011). Sport Industry Promotion Law. October 4th, 2012 retrieved from:

http://www.sac.gov.tw/sport_estate/industry_1.html.

Sport Affairs Council. (2012). The sport city survey. Taipei: Sport Affairs Council, Executive Yuan.

Yeh, K. T. (2001). The economic value of sport industry. *Taiwan Society for Sport Management Journal.* Vol. 1. Pp 6-12. Taiwan: Taiwan Society for Sport Management.

# The Future Development of Asian Sports Law*

KEE-YOUNG YEUN**

*In this paper, the author will present a strategy for developing Asian Sports Law. First, it is necessary to define and provide a brief background of Asian Sports Law. The author will then present the following recommendations for developing Asian Sports law:*
  *1. Supporting the Development of the Asian Sports Law Association;*
  *2. Unifying and Harmonizing Asian Sports Law;*
  *3. Promoting Exchanges and Cooperation of Asian Sports;*
  *4. Establishing Educational Organizations and Programs;*
  *5. Establishing a Financial Support for the Research and Education of Asian Sports Law;*
  *6. Studying Norms and Conventions to Develop Governmental and Non-Governmental Organizations in Asia; and*
  *7. Establishing an Asian Sports Arbitration Organization.*

*It is necessary for Asians to establish the identity of Asian law through introspection and rediscovery of Asia in the world. Despite the pluralistic circumstances in Asia, it seems to be easy to create comparatively consistent norms in sports because sports are part of our universal cultural norms. Most of Autonomic Sports Law is internationally consistent; Fundamental Rights of Sports consist of the right to pursue happiness which is one of the fundamental human rights. It is necessary to broaden interchange and cooperation of people and material resources, and to share the legal regimes of each Asian country in order to unify and harmonize the Asian*

---

* This article was originally published in 『The Korean Journal of Sports and Law』 Vol 11 No.3(Aug. 2008) by Korean Association of Sports & Entertainment Law Inc.. I also would like to thank Professor John Riley, Dongguk University College of Law, for his review of this work.
** Professor of Law, Dr. jur.(Unversity of Göttingen, Germany), Dongguk University College of Law in Seoul, Korea

*Sports Law.*

Key word: sports law, asian sports law, Establishment of Asian Sports Arbitration Organization, Agenda of Sports Law, Rules of Sports Arbitration, Unification of Asian Sports Law, Interchange and Cooperation of Asian Sports

## Introduction

Sport are part of the global cultural heritage that people enjoy. The whole world pursues happiness and higher quality of life through participation in sports, which play a fundamental role in world peace and cooperation; the world unites through participating in international sporting events such as the Olympics and Asian Games. Recognizing the important role sports play, sports law scholars in Asian nations, including Korea, China and Japan, founded the Asian Sports Law Conference in October, 2005, in Seoul, Korea. Since its foundation, the conference has been held every year to stimulate collaboration and friendship, laying the framework for the legal basis and studies for agreements of sports law among Asian countries.

The development of a new legal system in Asia based on traditional Asian norms is necessary especially during the acceleration of internationalization and globalization. Asian Sports Law should be studied by various groups cooperating in order to establish laws based on Asian identity in a way harmonious with the rest of the world.

The interchange of sports has been acknowledged as an effective means of exchange regardless the differences of politics, languages, and religions throughout the world. The 2002 Korea-Japan World cup demonstrates the importance of sports; the games influenced both countries' sports industry, laws and policies. The enormous cooperation and promotion of mutual understandings among Asian nations during the Asian Games also demonstrates the influence of sports.

The purpose of this essay is to present a strategy for developing Asian Sports Laws. First, it is necessary to define and provide a brief background of Asian Sports Law.

## The Conception and the Contents of Asian Sports Law.

### The Conception of Asian Sports Law

It is hard to say that the legal systems of many Asian countries have been founded coherently. According to the theory of legal family, used frequently in comparative law[1], Asian laws do not have a consistent legal system. In order to categorize the legal family, the standards should be defined clearly; dividing such standards is not easy.[2] Many comparative law scholars in the United States and England even take a negative attitude toward the theory of legal family.[3] Some scholars claim it is easier to achieve the goal of comparative law by studying various regions. European scholars, on the other hand, usually take the positive approach.

Adolf F. Schnitzer, a Swiss scholar, has insisted that racial traits, language, politics, economy and religion are standards to classify legal families.[4] R. David, a French scholar, has proposed classifying the legal family with considerations of technical and ideological factors of law.[5] Also, Konard Zweigert and Hein Kötz insist on considering the formation of law in classifying the legal sphere.[6]

---

1) It is called "legal system, family of law (Rechtssystem, Rechtsfamilie, Rechtskreis) or legal culture(Rechtskultur)".
2) Let us give an example of India Law. The Indian Obliegation Law adopted a English Law and Family Law and Succession Law was based by Chinese Law. Therefore, it is very difficult to classify the legal family, whether belong to continental law, anglo-american law or asian law. As we know, Korean Law is influenced by many legal systems cf. Choi Chong-Ko, *Korean Law and World Law*, Kyoyuk-Kwahak-sa, 1989, p. 8.
3) See Rudolf Schlesinger, *Comparative Law*, 1988; Choi Ghong-Ko, op.cit. p.10.
4) He divides it by racial law, the law of the antiquity race, the law of the Latin domain, the law of the German domain, the law of the Slavic domain, anglo-american law, the law of religion, African - Asian Law. Schnitzer, *Vergleichende Rechtslehre I, 2.Aufl.* 1961; Choi Ghong-Ko, *op.cit.*
5) He classified Western Law, Soviet Law, Islam Law, Hindu Law and Chinese Law in his book 'Traité elementare dedroit civil comparé' But later, he changed his mind and classified Roman-German Law Family, Socialist Law Family etc. in his book 'Les grands Systrmes de droit contemporains' in 1966; See detailed Choi Ghong-Ko, op.cit. p.16-18.
6) They classified Latin Law, German Law, Nord-europe Law, Anlo-amerikan Law, Socialist Law, East Asian Law, Islam Law, Hindu Law etc. See Konard Zweigert/Hein Kötz, *Einführung in die Rechtsverglieichung, auf Gebiete des Privatrechts I*, 1971; Choi Ghong-Ko, op.cit. p. 18-23.

These western scholars understanding of Asian legal systems lack depth due to several misunderstandings, primarily in analyzing these systems from the viewpoint of western legal thought and a sense of superiority.[7]

As a result, many of the legal scholars in Asia began to put effort to establish the correct and appropriate Asian Law studies. In Japan, the theory of Asian Law History by Masao Samada is being spotlighted.[8]

Even though Asian countries have created their legal system based on Western systems during the modernization period, they did not adopt fully the western attitude vis-à-vis the law.[9] Also, it is debatable whether Asian countries with diverse legal, social, and economic ideologies and customs can create an Asian Sports law that is consistent throughout the region. Of course the answer is yes; as mentioned above, Asian legal scholars have already been trying to establish a unique legal system that fits social, economical, and regional characteristics of Asia. Asian Sports Law is easier to develop compared to other areas of law since it is less subject to political, religious, and regional factors that could undermine its progress.

## The Contents of Asian Sports Law

There are two types of Sports Law in Asia: Autonomic Sports Law and Sports Law by State. Autonomic Sports Law is mostly consistent since it is

---

7) As a result of such effort, See Masashi Chiba, *Structure of multi dimensions of Asia Law*, Semondoh, 1988; Kiyoshi Igarashi, *Several aspects of the modern comparative law*, [Tokyo] : Shinzansha, 2002.6., *same person, Introduction to comparativ law*, Tokyo: Nippon Hyoron-Sha Co., 1968.5; same person, *History and Theory of the compariative law*, Tokyo: Ichiryubu-Sha, 1977.8; same person, *Problems of Comparative Civil Law*, Tokyo:Ichiryubu-Sha, 1976; Nobuyuki Yasuda, *ASEAN Law: An introduction to ASEAN law*, Tokyo:Nippon Hyoron-Sha Co., 1996.8.; same person, *Asian law and Society*, Tokyo: Sanseido Co., Ltd., 1987; Yamazaki, Nobuyuki Yasuda edition: *Legal System of Asian Countries*, Tokyo: Asian Economy Institute, 1980.3. (Materials of Economic Cooperation No. 97).

8) See Masao Shimada, *History of Orient law*, Tokyo: Tokyo Kyohaku-Shae, 1976. He wrote a conclusion in this book that it is better to call <History of Asian Law> in a title called 'History of law in World history' ; the Korean translation version.: See Im Dae-Hee and others, *History of Asian Law*, Seokyung, 2000.

9) The same discussion; see Kim Sany-Yong, "Necessity and Method and of Studies on Asian Legal System", *Studies on Asian Legal System*, 2004, Vol. 1, pp. 10-14.

related to international sports games. On the other hand, Sports Law by State requires comparative studies in establishment and development of each country, its current status, and political considerations such as each nation's legislative, judicial, and administrative bodies. It is recommended to perform cooperative and educational studies of security of Fundamental Rights of Sports, actualization of Autonomic Sports Law, and improvement of Relational Sports Law for each Asian nation. In particular, studies of legal policies including the enactment of Fundamental Sports Act and Sports Industry Promotion Act, consolidation of Relational School Sports Law, security of Autonomic Sports Law, and Administrative Sports Law as well as Alternative Dispute Resolution (ADR) and Sports Criminal Law and Sports Accident Law.

Also, United Asian Sports Law, which will be applied in every Asian country, requires studies in depth. The object of this study will be the unification of Autonomic Sports Law and National Sports Law. The unification and harmonization of laws are required in order to promote the interchange and cooperation of sports among Asian nations. It is necessary to establish a restatement of law or model law so that the Asians can benefit from the participation in sports.

## Strategy for Developing Asian Sports Law

### Supporting the Asian Sports Law Association

The Asian Sports Law Association(ASLA) seems to have the most important and effective human resources for studying Asian Sports Law and for exchange and cooperation among Asian nations. Since it is an academic organization with diverse sports law scholars from Korea, China, and Japan, it is a suitable forum for studying Asian Sports Law. It is necessary for scholars from different nations to put endless effort to constantly collect, exchange, and study the information of Sports Laws together for the development of Asian Sports Law.

If Asian legal conferences are promoted, the study of Asian Sports Law will be successful. In order to promote Asian legal conferences, it is necessary to prepare the financial foundation and expand research funds. This necessarily requires close cooperation from related governmental organization, the sports industry, and sports association.

## Unifying and Harmonizing Asian Sports Law

The necessity to promote the unification and harmonization of Asian Sports Law through comparative studies is fundamental. The establishment of organizations such as an Asian Union or Asian Economic and Social Community as well as governmental and nongovernmental organizations for interchange and cooperation of Asian sports will soon come to fruition. Studies of conventions to develop the legal bases of such organizations are urgently required.

Europe provides a good model for such development. European countries developed modern European law by combining both Roman and Germanic laws. Also, England and Scandinavian Empire have developed their own unique laws. After the Second World War, European countries including Germany, France, Italy, Belgium, Netherland, and Luxemburg established the ECSC (European Coal and Steel Community) in 1951. In 1957, ECSC further developed the EEC (European Economic Community) and merged with EURATOM (European Atomic Energy Community). Finally in 1967, the EEC unified itself into the EC (European Community) which became the basis for the European Union. The successful operation of the EC led England, Denmark, and Ireland to join the community in 1973, followed by Greece in 1981, and Spain and Portugal in 1986. The European Union Agreement was concluded in 1991 and was announced in 1993. Based on this agreement, the unification of European economies, politics, society and other systems was actively propelled. Starting in May 2005, 27 European nations joined the EU, allowing for the unification of pan-Europe.[10] The EU is now putting effort to unify European politics through development of a single currency and establishing a united constitution.

Numbers of European legal scholars are putting much effort to accomplish

---

10) For more information about the development of Eropean Union See at http://www.europa.eu.int/; http://www.eu.or.kr/; http://www.delkor.cec.eu.int/ .

the unification and harmonization of European law in order to accelerate the unification of the European economy, society, and politics. They are supporting the EU by studying European Tort Law and Contract Law and proposing restatement and Unification Law. The EU established Directives and Regulations to support the establishment of a unified European Law.[11]

Based on the European success, Asian legal scholars should acknowledge the necessity of cooperation and putting effort to support Asian unification and development. Through comparative studies, it is possible to unify and harmonize Asian Law.

## Promoting Exchanges and Cooperation of Asian Sports

History shows how sports have played a fundamental role in promoting understanding and improving relations between nations. Even during the Cold War, sports, before any other sphere, served as an important bond between nations. Sports allow people to have a mutual understanding and build trust instead of hostility caused by cultural differences. Moreover, sports, unlike political exchanges, are accessible and have an enormous influence because they facilitate economic cooperation and tourism.

Asian Sports Law should serve as the basis to stimulate such exchange and cooperation. The support of Asian Sports Law is essential in developing the Asian sports industry that can benefit prosperity, using both human and material resources in Asia. Through studying and developing Asian Sports Law, it is possible to prepare the legal foundation that allows for exchange within Asia. It is possible that Asian nation governments can gain a deeper sense of their legal system and laws better, as well as that of other nations, thus promoting mutual understanding and cooperation.

---

11) See Jochen Taupitz, *Europäische Privatrechtscereinheitlichung heute und morgen*, Tübingen: Mohr, 1993; Kim Sang-Yong, *Comparative Contract Law*, Pub-Young-Sa, 2002; European Committee on Contract Law, Principles of European Contract Law; www.lexmercatoria.org .

## Establishing Educational Organization and Programs

It is hard to expect continuous development of scholarly achievement without training future generations through education, study and networking. The organization for training future scholars, developing related teaching materials, and supporting research is necessary in order to continue scholarship of Sports Law. In order to achieve this goal, first, Sports Law programs should be established in universities and research organizations. Currently in Korea, some colleges of physical education and related departments have opened courses such as *Sports Law or Sports Law and Policies*. The Judicial Research and Training Institute of Korea also offers Special Contract Law courses as an elective. However, these developments are hardly sufficient to correctly educate young scholars.

Secondly, the construction a Sports Research Center, for example, is required to promote long-term scholarship. The Korea Institute of Sport Science, an organization affiliated with the Seoul Olympic Sports Promotion Foundation, is researching and developing new sports policies; it is difficult to find other such organizations that study sports law even though there are several sports science research centers. The Sports Law Research Center at Dongkuk University's Comparative Law and Culture Research Institute, located in Seoul, is the only organization that functions as a research center in this area.

Moreover, research papers and teaching materials for Sports Law are very difficult to find. Materials published in Korea are insufficient.[12] In Japan, only about ten books have been published.[13] Annual periodicals are published

---

12) See Sohn Seok-Jong, *Theory and Practice of Sports Law*, Taekun-Munwha-Sa, 2007; Chung Myeong-Su, *Essay to Sports law*, 2007; Chung Sung-Jae, *Introduction to Sports Law*, Korean Haksuljeongbo, 2007; Ryu Dong-Gyun, *Sports Law*, Taekyung Books, 2006; Shin Hi-Jun and ohters, *Sports Law*, Bupryul-Seowon, 2004; Son Kyung-Han/Kim Yong-Sup, *Sports law*, Bupyoung-Sa, 2002; Sohn Seok-Jong, *Sports Law*, Taekun-Munwha-Sa, 2000, etc.

13) See Masashi Chiba, Hamano Yoshio edition, *Introduction to sports law*, Tokyo: Japan Physical education institution publication, 1995.12; Yoichi Inoue, Tadashi Ogasawara supervision, *Sports Law of Takashi Ito by introduction talks*, Tokyo: Fumashobo, 2005; Hamano Yoshio, *Problems of physical education and sports law*, Tokyo, Maeno Bookstore, 1983.9; Takashi Sato, (an enlarged and revised edition) Studies on cases of physical education and sports accident precedent, Tokyo: Doyashoin Books, 1995.7.; A.J.

in Korea and Japan, e.g., Sport and Law by Korea Sports Law Institute in Korea[14], and annual report of the Japan Sports Law Institute. Model texts and prudent research results should be promoted and publishes as they are in the United States and Germany.

### Establishing Financial Support for the Research and Education of Asian Sports Law

Financial support for research and education of Asian Sports Law is urgently needed. In order to attain financial resources, the involvement of sports-related government bodies is important. So far, the budget used in the sports industry is rarely distributed to the study of Sports Law. Public awareness of the importance of Sports Law is necessary in this regard. Support and cooperation of the sports industry and other sports organizations are also needed. The establishment of a tentatively named Institute of Asian Sports Law and Policies can be expected in the long term.

Finally, it is necessary to construct a network of human and material resources related to information on Asian Sports and Sports Laws. Collecting and organizing laws, ordinances, leading cases, official gazettes and other information as well as exchanging information in conferences is needed.[15] In

---

Schwarz, Norio Takahashi(translated), *Polish criminal law and sports law*, Tokyo: Semondoh, 2000.5; Tetsuro Sugawara, *Spcial crisis control studies on sports law::for sporting house / sports manager / sports leaders.* Tokyo: Ray Dell Institute, 2005.1; Kmiya Sounozhuke, *Sports Law* Tokyo: Sanseido Co. Ltd., 2005.10; Mitsuru Irisawa, *An introduction to law of sports: For Risk management of the leader answering an on-site trouble in a question and answer*, Tokyo: Mountains and seas Books, 2004.2; Keiji Kawai, *Legal position of the professional athlete*, Tokyo: Sanseido Co. Ltd., 2003.6; *Study Group of Sports, Issue of sports meeting for the study, Question and Answer: The legal problems of Sports: Required knowledge about professional player*, Tokyo: Study Group of Civil Law, 2003.11; etc.

14) Specialized academic journal <*Sports and Law*> was founded in 2000 by the Korean Association of Sports & Entertainment Law and was chosen as registered Journal Lists from the Korea Research Foundation in 2006. It is pubishesd 4 times a year from 2007.

15) Because it can be it in the foothold of collection and the study of the Asian laws and ordinances information if it may be said that it is terrible to carry out an ALIN(Asian Legal Information Network) business at the Korean Legislation Research Institute from 2004. If it would be an encouragement mark, and this network would be built, could

order to aid researchers and promote seminars and colloquiums, a robust support system is necessary.

### Studying Norms and Conventions to Develop Governmental and Non-Governmental Organizations in Asia

The future of Asia can be predicted as being an Asian Union or Asian Economic Union. Korea already has proposed a regional cooperative community in order to attain mutual understandings and prosperity in Northeast Asia. This requires mutual effort to understand and fairly.

The future of Asia can be predicted as being an Asian Union or Asian Economic Union. Korea already has proposed a regional cooperative community in order to attain mutual understandings and prosperity in Northeastern Asia. Such purpose requires a prerequisite of mutual effort to understand and fairly exchange ideas.

Comparative and political studies within Asia are urgently required to achieve the unification and harmonization of Sports Law. Also, the study of legal status and foundations of organizations that are already established will be needed. The Olympic Council of Asia (OCA) is currently administrating support for games held in Asia including the Summer and Winter Asian Games. Affiliated with the OCA is the Asian Federation, which has strong political characteristics even though it is defined as a non-governmental organization.[16] Accordingly, changing such institutes into governmental organizations should be the subject of further research. Also, research on agreements and conventions in Asia should be openly promoted with more enthusiasm.

---

be big for the research of the field of sports method; seem to be helpful.

16) The Olympic Council of Asia (OCA) is the apex sports body controlling the sports in Asia. It is one of the five continental associations recognized by the IOC. The OCA was formed in 1982 and has its permanent headquarters in Kuwait. The main objective of the Olympic Council of Asia is to develop sport, culture and education of Asian youth and to promote international respect, friendship, goodwill & peace through sports. See at http://www.ocasia.org.

## Establishing Asian Sports Arbitration Organization

### The Necessity of an Asian Sports Arbitration Organization

The field of sports has strong professional and distinct aspect of autonomic laws since it follows rules of games and regulations of competing groups. The right of autonomy in sports is the result of practicing the right of self-determination. The free operation through self-regulating rules and decisions are guaranteed in sports. As each sporting event has different rules that are unified worldwide and are organized independently, the legitimacy and binding force of sports rules are accepted.

Each sports association acts on behalf of their self-interest. However, as competition intensifies, emerging conflicts are inevitable – quick and satisfactory resolutions are paramount.

In order to settle such conflicts rationally, it seems better to consent to resolve disputes within the realm of the autonomic sports domain rather than involving governments. Therefore, the means to resolve conflicts among sports institutes or players in arbitration should be considered. One solution is to establish an independent arbitration institute that would operate according to self-autonomic rights of sports.

As numerous amateur and professional games including the Asian Games have been held in Asia for many years, the necessity of an Asian Sports Arbitration Institute seems to be urgently necessary in order to resolve potential conflicts. Even though there has been an arbitration organization involved in the Olympics, the role and function of the Court of Arbitration for Sport (CAS)[17] operated by the International Olympic Committee (IOC)[18] has limited power. The establishment of an independent arbitration court for sports should be developed with cooperation of the Olympic Council of Asia (OCA) and other Asian Federations.

### The Authority of the Arbitration Organization

Studies needed to establish the Arbitration Organization should be provided

---

17) See www.tas-cas.org
18) See http://www.olympic.org

by the Asian Sports Law Conference. The results should be provided to the OCA and other Asian Federations so that the representatives of such organizations can establish the authority and jurisdiction of the Arbitration Organization. A plan that persons related to sports confer and make decisions can also be considered.

## Jurisdiction of Arbitration

### 1) Doping

Doping issues are likely to frequently occur in sports arbitration. Doping substances differ depending on games and events. Marijuana is not banned in every game. Also, not all doping substances are included in the doping list.

### 2) Qualification of Players

The issue is important because there are many cases where a player changes his nationality to play for another country. In this case, conflicts may emerge regarding a player's qualifications.(3) Major jurisdiction

### 3) Events Related to Professional Leagues

The events related to professional leagues, draft systems, sponsor contracts, production contracts, publicity rights, and other intellectual and property rights will be important issues.

### 4) Other Conflicts

Other conflicts such as qualifications, conflicts between competitors, and a competing group's claim for a player are predicted.

## Establishing Rules of Sports Arbitration

The rules related to the subject of arbitration, qualifications of applicants, procedures, appointing arbitrators, and expenses should be settled. It is preferable to establish an organization that can both arbitrate and mediate disputes.

Composition of Officials and Funding

The officials should be composed of persons who are recommended by the main body of foundation and who have professional erudition and morals with neutral opinions.

Funding should be supplied by the main body of the foundation and a membership fee collected from cooperative organizations and individuals.

The arbitration body should be composed of professional legal persons such as jurists and lawyers as well as persons involved in sports such as professional sports players.

Location of Headquarters

The headquarters should be established in Jejudo, an international city that connects China, Japan, and Korea.

## Conclusion

It is necessary for Asians to establish the identity of Asian law through introspection and rediscovery of Asia and its current place in the world. Despite the pluralistic environment of Asia, it seems relatively to create comparatively consistent norms in the field of Sports Law. It is necessary to broaden exchange and cooperation of human and material resources as well as sharing legal information of each of the Asian counties in order to unify and harmonize Asian Sports Law.

It is difficult to predict the future of Asia due to the drastic growth of European and American power. The regionalization of Asia should be fostered in order to build an Asian Community. In 2004, 10 ASEAN nations and Korea, China, and Japan agreed to economically cooperate by founding a regional Asian bank. Such economic cooperation will be greatly enhanced when exchange and cooperation of culture, including sports, are promoted. It is readily apparent that sports play a crucial role in Asian economies. If the study of sports law is promoted within the academic community, the laws of each country and the Asian Sports Law will naturally develop an identity and independence and benefit the Asia as a whole.

## References

Chiba, Masashi, *Structure of multi dimensions of Asia Law*, Semondoh, 1988.

Chiba, Masashi/ Yoshio, Hamano edition, *Introduction to sports law*, Tokyo: Japan Physical education institution publication, 1995.12.

Choi Chong-Ko, *Korean Law and World Law*, Kyoyuk-Kwahak-sa, 1989.

Chung Myeong-Su, *Essay to Sports law*, 2007.

Chung Sung-Jae, *Introduction to Sports Law*, Korean Haksuljeongbo, 2007.

Igarashi, Kiyoshi, *Several aspects of the modern comparative law*, [Tokyo]: Shinzansha, 2002.6.

Igarashi, Kiyoshi,, *Introduction to comparativ law*, Tokyo: Nippon Hyoron-Sha Co., 1968.5.

Igarashi, Kiyoshi, *History and Theory of the compariative law*, Tokyo: Ichiryubu-Sha, 1977.8.

Igarashi, Kiyoshi, *Problems of Comparative Civil Law*, Tokyo:Ichiryubu-Sha, 1976.

Inoue, Tadashi, Ogasawara supervision, *Sports Law of Takashi Ito by introduction talks*, Tokyo: Fumashobo, 2005.

Irisawa, Mitsuru, *An introduction to law of sports: For Risk management of the leader answering an on-site trouble in a question and answer*, Tokyo: Mountains and seas Books, 2004.2

Kawai, Keiji, *Legal position of the professional athlete*, Tokyo: Sanseido Co. Ltd., 2003.6;

Kim Sang-Yong, *Comparative Contract Law*, Pub-Young-Sa, 2002.

Kim Sany-Yong, "Necessity and Method and of Studies on Asian Legal System", *Studies on Asian Legal System*, 2004, Vol. 1, pp. 10-14.

Ryu Dong-Gyun, *Sports Law*, Taekyung Books, 2006

Sato, Takashi (an enlarged and revised edition) *Studies on cases of physical education and sports accident precedent*, Tokyo: Doyashoin Books,

1995.7.

Schlesinger, Rudolf, Comparative Law, 1988;

Schnitzer, *Vergleichende Rechtslehre I, 2.Aufl.* 1961

Schwarz, A.J., Norio Takahashi(translated), *Polish criminal law and sports law*, Tokyo: Semondoh, 2000.5;

Shimada, Masao, *History of Orient law*, Tokyo: Tokyo Kyohaku-Shae, 1976(the Korean translation version.: See Im Dae-Hee and others, History of Asian Law, Seokyung, 2000)

Shin Hi-Jun and ohters, *Sports Law*, Bupryul-Seowon, 2004

Sohn Seok-Jong, *Theory and Practice of Sports Law*, Taekun-Munwha-Sa, 2007.

Sohn Seok-Jong, *Sports Law*, Taekun-Munwha-Sa, 2000.

Son Kyung-Han/Kim Yong-Sup, *Sports law*, Bupyoung-Sa, 2002.

Sounozhuke, Kmiya, *Sports Law*, Tokyo: Sanseido Co. Ltd., 2005.10.


Sugawara, Tetsuro, *The spcial crisis control studies on sports law::for sporting house / sports manager / sports leaders.* Tokyo: Ray Dell Institute, 2005.1.

Study Group of Sports, Issue of sports meeting for the study, Question and Answer: *The legal problems of Sports: Required knowledge about professional player*, Tokyo: Study Group of Civil Law, 2003.11.

Taupitz, Jochen, *Europäische Privatrechtscereinheitlichung heute und morgen*, Tübingen: Mohr, 1993;

Yamazaki, Nobuyuki Yasuda edition: *Legal System of Asian Countries*, Tokyo: Asian Economy Institute, 1980.3. (Materials of Economic Cooperation No. 97).

Yasuda, Nobuyuki, ASEAN Law: *An introduction to ASEAN law*, Tokyo:Nippon Hyoron-Sha Co., 1996.8.

Yasuda, Nobuyuki, *Asian law and Society*, Tokyo: Sanseido Co., Ltd., 1987

Yoshio, Hamano, *Problems of physical education and sports law*, Tokyo, Maeno Bookstore, 1983.9.

Konard Zweigert/Hein Kötz, *Einführung in die Rechtsverglieichung, auf Gebiete des Privatrechts I*, 1971.


www.tas-cas.org ; http://www.ocasia.org ;

www.wada-ama.org ; www.lexmercatoria.org

http://www.europa.eu.int/;http://www.eu.or.kr/ ;http://www.delkor.cec.eu.int/

# The Development of International Sports Arbitration Bodies and Challenges of Legislative Policy for Reestablishment of Sports Arbitration Agency in Korea*

KEE-YOUNG YEUN**

*As the Korea Sports Council and The Korean Olympic Committee (KOC) were integrated in June 2009, the Amended Articles expunged the applicable provisions of the e Korea Sports Arb itration Committee (KSAC), which was established in Markch 2006. To successfully host international sports events, such as 2014 Incheon Asian Games and PyeongChang 2018 Winter Olympics, the Korea Sports Arbitration Committee (KSAC) must be restored immediately. In this sense, this thesis places emphasis on the necessity of precise legal basis with the purpose of the revitalization of sports dispute settlement as well as the enhancement of the Korea Sports Arbitration Committee.*

Key Word: Court of Arbitration for Sport(CAS), Korea Sports Arbitration Committee (KSAC), Sports Arbitration, Sports Mediation, Med–Arbitration

## Introduction

At the turn of the 21st century, the establishment of the Sports Arbitration Agency is being actively promoted based on research results of the sports law circle.[1] With the purpose of fulfilling sports autonomy, the

---

\* This article was originally published in 『Journal of Arbitration Studies』 , Vol 23 No. 3(September 2013) pp 101-126, by the Korean Association of Arbitration Studies in Seoul, Korea.

\*\* Professor of Law, Dr. jur.(Unversity of Göttingen, Germany), Dongguk University College of Law in Seoul, Korea

1) Detailed contents can be found in: YEUN Kee-Young, "Establishment and Activities of

International Olympic Committee (IOC) has already accepted public opinion that the Sports Arbitration Agency is necessary and founded the Court of Arbitration for Sport (CAS) in 1984. In 1994, the IOC guaranteed the independence and neutrality of the organization; it institutionalized activation plans and made it public to all nations that the Sports Arbitration Agency is needed. Furthermore, Korea started paying attention to the Sport Dispute Institution as Korean athletes were directly disadvantaged at the 2002 Winter Olympics in Salt Lake City and the 2004 Olympics in Athens. Taking these events of misjudgments of sports refereeing as an opportunity, the damage to "fairness" - the ground rule of the Olympic Charter - was considered pitiable and we all realized the significance of the Court of Arbitration for Sport, including the settlement body of sports entanglement.[2] In 2003, Japan established the Japan Sports Arbitration Agency (JSAA) and operated it as a general corporate body starting in April 2009. The JSAA started operating as a public corporate body after receiving recognition as one in April 2013.[3]

By fairly and rapidly solving conflict between the contestants and sports groups through adjustment or arbitration, the Korea Sports Council (KSC) specified a foundation in March 2006 in Art. 54 in Articles of KSC, and established and operated the Korea Sports Arbitration Committee (KSAC), with the means of contributing advancement of Korean sports. After the consultation, between the Ministry of Culture, Sports and Tourism and the KSC, which, to persuade the IOC members, have shared the understanding

---

Korea Sports Arbitration Committee", *The Korean Journal of Sports and Law,* Vol. 5, The Korean Association of Sports and Entertainment Law(KASEL), 2004, pp. 65-82; YEUN Kee-Young, "Proposal for Establishment of Sports Arbitration Organization" *The Korean Journal of Sports and Law,* Vol. 10 No.4, The Korean Association of Sports and Entertainment Law(KASEL), 2007, pp. 415-433.

2) On these two incidents, see YEUN Kee-Young, Id, pp417-418; on Dong-Sung Kim incident, see especially Arbitration CAS ad hoc Division (OWG Salt Lake City 2002) 007 Korean Olympic Committee(KOC) v. International Skating Union(ISU), award of 23 Feb. 2002, Matthieu Reeb(eds), Digest of CAS Awards III 2001-2003(2004),6.1.1; on Yang Tae Young incident, see CAS 2004/A/704 Yang Tae Young v. FIG, para 1.1.1.-1.1.5.

3) On JSAA, see http://www.jsaa.jp/doc/gaiyou.html (visited 2013. 8. 5); Dogauchi, Masato, "The Activities of Japan Sports Arbitration Agency" *The Korean Journal of Sports and Law,* Vol. 5, 2004.

that the KSAC is necessary to attract attention to the PyeongChang Olympic Winter Games and other international competitions, the KSAC was founded. Nonetheless, in June 2009, as the KOC and the Ministry of Culture, Sports and Tourism have combined, Amended Articles have expurgated the regulation that is the basis of the KSAC and led to the discontinuation of budget support since 2010. These decisions are ignoring the foundation's purpose. In particular, it will likely act as an obstacle to hosting Asian Games Incheon 2014 and the 23rd Olympic Winter Games in PyeongChang, as well as many other upcoming international competitions. This will retrogress international trend and sports advancement, so either the KSAC should be reestablished or a new sports arbitration agency should be established.

In this paper, legal strategies to properly conduct the functions of the Korea Sports Arbitration Agency, which will be newly founded in the future, are proposed. The paper will discuss the measures to settle the arbitration agency as an activated organization. These kinds of theoretical and institutional bases are to be found in the foundation background and system reform process of the CAS.

## The Distinctive Characteristics of the Sports Arbitration Agency and the Present Condition of International Sports Arbitration Bodies

### Conception and the Process of Arbitration in the Arbitration Act

The Korean Arbitration Act (KAA) was revised in 1966 and was partly modified in 1973; however, it has been criticized for its inadequacy to adapt to the international legislation environment. Thus, the current Arbitration Act (Law No. 6083), revised entirely in 1999, drastically embraced the content of UNICITRAL's Unicitral Model Law with the purpose to correspond to international tendencies. Such effort can be acknowledged to have restored trust from the international community and is still attempting to secure universality of dispute settlements. In other words, the KAA has procured international clarity, fairness, and legal stability.[4] In 2010, conforming to the 'easy-to-understand law making project' of the Legislative Office, the

Arbitration Act was revised into a simpler and easier wording and has been operating since.[5)]

The Arbitration system is an autonomous dispute settlement system which solves conflicts by selecting a third party arbitrator following the terms of the Arbitration Agreement.[6)] It acknowledges the adjudication of the arbitrator, not the verdict of the court.[7)] It is one type of ADR system which can rationally and rapidly settle conflicts in professional and technical areas. Although this is an independent legal system, the national governmental authority's right to execute with force is guaranteed by Arbitrary Act (Art. 1, 8, 9, 13, 35, 37 KAA).

The "Arbitration Agreement," disregarding whether it is a contractual dispute or not, is a consent between the concerned parties to solve all the conflicts, or partial consent that has already occurred or will occur in the future by arbitration (Art. 3, No. 2 KAA).

---

4) To see international trend of arbitration act, centering around UN, the reality of arbitration and issues of arbitration act and harmony of each country was rendered; in 1958, New York Convention for approval and execution of foreign arbitral award was held (Korea ratified in 1973. 5. 9). UNCITRAL adopted Model Law in 1985. 6.21 And advised each nation to apply the amendment to the arbitration act and accelerated international unification of arbitration act. Accordingly, since 1986 numbers of nations around the world established and reorganizing arbitration agencies with the purpose to attract international arbitration while reforming and enacting arbitration act. Korea was also influenced by this international tendency; the necessity for reforming arbitration act was raised from academia and business circles; there was also a need to quickly amend the arbitration act in a circumstance where international arbitral environment were radically changing. Eventually in 1999 arbitration act was entirely revised with the purpose to arrange international-level arbitration act, accommodating advanced foreign countries' examples of legislation and international standards to invite international arbitration.

5) http://www.law.go.kr/lsInfoP.do?lsiSeq=103956&lsId=&viewCls=lsRvsDocInfoR&chrClsCd=010102#0000 (visited Aug. 3, 2013).

6) Kim Yong-Kil, "A Study on the Scope of Effect in Arbitration Agreements" The Journal of Arbitration, Vol. 23 No 2, The korean Association of Arbitration Studies, 2013, pp.11-12;Sohn Kyung-Han /Shim Hyun-Joo "A New Approach on the Arbitration Agreement" The Journal of Arbitration, Vol. 23 No1, The korean Association of Arbitration Studies, 2013, p. 57.

7) Takeshi Kojima, *Civil Procedure and ADR in Japan,*, Series of the Institute of Comparative Law in Japan 65, Tokyo: Chuo University Press, 2004, pp. 265‑344, especially see pp. 321‑344.

The Arbitration Agreement can either be an isolated agreement or a form that includes an arbitration clause in the contract. It is the principle to complete the Arbitration Agreement in document. However, if the signed documents from the concerned parties contain the Arbitration Agreement, or if the Arbitration Agreement is included in the documents exchanged by letter, telegram, telegraph, fax or any other means of communication, or if one party claims that the party has the Arbitration Agreement and the other party does not argue about the claim, it ought to be considered as a settled arbitration (Art. 4 KAA). Arbitration is the concerned parties' expression of will to obey the decision made by the arbitrator. Arbitral Award is recognized to hold the same effect as the final ruling of the court.

The Arbitration procedure includes progress from the incident being charged to the incident being resolved by settled decision. When no negotiation appears during the process, the Arbitration agency applies the KAA's Arbitration Act and proceeds with proper procedure and methods of arbitration. In this case, the tribunal holds the right to judge the admissibility, relevance, and credibility of evidence (KAA Art. 20). When there is no separate negotiation or firm declaration of will from the concerned party, the procedure is decided upon the Arbitration Rules which the arbitration body had enacted.

## Right of Sports Autonomy and the Distinct Characteristics of a Sports Arbitration Body

Sports hold distinct characteristics and professionalism of autonomy law in accordance to the game rules and regulations of the game group. To sports, autonomy law is the product of exercising self-determination. The rights to decide a sport group, to legislate self-regulating rules, and to operate them are guaranteed. Sports work independently, holding internationally agreed upon game rules. The legitimacy and binding power of sports rules are acknowledged in that they are followed in regional tournaments, international games, and even in the Olympics; as such, sports can be shown to be organized.

Each sports organization works for the benefit of the sports people which belong to it, as well as for the development of the sport. However, in verified competitions occur collisions of interest among different sports people and organizations; speedy and amicable resolutions are required.[8]

In order for a sensible resolution of sports disputes, it is ideal for the disputes to be resolved within the self-autonomy of sports and avoid the intervention of nations. Therefore, the best option for resolving sports disputes is to establish an independent arbitration organization and not to file a lawsuit to a court that is a governmental institution.[9]

## International Sports Arbitration Organization

### The Disciplinary Committee and Appeal Panel of FIFA

The disciplinary committee and appeal panel of FIFA is comprised of a chairperson, a vice-chairman, and a set number of members; the chairperson must have a qualification in law. The disciplinary committee applies the rules that the executive committee has set and decides on detailed bylaws. The disciplinary committee withholds the right to take disciplinary action when each nation's soccer associations and organization, executives and staff, coaches, and athletes violate FIFA's regulation and game rules, orders and decisions. However, it does not hold the right to take part in the athlete's qualifications transfer or halt memberships for soccer associations.

Conflicts among FIFA, national soccer associations, soccer clubs, and the members of the clubs are bound to the obligation not to file a lawsuit to a court that is a governmental institution but to let the autonomic arbitration body (internal organizations such as disciplinary committees) handle arbitrations. If conflict arises between two or more associations and thus agreement on organizing a tribunal, the FIFA executive committee is to decide on the matter.[10] It is regulated in FIFA rules not to request

---

8) Kim Yong-Kil, "A Study of Alternative Dispute Resolution for Sports Dispute - Focus on Arbitration System -" *The Journal of Arbitration*, Vol. 21 No 1, The korean Association of Arbitration Studies, 2011, pp.111-112.

9) Kim Yong-Kil, Id,.*The Journal of Arbitration*, Vol. 21 No 1, 2011, pp.113-114.

10) FIFA Rule Art. 40 defines the list of disciplinary actions; in occasion of insubordination, the club cannot participate in title match nor goodwill match and every international

arbitration to the CAS.

### International Olympic Committee

The IOC is an NGO by international law; however, it is also acknowledged as a corporation in accordance with convention with the Swiss government November 1, 2000.[11] The headquarters are located in Lausanne, Switzerland.[12]

The IOC Executive Board assumes general overall responsibility for the administration of the IOC and the management of its affairs. In particular, it performs the following duties: it monitors observance of the Olympic Charter; it submits to the Session the names of the persons whom it recommends for election to the IOC; it establishes and supervises the procedure for accepting and selecting candidatures to organize the Olympic Games; it takes all decisions, and issues regulations of the IOC, which are legally binding, in the form it deems most appropriate; for instance, codes, rulings, norms, guidelines, guides, manuals, instructions, requirements and other decisions, including, in particular, but not limited to, all regulations necessary to ensure the proper implementation of the Olympic Charter and the organization of the Olympic Games.[13] The IOC Executive Board may delegate powers to one or more of its members, to IOC commissions, to members of the IOC administration, to other entities or to third persons.[14]

## The Development Process of the Court of Arbitration for Sport (CAS)

### Foundation Background

The Court of Arbitration for Sport (CAS) was founded as an ADR Organization by the IOC in 1984.[15] In 1981, Antonio Samaranch was elected

---

match sponsored by national associations and/or clubs.

11) Olympic Charter Rule 15.1. "The IOC is an international non-governmental not-for-profit organization, of unlimited duration, in the form of an association with the status of a legal person, recognised by the Swiss Federal Council in accordance with an agreement entered into on 1 November 2000".

12) Olympic Charter Rule 15.2.

13) Olympic Charter Rule 19.3.

14) Olympic Charter Rule 19.4.

as IOC chairman; he drew up an arbitration body, insisting on the necessity of a specialized body for Sports Arbitration.[16]

The history of the CAS dates back to the 1982 Session of the IOC in Rome. At this session, at the instigation of President Antonio Samaranch, the IOC accepted the idea of creating a court of arbitration, the jurisdiction of which would encompass activities linked more or less directly with sports. Thereafter, a draft of a statute was elaborated by three jurist members of the IOC, among them Keba Mbaye (Senegal), at that time a judge of the International Court of Justice (ICJ) at the Hague. This draft statute was subsequently adopted by the IOC on the recommendation of its Executive Board at its New Delhi Session in March 1983. The Statute entered into force on June 30, 1984.[17]

### The Independence and Reform

Since its establishment in 1984, the independency and fairness of the CAS as an arbitration body has been questioned. The chairman of the CAS doubled as an IOC member; the IOC elects 30 out of the 60 committee members of the CAS while 15 people among those 30 members doubled as IOC member. Also, they artificially made two-thirds of the CAS committee members approve of the reformation of CAS regulations through the instruction of the IOC executive committee during an IOC session.[18] Although the CAS was under the direct control of the IOC at the time of its establishment, the necessity for the body to turn into a more neutral organization was addressed since there was a possibility of a situation in which the IOC would file a case. However, it reached the point where a consensus that the CAS should be reformed as an independent organization

---

15) http://www.tas-cas.org/en/histoire/frmhist.htm(visited Aug. 3, 2013).
16) http://www.tas-cas.org/en/histoire/frmhist.htm(visited Aug. 3, 2013).
17) Bruno Simma, "The Court of Arbitration for Sport", in: *The Court of Arbitration for Sport 1984-2004* (ed. by Blackshaw/ Robert C.H. Siekmann/ Janwillem Soek), T.M.C. Asser Press, 2006, p. 21.
18) Matthiew Reeb, "The Role and Functions of the CAS", *The Court of Arbitration for Sport 1984-2004* (ed. by Blackshaw/ Robert C.H. Siekmann/ Janwillem Soek), T.M.C. Asser Press, 2006, p. 33.

from the IOC.[19]

On the other hand, in February 1992, a German horse rider named Elmar Gundel lodged an appeal for arbitration with the CAS on the basis of the arbitration clause in the International Federation for Equestrian Sports (FEI) statutes, challenging a decision pronounced by the federation. This decision, which followed a horse doping case, disqualified the rider, and imposed a suspension and fine upon him. The award rendered by the CAS on October 15, 1992 founded partly in favor of the rider (the suspension was reduced from three months to one month).[20] Then, Elmar Gundel filed a public law appeal with the Swiss Federal Court. He disputed the validity of this award; the fact that his claim was rendered by a court did not meet the condition of impartiality and independence needed to be considered a proper arbitration court. In its judgment of March 15, 1993, the Swiss Federal Tribunal (Court) recognized the CAS as a true court of arbitration. However, the Swiss Federal Tribunal (Court) drew attention to the numerous links which existed between the IOC and the CAS: the CAS was financed almost by the IOC; the IOC was able to modify the CAS Statute; and the real power given to the OOC and its president to appoint members of the CAS. In the opinion of the Swiss Court, the CAS had to be made more independent of the IOC both organizationally and financially[21].

This Gundel judgment led to the reform of the CAS.[22] Accordingly, CAS rules were drastically reformed in 1993. First of all, the CAS Statute and Rules were completely revised to make it independent of the IOC.[23] After the International Conference 'Law and Sport' in Lausanne, the International Council of Arbitration for Sport (ICAS) was created by the Paris Agreement.[24] Practically speaking, the operating fund of the ICAS is provided by three organizations: the IOC; the Ifs, including the Association of Summer Olympic

---

19) James Nafziger, *International Sports Law* 2nd ed., Transnational Publishers Inc., 2004, p.43.
20) Matthiew Reeb, Id.,p.33.
21) Matthiew Reeb, Id.,pp.33~34; Jan Paulssion, "Arbitration of international Sport Disputes", *The Court of Arbitration for Sport 1984-2004* (ed. by Blackshaw/ Robert C.H. Siekmann/ Janwillem Soek), T.M.C. Asser Press, 2006, p. 47.
22) Matthiew Reeb, Id.,p. 34; Jan Paulssion, Id., 47.
23) Matthiew Reeb, Id.,p. 34.
24) http://www.tas-cas.org/en/histoire/frmhist.htm(visited Aug. 3, 2013).

International Federations (ASOIF) and the AIWF; and finally the Association of National Olympic Committees (ANOC). There are 20 committee members in the ICAS.

The purpose of the ICAS is to facilitate the resolution of sports-related disputes through arbitration or mediation and to safeguard the independence of the CAS and the rights of the parties involved. It is also responsible for the administration and financing of the CAS.[25]

The disputes to which a federation, association or other sports -related body is a party are a matter for arbitration pursuant to this Code, only insofar as the statutes or regulations of the bodies or a specific agreement so provide.[26]

The seat of both the ICAS and the CAS is Lausanne, Switzerland.[27]

The term of ICAS members is four years and reappointment is allowed. Upon their appointment, the members of the ICAS sign a declaration undertaking to exercise their function personally, with total objectivity and independence, in conformity with this Code. They are, in particular, bound by the confidentiality obligation provided in Article R43 of the CAS. Members of the ICAS may not appear on the list of CAS arbitrators or mediators nor act as counsel to any party in proceedings before the CAS.[28]

The ICAS exercises the following functions[29]: It adopts and amends this Code; it elects from among its members for one or several renewable period(s) of four years the president, two vice-presidents who shall replace the president if necessary, by order of seniority in age; if the office of president becomes vacant, the senior vice-president shall exercise the functions and responsibilities of the president until the election of a new president, the president of the Ordinary Arbitration Division and the president of the Appeals Arbitration Division of the CAS, the deputies of the two division presidents who can replace them in the event they are prevented from carrying out their functions. The election of the president

---

25) Art. S2 Code of Sports-related Arbitration. "S" is Statues of the Bodies Working for the Settlement of Sports-related Disputes.
26) Art. S1 Code of CAS.
27) Art. S1 Code of CAS.
28) Art. S5 Code of CAS.
29) Art. S6 Code of CAS.

and of the vice-presidents shall take place after consultation with the IOC, the ASOIF, the AIOWF and the ANOC.

The ICAS exercises its functions itself, or through its board, consisting of the president, the two vice-presidents of the ICAS, the president of the Ordinary Arbitration Division and the president of the CAS Appeals Arbitration Division.30)

### The Basis of Arbitration

1) The Olympic Charter Article 59 (Dispute-Arbitration):

All disputes related to Olympic Games are obligated to only be filed to the CAS in accordance with the sports related arbitration rules. The CAS's so-called exclusive jurisdiction is acknowledged.31)

Also, all Olympic athletes can only ask the CAS for judgment if they have written a pledge acknowledging the jurisdiction of a temporary arbitration court.

2) Olympic anti-doping code Art 3.1: The recipient of the decision made by competent authorities such as the IOC, the IF, the NOC, and other organizations applying the rules can appeal to the CAS.32)

### Main Cases under Jurisdiction

The CAS constitutes panels which have the responsibility of resolving disputes arising in the context of sport by arbitration and/or mediation pursuant to the Procedural Rules.33) For such purposes, the CAS provides the necessary infrastructure, effects the constitution of Panels and oversees the efficient conduct of the proceedings.34)

### 1) *Doping*

The most frequently brought up issue in sports arbitration is doping. In

---

30) Art. S7 Code of CAS.
31) Olympic Charter Article 59.
32) Olympic anti-doping code Art 3.1
33) Art. R27 Code of CAS.
34) Art. S12 Code of CAS.

the case of the Nakano Olympics, the IOC decided on depriving an athlete who inhaled marijuana of a gold medal. The athlete appealed to the CAS; the CAS returned the gold medal to the athlete, acknowledging that marijuana is not a doping substance. The measure of doping substances varies game by game; Marijuana is not considered to be a doping substance restricted from all games. On the other hand, not all the doping substances are on the doping list. In the Atlanta Olympics, there was an arbitration in which the athlete was deprived of a bronze medal for using a substance that has a stimulating effect. This substance was invented in the former Soviet Union for military purposes; although it has a stimulating effect, it is not included on the doping list. The CAS returned the medal to the athlete, adjudicating so because the chemical effect of the substance is quite different and the data for the effect of the substance was insufficient.

### 2) Qualification as Representative

The qualification as representative is not a typically expected dispute for the CAS. It is because the qualification as representative is not a problem between international sports leagues and athletes; it is rather a dispute between each nation's Olympic Committee or domestic sports leagues and the athlete. In other words, it is categorized to be a domestic sports dispute. The CAS holds the right to judge for the qualification as representative for Olympic Games only in Australia. In the United States, the American Arbitration Association categorizes it as general arbitration.

### 3) Qualification as Representative Athlete.

In the case of South Korea, nationality does not cause much issue. However, in other nations, changing nationality to become a representative athlete is often discussed. In such cases, the legitimacy of qualification as athlete can cause a dispute.

### Current Processing Situation of the CAS's Dispute Settlement

Numbers of deputes brought up to CAS is increasing annually. There were 76 cases in 2000, 42 in 2001, 86 in 2002, 109 in 2003, 271 in 2004, 198 in

2005, 204 in 2006, 252 in 2007, 313 in 2008, 275 in 2009, 298 in 2010, 365 in 2011, 374 in 212. In the case of Ad hoc Division that executes during Olympic season, there were 6 in 1996, 5 in 1998, 15 in 2000, 8 in 2002, 10 in 2004, 12 in 200, 9 in 2008, 5 in 2010, 11 in 2012. Detailed statistics are contained in the following chart:[35]

[STATISTICS]

TABLE 1

This table lists the cases submitted to the CAS since its creation. The year refers only to the date when the requests were filed, not when the awards or advisory opinions were published.

| Année / Year | Demandes d''arbitrage enregistrées / Requests for arbitration filed | Demandes d''avis consultatif enregistrées / Requests for advisory opinions filed | Total | Demandes d''arbitrage ayant abouti à une sentence / Requests for arbitration leading to an award | Demandes d''avis consultatif ayant abouti à un avis / Requests for advisory opinions leading to an opinion | Total |
|---|---|---|---|---|---|---|
| 1986 | 1 | 1 | 2 | 1 | 1 | 2 |
| 1987 | 5 | 3 | 8 | 2 | 1 | 3 |
| 1988 | 3 | 9 | 12 | 0 | 1 | 1 |
| 1989 | 5 | 4 | 9 | 1 | 0 | 1 |
| 1990 | 7 | 6 | 13 | 1 | 0 | 1 |
| 1991 | 13 | 5 | 18 | 4 | 1 | 5 |
| 1992 | 19 | 6 | 25 | 12 | 0 | 12 |
| 1993 | 13 | 14 | 27 | 6 | 1 | 7 |
| 1994 | 10 | 7 | 17 | 5 | 1 | 6 |
| 1995 | 10 | 3 | 13 | 6 | 2 | 8 |
| 1996 | 20 | 1 | 21 | 16 | 0 | 16 |
| 1997 | 18 | 2 | 20 | 10 | 0 | 10 |

---

35) http://www.tas-cas.org/en/stat/frmstat.htm(visited Aug. 3, 2013).

| Année / Year | Demandes d"arbitrage enregistrées / Requests for arbitration filed | Demandes d"avis consultatif enregistrées / Requests for advisory opinions filed | Total | Demandes d"arbitrage ayant abouti à une sentence / Requests for arbitration leading to an award | Demandes d"avis consultatif ayant abouti à un avis / Requests for advisory opinions leading to an opinion | Total |
|---|---|---|---|---|---|---|
| 1998 | 42 | 3 | 45 | 33 | 2 | 35 |
| 1999 | 32 | 1 | 33 | 21 | 1 | 22 |
| 2000 | 75 | 1 | 76 | 60 | 1 | 61 |
| 2001 | 42 | 0 | 42 | 28 | 0 | 28 |
| 2002 | 83 | 3 | 86 | 70 | 3 | 73 |
| 2003 | 107 | 2 | 109 | 82 | 1 | 83 |
| 2004 | 271 | 0 | 271 | 178 | 0 | 178 |
| 2005 | 194 | 4 | 198 | 133 | 3 | 136 |
| 2006 | 204 | 0 | 204 | 128 | 0 | 128 |
| 2007 | 252 | 0 | 252 | 183 | 0 | 183 |
| 2008 | 311 | 2 | 313 | 220 | 2 | 222 |
| 2009 | 270 | 5 | 275 | 188 | 5 | 193 |
| 2010 | 298 | 0 | 298 | 209 | 0 | 209 |
| 2011 | 365 | 0 | 365 | 246 | 0 | 246 |
| 2012 | 374 | 0 | 374 | 90 | 0 | 90 |
| Total | 3,044 | 82 | 3,126 | 1,933 | 26 | 1,959 |

Comments:

1) the consultation procedure was deleted on January 1, 2011

2) the table includes the cases submitted to the CAS ad hoc divisions.

\* \* \* \* \* \* \*

## TABLE 2

Affaires soumises au Tribunal Arbitral du Sport depuis l"entrée en vigueur du Code de l"arbitrage en matière de sport (22 novembre 1994) jusqu"au 31 décembre 2012

Cases submitted to the Court of Arbitration for Sport from the entry into force of the Code of Sports-related Arbitration (November 22, 1994) until December 31, 2012

| | O | A | C | AcHoc | TOTAL | F | D | W | P |
|---|---|---|---|---|---|---|---|---|---|
| 1995 | 2 | 8 | 3 | 0 | 13 | 8 | 4 | 1 | 0 |
| 1996 | 4 | 10 | 1 | 6 | 21 | 16 | 2 | 3 | 0 |
| 1997 | 7 | 11 | 2 | 0 | 20 | 10 | 4 | 6 | 0 |
| 1998 | 4 | 33 | 3 | 5 | 45 | 35 | 4 | 6 | 0 |
| 1999 | 8 | 24 | 1 | 0 | 33 | 22 | 3 | 8 | 0 |
| 2000 | 5 | 55 | 1 | 15 | 76 | 61 | 4 | 11 | 0 |
| 2001 | 10 | 32 | 0 | 0 | 42 | 28 | 3 | 11 | 0 |
| 2002 | 9 | 66 | 3 | 8 | 86 | 73 | 6 | 7 | 0 |
| 2003 | 61 | 46 | 2 | 0 | 109 | 83 | 18 | 8 | 0 |
| 2004 | 9 | 252 | 0 | 10 | 271 | 178 | 58 | 35 | 0 |
| 2005 | 9 | 185 | 4 | 0 | 198 | 136 | 25 | 37 | 0 |
| 2006 | 17 | 175 | 0 | 12 | 204 | 128 | 44 | 32 | 0 |
| 2007 | 22 | 230 | 0 | 0 | 252 | 183 | 33 | 36 | 0 |
| 2008 | 26 | 276 | 2 | 9 | 313 | 222 | 20 | 69 | 2 |
| 2009 | 25 | 245 | 5 | 0 | 275 | 193 | 4 | 72 | 6 |
| 2010 | 49 | 244 | 0 | 5 | 298 | 209 | 13 | 70 | 6 |
| 2011 | 71 | 294 | 0 | 0 | 365 | 246 | 23 | 74 | 22 |
| 2012 | 62 | 301 | 0 | 11 | 374 | 90 | 17 | 73 | 194 |
| TOTAL | 400 | 2,487 | 27 | 81 | 2,995 | 1,921 | 285 | 559 | 230 |

Abréviations/Abbreviations:

O : Procédures ordinaires / Ordinary procedures

A : Procédures d' 'appel / Appeals procedures

C : Procédures consultatives / Consultation procedures

AdHoc : Procédures ad hoc / Ad hoc procedures

F : Procédures ayant abouti à une sentence ou un avis / Procedures leading to an award or an opinion

D : Procédures terminées par une décision du TAS autre qu' 'une sentence / Procedures terminated by a CAS decision other than an award

W : Affaires retirées / Cases withdrawn

P : Affaires en cours au 31.12.12 / Pending cases on 31.12.12

## The Necessity and the Role of the Korea Sports Arbitration Agency

### Guarantee of Basic Sports Rights and Sports Autonomous Rights.

Issues about sports-related rights are hardly ever found in the history of the development of basic rights since sports began to play a role in human life in modern society. In that sense, foreign legislation cases show changes in the basic rights of many nations, as the constitution was legislated or reformed after World War II. Among those changes appeared sports rights as a constitutional right; in the 1970s, sports became a major part of a nation's policies, and was starting to be addressed constitutionally.

Sports rights, although not part of constitutional regulation, hold a position equivalent to the basic law since they are rights that are essential to the development of human culture and happiness. As a constitutional right, sports rights hold a variety of legal characteristics. The basic rights were expanded as they have been developed from the right of freedom to social rights.

One of the nations that has a constitution containing rules on sports is Greece. Greece introduced rules on sports in the constitution during the 1970s. Greek Constitution Art.16.1 codes the freedom of art and scholarship; in second provision states "Education is a nation's fundamental task with the purpose of educating people of Greece morally, mentally, professionally, and physically," defining sports in an educational perspective. Also, provision 9 of the same article states that "Sports is under the nation's protection and regulation; the country financially supports and regulates all sports leagues that belong to each and every sports organization in accordance to the legislation. The constitution regulates the application of guarantee of each financial support in accordance to the aimed provision of the supported organization."

Similar to Greece's case, constitutions of numerous nations regulate basic sports rights as express provisions in the constitution; such nations include Portugal, Spain, Switzerland, Netherlands, and many states of Germany and South Africa.

The Korean constitution surely allows the relief of rights in sports disputes through trial, guaranteeing the right of access to courts.[36]

Such regulation of our constitution is coded in the same way in every democratic country. It is proper for the ideology of a constitutional state which guards the dignity and value of people and guarantees a living worthy of human dignity that sports people conform to a sports group, legislate rules, and join and participate in that group. Also, disputes occurring in such autonomic and self-regulating sports activity ought to be resolved by its own resources; it coincides with sportsmanship. It is rather natural considering the special characteristics of sports disputes. Therefore, establishing the Korea Sports Arbitration Association and operating an autonomic ally, within the boundaries of positive law, is advisable and adequate.

## Distinct Characteristics of the Rights of Sports Autonomy and Sports Arbitration Bodies

The field of sports has strong professionalism and specialty in legislation of self-government by the rights of sports autonomy in game rules as well as the rules of the game group. In sports, the right of autonomy is the product of practicing autonomous determination. It is guaranteed to form a sports group, set up rules for the organization, set game rules, and operate via an autonomic ally. Each sport operates independently with internationally unified game rules. The legitimacy and binding power of the rules are acknowledged in local tournaments, international tournaments and even in the Olympics.

Each sports group works for the benefit of the concerned sportspeople and for the development of the sport. However, collision of interest occurs among different sportspeople and organizations as competitions gradually increase; speedy and amicable resolution is required.

In order to have reasonable resolutions of sports disputes, it is ideal for the disputes to be resolved within the self-autonomy of sports and avoid the intervention of nations. Therefore, it is the ideal option for resolving sports disputes to establish an independent arbitration organization and not to file a lawsuit to a court that is a governmental institution. To satisfy this, an international organization, the Court of Arbitration for Sport was established

---

36) Art. 10, 37(1) Korean Constitution.

in 1984; sports arbitration organizations are installed and are operated in numerous countries including Japan, United Kingdom, United States, Germany, Netherlands, Canada, Hungary, and New Zealand.

The systems that allow arbitration without judicial dispute are: negotiation, intercession, adjustments, arbitration, and reconciliation. When a dispute arises, first the directly involved parties endeavor to resolve it on their own. When such an endeavor collapses, each person requests and counsels with professionals and hopes for the dispute to be resolved through deputies. If the settlement still fails at this point, then the case is filed in an official organization such as a court for a fair settlement.

When the settlement is handed to the hands of the national organization, court, the winner and the loser are clearly divided; however, usually the conflict and confrontation of the directly involved parties deepens. That is the reason why various ADR systems are applied in each field to reconcile conflicts and confrontation with the purpose of social unification. Moreover, the importance of scholarly research on the method of arbitration and establishment of the organization which can maximize the proper function of such an institution is increasing.[37]

## Special characteristics of sports dispute

Sports disputes have to be resolved fairly in a prompt, friendly, and inexpensive manner. Procedures for general trials are processed in accordance to the strict procedure of legal procedure law; if the trial proceeds to the third trial, it takes too much time. Sports disputes must be resolved quickly and in amity. Adjustment and arbitration systems can contribute to making social unity, relaxing and resolving the conflicts and oppositions because the procedure is closed to the public and comprised of sufficient conversation and consultation with amity. It also results in economic advantage for the sports arbitration utilizing a single-trial system, a concentrated trial, and preliminary discussions; the time and expenses consumed during the procedure are inexpensive.

---

37) Hirota Manabu, *Handbook of Dispute Resolution*, Shinsan Publish Co., 2002, Tokyo, Japan, pp. 3⁻17.

While general civil suit procedures are achieved by strict legal procedure law, thus comparatively guaranteeing propriety and fairness, the arbitration of the arbitration agency can be found to be less fair because of its special characteristics of being speedy and of being founded on the autonomy of the parties directly involved.

The system of arbitration or adjustment must be able to minimize the aftereffects of the dispute arbitration compared to the trials, especially because such a system allows conflict to be resolved or relaxed through offering opportunities to sufficiently stating the point of the issue and depends on mutual negotiation to draw a conclusion.

The system of arbitration and adjustment holds, as unofficial procedure, rapidness and elasticity, excluding the strict regulation application of evidence rule.

Generally, in the procedure of resolving disputes, the system of arbitration and adjustment has great significance in the sense that it actively utilizes a single-trial system, a concentrated trial, and preliminary discussions to minimize the time period until a conclusion is deduced; expenses consumed by the parties directly involved in the dispute can be reduced drastically using this system.

For example, if the dispute is about an athlete's qualification, even if the arbitration agency adjudges to admit the qualification of the athlete, the decision may hold no meaning to the athlete if he misses the game in question. Therefore, sports disputes lean to the tendency of requiring the arbitration agency to speedily draw conclusions.

## Necessity according to International Tendency

It is almost impossible not to follow the international tendency of sports. The Korea Sports Arbitration Committee was established upon the emphasis of the need for a sports arbitration agency along with successful hosting of the Seoul Olympic Games in 1988 and World Cup 2002. Also, the direct disadvantages the Korean athletes had to endure during the 2002 Salt Lake City Winter Olympics and the 2004 Athens Olympics, the interest in the CAS and international sports dispute systems increased sharply. The KOC requested the CAS for an arbitration, however, the case was dismissed; this unfortunate incident became an opportunity for renewing the realization of the necessity and the significance of a sports arbitration agency.

When the CAS was established in 1984, the organization was unable to resolve any dispute for the first two years; the number of cases resolved increased to one in 1986, and five in 1987; however, until 1993, for about ten years the organization only settled 76 cases (seven cases per year). After the reformation that acknowledged the priority rights and exclusive jurisdiction in sports arbitration area for the organization, the CAS succeeded to stimulate itself and escaped the danger of revocation. As a result, the CAS is now settling an average of 200 cases every year since the increase of cases in 1994.

Japan established the Japan Sports Arbitration Agency in 2003 and has been operating the organization since then. Although the number of cases settled in this agency seems inadequate (three in 2003, two in 2004, one in 2005, one in 2006, none in 2007, and three in 2008), in April 2009 the agency rather constituted itself as a general incorporated foundation. In April 2013, the agency was approved as a public utility foundation and constructed a firmer legal foundation for itself.

The United Kingdom, the United States, Canada, New Zealand, Hungary, Netherlands, Germany, and South Africa have also established and reformed basic sports law or similar applicable Acts, supporting the sports arbitration agencies' operations.

## The Necessity of Sports Advancement

The Korea Sports Arbitration Agency is essential for the sports advancement of Korea as a sports powerhouse. It has become more obvious that Korea is now a sports powerhouse, ranking 7th at the 2008 Beijing Olympics and 5th at the 2012 London Olympics. It is a commonly held opinion among all parts of society that Korea should be a developed sports country. It is necessary to achieve a true sports advancement that can act as a foundation for creating economical profit and national integration. It should be noted that the majority of sports advanced countries have established an active sports arbitration agency.


## Challenges of Legislative Policy

Fundamental Principles for Reestablishment: Granting Priority Rights
and Exclusive Rights to Sports Dispute Arbitration.

Regarding the issue of granting priority rights and exclusive rights of
sports dispute arbitration to a newly established Korea Sports Arbitration
Agency in accordance with the special characteristics of sports disputes, a
question arises as to whether this might violate the right of access to courts,
as guaranteed in Art. 27 of the Korean Constitution.[38]

Considering the need for speedy and fair resolutions of sports disputes,
sportsmanship, and sports autonomy, an arbitration system that does not
oppose good social customs and public order exhibits justification and
legitimacy.

Therefore, to invest preferred and exclusive arbitral rights to the Korea
Sports Arbitration Agency cannot be seen as violating the rights of access to
courts of people since the agency is an arbitration body founded on sports
autonomy that is constitutionally guaranteed through the approval and
agreement of relevant parties, including the Korea Sports Council and
affiliated bodies, as well as district subdivisions.


Legislative Measures for Reestablishment

A Measure Coding Basic Sports Law

The necessity of clearly defining a legal basis to enhance the position of
a sports arbitration body and to stimulate sports arbitration through enacting
a Basic Sports Law or a National Sports Law is emphasized once again.

The following summarizes the necessity of the enactment of a Basic

---

38) Jung Seungjae, "Sports Autonomy and Sports Dispute", *The Korean Journal of Sports
and Law* Vol. 5,The Korean Association of Sports and Entertainment Law(KASEL),
2004, p. 47.

Sports Law, as mentioned numerous times above: First, there are 50 laws related to sports; however, there is no basic law that embraces and organizes these laws. The National Sports Promotion Act, which serves such a function, is insufficient to fill the role of a basic law.[39]

Second, it is natural to include sports in the major policies of a country. It is a commonly approved fact that sports plays a significant role in enhancing national prestige, national harmony and each individual's life through a number of events, such as the Olympics. However, not to mention the current poor legal support for sports, it is not even included in 50 major government administrational tasks. The sports administration realm is dispersed among many departments; it is difficult to plan and execute policies.

Third, a fundamental law that systematically and synthetically regulates and manages the business in the field of sports is needed because it is urgently required to define general principles of other sports-related laws.

A fundamental law generally directs itself through systemizing and integrating many other principles of laws. It is common that a fundamental law leads to greater effectiveness of other relevant laws.

Such fundamental laws began to be enacted in 1966, starting with the Minor Enterprises Act; as of December 10th, 2009, there are 51 fundamental laws enacted and enforced. After 1987's democratic contention, the national consciousness of rights increased and the numbers of fundamental laws increased correspondingly. After 2000, numerous fundamental laws were enacted following the trend of changing social structure and national consciousness. A Basic Sports Law ought to regulate, ideally, fundamental aspects related to a Basic Law of Sports, the responsibility of the government, basic guidelines for sports industry promotion and sports promotion, and sports and international cooperation.

---

39) Detailed contents can be found in: Yeun Kee-Young, "Structure for the Enactment of Fundamental Law of Sport in Korea", *The Korean Journal of Sports and Law* Vol. 11 No. 4, The Korean Association of Sports and Entertainment Law(KASEL), 2008, pp. 113-143.

Policy Regulating the National Sports Promotion Act

Until the Basic Sports Law is enacted, it is worth considering reforming the National Sports Promotion Act to regulate necessary respects. As long as the National Sports Promotion Act is enforced, it would be desirable to define it as a corporation having a special status, such as the Korea Anti-Doping Agency. I would like to suggest the draft proposal for the reformation of this act as follows:

Draft Proposal for Amendment to the National Sports Promotion Act

Article 35. 2 (Establishment of a Korea Sports Arbitration Committee)

① In order to bring a peaceful, satisfactory and reasonable settlement to sports disputes through professional mediation and arbitration, with consideration of its distinct characteristics, and to allow each of the following businesses and activities to be enacted, hereby the Korea Sports Arbitration Committee (KSAC) is founded with the approval of the Minister of Culture-Sports.

1. Establishment and execution of planning consultation, mediation, and arbitration of sports dispute.

2. Installation and operation of a tribunal of sports arbitration.

3. Education, public relations, collecting information, and study for sports arbitration.

4. International and domestic cooperation for sports arbitration.

5. Other businesses and activities for the sake of sports arbitration.

② The KSAC must be established as a corporate body.

③ The KSAC is composed of 11 committee members, including one chairman and one vice chairman. The method for the election and terms of the members are defined in articles of the association.

④ The KSAC is allowed to operate as a for-profit business as defined by a presidential decree, with the purpose of arranging necessary expenses for businesses and activities in accordance to Provision 1.

⑤ Any matter other than defined in this act about the KSAC should apply with codes about a juridical foundation defined in Civil Law.

⑥ The KSAC may demand public officials of the relevant administration and executives and staffs of the relevant organization and/or group to be dispatched upon necessity.

⑦ Prior to a lawsuit claim, parties involved in sports disputes must preferentially apply mediation or arbitration to the KSAC as defined by presidential decree.

Enactment for Special Law

It is possible to consider a method of enacting a "Sports Med-arbitration Act" with consideration of the distinct characteristics of sports arbitration. This Law may define the KSAC's establishment, activities, its procedure for mediation and arbitration, and its effectiveness. Sports-related arbitration requires immediacy and professionalism more than anything. Because of its short history, the KSAC operates under a limited budget and less stimulated activities.

## Conclusion

Sports disputes require immediacy and professionalism more than anything else. The Korea Sports Arbitration Committee has a short history; the lack of organization, budget, and stimulated activities seems inevitable. Enacting a more definite legal basis for the new, soon-to-be-established Korea Sports Arbitration Agency is strongly recommended in order to stimulate sports arbitration and to enhance the Korea Sports Arbitration Agency's position. Establishment of a National Sports Law and a Fundamental Law of Sports are urgently called for. Defining aspects related to a Basic Law of Sports, the responsibility of the government, basic guidelines for sports industry promotion and sports promotion, and sports and international cooperation, as well as coding a basis for establishment of sports arbitration organizations, are demanded. Legislating a Sports Arbitration Act as a special law of the Arbitration Act currently in force is also proposed. It is also desirable to first define such aspects through reforming the current National Sports Promotion Act until a Basic Sports Law or a special law is enacted.

When a Korea Sports Arbitration Agency is established with the arranged legal basis, it will be required to enact "Sports Arbitration Rules" or "Sports

Mediation Rules." Methods to apply for dispute settlement without arbitral agreement as well as a "Med-Arbitration" system that allows simultaneous processing of mediation and arbitration should be considered through applying supplements and amendments to the articles of association of the KOC and the affiliated organizations when establishing the rules mentioned above.

Such reformation of the institution can emulate the CAS's reformation of related laws to allow the organization have exclusive jurisdiction in 1990. Olympic Charters Article 59 states, "The Olympic Games or any dispute arising related to it should apply only to the CAS for settlement in accordance to the Sports Arbitration Rules," approving the exclusive jurisdiction of the CAS. The fact that the majority of international sports federations approve of the CAS's exclusive jurisdiction must be recognized.


# References

Beloff, Michael, "The CAS Ad Hoc Division at The Sydney Olympic Games", *I.S.L.R.*, 1(Mar), 2001, p. 105.

Beloff, Michael, "Editorial", *I.S.L.R.*, 4(NOV), 2004, p.77.

Dogauchi, Masato, "The Activities of Japan Sports Arbitration Agency" *The Korean Journal of Sports and Law* Vol.5, 2004.

Ettinger, David J., "The Legal Status of The International Olympic Committee", 8 Pace.Y.B.Int'l.L., 1992, p. 97.

Haas, Ulrich, "Die Sportgerichtsbarkeit zwischen Individualrechtsschutz und Verbandsautonomie", *The Korean Journal of Sports and Law* Vol.5, The Korean Association of Sports and Entertainment Law(KASEL), 2004.

Honsell, Heinrich, Vogt Nedim P., Schnyder, Anton K., *International Arbitration in Switzerland,* 2000.

Jung Seungjae, "Sports Autonomy and Sports Dispute" [In Korean], *The Korean Journal of Sports and Law,* Vol.5, 2004.

Kim Yong-Kil, "A Study of Alternative Dispute Resosslution for Sports Dispute: Focus on Arbitration System" [In Korean], *The Journal of Arbitration,* Vol.21 No.1, 2011.

Kim Yong-Kil, "A Study on the Scope of Effect in Arbitration Agreements" [In

Korean], *The Journal of Arbitration,* Vol.23 No.2, 2013.

Kojima, Takeshi, *Civil Procedure and ADR in Japan,* Series of the Institute of Comparative Law in Japan 65, Tokyo: Chuo University Press, 2004.

Leaver, Peter, "The CAS Ad Hoc Division at the Salt Lake City Winter Olympic Games 2002", *I.S.L.R.* 2002 2(Jul), 50.

Lionnet, Klaus, Handbuch der internationalen and nationalen Schiedsgerichtsbarkeit, 2. Aufl., 2001.

Locklear, R. Jake, "Arbitration in Olympic Disputes: Should Arbitrators Review The Field of Play Decisions of Officials?", *4 Tex. Rev. Ent. & Sports L.* 199, 2003.

McLaren, Richard H. and Clement, Patrick, "Court of Arbitration for Sport: The Ad Hoc Division at the Salt Lake City Winter Olympic Games", I.S.L.R. 2(May), 51, 2004.

McLaren, Richard H., "Introducing the Court of Arbitration for Sport: The Ad Hoc Division at the Olympic Games", 12 *MARQSLR* 515, 2001.

McLaren, Richard H., "The Court of Arbitration for Sport: An Independent Arena for the World's Sports Disputes", 35 *VAL.U.L.R* 379, 2001.

Nafziger, James, *International Sports Law,* 2nd ed., Transnational Publishers Inc., 2004.

Panagiotopoulos, Dimitrios, "Court of Arbitration for Sports", 6 Vill. *Sports & Ent. L.J.* 49, 1999.

Polvino, Anthony T., "Arbitration as Preventative Medicine for Olympic Ailments: The International Olympic Committee's Court of Arbitration for Sport and the Future for the Settlement of International Sporting Disputes", 8 *Emory Int'l L. Rev.* 347, 1994.

Raber, Nancy K., "Dispute Resolution in Olympic Sport: The Court of Arbitration for Sport", 8 *Seton Hall J. Sport L.* 75, 1998.

Reeb, Matthiew, "The Role and Functions of the CAS", *The Court of Arbitration for Sport 1984-2004* (ed. by Blackshaw/ Robert C.H. Siekmann/ Janwillem Soek), T.M.C. Asser Press, 2006.

Reeb, Matthieu(eds), *Digest of CAS Awards II* 1998-2000, 2002.

Reeb, Matthieu (eds), *Digest of CAS Awards III* 2001-2003, 2004.

Simma, Bruno, "The Court of Arbitration for Sport", in: *The Court of Arbitration for Sport 1984-2004,* ed. by Blackshaw/ Robert C.H. Siekmann/ Janwillem Soek, T.M.C. Asser Press, 2006.

Sohn Kyung-Han /Shim Hyun-Joo, "A New Approach on the Arbitration Agreement" [In Korean], *The Journal of Arbitration,* Vol.23 No.1, 2013.

Schmitthoff, Clive M., Export Trade : *The Law and Practice of International Trade,* 9th ed., Stevens & Sons, 1990.

Yeun Kee-Young, "Establishment and Activities of Korea Sports Arbitration Committee" [In Korean], *The Korean Journal of Sports and Law,* Vol.5, 2004.

Yeun, Kee-Young, "Proposal for Establishment of Sports Arbitration Organization" [In Korean], *The Korean Journal of Sports and Law,* Vol. 10 No.4, 2007.

Yeun Kee-Young, "Structure for the Enactment of Fundamental Law of Sport in Korea" [In Korean], *The Korean Journal of Sports and Law,* Vol.11 No.4, 2008.

Zöller, Richard, *Zivilprozessordnung,* 24. Aufl., 2004..

# Die Europäische Union und neuere Entwicklungen im Internationalen Privatrecht (IPR)

WOLFGANG HEINRICH*

*The European Union and recent developments in Private International Law*

*According to the head the judicial Department of the Commission of the European Union (Mrs. Reding) about 12 millions of citizens of the Union are involved in factual situations which are influenced by the rules of Private International Law e.g.:*

*a) those who work in a country different from their home country,*

*b) those who are married with a person with a different nationality than their own, and*

*c) those who have movable or immovable property in different countries of the Union.*

*For these or similar reasons they come necessarily into contact with Conflict of Law rules. That is why - at least within the European Union –you should have some basic knowledge of legal terms like "applicable law", "renvoi", "characterization", "ordre public" and some others.*

*But apart from the national Conflict of Laws regulations of each of the 28 member states of the European Union there are guidelines and statutory orders of the Union which are penetrating into the respective national bodies of law and their legal terms thus pushing aside or at least influencing the respective national regulations like e.g. the statutory order on inheritance law or the tentative to create a uniform law of sales of goods for the Union.*

*The problem of the overprotection of the "Consumer", too, is*

* Rechtsanwalt und Notar in Frankfurt, Germany

*addressed.*

*In conclusion three recent court decisions dealing with the application of basic standards in International Private Law are reported.*

**Key word:** International Private Law (= I PR), Conflict of Law, Renvoi, Characterization, Ordre Public, European Union (= EU), Ordonances on Family and Inheritance Law, and Consumer protection in the EU.

## Einleitung

Nach Aussage der Justizkommisarin der Europaeischen Union (EU) in ihrer Begruessungsansprache anlaesslich der Konferenz ueber die Verordnungsvorschlaege zum Gueterkollisionsrecht am 17.10.2011 stehen in der EU etwa 12 Millionen Unionsbuerger mit einem Bein oder gar mit beiden Beinen im Internationalen Privatrecht (IPR), zum Beispiel:

a) weil sie in einem anderen Land der EU als ihrem Herkunftsland wohnen und arbeiten (ein Spanier wohnt und arbeitet in Frankreich),

b) weil Eheleute, Lebenspartner oder Kinder verschiedene Staatsangehöigkeiten haben oder

c) weil Unionsbuerger Vermoegensgegenstaende (zum Beispiel Aktienfonds oder eine Ferienwohnung) in verschiendenen Laendern der EU haben.

In allen diesen Faellen koennen Sachverhalte rechtlich zu beurteilen sein, die mehr als eine nationale Rechtsordnung –noch sind die Mitglieder der Union ja alle souveraene Staaten- beruehren.

Welche Rechtsordnung nun zur Regelung des in Frage stehenden Sachverhalts berufen ist, entscheiden die Vorschriften des sogenannten

**Internationalen Privatrechts.**

Nachdem vor etwa fuenfzig Jahren in Deutschland und vielen Laendern, die heute Mitglieder der EU sind, das Internationale Privatrecht und das Europaeische Recht mehr ein Nischendasein fuehrten und unter die sogenannten „Orchideen-Faecher" zu rechnen waren, fuer die sich kaum jemand an der Universitaet und in der Praxis fast gar keiner interessierte, hat sich das mit der Entwicklung der europaeischen Einigung und allgemein mit der immer groesseren Buntheit der Bevoelkerung in den Laendern Europas wesentlich veraendert.

Wer heute erklaeren wuerde, er interessiere sich weder fuer IPR noch fuer Europarecht, die sich seit langem gegenseitig mehr und mehr beeinflussen, riskierte zum Beispiel als Rechtsanwalt wohl sehr haeufig infolge seiner mangelnden Rechtskenntnisse grosse Haftungschaeden.

Leider fristet dieses Rechtsgebiet auch in Korea noch immer ein Schattendasein in der Lehre der Universitäten, und es ist auch kein Thema in den Prüfungen.

Was aber hat es auf sich mit dem Internationalen Privatrecht?

Schon der Name ist leider irrefuehrend; denn es geht nicht um internationales, sondern nationales Recht.

Es gibt das deutschen IPR, das im EGBGB, dem Einfuehrungsgesetz zum Buergerlichen Gesetzbuch, niedergelegt ist, ebenso das franzoesische IPR, das man im Code Civil (CC) findet, der vor etwa 200 Jahren als Code Napolén geschaffen wurde. Und so hat wohl jedes Land hat seine Vorschriften des IPR.

Und es ist auch kein Privatrecht, das dispositiv ist und also von den Beteiligten Personen einvernehmlich veraendert werden koennte; es ist zwingendes oeffentliches Recht.

Insoweit ist die Bezeichnung „Conflict of Laws", die in den U.S.A. oft an Stelle von „International Private Law" (den Begriff gibt es dort auch) gebraucht wird, „richtiger"; denn es geht ja immer darum, welches nationale Recht einen Sachverhalt regeln kann oder darf, an dem natuerliche oder juristische Personen oder Sachen mit Bezug zu verschiedenen Rechtsordnungen beteiligt sind.

Und so, wie das IPR die Frage beantwortet, welches nationale Recht zur Regelung „bei Sachverhalten mit einer Verbindung zu einem auslaendischen Staat" (so Artikel 3 des Einfuehrungsgesetzes zum Buergerlichen Gesetzbuch (= EGBGB) am Ende) berufen ist, so gibt es gleichermassen Vorschriften, die regeln, welches Gericht für die Entscheidung eines solchen Sachverhaltes zustaendig ist.

Nachdem aber schon das Internationale Privatrecht nahezu uferlos und selbst fuer Fachleute kaum noch zu ueberschauen ist, werde ich in diesen Ausfürungen keine Hinweise zum internationalen Verfahrensrecht geben koennen.

In dem vorbezeichneten Art. 3 EGBGB ist zwar gesagt, dass die Sachverhalte zu einem auslaendischen Staat sich nach den Vorschriften des Zweiten Abschnittes, also den Artikeln 3 bis 46 EGBGB regeln; dies wird aber gleich wieder eingeschraenkt:

„Soweit nicht

1. unmittelbar anwendbare Regelungen der Europaeischen Gemeinschaft in ihrer jeweils geltenden Fassung, insbesondere

(1) die Verordnung (EG) Nr. 864/2007 des europäschen Parlaments und des Rates vom 11. Juli 2007 ueber das auf ausservertragliche Schuldverhaeltnisse anzuwendende Recht (Rom II) (ABl. L 199 vom 31.7.2007, S. 40) sowie

(2) die Verordnung (EG) 593/2008 des Europaeischen Parlaments und des Rates vom 17. Juni 2008 ueber das auf vertragliche Schuldverhaeltnisse anzuwendende Recht (Rom I) (ABl. L 177 vom 04.07.2008, S. 6) oder

2. Regelungen in voelkerrechtlichen Vereinbarungen, soweit sie unmittelbar anwendbares innerstaatliches Recht geworden sind, ..." anwendbar sind.

Das heisst, dass im Bereich „ausservertragliche Schuldverhaeltnisse" fuer Deutschland im Verhaeltnis zu den anderen Unionslaendern nicht die

Artikel 38 bis 42 EGBGB gelten, sondern vorgenannte Verordnung Nr. 864/2007 der EU und im Bereich „vertragliche Schuldverhaeltnisse" die Verordnung Nr. 593/2008 und auch hier nicht die Artikel 38 bis 42 EGBGB.

Die Bestimmungen des EGBGB werden auch verdraengt, wenn die Bundesrepublik Deutschland binationale oder multinationale Abkommen abgeschlossen hat, wie zum Beispiel das Deutsch- Iranische Niederlassungsabkommen vom 17.02.1929 (RGB[1]) 130 II 1002 sowie vom 28.05.1929 mit der Tükei –[2]) oder alle Haager Abkommen, die die Bundesrepublik Deutschland gezeichnet hat, wie z.B. das Haager Uebereinkommen ueber das auf Unterhaltsverpflichtungen gegenueber Kindern anzuwendende Recht vom 24.10.1956 (BGBl[3]) 61 II 1012, nebst Ergaenzungsgesetz vom 02.06.1972 (BGBl II 589 (Art. 1 a).

Das hat unter anderem dazu gefuehrt, dass zum Beispiel der Kommentar zum Buergerlichen Gesetzbuch von Palandt (Er umfasst auch die Kommentierung des EGBGB.) neben der Kommentierung der Artikel 38 bis 42 EGBGB auch die Kommentierung zur Verordnung (EG) Nr. 864/2007 aufgenommen hat, also „weispurig" faehrt: Es geht ja auch insoweit um deutsches Recht, denn das Verordnungsrecht der EU ist unmittelbar geltendes deutsches Recht.

Bis dahin mag es ja noch ganz uebersichtlich sein, was die Regelungen des IPR angeht.

Das wird aber verwickelter und unuebersichtlicher, wenn wir uns den weiteren wichtigen Grundregeln dieses Rechtsgebiets zuwenden, auf die einzugehen deshalb noetig ist, weil sonst die Hinweise auf einige Beispiele aus der neueren Rechtsprechung gar nicht verstaendlich werden koennen:

## Rück- und Weiterverweisung

So bestimmt Artikel 4 Absatz 1 EGBGB, dass eine Verweisung auf das Recht eines anderen Staates (innerhalb oder ausserhalb der EU) immer auch

---

1) RGBl=Reichsgesetzblatt
2) vgl. Palandt/Thorn, 72. Aufl., 2013, RdNr.. 5 zu Artikel 14 EGBGB und Palandt/Thorn RdNr. 1 zu Art. 13 EGBGB)
3) Bundesgesetzblatt

eine Verweisung auf das Internationale Privatrecht dieses Staates enthät. Man spricht insoweit von einer „Gesamtverweisung".

Bei der neuen Erbrechts-VO, auf die ich noch eingehen werde, ist dies nicht so!

So kann es sein, dass das deutsche Recht in einer Ehescheidungssache auf das Recht eines USBundesstaates verweist, das das Heimatrecht einer Prozesspartei ist. Das Recht dieses US-Bundesstaates kann in seinen IPR-Bestimmungen aber eine Vorschrift enthalten, die nicht an die Staatsangehoerigkeit anknuepft, sondern an den tatsaechlichen Aufenthalt im Zeitpunkt der Klageerhebung und deshalb auf das Recht an diesem Aufenthaltsort zum Beispiel in Deutschland zurueckverweist ("Renvoi") oder bei einem Aufenthaltsort in Italien an das italienische Recht „weiterverweist".

Auch wenn das deutsche Gericht - etwa weil die Kinder in Deutschland leben –in einem Scheidungsfalle dann zustaendig waere, muesste das deutsche Familiengericht italienisches materielles Scheidungsrecht anwenden, wenn der Vater aus dem US-Bundesstaat seinen tatsaechlichen Aufenthaltsort in Italien haette.

Wird nur auf Sachvorschriften einer massgebenden auslaendischen Rechtsordnung verwiesen („Sachnormverweisung"), so wird gemaess Artikel 3 a EGBGB die Anwendung der Normen des Internationalen Privatrechts dieser Rechtsordnung ausgeschlossen.

Bei sogenannten Doppel- oder Mehrstaatern (vergleiche Artikel 5 EGBGB) ist fuer die Rechtswahl entscheiden, zu welchem der in Frage kommenden Staaten die Person die engeren Beziehungen hat.

## Der Ordre Public

Wohl alle nationalen Rechtsordnungen haben in ihrem IPR eine „Notbremse" eingebaut:

Die Anwendung auslaendischen Rechts ist gemaess Artikel 6 EGBGB dann ausgeschlossen, „wenn ihre Anwendung zu einem Ergebnis führt, das mit wesentlichen Grundsaetzen des deutschen Rechts offensichtlich unvereinbar ist" oder gemaess Satz 2 Grundrechte verletzen wuerde. Wann im Einzelfall gegen die „Öffentliche Ordnung" (den „ordre public") verstossen wird, so dass das eigentlich zur Anwendung berufene fremde Recht nicht angewendet wird, ist allerdings oft sehr streitig.

So wurde zum Beispiel die Stammesehe zwischen einem Deutschen und einer Nigerianerin wegen Verstosses gegen den ordre public nicht anerkannt (vgl. Palandt/Thorn, a.a.O. Anm. 20 zu Artikel 6 EGBGB). Ebenso die Benachteiligung weiblicher gesetzlicher Erben nach islamischem Recht (OLG Frankfurt am Main, ZEV 11, 135; a.A. Landgericht Hamburg, IPRspr. 91, Nr. 142, beide zitiert nach Palandt/Thorn, a.a.O. Anm. 30 zu Artikel 6 EGBGB).

## Veränderungen in der Systematik des IPR

Wärend frueher der Grundsatz galt, dass auf eine unerlaubte Handlung (etwa einen verschuldeten Verkehrsunfall) das Recht des Ortes des Unfalls anzuwenden ist (wenn auch mit der Einschraenkung des Artikels 12 EGBGB, dass in Deutschland gegen einen Deutschen keine weitergehenden Ansprühe geltend gemacht werden konnten, als das deutsche Recht vorsah), ist die Lage heute ein wenig komplizierter geworden, wie ueberhaupt das von Friedrich Carl von Savigny begruendete kollisionsrechtliche System, das in Band VIII seines Werkes „System des heutigen roemichen Rechts"[4] von 1849 enthalten ist und welches das ganze neuzeitliche IPR gepraegt hat[5] viel unuebersichtlicher geworden ist, was zum Teil wohl dem Diktat der sogenannten „Einzelfallgerechtigkeit" zu verdanken ist.

Die Regel, dass auf unerlaubte Handlungen das Recht am Ort der Handlung des Schadensersatzpflichtigen anzuwenden ist, wurde in Artikel 40 Absatz 1 EGBGB zwar in Grundsatz beibehalten, sie wurde aber durch ein Rechtswahlrecht des Geschäigten fü das Ortrecht des Schadenseintritts und -in Absatz 2 - die Sonderregel fuer den Fall des gleichen gewoehnlichen

---

4) Friedrich Carl von Savigny, Das System des heutigen römischen Rechts, Band VIII
5) vgl. Weller, Anknuepfungsprinzipien im Europaeischen Kollisionsrecht: Abschied von der „'klassischen," IPR-Dogmatik in *IPRax* 2011, Seite 429 bis 437

Aufenthaltsortes von Schaediger und Verletztem sowie eine Reihe weiterer Modalitaeten aufgeweicht.

Als eine aehnliche Aufweichung von Grundsaetzen und klaren Regeln erscheint Artikel 41 EGBGB, nach welchem ein an sich berufenes auslaendisches Recht verdraengt wird, wenn eine wesentlich engere Verbindung zu einem anderen Recht besteht, als dem Recht, das nach den Artikeln 38 bis 40 Abs. 2 EGBGB eigentlich zur Entscheidung eines Falles berufen waere.

Und wer die „alten" Artikel des EGBGB mit den sehr viel mehr ins Einzelne gehenden Vorschriften der Verordnungen Rom-I und Rom-II vergleicht, kann leicht versucht sein, dem „alten", aber viel uebersichtlicheren EGBGB nachzutrauern.

## Und nun die EU:

Die Vereinheitlichungswut der Eurokraten in Bruessel macht selbst den Unionsbuergern Angst, die im Grunde eigentlich sehr fuer Europa eingestellt sind, denen aber die Eile, mit der manche Gesetzesvorhaben angegangen und weitere Vorhaben geplant und teilweise „durchgepeitscht" werden, missfallen.

Die Einigung Europas begann in den 50er Jahren des vergangenen Jahrhunderts mit den sogenannten Roemischen Vertraegen (EWG und Euratom). Ihnen waren 1951 die Montanunion, die Europaeische Gemeinschaft fuer Kohhle und Stahl (EGKS), vorangegangen, der Frankreich, Italien, die Bundesrepublik Deutschland und die sogenannten Benelux-Staaten Belgien, Niederlande und Luxemburg angehoerten.

Die EWG entwickelte sich weiter zur EG und diese zur EU - mit all den Zwischenfaellen und Umwegen wie sie durch Begriffe wie Vertrag von Maastricht, Vertrag von Nizza, Schengener Abkommen, Verfassungsvertrag und schließlich Vertrag von Lissabon bezeichnet werden.

Ausgangspunkt war das Zusammenwachsen eines „Europas der Vaterlaender", und deshalb ist von Anfang an weder ein Staatenbund noch ein Bundesstaat geplant worden, vielmehr spricht man zu Recht noch immer von einem

„Staatenverbund", der zwar Elemente von beiden in seinen Strukturen eingebaut hat, aber doch mit keiner der beiden anderen Staatenformen identisch ist.

Regelten die Verordnungen, die mit Erlass unmittelbar in den einzelnen Laendern der Gemeinschaft als nationales Recht gelten, und Richtlinien, die in das jeweils nationale Recht umgesetzt werden muessen, zunaechst nur agrarrechtliche und den freien Warenverkehr betreffende Bereiche, so haben die Kommission und der Rat - seit einiger Zeit auch das Europaeische Parlament - immer mehr auch Regelungsbereiche fuer sich reklamiert, die sich ueber den Agrarbereich und den Gueterverkehr hinaus in viele andere Bereiche ausdehnten und noch immer weiter ausgreifen.

Das ist sogar drucktechnisch klar zu erkennen, wenn man in der Kommentierung von Palandt die Ausfürungen zu Rom-I und Rom-II sieht, die zwischen die Kommentierungen zu Artikel 42 und Artikel 43 EGBGB „hineingequetscht" wurden.

Mit Blick auf die inzwischen erlassene Erbrechtsverordnung und das geplante europaeische Kaufrecht gibt es auch unter den EU-Befuerwortern viele, die in städiger Angst davor leben, dass die europaeischen Instanzen die Vereinheitlichung des Rechtes in Europa mit aller Macht und in grosser Eile betreiben. Man hat den Eindruck, das die „Eurokraten" in Brüsel (Kommission und Rat), Strasbourg (Europaeisches Parlament) und Luxembourg (Europaeischer Gerichtshof) lieber heute als morgen die „Vereinigten Staaten von Europa" ausrufen wuerden, in denen in allen heutigen nationalen Unionsstaaten per Verordnung nur noch ein, naemlich das von den Eurokraten gemachte Recht gelten duerfte –natuerlich bei gleichzeitiger Kraftloserklaerung aller bis dahin geltenden und in Jahrhunderten, ja manchmal Jahrtausenden gewachsenen nationalen Rechtsordnungen der derzeit 27 Mitgliedstaaten. (So hat man es ja z.B. um 1880/1890 zur Zeit der Meiji Dynastie in Japan mit deutschen und anderen europäischen Rechtsvorschriften unter Missachtung der jahrhundertealten japanischen Rechtskultur gemacht.)

## Die Erbrechts- und die Kaufrechts-Verordnung

A) Nachdem der Rechtsausschuss des Europaeischen Parlaments am 11.10.2011 seinem Berichterstatter ein detailliertes Mandat zu Verhandlungen mit Kommission und Rat der Europaeischen Union zu einer Erbrechtsverordnung erteilt hatte, ist zwischenzeitlich die „erordnung (EU) Nr. 650/2012 des Europäischen Parlaments und des Rates üer die Zuläsigkeit, das anzuwendende Recht, die Anerkennung und die Vollstreckung von Entscheidungen und öentlichen Urkunden in Erbsachen sowie zur Einfuehrung eines europaeischen Nachlasszeugnisses" erlassen worden, und sie tritt am 17.08.2015 in Kraft.

Zunaechst einmal ist bedeutsam, dass diese Verordnung von den Gerichten der Mitgliedstaaten nicht nur dann angewendet werden muss, wenn es um Lebenssachverhalte mit Beruehrung zu anderen Mitgliedsstaaten geht, sondern auch –als „loi uniforme" auch für Sachverhalte mit Drittstaatenberuehrung.

Die Verordnung ersetzt insoweit die Vorschriften des EGBGB (Artt. 25 pp.) und bringt die Neuerung, dass (was im Erbrecht des EGBGB nur eingeschreankt bezueglich Grundstuecken gegeben ist) die Beteiligten eine- Rechtswahlmoeglichkeit erhalten, also eine Vereinbarung treffen koennen, welches nationale Recht auf ihren Nachlass Anwendung finden soll:

Der gesamte Nachlass soll danach einem nationalen Recht unterworfen werden. Anknuepfungspunkt soll das jeweilige nationale Recht am Ort des letzten gewoehnlichen Aufenthaltes des Erblassers sein.

Derzeit, seit Beginn der Geltung des EGBGB und bis zum 17.08.2015 knüft in Nachlassangelegenheiten der Artikel 25 Absatz 1 EGBGB an die Staatsangehoerigkeit, also das Heimatrecht des Erblassers an, weshalb der DAV (Deutscher Anwaltsverein) die Neuregelung zu einem frueheren Zeitpunkt auch bemaengelt hat, weil eine Feststellung der Staatsangehoerigkeit durch einen einfachen Blick in den Pass des Erblassers moeglich ist, die Ermittlung des letzten gewoehnlichen Aufenthaltes in vielen Faellen aber ungleich aufwaendiger und zeitraubender werden duerfte.

Und auch wenn der Entwurf ein Wahlrecht (in Form eines sogenannten „opt out") gewaehrt, ist die geplante Regelung aus meiner Sicht keine gute Loesung. Denn wir haben seit ueber hundert Jahren in sehr vielen

Rechtsbereichen, natuerlich auch im Erbrecht, die Anknuepfung an die Staatsangehoerigkeit, so dass der umgekehrte Weg praxisgerechter waere: Anknuepfung an die Staatsangehoerigkeit und Wahlmoeglichkeit fü das Recht am Ort des letzten gewoehnlichen Aufenthaltes.

Wenigstens hat die Erbrechtsverordnung den Rechtsunterworfenen EU-Buergern aber erlaubt, in von ihnen errichteten letztwilligen Verfuegungen (Testamenten und Erbvertraegen) die Anwendung ihres Heimatrechtes zu waehlen.

Einschneidend ist die Verordnung vor allem aber auch, weil die sogenannte Nachlassspaltung wegfällt:

Denn das qua Wohnsitz oder Rechtswahl auf den Nachlass anwendbare Recht umfasst alle zum Nachlass einer Person gehoerenden Vermoegenswerte, seien sie beweglicher oder unbeweglicher Natur:

Wenn ich als Deutscher meinen Nachlass meinem deutschen Heimatrecht unterstelle, werden zwangslaeufig auch mein Haus in Frankreich (dort wuerde nach der bisherigen Regelung die „lex rei sitae", also franzoesisches Recht Anwendung finden) und meine Rechte an einem U.S.- amerikanischen Fonds (derzeit Recht z.B. des Staates von New York) dem deutschen Erbrecht unterstellt.

B) Das geplante „einheitliche europaeische Kaufrecht" ist ein weiteres Beispiel fuer das Bemüen der „Eurokraten", moeglichst viele Rechtsgebiete unter Verdraengung nationaler Regelungen EU-einheitlich zu machen.

Das soll mit einem Retortenbaby versucht werden, das euphorisch „28. Regime" genannt wird, und dessen Vaeter fast ausschliesslich Wissenschaftler und keine Praktiker sind.

Argumentiert wird, der Binnenmarkt wuerde noch enger und besser, wenn gerade die Kaufleute mittlerer und kleiner Unternehmen ein einheitliches, uebernationales, also europaeisches Kaufrecht haetten, auf das sie ihre Vertraege gruenden koennten und sich nicht mehr wie derzeit mit 27 verschiedenen nationalen Kaufrechten „abmuehen muessten".

Dagegen wandten sich von Anfang an sowohl Wirtschaftsvertreter als auch Verbraucherschuetzer, vor allem die Notare, die erklaerten, sie haetten zwar nichts gegen eine Vereinheitlichung des Kaufrechts. Was die Kommissionsvizepraesidentin Reding jedoch vorgelegt habe, sein ein „Ausfluss obrigkeitsstaatlichen Regulierungseifers, der ueberhastet zusammengestellt und voller unbestimmter Rechtsbegriffe" sei[6] Der Bundesverband der Deutschen Industrie (BDI) befuerchtete ueberdies, dass dieses Gesetzeswerk, das nur als „Toolbox" verstanden werden will, „über kurz oder lang aber dann doch noch fuer alle verpflichtend" werden und kein reines Wahlrecht der Parteien bleiben wird.

Es kommt hinzu, das die Kommission offenbar uebersehen hat,[7] das ein neuer Rechtssatz nicht nur einen alten ersetzt, es wird dadurch auch der „Wissensschatz des Richterrechts" ausgeloescht.

Und obwohl er selbst Rechtsprofessor ist, befuerchtet Grigoleit, dass eine neue Regelung, wie sie geplant ist und im Entwurf vorliegt, ueber viele Jahre unter der Unsicherheit hinsichtlich der Auslegung ihrer Bestimmungen durch die Rechtsprechung leiden muesste, waehrend bei den bestehenden nationalen Regelungen jeder damit Befasste seit Jahren „eine" Rechtsprechung und die nationalen Besonderheiten der Rechtsanwendung genau kenne. Es komme hinzu, dass der Entwurf absichtlich Luecken enthielte und auf die jeweiligen nationalen Regelungen als Ergaenzungen verweise.

Darueber hinaus haben einzelne Praktiker auf den Umstand verwiesen, dass auch das UN-Kaufrechtsuebereinkommen, das mit aehnlichen Vorzuegen angepriesen wurde wie der Entwurf der EU, vergleichsweise recht selten von den Vertragsparteien gewaehlt werde.

## Noch ein Wort zum Verbraucher

Auch der Verbraucher soll im „28. Regime" gebuehrend beruecksichtigt werden.

Wer glaubt, das Wichtigste in der EU, die sich bekanntermassen aus der EWG ueber die EG entwickelt hat, sei der Binnenmarkt und seine behinderungsfreie Entwicklung, ist sicherlich einem Irrtum erlegen.

Die „heilige Kuh" der EU ist der Verbraucher bzw. (Wir wollen ja politisch korrekt sein.) die Verbraucherin.

---

6) vgl. Bericht in der FAZ (Frankfurter Allgemeine Zeitung) vom 12.10.2011)
7) vgl. Grigoleit – Professor an der Uni Müuenchen - in FAZ vom 02.11.2011)

Der Verbraucher wird in Watte gepackt und geradezu entmuendigt vor lauter Fuersorge; denn er kann auf den ihm von den Vorschriften der EU-Gesetzgebung (vgl. zum Beispiel Art. der Rom-I Verordnung) aufgezwungenen Schutz in keiner auch noch so eingeschraenkten Form verzichten.

Auf Eigentumsrechte, sein Wahlrecht oder jede Art von Rechtsmitteln, Erbschaften und sonstigen Rechten kann der Verbraucher jederzeit verzichten, nicht aber auf den ihm von der EU „verordneten" Verbraucherschutz.

Es ist leicht festzustellen, dass wir als Unionsbuerger im Grunde also zwei Internationale Privatrechtsordnungen haben, eine, die wir mit Abaenderungen im Laufe der letzten 110 Jahre schon immer hatten, und eine aufgepfropfte, die in jedem Fall dann gilt, wenn der Sacheverhalt nicht mit Drittstaaten (Auch hier gibt es Ausnahmen.) verbunden ist, sondern mit anderen Mitgliedsstaaten der Europaeischen Union.

Die Reibereien zwischen den einzelnen Mitgliedsstaaten der EU und den Organen der EU spiegeln sich auch ein wenig im Verhaeltnis zwischen dem deutschen Bundesverfassungsgericht und dem Europaeischen Gerichtshof in Luxemburg; indessen erlaubt es der zur Verfuegung stehende Raum nicht, auf dieses Problematik naeher einzugehen.

Im Folgenden moechte ich noch ein paar Beispiele aus der neueren Rechtsprechung vorstellen, die sich mit Fragen des IPR befassen:

1. Personalstatut = Heimatrecht
   In drei Verfahren hatten die Vorinstanzen unter Bezug auf Artikel 1, 2 des Haager Minderjaehrigenschutzabkommens (MSA; in Kraft fuer Deutschland seit dem 17.09.1971 –K BGBl II 1150) die Frage der Beendigung des Schutzes von minderjärigen Asylbewerbern bei Erreichen der Volljaehrigkeit dem deutschen Recht unterstellt. Das OLG Müchen berichtigte dies dahingehend, dass mit Erreichen der Volljaehrigkeit nach deutschem Aufenthaltsrecht das MSA (Es wird demnaechst durch das Haager Uebereinkommen ueber die Zustaendigkeit, das anzuwendende Recht, die Anerkennung, Vollstreckung und Zusammenarbeit auf dem Gebiet der elterlichen Verantwortung und der Massnahmen zum Schutze von Kindern vom 19.10.1996

(KSUE) ersetzt werden.) nicht mehr anwendbar ist (Artikel 12 MSA) und dass statt dessen Artikel 24 EGBGB als Vormundschaftsstatut und Artikel 7 EGBGB als Geschätsfäigkeitsstatut eingreifen[8]vgl. OLG Muenchen FamRZ 2009, 1602: FamRZ 2010, 1095 und FamRZ 2010, 1096).

2. Rueckverweisung

Das OLG Duesseldorf[9] konnte aufzeigen, dass selbst die Familiengerichte in erster Instanz manchmal nicht ausreichend vertraut sind mit dem EGBGB: Die Eheleute waren urpruenglich beide Togolesen, hatten in Togo geheiratet und waren dann beide nach Deutschland gekommen, wo der Ehemann eingebuergert wurde. Das Familiengericht hatte zwar gem. Artikel 17 Absatz 1 Satz 1 EGBGB i. V. mit Artikel 14 Abs. 1 Nr. 1 EGBGB das Recht von Togo als das Recht des Staates mit der letzten gemeinsamen Staatsangehöigkeit erkannt, und es hatte deshalb die Ehe nach togolesischem Recht geschieden. Das war jedoch falsch; denn der Verweis auf das togolesische Recht in Artikel 17 Absatz 1 Satz 1 EGBGB und 14 Absatz 1 Nr. 1 EGBGB ist ein sogenannter Gesamtverweis (vgl. Artikel 3 a Absatz 2 EGBGB), also ein Verweis auf die gesamte Rechtsordnung und damit auch auf das togolesische IPR. Das togolesische IPR verweist jedoch wegen des gemeinsamen Aufenthaltes der Parteien zurueck auf das deutsche Recht, das diese Rueckverweisung auch annimmt (vgl. Art. 4 Absatz 1 EGBGB), so dass das Scheidungsverfahren nach deutschem Recht durchgefuehrt werden muss.

3. Deliktsrecht

Bei der Frage, welches der für die Anknuepfung relevante Handlungsort bei einem Deliktsanspruch (vgl. Artikel 40 Absatz 1 Satz 1 EGBGB) gegen einen auslaendischen, von den USA aus operierenden Broker ist, hat der BGH (=Bundesgerichtshof)[10] nicht nur in den USA, sondern auch in Deutschland einen Handlungsort angenommen; denn dort waren dem Kunden Kontoeroeffnungsformulare

---

8) vgl. OLG Muenchen FamRZ 2009, 1602: FamRZ 2010, 1095 und FamRZ 2010, 1096).
9) OLG Düseldorf in NJW-RR 2009, 1515
10) BGH, NZG 2010, 550 = RIW 2010, 391)

vorgelegt und von ihm auch unterzeichnet worden. Diese Taetigkeit des Kunden sieht der BGH als „prägende Ausfuehrungshandlungen" in Deutschland an, so dass nach Artikel 41 Abs. 1 EGBGB deutsches Recht anzuwenden sei. Heute waere auf diesen Fall Artikel 4 Absatz 1 der Rom-II Verordnung anzuwenden und deshalb nicht mehr auf den Handlungsort, sondern auf das Recht am Ort des Schadenseintritts abzustellen.

4. Sachenrecht –Anknuepfung an die „lex rei sitae"

Schon lange vor der Schaffung des Artikels 43 EGBGB galt im Internationalen Privatrecht der Grundsatz, dass auf bewegliche und unbewegliche Gegenstaende (letztere meist Grundstuecke) das Recht des Ortes Anwendung findet, an dem sich der Gegenstand befindet. Im Gegensatz zu Grundstuecken haben bewegliche Gegenstaende, wie der Name sagt, die Eigenschaft, beweglich zu sein, so dass sie auch vom Bereich einer Rechtsordnung in den einer anderen Rechtsordnung gebracht werden koennen. Einen solchen „Statutenwechsel" hat ein Urteil des BGH[11] zum Gegenstand: Ein deutscher Vertragshaendler verkaufte einen Pkw Opel unter Eigentumsvorbehalt und mit Weiterverfuegungsverbot an die deutsche Firma X. Die Fahrzeugpapiere blieben bei der Verkaeuferin. Die Firma X verkaufte (trotz des Verbots) den Pkw an eine Kaeuferin in Frankreich und lieferte ihn auch nach Frankreich. Die franzoesische Kaeuferin gab den Pkw wegen einer Nachruestung an die Vertragshaendlerin, die den Pkw nicht mehr herausgab, sondern ihn weiterverkaufte, weshalb die franzoesische Kaeuferin auf Schadensersatz klagte. Der BGH stellte zunaechst fest, dass der Artikel 43 EGBGB zwingendes Recht und nicht abdingbar sei. Er erklaerte weiterhin, dass der Eigentumserwerb der franzoesischen Kaeuferin französischem Recht unterstehe; denn der Versendungskauf habe dieser keine Besitzposition gemaess § 929 BGB vor Ablieferung und damit erst nach Eintritt des Statutenwechsels verschafft. Ein gutglaeubiger Eigentumserwerb der franzoesischen Kaeuferin sei deshalb nur nach franzoesischem Recht moeglich gewesen. Eine

---

11) BGH in NJW 2009, 2824

Anwendung der §§ 932 ff. BGB oder des § 366 HGB scheide deshalb aus.

Der Schadensersatzanspruch unterstehe jedoch wiederum dem deutschen Recht, weil sich das Fahrzeug wieder in Deutschland befinde.

Die vorstehend aufgefürten Faelle aus der Rechtsprechung habe ich dem Aufsatz von Rauscher und Pabst, Die Rechtsprechung zum Internationalen Privatrecht 2009 –2010 in NJW 2010, S. 3487 bis 3494[12)] entnommen.

Zusammenfassung und Schluss

In den vorstehenden Ausfuehrungen war es naturgemaess nicht moeglich, alle Facetten des IPR auch nur anzusprechen. Ich wollte mit meinen Ausfuehrungen einige wesentliche Grundsaetze des IPR (Den schwierigen Bereich der Qualifikation habe ich absichtlich nicht angesprochen, weil er nahezu „uferlos" ist.), den Einfluss der EU-Rechtssetzung auf das deutsche IPR und einige wenige Entscheidungen aus diesem immer wichtiger werdenden Rechtsgebiet vorstellen.

## References

(1) RGBl = Reichsgesetzblatt
(2) Palandt/Thorn, 72. Aufl., 2013, RdNr.. 5 zu Artikel 14 EGBGB und Palandt/ Thorn RdNr. 1 zu Art. 13 EGBGB)
(3) Bundesgesetzblatt
(4) Friedrich Carl von Savigny, *Das System des heutigen röischen Rechts*, Band VIII
(5) Weller, Anknuepfungsprinzipien im Europaeischen Kollisionsrecht: Abschied von der „lassischen" IPR-Dogmatik in *IPRax* 2011, Seite 429 bis 437

---

12) Rauscher und Pabst, *Die Rechtsprechung zum Internationalen Privatrecht* 2009 – 2010 in NJW 2010, S. 3487 bis 3494

(6) Bericht in der FAZ (Frankfurter Allgemeine Zeitung) vom 12.10.2011)

(7) Grigoleit –Professor an der Uni Müchen - in FAZ vom 02.11.2011)

(8) OLG Muenchen *FamRZ* 2009, 1602: *FamRZ* 2010, 1095 und *FamRZ* 2010, 1096).

(9) OLG Düseldorf in NJW-RR 2009, 1515

(10) BGH, NZG 2010, 550 = RIW 2010, 391)

(11) BGH in NJW 2009, 2824

(12) Rauscher und Pabst, Die Rechtsprechung zum Internationalen Privatrecht 2009 –2010 in *NJW* 2010, S. 3487 bis 3494

# How Sports Law to Support the Combination of Physical Education Policy

## 我国现行体育法如何为"体教结合"保驾护航

YI LI(李 怡)*

*Sports Talent Reserve Force forms have become more diversified. Combination of physical education is one of them. However, due to the lag law, imperfect system and related managemen's behavior makes any whom "Combination" has become a piece of paper talk. Proposed approach to the important details into sports law, specifically sports federations registered administrative privileges. To ensure that the combination of physical education policy in Chinahealthy development. To ensure registered athletes in the stable exchange system, in good legal environment, safely enjoy fair competition, learning and training rights.*

**Key word:** Sports law；Combination；Athlete registration and management system；

## Ⅰ. 前言

"体教结合"是新的历史条件下加强学校体育工作、推动素质教育、促进青少年训练、为国家培养和造就高素质劳动者和优秀体育后备人才的一项新的重要举措，是整合体育、教育等资源而实施的人才培养战略的重要措施，体现了体育、教育事业最根本的培养目标，符合

---

\* Teacher @ Physical Education Department, China University of Political Science and Law；and Member of Sport law Research Centre, China University of Political Science and Law

人才培养的内在要求。

"注册制度"是我国对运动员实行管理、交流、确定运动员归属单位和参赛资格的根本制度。

既然体教结合制度是国家提出的培养体育优秀后备人才的新举措。那么就不应该出现学校体育培养出的体育后备人才因为注册制度的不完善而四散流失的现象。但是目前由于我国体育法的滞后，管理部门监管不力，导致出现抢注、伪注、撤注等丑陋现象的发生。法律上的缺失导致制度上的不稳定。朝令夕改以及对注册材料的任意造假，严重损害了运动员的相关权益。比如运动员的参赛权以及接受良好教育的权利。有必要通过完善体育法使其稳定化，公平化、人性化、合理化。从而促进、保护我国体育事业朝着"体教结合"这个改革方向健康发展。

## II. 讨论与分析

全国运动员注册与交流管理办法(试行)以下简称"办法"，自颁布实施以来的确出现了一些问题。尤其是在竞技体育人才后备力量培养机制出现多元化以后，(本文主要指"体教结合"培养模式)出现了抢注、伪注和撤注的现象。最令人关注的莫过于"体教结合"培养模式的"领头羊"-清华大学跳水队。

2001 年10 月，国家体育总局游泳运动管理中心取消了"运动员双注册制"，即每名运动员只能注册成为一个省(市)的队员。"运动员双注册制"即运动员既能在清华大学跳水队注册，同时也可以注册到省(市)队。当时一些已经注册的省(市)的队员在清华跳水队训练时，要向清华缴纳一定数额的培养费、伙食住宿费等，运动员可代表所注册省(市)参赛。

取消"运动员双注册制"，意味着在清华跳水队注册的队员就不能再代表各省市参赛。一些地方队为了争夺运动员，开始"抢注"清华跳水队的队员。而为了进国家队，清华队员只能离开清华回到省市队里。"运动员双注册制"是"体教结合"培养模式这个刚出生的新生儿遭遇的第一个致命打击。根据资料查阅，至今，游泳运动管理中心也没有就取消"运动员双注册制"给出过合理的解释。[1]

2005 年，清华跳水队将私自离队的王鑫及其家长告上法庭，舆论一片哗然。但此举并未遏止自主培养的队员被抢注的情况， 清华跳水队也曾向国家体育总局游泳运动管理中心和竞体司申诉，并不断和地方抢注单位协商，但结果往往不尽如人意。从此，清华跳水队每况愈下，曾经的4 级梯队有3 级被先后解散，很多教练和队员离去，辅导员制也于2008 年4 月被取消。2)

虽然清华跳水队在国内比赛中多次取得优异成绩，但是却很少有机会参加国际大赛。根据我国体育法第二十六条：“参加国内、国际重大体育竞赛的运动员和运动队，应当按照公平、择优的原则选拔和组建。具体办法由国务院体育行政部门规定。”所以根据该条款，国家体育总局应该设立一套统一、公平、严格的比赛选拔机制， 保证所有的运动员都享有公平的被选拔参赛资格。而不应该考虑这个运动员是来自高校还是地方专业队。同样作为国家竞技体育后备人才，应该给予同样的机会。

其实， 现在有很多项目的国家队都与学校合作， 例如射击队就在清华设立了一个基地，平时没有比赛时，清华队的队员就在学校里学习和训练，等有选拔赛时，再到射击队参加选拔，如果成绩合格就可以代表国家队参加比赛。这样，既没有耽误学习，也可以让队员以学生的身份在国际大赛中一展身手，为国家争光，何乐而不为呢？

另外， 根据体育法第二十九条：“全国性的单项体育协会对本项目的运动员实行注册管理。经注册的运动员，可以根据国务院体育行政部门的规定，参加有关的体育竞赛和运动队之间的人员流动。”

“办法”第一条：“为了加强运动员队伍管理，保证训练竞赛工作质量，促进运动人才资源合理配置， 推动体育事业发展， 根据≪中华人民共和国体育法≫制定本办法。”既然“办法”是国家体育总局依据体育法制订的，那么根据上述体育法的规定，“游泳运动管理中心”并不是法律规定的运动员注册与交流管理的主体。按照下位法服从上位法的立法原理， 体育规章、规范性文件等的制定必须以≪体育法≫为依据，在内容上不得与≪体育法≫的规定相抵触。但是“ 办法”在规定运动员注册管理主体时，仍然将单项体育协会与运动项目管理中心相混淆，违反了≪体育法≫对运动员注册管理主体的规定。3)

1) ≪中国新闻周刊≫文章：“落难”的清华跳水队http://www.chinanews.com.cn/ty/zhty/news/2009/01-22/1539417.shtml
2) 人民日报：迷茫的清华跳水队2010-07-29 17:05:00 http://www.sports.cn/qinghua/xun/2005-04-18/540515.html

现行体制下，体育部门掌控着国内的运动竞赛举办权、国际赛事的参与权、优秀选手的选拔权等资源，这使得学校培养的高水平运动人才很难进入国家竞赛体系。学生运动员从学校途径是报国无门，从某种角度是对高校践行"体教结合"的一种压制和不认可。在清华跳水队中，这种现象颇为明显，很多选手为了能够进入国家队，不得不选择出走到省队，然后迂回到国家队的路线。而培养了大量优秀人才的清华跳水队，却两手空空，遭遇人才的流失。4)

此外游泳运动管理中心撤销"双重注册"与"办法"第三条："运动员注册与交流应本着自愿、公开、合法、有序的原则进行。"也不相符。当运动员选择去清华训练时是因为"办法"的"双注册制度"的存在。为了能有更好的学习和训练条件，运动员选择了清华大学跳水队。游泳运动管理中心突然撤销该制度使得运动员只能被迫离开清华大学跳水队。在没有选择的情况下，这种"自愿"是牵强的。

由于现行体育法在程序法上的不完善导致出现上述纠纷时受害方，比如该案的清华跳水队，只能采取默认的态度，因为申诉无门。尽管在"办法"第七章，专门为注册管理纠纷的"裁决"做了以下规定：

第四十九条运动员注册和交流过程中发生争议问题或出现违规行为，任何单位或个人均可以书面形式向国家体育总局、全国性单项体育协会运动或运动项目管理中心提出申诉或进行举报。

第五十条全国性单项体育协会或运动项目管理中心须在接到申诉或举报30 天内做出裁决。

第五十一条当事人对全国性单项体育协会或运动项目管理中心的裁决或处罚有异议，可在裁决公布之日起20 天内，向国家体育总局提出书面夏议申请，国家体育总局须在收到夏议申请之日起30 天内做出最终裁决。"

众所周知，全国性单项体育协会和运动项目管理中心是"一套人马，两块牌子"。而国家体育总局作为政策的制订部门也难以有让人信服的裁决公正性。我们更多的需要借助外部纠纷解决机制，比如公正的仲裁机构和法院，需要他们的宣告性判决来打破体育界这种"一

---

3) 王小红《我国运动员注册管理相关问题探讨》湖北体育科技 2009 年11 月第28 卷第6 期 625 −640 页
4) 人民日报关注体教结合清华跳水培养模式何去何从2010-08-02 09:48:00 来源：中国新闻网(北京)

言堂"的不公正状态。

运动员原本短暂的运动生涯就这样在没有权利保障的情况下一再蹉跎。错过了一个又一个宝贵的参赛机会。相比之下，国外运动员面对被剥夺的参赛资格，往往会选择诉讼的途径来解决。他们这样认为："一心想参加体育竞赛的当事人试图通过诉讼来获得参加某一体育赛事临时或完全的资格。私法权利受到某一限制实施的影响的原告可以向法院申请一项宣告性判决，宣告该限制无效，他还有可能获得一项禁令，阻止该限制发生效力。在从前，人们认为并非基于所有的诉因都可以获得宣告性判决。但是现在已经确立，当私法权利受到影响时，获得宣告性判决的自立式权利(free standing right)本身就是一种诉因，足够获得宣告性救济。"

在美国，法院已经将体育协会制定和执行规则时未能遵守正当程序作为裁决该规则无效的理由。在修改规则之前，未能接受可能受到影响的人的听证，也可能导致该规则无效。甚至一项规则本身是合理的，而且是在经过公正的程序考虑后制定的，但如果未能制定对之进行适用的细则，或者未能让受影响的当事人进行听证的话，也可能会被视为无效。

在英格兰，公平行事义务的内容至少包括这样一项，那就是不得以可能被定性为武断和反复无常的理由来拒绝一项成员资格申请或者许可证申请。当参加某一体育赛事的权利或从事体育来谋生的权力产生疑问时，英格兰法院将支持那些显然是武断的、反复无常的决议而引起的诉讼，以及那些根据当时的情形应当进行听证而未能举行听证而引发的诉讼。5)

笔者认为，相对运动员的艰苦付出和短暂的运动生涯，要求管理方的公平义务尽到完善是非常必要的。我们有责任为运动员提供良好的法律环境和司法救济。

禁令也许是在体育纠纷中最有用的救济。一项禁令能够迫使某一不情愿的赛事组织者允许一名合格的参赛者参加该赛事。尽管禁令不能强迫一名不情愿的参赛者参加比赛。禁令也许最好地代表了法律的能力，即帮助弱者反抗强者，禁令对法律面前人人平等的概念给出了鲜明的表达，矫正最谦卑的个人与有权势的机构(或者，在偶然的情况下，是倒过来)之间的不平衡。6)

---

5) ≪sports law≫Michael J. Beloff ;郭树理译，武汉大学出版社，武昌珞珈山，2008.7 第一版，41－50 页
6) ≪sports law≫Michael J. Beloff ;郭树理译，武汉大学出版社，武昌珞珈山，2008.7 第一版258 页

## Ⅲ. 结论与建议

1. 建议体育法修改时规定，在管理方修改或制定规则时，建立并履行听证程序。将公平行事义务尽到完善，这样对规则修改的受影响方才是公平的。否则法院可以依法认定该规则无效。

2. 建立完善外部体育纠纷解决途径，依法设立体育仲裁调解机构。为当事人提供申诉通道。

3. 建议将运动员注册与交流办法中的重要细则纳入体育法，明确单项体育协会注册管理权限。杜绝朝令夕改。确保运动员在稳定的政策制度下实现真正的"自愿"选择注册单位。

4. 对体育竞技后备力量人才培养模式的多元化给予法律上的保护和政策上的支持。

‧ **摘要** ‧

我国体育人才后备力量培养形式日趋多元化，体教结合是其中之一。但是由于法律的滞后，制度的不完善以及相关管理部门任意为之的行为使得"体教结合"成为一纸空谈。建议将办法中的重要细则纳入体育法，明确单项体育协会注册管理权限。以确保体教结合政策在我国健康发展。使运动员在稳定的注册交流制度下，在良好的法律环境下，公平放心地享受参赛、学习和训练的权利。

关键词：体育法；体教结合政策；运动员注册与管理办法；

**参考文献**

1. ≪sports law≫Michael J. Beloff ;郭树理译, 武汉大学出版社, 武昌珞珈山, 2008 年7 月第1版, 41 −0 页, 258 页。

2. 王小红≪我国运动员注册管理相关问题探讨≫湖北体育科技 2009 年11 月第28 卷第6期 625− 40 页。

3. ≪全国运动员注册与交流管理办法≫(试行)。

4. ≪中华人民共和国体育法≫。


**Reference**

1. <sports law> Michael J. Beloff 2008/7 the 1th edition, 41−0pages, 258pages.

2. WangXiaoHong ≪On the Issues of Chinese athletesregistration management≫ Journal of HubeiSports Science, 2009/11.

3.≪National Athlete Registration and exchange management approach≫ (Trial)

4.≪The sports law of the People's Republic of China≫

# Negative Competition and its Governance

## 消极比赛及其治理研究

JIAN-CHUAN MA (马建川)*

*Negative competition is the biggest trouble for the development of the big sports events such as soccer, badminton, etc. At the 2012 Olympic Games in London, for the sake of strategic gains, a Chinese double- player team, an Indonesian one, and two South Korean ones together played negative matches of competing for defeats. As a result, they were disqualified by the Badminton World Federation. This incident is detrimental to the reputation of Olympic Games and has aroused widespread controversies both at home and abroad. Identify and punish the negative competition is difficult, it is not only related to sports organizations, more related to the specific country's social public perception attitude. Therefore, systematically research the negative competition forms, its causes and governance has great value to improve the social public's perception, prevention and governance of negative competition.*

*Using normative and empirical analysis, and combed with the negative phenomena analyze the negative competition's characteristics, manifestation, it's cause and harm, and put forward some suggestions. This article is organized into five sections. Section one analyzes the negative game's subject, subjective aspect and objective behaviors, harmfulness, serious violation of sports rules and ethics. Section two proposed the forms of the negative competition, including for advantageous position, "let the ball" for good registration, the tacit understanding ball deliberately lose and other negative behavior, etc. The third section points out the cause of the negative competition, including the gold medal, for competition interests, obtain economic benefits of other interests, etc.; Section four points out how negative competitions harm the sports, Olympic spirit, affect athletes and the public, and damage the national image of*

---

* Professor at China university of political science and law

*member countries. Section five proposes some aspects of governance to transform the ideas in sporting events, eliminate the cognitive misconception of negative competition, strengthen the accountability mechanism on negative matches, and perfect the competing rules.*

**Key word:** Negative Competition, Competition Rules, Sports theory

在2012年伦敦第30届奥林匹克运动会上，羽毛球女子双打比赛出现了中国、韩国、印度尼西亚三个国家的4 对选手相互"竞输"的消极比赛现象，引起了现场观众的强烈不满，被世界羽联(BWF)取消了比赛资格。到底是"合理利用规则"，还是"消极比赛"也引发了三个国家舆论与公众以及国际上的广泛争议。消极比赛是长期以来困扰足球等球类大型体育赛事的一种丑恶行为，阐明消极比赛的形式、成因、危害和治理之道，对厘清消极比赛和合理利用规则的界限，提高体育竞赛选手和公众的认知能力，维护体育赛事的纯洁性、信誉和市场吸引力，防范和有效治理消极比赛都有较大的应用价值。

## I. 消极比赛的定义与特征

由于体育运动项目众多，规定繁杂，对消极比赛很难下一个准确的能够包含所有消极比赛形式的定义。人们往往从一个具体的体育项目发生的消极比赛事件出发，结合该事件的表现形式，对消极比赛进行描述，主要集中在球类项目方面。针对足球等项目，熊文等人认为，"消极比赛是在特定情景下，参赛选手(队伍) 为了达到某种目的－－最终获得好的名次或经济利益等，故意输给(或弃权于)对方，并损及第三方利益的行为。"[1] 针对奥运会的羽毛球消极比赛事件，"消极比赛，指为了避开提前与本方队友在淘汰赛中相遇，而选择在小组赛中故意输球，从而为夺取更大胜利创造有利条件。"[2] 世界羽联(BWF)处罚中国、韩国、印尼4 对消极比赛选手的理由是违反了《BWF 运动员守则》的4.5 和4.6 两项条款－－"没有尽

---

1) 熊文等：《竞技体育不道德现象的表现、特点及危害》，载《浙江体育科学》2007 年11 月，第29 卷第6 期。

2) 百度百科：《消极比赛》，baike.baidu.com/linkurl＝1mCwjYB2YJue-fhfB3tVQErwGbuhsv2-WEXK53RJhMI0OT Q3cVK0n25pYAQ5x0pT，2013/08/26，。

自己的最大努力去赢得比赛"和"举止羞辱和伤害了羽毛球运动"。2012 年12 月初, NBA 官方针对圣安东尼奥马刺队在当地时间11 月29 日对阵迈阿密热火队的比赛中雪藏了大部分主力队员, 让他们提前返回圣安东尼奥休息的行为, 宣布对圣安东尼奥马刺队处以25 万美元的罚款。联盟希望每支球队在每场比赛中都能够拼尽全力为球迷们奉献最精彩的比赛, NBA 总裁大卫·斯特恩称马刺队的行为"伤害了NBA 联盟以及我们的球迷"。

笔者认为, 所谓消极比赛是指体育比赛选手(或球队)在体育比赛中, 为了最终获得好的名次等比赛利益或经济利益等其他比赛以外的利益, 而故意不尽全力去比赛或不尽最大的努力去赢得比赛, 并损害第三方利益, 严重违反体育规则和体育伦理的行为。

消极比赛具有以下特征:

1. 消极比赛的主体一般是体育比赛选手(或球队), 特定情景下, 如果作为一个比赛战术进行强制应用, 则教练也会成为消极比赛的责任主体。

2. 消极比赛的主观方面应该是一种故意的心理状态, 其目的是为了通过消极比赛获得好的名次等比赛利益或经济利益等其他比赛以外的利益, 是一种故意放弃比赛的行为。

3. 消极比赛的客观方面主要表现为不尽全力进行比赛或未尽全力去赢得比赛, 未尽全力去争胜是消极比赛的核心特征。至于如何未尽全力进行比赛, 有着许多不同的表现形式。

4. 消极比赛具有严重的危害。无论是对第三者的公平竞赛权利, 还是对体育赛事、观众与社会公众、甚至于体育伦理与社会道德的教育传承等都产生了严重危害。

5. 消极比赛行为是一种严重的违反体育规则和体育伦理的行为, 比较离经叛道, 其行为往往突破了社会的道德底线, 不被体育规则、体育伦理、社会道德、赛事比赛传统等容忍, 也不被赛事举办者、同行和社会舆论、社会公众认可。

## Ⅱ. 消极比赛表现形式

根据体育比赛当局处罚过的消极比赛事件和事后披露的消极比赛事件, 消极比赛的表现形式主要有:

1. 争取有利排位。消极比赛一般发生在循环式的小组赛事中, 比赛中体育比赛选手(或

球队)为了避开强大的对手, 通过进行消极比赛, 故意输掉比赛, 来选择淘汰赛甚至半决赛有利于己方的对手, 以便最终取得好的名次的行为。比如, 在上文提到的4 对羽毛球选手的消极比赛事件中, 不是比赛的一方放弃比赛, 而是比赛的双方都放弃比赛, 为了争取后续比赛的有利排位, 相互"竞输", 引起了裁判的制止和现场观众的一片哗然, 而成为丑闻。

2. "让球"争取有利对位。特定情况下, 在进入淘汰赛后, 如果一个国家的选手有两个以上, 并且这两个选手又在进行的淘汰赛中、甚至半决赛中对位, 则在谁可以更有利的战胜他国选手上进行选择, 安排"让球", 以便安稳的赢得比赛, 获得锦标。例如, 在第39 届世乒赛期间, 中国乒乓球队内部出现的何智丽"让球风波", 何智丽在1 / 4 决赛中接受了同队选手的"让球", 而在半决赛中拒绝了教练让其输给同队其他选手的"让球" 安排。"让球"事件一经公开, 在国际国内均产生了较大的质疑与批评。

3. 假赛, 即俗称的"假球"。在足球比赛中比较常见, 指在比赛的一方需要平局或大比分获胜才能够保级、晋级、出线或获得较好名次时, 比赛的另一方故意放弃全力争胜, 配合对方, 甚至大比分输给对方的情况。世界上许多国家的足球联赛都产生过假球事件, 例如意大利从 1949 年足球实行新赛制以来, 意大利足坛先后发生过10 多起违反体育道德的事件, 在公众中引起极坏的影响。2006 年著名的"电话门"事件, 使得尤文图斯队、拉齐奥队和佛罗伦萨队降入乙级并被扣分, 其中尤文图斯队还被剥夺了2005 至2006 赛季的联赛冠军头衔。中国近年来也频出假球风波, 1999 年"渝沈之战"、 2001 年"甲B 五鼠"事件等恶劣影响都非常大, 在随后的足坛廉政风暴中一些足协官员、裁判、俱乐部官员、运动员等被问责。消极比赛的"假球"与操纵比赛的区别在于, 在不能够证明其操纵比赛结果时, 即是一般意义上的消极比赛, 在操纵比赛结果证据充分的情况下则构成了刑事犯罪。

4. "默契球"。在足球等球类比赛中, 当遇到比赛的一方需要获胜才能晋级或保级, 另一方小比分输球也可以晋级或保级的情况, 或比赛的双方需要以平局或一定比分的平局均可以获得晋级或保级时, 双方往往打出心照不宣的"默契球", 以比赛双方需要的小输赢或平局终局。双方放弃全力争胜, 甚至以放弃进攻的方式来消磨比赛时间, 引起了媒体与观众的不满和质疑。例如在1982 年第12 届西班牙世界杯上, 第二小组小组赛, 与联邦德国、奥地利同组的阿尔及利亚队出线与否完全取决于前两者最后一轮的比赛结果, 只要最后一轮西德

队不击败奥地利，那么阿尔及利亚将能确保进入下一轮赛事。比赛开始10 分钟德国队就攻进一球，剩下的80 分钟比赛，双方均知道当前的比分会让他们两队都晋级，于是根本不打算进攻，不断的在球场上毫无目的的来回奔跑、后场倒脚，尽管全场嘘声一片，甚至有联邦德国球迷愤怒地焚烧德国国旗，两队还是成功地完成了这份"默契"，挤掉了阿尔及利亚。这次比赛在西班牙小城希洪进行，因此事件被称为"希洪之耻"。

5. 故意认输。运动员在比赛中，因为对裁判、教练、俱乐部、球迷、对手等不满，甚至对比赛举办地、场馆、举办国的文化传统、天气等因素不满，而选择放弃比赛，甚至主动认输。例如在台球项目上，2006 年，英锦赛1/4 决赛中，奥沙利文对阵亨德利4 : 1 领先的时候，在第6局比赛中突然与亨德利和裁判握手表示认输，并走进休息室，留下场上不知所措的亨德利，国际台联认定奥沙利文消极比赛，并处以 20800 英镑的罚金。2010 年10 月23 日欧洲球员巡回赛第三站，丁俊晖在不敌梁文博的比赛中，开杆即打散红球，国际台联认定丁俊晖消极比赛，并向丁俊晖开出了2000 英镑的罚单。

6. 其他消极比赛行为。指在上述典型的消极比赛形式以外，其他违反特定体育规则和体育伦理，不被赛事管理当局和公众容忍的消极比赛行为。例如在世界羽联(BWF) 制定的《BWF 运动员守则》中，除了第4.5 款和4.6 款，"未尽全力去赢得比赛"和"做出了明显有辱于或有害于羽毛球运动的行为"都属可处罚的不当行为外，其第10.6 款还进一步规定"球员不得采取其他未包含在本规则内的不当行为"，这实际上是以概括的方式赋予了世界羽联自由裁量权，来裁定运动员的行为是否涉嫌违规。再比如上文NBA 官方针对圣安东尼奥马刺队在对阵迈阿密热火队的比赛中雪藏大部分主力队员的行为进行处罚时，其理由就是未拼尽全力为球迷们奉献最精彩的比赛，伤害了NBA 联盟以及买票等着观看球星比赛的球迷。

以上的消极比赛形式，有的随着消极比赛事件的出现并被问责而被公众熟知；而有的则在隐秘发生多年以后，才被媒体披露出来，虽然未被问责，但也饱受质疑，并随着社会的发展进步而日渐式微。

## Ⅲ. 消极比赛的成因

### 1. 金牌主义

自中国参加洛杉矶第23 届奥运会以来, 伴随着国家改革开放后国力的不断强大, 体育事业也得到了长足的发展, 国民心理也更加自信。北京奥运会的成功举办和金牌数量第一, 极大的满足了国民的成就欲望, 增强了民族自豪感。奥运会成绩与金牌排序已经被赋予可以代表国家强大与否的指标意义, 引发了国民对金牌的强烈预期, 金牌也成为政府、体育管理者和参赛运动员的不懈追求。东亚民族国家独立和发展的历史, 以及相似的集体主义文化背景, 对国家成就感和民族自豪感极其热望, 形成了政府和社会对奥运会金牌的狂热追求。金牌代表着获奖者、组织者、管理者以及国家和国民的无尚荣誉。包括中国在内的许多国家都制定了奥运金牌战略, 力图以各种资源保障其优势项目能够获得金牌。

对参赛选手和教练员来说, 金牌还可以带来巨大的利益。由于金牌被赋予了特定的社会意义, 是否获得金牌对参赛选手和教练员影响很大。虽然银牌和铜牌也可以获得一定的奖励, 但与金牌相比差距极大。各种政府奖励、社会奖励和商业利益以及社会地位会伴随着金牌纷至沓来。而银牌和铜牌则相差甚远, 不可比拟。因此, 参赛队伍和参赛选手有着强烈的获取金牌动机, 甚至不惜违背体育道德, 以获得不当利益。

特别是就羽毛球来说, 中国、韩国、印尼是羽毛球强国, 都有获取金牌的机会。羽毛球往往已经被社会公众列入本国的强势项目和应该获得奖牌或金牌的范围, 造成了巨大的社会压力。面对压力、荣誉与利益的诱惑, 参赛者的竞赛行为可能会发生扭曲, 形成对体育伦理的背离和强烈冲击。

### 2. 获取比赛利益

2002 年9 月, 在德国举行的世界女排锦标赛上, 中国女排教练陈忠和经过精密考量, 率领中国女排先是在小组赛中以0∶3 让球给希腊队, 进入复赛后再以0∶3 让球给韩国队, 先后避开中国女排的强敌俄罗斯队和意大利队。这两场"让球"确实把中国女排"让"进了四

强。这是中国女排当时5 年来在国际大赛中获得的最好成绩。但中国公众并不领情,纷纷指责中国女排打"假球"、打"黑球",引发了人们"到底是尊重体育道德重要,还是注重体育成绩重要"的尖锐质疑。

在2012 年伦敦第30 届奥林匹克运动会上,羽毛球女子双打比赛中,由于D 组的中国选手获得小组第2 名,A 组的中国选手为了避免获得A 组第1 名,使得两对中国选手同处一个半区而在决赛前提前交手,意图通过输掉比赛,获得小组第2 名而避开D 组的本国选手。而A 组的韩国选手也不想赢这场比赛,她们想获得小组第二,这样,她们的队友力争C 组第一,从而保证至少有一对韩国组合能够进入四强。因此,双方不是积极争胜,而是相互"竞输"。按照规则C 组的第1 名将对A 组第2 名即中国排名世界第一的选手,C 组最后一轮比赛前对阵的两对选手面临输掉比赛也照样出线并可以避开强敌的情景,韩国选手和印尼选手都不愿全力争胜,意图输掉相互之间的比赛。因此,4 对选手相互"竞输",通过频频失误竞相失分,受到了现场观众的强烈反对和裁判的干涉与警告。

伦敦奥运会羽毛球女双比赛改变了以往的淘汰赛竞赛规则,实行了先小组赛、后淘汰赛的新赛制。导致事实上出现在小组赛最后一轮,已经出线的选手有根据自己的意愿,来决定比赛结果,进而挑选淘汰赛对手的可能。因此,"合理利用规则"成为消极比赛的借口,通过相互"竞输"以获得比赛利益,违背了体育的道德底线,也震惊了体育界和奥运会场馆内外的社会公众。

### 3. 获取经济利益等比赛以外的其他利益

除了通过消极比赛获得比赛利益以外,还可能为获得比赛以外的经济利益等其他利益而放弃比赛。比如2010 年4 月台球三届世界冠军希金斯与经纪人帕特·穆尼去乌克兰首都基辅商讨举办一项比赛的事宜,在那里他们遇到了假扮成赌博公司的《世界新闻报》记者,《世界新闻报》宣称希金斯同意在未来的某项比赛中输掉指定的某4 局球,以得到30 万欧元的报酬。世界新闻报称希金斯收了26100 欧元的贿赂,并将与希金斯接触时偷拍的画面上传到了网上。希金斯随后否认了世界新闻报的指控,并表示,当时他和经纪人以为面临俄罗斯

黑手党的威胁，为了自己人身安全，不得不虚与委蛇。经过体育仲裁委员会举行听证会，接受贿赂以及同意参与赌球这两项甚为严重的指控被世界台联撤回，希金斯被处以禁赛6 个月和罚款75000 英镑的处罚，其经纪人被永久禁止参与斯诺克运动。在听证会上，希金斯承认在受到威胁的情况下说了一些有损比赛公正的话，而且违反职业道德违规探讨赌球行为，不过希金斯最大的过错就是没有将这些情况及时向国际台联反馈，媒体爆料后给斯诺克运动蒙羞。

在上文提到的意大利和中国足球的"假球"事件中，一些消极比赛就是为了获得经济利益等比赛以外的利益(贿赂、赌球等)而产生的。2011 年6 月意大利警方逮捕了前著名球星西格诺里等16 名涉嫌操纵意大利联赛的犯罪嫌疑人，警方调查发现，西格诺里涉嫌为一些赌博集团服务，帮助他们操纵意大利联赛。意大利警方表示，并未发现意甲联赛遭到操纵，但意乙和更低级别联赛的个别赛场，的确有被场外势力操纵。2012 年5 月意大利警方认为包括多场意甲比赛等赛事需要调查，警方问询150 人，批捕19 人，其中10 位球员来自意甲，拉齐奥副队长毛里等人以体育欺诈的罪名被逮捕，据称他们都受到来自新加坡等跨国赌球集团的收买和贿赂。

## Ⅳ. 消极比赛"的危害

### 1. 严重危害了体育赛事的声誉、公信力与市场效应

奥运会是世界上最高等级的综合性体育盛会，不但其对"更快、更高、更强"的全力争胜的追求，使其成为最为盛大和精彩的体育竞赛平台，而且其倡导的 "团结、和平、进步"的理念，使其受到了世界上不同国度、不同种族、不同语言、不同宗教信仰的人广泛热爱和积极参与。"每一个人都应享有从事体育运动的可能性，而不受任何形式的歧视，并体现相互理解、友谊、团结和公平竞争的奥林匹克精神"。[3]

对奥运赛事等体育大型赛事来说，能够坚守其高贵的品质和公平竞赛的精神，是其长盛

---

3) 国际奥委会：《奥林匹克宪章》, http://en.wikipedia.org/wiki/Olympic_Charter, 2013/08/26。

不衰的保证。国际奥委会主席罗格在伦敦奥运会开幕式上说"不在于你是否获胜，而在于你怎样去比赛，品德远比奖牌重要。"[4] 为了争取有利的排位而进行消极比赛，是对奥运会声誉的最大损害。

消极比赛将损及体育赛事的公信力，动摇与瓦解公众对赛事的品质和公平竞赛能力的信心，影响到公众买票进入体育场馆观看比赛的热情、票房和收视率，并进一步影响到市场等资源对赛事的赞助等支持行为，最终致使体育赛事举办艰难，伤及体育赛事本身。

## 2. 损害了以奥林匹克为代表的体育精神

奥运会不仅体现了体育意义，而且体现了文化和教育意义。奥林匹克精神不仅是公平、公正、平等、自由，追求"更快、更高、更强"的体育竞技精神，而且是一种生活态度和生活哲学，奥林匹克精神强调人通过自我锻炼、自我参与而拥有健康的体魄、乐观的精神和对美好生活的热爱与追求。"奥林匹克主义是将身、心和精神方面的各种品质均衡地结合起来，并使之得到提高的一种人生哲学"。[5] 奥林匹克精神还是一种和谐，自由，健康，积极的现代伦理。奥林匹克主义通过从奋斗中体验到的乐趣、积极的进取精神、优秀榜样的教育价值和对社会公平正义伦理的恪守来启迪社会和青年，以传承和发扬人类的优秀文化和基本伦理。因此，突破道德底线进行消极比赛，会树立损害社会基本价值和伦理的坏榜样，损害奥林匹克为代表的体育精神的传承和发扬。

## 3. 损害了参赛选手和公众的权益

消极比赛既损害了参与消极比赛的选手自己的权益，也损害了其他参赛选手的权益。对参与消极比赛的选手来说，如果能够进入奥运会等大型赛事，都是经过长时间系统的艰苦训练，克服了伤病等困难，获得了优异的竞赛能力。无论是以自己的意愿还是接受教练等人的

---

4) 国际奥委会主席罗格：《伦敦奥运会开幕式致辞》, http://www.kouyi.org/field/sport/1833.html, 2013/08/26。

5) 国际奥委会：《奥林匹克宪章》, http://en.wikipedia.org/wiki/Olympic_Charter, 2013/08/26。

安排进行消极比赛, 不但失去了通过公平竞争带来的荣誉和利益, 而且受到处罚, 一定程度上丧失了进行比赛的资格。对其他参赛选手来说, 消极比赛损害了他们公平竞赛的权益, 使他们成为"陷阱"设置的对象, 损害了他们通过公平竞赛可能得到的利益。

消极比赛还损害了公众的权益。奥运会等赛事不仅吸引了本国观众, 而且吸引了大量的世界观众, 漂洋过海前去观看。各国的公众也通过电视转播, 享受高水平的体育竞赛和体育文化。但消极比赛既损害了现场观众欣赏真实的高水平比赛的权利, 也损害了现场以外公众的观赏权和破坏了他们眼中的体育文化盛宴, 扭曲了社会正常的价值观念。

### 4. 损害了消极比赛参与国的形象

历次"让球"等消极比赛事件都让国际舆论对参与消极比赛选手所属国家的形象产生了非议与质疑。特别是2012 年伦敦第30 届奥运会上羽毛球女双选手消极比赛事件, 由于相互"竞输", 表现十分恶劣, 影响重大, 还受到了被驱逐出赛事的处罚, 开创了奥运会的不良先例。而且, 实施过程极其难堪, 事中和事后还产生了推卸责任的表现等, 损害了国际上对运动员所属国家人民品格的认知, 损害了所属国的国家形象, 混乱了人们的观感。对处于国力上升时期, 志在让世界接受自己经济地位的同时, 接受自己文化价值和政治地位的东亚国家来说, 损害尤其突出。

## Ⅴ. 治理消极比赛的建议

### 1. 转变体育比赛理念

2012 年 8 月1 日国际羽联取消4 对参与消极比赛的奥运会羽毛球女双选手继续参赛资格后, 中国的人民网与新华网两大网站推出调查, 统计结果如下:

人民网: 我羽毛球队员因消极比赛被取消奥运资格, 您咋看?

截止2 日23 时, 共有4515 人次参与调查。图1 所示, 35.3%的网友(1596 票)表示"理解,

消极比赛有违体育道德，实不可取"；41.3%的网友(1863 票)表示"反对，比赛制度设置不完善，有漏洞缺陷"；22.3%的网友(1007 票)表示"建议，赛制应完善，但奥运精神更不可丢"。此外，还有1.1%的网友(49 票)选择"其他看法，我有话说"。6)

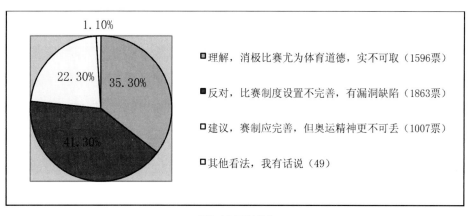

图1 人民网调查图

新华网：你如何看待运动员"消极比赛"？

截至8月3日上午8时，共有近4000网民参与调查。图2所示，参与投票的网友中，41.5%(1655票)的网友认为是制度设置缺陷，不应取消资格，还有约31.1%的网友(1242票)认为"违背了体育道德和奥运精神"。另外约20.9%的网友(836 票)认为"不尊重观众"，约3.56%的网友(142票)认为"战术设计需要，不需过分责怪运动员"，约2.81%的网友(112票)认为"为了更好的成绩，做法可以理解"。7)

---

6) 人民调查：《超四成网友反对我羽毛球队员因消极比赛被取消奥运资格》，http://society.people.com.cn/n/2012/0802/c1008-18659372.html。

7) 《新华调查：你如何看待消极比赛》，http://news.xinhuanet.com/politics/2012-08/02/c_123513346.htm。

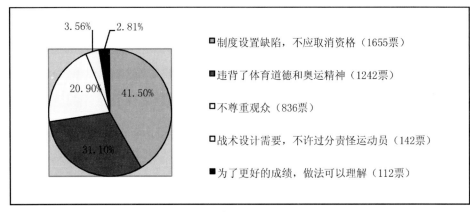

图2 新华网调查图

羽毛球的消极比赛事件涉及到3 个国家, 4 对8 名选手, 说明金牌主义的影响极为广泛。事件发生后, 在运动员所在国和国际上都产生了支持、反对、同情的冲突态度, 表明了体育伦理问题存在的群众性和普遍性。也表明参与体育比赛的观念应该转变。

价值观念的转变是有效治理的重中之重。应该转变随意可以利用规则的观念, 不能说规则有漏洞就可以违反伦理要求去利用规则获得不道德的利益。应该提倡在恪守伦理的前提下, 去遵守规则和利用规则, 拿"道德"的金牌, 反对损害道德的金牌。应该改变"国内练兵, 一致对外"的比赛传统, 摒弃通过"让球"等获得比赛有利排位的做法, 无论是在不同国家的对手之间, 还是相同国家的对手之间进行比赛, 都应该公平竞赛, 全力争胜。

还应该转变参与比赛的态度, 摒弃"唯金牌论"。虽然获取金牌, 体现了"更快、更高、更强"的奥林匹克精神, 但是, "参与比取胜更重要"也是奥林匹克的基本信念。"生活中重要的不是凯旋而是奋斗, 其精髓不是为了获胜而是使人类变得更勇敢、更健壮、更谨慎和更落落大方"。[8] 参与的可贵之处在于通过参与, 运动员可以不断地超越自己, 达到新的境界, 在更快、更高、更强之中寻找自我, 实现自我。通过参与培养了参与者高尚的品质、真诚的态度、奉献的精神和对理想的追求, 使人得到全面的发展, 其意义远远超过了名次和奖牌。

近年来中国在世界的发展经历使我们发现, 仅仅是国力的强大, 并不能成为世界眼中的

---

8) 维基语录:《皮埃尔·德·顾拜旦》, http://en.wikiquote.org/wiki/Pierre_de_Coubertin, 2013/08/26。

大国强国，必须伴随着文化的强大，强大的国力才能被国际上所接受。同样，仅仅是金牌领先，并不代表是体育强国，必须使人民参与体育和享受体育，并促进国民的全面发展才能成为真正的体 育强国。转变观念正当其时。

### 2. 消除对消极比赛的认识误区

一些消极比赛参与者往往以"合理利用规则"为借口。一般来说，规则是体育比赛的行为依据，伦理是体育比赛的价值导向，在规范意义上两者应该和谐一致，以引导参赛者的行为。参赛者参加体育比赛，应该遵守比赛规则，信守体育伦理。但在消极比赛事件中参赛选手以利用规则为借口，不是积极争取比赛的胜利，全力战胜对手，而是以输掉比赛为目的，甚至相互"竞输"，以获取比赛利益。在此，规则与伦理产生了极大的背离，引起了认知和行为的极大混乱。是利用规则获利，甚至消极比赛，还是守护体育精神、体育伦理，积极进取、公平竞赛，发生了严重的冲突。消极比赛是规则问题还是伦理问题，如何在遵守伦理的前提下选择规则，对体育运动至关重要。从实质上说，能否"合理利用规则"其前提是遵守奥林匹克等体育精神、体育道德和人们的认知底线。在商业化、市场化不断侵蚀体育运动的当下，呵护奥林匹克精神，自觉捍卫最起码的体育精神和体育道德应该成为体育参赛选手和其他参与者、以及社会的重要价值。

查阅一些消极比赛事件参与者和其教练的言论，他们之所以这样做，是把一些规则、道德、传统等允许的利用规则的行为误当为"消极比赛"，因此毫无顾忌的违反体育道德。

比如，举重选手根据所报的级别，称体重前减体重、称体重后适当进食，以保持体力，就属于"合理利用规则"。NBA 篮球比赛中，当临近结束而比分领先过多时，一般是比分低的球队先换下主力队员，以示放弃取胜机会，而领先的球队也换下主力队员，比赛进入"垃圾时间"。但这已经成为比赛的传统，而且被竞赛者和公众所接受，并不违反体育精神和体育道德。即使是足球比赛小组出现后，在不需要分数的最后轮次，更换一些主力队员，以防止伤病或红黄牌减员，也不能认为是消极比赛。因为它是人员可以更换和替代的比赛项目，况且双方没有因此就放弃 比赛或相互"竞输"，仍属正常比赛。

还有一些人常常将"消极比赛"与历史典故中的"田忌赛马"相比较，并为之开脱，也是极不妥当的。"田忌赛马"虽然用了计策，以错位排阵获得了比赛胜利，但该赛马比赛可以自由选择己方参赛的马匹，并可以自由决定马匹的比赛对位。因此，"田忌赛马"是合理利用规则，是智慧的象征，也是符合道德和正义要求的，是被社会伦理认可和接受的。

但伦敦奥运会的羽毛球女子双打项目，在比赛人员不能更换替代的规则约束下，为了选择比赛对手而相互"竞输"，已经严重脱离了"合理利用规则"的范围，且此行为不为体育精神、体育道德、项目比赛传统、社会伦理等所允许。

### 3. 加强对消极比赛的问责

消极比赛之所以肆无忌惮，就是因为缺乏有力的问责。因为伦敦奥运会羽毛球女双消极比赛而取消选手的比赛资格，在历届奥运会中还属首次。世界羽联(BWF)依据≪BWF 运动员守则≫的4.5 和4.6 两项条款－－"没有尽自己的最大努力去赢得比赛"和"举止羞辱和伤害了羽毛球运动"对所涉选手进行了处罚，取消了消极比赛四对组合的奥运会比赛资格。国际奥委会支持世界羽联的处罚，为了有效控制消极比赛，要求相关队伍的国家奥委会展开调查，以确 定除当事运动员外是否还有其他人员应承担责任。并希望此事给所有项目、所有人都敲响警钟。警告说"如果此类事件再次发生，我们必会采取行动。"

认定和处罚消极比赛的困难在于，无论是国际体育组织，还是主权国家的法律或体育组织的赛事规则，对消极比赛的责任主体、责任认定和处罚等缺乏规定，致使缺乏足够的法规依据来进行问责，证据的难于取证，也使得认定和处罚难以深入进行。

应该加强对消极比赛的立法，完善对其问责的制度体系。在责任主体方面，一般情况下实施消极比赛的参赛选手是责任主体，但如果属于教练安排或唆使队员进行消极比赛，则应该将教练列入责任主体，处罚教练。在责任构成方面，应该强调两个核心特征，一个是有故意不尽全力进行比赛或未尽全力去赢得比赛的行为与心理状态， 另一个是严重的违反了体育规则和体育伦理，其行为比较离经叛道，突破了社会的道德底线，不被体育规则、体育伦理、社会道德、赛事比赛传统等容忍，不被赛事举办者、同行和社会舆论、社会公众认可。

对一般的违反体育规则与体育伦理的行为，如果没有达到严重的程度，只进行道德谴责即可，没有必要对其进行处罚。在问责程序方面应该强化听证程序，实现程序正义。在处罚措施方面应该完善停止比赛资格、禁赛、罚款、降级、扣分等处罚措施，使处罚有明确的依据。在证据方面，如果属于严重的为追求比赛利益不尽全力进行比赛，应该结合未尽全力去赢得比赛和违反体育精神和体育伦理的严重情况，来确定消极比赛性质；如果属于为了追求经济利益等体育以外的不当利益，在没有充分的证据以前，应该以消极比赛来查处，如果能够获得充分证据，则转入司法程序，以操纵比赛结果等刑事责任来处理。

由于消极比赛的违规性特别是违反道德性是一个争议较大的问题，具有一定的相对性，不同的国家、不同的利益主体、不同的文化和社会环境、不同的项目、不同的动机等会使人们对一个比赛行为是否违规特别是违反体育道德，往往会产生不同的认知态度。伦敦奥运会羽毛球消极比赛事件发生后，中国、韩国、印尼三个国家的舆论和公众并不是一边倒的去指责消极比赛，也都对世界羽联(BWF)取消四对组合的奥运会比赛资格有所非议甚至抗议，但印尼对所涉人员进行了禁赛处罚，韩国对所涉人员进行了禁赛处罚，对所涉教练进行了取消比赛资格的处罚。中国代表团和主教练当时也进行了道歉，并表示要进行调查，并追究或承担责任，但奥运会后并没有公布调查结果和进行责任追究。可见，相比于对消极比赛缺乏认定标准，转变体育比赛理念，并具有调查和处罚消极比赛的政治意愿则更为关键。

## 4. 合理完善体育比赛赛制与规则

完善的体育比赛赛制和竞赛规则是良好的体育赛事的基础，赛制与规则的不足与漏洞，往往为"合理利用规则"进行消极比赛提供了借口。伦敦奥运会中，羽毛球比赛之所以会出现消极比赛，虽然主观上有所涉选手违反体育精神和体育道德的情况，但不合理的比赛规则也为"合理利用规则"挑选比赛对手，争取比赛的有利排位提供了可能的机会。世界羽联一改前五届奥运会的单败淘汰赛制，为了让低水平选手多打几场比赛，采用了先小组赛、后淘汰赛的赛制。而且，最后一轮各组比赛时间不一致，时间的差异可能会导致对手的选择。建议要么取消小组循环赛制，直接进行单败淘汰赛，要么在小组赛后，四分之一比赛的对手以一定

的等级对应, 进行抽签决定, 以避免消极比赛。

在足球比赛中, 不少国家甚至是足球项目发达的国家都因为联赛最后一轮频频产生一些可笑的不可理解的消极比赛事件而困扰, 一些球队也因此受益, 获得了冠军等好的名次或晋级、保级等利益。因此, 许多国家的联赛统一了最后一轮的比赛时间, 尽可能杜绝根据他人比赛的结果来决定自己比赛结果的消极比赛现象, 以保证公平竞赛。

美国职业篮球联赛(NBA)为了保证各个球队的实力接近, 使得比赛竞争激烈而精彩, 出台了根据比赛成绩, 由成绩差的球队优先挑选新秀队员的制度, 产生了较好的作用。但也出现了一些球队通过"摆烂", 以获得优秀新秀的情况。为了防止差队在赛季中为赢得优先选秀权故意输掉更多比赛, 完善赛制, 上世纪80 年代NBA 引入了选秀抽签制度, 以更合理的赛制来保证公平竞赛, 保证联盟的吸引力和观众的利益, 带来了较好的效果。

伦敦奥运会上, 世界羽联处罚以后, 本已出炉的女双8 强对阵表立刻变得支离破碎, 比赛质量严重降低。可见, 虽然进行了责任追究, 但不合理规则的破坏力巨大, 对体育比赛来说, 必须制定和完善合理的赛制和竞赛规则。

· 摘要 ·

消极比赛是长期以来困扰足球等球类大型体育赛事的一种丑恶行为, 对体育运动危害极大。特别是2012 年伦敦第30 届奥林匹克运动会上, 羽毛球女双比赛中一对中国组合、一对印尼组合和两对韩国组合为了获得比赛利益, 进行了相互"竞输"的消极比赛, 被世界羽联取消了比赛资格。这一事件严重危害了奥运赛事的声誉, 也引发了国内外广泛的争议。认定和处罚消极比赛较为困难, 这不仅与体育组织有关, 更与特定国家社会公众的认知态度有关。因此, 系统地探讨消极比赛的形式、成因与治理之道, 对提高体育界、社会公众对消极比赛的认知能力, 防范与治理消极比赛有着重要的应用价值。

论文运用规范分析和实证分析方法, 系统梳理了消极比赛现象, 剖析了消极比赛的特点、表现形式、成因、危害等, 提出了治理消极比赛的一些建议。论文分为五个部分, 第一部分分析了消极比赛的定义与主体、主观方面、客观行为、危害性、严重的违反体育规则和体育伦理等特征; 第二部分提出了消极比赛的表现形式, 包括争取有利排位、"让球"争取有利对位、假赛、默契球、故

意认输、其他消极比赛行为等；第三部分指出了消极比赛的成因，包括金牌主义、获取比赛利益、获取经济利益等比赛以外的其他利益等；第四部分阐述了消极比赛对体育赛事的声誉、公信力与市场效应、以奥林匹克为代表的体育精神、运动员和公众的权益、消极比赛参与国的形象产生了危害；第五部分提出了转变体育比赛理念，消除消极比赛认识误区，加强对消极比赛的问责，完善体育比赛规则等治理建议。

**关键词：消极比赛竞赛规则体育伦理**

# 參考文獻 (References)

熊文等：《竞技体育不道德现象的表现、特点及危害》，载《浙江体育科学》2007 年11 月，第29
    卷第6 期。

百度百科：《消极比赛》，baike.baidu.com/linkurl＝1mCwjYB2YJue-fhfB3tVQErwGbuhsv2-　WEXK5
    3RJhMI0OTQ3cVK0n25pYAQ5x0pT，2013/08/26。

国际奥委会：《奥林匹克宪章》，http://en.wikipedia.org/wiki/Olympic_Charter，2013/08/26。

国际奥委会主席罗格：《伦敦奥运会开幕式致辞》，http://www.kouyi.org/field/sport/1833.html，2013/
    08/26。

人民调查：《超四成网友反对我羽毛球队员因消极比赛被取消奥运资格》，http://society.people.com.
    cn/n/2012/0802/c1008-18659372.html 。

《新华调查：你如何看待消极比赛》，http://news.xinhuanet.com/politics/2012-08/02/c_123513346.htm。

维基语录：《皮埃尔·德·顾拜旦》，http://en.wikiquote.org/wiki/Pierre_de_Coubertin，2013/08/26。

韩新君等：《对奥运会中越轨行为的研究》，载《天津体育学院学报》，2013 年，第28 卷第1期。

金晶：《竞技体育"让球"现象透析》，载《南京林业大学学报》，2007 年12 月，第7 卷第4 期。

刘淑英、王建平：《运动竞技规则评价之合理向度》，载《成都体育学院学报》，2013 年，第39 卷
    第6 期。

梁汉平、袁古洁：《假球黑哨赌球行为法律分析》，载《体育文化导刊》，2011 年第10 期。

张磊：《中国足坛"假、赌、黑"三大顽症的主要成因及遏制策略》，载《河北体育学院学报》，2010

年 第5 期。

王利宾：《操纵体育比赛的刑法规制分析》，载《体育文化导刊》，2013 年第1 期。

王栋：《增设操纵体育比赛罪的初探》，载《体育世界》，2011 年第11 期。

于善旭、李先燕：《中国体育竞赛赛风赛纪的法律规制》，载《西安体育学院学报》，2009 年 第3
期。

# Research about Online Football Gambling Crimes

## 关于网络赌球的犯罪研究

ZHONG-QIU TAN (谭仲秋)*

*The online football gambling, as a new form of gambling, unlike traditional gambling, its gambling sites are virtual network, rather than the real space with characteristics of cross-regional, convenient links, simple operation and quick, strong funds transfer with concealment, which is of great social harmfulness. The online football gambling crimes are of cross-border ,also,the criminal legislation is relatively lacking, which,of course,leading tothe unavoidable criminal jurisdiction conflicts. This article attempts to do a research about online football gambling crime`s characteristicsand constitutions,and to put forward legislative proposals inonlinefootball gambling.*

Key word: Online Football Gambling ; Crime ; Constitutions ; Laws Application

网络赌球作为一种新的赌博形式，不同于传统的赌博犯罪，其赌博场地是虚拟网络而非现实空间，具有跨地域、链接便捷、操作简单、资金划拨迅速、隐蔽性强等特点，具有极大的社会危害性。其犯罪构成要件也具有自身的独特性。网络赌球犯罪的跨国界性以及当前立法的滞后导致了难以避免的刑事管辖权冲突。迫切需要从司法实践的角度出发，在事实认定和法律适用上尽快完善网络赌博罪的相关立法。

\* Professor at Chengdu Sport University, in P.R.C. China

# I. 网络赌球犯罪的特点

网络赌球犯罪实际上是传统赌博犯罪在网络空间的延伸，是网络犯罪的一种具体表现形式。根据立法精神及司法解释，网络赌球犯罪是指以谋取利润为目的，利用网络技术和金融支付手段，聚众赌球、开设赌场、或以赌球为业，违反有关禁赌法规的赌博行为。

相对于传统赌博犯罪，网络赌球犯罪具有以下特点：

## 1. 网络赌球犯罪空间的虚拟性、隐蔽性、诱惑性、跨越性和快速传播性

网络赌球犯罪以互联网为平台，不需要传统赌博的那种固定的能容纳不定数赌客的物理空间，参赌人员的投注行为是在虚拟空间内进行的，他们可以处于全球的各个角落，轻点鼠标即可完成跨地域、跨国界的赌博行为，时空跨越性极强。[1] 它的犯罪行为地和犯罪结果地也不处于"共生体状态"，而往往是分离的，具有无限性。因此，网络赌球相比一般赌博更具有隐蔽性、诱惑性、快速传播性。

## 2. 网络赌球犯罪的低成本和低风险

由于网络赌球的隐蔽性，无论对于网络赌球运营者还是参与者，都是低成本和低风险的。对于运营者而言，他们不需任何物理建设投入，只需架设一台服务器、开办一个网站就能够在内容和形式上做到与传统赌博基本一致。同时严密的组织机构和网络的虚拟性使得运营者之间在现实社会中很少相识，这就必然减少内部道德风险。而对于赌客而言，网上赌博不像传统赌博那样聚众显眼，只要有一间小屋、一部可以上网的电脑，赌博者轻点鼠标就能完成一次赌博过程；甚至拎一台手提电脑，随时随地便能完成一次赌博。赌徒在投注时不需要现金即可过足赌瘾。

---

1) 王君. 广东地下赌球的危害、原因及对策[J]. 体育学刊，2005，(7)

### 3. 网络赌球呈现集团化、公司化趋势，组织严密，境内外勾结情况日渐突出

网络赌球集团有着严密的组织结构，多采用金字塔式的传销经营模式。塔顶是赌博公司、中间是各级代理，塔基是赌客。位居顶端的赌博公司掌握整个赌球组织并物色代理。根据所代理的资金规模和信誉度，代理分为多个级别，他们受控于赌博公司和上级代理，拥有自己的帐号和供发放的帐号，具有一定资金实力。各级代理大都通过网络结识，互不知道对方的真实身份。赌客则向代理交纳保证金取得帐号或者利用他人帐号直接进行赌球。这样相对逐级发展的内部结构有利于赌博公司对整个赌球网络的控制。[2] 当前，网络赌球利用互联网的技术条件，境外渗透和境内活动猖獗。北京市公安局治安总队行动支队副队长任鹏告诉记者，"从一个标准的赌球网络结构图上看，目前境内赌球网络几乎都是由境外赌博公司操控的，他们首先在境内发展一个大庄家，然后再由这个大庄家向下发展二级庄家，二级庄家再向下发展级别更低但数量更多的三级庄家，由三级庄家来出面负责联系普通赌徒，这个赌球网络是一个金字塔结构。"内地不法人员也在积极效仿境外赌博公司，开设网上赌博公司。

### 4. 涉案面广、涉案赌资大、社会危害极其严重

当网络技术和传统赌博犯罪结合而成为网络赌博犯罪时，其危害性愈发明显。首先，北京大学中国公益事业彩票研究所执行所长王薛红博士经过研究和调查，国内每年的非法赌资和彩票的资金比例大概是10∶1。2008 年，我国彩票销售额为1059 亿元人民币。按此类推，去年我国的非法赌资就可能高达1 万亿元左右。[3] 其中，地下赌球和网络赌球的赌资相当恐怖。其次，由于全球已有50 多个国家赋予网络赌博以合法地位，网络赌球也成为被经常利用的隐蔽的洗钱方法。[4] 据估计，每年犯罪分子利用全球数以千计的赌博网站洗白的黑钱约在6000亿至15000 亿美元之间。为获取高额利润，网络赌博集团通过贿赂或恐吓等手

2) 王道春.网络赌博犯罪的特点、构成要件及立法完善［J］.湖南公安高等专科学校学报，2005,(6)

3) 王五一. 世界赌博爆炸与中国经济利益[M]. 北京：经济科学出版社，2005.

4) 束剑平.关注利用网络赌博洗钱［J］.人民公安，2005,(5)

段、控制比赛、通过打假球等来操纵比赛输赢结果，严重影响了体育事业的健康发展。

### 5. 网络赌球案件取证、查处难度大

由于网络赌球犯罪内部结构严密、犯罪手段隐蔽，使得侦查人员感到线索难觅、取证困难、查处难度大。[5] 网络赌博公司通常利用各国对赌博行为的立法不同，在法律上不禁止赌博的国家或地区注册成立，采用专门的网络赌博软件，将赌博网站建立在国际互联网上。同时在境内实行多级代理模式，使用圈内的行话、暗语进行交易，从事网络赌球。另外，由于网络赌博的参与人员仅通过一台计算机就可以完成所有操作，并采用信用卡投注、电子划账的方式进行资金转移，留下的线索往往只有一个IP地址，查证起来十分困难，而且我国目前对电子证据的审查缺乏清晰的标准，缺少成熟的经验。与普通的物证、书证的单一性相比，电子证据具有无形性、多样性等特征，并且容易被篡改、破坏或毁灭，收集和固定的难度很大。因此打击追究此类犯罪的难度更大。

### Ⅱ. 网络赌球犯罪的构成要件

网络赌球犯罪与传统赌博犯罪，两者虽本质相同，但网络赌球犯罪的构成要件有其自身的特殊性。

### 1. 网络赌球犯罪构成的主体

犯罪主体从自然属性上可以分为自然人犯罪主体和拟制人(即法人单位)犯罪主体；自然人犯罪主体从法律属性上可以分为一般主体和特殊主体。本罪为一般主体。根据我国刑法规定，自然人犯罪的一般主体是指达到一定刑事责任年龄，具有刑事责任能力，而实施了

---

5) 张平. 网络赌博活动的特点与防治对策[J]. 北京人民警察学院学报，2005(4)

犯罪行为的自然人。本罪犯罪嫌疑人主要有四种：(1) 网络赌球的组织者和代理，包括赌博网站的管理者、经营者、服务商和境内赌博网站代理人；(2) 以赌球为业的赌客和聚众赌球者；(3)赌资提供者；(4)协助开设、经营境外赌博网站者，网络赌球员工、参赌人员的介绍或引诱、组织者。在网络赌球犯罪中，单位实际上也可能实施，特别是开设赌场的行为或者帮助他人开设赌场的行为。另外，单位也可以实施帮助他人提供网络接入服务、服务器托管、网络存储空间、通信传输通道、费用结算、广告信息等条件或者服务，对赌球活动起直接帮助作用。单位实施的上述行为虽具有严重的社会危害性，但国内刑法并没有将单位规定为赌博犯罪主体。依据罪刑法定原则，网络赌博罪的犯罪主体是自然人而不包括单位。

## 2. 网络赌球犯罪构成的主观方面

本罪的主观方面表现为直接故意，即行为人在主观上具有通过实施赌博活动营利的犯罪故意。一般来说，组织者和代理者的主观恶性要比聚众赌球者和赌客大，因此笔者认为可以借鉴原赌博罪已分成开设赌场罪和赌博罪的情况，将网络赌球犯罪中开设网络赌场的行为与其他行为分别定罪。

## 3. 网络赌球犯罪构成的客体

我国《刑法》将赌博罪归类于"妨害社会管理秩序罪"，表明本罪侵犯的客体是社会正常管理秩序。但笔者认为，由于网络赌球犯罪不仅败坏社会风气，滋长不劳而获的思想，而且诱发其他犯罪，如赌徒用贪污、盗窃、抢劫、诈骗等方式获取赌资；赌球团伙采取非法拘禁、故意伤害等方式逼欠赌债者还钱；犯罪集团利用赌球网站开设的账户洗钱等。此罪触及的社会关系复杂，涉及社会管理秩序、国家货币出入境管理、金融安全、公私财产及人身安全，因此，网络赌球犯罪的客体区别于传统赌博罪的单一客体，具有侵犯社会管理秩序、金融秩序、治安秩序的多重属性，为复杂客体。

### 4. 网络赌球犯罪构成的客观方面

本罪客观方面表现为行为人实施了在网络上开设赌场、聚众赌球或以赌球为业的行为。

(1) 对"在网络中聚众赌球"的理解。

在传统的赌博方式中，聚众赌博的认定是比较容易的，因为赌徒们的聚众赌博行为发生在同一时空，赌资的清算、支付大都以现金方式当场进行。然而，网络赌博行为是依托于国际互联网进行的，突破了时空界限，赌徒们可以在任何时间、任何地点借助现代通讯工具和网络直接或间接投注进行赌博，赌资的支付也大都通过银行的电子结算系统进行。这就给网络赌球中"聚众赌博"的认定带来一些困惑。

1) 对"组织三人以上"的认定。

根据《关于办理赌博刑事案件具体应用法律若干问题的解释》(以下简称"赌博解释")第一条第(1)(2)(3)项规定，以营利为目的"组织三人以上赌博"，抽头渔利、赌资数额、参赌人数达到一定数额的属于"聚众赌博"(可称为聚众型赌博罪)。由此可见，我国刑法惩治的是赌博行为的组织者，组织三人以上赌博是聚众赌博的本质特征。根据《赌博解释》第二条的规定，网络赌球中的庄家和代理属于"开设赌场"(可称为代理型赌博)，网络赌球中的"聚众赌博"主要存在于赌客之中，即具有"组织三人以上赌博"行为的赌客。聚众赌博的组织行为主要有，招引他人参加网络赌球并为其在网上投注，在赌博结束后为其清算、交割赌资。在认定聚众赌博时，要注意把一般的介绍行为和组织行为加以区别。如果只是单纯的介绍他人参加赌博，不宜认定为聚众赌博。

《赌博解释》中的"组织三人以上"是指在同一时间内组织三人以上，还是在不同的时间先后组织三人以上，认识是有分歧的。有人认为，组织三人以上是指"每次被组织参与赌博的人数至少应在三人以上。"笔者认为，这种观点忽视了网络赌博的特点。在网络赌博中，就是在一天之内，世界各地的球类赛事和场次繁多，仅足球比赛就有"意甲"、"德甲"、"英超"等多项比赛，具体的比赛场次更是众多。赌徒们投注赌博的时间和球赛场次各不相同，"每次"该如何计算？一天算一次，还是同一场次的球赛算一次。笔者认为，《赌博解释》

中"组织三人以上"应当是，行为人一次组织三人以上或者先后组织三人以上。这里的三人，是不同的三个人，不是三人次。而且三人中，不包括组织者本人。

2）对"抽头渔利"和"赌资"的认定。

"抽头渔利"即俗说的"返水""抽水"。是指网络赌球的组织者从其上线(代理)处，依照一定比例提取的"佣金"、"红利"和从参赌者赢取的赌金中抽取的"提成"。"抽头渔利"来源于两部分，一部分来自上一级代理，另一部分来自被其组织的参赌者。赌博公司和各级代理为了吸引和鼓励他人组织、参与赌博，都按投注数额和赌输数额的一定比例(1％到2％不等)提取佣金、红利返还给下级组织者。有的组织者(代理)还从参赌者赢取的赌资中，依照一定比例提取赌金，这也属于"抽头渔利"的一部分。

"赌资"，即用于赌博的款物。赌资数额反映出赌博规模的大小，也反映出赌博行为社会危害性的大小。《赌博解释》第八条规定："赌博犯罪中用作赌注的款物、换取筹码的款物和通过赌博赢取的款物属于赌资"。上述规定将赌资分为两类，直接被用作赌注的款物(或用作换取筹码的款物)和赌博赢取的款物。鉴于网络赌博的特点，《赌博解释》第八条同时又对网络赌博的赌资作了规定："通过计算机网络实施赌博犯罪的，赌资数额可以按照在计算机网络上投注或者赢取的点数乘以每一点实际代表的金额认定"。如果我们仔细分析就会发现，《赌博解释》第八条对非计算机网络型赌博中的赌资和计算机网络赌博中的赌资的规定是不相同的。在非网络型赌博中，赌资是由赌徒的"本金"(用作赌注的款物或换取筹码的款物)和"利润"(赌博赢取的款物)合计构成；而网络赌博的赌资则是由"虚拟本金"(投注数额)或者"利润"(赢取数额)分别构成。

笔者认为，如此规定值得商榷。在认定网络赌球中的赌资数额时，涉及到以下三种数额(金额)，一是投注数额(点数)，根据赌博公司规定，投注数额就是投注金额，在大陆地区就是等值的人民币；二是赌输金额；三是赢取金额。实际上，在每一局(场)赌博中，赢取金额很有可能小于投注数额，也可能为零。这种情况下，如何计算赌资数额？如果根据适用法律的一般原则，有利被告原则，在认定赌资数额时应当就低不就高，当出现投注数额巨大，远远超过定罪标准，但赢取金额较小、尚未达到定罪标准时该如何处理？况且，赌博

的一般规律也是输多赢少，将赢取金额作为认定赌资数额的标准也是不科学的。那么，是否可以将投注数额和赢取金额的合计作为认定网络赌球赌资的标准呢？也不行。因为，赌徒们常常把赢取的"利润"重复投入到赌博中，如果将两者合计会导致重复计算。例如，某人网络赌球，第一次投注二万元，赢取了二万元；再赌，投注一万元，全部输掉；第三次投注三万元，输掉一万元；第四次投注二万元，输掉二万元。本例中，行为人投注四次，累计投注数额八万元；赢取金额二万元，赌输金额四万元；实际赌输金额为二万元；赌博涉及现金数额(赢取金额和赌输金额)共计六万元，实际投入现金二万元。由于网络赌球，投注不需要现金，往往投注数额呈虚高状态，这在已查处的案件中反映的特别突出。相对来说，现金数额(输、赢金额的合计)更准确地反映出网络赌球行为的危害性。

所以，在网络赌球中，应当将参赌人员输、赢金额的合计数额，认定为赌资数额。而且必需要明确，认定"赌资"数额，仅限于被组织者的投注数额的累计，不应包括组织者本人的投注数额。同样，"抽头渔利"数额，也不包括组织者本人参赌所产生的佣金和赢取的金额。

(2) 对"开设网络赌场"的理解。

与传统的营业性地为赌博者提供场所，设定赌博方式，提供赌具、筹码，接受赌客投注以供他人赌博不同，对于通过互联网做庄的赌博行为，《赌博解释》认为，属于《刑法》第303 条规定的"开设赌场"。根据司法解释，除了开设网上赌球的庄家，那些明知他人实施赌博犯罪活动，而为其提供资金、计算机网络、通讯、费用结算等直接帮助的，以赌博罪的共犯论处。也就是说，除了在互联网上建立赌博网站的庄家，其他包括为赌博网站担任代理，接受投注的甚至为其提供域名和服务器的，只要是明知他人在从事赌博活动的，就构成共同犯罪。

(3) 对"以网络赌球为业"的理解

理论界通常认为，以赌球为业是指以赌球所得为主要生活来源或挥霍来源，而不论赌球者有无正当职业。也有学者认为是指在较长时间内，赌球活动成为其个人生活的主要内容，输赢金额在其经济生活中占主要部分，并以赌球收入为其生活挥霍的主要来源。这样

的理论解释对司法实践的指导意义似乎不大。因为从打击网络赌球犯罪的司法实践看，不少人都是私营企业或经商者，他们都具有较强的经济实力，也就不是以赌球所得为主要生活来源或挥霍来源。按照上述标准意味着这些具有赌博恶习的富人一般都不能构成"以赌球为业"的犯罪，这显然是不合理的。[2] 针对这种现象，笔者认为可以借鉴日本刑法中"常习赌博罪"的相关规定。[6] 以行为人已经具有反复实施赌球行为的习癖、行为人存在赌球的前科和反复累行赌球行为的事实等标准来判断行为人是否为赌球的常习者，并通过相关解释以明确判断标准。

## Ⅲ. 关于网络赌球的立法建议

### 1. 以司法解释的形式，对网络赌球的罪与非罪进行补充界定

　　我国的刑法典及相关司法解释虽然将网络赌球行为归于"开设赌场罪"这一罪名之下。但"开设赌场"行为在学理上，通常理解为以营利为目的，营业性的为赌博提供场所、设定赌博方式、提供赌具、筹码、资金等组织赌博的行为。"开设赌场"是一个按照传统赌博所设立的罪名，将网络赌球归于这一罪名之下，在犯罪行为的规定上，并不能完全对号入座。因为由于互联网的虚拟性，将建立赌博站点解释为开设赌场的行为，似乎有类推解释之嫌，与罪刑法定原则不完全一致。

　　网络赌球行为，从行为内容上看，可以分为三种：(1)开设、组织、经营赌博网站的行为，这类行为的主观恶性最大，危害也最直接、最严重，应当成为重点打击的对象；(2)提供服务以便于网络赌球行为的进行，如提供赌资支付服务、宣传或引诱他人赌球、帮助开发赌球软件系统等；(3)参与赌球并以赌球为业的赌客，这一类涉及人数往往最多，但"以赌球为业"这一标准，笼统模糊，缺乏可操作性。有人主张为网络赌球设立新罪名，以适应网络赌博的特殊性；也有人主张将网络赌球看作赌博的一种新的形式。前者强调了问题的特殊性，后者指出了问题的普遍性和一般性。前者主张为网络赌博犯罪设立明确的特别规

---

6) [日]大冢仁.刑法概说(各论) [M].冯军译.北京：中国人民大学出版社，2003.

定，以体现罪刑法定的原则。但是，若在未来另设网络赌球的独立罪名，则无形中肯定了目前网络赌球行为的非违法性，给目前查处网络赌球的司法实践造成操作上的困难。后者则抓住了网络赌球的本质，仍然与传统赌博相同。但是，由于互联网的特性，若不对网络赌球行为作出界定，很难使形形色色的网络赌球行为原形毕露。笔者的建议是，保持目前刑法的规定，而以司法解释的形式，对网络赌球的罪与非罪进行补充界定。将使用互联网等设备从事赌球活动，作为从重处罚的情节。具体体例，可以比照≪最高人民法院、最高人民检察院关于办理利用互联网、移动通讯终端、声讯台制作、复制、出版、贩卖、传播淫秽电子信息刑事案件具体应用法律若干问题的解释≫的形式。该≪解释≫第一条通过对涉案违法淫秽信息数量、被点击次数、注册会员数量、违法所得金额及造成后果的规定，对以牟利为目的，利用互联网、移动通讯终端制作、复制、出版、贩卖、传播淫秽电子信息的行为中，罪与非罪的界限加以确定。

## 2．设置科学有效的法定刑

2006 年6 月底颁布生效的≪刑法第修正案≫(六)将"开设赌场罪"的刑罚由原先的"三年以下有期徒刑、拘役或者管制，并处罚金" 扩大到"三年以下有期徒刑、拘役或者管制，并处罚金；情节严重的，处三年以上十年以下有期徒刑，并处罚金" 这就使网络赌博的量刑幅度实际上扩大到了"十年以下有期徒刑、拘役或管制，并处罚金"。但对于"情节严重"及"罚金"的解释尚未明确。

### (1) 将犯罪结果纳入构成要件

目前立法上的开设赌场罪，属于行为犯，即无论其规模大小、汇集赌客和涉赌金额的多少，社会危害轻重，都属于开设赌场的犯罪，受刑法制裁。这样一来，只要开设、经营赌博网站，无论危害大小、或是否造成了危害，都属于开设赌场的犯罪。笔者认为这样的规定从行为上看，网络赌球并不像传统的开设赌场那样，提供全套赌博用具和现实场所，网络赌球参与者必须另外自备电脑、网络等硬件设备以及使用它们的物理空间。换而言之，

网络赌球犯罪的实施，较之传统开设赌场的行为，更多地依赖于赌博参与者的积极行为。若照此规定，可能造成轻罪重罚的结果。笔者建议，对于网络赌球犯罪构成的规定，应仿照≪最高人民法院、最高人民检察院关于办理利用互联网、移动通讯终端、声讯台制作、复制、出版、贩卖、传播淫秽电子信息刑事案件具体应用法律若干问题的解释≫的规定，把犯罪行为造成的客观结果作为判断罪与非罪的标准之一。

### (2) 明晰"情节严重"

从司法实践上来看，由于缺乏统一的规定，各地区法院对"情节严重"的认定大相径庭。≪赌博解释≫规定，聚众赌博，抽头渔利数额累计5000 元以上；赌资数额累计5 万元以上；参赌人数累计20 人以上，即可定罪处罚。笔者认为，可以将"情节严重"定义为：实施≪赌博解释≫规定的行为，数量或者数额达到规定标准十倍以上的，应当认定为刑法第三百零三条第二款规定的"情节严重。"我国刑法第三百零三条第二款中，并没有"情节特别严重"的规定。但笔者认为，以有期徒刑五年或七年为分界点，再将"情节严重"划分为一般的"情节严重"和"情节特别严重"，将会使刑罚的阶梯性得到更好的体现。当然，这也可以采用立法或司法解释的方式达到这样的目的。

### (3) 细化罚金刑

≪刑法第修正案≫(六)，对于开设赌场罪规定了一种附加刑，即罚金。罚金是人民法院判处犯罪分子向国家机关交纳一定数额金钱的刑罚方法，主要是用于贪图财利或与财产有关的犯罪。7罚金所适用的标准，目前，罚金数额的确定标准有三种情况：(1)比例和倍数制，不规定具体的罚金数额，即根据犯罪数额的一定比例和倍数确定罚金的数额；(2)特定数额制，即明确规定罚金数额；(3)抽象罚金制，即只抽象地规定判处罚金，本文所讨论的关于赌博的刑罚规定，就属于这一类。这样无限额罚金的规定，赋予了法院过大的自由裁量权，缺乏科学性，不利于公民权利的保障，也不符合罪刑法定的原则，容易滋生弊端。笔者认为应当细化关于罚金的规定，具体到网络赌球，同样可以用司法解释的形式予以规定。在设立规定时，至少应当考虑以下因素：(1)网络赌球的非法所得；(2)造成的危害结

果；(3)犯罪者的现实情况；(4)主刑(主要是自由刑)的轻重；(5)通货膨胀等其他的影响。

### (4) 增设没收财产刑

没收财产刑，是一种附加刑、财产刑。[7] 对于网络赌球这样的犯罪，没收财产刑的优势不言而喻。它不仅能像罚金一样，针对犯罪者的贪欲进行处罚，并且还具有其他优势：第一，没收财产的范围是犯罪分子的个人财产，而不包括其家属的财产。这就避免了当犯罪分子无法支付罚金时，其家属为其承担罚金的现象，体现了罪责自负、罚不及于无辜的刑法原则。第二，没收财产的范围包括金钱和其他财产。这就赋予了司法机关相当大的斟酌权衡的余地，保证了刑罚的充分性，能够体现罪刑相适的原则。第三，没收财产的范围限于犯罪分子的现有财产，不包括其未来财产。这就增强了刑罚的可执行性，避免了判决执行不能的困难。因此，在网络赌球"情节严重"的情况下，增设没收财产的刑罚，则更显得合情合理。

### 3. 承认单位犯罪

单位犯罪是相对于自然人犯罪而言的一个概念，只有法律明文规定单位可以成为犯罪主体的犯罪，才成立单位犯罪，才能令单位承担刑事责任。我国刑法第303 条的规定中没有涉及赌博之单位犯罪，故依照罪刑法定，单位参与网络赌球并不能课以刑罚。[8] 1999 年《最高人民法院关于审理单位犯罪案件具体应用法律有关问题的解释》第2 条规定："个人为进行违法犯罪活动而设立的公司、企业、事业单位实施犯罪的，或者公司、企业、事业单位设立后，以实施犯罪为主要活动的，不以单位犯罪论处。"故若专为网络赌球犯罪而设立的单位或设立后以其为主要活动的，直接认定为有关个人的赌博罪。

但在司法实践中，确有一些单位为了非法利益通过集体决定或负责人员决定进行网络赌球犯罪(开设赌场等)，故而对涉及网络赌球的单位进行刑法控制是有必要的。即由单位的

---

7) 高铭暄,马克昌.刑法学 [M] .北京：北京大学出版社、高等教育出版社，2002.
8) 战秋萍. 中国网络赌博法治现状分析[J]. 信息网络安全，2007,(12)

主管人员决策、由直接责任人员组织、策划、实行，使单位中的其他人员，对其组织赌博的犯罪意图和手段并不明了，也没有了解的义务，却以自己的行为协助了犯罪行为。双罚制能够在无形中加重对赌博犯罪的刑罚，因为对单位的罚金刑与对犯罪人的自由刑并处罚金，能够在经济上对犯罪者予以双重打击，从而更加降低了犯罪主体的经济能力，增加了其犯罪成本。明确赌博罪中单位犯罪的存在，也可以避免使单位之中的非主管或直接责任人受到刑事处罚，体现了法律的公正原则。但同时，由于单位和其所属自然人的隶属关系，对于单位的罚金刑，必然也能影响到单位中的非主管或直接责任人的利益，从而起到警示的作用，使其对单位从事的网络赌球等违法行为提高警觉，一旦发现单位行为的违法性，能够积极地纠正单位行为，从而避免犯罪危害的扩大。对于网络赌球这样一个监督和查处都有相当难度的行为，利用公检法系统之外的社会力量协助监督，便显得更加重要。

## 4. 积极寻求刑事法律冲突的国际协调和合作

由于网络能够在全球范围内实现赌球活动的信息化与智能化，中国司法机关在打击网络赌球犯罪过程中必须解决国际、区际法律冲突等问题。加强国际协作，积极促成各国在侦查、起诉、判决网络赌球犯罪方面达成相关协议，解决好司法管辖权、证据收集、承认生效判决等问题。

▪ 摘要 ▪

网络赌球作为一种新的赌博形式，并不同于传统的赌博犯罪，其赌博场地是虚拟网络而非现实空间，具有跨地域、链接便捷、操作简单、资金划拨迅速、隐蔽性强等特点，具有极大的社会危害性。网络赌球犯罪的跨国界性以及当前立法的滞后导致了难以避免的刑事管辖权冲突。本文拟对网络赌球犯罪的特点、构成要件加以研究，并就网络赌球提出立法建议。

关键词：网络赌球 犯罪 构成要件 法律适用

## 參考文獻 (References)

[1] 王君. 广东地下赌球的危害、原因及对策[J]. 体育学刊, 2005, (7)

[2] 王道春.网络赌博犯罪的特点、构成要件及立法完善 [J] .湖南公安高等专科学校学报 2005,(6)

[3] 王五一. 世界赌博爆炸与中国经济利益[M]. 北京：经济科学出版社, 2005.

[4] 束剑平.关注利用网络赌博洗钱 [J] .人民公安, 2005,(5)

[5] 张平. 网络赌博活动的特点与防治对策[J]. 北京人民警察学院学报, 2005(4)

[6] [日]大冢仁.刑法概说(各论) [M] .冯军译.北京：中国人民大学出版社, 2003.

[7] 高铭暄,马克昌.刑法学 [M] .北京：北京大学出版社、高等教育出版社, 2002.

[8] 战秋萍. 中国网络赌博法治现状分析[J]. 信息网络安全, 2007,(12)

# On the Sports Law of the People's Republic of China Amended

−The transition from "Basic Law on Sports" to "Law on Promotion of Sports"−

## 论《中华人民共和国体育法》的修改

−从"体育基本法"向"体育事业促进法"的转型−

SI-YUAN TIAN(田思源)*

*Sports Law should not be Basic Law on Sports. Sports Law has historical limitations when being enacted, which decided that it can only enhance functions on sports' administration when it acted as Basic Law on Sports; It comes to obstacles in legislative technology when constructing sports rules of law with core of Basic Law; meanwhile, practice of construction on sports rules of law doesn't reflect the commanding position of Basic law; In modification of "Sports Law" whose core is protection and realization of civil rights on sports, it is not the right time to reshape 'sports law' as status of 'Basic law' and faces the difficulty in modifying 'sports law'. The way to solve the problem above is to promote the ideal of 'Law on Promotion of Sports' and fulfill the transition from 'Basic Law' to 'Promote Law' in the modification on Sports Law.*

Key word: Sports Law; Modification on Sports Law; Basic Law on Sports; Law on Promotion of Sports; Law on Promotion of Sports Career

## Ⅰ. 关于《体育法》的修改

《中华人民共和国体育法》(以下简称《体育法》)是1995 年8 月29 日第八届全国人民代表大会常务委员会第十五次会议通过, 同年10 月1 日起实施的, 至今已有17 年。作为新中国成立以来第一部体育领域的"基本法", 其颁布实施在中国体育法治建设中具有里程碑

---

* Professor, School of Law, Tsinghua University

的意义。[1] 17 年来,《体育法》在保证体育事业持续、快速、健康发展,增强人民体质,提高运动技术水平,扩大体育对外开放,促进社会主义物质文明和精神文明建设,推进"依法治体"等方面,都发挥了积极的作用。但是,由于《体育法》制定的历史背景,决定了其历史的局限性。其一,"由于《体育法》带有明显的计划经济的历史印记,作为'体育基本法'、'体育管理法'、'体育大全法'、'体育政治法'的《体育法》,在制度变迁、社会进步、时代发展的大背景下,在市场经济发展、公共行政改革、政府职能转变过程中,面对体育的市场化、职业化、产业化和社会化,面对如何推动、深化体育改革,巩固体育改革的成果,并进一步促进体育事业蓬勃发展等问题,难于应对、无力承载。"[2] 其二,中国《体育法》"其立法价值取向更多的是倾向于'以义务为本位',重视各个调整主体的义务规定,大部分条款是针对各方面的体育管理而制定的管理性规定,管理效力是当时立法的关注,立法目的在当时偏重国家和社会利益。"[3] 其三,"《体育法》作为一部部门法,它所具有的一般法的滞后性、机械性也日益显示出来,并且已经影响到我国体育事业的健康发展。"[4] 等等。《体育法》的修改势在必行。

早在2005 年,国家体育总局局长刘鹏在全国体育局长会议上的讲话中就提出:要"推动现有《体育法》的修改工作,争取早日列入全国人大常委会的工作议程。"[5] 2005 年9 月国家体育总局政策法规司发出了《关于征集修改<中华人民共和国体育法>有关论文的通知》(体政字[2005]81 号),[6] 并于2006 年2 月27‐28 日,在天津体育学院召开了"修改《中华人民共和国体育法》理论研讨会"。之后,2010 年11 月29‐12 月1 日,中国政法大学也组织召开了"《体育法》修改国际研讨会"。2005 年1 月,北京市人大代表沈梦培、王玉梅向北京市人大提出《修改体育法,推进体育产业化进程‐‐以中国足球为例》的议案。[7] 国家体

---

1) 参见伍绍祖:《依法行政、以法治体的基本纲领》,载自《求是》,1995 年第23 期,第22 页。

2) 田思源:《我国<体育法>修改理念分析‐‐兼论<体育事业促进法>的制定》,载自《法学杂志》2006年第6 期,第68 页。

3) 李先燕、于善旭、韩宝:《后奥运时期我国<体育法>修改理念的再思考》,载自《成都体育学院学报》 2009 年第1 期,第18 页。

4) 秦毅、周爱光:《<中华人民共和国体育法>价值的探讨与反思》,载自《体育科学》2008 年第12 期,第69 页。

5) 华奥星空网(http://www.sports.cn)。

6) 中国体育信息网(http://www.sport.gov.cn)。

7) 参见谢文英:《发展中国足球须从修改体育法入手‐‐按照体育法第三十一条规定,由足协管理足球比赛违背依法行政原则》,载自《检察日报》2005 年12 月22 日。

育总局在≪体育事业"十一五"规划≫(2006 年)和≪体?育事业发展"十二五"规划≫(2011 年)中, 也都明确了≪体育法≫的修改任务。

2009 年12 月2 日, 全国人大教科文卫委员会召开第19 次会议, 审议了第十一届全国人大第二次会议主席团交付审议的代表提出的议案, 并提出了审议结果的报告。报告在"需要尽快立法, 建议国务院有关部门加强调研起草工作, 待条件成熟时列入全国人大常委会立法工作计划"中, 将≪体育法≫的修改纳入其中。2010 年1 月1 日, 国务院办公厅发布了关于印发国务院 2010 年立法工作计划的通知,[8] 在国务院2010 年立法工作计划中, 将修订体育法纳入"保障和改善民生, 加强社会建设和公共服务, 维护社会和谐稳定需要提请全国人大常委会审议的法律草案、法律修订草案和需要制定、修订的行政法规"中。由此, ≪体育法≫的修改工作终于列入了国家的立法计划中, ≪体育法≫的修改工作正式启动。

2010 年3 月22 日, 国家体育总局召开了"修改≪体育法≫研究工作小组"第一次会议, 会议以"修改≪体育法≫研究中涉及的若干问题"为题进行了讨论, 确立了修改研究工作的总体思路和具体工作安排。三年多来, 关于修改≪体育法≫的理论研讨、调研、草案形成、征求意见等工作紧锣密鼓地进行, 在如下重要问题上基本达成共识:(1)以现有≪体育法≫为基础, 进一步补充、修正和完善, 增强条款的可操作性;(2)明确规定公民享有"体育权利", 并规定保障公民体育权利实现的具体措施;(3)改变重管理轻服务的观念, 尊重体育规律, 强调政府责任;(4)明确体育纠纷的解决机制和权利救济制度。

但≪体育法≫修改工作还面临着许多困难, 一些重大的理论问题还没有解决。主要有:(1)立法与改革的关系;(2)体育相关主体(如政府、行业部门、社会团体、中介组织等)在推动体育事业发展中的权利义务及相互关系;(3)体育事业和体育产业的关系;(4)对职业体育的定位与规范, 包括职业体育发展战略目标模式, 职业体育的概念、范围、性质、地位、作用、基本要件要素、投资者的权利、运动员合同、培训与补偿, 等等;(5)如何将全民健身活动落实到实处;(6)如何推动竞技体育的科学发展。包括部分项目发展基础薄弱, 机制不顺畅, 项目发展不均衡, 后备人才培养体系面临困难和冲击等;(7)体育社会团体的规范与发展。如体育社团登记门槛高, 大量社会团体活动频繁但无法登记, 涉外社团增加但现行立法

---

8) 国办发［2010］3 号。

没有规定, 监管监督操作性不强等。(8)体育纠纷的解决和救济机制问题。(9)立法衔接问题。
如民政部修订的≪社会团体登记条例≫与现有体育社会团体法律规定的衔接等。

## Ⅱ. 如何理解≪体育法≫是"体育基本法"

### 1. 中国法律体系中的"基本法"

在中国, 所谓的基本法, 一般是指广义的立法意义上的"基本法律"和狭义的香港、澳门
两个特别行政区的≪基本法≫。

#### (1) 宪法意义上的"基本法律"

在中国, 法律是由最高国家权力机关制定的。1954 年宪法规定全国人民代表大会享有
制定法律的国家立法权。1955 年将国家立法权扩展至全国人民代表大会常务委员会, 但全
国人民代表大会常务委员会的国家立法权不同于全国人民代表大会, 其所制定的法律规范
称之为"法令", 效力低于"法律"。1982 年宪法取消了"法令"的立法层级及其称谓, 全国人民
代表大会常务委员会制定的法律规范和全国人民代表大会一样, 统称之为"法律"。但1982
年宪法同时规定, 全国人民代表大会制定"基本法律", 全国人民代表大会常务委员会制定
"基本法律"以外的"其他法律"(学理上称之为"普通法律"或"一般法律"), ≪中华人民共和国
立法法≫对此也予以确认。可见虽然全国人民代表大会常务委员会和全国人民代表大会一
样享有国家立法权, 同样享有法律的制定权, 但实际上二者是有立法权限的分工的。≪体育
法≫是全国人民代表大会常务委员会制定的, 不是"基本法律"而是"基本法律"以外的"其他
法律", 是"普通法律"或"一般法律"。

#### (2) 法律意义上的≪基本法≫

中国法律上可以称之为≪基本法≫的有两部法律, 即≪中华人民共和国香港特别行政区
基本法≫和≪中华人民共和国澳门特别行政区基本法≫。两个≪基本法≫是以≪宪法≫第

31 条"国家在必要时得设立特别行政区。在特别行政区内实行的制度按照具体情况由全国
人民代表大会以法律规定。"为依据, 按照"一个国家, 两种制度"的方针, 规定香港、澳门特
别行政区所实行的制度, 保障国家对香港、澳门基本方针政策实施的授权立法。《体育法》
显然也不是这种意义上的《基本法》。


### 2. "体育基本法"的提出

1995年《体育法》通过、实施前, 中国的体育立法可谓是一有、二无、三少、四多。"一
有"是有宪法第21 条关于"国家发展体育事业, 开展群众性的体育活动, 增强人民体质"的体
育方面内容的宪法规定;"二无"是没有将宪法上述原则规定具体化的专门体育法律;"三
少"是国务院的行政法规少, 当时只有3 项;"四多"是国家体育主管部门的行政规章多。9)
《体育法》的制定填补了体育立法中没有法律的空白, 《体育法》历史地成为了体育法领域
和体育法律体系中的"基本法"。对此时任国家体委主任的伍绍祖同志指出:"《体育法》是
新中国成立以来的第一部体育部门的基本法。""《体育法》作为国家的体育基本法, 确定了
国家发展体育事业的一些基本方针、基本原则和基本措施, 有些具体问题的规范则有待于
在配套立法中加以解决。"10) 并进一步提出, 力争在20 世纪末21 世纪初, "初步建立起一个
符合我国宪法原则、以《体育法》为龙头、以行政法规为骨干、以部门规章制度和地方性
法规为基础的体育法规体系。"11) 由此, 《体育法》成为了"体育法"意义上的"体育基本法"。


### Ⅲ. 以"体育基本法"为核心难以构建体育法体系

以作为"体育基本法"的《体育法》为核心建构体育法体系, 是一直以来体育法学者和体
育主管部门在体育立法和体育法治建设方面的基本思路。"《体育法》作为体育基本法, 在
专门体育立法中具有最高的法律地位和效力等级, 整个体育法规体系的建立必须以《体育

---

9) 伍绍祖:《依法行政、以法治体的基本纲领》, 载自《求是》1995 年第23 期, 第22 页。
10) 伍绍祖:《依法行政、以法治体的基本纲领》, 载自《求是》1995 年第23 期, 第23、24 页。
11) 伍绍祖:《依法行政、以法治体的基本纲领》, 载自《求是》1995 年第23 期, 第25 页。

法≫为依据、为核心, 不得与其相抵触、相违背。≪体育法≫中的体育法治精神和各项原则规定与授权规定, 将具体体现为一系列与之配套的低位阶法规。所以, 今后建立的我国体育法规体系, 应是一个≪体育法≫的配套立法体系。"12) "在≪体育法≫的基础上加强体育立法, 就是完善≪体育法≫的配套立法。我们对体育立法工作的认识和思考, 当然就不能离开配套体育立法的角度。体育立法意识的增强, 必然具体体现为配套体育立法自觉性的提高。"13) 这样的一个以"体育基本法"为核心, 其他立法为配套的中国体育法体系的建构模式和立法思路, 在当时无疑是一个理想的选择。然而, 中国体育法治建设的理论和实践告诉我们, 这种立法思路只是一个"理想化"的理想。

## 1. ≪体育法≫的先天不足难负"核心"之重

≪体育法≫是在当时中国体育事业发展中面临的诸多困难和问题, 急待通过体育立法加以解决而制定的。如群众参加体育活动的权利没有得到充分的保障, 公民体质状况不容乐观;体育基础设施落后的状况没有得到根本改变, 场地不足, 又大量被占;市场经济体制下体育行政部门对体育事业的领导、协调、监督职能尚未充分发挥等。14) 在≪体育法≫制定过程中, "体育改革"问题提上日程。1993 年5 月24 日国家体委发布了≪关于深化体育改革的意见≫提出了体育改革的十项目标和要求。但由于"体育改革"刚刚起步, ≪体育法≫既要解决中国体育事业发展中的困难和问题, 又要体现改革要求, 而改革又没有成熟的经验, 所以, 可以说≪体育法≫是以原则性立法为指导, 在不失规则性的前提下, 尽可能使≪体育法≫的规定拥有较大的空间, 或者是为了尽快出台≪体育法≫而有意放大了≪体育法≫的弹性。15) ≪体育法≫既没有预见性又没有可操作性的先天不足, 使其在体育的市场化、职业化、产业化、社会化等层出不穷的新的问题面前无能为力。体育管理体制转轨困难重重, 体育事业

12) 于善旭、张剑、陈岩:≪建立以<体育法>为核心的我国体育法规体系的框架构想≫, 载自≪中国体育科技≫ 1999 年第1 期, 第4 页。

13) 于善旭、陈岩, 李雁军:≪完善<中华人民共和国体育法>配套立法的对策探讨≫, 载自≪体育与科学≫ 1999 年第1 期, 第6 页。

14) 参见伍绍祖:≪关于<中华人民共和国体育法(草案)>的说明≫。

15) 刘凤霞:≪对现行<体育法>修改之思考≫, 载自≪浙江体育科学≫2003 年第4 期, 第4 页。

改革举步维艰，竞技体育独木成林，以≪体育法≫为"基本法"的配套立法难以跟进，体育法治建设步履蹒跚。≪体育法≫难负"核心"之重。

### 2. ≪体育法≫在配套立法中的"基本法"作用并不明显

#### (1) 体育立法和体育法体系建设不尽如人意

≪体育法≫颁布实施后，我们立即着手体育法体系的建构工作。1996 年国家体委召开了第一次全国体育法制工作会议，首次公开提出我国体育法制工作目标问题。1997 年国家体委做出了≪关于加强体育法制建设的决定≫，明确提出在20 世纪末21 世纪初，初步建立起适应中国社会主义市场经济需要、符合现代体育运动规律的，以宪法为指导、体育法为龙头、行政法规为骨干、部门规章和地方性法规为基础的结构合理、层次衔接有序的体育法规体系，以及与此相适应的体育执法监督和法律服务体系，争取在2010 年前后，使体育工作全面纳入规范化、法制化的轨道的我国体育法制建设目标。然而，纵观中国的体育立法和体育法体系现状，法律仍仅为≪体育法≫一部，与其配套的行政法规寥寥可数，一些亟待规范的诸如体育仲裁等重要立法尚未出台，立法层级偏低，≪体育法≫制定当时的"三少、四多"现象并未改变，"体育基本法"在建构体育法体系中的理想作用并没有发挥出来。

#### (2) 体育配套立法鲜有以"基本法"为制定依据的

以≪体育法≫为"基本法"、为"核心"的体育配套立法，理应以≪体育法≫为其制定依据，但事实并非如此，参见表1。

表1 ≪体育法≫及其"配套"行政法规一览表(通过时间先后为序)：

| 法律、行政法规名称 | 制定机关 | 通过时间 | 制定依据 |
|---|---|---|---|
| 中华人民共和国体育法 | 全国人大常委会 | 1995 年 | 宪法 |
| 奥林匹克标志保护条例 | 国务院 | 2002 年 | 无 |
| 公共文化体育设施条例 | 国务院 | 2003 年 | 无 |
| 反兴奋剂条例 | 国务院 | 2003 年 | 体育法和其他有关法律 |

| 法律、行政法规名称 | 制定机关 | 通过时间 | 制定依据 |
|---|---|---|---|
| 北京奥运会及其筹备期间外国记者在华采访规定 | 国务院 | 2006 年(已失效) | 无 |
| 彩票管理条例 | 国务院 | 2009 年 | 无 |
| 全民健身条例 | 国务院 | 2009 年 | 无 |

从表1 我们可以看到《体育法》配套立法的几个特点：一是配套立法速度慢。《体育法》颁布实施后的第七个年头才产生了第一个配套立法－－《奥林匹克标志保护条例》；二是配套立法数量少。其中的《北京奥运会及其筹备期间外国记者在华采访规定》是一个临时性的行政法规，2007年1月1日开始施行，北京奥运会结束后2008年10月17日自行废止；《彩票管理条例》不是专门的体育立法，虽然体育彩票要依其管理规定。所以，《体育法》颁布实施17年的配套立法，严格意义上说只有《奥林匹克标志保护条例》、《公共文化体育设施条例》、《反兴奋剂条例》和《全民健身条例》4 部行政法规，且也是借助了举办北京奥运会的推动力量。三是配套立法鲜有明确规定是以《体育法》为制定依据的。就配套立法的制定依据而言，仅有《反兴奋剂条例》明示了以《体育法》为其制定依据，其他几部行政法规则没有法律上的制定依据的规定。而即便是《反兴奋剂条例》， 其制定依据也不仅限于《体育法》，还包括了"其他有关法律"。

显然，中国《体育法》的定位和内容上的缺失，使其他体育立法难以直接规定以《体育法》为其制定依据，难以实现以"体育基本法"为核心的体育法体系建构的预期目标。

### 3. 立法技术角度的分析

#### (1) 《体育法》能否统领体育立法

在中国，还没有一个领域是通过一部全国人民代表大会常务委员会的立法来统领整个领域的法体系建构的。因为即便是在同一领域， 其社会关系也呈现出多面性、复杂性的特点，难以用一部所谓的"基本法"予以涵盖。我们知道，法律部门和法律学科的划分是基于调整社会关系的对象的特定性以及在调整对象交叉时的调整方法的特殊性， 体育法之所以能够成

为一门独立的法律学科, 成为法律体系中的一个部门法, 即在于它所具有的特定的调整对象
－－体育关系。体育关系是一个非常广泛而复杂的社会关系, 有不同的关系主体、不同的权
利义务内容、不同的关系侧面和分类, 《体育法》并不能调整所有的体育关系, 解决所有体
育关系中的问题。所以《体育法》并非"体育法", 《体育法》只是"体育法"的一部分。

当然, 《体育法》是"体育法"中最重要的一部分, 它调整着最基本的体育关系。但问题
在于, 是否其他的体育立法都要以《体育法》为立法依据呢？《体育法》是全国人民代表大
会常务委员会制定的法律, 体育行政法规当然不能与其相抵触, 而在是否作为立法依据问题
上, 前述的立法实践已经给出了答案。更进一步而言, 在《体育法》之外, 全国人民代表大
会常务委员会是否还可以以《体育法》为依据制定其他的体育法律呢？如果可以, 同一立法
主体制定的法律怎么可能出现A 法依据B 法而制定的情形呢？如果不可以, 是否意味着"体
育法"就永远只能有《体育法》这一部法律了呢？

强调《体育法》的"基本法"地位的观点, 是为了建构统一、协调、完备的体育法体系,
而并非排斥其他体育法律的制定, 如建议制定《社会体育管理法》(或《全民健身保障法》)、
《学校体育法》、《体育设施法》等。16) 虽然中国《立法法》并没有规定同一立法主体同
一位阶立法间的制定依据问题, 但立法要遵循和依据上位法则是《宪法》和《立法法》的明
确 要求, 也是立法的基本原则之一, 依据宪法和上位法而不能依据同主体的同位阶立法, 在
立法实践中也得到了验证。

所以笔者认为, 在立法技术上《体育法》也难以统领体育立法, 《体育法》成为"体育基
本法", 其他体育立法都要以其为核心、为依据, 这在立法技术上是存在障碍的。当然, 如果
《体育法》是全国人民代表大会的立法那就另当别论了, 在其之下全国人民代表大会常务
委员会制定其他体育法律就也就顺理成章了。


### (2) 其他领域立法模式的借鉴

如前所述, 中国还没有一个领域像体育法这样以一个全国人民代表大会制定的法律作为

---

16) 于善旭、张剑、陈岩：《建立以<体育法>为核心的我国体育法规体系的框架构想》, 载自《中国体育科技》 1999
年第1期, 第6、9页。

"基本法"来建构其法律体系。也许有人会说， 这是因为体育立法中≪体育法≫出台的比较早，又规定了基本的体育制度，所以之后的其他立法就应该以其为依据。这种说法有一定道理，但体育立法的这种立法模式并不是唯一的。如2005 年颁布的≪治安管理处罚法≫并没有规定以1996 年颁布的≪行政处罚法≫为其制定依据，虽然治安管理处罚是行政处罚的一种。再如我国的农业立法中有≪农业技术推广法≫(1993 年)、≪农业法≫(1993 年，2002 年修订)、≪种子法≫(2000年，2004年修订)、≪农村土地承包法≫(2002 年)和≪农业机械化促进法≫(2004年)等5 部法律，都是全国人民代表大会常务委员会的立法，其中只有≪农村土地承包法≫规定了依宪法制定，而其他4 部法律没有规定制定依据。如果按照体育立法的思路，这其中的≪农业法≫理所当然地应当成为农业"基本法"，其他农业立法都应以此为立法依据，是其下位法。如此，上述的其他农业立法也就只能是行政法规了。特别需要指出的是，≪农业技术推广法≫和≪农业法≫都是第八届全国人民代表大会常务委员会第二次会议于1993年7月2日通过的，显然并没有时间先后顺序的考虑和影响。

为了进一步说明问题，这里我们选取与体育相关的教育和科技领域的立法，分析其立法模式，以供体育立法参考。

表2 教育法律一览表(通过时间先后为序)：

| 法律名称 | 制定机关 | 通过时间 | 制定依据 |
|---|---|---|---|
| 中华人民共和国学位条例[17] | 全国人大常委会 | 1980年、2004年修订 | 无 |
| 中华人民共和国义务教育法 | 全国人大 | 1986年、2006年修订 | 宪法和我国实际情况 |
| 中华人民共和国教师法 | 全国人大常委会 | 1993年 | 无 |
| 中华人民共和国教育法 | 全国人大 | 1995年 | 宪法 |
| 中华人民共和国职业教育法 | 全国人大常委会 | 1996年 | 教育法和劳动法 |
| 中华人民共和国高等教育法 | 全国人大常委会 | 1998年 | 宪法和教育法 |
| 中华人民共和国国家通用语言文字法 | 全国人大常委会 | 2000年 | 宪法 |
| 中华人民共和国国防教育法 | 全国人大常委会 | 2001年 | 国防法和教育法 |
| 中华人民共和国民办教育促进法 | 全国人大常委会 | 2002年 | 宪法和教育法 |

---

17) 根据1987 年≪行政法规制定程序暂行条例≫和2002 年≪行政法规制定程序条例≫的规定，"条例"属于行政法规的名称。但由于≪中华人民共和国学位条例≫是在此之前的1980 年制定的，所以虽称为"条例"，但因其为全国人民代表大会常务委员会的立法，性质上属于法律。2004 年≪中华人民共和国学位条例≫修改时沿用了"条例"的表述，实则改为≪中华人民共和国学位法≫应该更为妥当。

　　从教育立法的情况看，有9 部法律，[18] 其中两部是全国人民代表大会的"基本法律"，7 部是全国人民代表大会常务委员会的"普通法律"。教育立法并不是以《教育法》为唯一的法律，而是一个系列的教育法律体系。《教育法》在教育法律体系中不具有类似于《体育法》那样的"基本法"地位，虽然在《教育法》颁布后，《职业教育法》、《高等教育法》、《国防教育法》和《民办教育促进法》在制定依据上都明确规定是依据《教育法》制定的，但这里有两个前提：其一，职业教育、高等教育、民办教育等都属于教育关系中的同一类关系，依据《教育法》制定在法律规范内容和调整对象上具有统一性和一致性；其二，《教育法》是全国人民代表大会制定的"基本法律"，《职业教育法》、《高等教育法》和《民办教育促进法》都是全国人民代表大会常务委员会制定的"普通法律"，是依据全国人民代表大会的法律制定的，并不存在全国人民代表大会常务委员会制定的法律之间作为立法依据的问题。

表3 科技法律一览表(通过时间先后为序)：

| 法律名称 | 制定机关 | 通过时间 | 制定依据 |
|---|---|---|---|
| 中华人民共和国科学技术进步法 | 全国人大常委会 | 1993年、2007年修订 | 宪法 |
| 中华人民共和国促进科技成果转化法 | 全国人大常委会 | 1996年 | 无 |
| 中华人民共和国科学技术普及法 | 全国人大常委会 | 2002年 | 宪法和有关法律 |

　　从科技立法的情况看，也并没有一部统一的作为"基本法"的"科学技术法"，而是分解成"科技进步"、"成果转化"和"科技普及"等3 部法律，且都由全国人民代表大会常务委员会制定，相互间此法也不作为彼法的制定依据。

## Ⅳ. 《体育法》的修改难塑"体育基本法"之地位：《体育法》修改面临的问题和"体育基本法"的标准

　　如果说《体育法》和制定和实施中的问题使《体育法》未能成为我们所希望的"体育基本法"的话，我们可否通过《体育法》的修改来重塑其"基本法"之地位呢？答案是否定的。

---

18) 也有人将《国家通用语言文字法》列入文化法系列；将《国防教育法》列入国防、军事法系列。

就此，笔者仅就《体育法》修改中所面临的几个宏观问题，结合《体育法》成为"体育基本法"所应具备的条件和应有标准予以论述。

### 1. 《体育法》定位的科学性和预见性

《体育法》定位的科学性和预见性是其成为"体育基本法"的一项重要标准和条件。如果其定位不准，以"体育基本法"为核心的体育法治建设将全面偏离正确的轨道；如果其预见性不够，当社会关系发生变化时，配套立法无以是从，体育执法、司法都将陷于被动。

修改《体育法》的一个重要理由，是《体育法》作为"管理法"的定位不准和对体育改革发展的复杂程度预见性差。从《体育法》的制定到《体育法》的修改，中国社会政治、经济、文化等各方面都发生了巨大的变化，《体育法》的定位也将从"计划"向"市场"、"管理"向"服务"、"义务"向"权利"转变。对此学界已基本达成共识。但由于中国体育体制改革进展缓慢，体育市场化机制极不成熟，职业体育发展偏离轨道，公共体育服务难以落实，依法治体还面临着受传统体育管理模式制约的体制性障碍，对立法与改革的关系、中国特色的"举国体制"、"体育强国"建设、社会主义文化大发展大繁荣中体育的功能和作用、新时期体育社会团体的规制与发展等重大理论问题还缺乏深入研究，通过理论创新和制度创新解决实践难题的能力还有很大的差距，准确实现《体育法》的定位还会有阻力和障碍，过多的未知也会使《体育法》的预见性大打折扣。

### 2. 《体育法》规范的原则性和可操作性

对于《体育法》的修改，比较集中的意见是改变"宜粗不宜细"立法原则指导下的《体育法》内容过于原则，可操作性差的问题。笔者认为，《体育法》未能很好实施的关键并不在于其过于原则，而在于其立法的科学性、预见性以及相关立法配合方面的欠缺。《体育法》作为法律的立法层级、立法的迫切性和立法当时体育改革刚刚起步的客观状况，决定了其规定的"原则性"。我们设想如果当时《体育法》不采取"宜粗不宜细"的立法原则，而是尽可

能具体详尽地予以规定, 增强其"可操作性", 那岂不是更加无法适应迅速发展、变化的体育改革的形势吗？

任何一部立法都要平衡其规范的原则性和内容的实效性的关系, 但一般而言, 层级高的立法原则性、概括性较强而操作性较低, 反之, 层级低的立法原则性、概括性较低而操作性较强。《体育法》的重点应是确立规则而非规则的具体执行。一方面强调《体育法》的"基本法"地位, 另一方面又强调其可操作性, 这本身就是一个悖论。

### 3. 《体育法》内容的全面性和适度性

如前所述, 《体育法》只是广义的体育法的一部分, 它并不能调整所有的体育关系, 解决所有体育关系中的问题。而且, 随着社会的发展和法治的进步, 体育关系日趋复杂和广泛, 体育法的内容不断扩张和膨胀。体育法治需要全面建设与重点建设的统一, 需要全方位推进与渐进性推进的统一,[19] 如果《体育法》的修改以"体育基本法"为定位, 其内容范围将大大超出现有《体育法》所涵盖的范围。从横向上说, 《体育法》成为面面俱到、包罗万象的"体育大全法"并不现实；从纵向上说, 在不断丰富体育法治内容的过程中, 《体育法》即便怎样地不断修改, 也仍将滞后于实践的需要。《体育法》的内容应当具有适度性和可控性, 这也是《体育法》的稳定性所需要的。

### 4. 《体育法》调整体育社会关系的成熟性和稳定性

体育社会关系表现在不同的方面, 有一些相对成熟和稳定, 比如学校体育、社会体育等, 有一些则还没有形成规律性的认识, 有待理论、实践的进一步发展予以解决, 如体育产业、职业体育、体育仲裁等。立法不仅仅是社会需用的反映, 还需有以社会关系的成熟度和稳定性为前提, 特别是层次较高的立法更当如此。就《体育法》的修改而言, 以"基本法"定位尽可能地调整更广泛的体育关系, 必将使《体育法》体系和内容因不同的社会关系成熟度

---

19) 田思源：《改革开放三十年我国体育法治的回顾与展望》, 载自《法学杂志》2009 年第9 期。

和稳定性的不同，而无法统一和协调一致。对那些成熟度和稳定性较好的体育社会关系就可以规定的较为具体详尽，而对于那些成熟度和稳定性较差的体育社会关系则只能规定的较为原则、概括。例如，《体育法》第33条规定竞技体育纠纷由体育仲裁机构负责调解、仲裁，而体育仲裁的机构和范围则授权"由国务院另行规定"。即便如此原则的规定，由于其所调整的社会关系并不成熟，国务院至今也未能就体育仲裁问题作出相应规定。

综上所述，《体育法》修改中所面临的问题决定了其修改不过是权宜之计，具有过渡的性质。我们也无法通过《体育法》的修改来重塑《体育法》的"基本法"地位。

## Ⅴ. 以《体育法》修改为契机，实现《体育法》从"体育基本法"向"体育事业促进法"的转型

### 1. 《体育法》修改的理念和"体育事业促进法"的提倡

《体育法》修改的理念和思路应该是：

1）《体育法》的修改必须适应社会主义市场经济的基本要求，顺应政府职能从"全能政府"向"有限政府"、从"管理政府"向"服务政府"转变的时代潮流，科学反映现代体育运动的基本规律，准确体现体育事业改革和发展的方向。《体育法》的修改需要强调政府责任，"以人为本"，"权利本位"，以保障公民体育权利实现为核心；需要指引、引导、推动和促进体育事业积极、健康、可持续的发展。为此而要求《体育法》的"脱政府化"、"脱政治化"，改"管理法"为"服务法"，确立"体育为民"的理念，为体育的市场化、职业化、产业化和社会化服务。

2）体育事业的发展，不断丰富体育法治的内容，使以"基本法"为其定位的《体育法》的内容也必将不断的调整和充实。由此而导致《体育法》内容的扩张和膨胀，这样即便不断地修改《体育法》，它也仍将滞后于实践的需要，造成《体育法》及其配套立法制定和执行上的困难。为此我们应该改变《体育法》的"体育大全法"、"体育基本法"的定位，加强体育领域其他法律法规的制定和执行工作，使体育法律法规(包括《体育法》)相互配合，共同发挥作用。

3）中国体育事业的发展，由于受"奥运战略"的影响，竞技体育、"举国体制"被高度重视，

与群众体育未能平衡、协调地发展，有违《体育法》确立的体育方针。为此，《体育法》的修改应该充分考虑"后2008"时代中国体育战略的调整，[20] 强调群众体育的重要性，强调公民心身健康、愉悦的重要性，推动和促进体育事业积极、健康、可持续地发展。

根据上述对《体育法》修改理念和思路的分析，我建议在《体育法》修改时，将《体育法》改称为《体育事业促进法》)。[21]

## 2. 关于制定《体育事业促进法》的建议

### (1) 关于法的名称

这涉及到《体育法》的定位。如前所述，《体育法》如果作为"管理法"，与体育市场化、职业化、产业化和社会化的改革，与政府体育行政管理职能的转变和建立服务政府的理念，与体育自身的特点和发展规律等不相适应；《体育法》如果作为"基本法"，也只能限于原则性的规定，且体育改革方兴未艾，体育法制范围日益扩大，体育法学理论研究刚刚起步，很多新情况、新问题还有待我们进一步认识、研究并逐步加以解决，从而导致"基本法"配套立法制定上的困难，使"基本法"无法贯彻落实。如果"基本法"的很多原则规定都像前述《体育法》第33 条规定的体育仲裁的配套立法无法实现那样，"基本法"的权威和体育法治的建设势必受到极大的影响。鉴于以上问题的存在，我们应该改变《体育法》修改、完善的立法思路，强调政府在推动和促进体育事业发展中的作用和责任，用《体育事业促进法》代替《体育法》，或者说是制定《体育事业促进法》，这样就既限定了《体育法》的范围，适应了时代发展的需要，解决了"管理法"和"基本法"的弊端，同时又能够更好地促进体育事业的发展。

---

20) 参见陈季冰：《勾画"后2008"时代的中国体育体制》，载自《东方早报》2005年10月24日。笔者无意否定2008 年北京奥运会前"奥运战略"、"举国体制"的重要意义，但这毕竟是这一特殊阶段的特殊政策，我们不能以此作为体育立法的指导准则，恰恰相反，我们的体育立法更应该考虑的是如何更好地为"后2008"时代中国体育的战略调整、改革和发展服务。所以笔者非常赞同这篇论文的提法。

21) 参见田思源：《我国<体育法>修改理念分析－－兼论<体育事业促进法>的制定》，载自《法学杂志》2006年第6期，第68-70页。

(2) 关于≪体育事业促进法≫的立法宗旨和体育事业发展的基本方针

中国≪体育法≫的立法宗旨和立法依据是："为了发展体育事业，增强人民体质，提高体育运动水平，促进社会主义物质文明和精神文明建设，根据宪法，制定本法。"(第1 条)这里的"根据宪法"是指宪法第21 条第2 款"国家发展体育事业，开展群众性的体育活动，增强人民体质"的规定。≪体育法≫的立法宗旨是否准确反映了宪法的上述原则规定呢？宪法的这一原则规定包含有三层含义：一是"发展体育事业"是国家的积极义务；二是"开展群众性的体育活动"是体育事业的核心内容；三是"增强人民体质"是体育事业的根本目的。层次分明，逻辑严密。而≪体育法≫规定了三项并列的立法宗旨：一是"增强人民体质"，二是"提高体育运动水平"，三是"促进社会主义物质文明和精神文明建设"。甚至还可以认为"增强人民体质"和"提高体育运动水平"是为了"促进社会主义物质文明和精神文明建设"，从而将"促进社会主义物质文明和精神文明建设"作为≪体育法≫立法的根本宗旨。

≪体育法≫规定的立法宗旨显然有违宪法规定的精神，它增加了"提高体育运动水平"的规定，并将其与"增强人民体质"相并列，同时又规定了"促进社会主义物质文明和精神文明建设"的宗旨。这样就使体育承载了更多的社会、政治意义，虽然我国"实行普及与提高相结合"的体 育事业发展方针是以"全民健身活动为基础"的，[22] 但由于没有以"普及"为核心，在"普及"与"提高"相结合、相协调的过程中，"提高"成了我们体育工作实际上的中心，使我们"竞技体育在国际赛场上高歌猛进的时候，国民体质却出现了下滑的势头，"[23] 形成了竞技体育优先于、优越于、优位于群众体育的局面。

2002年7月22日，中共中央、国务院在≪关于进一步加强和改进新时期体育工作的意见≫(以下简称≪意见≫)中指出， 新时期发展体育事业的指导思想是："高举邓小平理论伟大旗帜， 全面贯彻党在社会主义初级阶段的基本路线和基本纲领，认真实践江泽民同志'三个代表'重要思想，以举办2008 年奥运会为契机，以满足广大人民群众日益增长的体育文化需求为出发点，把增强人民体质、提高全民族整体素质作为根本目标，积极开创体育工作新局面，

---

22) 参见≪体育法≫第2 条。

23) 郭奔胜、王恒志、张泽远：≪夺金潮，难掩国民体质下滑的尴尬－－"竞技体育腿长、群众体育腿短"，一份"清单"说话≫，新华每日电讯2005 年10 月22 日，新华网(http://news3.xinhuanet.com/mrdx/2005-10/22/content_3666600.htm)。

为实现新世纪我国经济、社会发展的战略目标和中华民族的伟大复兴做出应有的贡献。"[24)]
该《意见》非常明确地把"增强人民体质、提高全民族整体素质"作为新时期我国发展体育
事业的指导思想和根本目标，并把举办2008 年奥运会作为实现上述根本目标的"契机"。这
样的表述是准确的，是符合宪法的原则规定的，同时也被2006年7月25日国家体育总局发布
的《体育事业"十一五"规划》(以下简称《规划》)所认可。[25)]

关于我国体育事业发展的基本方针，《体育法》第2 条作了如下规定："国家发展体育事
业,开展群众性的体育活动， 提高全民族身体素质。体育工作坚持以开展全民健身活动为基
础，实行普及与提高相结合，促进各类体育协调发展。"该规定的前半部分，即"国家发展体
育事业，开展群众性的体育活动，提高全民族身体素质"实则应为第1 条立法宗旨的内容。
《体育法》第1 条立法宗旨和第2 条体育事业发展方针的规定内容有重合，条文间的界分不
够明晰。另外，如前所述，虽然在《体育法》审议过程中对群众体育和竞技体育的关系有许
多的讨论，立法中也体现了对群众体育的偏重，但并没有将群众体育摆在核心位置上。

《意见》在对我国体育事业发展的基本方针(《意见》中称为"工作方针")的规定上则比
较具体、明确， 即："坚持体育为人民服务、为社会主义现代化建设服务的方针， 坚持普及
与提高相结合，实现群众体育与竞技体育的协调发展和相互促进；坚持以改革促发展，强化
体育制度创新，努力推进体育体制改革和运行机制转变，增强体育发展的活力和后劲；坚持
依法行政，加强体育工作的法制建设，依靠科技力量,保障体育事业持续、健康发展。"并进
一步提出体 育事业发展的"总体要求"是："从我国国情出发,坚持体育事业与经济、社会协
调发展"。

我们在修改《体育法》，抑或是制定《体育事业促进法》时，必须明确其立法宗旨，明确
我国体育事业发展的基本方针和方向，而这又是与我们对体育的理解，对体育的功能、性质
的认识分不开的。纵观世界各国的体育法,[26)] 多数国家不仅阐明了体育健身娱乐的目的，也

---

24) 中发[2002]8 号。中国奥委会官方网站(http://www.olympic.cn/rule_code)。
25) 《规划》规定：我国"'十一五'时期体育事业发展的指导思想是：高举邓小平理论和'三个代表'重要思想的伟大旗帜，以
科学发展观为统领，认真贯彻落实《中共中央、国务院关于进一步加强和改进新时期体育工作的意见》，以筹办2008
年奥运会为契机，以满足群众日益增长的体育文化需求为出发点，把提高全民族健康素质作为根本目标，积极开创体育
事业发展的新局面，为全面建设小康社会和构建社会主义和谐社会服务，为中华民族的伟大复兴做出贡献"。载自《中
国体育报》2006年7月27日。《规划》与《意见》规定的精神和内容基本一致，它是以《意见》为基础，同时又赋予
了"科学发展观"和"和谐社会"等时代内容。

强调了其提高生活质量、塑造国民精神的社会、文化意义。西班牙《体育法》规定："体育是一种自由、自愿的活动。作为一种教育和人们全面发展的基本要素，它构成的文化现象应该受国家公众权力机关的保护和鼓励。"俄罗斯《体育法》规定：体育"是人民文化的重要组成部分，也是社会为增进俄联邦人民健康，在体育过程中创造、发展和使用的精神和物质财富的总和。"乌克兰则规定："体育是社会文化的组成部分，其目的在于增强人的体质、道德意志与文化智力，以形成协调和个性。"关于立法目的，俄罗斯联邦体育立法原则规定："保护和保证公民从事体 育运动的权利；为俄联邦体育运动体制的发展和职能的行使提供权利保障；确立体育领域中的自然人和法人的权利、义务和责任，对其相互关系作权利调整。"日本《体育振兴法》规定："体育以促进国民的身心健康发展及形成愉快活泼的国民生活为目的。"韩国《国民体育振兴法》规定："本法律的目的是通过振兴国民体育，增强国民体力，培养健全的精神，形成明朗的国民生活，以及通过体育为国争光"。

从中国宪法、《意见》、以及世界一些国家体育立法的相关规定，我们可以看到促进竞技体育的发展，提高体育运动水平并非体育法制定的宗旨、目的和体育事业的发展方向。同时，国外对体育的理解也不仅仅是身体的健康。体育具有深刻的文化内涵，体育是国民精神的塑造和体现，体育是健康、愉悦、丰富的国民生活。

《体育事业促进法》在立法宗旨的规定上，应该以宪法为依据，纠正《体育法》规定上的偏差，强调促进和发展体育事业是国家和政府的责任,[27] 强调发展体育事业在提高和增强人民的身体素质的作用的同时，还应强调其对公民心身的健康、愉悦的生活方面的作用,[28] 强调体育文化的传承和体育精神的弘扬；在体育事业发展的基本方针的规定上，改变《体育法》混淆立法宗旨与体育事业的发展方针的做法，在"体育为民"理念的指导下，将"体育工作坚持以开展全民健身活动为基础"，修改为"开展全民健身活动是体育工作的基础和核

---

26) 以下各国体育法的规定，引自徐伟：《形形色色的外国体育法》，载自《政法论丛》2000年第4期，第4页。

27) 如果用"国家促进体育事业的发展"代替"国家发展体育事业"，是非常能够体现《体育事业促进法》与《体育法》立法理念的不同的。

28) 日本的《体育振兴法》第1 条规定了促进"国民身心健全的发展和形成愉悦丰富的国民生活"的体育振兴政策的基本方针(参见周爱光、周威、吴兴华、刘凤霞：《中日两国体育法的比较研究》，载自《体育学刊》，2004年3月第11卷第2期，第2页)，这是值得我们借鉴的。虽然我国《体育法》 第5条有"增进青年、少年、儿童的身心健康"，第10条有"国家提倡公民参加社会体育活动，增进身心健康"的规定，但这些规定并没有与体育事业的发展方针相联系，没有把公民心身的健康、愉悦与提高、增强身体素质相联系。

心", 将"实行普及与提高相结合"修改为"以普及促提高", 在"促进各类体育协调发展"的规定后增加"促进体育事业与经济、社会协调发展"的规定, 同时增加体育体制改革和体育制度创新, 发展体育产业和培养体育市场, 发展体育科技、教育, 科学治体、依法治体, 保障体育事业全面、协调、可持续发展的规定。

### (3) 关于《体育事业促进法》的具体内容

以上述的《体育事业促进法》确立的立法宗旨和体育事业发展的基本方针为指引, 以现行《体育法》为蓝本, 参照《规划》, 从"促进"的视角, 在明确"体育"、"体育事业"基本含义的前提下, 规定国家和政府在"促进"体育事业发展中的基本政策、措施、手段、保障、责任、权利义务等内容。有些内容可以规定的具体、明确一些。比如关于奖励问题, 《体育法》仅仅在第8条做了原则规定, 即"国家对在体育事业中做出贡献的组织和个人, 给予奖励"。作为体育"基本法", 这样的原则规定是可以的, 具体的奖励制度由配套法律法规去落实, 但作为"促进法", 则可以把"奖励"作为促进体育事业发展的政策措施, 明确规定"奖励制度"。

### (4) 关于《体育事业促进法》与体育法治建设的关系

《体育事业促进法》是国家促进体育事业发展的方针、政策的"基本法", 而不是体育"基本法", 在体育法治建设中, 其他立法可以是它的配套立法, 也可以是"独立"立法, 根据社会需要和可能, 大力推进体育法律规范的制定工作, 逐步形成我国的体育法体系, 从而改变以《体育法》这个"基本法"为核心, 其他立法为配套立法来建立我国体育法体系的现有思路,[29] 解决在原思路指导下的《体育法》修改中的困境和配套立法中的困难, 实现《体育法》从"管理法"到"服务法", 从"基本法"到"促进法"的转型, 逐步完成中国体育法治建设的繁重任务。

---

29) 参见于善旭、张剑、陈岩:《建立以<体育法>为核心的我国体育法规体系的框架构想》, 载自《中国体育科技》, 1999年(第35卷)第1期, 第3-11页;于善旭、陈岩、李雁军:《完善<中华人民共和国体育法>配套立法的对策探讨》, 载自《体育与科学》, 1999年1月(第20卷), 第5-10页。此外, 《规划》在"加强体育法制建设"方面也是这样的思路, 提出要"做好《中华人民共和国体育法》的修改工作。加强体育配套立法, 抓紧进行全民健身、体育纠纷处理、体育市场管理、体育竞赛秩序等领域行政法规和规章的起草工作。进一步健全符合体育改革和发展要求的体育法规体系。"载自《中国体育报》2006年7月27日。

### 3. 关于≪体育事业促进法≫的争论

笔者所提倡的"体育事业促进法"的理念和观点，体育法学界给予了高度的关注和积极的回应，并将其评价为是体育法修改理念研究中的具有"颠覆性"的观点。[30] 有学者对管理型立法和促进型立法作了比较分析，指出：所谓管理型立法，其基本特征就是立法服务于政府管理，主要表现在管理型立法通常发生在这类立法所调整的社会关系已发展到一定程度，形成一定的市场规模、甚至出现市场的过度竞争，国家不得不加以干预的情况下，即管理型立法主要解决需求问题，在整个社会运行和政府干预的意义上，属于后置性的。促进型立法则较多强调政府的服务功能，受阶段性、补充性或者政策性特征制约，通常是针对那些在社会关系尚未得到良好发育、市场规模并未形成而急需鼓励形成市场规模的领域。因而，促进型立法主要解决供给问题，具有积极的和主要的促进导向，对社会的发展具有引导意义。在此基础上进一步认为："促进型立法是体育法修改的方向"，而现行≪体育法≫"实际是管理型立法和促进型立法的混合体"。"同意≪体育事业促进法≫的观点(当然也可以不更换名称)，但仍认为其是体育基本法。建议≪体育法≫修改朝向促进型立法发展。" "促进型立法是管理型立法的前奏"，"当促进型体育法在所调控的体育领域走向成熟的时候，再将其所调控的范围让渡给管理型立法，由其运用'规制'的方法让体育发展有序运行。"[31] 有学者将上述观点称之为"折中派"，并坚持"基本法"，反对"促进法"。指出中国体育事业需要一部体育基本法，≪体育法≫应该坚持"基本法"的性质，这样更利于体育事业的可持续发展。≪体育法≫作为中国目前唯一的体育法律，体现国家最高意志对全国体育进行全面规范调整的体育基本法，是所有其他体育立法的基础。≪体育法≫的修改也必将坚持"基本法"的性质，以"权利本位"为修改理念。认为≪体育法≫所调整的社会关系的主体并未发生根本性的变化，发生变化的主要是在客体和内容上，但这并不能否认其"基本法"的功能定位。不赞同将≪体育法≫按照"体育事业促进法"的方向修改的意见，因为"促进法"不能调制体育整个社会关

---

30) 贾文彤、梁灵艳：≪对<中华人民共和国体育法>修改研究的思考≫，载自≪中国体育科技≫ 2007年第6期，第11-13；李先燕、于善旭、韩宝：≪后奥运时期我国<体育法>修改理念的再思考≫，载自≪成都体育学院学报≫2009年第1 期，第16-19 页。

31) 贾文彤、梁灵艳：≪对<中华人民共和国体育法>修改研究的思考≫，载自≪中国体育科技≫ 2007 年第6 期，第11-13 页。

系, 无法起到"基本法"的宏观指导作用。[32]


## 4. 对≪体育事业促进法≫质疑的回应和≪体育事业促进法≫理念的再提倡

### (1) 对≪体育事业促进法≫不同观点的简要回应

关于"体育基本法"存在的问题我们已从多个角度予以论述, 对于上述关于"体育促进法"的不同观点和意见也还有待于理论和实践的检验。这里我们需要特殊强调的是, 如果我们承认现行≪体育法≫重管理轻服务, 重义务轻权利的历史局限性, 那么这样的"体育基本法"是与"体育政治法"、"体育管理法"、"体育大全法"相联系的, 是以"体育义务本位"为核心的, 长期以来我们所强调的"体育基本法"地位实则是在强调≪体育法≫政治功能、管理功能对体育关系的全面作用, 是不符合体育体制改革、人权保障、民主法治建设的时代潮流的。在这样的背景下改"体育基本法"为"体育促进法", 也就不存在泛泛意义上的"促进型立法是管理型立法的前奏"之说了。如果说在≪体育法≫修改中确定"体育权利本位"的理念, 并以此强调≪体育法≫"基本法"的地位, 这当然有利于公民体育权利的实现和保障, 但如前所述, 由于各种因素使≪体育法≫并不具备成为这样的"体育基本法"的条件。而且笼统地说"≪体育法≫的修改将在坚持'基本法'的基础上, 以'权利本位'为立法理念"[33]的观点, 没有区分现行≪体育法≫和≪体育法≫修改中"基本法"意义上的不同, 没有考虑≪体育法≫作为"基本法"所应具备的条件, 也会给人以反对"基本法"就是反对"权利本位"的错觉。"基本法"的定位和"权利本位"是两个不同的问题, ≪体育法≫是"基本法"并不意味着就是权利保护之法, 现在的"义务本位"下的≪体育法≫不也被称之为"基本法"吗?


### (2) ≪体育事业促进法≫理念的再提倡——理想与现实之间

定位为"基本法"的≪体育法≫, 其实施面临困难, 其修改也同样面临困难, 那么在此重提

---

32) 李先燕、于善旭、韩宝：≪后奥运时期我国＜体育法＞修改理念的再思考≫, 载自≪成都体育学院学报≫ 2009 年第 1 期, 第19 页。

33) 李先燕、于善旭、韩宝：≪后奥运时期我国＜体育法＞修改理念的再思考≫, 载自≪成都体育学院学报≫ 2009 年第 1 期, 第19 页。

《体育事业促进法》具有怎样的意义呢？首先，它可以解决困扰着我们的《体育法》修改中所面临的科学性与预见性、原则性与可操作性、全面性与适度性等问题； 其次，它可以破解"基本法"立法技术上的障碍， 加快整体推进和重点突破相结合的体育法治建设进程；第三，它有助于我们正确认识体育规律，定位体育功能，改革体育管理体制，厘清政府体育职能界限，从而有效地保障和实现公民的体育权利。

《体育事业促进法》替代《体育法》的方案在《体育法》修改实践中是否可行呢？《体育法》的修改既要创新又要稳妥，在多数人持"基本法"观点的时候，用"促进法""颠覆性"地重构体育法治显然并不现实，但我们并不能以此否定《体育事业促进法》的意义，《体育法》的名称可以不改，但"促进法"的理念应予提倡，在《体育法》修改中应当体现从"体育基本法"向"体育促进法"的转型。

· **摘要** ·

《体育法》不应是"体育基本法"。《体育法》制定时的历史局限性， 决定了其作为"体育基本法"只能是对体育行政管理功能的强化；以"体育基本法"为核心建构体育法治在立法技术上存在障碍，体育法治建设的实践也并没有体现出"体育基本法"的统领地位；在以保障和实现公民体育权利为核心的《体育法》修改中，重塑《体育法》的"基本法"地位条件并不具备， 并使《体育法》修改面临困难。解决上述问题的途径是提倡"体育促进法"的理念，在《体育法》修

关键词： 体育法；体育法修改；体育基本法；体育促进法；体育事业促进法

## 参考文獻 (References)

参见伍绍祖：《依法行政、以法治体的基本纲领》，载自《求是》，1995 年第23 期 第22页。

田思源：《我国<体育法>修改理念分析－－兼论<体育事业促进法>的制定》，载自《法学杂志》 2006 年第6 期 第68 页。

李先燕、于善旭、韩宝：《后奥运时期我国<体育法>修改理念的再思考》，载自《成都体育学院 学报》 2009 年第1 期 第18 页。

秦毅、周爱光：《<中华人民共和国体育法>价值的探讨与反思》，载自《体育科学》 2008 年 第 12 期 第69 页。

华奥星空网(http://www.sports.cn)。

中国体育信息网(http://www.sport.gov.cn)。

参见谢文英：《发展中国足球须从修改体育法入手－－按照体育法第三十一条规定，由足协管理 足球比赛违背依法行政原则》，载自《检察日报》 2005 年12 月22 日。

国办发〔2010〕3 号。

伍绍祖：《依法行政、以法治体的基本纲领》，载自《求是》 1995 年第23 期 第22 页。

伍绍祖：《依法行政、以法治体的基本纲领》，载自《求是》 1995 年第23 期 第23、24 页。

伍绍祖：《依法行政、以法治体的基本纲领》，载自《求是》 1995 年第23 期 第25 页。

于善旭、张剑、陈岩： 《建立以<体育法>为核心的我国体育法规体系的框架构想》， 载自《中 国体育科技》 1999 年第1 期 第4 页。

于善旭、陈岩, 李雁军：《完善<中华人民共和国体育法>配套立法的对策探讨》，载自《体育与 科学》 1999 年第1 期 第6 页。

参见伍绍祖：《关于<中华人民共和国体育法(草案)>的说明》。

刘凤霞：《对现行<体育法>修改之思考》，载自《浙江体育科学》 2003 年第4 期 第4 页。

于善旭、张剑、陈岩：《建立以<体育法>为核心的我国体育法规体系的框架构想》， 载自《中国 体育科技》 1999 年第1 期 第6、9 页。

田思源：《改革开放三十年我国体育法治的回顾与展望》，载自《法学杂志》 2009 年第9 期。

参见陈季冰：《勾画"后2008"时代的中国体育体制》，载自《东方早报》 2005 年10 月24日。笔 者无意否定2008 年北京奥运会前"奥运战略"、"举国体制"的重要意义, 但这毕竟是这一特殊阶 段的特殊政策, 我们不能以此作为体育立法的指导准则, 恰恰相反, 我们的体育立法更应该考

虑的是如何更好地为"后2008"时代中国体育的战略调整、改革和发展服务。所以笔者非常赞同
这篇论文的提法。

参见田思源：《我国<体育法>修改理念分析－－兼论<体育事业促进法法>的制定》，载自《法
　　学杂志》2006 年第6 期　第68-70 页。参见《体育法》第2 条。

郭奔胜、王恒志、张泽远：《夺金潮　难掩国民体质下滑的尴尬－－"竞技体育腿长、群众体育腿
　　短"，一份"清单"说话》，新华每日电讯2005 年10 月22 日，新华网(http://news3.xinhuanet.com/
　　mrdx/2005-10/22/content_3666600.htm)。

中发[2002]8 号。中国奥委会官方网站(http://www.olympic.cn/rule_code)。

以下各国体育法的规定，引自徐伟：《形形色色的外国体育法》，载自《政法论丛》 2000 年第4
　　期　第4 页。

贾文彤、梁灵艳：《对<中华人民共和国体育法>修改研究的思考》，载自《中国体育科技》 2007
　　年第6 期　第11-13；李先燕、于善旭、韩宝：《后奥运时期我国<体育法>修改理念的再思考》，
　　载自《成都体育学院学报》2009 年第1 期　第16-19 页。

贾文彤、梁灵艳：《对<中华人民共和国体育法>修改研究的思考》，载自《中国体育科技》 2007
　　年第6 期　第11-13 页。

李先燕、于善旭、韩宝：《后奥运时期我国<体育法>修改理念的再思考》，载自《成都体育学院
　　学报》 2009 年第1 期　第19 页。

李先燕、于善旭、韩宝：《后奥运时期我国<体育法>修改理念的再思考》，载自《成都体育学院
　　学报》 2009 年第1 期　第19 页。

# On Determination of Infringement
# in the Competitive Sports Field

## 论竞技体育中侵权行为的认定

YU-MEI WANG(王玉梅)*

*The athletes can't realize their interests during the sports process under the undeveloped insurance policy and without the protection of the law of torts at same time. Combining the legislation practice and the theories both domestic and abroad, this article analyzes the particularity of the elements of a tort action in the competitive sports field, including the damages, intents, illegal act, causation and the impediment of illegality. It proposes to build and perfect the system of the compensational liabilities of civil tort and infringement, balancing the sports fierceness and the protection of athletes.*

**Key word：** Competitive sports, Torts

在体育运动尤其是身体接触类的运动中，　因他人故意或者过失导致的各种损害层出不穷。以足球为例，有媒体列出中国足坛中的十大伤害事件[1]：从1994 年张海涛(右膝关节被对方球员踢成重伤)24 岁梦断职业联赛，到2004 年杜苹血洒绿茵场：从于涛争球中险些丧命到班古拉右眼被踢裂导致失明。

一幅幅的惨剧[2]警示竞技体育中所面临的风险。在这些改变他们一生的伤害面前，　运动

---

* Proferssor at China University of Political Science and Law

1) 《谁是"中国西塞"--国内足坛意外伤害事件TOP10》，载 http://sports.sohu.com/20060711/n244192821.shtml，最后访问时间：2013 年7 月7 日。

2) 对于运动员的受伤比例，笔者未找到国内的相关数据，而在美国，一个名为"America sports data inc."的机构发表的调查报告显示：2002 年，美国有17,641,000 人参与篮球运动，其中1,063,000 受伤，比例为7.6％；橄榄球运动的受伤比例是9.3％；而冰球和足球中运动员的受伤率更是分别高达15.9％和18.8％。当然这些数据不仅限于赛场上的，还包括训练等其他情形。但可以推测，像足球这类身体接触类的运动，竞技性和激烈程度导致运动员受伤的可能性更大。转引自

员却无法获得普通人在受到伤害时的侵权损害救济。在竞技体育领域, 侵权法的适用几乎是空白的, 理论上的探讨也很鲜见。运动员可能有的选择只是尚处于发展初期的商业保险和国家的福利, 但很多情况下, 这些对于他们所受到的伤害的救济来说只是" 杯水车薪"。笔者认为, 应当在职业竞技体育中引入侵权损害赔偿机制, 为受到伤害的运动员提供更有力地保障。

## Ⅰ. 侵权行为法在竞技体育运动中的角色

通常, 人们认为在竞技体育中引入侵权损害赔偿机制会伤害运动员的在赛场上的运动积极性, 导致他们在赛场上畏首畏尾, 妨碍运动的顺利进行, 减少它的激烈性和可视性, 进而阻碍竞技体育事业的发展。同时, 一些业内人士认为体育保险的发展已经能够让运动员在受到伤害后获得足够的保障。[3] 的确, 2006 年世界杯期间, 贝克汉姆给他的右脚投保千万欧元保险；欧文所投的保险不仅保证了他的受伤的治疗和康复费用, 而且保证他在养伤期间能有正常的工资收入(由保险公司负担受伤期间的工资), 在病床上还能收到了价值百万欧元的理赔金。[4] 然而, 中国的竞技体育保险事业远没有达到这种保障程度。

在国内, 运动员受伤后可以获得补偿的方式主要有三种: 一是工伤保险。运动员受伤可以认定为工伤(球员和俱乐部之间的关系被视为劳动关系), 但从《工伤保险条例》的赔偿标准看这种补偿金额非常少,[5] 对受伤的运动员来说是微不足道的。二是商业保险。我国的

---

Dean Richardson: "PlayerViolence :An Essay on Torts and Sports", 载westlaw 数据库。该报告(A Comprehensive Study of Sports Injurise in the U.S.)的内容亦可在下列网页中获得：http://www.americansportsdata. com/sports_injury_spec4.asp, 最后访问时间：2013 年7月7 日。

3) 在金德俱乐部准备起诉吕刚恶意伤害班古拉时, 吕刚所在俱乐部的高层认为这种起诉是毫无道理的, 不符合相关规定和国际惯例, 应当由俱乐部在事前替球员购买意外伤害险而由保险公司承担责任。载 http://sports.sohu.com/20060713/ n244244973.shtml, 最后访问时间：2013 年7 月8 日。

4) "贝克汉姆保单创天价, 签定总价一亿英镑保险合同", 载 http://www.chinanews.com.cn/ty/gjzq/news/2006/12-19/ 840367.shtml , 最后访问时间：2013 年7 月9 日。

5) 《工伤条例》第31-38 条规定的对工伤的赔偿包括：停薪留职期间内的工资和福利、生活护理费、伤残补助, 发生死亡事件的还包括丧葬补助金、抚恤金和工亡补助金。看似完备的赔偿范围, 仔细研究会发现, 《工伤条例》中规定的赔偿标准较低, 相较于运动员因伤不能参加比赛所丧失的收入、可能的广告费等收入几乎是杯水车薪。第31 条："职工因工作遭受事故伤害或者患职业病需要暂停工作接受工伤医疗的, 在停工留薪期内, 原工资福利待遇不变, 由所在单位按月支付。停工留薪期一般不超过12 个月……"第32 条："工伤职工已经评定伤残等级并经劳动能力鉴定委员会确认需要生

体育商业保险尚不能给运动员提供充分的保障。一方面, 相对其他国家而言, 国内的体育保险领域尚未得到足够的开发, "运动员能够购买的险种和普通人的没有太大的差别, 而针对职业特点的险种根本没有"。[6] 另一方面, 运动员本身对保险意识的薄弱也使得保险作为运动员受伤后可寻求的救济机制不那么"保险"。运动员在签合同时往往只关注自己的收入, 而不注意俱乐部是否给自己上了保险。[7] 三是互助保险。2002 年9 月27 日, 国家体育总局颁行《优秀运动员伤残互助保险试行办法》,[8] 在一定程度上加强了对运动员的保护程度, 但其所承保的范围过于狭窄, 仅限于全国各省、市、自治区及计划单列市所属正式在编、享受体育津贴奖金制并从事奥运会和全运会项目的运动员, 其他类型的运动员则被排斥在外, 而且其最高的赔偿额仅为30 万。

可见, 我国体育保险事业尚不能为运动员提供真正的保险机制, 远不能让运动员受到伤害后无"后顾之忧"。因此, 为了保护运动员受到伤害后能够维持起码的生活水平和生活的尊严, 侵权损害赔偿机制的引入非常必要和急迫。退一步讲, 即使体育保险已经足够完善, 也并不妨碍侵权行为法在竞技体育中的规制作用。正如投保了人身伤害保险的人在权利受到侵害时同样可以主张侵权人承担侵权责任一样, 保险机制和侵权赔偿机制并不是水火不容的关系。[9]

---

活护理的, 从工伤保险基金按月支付生活护理费……"第33 条至37 条分别规定不同级别的伤残补助标准。第37 条: "职工因工死亡, 其直系亲属按照下列规定从工伤保险基金领取丧葬补助金、供养亲属抚恤金和一次性工亡补助金……" 第38 条: "伤残津贴、供养亲属抚恤金、生活护理费由统筹地区劳动保障行政部门根据职工平均工资和生活费用变化等情况适时调整。调整办法由省、自治区、直辖市人民政府规定。"

6) 《辽宁日报》2006 年7 月21 日, 载http://sports.sohu.com/20060721/n244382091.shtml, 最后访问时间: 2013 年7 月7 日。

7) 《沈阳日报》2007 年7 月20 日, 载http://sports.sohu.com/20060720/n244358936.shtml, 最后访问时间: 2013 年7 月7 日。

8) 该试行办法规定, 由体育基金会设立伤残互助保险基金。该基金以运动员个人交纳的保费、体育基金会通过相关活动募集的资金和社会捐赠为主要资金来源。运动员缴纳保费后, 在发生伤残事故时根据鉴定机构鉴定的伤残等级, 按规定的保险待遇向该基金申请领取伤残保险金。该伤残互助保险将伤残互助保险待遇标准分为十二级, 特级为30 万元, 十一级为2000 元, 而特级的认定标准为"死亡或者成为植物人"。同时将运动员在训练、比赛过程中, 或者在训练、比赛的规定时间和必经路线上受到意外伤害, 也归属于该保险的认定范围。这种互助保险是对国家职工工伤保险的一种补充, 象征性地收取一定费用, 属于福利性保险, 只是一种特殊的抚恤金。

9) 财产和责任保险属于补偿性保险, 补偿性保险的出发点是弥补被保险人实际所遭受的损失。因此, 保险法律都会赋予保险公司在对被保险人履行完保险责任后取得对造成保险事故人代位求偿权。而人的生命和健康则不同于财产, 人的生命和健康是不能用金钱来衡量的, 人的伤痛也是不能用金钱来表示的。人身保险不是为了补偿被保险人所受到的损失, 也就使保险公司的代位求偿权失去了存在的基础。在体育竞技中, 运动员购买的人身意外伤害保险基本上被划入人身保险范畴。参见陈欣: 《保险法》, 北京大学出版社2002 年12 月。我国《保险法》第4 条赋予财产保险中的保险人代位

此外，保险的作用仅在于填补受害者所遭受的损失，而没有损害的预防功能，容易引发道德风险。而侵权损害的赔偿机制则不一样。传统理论上认为， 侵权行为法的机能不仅包括填补损害，还有预防损害的作用。"损害的预防胜于损害的补偿"。[10] 因为损害一旦造成，对于遭受到严重的伤害的运动员来说， 无论赔偿多少都很难以恢复其竞技运动能力。损害的补偿只能是事后的救济机制，如果能够预防这种损害的发生，无论对于运动员还是竞技体育事业发展都具有一种更为积极的意义。在没有伤害的竞技体育运动场上， 运动员可以更加充分的发挥技能而不需要考虑伤病的困扰。 竞技体育事业也会因此得到更长远的发展。侵权损害赔偿机制让侵权人为其伤害行为而付出沉重的代价， 以此告诫其他运动员在比赛中约束自己不为体育规则和体育道德所不能容忍的行为， 从而起到净化体育赛场、预防伤害的功能，让真正的体育精神得以发扬。

## Ⅱ. 竞技体育中侵权构成要件的认定

依据一般的民法原理，侵权行为的构成要件包括主观过错、违法行为、损害事实和违法行为与损害事实之间存在因果关系。

体育的竞技性容忍一定"侵害"行为的存在，有些体育活动甚至就包含着一定"暴力"行为，如拳击等运动。一些在日常生活中的侵权行为在竞技场上被视为合理。如果将竞技体育中侵权标准界定过于严格则会导致竞技失去激烈性而影响体育事业的发展， 但不引入侵权责任或侵权责任构成要件过松， 将导致运动员一旦进入竞技场就意味着丧失基本的身体权利保障。因此， 判断竞技场上某种行为是否构成侵权与判断日常生活中的普通行为是否构成侵权的标准是不相同的。在竞技体育中引入侵权损害赔偿机制， 需要对传统侵权的构成要件做出特殊的认定标准，以求在体育竞技性和运动员保护的两极之间找到平衡点。

---

求偿权，"因第三者对保险标的的损害而造成保险事故的，保险人自向被保险人赔偿保险金之日起，在赔偿金额范围内代位行使被保险人对第三者请求赔偿的权利。"第68 条则明确规定代位求偿权不适用于人身保险，"人身保险的被保险人因第三者的行为而发生死亡、伤残或者疾病等保险事故的，保险人向被保险人或者受益人给付保险金后，不得享有向第三者追偿的权利。但被保险人或者受益人仍有权向第三者请求赔偿。"

10) 王泽鉴：《侵权行为法》(第一册), 中国政法大学出版社2001 版, 第8 页。

### 1. 损害事实

损害事实的有无是侵权行为的逻辑起点,[11] 有损害就应当有补偿。换言之, 不管损害大小均应得到侵权法的救济。但是在体育竞赛过程中, 特别是在对抗激烈的运动中, 受伤几乎是难免的。如果任何形式、任何程度的损害都构成侵权的话, 将导致运动员在场上畏首畏尾, 运动竞技也就失去了其内在的魅力。

为此, 需要法律从竞技体育的特殊性出发, 来判断哪些伤害是参赛者必须容忍的。只有重大的或者不合理的损害, 才可能构成体育侵权。在判断竞技体育中的伤害是否重大、是否不合理时应当考虑的因素包括：此种伤害在该项竞技体育运动中发生的可能性, 运动员在参赛时是否应当预见到这种伤害, 是否属于运动员应当容忍的危险。不同的竞技体育类型所包含的风险不同, 运动员所应当容忍的伤害度也不一样。例如, 同样是骨折, 在足球比赛中和在高尔夫球比赛中发生的机率就很不一样。在高尔夫球比赛中发生骨折则应当是该项运动所能" 容忍" 的。美国的理论和实践将运动分为身体接触类运动和非接触类运动, 以此为基础考虑某种伤害是否构成侵权。[12] 这一区分值得我们借鉴。

可见, 在竞技体育中, 并非有损害即构成侵权, 而是需要根据具体的竞技体育类型来判断该等损害是否重大、不合理及不可预见。正因为如此, 某种伤害是否构成侵权, 需要依据各类竞技体育运动的规则并参考相关专业人士的意见作出判断。

### 2. 主观过错

一般侵权的构成要件中, 主观过错包括故意和过失。认定竞技体育中的侵权行为是否应当限于主观故意, 理论和司法实践的意见并不一致。

美国作为世界上的体育大国, 在体育侵权方面的实践值得我们借鉴。过去美国法院认为运动员参与竞技比赛就要承担因此产生的危险, 即实行风险自担原则, 因而运动员对于职业体育比赛中发生的"侵权行为"不能请求损害赔偿。直到1977年Hackbart v. Cincinnati Bengals,

---

11) 张俊浩主编：《民法学原理》, 中国政法大学出版社2000 年版, 第908 页。
12) Walter T. Champion, JR: "Sports Law", Thomson West Press 2005, pp117.

inc[13] 一案，上诉法院推翻了联邦地区法院的判决，建立了体育侵权中的过错标准－－Recklessness。[14] Reckless 的标准相当于重大过失(gross negligence),[15] 是指鲁莽、不顾一切的；指已经认识到并且自觉漠视可能发生的实质性危险， 不仅是纯粹的疏忽更是严重偏离了理性人的行为标准。[16] 在体育侵权中， 重大过失标准被解释为一个理性的人在采取某种行为时知道或者有足够的理由知道他的这种行为不仅将给他人带来不合理的身体伤害风险， 而且这种风险要远大于他的一般的过失行为带来的风险。[17] 根据这一标准， 只有当侵害人一味追求比赛的结果，而对于自己的行为给对方造成的可能的损害抱着极其冷漠的态度时， 侵权人才应当承担赔偿责任， 而一般的过失(negligence)不能构成体育侵权。因为在体育场上激烈的竞技行为中， 某些因为身体的接触导致的伤害是不可避免的。如果责任标准过严导致运动员在场上因为害怕"动辄得咎"而畏首畏尾，则与体育竞技本身的"竞技"的性质不符，不利于体育事业的发展。

实际上，美国并没有统一的认定体育侵权的主观过错的标准。各州基于各自政策、对体育产业的保护的考虑而采用各自认为合适的标准。[18] 有些州( 如威斯康辛州) 采取过失标准。

过失在法律上的涵义是未达到一个通情达理的人在当时的情况下根据法律所应达到的注意标准。[19] 或者说是"一个理智的人没有去做他应该做的事情，或者一个文雅和理智的人做了他不应该做的事"。[20] 采取过失标准作为体育侵权的主观要件的理由主要是：首先， 在社会的其它一般领域的侵权行为都是以过失来认定，体育场上不应当有例外；其次，过失标

---

13) 该案中，原告在比赛中被被告恶意用前臂撞伤头部后面。科罗拉多州地区法院认为暴力是职业橄榄球赛的本质特点之一， 传统的侵权责任不适用于职业球赛。上诉法院推翻了地区法院的判决，认为橄榄球的普遍习惯并没有允许故意的撞击行为，法律也没有将职业比赛中受到的伤害排除其规制范围，侵权法仍然可以为职业运动员提供保护，否则他们将只能用"报复"去解决问题。601 F.2d 516

14) Walter T. Champion, JR: "Sports Law", Thomson West Press 2005, pp115-116.

15) Michael Mayer : "Stepping In to Step Out of Liability : The Proper Standard of Liability for Referees in Foreseeable Judgment-call Situation", 3 DePaul J. Sports L.& Contemp. Probs 54.

16) 《元照英美法律词典》，法律出版社2003 年版，第1156 页。

17) 709 N.E.2d.1241 (1998)

18) 参见：Erica K. Rosenthal : "Inside The Line : Basing Negligence Liability In Sports For Safety-Based Rule Violations On The Level of Play", 72 Fordham L. Rev. 2631 ；Michael F. Taxin : "The Changing Evolution of Sports : Why Performance Enhancing Drug Use Should Be Considered in Determining Tort Liability of Professional Athletes", 14 Fordham Intell .Pro. Media & Ent. L.J.817; Dean Richardson : "Player Violence: AN Essay on Torts and Sports", 15 Stan .L .&Pol'y Rev.133.

19) 《元照英美法律词典》，法律出版社2003 年版，第955 页。

20) 徐爱国：《英美侵权行为法学》，北京大学出版社2004 年版，第54 页。

准比起重大过失标准能够更好地保护运动员的权利, 净化体育场上的不良风气, 减少场上的"报复"行为 ; 最后, 过失标准并不会像有些学者担心的会造成诉讼泛滥。因为运动员之间存在" 体育场上的纠纷在体育场上解决", 而不需要让法院解决的"潜规则" : 在体育侵权的过失的认定上, 法院会参考很多因素, 甚至包括运动员本身的素质、从事体育的年限、经验等,21) 而不会轻易认定侵害者构成过失。

可见, 即使是采取过失标准的州在对侵权人是否构成过失的认定上也并不宽松, 在判断侵权人是否违反了对受害人的注意义务而构成" 过失" 时, 法院会考虑各种因素防止运动员会"动辄得咎"。正如威斯康辛州最高院的法官所言, "过失标准如果被正确的理解和运用, 同样能够实现重大过失标准所主张的目标和信念"。22)

笔者主张对身体接触类或者对抗性激烈的运动中的伤害行为是否构成侵权以故意或者重大过失为标准 ; 对于非身体接触类的对抗性不强的运动中的伤害行为是否构成侵权采取过失标准。即根据运动类型的不同对运动员施加不同的注意义务。因为在对抗性很强的比赛中, 运动员没有可能非常谨慎地考虑自己的行为是否可能会给对方造成伤害。"当比赛在有限的空间里高速地进行着, 那么谨慎的注意标准就会使这一体育的本质和目的泡汤"。23)

然而, 如何区分重大过失和过失, 仍是个非常复杂的问题。需要考虑的因素包括但不限于比赛的类型和激烈程度 ; 赛场上行为的惯例 ; 运动内在的风险 ; 运动员自身的特征(包括运动员的运动经历)等。

## 3. 违法行为

侵权行为的可责难性在于这些行为"违法性", 导致"法"所保护的利益受到了侵害。为了

---

21) 538 S.W.2d 737 (1976) , Niemczyk v. Burleson ; 在另一个案件中法院还具体列举了构成过失的九大要素 : 身体的接触和损害可预见的程度对侵权人行为方式的影响 ; 比赛的规则(rules)和规章(regulations) ; 被广泛接受的运动中的惯例和常规和通常的暴力程度 ; 比赛的内在风险和预期之外的风险 ; 运动的保护措施和具体案件中的事实和环境(包括运动员的年龄和身体特征 ; 运动员自身的特殊技能 ; 和运动员对比赛惯例和规则的认知。501N.W.2d33 (1993)

22) Dean Richardson : "Player Violence: An Essay on Torts and Sports", 15 Stan .L .&Pol'y Rev.133.

23) [加]约翰·巴勒斯 : "体育伤害的民事责任", 高燕竹译, 载≪民商法论丛≫第26 卷, 金桥文化出版有限公司2003 年版, 第509 页。

树立"法"的权威性, 应当对这种侵权行为进行法律评价。但是在竞技体育中什么样的行为构成"违法"?这里的"法"除包括一般的法律、行政法规外, 是否应当包括各种竞赛规则?

"竞赛规则"是体育组织所制定的适用于某项体育运动的, 为该运动所涉及的相关人员所认同的, 旨在实现保护相关人员的利益, 保证赛事顺利进行等目的的规定, 如国际足协制定的《足球竞赛规则》。笔者认为, 体育侵权中的"法"应当包括体育的竞赛规则, 没有违反规则的行为导致的损害不应当构成侵权。在体育赛场上包含着不为正常生活状态所容纳的激烈的竞技性。体育竞赛规则是针对这种特殊领域, 照顾到该领域中不同于正常生活状态下的特点而制定的。因此如果某种侵害行为并没有违反竞赛规则, 符合该领域的"特殊性", 则不应依一般的标准将其认定为侵权。比如篮球比赛的卡位, 通过脚步动作用身体去阻挡别人于自己身后, 来占据篮下先机从而抢到篮板球。此时被阻挡于背后的人如果因此摔倒受伤, 卡位的人无需承担侵权责任。因为这是篮球竞赛规则所允许的合理冲撞, 而对方所受到的伤害也不是不可预见的。而柔道比赛中甚至允许以扭脱关节制胜。

制定体育竞技规则的目的是为了保护运动员安全, 也是为了保证运动顺利进行。只有违反以保护运动员安全为目的的规则时才有侵权成立的可能。[24] 虽然在运动场上运动员没有保障对方运动员安全的义务, 但是他应当负有不使自己的行为导致对方危险增加的注意义务。而这种义务的具体表现就在于遵守比赛规则中旨在保障运动员安全的规则。运动员参赛就意味着其对竞赛规则的认可, 负有在比赛中遵守竞赛规则的义务。运动员违反竞赛规则, 就应当为其违反义务的行为承担责任。

但是, 并非违反比赛规则的行为都应承担侵权责任。运动员无须为一些轻微的违规行为造成的其他运动员的损害承担侵权责任, 否则会使得比赛丧失激烈对抗带来的魅力。例如在足球等身体接触类体育比赛中, 裁判员依运动员不同程度的违规行为分别做出口头警告、黄牌警告、红牌罚下、停赛、禁赛等相应的处罚。判定运动员的违规行为是否构成体育侵权行为时, 应当考虑违规行为的严重程度, 只有严重的违规行为才应承担侵权责任。

---

24) Walter T. Champion, JR: "Sports Law", Thomson West Press 2005, pp117.

## 4. 侵害行为和损害后果之间的因果关系

在因果关系的判断中, 在体育侵权中不具有特殊性, 故不再赘述。

综上所述, 判断竞技体育中的行为是否构成侵权的要素包括：该行为是否造成了该类运动所容忍范围之外的健康或者生命的损害,  行为人是否违反了保护运动员安全为目的的规则。根据不同的体育类型,  在主观过错的认定上应当采用不同的标准：在身体接触类的或者对抗激烈的竞技体育中,  以故意或者重大过失为要件；而非身体接触类的或者对抗性不强的竞技体育中,  以行为人的过失为要件。

## Ⅲ. 违法阻却事由

即使某一行为满足了侵权的构成要件, 但因为存在某些事由而使该行为不被认定为侵权行为, 这些事由在学理上称之为违法阻却事由。一般包括正当防卫、紧急避难、自助行为、无因管理、权利行使、被害者的允诺。在体育侵权中的违法阻却事由一般是指被害者允诺, 或称被害人同意。也有学者认为自愿参加带有危险性的体育活动属于甘冒风险。[25] 英美法上则主要以受害人"风险承担"(assumption of risk)作为抗辩理由。对于两者的关系, 有学者认为两者是相似的,[26] 也有学者认为两者是有区别的。[27]

风险承担是指, 受害人明知可能遭受来自于特定危险源的风险, 却依然冒险行事。[28] 在美国司法中, 风险承担的形式包括明示的(expressed)和默示的(implied)。明示的风险承担能够完全阻止原告的赔偿请求,  免除加害人的责任。默示的风险承担通过原告知道风险的存在仍然继续参与该比赛而成立。[29]  后来很多州通过立法取消了默示的风险承担,  代之以比较过

---

25) 杨立新：≪侵权行为法案例教程≫, 知识产权出版社2003 年版, 第47 页。

26) 杨立新：≪侵权行为法≫, 夏旦大学出版社2007 年版, 第128 页。

27) 王泽鉴：≪侵权行为法≫第一册, 中国政法大学出版社2001 版, 第242 页；程啸："论侵权行为法中的受害人同意", 载≪中国人民大学学报≫2004 年第3 期。

28) 程啸："论侵权行为法中的受害人同意", 载≪中国人民大学学报≫2004 年第3 期。

29) Walter T. Champion, JR："Sports Law", Thomson West Press 2005, pp117; 121 HVLR 1253, "Tort Law --Sports Torts--California Supreme Court Extends Assumptionof Riskto Noncontact Sports." Harvard Law ReviewFebruary, 2008.

错(comparative fault)[30] 原则进行规制。[31] 比较过错原则主张即使原告存在风险承担的行为，被告也不能因此完全免责，而是根据具体案例中双方当事人之间的过失的轻重，将双方当事人的过错比例化和数量化。在该规则的调整下， 即使原告在承担不合理风险时被法院认定存在过错，他仍能够获得一定的赔偿，只是他的赔偿数额要根据其过错的程度减少。[32] 在德国法上，对自甘冒险( 风险承担) 的理论见解也发生过变化。早期认为是默示合意免除责任，后来解释为被害者的允诺，具违法阻却性，而最近则强调属于"与有过失"[33]的问题。[34] 台湾学者也有建议将自甘冒险纳入与有过失的范畴， 由法院衡量当事人对损害或者扩大的原因力，以合理分配其责任。从上述各国理论的发展过程不难发现，对于风险承担的责任承担问题都经历了从完全排除加害人的责任到根据受害人和加害人的过错来进行责任的分担。但该学者也认为，如果自甘冒险的情形严重时也可排除加害者的责任，不过要对具体案情进行分析。[35]

受害人同意是指受害人事前作出自愿承担某种损害结果的意思表示。[36] 其表现形式也包括明示的和默示的同意。对于受害人同意所产生的法律效果， 认识并不一致。大陆法系的瑞士、德国认为，受害人同意只要不违反法律或者公共秩序，就可以作为一种正当的理由构成违法阻却事由，故加害人无须承担损害赔偿责任。[37] 但是在法国则不然，他们认为受害人的同意并不能除去加害人行为的过错， 因为"一个谨慎的人不会从事一项可归责的行为，即使受害人同意时亦如此。倘若受害人明确向他表示，请求他造成伤害，他也应当依法予以抵制"。[38] 但同时受害人的同意表明了在招致损害方面同样具有过错。而我国民法没有明确

---

30) 比较过错是指在损害赔偿诉讼中，将原告的过失与被告的过失进行比较，以尽少被告应承担的赔偿份额。≪元照英美法律词典≫，法律出版社2003 年版，第268 页。

31) Erica K. Rosenthal： "Inside The Line : Basing Negligence Liability In Sports For Safety-Based Rule Violations On The Level of Play", 72 Fordham L. Rev. 2631

32) 徐爱国：≪英美侵权行为法学≫，北京大学出版社2004 年版，第88 页。

33) 杨立新先生认为，侵权行为法上的"与有过失"是指侵权行为所造成的损害结果的发生或扩大，受害人也有过错，受害人的行为和加害人的行为对损害的发生均有原因力的侵权形态。杨立新：≪侵权行为法≫，夏旦大学出版社2005 年版，第192 页。

34) BGHZ 34, 355 .转引自王泽鉴：≪侵权行为法≫(第一册)，中国政法大学出版社2001 版，第242 页。

35) 王泽鉴：≪侵权行为法≫(第一册)，中国政法大学出版社2001 版，第242 页。

36) 王利明：≪侵权行为法研究≫(上)，中国人民大学出版社2004 年版，第563 页。

37) 江平主编：≪民法学≫，中国政法大学出版社2000 年版，第785 页。

38) Jean Limpens, "Liability for One's Act", International Encyclopedia of Comparative Law · Torts , Chapter 12, at 90.转引自王利明：≪侵权行为法研究≫(上)，中国人民大学出版社2004 年版，第564 页。

规定受害人同意是否可以作为完全的抗辩事由。

从上述两种违法阻却事由适用的范围和情形及产生的后果来看，两者似乎没有实质的区别。无论是受害人同意还是风险的承担，都体现法律对人的自我处分权利的一种尊重，使得人们可以根据自己意愿来对某种不利进行价值衡量，从而获得对自己最有利的后果。只不过受害人同意更加侧重对当事人意思自治的尊重，而风险承担则比较侧重平衡当事人在利益和风险之间的选择。

在我国现有的法律框架内，如果用受害者同意来作为体育侵权的违法阻却事由应当满足下列条件：首先这种同意或者承担风险应当是事先的表示， 事后的承认属于对已发生的损害赔偿请求权的放弃。[39] 而且这种事先的同意必须是自愿、真实的， 受诈欺或者胁迫而为的承诺则不生效力。

其次，同意受到不利益或者承担的风险的范围应当仅限于该种竞技体育内在的或者固有的风险，其他人为的风险不属于同意的范围。如上文所述，这种固有风险的界定应当根据不同的体育类型来具体判断，考虑各种竞技体育运动本身所要求的对抗性程度，伤害在运动中的出现的概率，是否违反比赛规则，风险的可预见性、大小，比赛中的惯例和常规等各种因素。需要注意的是，事先"知道"风险的存在不意味着"同意"承受这种风险。如比赛中运动员都能预见到可能会有违规行为的出现， 但并不等于运动员同意受到因违规而带来的伤害后果，否则这些比赛规则也将会失去意义。[40] 此外，同意的内容亦不得违反法律的强制性规定和社会善良风俗，人身权利具有专属性，不得处分，也不允许他人任意侵害。[41]

最后对于受害人同意或者风险自担的法律后果，笔者认为如果把这种同意或者风险的范围限制在体育运动固有的风险及法律和社会善良风俗许可的范围内， 则这种风险导致的损害是合理的，是运动员在选择走上赛场的那一刻必须承担的不利益，故而应该将其作为完全地抗辩事由。在出现这种合理的损害时， 侵害者可以主张受害者同意或者风险自担来免责。否则将会约束运动员在赛场上的行为而影响体育运动的竞技性。结语体育竞技本身具有风险性，也正是这种风险带来了体育的激情和魅力，让观众和运动员从中获得刺激和愉悦。但

---

39) 王泽鉴：《侵权行为法》(第一册)，中国政法大学出版社2001 版，第242 页。

40) Walter T. Champion, JR: "Sports Law", Thomson West Press 2005, pp117.

41) 王利明：《侵权行为法研究》(上)，中国人民大学出版社2004 年版，第564 页。

也正是这种风险导致一些运动员受到严重的伤害而断送自己的运动生涯，甚至为此失去生命。如何在不伤害体育这种"本性"的同时保障运动员的人身权利，法律面临两难的选择。但法律作为维护社会公平和正义的手段，必须在竞技体育的发展和人的尊严中间寻求平衡点。清楚地界定体育侵权的构成要件及其阻却违法的事由，不仅有利于彰显"有损害就有救济"的法律理念，也是为了预防更加重大的伤害，保障竞技体育运动的自由和安全。

中国政法大学民商经济法学院教授

王玉梅

2013年9月26日

· 摘要 ·

侵权行为法在体育竞技规制中的缺失，体育保险制度的不完善导致运动员的合法权益得不到充分的保障。文章结合国内外体育立法实践和理论，通过对竞技体育中侵权行为的构成要件（损害事实、主观过错、违法行为和因果关系）及其阻却违法事由的特殊性分析，主张在我国竞技体育中建立和完善侵权损害赔偿机制，达到体育竞技性和运动员保护两极之间的平衡。

关键词：竞技体育，侵权行为

## 參考文獻 (References)

陈欣：《保险法》，北京大学出版社2002 年12 月。

王泽鉴：《侵权行为法》(第一册)，中国政法大学出版社2001 版。

张俊浩主编：《民法学原理》，中国政法大学出版社2000 年版，第908 页。

徐爱国：《英美侵权行为法学》，北京大学出版社2004 年版。

杨立新：《侵权行为法案例教程》，知识产权出版社2003 年版。

杨立新：《侵权行为法》，夏旦大学出版社2007 年版。

徐爱国：《英美侵权行为法学》，北京大学出版社2004 年版。

王利明：《侵权行为法研究》(上)，中国人民大学出版社2004 年版。

江平主编：《民法学》，中国政法大学出版社2000 年版。

《元照英美法律词典》，法律出版社2003 年版。

[加]约翰·巴勒斯："体育伤害的民事责任"，高燕竹译，载《民商法论丛》第26 卷，金桥文化出版有限公司2003 年版。

程啸："论侵权行为法中的受害人同意"，载《中国人民大学学报》2004 年第3 期。

Walter T. Champion, JR: "Sports Law", Thomson West Press 2005.

Michael Mayer : "Stepping In to Step Out of Liability : The Proper Standard of Liability for Referees in Foreseeable Judgment-call Situation", 3 DePaul J. Sports L.& Contemp. Probs 54.

Dean Richardson : "Player Violence: An Essay on Torts and Sports", 15 Stan .L .&Pol'y Rev.133.

Erica K. Rosenthal : "Inside The Line : Basing Negligence Liability In Sports For Safety-Based Rule Violations On The Level of Play", 72 Fordham L. Rev. 2631.

Michael F. Taxin : "The Changing Evolution of Sports: Why Performance Enhancing Drug Use Should Be Considered in Determining Tort Liability of Professional Athletes", 14 Fordham Intell .Pro. Media & Ent. L.J.817.

121 HVLR 1253, "Tort Law --Sports Torts--California Supreme Court Extends Assumption of Riskto Noncontact Sports." Harvard Law ReviewFebruary, 2008.

# Study on Legal Problems Relative to Doping Search

## 兴奋剂搜查若干法律问题研究

XUE-FENG YAN (闫旭峰)* · XIAO-XUE XIE (谢晓雪)

*With the method of data and comparison, we study several representative instances of the doping search which happened in the domestic or overseas. After discussing the difference of the doping search between Chinaand some other countries and the legal puzzle relative to the doping search in our country. And we put forward the inevitability of adopting the doping search on the background of the increasing grimness and complication of anti-doping position. Withthe trend of the doping nomocracy in the international community, we think it should be necessary and important to strengthen the construction of legal system on the doping search. So we suggest that the legislation of the doping search should be built upon the basis of the amendments of some laws in future, such as our criminal law and physical law. In details, we suggest that in our country the right subject of the doping search should be clear, the object and the right purview of the doping search should be definite, and the procedure of the doping search should be strict, and so on.*

Key word: Doping Inspection, Doping Search, Doping Nomocracy

随着反兴奋力度不断加大，兴奋剂搜查实例在国内外反兴奋剂斗争中已屡见不鲜，且成

---

* Beijing sport University, China, Graduate Student Supervisor, the President of Teaching Institute of Ideological and Political Theory Courses, Member of the University Academic Degree Committee, a Standing Director of Chinese Society of Law (Sports Law Branch), a Member of Chinese Sport Society (in Sports Sociology Branch), a Member of Committee Hearings by Anti-doping Commission, Vice Director of Sportsmanship and Lianzheng Risk Research Center of China.

功率极高，有效地震慑和打击了兴奋剂行为。然而，研判反兴奋剂行为的成功与否，不仅应当看其有效性，而且应当看其合法性。将反兴奋剂斗争纳入法制的轨道，加强反兴奋剂法制建设，完善兴奋剂检查和搜查的立法、执法环节，是顺应兴奋剂法治趋势，维护运动员权益，有效打击兴奋剂的必然要求。

从国际体育组织和世界各国来看，有关兴奋剂检查方面法律、法规、规章和制度建立的都比较完善，兴奋剂检查组织、队伍建立健全，实践中实施兴奋剂检查行为、程序也都较为规范。但有关兴奋剂搜查的法律制度，无论是国际奥委会，还是中国奥委会，大多没有这方面的立法。

本文试图运用文献资料和比较的方法，通过对国内外兴奋剂搜查的典型实例比较和法律分析，在阐述我国兴奋剂搜查制度的必要性的基础上，就我国兴奋剂搜查制度中搜查主体资格、搜查对象和权限范围和兴奋剂搜查实施程序等法律问题进行探讨。

## Ⅰ. 中外兴奋剂搜查典型实例之比较

实例一：四川省运动技术学院犀浦田径训练基地藏匿兴奋剂被查

2001年，中国奥委会反兴奋剂委员会陆续接到有关四川省运动技术学院犀浦田径训练基地藏匿并使用违禁药物的举报。8月9日，反兴奋剂委员会派出五名工作人员前往调查。在该基地某房间内查获了安雄、胰岛素样生长因子等大量违禁药物，随后，对十六名田径运动员分批进行了赛外检查。[1]

实例二：山西省九运会代表团田径队医生藏匿兴奋剂被查获

根据群众举报，2001年10月26日，中国奥委会反兴奋剂委员会和九运会反兴奋剂监督组派出的4名工作人员来到南方某省体工队招待所，对山西省九运会代表团田径队的4名太原市运动员进行赛外兴奋剂检查。在队医常歌华房间内查获了大量从国外进口的、属于违禁药物的生长激素(HGH)和促红细胞生长素(EPO)，另外还发现有成分不明的针剂若干。[2]

---

1) 四川体育界一连串兴奋剂丑闻相继被曝光 http://unn.people.com.cn/GB/channel2200/2205/200110/17/115311.htm
2) 群众举报查出大量违禁药物 山西九运田径队遭严惩 http://sports.sohu.com/10/42/sports_news 163644210.shtml

实例三：辽宁省鞍山市田径学校集体使用兴奋剂事件

2006年，接到有关鞍山市田径学校为了备战辽宁省十运会集体使用违禁药品举报后，8月8日，中国奥委会反兴奋剂委员会、国家体育总局监察局等单位组成兴奋剂检查组一行7人，前往突击检查。在运动队驻地发现该校一些人正在给多名运动员注射违禁药物，检查组还在现场收缴了大量促红细胞生成素、丙酸睾酮等违禁物质以及一次性注射器，并在该校校长邵会斌的房间内查获大量上述违禁物质。[3]

实例四：意大利警察搜查迈尔(Walter Mayer)驻地

2006年都灵冬奥会令举办期间，国际奥委会接到WADA有关曾因涉嫌使用兴奋剂而被禁赛的前奥地利越野滑雪队教练迈尔(Walter Mayer)出现在奥地利代表队的秘密通知后，立即通知意大利警方。2月18日，警方迅速对奥地利冬季两项和越野滑雪队在奥运村外的驻地进行搜查，结果搜出了100个注射器、30包无标签药品、一台血液分析仪和一台血液回输仪。[4]

实例五：意大利警察搜查药店、健身房和体育中心等案

2000年7月14日，意大利警察在巴勒莫等城市突然行动，对65家药店、健身房和体育中心等进行搜查，查获了1500多箱非法制造的兴奋剂，并对26人提出起诉。[5]

2002年，环意大利自行车赛期间，200名警察对所有参赛车队下榻的饭店进行了突击搜查，发现了很多违禁药物，从此开始了对80名车手长达12个月的司法调查。

2004年5月27日出动700名警察突击搜查了100多名运动员的家、办公室和饭店的房间，从而拉开了全国范围内兴奋剂调查的序幕。[6]

案例六：希腊警方和反兴奋剂机构突击检查特泽科斯的公司

2004年8月20日，希腊警方和反兴奋剂机构人员联合行动，对希腊田径教练特泽科斯的公司进行了突击检查。结果搜出了1400多瓶含有特殊成分的营养药片，其中大部分药片含有兴奋剂和麻黄素成分，而另外一些则含有合成的违禁药物。[7]

---

3) 辽宁省鞍山市田径学校 惊爆集体使用兴奋剂，华奥星空，http://www.sports.cn/ 2006年8月23 日

4) 郑 斌："都灵冬奥会兴奋剂检查综述"《反兴奋剂动态》2006年第3期

5) 中新社：《意大利破获一制贩兴奋剂的犯罪团伙》，http://www.sina.com.cn，2000年07月16日

6) 杜文杰："意大利警方围剿兴奋剂 全国大搜查找出违禁药物"，《中国体育报》2004年5月31日

7) 关注兴奋剂丑闻《京华时报》2004年8月22日 http://www.people.com.cn/GB/paper1787/12755/1146348.html

案例七：德、波警方联合行动藏匿德国的兴奋剂团伙突击搜查

2006年8月29日，德国和波兰的240名警方联合行动，对一个藏匿在德国的兴奋剂团伙进行了突击搜查。搜查目标是以德国人鲍里斯为首的兴奋剂贩卖团伙，他们从泰国进口药物，并在德国，波兰和瑞典等地销售，从中牟取暴利。警方当场逮捕鲍里斯，并获取大量兴奋剂药物和交易脏款。[8)]

表1：中外兴奋剂搜查实例比较情况：

| 发生国别、地点 | 行动名称 | 行为主体 | 参与人数 | 搜查对象范围 | 发生时间 |
|---|---|---|---|---|---|
| 中国四川犀浦 | 调查和赛外兴奋剂检查 | 行政人员、反兴奋剂机构人员 | 5人 | 犀浦田径训练基地某房间 | 2001.08.09 |
| 中国江西南昌 | 赛外兴奋剂检查 | 行政人员、反兴奋剂机构人员 | 4人 | 江西南昌某招待所山西田径队医房间 | 2001.10.26 |
| 中国辽宁鞍山 | 突击检查 | 行政人员、反兴奋剂机构人员 | 7人 | 鞍山市田径学校校长房间 | 2006.08.08 |
| 意大利都灵 | 搜查 | 警方 | 不详 | 奥地利冬季两项和越野滑雪队在奥运村外驻地 | 2006.02.18 |
| 意大利巴勒莫 | 搜查 | 警方 | | 65家药店、健身房和体育中心等 | 2000.07.14 |
| 环意大利自行车赛 | 突击搜查 | 警方 | 200人 | 参赛车队下榻的饭店 | 2002. |
| 意大利全国 | 突击搜查 | 警方 | 700人 | 运动员的家、办公室和饭店的房间 | 2004.05.27 |
| 希腊 | 突击检查 | 警方和反兴奋剂机构人员 | 不详 | 田径教练特泽科斯的公司 | 2004.08.20 |
| 德国、波兰 | 突击搜查 | 警方 | 240人 | 藏匿于德国的兴奋剂团伙 | 2006.08.29 |

上述前三起发生在中国的兴奋剂实例具有如下的共同点：(1)都是在中国反兴奋剂机构接到有关举报后采取的行为；(2)被派出的兴奋剂检查组成员都是行政工作人员和反兴奋剂机构人员，警方均未介入；(3)兴奋剂藏匿的地点都是在辅助人员房间；(4)发生藏匿和使用

8) 《德国波兰警方擒获兴奋剂贩卖团伙》北京电视台 http://www.btv.org/btvweb/ty/2006-08/30/content_93151.htm

事件都是在兴奋剂高危项目田径
中；(5)查获的结果与举报情报完
全相一致性；(6)均发生在全运会
或省运会之前。

六起国外的兴奋剂搜查实例
所具有的共同点是：(1)实施搜查
行为的主体都有警方介入，或者
是警方单独搜查，或者是警方和
体育组织合作进行；(2)搜查的地
域范围和对象较广泛，包括运动员、教练员和重点嫌疑人驻地，也包括销售、制造兴奋剂
的商店、药店等；(3)实施兴奋剂搜查行为的法律依据和搜查程序完善；(4)兴奋剂搜查所动
用的警力人数较多。

国外的兴奋剂搜查实例表明：愈演愈烈的兴奋剂事件使得警察的帮助成为国际社会防
范和打击兴奋剂的有力手段，随时出动依法实施搜查行动的警察也对利益驱动下的潜在兴
奋剂违法者产生了强大的威慑力。这恰恰就是我国反兴奋剂工作中值得借鉴的地方。另一
方面，这也说明兴奋剂搜查在反兴奋剂斗争中是必不可少的手段。

## Ⅱ. 兴奋剂突击检查和搜查之法律思考

应当肯定，中外反兴奋剂斗争中，实施兴奋剂突击检查、搜查行为，现场取证，人赃俱
获、水落石出，严厉有效地打击了集体藏匿、使用兴奋剂行为。但是从法律法规的视角分
析，我国在兴奋剂检查和搜查上存在着一些值得思考的问题：

比较中外兴奋剂搜查所有有关报道、通报、文件，我们发现对此类行为的描述，外国多
用搜查或突击搜查，而我国则慎重和一般不用"搜查"二字，多用词汇"调查" "检查" "突击
检查"。为什么行为性质相同、行为的目标一致、行为的方式一样，但描述用词不同呢？我
们以为这主要是由于实施此行为的法律依据所致。

外国警方介入兴奋剂搜查，具有明确的法律依据和严格的法律程序。意大利法律规定，运动员携带、服用禁药、教练提供禁药或指使运动员服用禁药都是犯罪行为，可被判处3个月至3年的监禁。因此警方可以突击搜查运动员驻地，并直接逮捕使用兴奋剂的人员。如2004年5月27日意大利警察突击搜查了100多名运动员的家、办公室和饭店的房间的行动，是根据第138号搜查令开展这次行动的，目的是搜集在各种业余体育项目中运动员使用和传播兴奋剂的罪证。2004年08月20日，希腊警方和反兴奋剂机构人员联合行动，对希腊田径教练特泽科斯的公司进行了突击检查后，警方犯罪调查科人员透露，一这次搜查警方具有齐备的搜查证。这次的搜查成果对于调查整个兴奋剂事件有着重大意义。9)

我国警方为什么不介入兴奋剂搜查？根据我国法学理论和有关法律规定，搜查是刑事侦查人员依法调查和搜集犯罪证据的行为。从目前我国刑法看，藏匿、携带、运输、销售和使用兴奋剂不是犯罪行为。因此，警方介入兴奋剂搜查目前无法可依。

那么，我国兴奋剂检查人员的权限和职责范围有多大？从我国的《反兴奋剂条例》和1998年国家体育总局发布的《兴奋剂检查工作人员管理暂行办法》看，兴奋剂检查工作人员应当按照兴奋剂检查规则实施兴奋剂检查；实施兴奋剂检查，应当有2名以上检查人员参加。检查人员履行兴奋剂检查职责时，应出示兴奋剂检查证件；向运动员采集受检样本时，还应出示按照兴奋剂检查规则签发的一次性兴奋剂检查授权书。检查人员履行兴奋剂检查职责时，有权进入体育训练场所、体育竞赛场所和运动员驻地。因此，兴奋剂检查人员的重要职责之一就是依照法律和有关规定采集受检样本。

我国法律法规并没有明确规定其检查、搜查运动员和辅助人员的身体、住所、物品的职权。

《反兴奋剂条例》39条规定了，"体育社会团体、运动员管理单位向运动员提供兴奋剂或者组织、强迫、欺骗运动员在体育运动中使用兴奋剂的，运动员辅助人员组织、强迫、欺骗、教唆运动员在体育运动中使用兴奋剂的，由国务院体育主管部门或者省、自治区、直辖市人民政府体育主管部门收缴非法持有的兴奋剂"。但并没有明确规定国务院体育主管部门或者省、自治区、直辖市人民政府体育主管部门如何行使收缴权，也没有规定通过搜查

---

9)《黑幕正在被揭开 希腊冠军教练藏有大量违禁药品》，http://sports.sina.com.cn，2004年08月21日

等手段、途径查获非法持有的兴奋剂。

因此，在我国发生的三起名为兴奋剂调查或兴奋剂突击检查，实为兴奋剂搜查的行为，从法律意义上判析是一种无搜查权的行为主体，在无法律依据的情况下超越法定检查权限，实施的搜查行为。这一行为的违法性虽然最终被查获兴奋剂并达到反兴奋剂"正义"目的的辉煌所掩盖，但仍然存在很大的风险：假如搜查无结果，很可能会引起诉讼。对非法搜查监督的薄弱，对非法搜查导致损害救济制度的不完善等问题，都给兴奋剂检查工作人员提供了很大的自由裁量空间，同时也留下了滥用权利的危险。

我国兴奋剂突击检查中实施搜查行为存在的问题，正是我国反兴奋剂法律法规中缺失的部分－－无论在实体权利还是程序制度上，都折射出我国兴奋剂搜查方面相关法律条款的缺失。

## Ⅲ. 我国兴奋剂搜查制度建设的法律困境

兴奋剂检查主要针对和解决的是运动员身体内是否含有兴奋剂的问题，而兴奋剂的搜查则是对社会上存在的兴奋剂问题进行打击。兴奋剂市场的禁止、兴奋剂的违法生产、运输和销售的查获，运动员、教练员和辅助人员私自购买、携带、藏匿兴奋剂及运动队和体育社团有组织地集体使用兴奋剂行为的禁止等，均需要兴奋剂搜查行为来完成。而要使得兴奋剂搜查行为合法化、科学化、规范化，必须建立兴奋剂搜查法律制度，这也是反兴奋剂工作适应当今世界兴奋剂违法行为所呈现出的多样性、复杂性、隐蔽性等特征的客观需要。

从我国法律体系的现有框架来看，有权行使搜查的主体仅限于侦查机关，具体人员主要是指警察或检察人员。我国刑事诉讼法第205条规定，搜查是指刑事案件中侦查机关在侦查过程中为查获犯罪证据和犯罪嫌疑人采取的一种强制性措施。"为了收集犯罪证据、查获犯罪人"，这是搜查的目的和前提。

但在我国刑事法律制度中，使用、投放或非法持有兴奋剂等恶劣行为并不是犯罪行为。原国家体育总局运动医学研究所副所长赵健曾说，鞍山体校集体服用兴奋剂的行为是相当

严重的，目前却只能按照行政法规来处理。但在欧美的司法体系中，对这种行为有严格的约束和监管。10)

仔细查阅美国禁药取缔管理机构的官方网站(U.S. Drug Enforcement Administration)，我们发现在美国对非法拥有类固醇等行为，可以被判刑。该药是未经医生处方不得买卖的药品，倘若违反，将受到长至七年的有期徒刑惩罚。同时对于一些辅助人员，如队医、教练等的非法持有、非法销售可能会受到行政的处罚，严重

的将被认定为非法经营罪。而在中国尚无这方面的规定。

在我国反兴奋剂斗争中，一方面，警察有搜查权，但没有兴奋剂搜查权，因此，我国司法机关基本不介入体育争议的解决。另一方面，兴奋剂检查人员有检查权，但没有搜查权。而现实生活中有着兴奋剂检查人员"违法"搜查却大获成效的案例。法律制度建设的滞后，使我国兴奋剂检查人员处于尴尬的境地，面对可能被隐藏的兴奋剂，欲深入搜查获取更多证据，却是无法可依。尴尬之际，我们看到兴奋剂搜查在我国体育法治建设中存在的法律困境

因此，为完善反兴奋剂的立法，建立兴奋剂搜查法律制度，是解决反兴奋剂斗争中兴奋剂搜查无法可依的客观必须。

## Ⅳ. 建立和完善兴奋剂搜查法律制度的设想

坚持依法治体的方针，加强兴奋剂法治，加快反兴奋剂立法步伐，填补空白，堵塞漏洞，是摆在我们面前亟待着手的重要课题。结合国内外相关的兴奋剂案例，以及兴奋剂问

---

10) 《探营中国反兴奋剂中心：兴奋剂已经走出体育界》http://2008.sohu.com/20071128/n253676646.shtml

题在体育领域中的严重危害，我们建议在在刑法体系中，以修正案的形式增设兴奋剂犯罪的罪名；在体育法的修正中，增加"非法制造、经营、贩卖兴奋剂行为，非法使用和持有兴奋剂行为、投放兴奋剂及组织、教唆、欺骗使用兴奋剂等行为，情节严重，构成犯罪的，应承担刑事责任"条款。

在相应《刑法》和《体育法》修正案出台的基础上，我们建议在反兴奋剂的专门立法中设立兴奋剂搜查的章节，明确具体地规定实施兴奋剂搜查行为的主体，兴奋剂搜查主体的权限，兴奋剂搜查的程序等内容。

## 1. 兴奋剂搜查权利主体

我们认为，我国实施兴奋剂搜查行为的主体可通过立法形成三种模式：一是确立兴奋剂刑事案件的侦查机关(公安机关和检察机关)为我国兴奋剂搜查制度中的搜查主体，使警察等侦查人员依法介入对兴奋剂行为的搜查；二是立法授权于国家反兴奋剂机构和兴奋剂检查人员实施兴奋剂搜查的主体资格，享有兴奋剂搜查权的反兴奋剂机构及其工作人员单独依法实施兴奋剂搜查；三是结合前两种模式，使享有兴奋剂搜查权的反兴奋剂机构及其工作人员与刑事侦查机关联合行使搜查权。考虑到我国目前现有法律体系的结构情况，我们建议我国兴奋剂搜查权利主体的立法可采用第三种模式。

## 2. 明确兴奋剂搜查对象和范围

兴奋剂检查主要是对运动员身体内部兴奋剂的监控。而兴奋剂搜查是对尚未进入运动员身体内的兴奋剂的控制。因此，我们认为，兴奋剂搜查的重点对象和范围应当针对药物生产企业、经营部门、医疗卫生机构等非法生产、销售、运输兴奋剂行为和体育团队组织、运动员、教练员和队医、科研人员等辅助人员非法藏匿、携带兴奋剂行为。

### 3. 严格兴奋剂搜查程序

兴奋剂搜查作为一种强制侦查措施，其对公民的潜在威胁是搜查人员在搜查过程中对公民财产权、人身权，尤其是个人隐私权的侵犯。

综观我国的搜查制度设计和侦查实践运作，其在价值取向上明显的倾向于如何有效地查控犯罪，而忽视了对犯罪嫌疑人等其他公民合法权益的保障，表现在从搜查证的获取到执行都缺乏一个正当程序的制约。这是我国搜查制度中的法律问题，也是建立我国兴奋剂搜查制度的法律难题。我们建议对兴奋剂搜查制度采取严格的司法令状主义，并建立严格的证据排除规则体系，对非法搜查所获得的利益予以剥夺，以保障公民合法权益不受侵害。

具体来说，建立严格的兴奋剂搜查程序，必须深入研究能体现兴奋剂搜查特征、有利于达到兴奋剂搜查目标、有利于搜查权利主体实施搜查行为、有利于维护被搜查方合法权益不受侵犯的各种程序，包括兴奋剂搜查证申请和审批程序、兴奋剂搜查规范的执行程序、对查获兴奋剂物品的扣押程序和兴奋剂搜查损害的救济程序等等。

## Ⅴ. 结论与建议

(1) 比较外国兴奋剂搜查实例，我们发现我国兴奋剂搜查的法律依据、主体、对象范围等方面都存在规范缺失的问题。国外有关兴奋剂犯罪的立法、警方介入兴奋剂搜查等值得借鉴。

(2) 兴奋剂法治是当今世界反兴奋剂斗争的发展趋势。加强我国兴奋剂搜查法制建设，是顺应兴奋剂法治趋势，做到兴奋剂搜查有法可依，维护被搜查者合法权益，打击各种兴奋剂行为的必然要求。

(3) 建议修正刑法，增设有关兴奋剂犯罪的罪名；建议修正体育法和相关配套法律法规，增加有关追究兴奋剂犯罪的刑事责任、兴奋剂搜查等内容的条款，为警方介入兴奋剂搜查搭建平台。

(4) 依法设定兴奋剂搜查的权利主体，授予反兴奋剂机构及其兴奋剂检查人员以兴奋剂搜查权；通过立法，明确规定搜查权的行使权限范围和兴奋剂搜查的对象。

(5) 严格兴奋剂搜查法定程序, 研究制定和完善兴奋剂搜查所必须的兴奋剂搜查证申请和审批程序、兴奋剂搜查规范的执行程序、对查获兴奋剂物品的扣押程序和兴奋剂搜查损害的救济程序等内容。

▪ **摘要** ▪

本研究运用文献资料和比较的方法, 通过对国内外发生的兴奋剂搜查典型实例的比较, 探讨了我国和一些国家在兴奋剂搜查方面存在的差异及我国在兴奋剂搜查问题上面临的法律困境；提出在反兴奋剂斗争形势日益严峻、复杂的背景下, 采取兴奋剂搜查行为的必然性；阐述了国际社会"法治兴奋剂"发展趋势下, 加强兴奋剂搜查法制建设的必要性和重要性；提出通过修正刑法、体育法等法律, 加强兴奋剂搜查立法, 设定我国兴奋剂搜查的权利主体, 明确兴奋剂搜查对象和权限范围, 严格兴奋剂搜查程序等设想和建议。

**关键词:** 兴奋剂检查   兴奋剂搜查   兴奋剂法治

## 参考文獻 (References)

1.  《反兴奋剂条例释义》, 国务院法制办、国家体育总局政策法规司、科技司、国家食品药品监督管理局政策法规司、安全监管司编写 , 新华出版社出版, 2004年6月第1版
2. 郑旭：《刑事诉讼法学》, 中国人民大学出版社, 2007年11月第1版
3. 郑斌：奥运会兴奋剂检查发展趋势, 体育科技文献通报, 2005年9月
4. 薛竑：完善我国现行搜查制度浅论, 《河南社会科学》2006年1月
5. 刘为源：浅论我国有证搜查制度的立法完善, 《科教文汇》2006年3月

# Research on Respective Torts

论分别侵权行为

LI-XIN YANG (杨立新)* · YING TAO (陶盈)**

*Respective tort is the modality of tortious act stipulated by article 11 and 12 in Tort Liability Law of the People's Republic of China. It's a part of the multi-torts system, together with the other three modalities of tortious act, which are joint act of tort, overlapping act of tort and the third party's act of tort. Respective tort means that two or more persons commit torts respectively with neither joint intention nor joint negligence, but causing the same damage only because of the objective connection between respective conducts. The legal characteristics of respective tort covers the following four aspects: 1) two or more persons commit torts respectively; 2) these two or more persons' conducts objectively aim at the same victim or the same object; 3) each person's conduct makes contribution to the final damage, either jointly or respectively; 4) causing the same damage which is divisible. Respective tort can be classified as the typical respective tort and the overlapping respective tort. And the latter can be furtherly divided into the wholly- overlapping respective tort and the partially- overlapping respective tort. As to the typical respective tort, the tortfeasors shall assume shared several liabilities. As to the overlapping respective tort, when the causative potency of each tortious conduct are added together, that will exceed 100 percentage. So the outcome of the added causative potency of all tortious conduct should be used to be divided by the amount of the tortfeasors, that will get to a average percentage of the causative potency, which will be the*

* Li-Xin YANG(杨立新), Professor of Law School and Director of Research Center for Civil and Commercial Jurisprudence of Renmin University of China. 中国人民大学民事法律科学研究中心研究员、中俄人文合作协同创新中心首席法律顾问，北京，100872，18610093822，ylx354@126.com。

** 陶盈，中国人民大学民商事法律科学研究中心民商法学博士研究生，北京，100872，15910693181，taoying0801@163.com

*standard of the several liability of each tortfeasor. As a result, each tortfeasor of wholly- respective tort will assume the whole liability of compensation, while each tortfeasor of partially- respective tort will assume the joint and several liability. However, the several liability among the tortfeasors will change correspondingly.*

**Key word:** Respective Torts; Concept; Connotation; Extension; Multi-torts

我国侵权责任法理论和实践通常将分别侵权行为称作无过错联系的共同加害行为或者无意思联络的数人侵权行为。我们依照《侵权责任法》第11 条和第12 条规定，主张将其改称为分别侵权行为，并与共同侵权行为、竞合侵权行为和第三人侵权行为一道，构成多数人侵权行为体系。本文对此概念的命名和界定提出以下新看法。

## I . 我国侵权责任法分别侵权行为概念的发展沿革

1949 年以来，我国侵权责任法关于分别侵权行为概念的发展，归纳起来，可以分为以下四个阶段：

### 1. "无名"侵权行为阶段

1949 年以来至1980 年代，在我国的侵权责任法理论中，没有分别侵权行为的概念。由于这个概念与共同侵权行为概念紧密相关，因而在研究共同侵权行为的理论中涉及分别侵权行为的概念。

在中央政法干部学校民法教研室编著的《中华人民共和国民法基本问题》一书中，有过对于分别侵权行为的描述，即"那些不具备共同致人损害的特征的几个违法行为，它们之间虽有联系，但也不能作为共同致人损害案件处理，不能让行为人负连带赔偿责任。例如，某企业因会计员擅离职守，被小偷偷去现款二百多元。会计员的擅离职守，固然是给小偷造成

了便利条件,与损害事实的发生有连系(应为联系－作者注),但会计员与小偷之间并无共同偷窃现款的意思联络,因此令会计员和小偷对企业负连带赔偿责任,显然是不合理的。会计员的擅离职守与小偷的偷窃行为应根据具体情节分别处理。"1) 这里所述的侵权行为, 显然是分别侵权行为, 与共同侵权行为相异。此外, 1989 年出版的《债权法》一书中也有类似的表述。2)

1980 年代初, 学者在讨论共同侵权的构成要件时, 有的否定意思联络为共同侵权行为的本质要件, 承认客观的"共同行为"为共同侵权行为,3) 认为共同侵权行为的"客观特征", 即"各主体的行为在客观上必须构成一体, 并成为损害后果的统一原因", 此外, "多因一果和偶然相合的侵权行为, 各行为主体只根据自己的过错, 分别承担, 而不承担连带责任。"4) 另一些学者则坚持意思联络说, 认为如无主体间的意思联络, 则各人的行为就无法在实质上统一起来, 因而也不构成共同侵权行为, 行为人之间虽有联系, 但不应视共同致人损害行为处理。例如某干部出差携带差旅费300 元, 在所住旅社洗澡时, 麻痹大意, 将300 元现金压于枕头下, 门不闭, 锁不上就出门了。结果所带300 元全部被小偷偷走。在这里, 某干部的麻痹大意, 固然是给小偷造成了便利条件, 与损害事实的发生有联系, 但某干部与小偷之间并没有共同偷窃现款的意思联络。因此, 某干部应对自己行为的过错负一定责任, 赔偿一定的损失, 但是, 如令其和小偷对单位负连带赔偿责任, 即全部由某干部赔偿损失, 显然是不合理的。"5) 这个案件的性质不是共同侵权行为, 也不是分别侵权行为, 而是与有过失。6) 这个评论显然不当。不过, 否定共同过失是共同侵权行为的本质要件, 使分别侵权行为的范围大大扩大, 这个意见倒是对的。

1986 年《民法通则》颁布之后, 通说认为共同过错是共同侵权行为的本质要件, 共同故意构成共同侵权行为, 共同过失也构成共同侵权行为, 《民法原理》一书对"共同致人损害"的分析,7) 《民法教程》8)、《中国民法教程》9)等著作都对共同侵权行为(共同过错)有深入

---

1) 中央政法干部学校民法教研室:《中华人民共和国民法基本问题》,法律出版社1958 年版, 第331 页。

2) 覃有土、王亘:《债权法》,光明日报出版社1989 年版, 第591~593 页。

3) 邓大榜:《共同侵权行为的民事责任初探》,《法学季刊》1982 年第3 期。

4) 沈幼伦:《试析共同侵权行为的特征》,《法学》1987 年第1 期。

5) 伍再阳:《意思联络是共同侵权行为的必要要件》,《法学季刊》1984 年第2 期。

6) 这个意见错误的根源在于, 将干部出差所带的费用作为单位的所有权对待。须知, 货币是动产, 干部借公款出差, 该公款的所有权已经转移为干部所有, 单位对干部的权利是债权, 而不是物权。

的讨论, 但对分别侵权行为则基本没有论及。这样的做法, 与大陆法系通行的作法相同, 即从逻辑上推论, 不符合共同侵权行为本质要件的数人侵权就是分别侵权行为。不过, 在这一时期中, 没有人这样去论述。

### 2. 提出"无意思联络的数人侵权"阶段

1990 年代初, 学界开始提出了"无意思联络的数人侵权"这一概念,10) 认为"无意思联络的数人侵权, 是指数人行为事先并无共同的意思联络, 而致同一受害人共同损害",11) 对于共同侵权行为与无意思联络的数人侵权之间的区别已经开始形成初步认识。学者认为, 由于数人在主观上无意思联络, 只是因为偶然因素使无意思联络人的各行为偶然结合而造成同一损害结果。使各行为人的行为结合在一起的因素, 不是主观因素, 而是行为人所不能预见和认识的客观的、外来的、偶然的情况,12) 个别行为偶然聚合而成为损害的原因, 每个人的行为只不过是损害产生的一个条件。对于无意思联络的数人侵权, 依过错程度确定责任, 意味着根据案件的具体情况确定各行为人在损害发生时所具有的不同程度的过错, 使过错程度重的行为人承担较重的责任, 过错程度轻的行为人承担较轻的责任, 而没有过错的人则应被免除责任。13)

### 3. 使用"无过错联系的共同致害"或者"无过错联系的共同加害行为"阶段

进入二十一世纪, 学者开始普遍使用"无过错联系的共同致害"或者"无过错联系的共同加害行为"等概念, 认为无过错联系的共同致害, 是指数个行为人事先既没有共同的意思联

---

7) 佟柔主编:《民法原理》, 法律出版社1986 年版。

8) 江平主编:《民法教程》, 中国政法大学出版社1988 年版。

9) 马原主编:《中国民法教程》, 人民法院出版社1989 年版。

10) 王利明:《侵权行为法归责原则研究》, 中国政法大学出版社1992 年版, 第293 页。

11) 王利明, 杨立新:《侵权行为法》, 法律出版社1996 年版, 第199 页。

12) 王利明:《民法侵权行为法》, 中国人民大学出版社1993 年版, 第366 页。

13) 王利明, 杨立新:《侵权行为法》, 法律出版社1996 年版, 第201 页。

络，也没有共同过失，只是由于行为的客观上的联系，而共同造成同一个损害结果。14) 这样，就避免了将共同侵权行为界定为意思联络的狭窄的领域， 限缩无过错联系的共同加害行为概念的外延。

2003年，最高人民法院《关于审理人身损害赔偿案件适用法律若干问题的解释》第3 条第2 款规定了既无共同故意又无共同过失的共同加害行为， 是我国在司法解释中第一次肯定了这个概念， 其中使用了"分别"一词， 等于承认了分别侵权行为的概念。该条款的内容是："二人以上没有共同故意或者共同过失， 但其分别实施的数个行为间接结合发生同一损害后果的， 应当根据过失大小或者原因力比例各自承担相应的赔偿责任。"这是当时最为权威的无过错联系的共同加害行为的规定。2009年，《侵权责任法》第11 条和第12 条使用"分别实施"的侵权行为这一概念，对此作出肯定的规定。在学说上，就将这种侵权行为称为无过错联系的共同侵权行为，15) 或者无意思联络的共同侵权行为中的原因力可分的侵权行为。16) 这些概念都比较冗长，使用起来不够方便，也不够简洁。

### 4. 提出"分别侵权行为"概念的阶段

《侵权责任法》公布实施之后， 对无过错联系的共同加害行为的研究开始了新阶段。2011年，就有学者使用"分别侵权"的概念。17) 2012 年，我们使用了分别侵权行为的概念，认为"分别侵权行为就是无过错联系的共同加害行为。将《侵权责任法》第12 条规定中的"分别实施"概念提炼出来， 确定无过错联系的共同加害行为就是分别侵权行为， 是非常贴切的。按照《侵权责任法》第12 条的规定，分别侵权行为的后果是发生按份责任，每个行为人只对自己的行为后果承担侵权责任，不存在连带责任的问题。"18) 2013 年，我们再次使用了这个概念，认为分别侵权行为在表现形式上，行为人在主观上不关联，在客观上也不关联，

---

14) 杨立新：《侵权法论》(上册)，吉林人民出版社2000 年版，第325~328 页。

15) 杨立新：《＜中华人民共和国侵权责任法＞条文释解与司法适用》，人民法院出版社2010 年版，第66 页。

16) 张新宝：《侵权责任法立法研究》，中国人民大学出版社2009 年版，第245~246 页。

17) 竺效：《论无过错联系之数人环境侵权行为的类型－－兼论致害人不明数人环境侵权责任承担的司法审理》，《中国法学》2011 年第5 期。

18) 杨立新：《多数人侵权行为及责任理论的新发展》，《法学》2012 年第7 期。

仅仅是损害后果相关联, 其后果是按份责任。[19] 在此基础上, 建立多数人侵权行为与多数人侵权责任之间的对应关系, 即共同侵权行为对应连带责任, 分别侵权行为对应按份责任, 竞合侵权行为对应不真正连带责任, 第三人侵权行为对应第三人责任, 形成了严密的逻辑关系体系。[20] 至此, 分别侵权行为概念被推到侵权责任法理论的前台, 接受理论和实践的检验。

## Ⅱ. 分别侵权行为概念的比较法研究

为了进一步准确揭示分别侵权行为概念的内涵和外延, 我们对这个概念进行比较法的研究, 为确立这一概念的论证提出更为准确的法理基础。

### 1. 德国法

传统的德国侵权法对数人侵权行为以连带责任为基础。1887 年公布的《德国民法典》第一草案第714 条规定, 数个行为人通过共同行为, 如教唆人、实行行为人、辅助人, 造成一项损害的, 他们作为连带债务人负责。当数个行为人造成了损害, 虽然他们没有实施共同行为, 但是各自损害的份额无法查明的, 亦同。[21] 反之, 以逻辑推论, 数个行为人既不是共同行为人, 各自的损害份额能够查明, 就不认为是共同侵权行为, 当然就不必承担连带责任。这种侵权行为其实就是分别侵权行为。

1900 年实施的《德国民法典》第830 条规定了共同侵权行为。德国的学说和判例通常认为该条中的"共同", 系指主观的共同, 即有共同意思联络,[22] 因而共同侵权行为的范围较窄, 不利于救济受害人。近几十年来, 德国法从扩大责任范围、及时填补受害人的损失出发,

---

19) 杨立新：《论竞合侵权行为》,《清华法学》2013 年第1 期。

20) 杨立新：《多数人侵权行为及责任理论的新发展》,《法学》2012 年第7 期。

21) Haben mehrere durch gemeinsames Handeln, sei es als Anstifter, Thäater oder Gehüulfen, eien Schaden verschuldet, so haften sie als Gesammtschuldner. Das Gleiche gilt, wenn im Falle eines von mehreren verschuldeten Schadens von den mehreren nicht gemeinsam gehandelt, der Antheit des Einzelnen an dem Schaden aber nicht zu ermitteln ist.

22) 参见王泽鉴：《民法学说与判例研究》, 第1 册, 北京大学出版社2009 年版, 第47 页。

也认为数人虽无意思联络, 但若各人对损害所产生的部分无法确定者, 应负共同侵权的连带赔偿责任。[23] 但是值得重视的是, 近年来出现了对于多家企业的经营活动造成的大规模损害案件中适用按份责任的讨论。这类产品责任、环境污染责任案件之所以不同于《德国民法典》第830 条第1 项第2 句规定的对"关系人"课以连带责任的情形, 是因为大规模侵权案件中的被告企业往往只是造成损害的部分侵权行为主体, 出于公平原则的考虑, 由其承担全部责任不利于企业成长和经济的发展。此外,《德国民法典》第830 条第1 项第2 句规定的情形主要是规范复数"关系人"与单个被害人之间的关系, 在大规模侵权案件中, 由于侵权人和受害人均规模庞大, 具有较明显的特殊性, 参考美国1980 年代出现的"市场份额原则", 德国理论界也出现了较多针对连带责任的反思。在医疗过失领域中适用按份责任的主张也引发了关注, 讨论基于医生的过失责任与患者的个人体质等差异性以及医学发展水平的限制之间的关系, 按照因果关系及原因力理论进行责任的划分。对于事先没有意思联络的多人同时或先后利用某一机会从事侵权行为, 而各个侵权行为并不能导致全部后果的, 例如哄抢、打砸行为, 虽无法查明每个参与侵权人所造成的具体损害份额, 但能够确定每个侵权人都只是造成最后损害后果的一部分, 适用《德国民事诉讼法》第287 条的规定,[24] 即法官通过自由裁量可以确定参与共同侵权人具体承担损害赔偿的份额。[25] 这显然与分别侵权行为有关。

共同侵权行为范围的扩大, 后果是分别侵权行为范围的缩小。尽管德国侵权法并无分别侵权行为的概念, 但实际情况必然如此。

## 2. 法国法

《法国民法典》在关于侵权行为和准侵权行为的规定中, 没有规定共同侵权行为和不构成共同侵权行为的数人侵权。但在法院的司法实践中, 认可共同责任人的整体(in solidum)债

---

23) 参见王泽鉴:《民法学说与判例研究》, 第1 册, 北京大学出版社2009 年版, 第47 页。

24)《德国新民事诉讼法》第287 条第1 款第1 句规定: "当事人对于是否有损害、损害的数额以及应赔偿的利益额有争论时, 法院应考虑全部情况, 经过自由心证, 对此点作出判断。"

25) 朱岩:《当代德国侵权法上因果关系理论和实务中的主要问题》,《法学家》2004 年第6 期。

务。1970 年4 月29 日, 最高法院第二民事庭认为, 同一损害的每一个责任人均应被判处赔偿全部损害, 而没有必要考虑本案法官在不同的责任人之间进行的责任分割。这种责任分割仅涉及不同责任人之间的相互关系, 而不涉及他们对受害当事人的债务的范围。[26] 可见法国的共同侵权行为的范围比较宽泛。同样, 《法国民法典》也没有对分别侵权行为作出规定, 依据逻辑推理, 不符合共同侵权行为的数人侵权, 应当就是分别侵权行为。

法国法系的其他各国民法差不多都采取法国法的这种做法, 但源自法国法系的《魁北克民法典》第1478 条却规定：“数人引起的损害, 依他们各自过错的严重程度的比例分担责任。”同样, 第1480 条规定：“数人共同参与了导致损害的过错行为或分别犯有可以导致损害的过错的, 在这两种情形, 如不能确定损害实际上由他们中的何人或诸过错中的何过错引起, 则他们就赔偿此等损害负连带责任。”按照这样的规定, 在多数人侵权行为中, 原则上是分别侵权行为, 由行为人分担责任, 在共同参与的共同侵权行为和共同危险行为中, 才承担连带责任。从立法逻辑上观察, 这样的作法与通常规定共同侵权行为, 将分别侵权行为作为例外的作法相反, 不仅与法国法系的作法有所区别, 与德国法系的作法也不相同, 值得认真研究。

### 3. 日本法

《日本民法典》对于共同侵权行为的规定基本与《德国民法典》一致, 而学界的解释论却深受法国因果关系理论的影响。《日本民法典》第719 条[27]只规定了夏数原因行为人引发损害中的三种情况, 即第一项前段的狭义共同侵权行为, 第二项的教唆、帮助行为, 以及第三项的加害人不明的情形, 并没有像《德国民法典》第830 条或日本旧民法第378 条那样, 设立一般性的夏数原因行为人引发损害的规定。《日本民法典》虽然通过第719 条规定共同侵权行为应当承担连带赔偿责任, 但是对于共同侵权行为的定义并不明确。对于该条

---

26) 罗结珍译：《法国民法典》, 法律出版社2005 年版, 第1091 页。

27) 第七百十九条数人が共同の不法行为によって他人に损害を加えたときは, 各自が连带してその损害を赔偿する责任を负う。共同行为者のうちいずれの者がその损害を加えたかを知ることができないときも, 同样とする。行为者を教唆した者及び帮助した者は, 共同行为者とみなして, 前项の规定を适用する。

第1 项前段的共同侵权行为的成立要件, 立法者认为有必要存在共同的意思, 但判例采纳了存在客观的关联共同性的认定标准, 如山王川诉讼(最高裁判所判决昭和43 年4 月23 日判例时报519 · 17)、四日市诉讼(津地四日市支判昭和47 年7 月24 日判例时报672 · 30)等判决结果, 认为不需要侵权行为人之间存在意思联络或共同的认识, 只需要客观上共同侵害了他人权利即可。但认为山王川诉讼是单独的侵权行为的观点也不在少数, 近年来学说中主张只有客观性要素并不充分, 还应当存在某些主观性要素的观点, 认为客观性要素和主观性要素应当并用的观点, 以及应当重视共同行为人的实质性关系的观点都是较为有力的主张。28) 可见, 日本侵权法尽管没有直接规定和特别研究分别侵权行为, 但不符合共同侵权行为要求的数人侵权就是分别侵权行为的见解, 则是一致结论。

### 4. 英国法

普通法国家没有共同侵权行为或分别侵权行为的概念, 但通过大量的判例形成了一系列裁判规则。英国学者约翰·萨尔曼德认为, 英国侵权法对此问题的观点是, "数人若没有共同实施不法行为, 但造成共同的损害结果, 应对此结果在法律上和事实上负责", 但只应"分别对同一损害负责, 而不是共同对同一损害负责"。29) 这一意见特别鲜明地表明了分别侵权行为的存在和地位。英国法学家帕特里克·阿蒂亚则总结了英国法中两种连带责任的情形, 即"协同行动的数侵权人对全部损害负责, 即使可以确定每个人对最终损害的贡献, 协助或鼓励他人请求的也是如此", 以及"对于数人虽非协同行动, 但因过错行为相结合导致损害的, 全体须对全部损害负责, 只要无法区分个人的贡献。"这一主张区分了协同行动致害与偶然结合致害, 认为前者承担连带责任, 而后者在可以区分出不同行为人导致之损害时, 不承担连带责任。30) 帕特里克·阿蒂亚的这个论述, 区分了共同侵权行为与分别侵权行为的基本界限。

---

28) 参考塩崎勤编著、『判例にみる共同不法行为责任』、新日本法规出版、2007 年3 月19 日、P436－439。

29) 王利明：≪侵权行为法归责原则研究≫, 中国政法大学出版社2004 年版, 第357 页。

30) See Patrick Atiyah, Peter Cane, Atiyah's Accidents, Compensation and the Law, Weidenfeld and Nicholson, London, 1980, 4th.pp.140-141.转引自叶金强：≪共同侵权的类型要素及法律效果≫,≪中国法学≫ 2010 年第1 期。

### 5. 美国法

美国侵权法上的连带责任适用范围经历了近代扩张和现代萎缩的起伏历史，近30 年来，美国各州的侵权法呈现了倾向对连带责任的废除与限制的趋势。2000 年美国法学会《侵权法重述·第三次·责任分担编》第11 条规定了单独责任的效力，[31] 第17 条规定了独立侵权行为人的连带责任或单独责任，[32] 第18 条则是关于数个侵权行为人对不可分伤害的责任的规定。[33] 由于损害的不可分性是适用连带责任的关键，而除了数个被告单独造成的损害，如下情况也被认为是可分损害：(1)一被告造成了全部损害，而另一被告只造成了部分损害；(2)被告造成了部分损害，而合法行为造成了其他损害；(3)数个相继造成的损害；(4)受害人自己行为造成的可分损害。[34] 如果属于可分损害，则先不考虑其侵权责任分担的问题，而是将可分损害分割为数个不可分损害后再讨论责任的分担，这在一定程度上限制了连带责任的广泛应用。单独责任的概念，就是按份责任的概念。美国侵权法关于数人侵权的单独责任的规定，就是分别侵权行为承担按份责任的规则。

值得重视的是美国侵权法提出的市场份额规则。美国加利福尼亚州上诉法院1980 年审理的辛德尔诉阿伯特制药厂案(Sindell V. Abbort Laboratories)，被告为制造安胎药之药商，该药物名为 diethylstilbestrol，简称DES，行销多年后发现其中含有致癌物质，服用该药之孕妇日后产出之女婴，易罹患癌症。原告辛德尔的母亲曾于怀孕期间经由医师处方服用该种药物，致使原告成年后患有癌症。原告以生产该药而市场占有率共计九成以上之五家药商为共同被告(实际生产厂商约有二百家)，起诉请求损害赔偿。一审事实审法院驳回原告之诉。上诉审法院判决原告胜诉，认定五家药商均有过失，每家药商须为损害之发生负全部之赔偿责任(连带责任)。阿伯特化工厂(Abbott Laboratories)上诉加州最高法院，判决原判决废弃，各个被告公司不须负全部之赔偿责任，仅须依其产品之市场占有率比例分担之(按份责任)。[35]

---

31) 第11 条："当依据适用的法律，某人对受害人的不可分损害承担单独责任时，该受害人仅可以获得该负单独责任者在该受害人应得赔偿额中的比较责任份额。"

32) 第17 条："如有两人或多人的独立侵权行为构成某一不可分损害的法律原因，将由该案司法管辖区的法律确定这些侵权人应否承担连带责任、单独责任或连带责任与单独责任的某种混合责任形态。"

33) 第18 条："如果两个或两个以上人的独立侵权行为构成一不可分损害的法律原因，每个人均对事实调查人分配给该人的原告损害赔偿的比较责任份额承担单独责任，适用本重述第12 条例外规定的除外。"

34) 参见王竹：《侵权责任分担论——侵权损害赔偿责任数人分担的一般理论》，中国人民大学出版社 2009 年版，第17~23 页。

加州最高法院确定五家药商对同一损害须负责任，但以按份责任确定，独具新意，引发了前述德国的讨论，以及我国《侵权责任法》第67 条规定的确立。

## 6. 我国台湾地区法

我国台湾地区民法第185 条第1 款规定："数人共同不法侵害他人之权利者，连带负损害赔偿责任。不能知其中孰为加害人者，亦同。"这一规定采自德国立法例，至为明显。在解释上，认为共同侵权行为者，数人共同不法侵害他人权利或利益之行为也。[36] 具体包括主观(意思联络) 共同加害行为和客观行为关联共同的共同加害行为，其后果都是由各行为人承担连带责任。[37] 在实务中认为，各行为人既无意思联络，其行为又无关连共同者，非共同侵权行为，例如他人所有物而为数人个别所侵害，若各加害人并无意思上之联络，只能由各加害人各就其所加害之部分，分别负赔偿责任。[38] 所谓的非共同侵权行为，自然就是分别侵权行为；分别负赔偿责任，当然是按份责任。这个结论自属当然。

## 7. 比较结论

### (1) 立法例

通过上述比较法的研究可以看到，各国规范分别侵权行为，主要采取以下方式进行：

一是间接承认分别侵权行为。这种作法是通过立法规定共同侵权行为，确定不符合共同侵权行为要件的数人侵权行为的数个行为人各自承担侵权责任的方式， 间接承认分别侵权行为，即非共同侵权行为。台湾地区司法实务关于各行为人既无意思联络，其行为又无关连共同者，非共同侵权行为，分别负赔偿责任的观点，特别具有典型性。

---

35) 该案参见潘维大：《英美侵权行为法案例解析》(上)，台湾地区瑞兴图书股份有限公司2002 年版，第270 页。

36) 郑玉波著、陈荣隆修订：《债法总论》，中国政法大学出版社2004 年版，第140 页。

37) 参见王泽鉴，《侵权行为》，北京大学出版社2012 年版，第356、360 页。

38) 台上字第1960 号判决书，见刘清景主编：《民法实务全览(上册)》，学知出版事业股份有限公司 2000 年版，第370 页。

二是直接确认分别侵权行为。这种立法例是直接承认分别侵权行为，并将共同侵权行为的连带责任作为特例规定。对此，《魁北克民法典》第1478 条和第1480 条规定是最具有特色的。第1478 条直接规定分别承担侵权责任的数人侵权即分别侵权行为，其中符合连带责任条件的，方承担连带责任。

三是判例法普遍承认单独责任的分别侵权行为。在英美法系侵权法中，对于承担单独责任的数人侵权行为，尽管没有界定其称谓，但明确认为数人若没有共同实施不法行为，但造成共同的损害结果，应对此结果在法律上和事实上负责，分别对同一损害负责，而不是共同对同一损害负责，是极为明确的。英美法上的单独责任，其实就是大陆法系侵权法的按份责任，承担按份责任的侵权行为当然就是分别侵权行为。

### (2) 立法发展趋向

经过比较法的分析可以看到，在立法上，英美法侵权法是确认承担单独责任的数人侵权的。在大陆法系，一方面，在更多的领域采用按份责任的方法，限制共同侵权行为的连带责任范围，例如市场份额规则的做法； 另一方面，出现单独规定承担按份责任的多数人侵权的直接的立法例，对分别侵权行为的间接立法例似乎也在变化中。我国《侵权责任法》不仅规定共同侵权行为及其连带责任，而且特别规定分别侵权行为及其责任，将两者并立于多数人侵权行为的概念体系之中，完全符合世界侵权法的发展趋势，应当继续坚持和发展，并且提出完善的理论，使之汇入世界侵权法发展的潮流中来，并发挥引导作用。

## Ⅲ. 分别侵权行为概念的内涵界定

### 1. 称谓的选择

对于《侵权责任法》第11 条和第12 条规定的、带有"分别"二字的多数人侵权行为类型，究竟应当如何称谓，我国学界有无意思联络的数人侵权责任、[39] 无意思联络的数人侵权行

---

39) 王利明：《侵权责任法研究(上卷)》，中国人民大学出版社2010 年版，第569 页；程啸：《侵权责任法》，法律出版社2011 年版，第270 页。

为、40) 数人承担按份的侵权责任、41) 无过错联系的共同加害行为42)以及分别侵权行为43)
等概念的不同主张。究竟应当用何种概念称谓这种侵权行为形态为妥，分析如下：第一，凡
是用"无意思联络"字样的概念，都不能界定这种侵权行为的特征，也不能以其与共同侵权行
为相区别。所谓无意思联络，就是指数行为人之间不具有共同故意。问题是，我国《侵权责
任法》第8 条规定的共同侵权行为并非以共同故意为界限， 而是包括客观的共同侵权行
为。其中"共同"的含义，一是共同故意，二是共同过失，三是故意行为与过失行为相结合，而
并非只包括共同故意。44) 既然如此，将这种侵权行为形态称之为"无意思联络"，就会与第8
条规定中的共同过失、故意行为与过失行为相结合的形态相混淆，无法区分其界限，因此不
宜使用。

第二，"数人承担按份的侵权责任"这种概念也有不当。一是这个概念过于冗长，不适宜
使用；二是"按份的"侵权责任不能包含第11 条规定的情形，将承担连带责任的分别侵权行
为排斥在外，只能包含第12 条规定的情形。

第三，无过错联系的共同加害行为或者无过错联系的数人侵权这两个概念都是比较准确
的,与分别侵权行为概念的内涵基本相等， 但其缺陷是概念称谓过于冗长，不如分别侵权行
为这个概念更为简洁，更为准确。

基于以上分析，对于《侵权责任法》第11 条和第12 条使用"分别实施"一词规定的侵权
行为形态，直接称其为分别侵权行为，既符合这两个条文的内容，又直接使用的是条文的"分
别"概念，应当是一个最好的选择。


## 2. 分别侵权行为概念内涵的界定

对分别侵权行为概念的界定，学者的意见各不相同。有的认为，所谓无意思联络的数人
侵权,指数个行为人并无共同的过错而因为行为偶然结合致受害人遭受同一损害。45) 有的认

---

40) 王成：《侵权责任法》，北京大学出版社2011 年版，第117 页。
41) 张新宝：《侵权责任法》，中国人民大学出版社2010 年版，第47 页。
42) 杨立新：《侵权责任法》，法律出版社2012 年第2 版，第123 页。
43) 杨立新：《多数人侵权行为及责任理论的新发展》，《法学》2012 年第7 期。
44) 王胜明主编：《<中华人民共和国侵权责任法>条文理解与立法背景》，人民法院出版社2010 年版，第47 页。

为，数人承担按份的侵权责任，是指数个责任主体承担共同侵权责任之情形，每一个责任主体只对其应当承担的责任份额负清偿义务，不与其他责任主体发生连带关系的侵权责任。[46] 有的认为，无过错联系的共同加害行为是指数个行为人事先既没有共同的意思联络，也没有共同过失，只是由于行为在客观上的联系而共同造成同一个损害结果。[47] 有的认为，无意思联络的数人侵权是指数个行为人并无共同的过错，但由于数个行为的结合而导致同一损害后果的侵权行为。[48]

上述这些概念界定，在基本问题上是一致的，都是有道理，但应注意的是，界定分别侵权行为不能特别强调按份责任，因为《侵权责任法》第11 条承担的责任不是按份责任而是连带责任，强调按份责任就将其排斥在分别侵权行为之外。

我们主张采用下述定义：分别侵权行为是指数个行为人分别实施侵权行为，既没有共同故意，也没有共同过失，只是由于各自行为在客观上的联系，造成同一个损害结果的多数人侵权行为。

分别侵权行为具有以下法律特征：

### (1) 两个以上的行为人分别实施侵权行为

分别侵权行为最基本的特征，是行为人为两人以上，因此符合多数人侵权行为的要求，属于多数人侵权行为的范畴。

两个以上的行为人实施的行为是分别进行的。所谓"分别"，与《侵权责任法》第8 条的"共同"相对应，含义是：第一，数个行为人各自进行，自己实施自己的侵权行为，客观上没有关联共同；第二，各个行为人在各自实施侵权行为时，没有主观上的联系，既没有共同故意，也没有共同过失。分别侵权行为人实际上对于其他各自实施造成他人损害的行为不知情，如果数个行为人有主观上的联系，就不构成分别侵权行为。

45) 王利明：《侵权责任法研究(上卷)》，中国人民大学出版社2010 年版，第569 页。
46) 张新宝：《侵权责任法》，中国人民大学出版社2010 年版，第47 页。
47) 杨立新：《侵权责任法》，法律出版社2012 年第2 版，第123 页。
48) 王成：《侵权责任法》，北京大学出版社2011 年版，第117 页。

(2) 数个行为人实施的行为在客观上针对同一个侵害目标

分别侵权行为的数个行为人在实施侵权行为时，尽管没有主观上的联系，但在客观上，每一个行为人实施的侵权行为实际上都针对同一个侵害目标。

所谓同一个侵害目标，一是指受害人是同一主体，二是指受到损害的是同一主体的民事权利，通常是同一个权利，也有特例。在数个行为人分别实施侵权行为时，受到侵害的是同一主体的同一个权利，当然是同一个侵害目标；受到侵害的是同一主体的不同权利，例如有的行为人侵害的是同一主体的人身权利，有的行为侵害的是同一主体的财产权利，由于受到侵害的权利的性质不同，不能构成分别侵权行为，而是不同的侵权行为；但在数个行为人实施的侵权行为侵害的是同一主体且性质相同的不同权利时，例如数个行为侵害了同一受害人的姓名权、名誉权，则构成分别侵权行为。

所谓的实际上，是说数个行为人实施的行为在客观上现实地目标一致。数个行为人在实施行为时，针对的同一个侵害目标并非出自行为人的本意，而是每一个行为人自己的主观选择，或者客观地针对着这个侵害目标。主观选择，是行为人故意实施的侵权行为，或者过失实施的侵权行为(懈怠)，对于侵害目标是有选择的，有明确的目的，或者存在侵害该目标的意向。客观地针对着该侵害目标，是实施过失行为(疏忽)或者在无过错责任原则情形下，侵权行为针对着该侵害目标。不论故意或者过失，数个行为人之间对于同一个侵害目标不是共同选择，而是分别针对，在主观上没有关联。

(3) 每一个人的行为都是损害发生的共同原因或者各自原因

分别侵权行为的数个行为人的行为都作用于同一侵害目标，是损害发生的共同原因，或者是损害发生的各自原因。共同原因，是数个行为人的行为结合在一起，共同作用于受害人的权利，集中地造成了受害人的同一个损害。各自原因，是数个行为人的行为分别作用于受害人的权利，造成了受害人同一权利的损害后果。前者例如，有缺陷的淋浴热水器与有缺陷的漏电保护器两件产品结合在一起，共同造成洗浴的人的死亡后果。[49] 后者例如，数个行为人中有的进行诽谤，有的进行侮辱，使同一个受害人受到名誉损害。

---

49) 王利明：《侵权责任法研究(上卷)》，中国人民大学出版社2010 年版，第569~570 页。

在分别侵权行为中，就数个侵权行为对于损害发生的原因力而言，有两种情形：一是数个行为人行为的原因力相加，等于百分之百；二是，数个行为人行为的原因力相加，超过百分之百。前者如淋浴器与漏电保护器的结合。后者例如两个行为人先后向他人饲料中投毒，均有百分之百的原因力，相加为百分之二百。在分别侵权行为中，前者的原因力比例对于分担责任具有决定性作用，原因力决定责任份额；后者的原因力将导致责任的连带承担，内部份额的确定应当按照原因力相加并处以行为人数的比例确定。

### (4) 造成了同一个损害结果且该结果可以分割

分别侵权行为的一个本质特点，是虽然造成了一个损害结果，但该结果可以分割。在对物的损害中，这种情形尤为明显。例如，甲用汽车运送的现金因肇事撒落，数人涌上争抢，每个人对受害人造成的损害就是可分的。如果受害人所受到的损害不能分割，就有可能属于客观关连共同的共同侵权行为，不构成分别侵权行为。

上述关于对分别侵权行为概念的法律特征的分析，都比较抽象。如果从司法实践的角度进行研究，实际上在数人实施的侵权行为中，排除了竞合侵权行为和第三人侵权行为之后，分为四个等级：(1)主观的共同侵权行为；(2)客观的共同侵权行为；(3)分别侵权行为；(4) 各行为人的单独侵权行为。对于那些不符合客观的共同侵权行为要求的二人以上的行为人实施的侵权行为，又不是各个行为人单独实施的侵权行为的，就是分别侵权行为。

## 3. 与其他多数人侵权行为的联系与区别

### (1) 分别侵权行为与共同侵权行为

分别侵权行为与共同侵权行为都是多数人侵权行为，其行为主体都是复数即二人以上，都是造成同一个损害结果。分别侵权行为与共同侵权行为的主要区别是：第一，行为人实施侵权行为的性质不同，一为分别实施，二为共同实施。分别者，为各自实施，行为人之间在主观上没有相互联系。共同者，为共同实施，数个行为人或者在主观上相联系，具有主观的意思联络，或者在客观上有联系，数个行为结合在一起，造成同一个损害结果。第二，造

成的同一个损害后果是否可分。损害后果可分的， 一般是分别侵权行为；损害后果不可分的， 一般是共同侵权行为， 通常是客观的共同侵权行为。主观的共同侵权行为不作此区分，因为主观方面已经能够将分别侵权行为和共同侵权行为相区别。

### (2) 分别侵权行为与竞合侵权行为

竞合侵权行为是指两个以上的民事主体作为侵权人， 有的实施直接侵权行为， 与损害结果具有直接因果关系， 有的实施间接侵权行为， 与损害结果的发生具有间接因果关系， 行为人承担不真正连带责任的多数人侵权行为形态。[50]   分别侵权行为与竞合侵权行为尽管都是多数人侵权行为， 行为人都是二人以上， 也都是造成同一个损害结果， 但二者的主要区别是：首先， 分别侵权行为的数个行为人实施的行为都是直接侵害被侵权人的权利的行为， 不存在具有间接因果关系的间接行为人； 而在竞合侵权行为的数个行为人中， 有的行为人实施的行为是直接行为， 有的实施的行为是间接行为。其次， 在竞合侵权行为中， 有的行为是损害发生的全部原因， 具有百分之百的原因力， 有的行为仅是损害发生的间接原因， 属于提供必要条件或者提供机会的性质； 而分别侵权行为的数个行为人的行为都是损害发生的直接原因， 都具有直接的原因力。再次， 竞合侵权行为造成的损害结果就是直接行为引发的，直接行为是损害发生的全部原因， 造成的损害结果不存在可分不可分的问题， 与分别侵权行为的同一损害结果须为可分的情形完全不同。

### (3) 分别侵权行为与第三人侵权行为

第三人侵权行为是指第三人由于过错， 通过实际加害人的直接行为或者间接行为， 造成被侵权人民事权利损害， 应当由第三人承担侵权责任、实际加害人免除责任的多数人侵权行为。第三人侵权行为的最主要特点是实际加害人造成损害， 第三人的过错是全部原因， 造成的损害行为只有这一个， 只有第三人承担责任， 实际加害人不承担责任；实际加害人的行为尽管是造成损害的原因， 但其对损害的发生毫无过错。而分别侵权行为中的每一个行为人都是造成实际损失的加害人， 每一个行为人对于损害的发生都有过错， 每一个行为人都是

---

50) 杨立新：《论竞合侵权行为》，《清华法学》2013 年第1 期。

责任人。因此，第三人侵权行为与分别侵权行为尽管都是多数人侵权行为，但在性质上有原则区别。

## Ⅳ. 分别侵权行为概念的外延界定

### 1. 分别侵权行为概念的外延

《侵权责任法》规定的分别侵权行为究竟包括哪些内容，学者的意见并不相同。

一种意见认为，分别侵权行为只包括第12 条规定的内容，即只有承担按份责任的分别侵权行为，第11 条规定的情形属于叠加的共同侵权行为，不属于共同侵权行为。[51] 这种意见的基础，是认为凡是分别侵权行为都承担按份责任，将承担连带责任的第11 条规定的情形放在共同侵权行为概念之中，使多数人侵权行为的类型以责任形态作为标准，划分比较整齐，逻辑更加清晰。

另一种意见认为，将《侵权责任法》第11 条和第12 条都作为一种类型的侵权行为形态划分，都是无意思联络的数人侵权，分别称之为"累积因果关系的无意思联络数人侵权"和"聚合因果关系的无意思联络数人侵权"，[52] 也有学者称之为"多数人无过错联系但承担连带责任的分别侵权"与"多数人无过错联系但承担按份责任的分别侵权"。[53]

这两种不同意见的焦点，在于将《侵权责任法》第11 条规定的侵权行为认定为共同侵权行为还是分别侵权行为。依据第11 条内容观察，对侵权行为的表述是"分别实施侵权行为"，对后果责任的表述是"连带责任"。如果依据责任后果的规定将其界定为共同侵权行为，没有特别的错误；依据对侵权行为的表述将其界定为分别侵权行为，则更为准确。将其界定为共同侵权行为的好处是，责任后果与共同侵权行为同属于一个类型，都承担连带责任，且与规定共同侵权行为、教唆帮助行为和共同危险行为相衔接，似乎顺理成章；同时，共同侵权行为增加一个类型，分别侵权行为减少一个类型。如果将其界定为分别侵权行为，则分

---

51) 杨立新：《侵权责任法》，法律出版社2012 年第2 版，第124、113 页

52) 王利明：《侵权责任法研究(上卷)》，中国人民大学出版社2011 年版，第572 页。

53) 竺效：《论无过错联系之数人环境侵权行为的类型——兼论致害人不明数人环境侵权责任承担的司法审理》，《中国法学》，2011 年第5 期。

别侵权行为的外延比较复杂, 将有两种不同的分别侵权行为, 分别承担按份责任或者连带责任 ; 同样, 共同侵权行为减少一个类型, 分别侵权行为增加一个类型。

经过比较分析研究, 将《侵权责任法》第11 条规定的侵权行为界定为共同侵权行为还是分别侵权行为的利弊相差无几。不过, 有一个重要的问题促使我们下决心, 那就是, 既然《侵权责任法》第11 条对侵权行为的表述是"分别实施侵权行为", 第12 条对侵权行为的表述也是"分别实施侵权行为", 因而从行为形态的角度进行界定, 应当认定第11 条和第12 条规定的侵权行为类型是同一种侵权行为形态, 即分别侵权行为。因此, 我们告别原来的主张, 采用现在的这种主张。

《侵权责任法》第11 条规定的分别侵权行为究竟应当怎样称谓, 有的称之为"累积的",[54] 有的称之为"叠加的",[55] 有的称之为"承担连带责任的"。[56] 我们认为, "累积的"表述只表述了行为原因重合的形式, 属于定性表述, 而不是定量表述。"承担连带责任"的表述则过于直白, 没有将这种侵权行为固定称谓。"叠加的"表述, 既有定性表述, 又有定量表述, 因此, 称之为叠加的分别侵权行为, 更为明确、准确。

《侵权责任法》第12 条规定的分别侵权行为, 由于过去我们将分别侵权行为只界定为这一种, 因此不存在命名的问题。[57] 将叠加的分别侵权行为归并为分别侵权行为之后, 对此必须命名, 以与叠加的分别侵权行为相区别。对此, 有的将其称之为"数人承担按份的",[58] 有的称之为"承担按份责任的",[59] 有的称之为"聚合的"或者"以部分因果关系表现的"。[60] 这些表述都对, 但是, 我们的意见是, 称作典型的分别侵权行为可能会更好, 因为在通常情况下, 凡是分别侵权行为就应当承担按份责任, 而叠加的分别侵权行为是分别侵权行为的非典型形态。不过, "典型的"表述与"聚合的"、"承担按份责任的"或者"以部分因果关系表现的"表述都没有实质的区别。

据此, 分别侵权行为概念的外延包括典型的分别侵权行为和叠加的分别侵权行为。在分

---

54) 王利明 :《侵权责任研究(上卷)》, 中国人民大学出版社2011 年版, 第535 页。

55) 张新宝 :《侵权责任法》, 中国人民大学出版社2010 年第2 版, 第45 页。

56) 王成 :《侵权责任法》, 北京大学出版社2011 年版, 第117 页。

57) 杨立新 :《多数人侵权行为与责任理论的新发展》,《法学》 2013 年第1 期。

58) 张新宝 :《侵权责任法》, 中国人民大学出版社2010 年第2 版, 第47 页。

59) 王成 :《侵权责任法》, 北京大学出版社2011 年版, 第117 页。

60) 王利明 :《侵权责任法研究(上卷)》, 中国人民大学出版社2010 年版, 第572、576 页。

别实施侵权行为的数人中, 一人的侵权行为足以导致全部损害的发生, 而另一人的侵权行为却仅能造成部分损害的情形,[61] 究竟属于叠加的分别侵权行为, 还是属于典型的分别侵权行为, 有的归之于典型的分别侵权行为,[62] 有的归之于叠加的分别侵权行为。[63] 我们认为, 这种情形尽管《侵权责任法》没有明确规定, 应当属于两种分别侵权行为类型的中间状态, 更侧重于原因力的叠加, 应当属于部分叠加或者半叠加的分别侵权行为。

故分别侵权行为的外延可以界定为: 分别侵权行为分为典型的分别侵权行为和叠加的侵权行为两种; 叠加的分别侵权行为分为全部叠加的分别侵权行为与半叠加的分别侵权行为。

### 2. 典型的分别侵权行为

#### (1) 典型的分别侵权行为的概念和特点

典型的分别侵权行为, 是指数个行为人分别实施侵权行为, 既没有共同故意, 也没有共同过失, 只是由于行为人各自行为在客观上的联系而造成同一个损害结果, 应当承担按份责任的分别侵权行为。

典型的分别侵权行为与共同侵权行为最为相似, 二者相比较, 显著区别有以下四点:

第一, 在主观上, 分别侵权行为人没有共同过错, 既不存在主观上的意思联络, 也不可能对自己的行为会与他人的行为发生结合造成被侵权人的同一损害有事先的预见, 既没有共同故意也没有共同过失。而共同侵权行为在主观方面有的是具有共同的意思联络, 或者具有共同过失。

第二, 在客观上, 分别侵权行为的数个行为人的行为是分别实施的, 尽管造成了同一个损害结果, 但该损害结果是可以分割的, 而不是不可分割。而客观的共同侵权行为中的数个行为人虽然也既没有共同故意或者共同过失, 但是他们的行为紧密关联, 构成了一个侵权行为, 造成了同一个损害, 而且该损害结果是不可以分割的。

---

61) 程啸:《侵权责任法》, 法律出版社2011 年版, 第274 页。
62) 程啸:《侵权责任法》, 法律出版社2011 年版, 第274 页。
63) 杨立新:《侵权责任法》, 法律出版社2012 年第2 版, 第113 页。

第三，在行为的表现形式上，分别侵权行为的每一个行为人实施的行为，都是一个个的单独的行为是行为人分别实施的数个侵权行为，只是由于行为在客观上造成了同一个损害结果。而共同侵权行为是一个侵权行为，即使数人实施，但该数个行为在主观上关连共同，或者在客观上关连共同，构成完整的、单独的、独立的侵权行为，在行为的数量上只是一个侵权行为。

第四，在后果上，分别侵权行为承担的法律后果是按份责任，每一个行为人只对自己的行为引起的损害后果承担按份责任，而不是对整体的行为后果承担连带责任。而共同侵权行为承担的法律后果是连带责任，每一个共同侵权人都对整体的损害后果承担全部的赔偿责任，实行对外连带对内也连带。

综合起来，认定典型的分别侵权行为的构成要件是：第一，行为人为二人以上；第二，数个行为人都分别实施了侵权行为；第三，数个行为人的行为不构成引起损害发生的同一原因，而是各个行为对损害后果的发生分别产生作用，具有原因力；[64]第四，数人的行为造成同一个损害结果，损害结果具有同一性。符合这些要件要求的，构成典型的分别侵权行为。可以得出一个结论，即数人侵权，行为人有共同故意的，对于损害后果不存在可分不可分的问题，都属于共同侵权行为；对于客观的共同侵权行为与典型的分别侵权行为，因无主观上的关连，因此，通常认为，同一损害后果不可分的，为客观共同侵权行为，同一损害后果可分的，[65]为典型的分别侵权行为。

### (2) 典型的分别侵权行为的按份责任

对于分别侵权行为的赔偿责任应当如何承担，历史上曾经有过不同主张。例如认为："数人主观上无意思联络，仅因行为偶合导致损害后果发生，若各人的加害部分无法单独确定，则应以共同侵权论，各人对损害应承担连带赔偿责任。"[66] 这是说，对无过错联系的数人致害，能确定各人的损害部分的，就单独承担责任；如果各人的加害部分无法单独确定，则承担连带责任。也有的认为，各人的损害部分能够单独确定行为人的，只对自己行为的后果

---

64) 张新宝：《侵权责任法原理》，中国人民大学出版社2005 年版，第82 页。
65) 美国侵权法关于单独责任的规则，实际上就是采用这样的标准。
66) 蓝承烈：《连带侵权责任及其内部求偿权》，《法学实践》1991 年第1 期。

负责；如果各行为人的加害部分无法单独确定，则应按公平原则，由法院根据案件的具体情况，令行为人分担适当的责任。[67] 这些不同意见，经过讨论和实践，后来都统一了，都认为既然构成分别侵权行为，就应当各自承担按份责任，并不实行连带责任。理由是，无过错联系的各行为人没有共同过错，不具备共同侵权行为的本质特征，因而也就不应当承担共同侵权行为的民事责任，而共同侵权行为的责任以连带责任为特点。如果令无过错联系的共同加害行为人承担连带责任，则是将其作为共同侵权行为处理了。反之，依照按份责任处理，则既考虑了这种行为与共同侵权行为的区别，也体现了这种行为本身对其责任形态的要求。《侵权责任法》第12 条采纳了这种意见，确定典型的分别侵权行为承担按份责任。

因而，确定典型的分别侵权行为的责任，应当依照以下规则处理：第一，各个分别侵权行为人对各自的行为所造成的后果承担责任。典型的分别侵权行为属于单独侵权而非共同侵权，各行为人的行为只是单独行为，只能对其行为所造成的损害后果负责。在损害结果单独确定的前提下，应当责令各行为人就其行为所造成的损害承担赔偿责任。这是按份责任的体现。

第二，依照分别侵权行为人各自行为的原因力确定责任份额。各行为人在共同损害结果无法确定自己的行为所造成的后果时，按照各行为人所实施行为的原因力，按份额各自承担责任。分别侵权行为的多数情况是有一个共同的损害结果。因此应当将赔偿责任确定为一个整体责任，依据各行为人的行为对损害后果的原因力划分责任份额，由各行为人按照自己的份额承担责任。第三，无法区分原因力的应当平均承担责任，确定各自应当承担责任份额。第四，不实行连带责任，各个行为人只对自己的份额承担责任，不对他人的行为后果负责赔偿。

### 3. 叠加的分别侵权行为

#### (1) 叠加的分别侵权行为的概念和特点

叠加的分别侵权行为是指数个行为人分别实施侵权行为，既没有共同故意，也没有共同

---

67) 王利明：《侵权行为法归责原则研究》，中国政法大学出版社1992 年版，第296 页。

过失, 每一个行为都足以引起损害结果, 或者部分行为足以引起损害结果部分行为具有部分原因力, 因行为叠加而造成同一个损害结果, 应当承担连带责任的分别侵权行为。

叠加的分别侵权行为与共同侵权行为相比较, 最突出的特点是行为人实施的侵权行为是分别实施, 是数个侵权行为的结合, 而不是一个侵权行为。而共同侵权行为不论是主观的共同侵权行为, 还是客观的共同侵权行为, 都是由于行为人的主观意思联络, 或者因共同过失, 或者因客观的关连共同, 而使数人实施的行为成为一个侵权行为, 因此是一个完整的连带责任。例如, 前一个肇事司机将行人撞成致命伤后逃逸, 后一个肇事司机将被侵权人轧死, 两个行为人的行为都足以造成被侵权人死亡的后果。又如, 一个人将他人的内脏刺伤, 另一个又刺伤其内脏, 两处刺伤均为致命伤, 造成死亡结果。这两种情形都构成叠加的分别侵权行为, 都与共同侵权行为不同。

《侵权责任法》第11 条规定的叠加的分别侵权行为, 与典型的分别侵权行为的主要区别在于, 典型的分别侵权行为是每一个行为人实施的侵权行为的原因力相加, 刚好等于百分之百的原因力。而叠加的分别侵权行为的每一个行为人实施的侵权行为的原因力相加, 高于百分之百的原因力, 甚至百分之二百, 或者更多。叠加的分别侵权行为, 每一个行为人实施的行为对于损害的发生都具有百分之百的原因力, 都足以造成全部损害。即使是半叠加的分别侵权行为, 部分人的行为具有百分之百的原因力, 部分人的行为不具有百分之百的原因力, 但是原因力相加, 仍然高于百分之百, 因而与典型的分别侵权行为完全不同。

## (2) 叠加的分别侵权行为承担连带责任

叠加的分别侵权行为中的数人承担连带责任。其基本规则是:

### 1) 对外的中间责任

连带责任的对外效力, 是一个侵权责任。被侵权人可以向数个行为人中的任何一个行为人请求承担全部赔偿责任, 每一个分别侵权行为人都应当就全部损害承担赔偿责任。对此, 应当依照《侵权责任法》第13 条规定的规则承担中间责任。

### 2) 对内的最终责任

连带责任的内部效力，是对数个连带责任人确定最终责任，应当按照份额确定。对此，应当按照《侵权责任法》第14条规定的规则进行。一是连带责任人根据各自责任大小确定相应的赔偿数额，难以确定责任大小的，平均承担赔偿责任。二是承担中间责任超过自己赔偿数额的连带责任人，有权向其他连带责任人追偿，实现最终责任。

在确定份额上，叠加的分别侵权行为的连带责任与共同侵权行为的连带责任的责任份额确定有所不同。构成共同侵权行为，其确定责任份额的基本方法是按照每一个共同侵权人的过错程度和行为原因力大小比例。事实上，每一个共同侵权人的过错比例和原因力比例是多少，就承担多大的份额责任。由于叠加的分别侵权行为的每一个侵权人的行为原因力相加超过百分之百，因此不能依照过错比例和行为的原因力确定责任份额，只能按照每一个人的行为的原因力相加，再按照行为人的数量相除，按照原因力的平均比例，确定每一个行为人的责任份额。

全叠加的分别侵权行为，两个以上的行为人分别实施的行为，每一个行为人对于损害的发生都具有全部的即百分之百的原因力，每个人都应当承担全部赔偿责任。而每一个加害人的行为都构成侵权行为，都对被侵权人承担全部赔偿责任，被侵权人的损害只有一个，每一个侵权人都承担全部责任，将会使受害人得到超出损害的不当赔偿，这不符合大陆法系侵权法填补损害的基本规则，因此只有承担一个全部赔偿责任，就能够保证被侵权人的损害赔偿请求权得到满足。只有按照连带责任确定数个侵权人的责任最为适当。每个行为人的行为的原因力均为百分之百，但责任份额不能都是百分之百，每个人的责任份额应当为百分之五十，在此基础上实行连带责任。

半叠加的分别侵权行为，是在分别实施侵权行为的数人中，一个人的行为具有百分之百的原因力，另外的人只具有百分之五十的原因力。对此，也应当看做叠加的分别侵权行为，不过叠加的原因力为半叠加而不是全叠加。其后果仍然应当承担连带责任，不过连带责任的内部份额应当随之改变。例如，一个行为的原因力是百分之五十，另一个行为的原因力是百分之百，将两个原因力相加，除以行为人的人数，得到的责任份额即为33.3%和66.7%，即为各自应当承担的责任份额。

## ∙ 摘要 ∙

分别侵权行为是《侵权责任法》第11 条和第12 条规定的侵权行为形态，与共同侵权行为、竞合侵权行为、第三人侵权行为一道构成多数人侵权行为体系。分别侵权行为是指数个行为人分别实施侵权行为，既没有共同故意，也没有共同过失，只是由于各自行为在客观上的联系，造成同一个损害结果的多数人侵权行为。分别侵权行为的外延可以界定为：分别侵权行为分为典型的分别侵权行为和叠加的侵权行为两种；叠加的分别侵权行为分为全叠加的分别侵权行为与半叠加的分别侵权行为。

关键词： 分别侵权行为；概念；内涵；外延；多数人侵权行为

## 参考文献 (References)

中央政法干部学校民法教研室：《中华人民共和国民法基本问题》，法律出版社1958 年版，第331 页。

覃有土、王亘：《债权法》，光明日报出版社1989 年版，第591~593 页。

邓大榜：《共同侵权行为的民事责任初探》，《法学季刊》1982 年第3 期。

沈幼伦：《试析共同侵权行为的特征》，《法学》1987 年第1 期。

伍再阳：《意思联络是共同侵权行为的必要要件》，《法学季刊》1984 年第2 期。

这个意见错误的根源在于，将干部出差所带的费用作为单位的所有权对待。须知，货币是动产，干部借公

款出差，该公款的所有权已经转移为干部所有，单位对干部的权利是债权，而不是物权。

佟柔主编：《民法原理》，法律出版社1986 年版。

江平主编：《民法教程》，中国政法大学出版社1988 年版。

马原主编：《中国民法教程》，人民法院出版社1989 年版。

王利明：《侵权行为法归责原则研究》，中国政法大学出版社1992 年版，第293 页。

王利明，杨立新：《侵权行为法》，法律出版社1996 年版，第199 页。

王利明：《民法侵权行为法》，中国人民大学出版社1993 年版，第366 页。

王利明，杨立新：《侵权行为法》，法律出版社1996 年版，第201 页。

杨立新：《侵权法论》(上册)，吉林人民出版社2000 年版，第325~328 页。

杨立新：《<中华人民共和国侵权责任法>条文释解与司法适用》，人民法院出版社2010 年版，第66 页。

张新宝：《侵权责任法立法研究》，中国人民大学出版社2009 年版，第245~246 页。

竺效：《论无过错联系之数人环境侵权行为的类型－－兼论致害人不明数人环境侵权责任承担的司法审理》，《中国法学》2011 年第5 期。

杨立新：《多数人侵权行为及责任理论的新发展》，《法学》2012 年第7 期。

杨立新：《论竞合侵权行为》，《清华法学》2013 年第1 期。

杨立新：《多数人侵权行为及责任理论的新发展》，《法学》2012 年第7 期。

Haben mehrere durch gemeinsames Handeln, sei es als Anstifter, Thäer oder Gehüfen, eien Schaden verschuldet, so haften sie als Gesammtschuldner. Das Gleiche gilt, wenn im Falle eines von mehreren verschuldeten Schadens von den mehreren nicht gemeinsam gehandelt, der Antheit des Einzelnen an dem Schaden aber nicht zu ermitteln ist.

参见王泽鉴：《民法学说与判例研究》，第1 册，北京大学出版社2009 年版，第47 页。

参见王泽鉴：《民法学说与判例研究》，第1 册，北京大学出版社2009 年版，第47 页。

《德国新民事诉讼法》第287 条第1 款第1 句规定："当事人对于是否有损害、损害的数额以及应赔偿的利益额有争论时，法院应考虑全部情况，经过自由心证，对此点作出判断。"

朱岩：《当代德国侵权法上因果关系理论和实务中的主要问题》，《法学家》2004 年第6 期。

罗结珍译：《法国民法典》，法律出版社2005 年版，第1091 页。

第七百十九条数人が共同の不法行為によって他人に損害を加えたときは、各自が連帯してその損害を賠償する責任を負う。共同行為者のうちいずれの者がその損害を加えたかを知ることができないときも、同様とする。行為者を教唆した者及び帮助した者は、共同行為者とみなして、前項の規定を適用する。

参考塩崎勤編著、『判例にみる共同不法行為責任』、新日本法規出版、2007 年3 月19 日、P436－439。

王利明：《侵权行为法归责原则研究》，中国政法大学出版社2004 年版，第357 页。

See Patrick Atiyah, Peter Cane, Atiyah's Accidents, Compensation and the Law, Weidenfeld and Nicholson, London, 1980, 4th. pp. 140-141. 转引自叶金强：《共同侵权的类型要素及法律效果》，《中国法学》2010 年第1 期。

第11 条：“当依据适用的法律，某人对受害人的不可分损害承担单独责任时，该受害人仅可以获得该负单独责任者在该受害人应得赔偿额中的比较责任份额。”

第17 条：“如有两人或多人的独立侵权行为构成某一不可分损害的法律原因，将由该案司法管辖区的法律确定这些侵权人应否承担连带责任、单独责任或连带责任与单独责任的某种混合责任形态。”

第18 条：“如果两个或两个以上人的独立侵权行为均构成一不可分损害的法律原因，每个人均对事实调查人分配给该人的原告损害赔偿的比较责任份额承担单独责任，适用本重述第12 条例外规定的除外。”

参见王竹：《侵权责任分担论－－侵权损害赔偿责任数人分担的一般理论》，中国人民大学出版社2009 年版，第17~23 页。

该案参见潘维大：《英美侵权行为法案例解析》(上)，台湾地区瑞兴图书股份有限公司2002 年版，第 270 页。

郑玉波著、陈荣隆修订：《债法总论》，中国政法大学出版社2004 年版，第140 页。

参见王泽鉴，《侵权行为》，北京大学出版社2012 年版，第356、360 页。

台上字第1960 号判决书，见刘清景主编：《民法实务全览(上册)》，学知出版事业股份有限公司2000 年版，第370 页。

王利明：《侵权责任法研究(上卷)》，中国人民大学出版社2010 年版，第569 页；程啸：《侵权责任法》，法律出版社2011 年版，第270 页。

王成：《侵权责任法》，北京大学出版社2011 年版，第117 页。

张新宝：《侵权责任法》，中国人民大学出版社2010 年版，第47 页。

杨立新：《侵权责任法》，法律出版社2012 年第2 版，第123 页。

杨立新：《多数人侵权行为及责任理论的新发展》，《法学》2012 年第7 期。

王胜明主编：《<中华人民共和国侵权责任法>条文理解与立法背景》，人民法院出版社2010 年版，第 47 页。

王利明：《侵权责任法研究(上卷)》，中国人民大学出版社2010 年版，第569 页。

张新宝：《侵权责任法》，中国人民大学出版社2010 年版，第47 页。

杨立新：《侵权责任法》，法律出版社2012 年第2 版，第123 页。

王成：《侵权责任法》，北京大学出版社2011 年版，第117 页。

王利明：《侵权责任法研究(上卷)》，中国人民大学出版社2010 年版，第569~570 页。

杨立新：《论竞合侵权行为》，《清华法学》2013 年第1 期。

杨立新：《侵权责任法》，法律出版社2012 年第2 版，第124、113 页

王利明：《侵权责任法研究(上卷)》，中国人民大学出版社2011 年版，第572 页。

竺效：《论无过错联系之数人环境侵权行为的类型――兼论致害人不明数人环境侵权责任承担的司法审理》，《中国法学》，2011 年第5 期。

王利明：《侵权责任研究(上卷)》，中国人民大学出版社2011 年版，第535 页。

张新宝：《侵权责任法》，中国人民大学出版社2010 年第2 版，第45 页。

王成：《侵权责任法》，北京大学出版社2011 年版，第117 页。

杨立新：《多数人侵权行为与责任理论的新发展》，《法学》2013 年第1 期。

张新宝：《侵权责任法》，中国人民大学出版社2010 年第2 版，第47 页。

王成：《侵权责任法》，北京大学出版社2011 年版，第117 页。

王利明：《侵权责任法研究(上卷)》，中国人民大学出版社2010 年版，第572、576 页。

程啸：《侵权责任法》，法律出版社2011 年版，第274 页。

程啸：《侵权责任法》，法律出版社2011 年版，第274 页。

杨立新：《侵权责任法》，法律出版社2012 年第2 版，第113 页。

张新宝：《侵权责任法原理》，中国人民大学出版社2005 年版，第82 页。

美国侵权法关于单独责任的规则，实际上就是采用这样的标准。

蓝承烈：《连带侵权责任及其内部求偿权》，《法学实践》1991 年第1 期。

王利明：《侵权行为法归责原则研究》，中国政法大学出版社1992 年版，第296 页。

# The Idea of Partnering and the New Development of Construction Contracts

## パートナリングによる建設請負契約の新しい発展

OSAMU KASAI (笠井修)*

*A new method of alliance, "Partnering" has been very quickly developed in the past decade in the field of major construction. It originates from a kind of construction management used in the United States and has become a contract type of construction as "Partnering Contract", adopted in Great Britain, Australia, Hong Kong and other countries to open new opportunities for the growth of dramatic reform for construction projects. The core idea of Partnering consists of mutual trust, information sharing and risk sharing among the companies of project to achieve a sort of business alliance. The concept of Partnering must be crucial for plant exportation as well as domestic construction projects.*

**Key word:** Partnering, Construction Contract, Risk Allocation, Risk Sharing, Mutual Trust, Information Sharing, Plant Exportation

## ▪ はじめに ▪

　今日の建設請負契約には、目覚ましい革新が見られるが、なかでも、「パートナリング」(partnering)の手法が、国際的に注目を集めている。これは、注文者・請負人・下請人という単純な構図ではなく、さらに設計者、資材提供者、コンサルタントなどの建設工事に関与する多数の当事者を取り込んだ、まったく新しい発想の建設請負契約であり、特に大規模な建設請負プロジェクトにおいて、その参加企業の相互信頼、情報共有をもとに、リスクの共有と一種の共同事業を実現する、注目するべき請負形態である。

---

* Professor at Chuo Law School in Tokyo, Japan

パートナリングの考え方は、建設工事のマネジメント手法としてアメリカで生まれたが、今日では、建設請負に關する獨特の契約類型となり、イギリス、オーストラリア、香港などにおいて多数のプロジェクトに採用されて大きな成果をあげつつある。これにより、多くのリスク分配の問題が、これまでとは異なる仕組みの中で解決されようとしている。そしてまた、それは契約法的にも新しい發展の方向と理論的なインパクトを生み出すものである。


## I. 大規模な建設請負契約におけるリスク

### 1. 大規模な建設請負契約における從來の当事者關係

今日の建設工事には、きわめて大規模なものが多くなっているが、そこにはリスクに關する問題も集約的に發生する。例えば、建設プロジェクト、特にプラント輸出[1]のような大規模建設事業は、韓國においても日本においても、ビジネスとしての大きな可能性とともに、プロジェクトの推進環境の予期せぬ変化やそこに参加する多くの企業間の利害對立をはじめとする様々なリスクをあわせもつものとなっている。すなわち、以下のような事情がある。

まず、そのような建設工事プロジェクトの多くは、その契約上の義務内容として、工場や發電所などの大規模施設の建設、機器の製作・据付け、技術の指導・移轉さらには操業の指導等を含む幅廣い業務を對象としている[2]。これらの多くは、請負契約またはそれとの

---

1) プラント輸出は、長く日本の経濟的プレゼンスを象徴する隆盛を維持してきたが、ここに至るには、大きく4期の國際環境の変遷がみられた。すなわち、海外におけるプラント輸出の幕開けとなる第1次石油危機までの黎明期(1970年代前半まで)、専業エンジニアリング會社に加え、造船、重機、重電等の各社エンジニアリング部門の創設やプラント輸出が本格化する成長期(1970年代後半～1980年代前半)、原油価格の低迷に伴う石化プラント等のプロジェクトの停滞、歐米や韓國のE.P.C コントラクターとの競合がはじまる轉換期(1980年代後半)と續いてきた。さらに1990年代に入ると、大手E.P.C コントラクターとの競争、韓國、中國等のE.P.C コントラクターとの価格競争が一層激しさを増すなか、既存分野での競争力の維持に加え、大手企業による寡占化が進展する世界市場での企業間提携の重要性が増大してきた。そして、今世紀に入り、先端技術分野において自らが新たな市場を開拓することやファイナンス技術を生かしたプロジェクト創造の重要性も増大している(1990年代以降)。
2) それは、プラント輸出契約(國際建設契約、エンジニアリング契約)そのものの、大きな変革の中で捉えることができる。しばしが、プラント輸出契約から國際プロジェクト契約への進化と理解されるものである。
具体的には、①契約当事者の複雑化が、國際ジョイントベンチャーやコンソーシアムという横の關係の擴大や、下請けや資材・機器提供者の多様化という縦の關係の変化をもたらしつつある。また、②契約内容の複雑化も急速に進んでいる。たと

混合契約・複合契約である。

　また、これらと同時に、發注者・受注者間の契約のみならず、下請、コンサルタント、資材の調達、保險、ファイナンスをめぐる契約もそれぞれの當事者間で結ばれるのが通常である。

　他方、このような中で、建設請負契約は、諸外國の事情をもながめれば、プロジェクトの推進に關與する複數の企業の一定の「提携」の中で結ばれることが多い[3]。それは建設工事の円滑な推進や、なによりもリスク分配、請負關係における相互補完などを目的とするものであるが、その形態については、プロジェクトの內容・規模によっていくつかの組み合わせの可能性がありうる。例えば、發注者と受注者(主契約者)が建設請負等の契約を結び、これを基本にして、受注者の下に多様な下請契約がなされる、いわゆるサブコン方式がとられることがあり、他方、發注者と企業連合(コンソーシアム)の契約により、複數の企業が共同して受注し、發注者に對して連帶責任を負う、いわゆるコンソーシアム方式が採用されることもある[4]。そして、それらの當事者は複數の國々にまたがることも多い。

　このような、契約構造の複雜さと關與者の多様性のもとで、大規模建設プロジェクトは、しばしば履行環境の変化をはじめとする様々なリスクにさらされることとなる。

---

えば、いわゆるターンキーを內容とする契約から、プロダクト・イン・ハンドという安定した製品の生産にまでを請け負う契約へと廣がり、さらには、BOT(Build, Operate, Transfer)という一定期間の操業による利益確保を可能にする形態も多くみられるようになってきた。他方、③資金調達の方法においても、公的借款の供与からプロジェクト・ファイナンスへと変化が見られる。そして、これらの変化に對応するべく、國際的な標準約款も改訂を繰り返しており、その規律が急速に發展しつつある。

このような、プラント輸出をめぐる契約の変化の一方で、これを規律する契約法のあり方については、その法的性質や準拠法をはじめとして、理論的整備を必要とする多くの論点が殘されており、それらの問題点を研究し、新しい時代のプラント輸出契約法を形成することは、今日、喫緊の課題となっている。

3)　企業間提携の目的、手段、起こりうる問題に對する判斷要素については、J.R.ハービンソン＝P.ピカーJr.『アライアンススキル』(ピアソン・エデュケーション、1999年)、德田昭夫『グローバル企業の戰略的提携』(ミネルヴァ書房、2000年)、ゲイリー・ハメル＝イブ・ドーズ『競爭優位のアライアンス戰略』(ダイヤモンド社、2001年)、石井眞一『企業間提携の戰略と組織』(中央経済社、2003年)、松崎和久(編著)『戰略提携アライアンス』(學文社、2006年)、安田洋史『競爭環境における戰略的提携』(NTT出版、2006年)参照。

4)　コンソーシアム方式にはさらに二通りあり、ひとつは、コンソーシアムを結成して連名で受注者となり、內部的取り決めとして各パートナーが自己の施工分担部分のみに責任を負うかたちである(分割施行型コンソーシアム)。もうひとつは、各パートナーが持分比率に応じて責任を共有するジョイントベンチャーを結成するが、業務については分擔責任とせずに一体の組織として共同施行するかたちである(共同施行型コンソーシアム)。これに加え、ライセンシー契約、ファイナンス契約などの各種付随契約が結ばれることが多い。絹巻康史『國際商取引』(文眞堂、2001年)169頁。

## 2.  二つの提携關係と研究の課題

　　当事者の提携關係にさらに注目すると、上の形式はいずれも、發注者・受注者(側)という對立構造を前提としていることに変わりはない。いずれも「受注者側の複數のプロジェクト關与者における提携」ということになる。

　　しかし、これらとは別に、「發注者・受注者間における提携」あるいは「發注者を含めた複數のプロジェクト關与者における提携」による請負工事の推進も、近時注目されるようになってきた。これは、本來對立關係(一方當事者が得るものを他方當事者は失うという關係)にあるととらえられる當事者間における提携である。大規模建設プロジェクトにおいて、一見提携の前提を欠くかに見えるこのような組み合わせが模索されるようになったのは、比較的最近のことである。

　　以下では、そのような提携の發展としての「パートナリング」の手法が、どのような背景のもとで登場し、今日どのような狀態にあるのかを、特に、建設請負のための提携契約としての法的側面(パートナリング契約)おける特質と今後解明されるべき課題について考察を試みたい。

## Ⅱ.  パートナリング導入の背景と理念

### 1.  從來のリスク分配の克服とパートナリングの導入の必要性

　　パートナリングの手法が比較的規模の大きな建設請負プロジェクトにおいて注目されるようになったのは、この10〜20 年のほどのことである。すなわち、1980〜90 年代、多くの國々において、發注者と受注者が、建設工事の推進や工事請負契約書の條項の解釋・適用、さらに多様なリスク負担をめぐって、嚴しく對立するケースや、契約後のいわゆる「クレーム」をめぐって紛糾するケースが頻發し、そられの多くが法的紛爭に發展する事態や、工事中斷や工期遅延、またコスト超過に陷る事例がしばしば發生した。それによる不利益の多くは發注者の負担となったが、同時に請負人の側も多くのリソースを費やすこととなり、特に大規模プ

ロジェクトにとっては、これがビジネス上の大きなマイナス要因となっていた。

そこで、このような問題を回避してプロジェクトを推進すること、投下したリソースに見合う利益を得ること、さらに發生した紛爭を從來の民事法の枠組みよりも效率的に解決することを考慮した新しい請負、企業間提携のあり方が、各國においても模索されてきたが、その中で考え出されたのが、「パートナリング」という手法である。それは、紛爭の發生を抑止するためのマネジメント手法から出發し、プロジェクトの效率的な推進、契約上の適切な利益分配・リスク負担に關する法的枠組み、さらに、紛爭が發生した場合に提携企業間において問題解決を図る仕組みにいたる廣い性格をもつものとして發展してきた。

パートナリングの導入は、アメリカから始まったが、以後、イギリス、オーストラリア、香港等における大規模工事(特に、公共工事)に次々に採用され、今日さらに廣い範囲の諸國において導入が檢討されているのである。


## 2. パートナリングの概念━━━新しい建設請負契約

パートナリングの廣範な性格と採用範囲の擴大により、今日ではその定義にも様々なものがみられる。たとえば、アメリカでは、パートナリングとは、「參畫者の経営資源のもっとも效率的な活用を図ることにより、一定のビジネス目的を達成するべく、複數の組織において交わされる誓約である。これは、旧來の關係から、組織の垣根を越えた文化共有への轉換を求めるものである」[5]　とされ、また、イギリスでは、「パートナリングとは、2つ以上の組織がそれぞれのリソースの効果を最大化することによりビジネス上の一定の目的を達成するために用いられるマネジメント手法である。この手法は、共通の目的、あらかじめ合意された問題解決の方法、そして継續的かつ測定可能な改善のための評価を基にするものである」[6]と表現されることがあった。

しかし、このような表現ではあまりに抽象的であって、パートナリングのイメージをつ

---

5) Construction Industry Institute(CII), Model of Partnering Excellence(1996).

6) J. Benett/S. Jayes(Centerf or Strategic Studiesin Construction), Trusting the Team: The Best Practice Guide to Partneringin Construction(1995).

かみにくい。そこでより具体的にいえば、パートナリングとは、一つの建設請負プロジェクトに關わる發注者、受注者、設計者、下請、コンサルタントなどの當事者が、できるだけ早期から、一つのチームのパートナーとして行動し、相互信賴、目標共有、情報共有を通じて、生じる可能性のあるリスクを未然に回避し、あるいは最小に食い止めつつ、工事品質の向上、コスト削減、工期短縮などの共通の目的・利益を實現するように工事を推進しようという考え方である。基本的には、上記のような問題を回避し、投入した資金に見合う價値(VFM: Value for Money)を可能なかぎり高めることを目的とする。そして、今日のパートナリングには、特定の工事のみを對象としたもの(Project Partnering)から、長期的な企業間提携に及ぶもの(Strategic Partnering)もみられるようになっている。實際に、近年これを採用した國々では、一種の「チームプレー型」の企業間提携を實現し、プロジェクト參加者全員がその利益を享受する手段として、それぞれ特色あるパートナリングを展開し、成果をあげている。

そして、パートナリングは、その由來においては、一種のマネジメント手法、あるいは企業の行動理念・行動指針として注目されたが、今日では、いくつかの國において、建設請負を目的とした企業間提携を實現するための獨特の契約類型としての內實をもつもの(さらには一種の問題解決手段としての機能をそなえるもの)　となっている。海外建設プロジェクトにおいてパートナリング方式の採用の可能性を探っている國にとって[7]、さらにその法的側面を分析し新しい企業間提携の可能性を明らかにすることは喫緊の課題となっている。また、近時は、國內工事についてもこのような請負方式の採用の得失が檢討されつつあり[8]、そこにおける契約構造と法的問題を明らかにすることも重要な意義を持つものと思われる。

---

7)　例えば日本では、國土交通省が廣汎な調査を行い、その成果が、たとえば、イギリスについては、『英國におけるパートナリングに關する調査報告(海外建設市場環境整備事業B)』(2003)としてまとめられている。また、この調査を受託した社團法人海外建設協會も、『海外に學ぶ建設業のパートナリングの實際』(鹿島出版會、2007 年)を刊行している。

8)　例えば、日本大ダム會議・海外における發注制度調査分科會「ダム事業への民間資金導入と新たな入札契約方式導入に關する檢討」大ダム196 号(2006 年)10 頁以下。

## Ⅲ. 各国におけるパートナリングの導入経緯と枠組み

### 1. 行動理念としてのパートナリング

そこで、各國におけるパートナリングの導入経過とその基本的性格を簡単にみわたせ
ば、それぞれにおいて、かなり異なった扱い、性格付けがなされているのを見て取ることが
できる[9]。

まず、パートナリングがはじめて提唱されたのは、アメリカにおいてであった。1980年代
のアメリカの建設業界では、激しい受注競争と契約当事者の對立、さらに、非効率的な施工
が、工期の遅延とコストの膨張を招いていた。そこで、1980 年代後半、對立的契約關係の
解消を目的として、プロジェクト参加者全員が、共通目標や行動原理を定めた「憲章」
(Charter)を作成するとともに、「パートナリング協定」(Partnering Agreement)を結び、プロジェ
クトの内容・計畫に關わるオープンな協議とリスクの共有のもとにプロジェクトの推進をめ
ざすという大きな轉換が試みられた。これは、まず、1988年、陸軍施設の建設工事において
取り入れられ[10]、その後多くの大規模工事、特に公共工事において採用されてきた[11]。

ただ、アメリカにおいては、パートナリングという概念は、その由來において法的概念
ではなかった。それは、既存の受注・施工のシステムにおいてプロジェクトを推進する上
で、發注者・受注者・下請などのステークホルダーが據るべきひとつの行動理念・行動指
針あるいはマネジメント手法として一般に理解されてきた[12]　(当事者間の契約に取り込ま
ないことについては、法的關係としての曖昧さが殘ってしまうことや、獨禁法上の問題が
生じうることが指摘されてきた)。實際にパートナリングの考え方を採用したプロジェクト
においても、これまで一般に用いられてきた工事請負契約約款(AIA、AGC、CMAA　など)
が、当事者間の法律關係を規律するものとしてそのまま使用されているのである。

---

9) 歴史的概觀として、Sally Roe/Jane Jenkins, Partnering and Alliancing in Construction Projects, 13(2003).
10) これは、米陸軍工兵隊(US Army Corps of Engineers)において導入されたとされる。その後、毎年陸軍の100 以上のプ
ロジェクトで採用されている。Roe/Jenkins, supra note 9, , at15.
11) たとえば、中村幸男＝桑原健『米國西海岸での下水處理場建設工事──パートナリング手法の適用について』電力土木284 号
(1999)155 頁参照。
12) もっとも、近時は、アメリカにおいても、Partnering やAlliance を契約として取り入れる可能性が論じられている。James J.
Myers, Alliance Contracting: A Potpourri of Proven Techniques for Successful Contracting, [2001]I.C.L.R.56.

　つまり、パートナリングは、直接の權利義務關係を導くものではなく、入札・發注後に、プロジェクトを圓滑に推進し、生じうる問題を解決するための理念として、取り入れられるべきものとされている[13]。


　2. 契約としてのパートナリング―――契約によるリスク共有

（1）イギリスにおけるパートナリング契約

**1）パートナリング方式のイギリスへの導入**

　パートナリングの考え方は、その後イギリスにおいて取り入れられた。イギリスでも、1980年代には、生産性の低下、施工品質の低下、安値受注に起因する發注者へのクレームの多さ、工期の遲延、最終工事費の膨張のような、建設請負契約の当事者間における、アメリカと類似の問題が大きくなっており、それを解決するためのさまざまな取り組みが試みられていた。そこへ、狀況打開の一つの切り札として登場したのが、パートナリングの手法であった[14]。

　イギリスにおけるパートナリングは、まず、北海油田における坑井掘削工事に取り入れられたが[15]、必ずしも廣く浸透したわけではなかった。

　しかし、その後、上記の建設業界の問題に關する政府・業界共同の調査が行われ、1994年にはレイサム卿が、この調査の報告書「チームを組む」[16]　を議會に提出した。これは、当時の建設業界の抱える多くの問題点を指摘し、これを解決するために工事關与者たる各企業の相互信賴と協力の必要性を說くものであった。そして提言として、發注者、設計技術者、施工業者、メーカーなどの關係をめぐる從來の生産システムの改革の必要性を

---

13) アメリカでは、入札時にパートナリングの方式を取り入れたいという發注者の意向が表示され、入札後に、法的拘束力のない憲章という形のパートナリングの理念をうたったフォームにより合意がなされる。Chris Skeggs, Project Partnering in the International Construction Industry, [2003]I.C.L.R.469.

14) 導入について、Roe/Jenkins, supra note 9, at13. また、杉山正「新しい契約方式――英國のパートナリング」土木技術 57 巻11 号(2002 年)77 頁以下(施工事例について79 頁以下)、海外建設協會、前掲注(7)11 頁も参照。

15) Roe/Jenkins, supra note 9, at15, 16.

16) Sir Michael Latham, Constructing the Team(HMSO, 1994).この報告書では、競争入札による最低価格者を契約の相手方として選択する方法では、コストに見合った価値がえられず、これをえるためには、「チームを組む」方法への切り替えが必要である、とされた。

指摘し、特にパートナリングの採用を推奨した[17]。次いで、レディング大學の「建設フォーラム」[18] が、日本の生産方式とアメリカのパートナリングに關する研究をもとに、パートナリング導入にともなう諸問題を、法律論を含めて檢討し、大きな影響を及ぼした。さらに、1998年にはイーガン卿を議長とする政府の建設タスクフォースが、報告書を公表して、建設工事の品質の向上と効率改善の必要性を訴え[19]、パートナリングの導入を促した（イーガン卿は、2002年の報告書[20]　でも、發注者を巻き込んだパートナリングの普及を加速するべきであるとした）。

　このような提言を受けて、パートナリング方式は徐々に實際の工事に採用され、建設の工程に關與する多數の企業が相互信賴、共通目標、情報共有のもとで効率性の高い生産を行い、プロジェクト參加者全員がWin/Win になる生産を實現しようとする考え方として効果を上げてきた[21]。レディング大學の「建設フォーラム」は、パートナリングの採用によって、工費を40%以上削減し、工期を50%短縮することも可能という驚くべき數字を出している[22]。

　イギリスのパートナリング方式の特長は、發注者を含む、設計者、總合工事會社、專門工事會社、下請者、資材業者など主要なプロジェクト參加企業が提携し、共通の目標を掲げるチームを作るとともに、設計はじめ諸々の情報共有と事前の綿密な打ち合わせのもとで施工し、目標を達成したときの利益と達成できなかったときの損失をチームの構成員全員で分配する点にある。作業効率、コスト削減、工期嚴守、リスクの適正配分などが共通目標になるのが通常であるが、これを達成するための、關係企業相互の信賴と協力、情

---

17) レイサムレポートにおいては、パートナリングの採用により、工費を30%削減し、工期を25%短縮することが可能としていた。また、契約に要する手間や費用も、2 当事者間の契約を積み上げるよりも1 本の契約によって行う方が、はるかに輕減できるとする。

18) John Bennett/SarahJayes, Trusting the Team: The Best Practice Guide to Partnering in Construction(1995). なお、日本の「系列」が、海外では「コスト管理能力、工期遵守能力、品質管理能力が非常に高い生産システム」として注目されており、パートナリングは、日本の實例に學んで、關係者間の信賴關係を構築して、高効率・高品質で顧客満足度の高い建設生産体制を作ることを試みたところから、その構想が始まったという説明が見られる。金多隆＝吉原伸治＝古阪秀三「建設業における系列とパートナリングの比較分析」日本建築學會第21　回建築生産シンポジウム論文集(2005)223頁以下参照。

19) Sir John Egan, Rethinking Construction(1998).

20) Sir John Egan, Accelerating Change: A Report by the Strategic Forum for Construction(2002).

21) Ellis Baker, Partnering Strategies: The Legal Dimension, Const. L.J. 2007, 23(5), 344; Roe/Jenkins, supra note 9, at29-31; 海外建設協會、前掲注(7)233 頁以下。

22) John Bennett and Sarah Jayes/Reding Construction Forum, The Seven Pillars of Partnering, 54(1998).

報の透明性[23]がこの手法の成否の鍵となるのである。


2) パートナリング契約

イギリスのパートナリング方式がアメリカのそれと決定的に異なるのは、イギリスで
は、パートナリングが、プロジェクト關与者の行動理念にとどまらず、法的責任を生ぜし
める当事者關係を成立させるところにある[24]。すなわち、イギリスでは、「パートナリング
契約」(Partnering　Contract)の概念が成立するとともに、パートナリング方式の当事者關係に
即した約款の整備が進んでいるのである[25]。

ⅰ) もっとも、パートナリングを推進するための形態としては、当初、契約というかた
ちをとらない、紳士協定的なアプローチが提唱されたこともあった[26]。パートナリング
は、協力的、紛争回避的、自己改善的なものであり、契約とは關わりなく行われうるもの
である、という立場である。必要となるのは、パートナリング憲章にとどまるとされた。

ⅱ) しかし、1990 年代に入ると、パートナリングにおける契約の役割が評価されるよ
うになった[27]。實際の利害對立が生じた場合に備え当事者の法的關係を明確にしてお
く必要が意識されるに至ったからである。パートナリング方式で契約をするという場合に、
まず考えられたのは、從來用いられている建設工事請負契約約款を基礎として、それを修
正し、建設請負契約を当事者間の協力の理念を反映したものとする手法である。これは、
あくまで2 当事者間の契約であり、そのなかにパートナリングの手法を取り込んだ條項を含
むものとなる。パートナリング方式に適合した條項を含んだ約款、たとえばICE(The

---

23) 情報の透明性・共有性を實現するひとつの手段として、プロジェクトにかかわる情報をウェブ上の特定サイトに集中させ、す
べてのステークホルダーにそれを供する試みについて、Gerald S. Clay/Ann L. Mac Naughton/John F. FarnanJr.,
Creating Long-Term Success through Expanded "Partnering", 59-APRDisp.Resol.J.42, 47(2004)参照。

24) Richard Honey/Justin Mort, Partnering Contracts for UK Building Projects: Practical Considerations, Const. L.J.
2004, 20(7), 361, 364.

25) その進展について、Honey/Mort, supra note 24, at365; AlanLedger, An Agenda for Collaborative Working
Arrangement:The Role of Partnering and Alliancein the U.K., 58-JULDisp.Resol.J.37, 42(2007); 海外建設協
會、前掲注(7)79 頁。

26) パートナリングの主唱者の一人であるイーガン卿も、当初は、パートナリングを契約化することに前向きではなかった。パー
トナリングの長所は、紛争を回避するところにあるのであり、その限りで契約は有用ではなく、コストもかかると考えていた。
Egan, supra note 20, at 30; Baker, supra note 21, at345.

27) Skeggs, supranote12, at469.

Institution of Civil Engineering)發行のNEC(The New Engineering Contract)[28] Option C や FIDIC(1999年版)などを用いたうえで、發注者・受注者以外の第三者(設計者、下請企業など)がパートナリング方式に適合した關與を行うことができるよう、パートナリング憲章によって約款を補うという形態である[29]。

　ただ、この手法による場合に、2 當事者を前提にした從來の約款が、パートナリングに参加しチームを作るすべての提携者の法律關係をカバーすることができるのか、という疑問が生じてくる[30]。傳統的な双務の契約關係と憲章とが矛盾した關係となる危險も殘される(パートナリング憲章は共通の目的と各當事者の利益實現の尊重を理念とするものであるが、傳統的な約款は對立的な當事者關係を對象にしており、憲章と對立しかねない)。このような点から、パートナリング契約に適した法的枠組みを正面から構成することの必要性が意識されるようになった。

　このような認識を廣げたのが、Birse Construction Ltd v St David Ltd 事件[31]であった。これは、1997 年にカーディフ湾にある施設を建設するにつき、原告たる建設會社と發注者がパートナリング憲章を作成したケースである。同年末までに契約に署名することとしていたが、實際には署名がなされず、新年に入り3 月になっても進展がなかったので、發注者は請負人に對し工事遲延の損害を請負報酬から控除すると通知して爭いとなった。同年夏には初期工事は實質的に完了したが、注文者は、請負人が工事現場を離れたことを捉えて放棄したものとした。請負人は、TCC(The Technology and Construction Court)に、「提供役務相當金額請求訴訟」(quantum meruit)を提起したが、退けられた。この経験の中で、パートナリングの合意を適切な法的枠組みによって支えること、特に契約關係を明確なものとすることが必要であるという認識が一般となった[32]。また、同時に、憲章の効力、支拂いの仕組みに對する疑問も生じてきた。

　iii) そこで、第3 段階として、「3 當事者以上のパートナリング契約」による、傳統的な

---

28) これは、本來パートナリング契約のためのものではないが、パートナリング契約の基礎とするのにはもっとも適合的な約款とされてきた。その、一般的なスタイルはパートナリングにもあてはまり、簡明な言葉遣いは革新的な契約方法にも適合するとされた。

29) Skeggs, supranote13, at469.

30) Baker, supra note 21, at347.

31) [1999]B.L.R.194.

32) Skeggs, supra note 13, at469.

契約の枠組みを脱皮した企業間提携が提案されるにいたり、今日では、むしろこの形態が一般的となっている。そして特に注目するべきは、イギリスにおいては、すでに、このようなパートナリング方式による建設請負契約約款として、ACA(The Association of Consultant Architects Ltd)によって策定されたひな形、PPC2000[33](The ACA Standard Form of Contract for Project Partnering)が2000 年9 月に發表され、また、ICE によるECC(The Engineering and Construction Contract) Option X12[34]も現われて、これらが實際の工事で利用されていることである。これらは「多當事者間パートナリング契約」[35](Multi-party Partnering Contract) であり、發注者、受注者、設計者、コンサルタント、下請等が直接の當事者となる一本の契約として構成されている。

iv)さらに、2007 年5 月には、民間の工事約款を策定するJCT(Joint Contracts Tribunal)が、新たなパートナリング方式の約款であるJCT-CE を發表した。これは、基本的に2 當事者間の契約として構成されているが、従來のパートナリング約款が法的に曖昧な表現を殘していたのに對し、明確な法的枠組みを示そうとしたものである[36]。これまでの、パートナリング方式の約款が、公共工事を念頭においていたのとは異なり、民間工事においてもパートナリング方式が本格的に取り入れられることも予想される。

ただ、これらの多當事者間の契約形態は、それ採用すると、多くのプロジェクト参加者の義務と責任に關わる法律關係が複雑になるという問題も指摘されている[37]。紛争を回避することを重要な目的としたパートナリングによって逆に新たな訴訟の嵐を誘發するのではないか、という懸念である。当面、種々の新しい約款を採用するプロジェクトが増加するなかで、パートナリングに關する法理論が固まるまでは、その選択・採用に試行錯誤が繰り返されるであろう[38]。

---

33) これは、イーガンの報告書(前掲注(18))を實現するべく策定されたものである。PPC2000 の解説として、David Mosey, Guide to the ACA Project Partnering Contracts PPC 2000 and SPC 2000(2003) 参照。なお、SPC 2000(The ACA Standard Form of Specialist Contract for Project Partnering)、TPC 2005(the ACA Standard Form of Contract for Team Partnering)も参照。Honey/Mort, supra note 24, at369.

34) 上の第2 段階の2 當事者間契約に付加して、複数のプロジェクト参加者の組織化をはかるアンブレラ契約を締結するという方法である。Honey/Mort, supranote24, n28.

35) これをAlliance と呼んで、Partnering と區別することもある。Ledger, supranote24, at38.

36) Baker, supra note 21, at354.

37) Skeggs, supranote13, at470;海外建設協會、前掲注(7)73 頁。

(2) その他の諸國におけるパートナリング契約

その他の諸國、たとえば、オーストラリアでも同様の理念、つまり信頼に基づく施工チームづくりをめざす取り組みが擴大している。オーストラリアには、まずアメリカから、法的拘束力を持たないパートナリング方式が導入されたが、これは必ずしも十分な成果をあげるにいたらなかった[39]。しかし、その後、Relationship Contracting の概念により、パートナリングの趣旨を契約中に取り込もうとする獨特の展開が現れ、さらにこれを發展させた形態としてのAlliance Contracting という契約類型が生み出されるに至っている[40]。

また、香港では、二つの報告書がパートナリングの導入を提唱し、獨自のパートナリング方式の約款が整備されつつある[41]。これは、實際にいくつかの大規模プロジェクトで採用されている。近時、日本の建設會社が、地下鐵工事において、香港初のパートナリング方式(ターゲットコスト方式)の契約を締結し、注目されたところである。

## IV. イギリスにおけるパートナリング契約の展開

### 1. イギリスのパートナリング契約の特徴

上記のような経緯を見ると、多当事者の提携による建設請負解約としてのパートナリングとしては、現在のところ、イギリスにおける展開がもっとも注目されるべきであろう(さらに、オーストラリア、香港における展開も興味深い)。イギリスにおいては、多当事者間における強制可能性のある(enforceable)契約としての「パートナリング契約」が登場するに至ったが、この契約内容を見ると(各約款による相違は見られるものの)、特に、プロジェクト参加者における「リスクと利益の共有」の仕組みが用意されていることと、プロジェクトの推進に「ワークショップ」と呼ばれるしくみが大きくかかわっていることが重要と思われる。

---

38) パートナリング契約に關するいくつかの約款の得失を比較檢討した研究として、Honey/Mort, supranote24 参照。

39) 海外建設協會、前掲注(7)16 頁。

40) DouglasJones, ProjectAlliances, [2001]I.C.L.R.411.

41) 香港におけるTang Report とGrove Report、およびパートナリングのひろがりについて、Philip Nunn/Ian Cocking, The Tang Report: Catalyst for Changein the HongKong Construction Industry, [2001]ICLR617;海外建設協會、前掲注(7)22 頁。

### (1) リスク共有の仕組み

すなわち、パートナリング契約においては、發注者と受注者が損失も利益も分け合う Pain/Gain Share の理念、およびその配分の比率が、契約中に明文をもって約定されている。そして、この配分のために、その基礎となる「目標価格」(Target Cost)の合意が行われる。この目標価格は、工事の請負価格ではなく、發注者、受注者、設計者、コンサルタントなどが協議し、標準的能力のある企業が通常建設に要する費用とありうるリスクの對處費用を考慮して措定した工事価格であり、一種の仮想の數値である。實際の工事費はこれを上回ることもあれば、下回ることもある。これをPain またはGain と見立てて、それを發注者と受注者との間において一定の比率で分かち合うというフィクションにより、プロジェクト参加者の最終的な負担と取り分を決めるのである。そして、この比率については契約においてあらかじめ取決めがなされることになる。これを基本的な枠組みとしてリスク共有がはかられるのである(下図参照)。

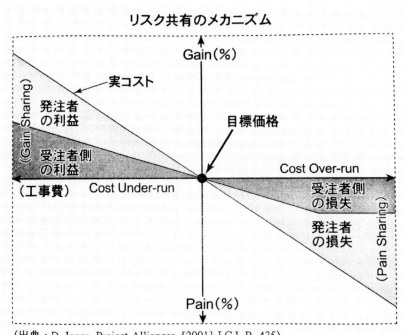

(出典：D. Jones, Project Alliances, [2001] I.C.L.R. 435)

このPain とGain の割合の取り決めを適用するにあたっては、原価の透明性を確保し、実際の工事費の中から正当に原価と評価されるべきコストだけを基にしてPain とGain を算出する必要がある。これを「實コスト」(Actual Cost)とよび、それをどのように評価するかについても契約上明確な定めが必要となるのである。たとえば、他の業者への過失による過拂い、不要資材の購入等によるコストなどは原価に算入されるべきではないとされる(これらは、建設請負契約約款に列擧されることが多い)。

また、特定のプロジェクト参加者の固有のリスク負担に委ねられるべき費目もあるはずであり、これは契約上明確にされなければならない。

なお、目標価格は、契約においてあらかじめ定められた事情が生じた場合には、増減額される余地がある。たとえば、設計変更によるコスト増は、目標価格の上昇に結びつくことがある。

### (2) ワークショップを中心としたプロジェクトの推進———一種の「共同事業性」

パートナリング方式によるプロジェクトは實際にはどのように進行することになるか。すでに述べたように、パートナリング契約には、發注者・受注者の2當事者間を前提にしたものから、下請、設計者、エンジニアなどを含むより多數の當事者間で締結されるものまで、その發展段階に応じて、いくつかの多様性があるが、そこでは、ワークショップ(パートナリング會議) と呼ばれるしくみにおいて、パートナリング構成員が十分な意思疎通を図りつつプロジェクトを推進して行くことになる。ここに一種の「共同事業性」を見て取ることができるように思われる[42]。それは、およそ次のような形態において推進される[43]。

---

42) パートナリングにおいては、プロジェクトの關係者のすべてがその役割と責任を組織・統合しあって、ひとつの「バーチャルカンパニー」が存在するかのように、お互いの信頼と自由な意見交換・批判の中で、共同作業と意思決定を行って、プロジェクトの運営が行われる。Clive T. Cain, Profitable Partnering for Lean Construction, 61(2004).

43) BevisMak, Partnering/Alliancing, Const.L.J.2001, 17(3), 218, 221;日本大ダム會議技術委員會、前掲注(7)42 頁参照。また、8段階に分けた説明として、Clay/MacNaughton/FarnanJr., supranote22, at45 参照。PPP やPFI との對比について、Skeggs, supranote13, at467.

### 1) 受注事業者の選定

まず、プロジェクトに参加する事業者の選定が必要になる。ここでは、契約当事者である事業者の選定自体がパートナリングの枠組みの中で行われる。すなわち、パートナリングの手法においては、受注事業者は、入札価格のみならず、過去の實績、信頼性、業績、施工品質、環境管理計畫や、過去のパートナリング實績、他組織との協調性も考慮のうえ決定される。入札価格のみならず、プロジェクトの成果を見通した選定が行われる。

### 2) ファシリテーターの選定

ファシリテーター(facilitator)は、パートナリングの手法がプロジェクトに適合するよう組織内の調整・コミュニケーションの円滑化をはかることを任務とする。参加企業がワークショップの場で議論するための調整約であり、發注者から選出される場合もあれば、第三者機關から選出される場合もある。

### 3) ワークショップを通じたパートナリングの展開[44]

① ワークショップの編成と憲章作成・契約締結

次いで、ワークショップが開催されそこにおいて、プロジェクトの各参加者(發注者、受注者、コンサルタント、下請業者など)の代表が、まず、プロジェクトの共通ミッションと行動規範に關する合意形成をおこない、それを表現した憲章[45] を作成する。また、多当事者間の約款を採用した場合には、プロジェクト参畫者がともに署名する一本の契約書によって、パートナリング契約が締結される。

② 共通目標の設定

ワークショップにおいて、施工方法、工事の工程、品質、環境、コスト、作業効率、工

---

44) Clay/MacNaughton/FarnanJr., supranote23, at42.
45)  憲章において盛り込まれるのは、たとえば、①パートナリングの原則を遵守する旨の誓約の一般的言明、②プロジェクトの成功のために共同にめざすべき中心的目標、③情報交換と共同作業の手續きおよび役割と責任、③モニタリングの推進と目標達成指標(KPIs)の利用を含む評価を活用した施工の手順、④問題の速やかな議論とその解決のための建設的協働の誓約、⑤問題解決の手順、⑥ワークショップ、セミナー、ファシリテーターに關する費用分担などの諸條項である。Roe/Jenkins, supra note 9, at2.

期、標準作業量、リスクの配分、設計情報の共有等の諸事項について目標が設定され、プロジェクト参加者がその目標の達成に向けて協力することになる。そして、この目標は、すべてのプロジェクト参加者について共通の利害となるように設定されている。

③ 目標価格の設定

先に述べた目標価格をワークショップにおいて決定することとなる。この数値の決定については、獨立したエンジニアの客觀的な査定を考慮するが、發注者とプロジェクト關与者の力關係が反映されるおそれもなお殘っている。

④ パートナリングによる施工の推進

パートナリングの進行も、当初のワークショップ(キックオフ・ワークショップ)に續いて、實績モニター、中間ワークショップ、最終レビューミーティングというプロセスで進められ、その過程では、ファシリテーターが、憲章に卽して、プロジェクト目的を達成するために、その進行中に發生する問題に關し關係者間の意見の調整をするなどの役割を果たす。

ワークショップにおいては、發注者から受注者、下請會社、資材供給會社に至る關係者のそれぞれが施工に關する情報を出し合って、その情報を共有する。相互に十分な情報開示をすることにより、ワークショップが、相互の信賴關係を醸成する場となり、また、一種の共同事業を推進する機能を備えたものともなる。

⑤ ワークショップの性格

なお、ワークショップは、プロジェクト遂行の中心的な「場」であるが、それ自体が、組織や機關ではないということは、注目される。そこで、パートナリング契約の約款では、ワークショップの性格が明らかでないことも多い。他方、約款によっては、パートナリングを代表する性格のグループを規定するものも見られるのである(たとえば、次に見るPPC2000 には、コア・グループというグループを置き一定の決議を行う權限を与えている)。

## 2. パートナリング方式の建設工事請負契約約款————PPC2000 を例にとって

では、パートナリング契約の建設工事請負約款はどのように構成されているであろうか。上に指摘したように、現在では、パートナリング方式のプロジェクトに利用されることを予定した約款がいくつか發表されているが、ここでは、それらの中から、PPC2000　の例を見てみよう[46]。

### (1) PPC2000 の特徴[47]

PPC2000　は、はじめての多當事者パートナリング契約約款であり、設計、資材供給、施工を視野に入れた規定を整備するものである。パートナリング合意書、パートナリング規定、付屬書からなり、パートナリング工程表、コンサルタントサービス概要、プロジェクト概要書、價格予算書、目的達成度指標なども付される。パートナリングのメンバーを一定の範囲で代表するコア・グループのしくみを導入し、施工の進捗に對する評價も擔わせている。また、利益の分配とともに、目標達成指標[48](KPIs: Key Performance Indicators)を目安とした報酬によるインセンティブにも配慮している。さらに、パートナリングアドバイザーを導入している点でも注目される。

### (2) 主な條文構成[49]

PPC2000　の條文構成について詳細な分析を試みるには別稿を要する。ここではその特質をなす條項を見渡すにとどめると、以下のようなものがあげられる。

### 1) 契約當事者

契約當事者として、發注者、請負人のほか、發注者代理人(FIDIC 等におけるEngineer)、

---

46) Mosey, supranote33.

47) Roe/Jenkins, supranote 8, at213;Mosey, supranote33, at6.

48) イギリスにおける建設工事の成果を測定する指標および契約方式の發展については、盛武建二＝芦田義則「英國における建設パフォーマンス改善の取り組みに關する調査研究」建設マネジメント研究論文集10 卷(2003 年)165 頁以下參照。

49) Mosey, supranote33, at21-48.

専門業者、サプライヤーが、署名する(合意書1.3 條、1.5 條)。

### 2) 利益損失按分比率

實コストが目標価格を下回った場合、あるいは上回った場合の、Pain Share, Gain Share と呼ばれる利益損失按分比率を規定する(合意書13.2　條)。これは、パートナリングの理念をもっとも反映したリスク共有と利益分配の條項である。この比率は、ファシリテーターの開催するワークショップにおいてリスク評価を行ったうえで決定された「目標価格」(Target Cost. PPC2000 ではAgreed Maximum Price と呼んでいる)をもとに、これを基準とした損益を發注者・受注者等が分かち合うための基準となるものである。それぞれが負担する損益の比率はプロジェクトごとに異なるが、その比率は事前に契約に盛り込まれることになる。

このPain またはGain を算定するには、原価の透明性の確保が必須となる。また、契約上、一定の事情が生じた場合に目標価格を増減することがありうる(プロジェクト實施前に評価できるリスクについてはワークショップで議論され相応のコストが割り振られる。事前に評価することが難しいリスクについて、約款上Shared Risk とされ、負担当事者が決定されることもある)。

### 3) 目標価格

上のリスク共有の前提となる目標価格を、「付屬書」において規定する。實際のコストがこれを下回ればその差額分を利益損失按分比率によって当事者間で分配し、實際のコストがこれを上回れば、その損失をやはりこの比率により当事者が負担する(前掲の図を参照)。

### 4) 役割と責任、注意義務

パートナリングの構成員が、信頼、公平、相互協力の精神に則って仕事を遂行すべきことが契約上の義務とされている(一般規定1.3 條)。また、自己の役割、技術経験等について合理的に期待される注意を拂うべきものとされている(同22.1 條)。

### 5) コア・グループ

PPC2000 は、工事の進捗狀況を評価しそれを促進するためのコア・グループを選出するものとし、このグループにプロジェクト推進の實質的運營の一部を委ねている(同3.3〜3.6 條)。

### 6) パートナリングの構成員への支拂い義務

パートナリング構成員(たとえば、コンサルタント、專門業者)に對する報酬等の支拂義務の所在を確定する(同1.5 條、1.6 條)。

### 7) 工事の遂行に關する權利義務

着工から始まる工事遂行を規律する權利義務關係を規定する(同8.3 條以下)。また、設計に關する請負人の異議も認められる(同8.11 條)。

### 8) リスク管理

リスク共有條項によって處理される場合以外は、請負人がリスク管理にあたる(同18條)。

### 9) 目標達成指標による評価

パートナリング構成員による施工の成果を目標達成指數( KPI s) によって定期的に測定し、パートナリングの成果を定期的に評価することとされている(同23 條)。その結果に問題がある場合には、ワークショップによる檢討に委ねられる。

### 10) 契約解除

發注者は、一般規定14.1 條に規定する契約の全體條件が充たされないか、予見できない狀況が發生したときは、契約を解除できることができる(同26 條)。また、パートナリング構成員が倒産した場合には、その構成員とのパートナリング契約は自動的に解除される。

### 11) 戰略的提携

PPC2000 は、本來個々のプロジェクト單位におけるパートナリングに關する約款である

が、これを超えて、複数のプロジェクトにわたる長期的なパートナリング關係を構成する戰略的提携(Strategic Alliance)がありうることを考慮し、パートナリングのメンバーがこれに合意しうることを規定している(同24 條)。

PPC2000 は、はじめての多当事者間パートナリング契約約款として登場し、おおむね肯定的な評価を得ている。韓國法や日本法において問題となるような、請負の危険負担や建築物の瑕疵の問題が獨特のリスク共有の枠組みの中で處理されているのを見て取ることができる。ただ、パートナリング構成員の責任範囲等になお不明確な部分を残しているという指摘も見られる。


### 3. パートナリングの鍵となる要素

イギリスの経驗から見て、パートナリング方式の建設工事請負契約約款が適切に機能するためのいくつかの重視するべき要素を指摘することができる。


① ひとつは、パートナリングを組む業者の選択において、その實績と能力に重点を置いた判斷を行う必要があるということである。「人札時の最低価格」から「完成時の最大価値」への視点の轉換が必要となる。

② また、ワークショップがその任務を果たすことが重要であり、そのためには、プロジェクトに参加する各当事者が協力しつつ利益の最大化をはかることめざす環境形成が必要となる。

③ さらに、情報の透明性が鍵となる。パートナリングの場合は、プロジェクトごとにリスク共有があらかじめ決められているが、それは、プロジェクトとその参加者に關する情報の透明性を前提とするものであり、それが信頼關係の前提となる。そして、情報の透明性は、しばしば、各参加企業のプロジェクトの工事原価に關する會計記録を相互に開示するオープンブック・アカウンティングを求めることが多い[50]。これは、他の参加企業に利得の秘匿がないとの信頼を確かにすることや、決濟プロセスの確實な実行においても、本質的

---

50) Baker, supra note 21, at354.

な意味を持つ(PPC2000　は、サプライチェーン・マネジメントを行うために、この点について規定を設けている)。また、實際上オープンブック・アカウンティングは、受注者からのクレームの發生を低減させる效果をも果たすものとなる。

## 4. パートナリング方式の建設請負からえられる成果

以上のように、イギリスのパートナリングは、工事の調達方法や契約方式、施工プロセスそのものに大きな變更を試みるものであるが、すでに指摘したように、そこからはいくつもの成果(および今後の期待)が見出される[51]。

### (1) 受注者の能力の有效な活用

たとえば、受注者がパートナーとして工事の計畫段階から參加することにより、そのノウハウと所有する人的・物的資源の有效な活用をはかることができる。

### (2) コスト削減

プロジェクトのコスト削減を期待することができる[52]。そして、その成果が、工事に參加する各当事者にインセンティブとして配分される。從來、コスト削減については、發注者と受注者の利害は對立するものとされてきたが、パートナリングは、それが兩当事者の利益となることを可能にする。

### (3) 工期短縮と品質向上

工期を短縮するとともに、工事の品質の向上ないし瑕疵發生率の低下を實現することができる。これによって同時に、法的紛爭の回避が期待される。

---

51) Skeggs, supranote13, at461, 462;Honey/Mort, supranote24, at362;Mak, supranote43, at229;海外建設協會、前揭注(7)30 頁。
52) 前揭注(20)(21)參照。Ledger, supranote 25, at39 も參照。

### (4) ビジネス上の予見可能性

さらに、工事計畫の段階で工事参加者がありうるリスクを徹底的に洗い出すので、施工段階で計畫が狂う可能性が低くなる。これによりビジネスとしての予見可能性を高めることもできる。

### (5) 適切な事業者の選択

パートナリングのプロセスの中で、受注者は、受注価格のみによって評価されるのではなく、施工能力・施工實績が業者選定の重要な要素となるため、よい工事を行うことが自己の評価を高めるものとなり、そのような業者の選定が結局は工事の品質の向上につながることが期待される。受注者は、入札時の価格競争から一定範囲で解放され、能力・實績重視の競争が可能となるとともに、繼續的な受注の可能性がえられる。

このような変化は、プロジェクト参加者に、發注者のパートナーとして脱皮することを求めるものとなる。パートナリングは、單に協調關係が實現されればよいという考え方ではなく、プロジェクトに關わる組織のパートナーとしての役割を、各メンバーに求めることになるのである。

## 5. 明らかにされるべき法律關係

しかし、パートナリングも、なお解決されるべき多くの問題点、課題を抱えている。特に、パートナリングをめぐる各当事者の法律關係については、約款上明確にされていない点が多く、理論的整備が急がれる狀況にある。

### (1) 法律關係の明確化の課題

今日の發展段階におけるパートナリング契約は、3当事者以上の多当事者間契約の形態をとっており、發注者、受注者、設計者、コンサルタント、下請等が直接の当事者となるが、このようなパートナリング契約から導かれる、当事者間の法律關係が、現在のとこ

ろ十分に明確ではない。パートナリング契約は、契約当事者間の紛争を予防するための仕組みとしては優れているが、契約の本質であるリスク負担と責任の關係が嚴密に明らかになっていない面もある。

そのため、パートナリング方式のプロジェクトにおいて紛争が生じた場合には、契約に基づく權利義務關係がはっきりしない場面が生じる可能性がある。

これまで、パートナリング契約については、實際の判例や仲裁事例による規範形成が現在のところ十分ではなく、學說による理論的整備もこれから本格化する段階にある。おそらくこの点がパートナリングのもっとも問題となるところであろう。

### (2) 理論的整備の課題

理論的には、特に、以下のような点が明確にされる必要がある。

### 1) パートナリングの法的性格

たとえば、「チームを組む」(レイサム)というパートナリングの本質の表現は、比喩的なものであるが、その「チーム」の法的性質[53]、チームとメンバーとの關係、メンバー相互の關係、チーム外の第三者との關係については、今のところあまり明らかになっていない[54]。

### 2) 契約の解除と清算

約款は通常、發注者は任意に契約を解除することができる旨の條項をおいているが、それによる最終的な清算のあり方については、未整理の部分も多く殘されている。

---

53) PPC2000 の一般規定25 條は、「パートナーシップ」と混同されないようにするべき旨を定めるが、パートナリングの性質については明らかにする規定は存しない。また、どこまでがenforceableな約束なのかがはっきりしない。Honey/Mort, supranote24, at362.

54) これは特に、伝統的な契約法理論との關係において、はっきりさせなければならない問題を提起している(プラント輸出の場合には、そのプロジェクトに適用になる法体系の相違により、論点も異なることになることはいうまでもない)。たとえば、パートナリング契約においては、契約上の義務内容と、パートナリングの過程における表示とが食い違うことがありうる。当事者は、そのような場合に、禁反言の法理や權利放棄の法理に基づく權利を行使することができるか、あるいは、信認關係上の義務は、パートナリング契約上の義務とどのような關係にたつのか、さらに、パートナリングの基本原理と信義則との關係はどのようにとらえるべきか、などの点である。Skeggs, supranote13, at463.パートナリングの法律關係については、特に、Roe/Jenkins, supranote 8, at69-193.

また、参加当事者の破産等による離脱に伴うボンド等による處理についても、未確定の部分は多い。

### 3) 契約の違反と再履行、契約違反の責任と損害賠償

プロジェクトによって建設された物が瑕疵を帯びていた場合等における、再履行や賠償責任の負担については、パートナリングの構成員の誰がいかなる責任を負うことになるのかをはじめ、きわめて大きな問題を殘しているのである[55]。

### 4) パートナリング內部の紛爭解決手段

パートナリング契約約款は通常その內部に問題解決に關する條項を含んでいる。そのような紛爭解決手段が適切な働きをするものかについても檢討が開始されている[56]。

### 5) 知的財産權

パートナリングはメンバー相互の情報の透明化と共有を重要な條件としている。他方で、建設工事においては、多様な知的財産權やノウハウ等にかかわる秘密保持も重要な要請となる。後者の要請に配慮しつつ、チームプレーとしてのパートナリングの實をあげるには、その法律上の枠組みが必要となる。この点に關する檢討も始まったところである[57]。

### 6) 競爭法上の規律

パートナリングにおける参加事業者の選定、契約內容の確定の方法が、競爭法上の問題と關連することも指摘され、その望ましい回避のあり方が議論されつつある[58]。

### 7) パートナリング約款の解釋

なお、パートナリング約款の條項解釋の指針も明らかにされる必要がある。すでにこの

---

55) Roe/Jenkins, supranote 8, at85-88.
56) これについてはすでに多数の研究が現れている。Ledger, supranote25.また、PPC2000 一般規定27.1-27.4 條も参照。
57) Roe/Jenkins, supranote 8, at121-133.
58) Roe/Jenkins, supra note 8, at135-162.

点が爭われたケースも目に付く[59]。特に、Pain/Gain Share の條項に關しては、契約上明確な取り決めをおき、法律關係の曖昧さを殘さないことが必要となる[60]。

## 6. その他の課題

### (1) 情報開示の必要性と範囲の確定

發注者、受注者とも、パートナリングの契約段階で、共有するべきリスクを正確に評價するために、自らの能力、技術等に關する情報を開示しなければならないが、この過程で、各企業の內部狀況が外部にさらされることになる。これが場合によっては企業としてのマイナスになる可能性もある。また、施工のノウハウ、コスト情報等が開示されることの不利益は、受注者側に大きな脅威となる。この情報開示の適切な範囲をパートナリング參加者の義務內容として明らかにする必要がある。

### (2) 競爭と協調のバランス

さらに、紛爭回避を目的とした協調と適切な競爭のバランスが必要となる。たとえば、パートナリングは、常にプロジェクト參加者の馴れ合いや官民の癒着の危險をはらんでおり、特に、公共調達の場合には、納稅者や入札者との關係において、客觀性ある運營が確保される必要がある。イギリスでは、目標價格に對する達成度によりこれに對應しており、目標價格の設定にも獨立的なエンジニアの評價を考慮している(当事者間の力關係が目標價格に反映されることを防ぐ)。また、入札者の評價の客觀性を高める指標の設定に努めている[61]。

---

59) たとえば、Alstom Sibnalling Ltd(t/a Alstom Transport Information Solutions)v. Javis Facilities Ltd([2004] EWHC 1285)事件では、当事者は Pain/Gain Sharing に合意し、コストが目標價格を下回れば、そのGain を發注者・受注者(Alstom)・下請人(Javis)が分け合うこととなっていた。また、コストが500, 000 ポンドを上回れば、發注者と受注者がそのPain を負担しあうこととなっていた。しかし、大部分の仕事を實際に行った下請人が損失の負担にいかなる範囲で參加すべきかという点については当事者間で十分に合意されておらず訴訟において爭点となった。当事者はPain/GainSharing が下請人にも及ぶことについては合意していたものの、それ以上の点については、明確な取り決めが存しなかったのである。受注者は、下請人の負担に關して默示の合意があったと主張したが退けられた。

60) Baker, supra note 21, at353.

　また、パートナリングにより、受注者は大きな損失を抱え込むことを避けることができるが、逆に、大きな利益、大きなリターンを期待しにくい面もある。すなわち、ローリスク・ローリターン(實コストが目標金額を超えた場合でも受注者の被害は少なく、下回った場合でも取分は少ない) のビジネスになりかねない。これを、インセンティブに欠けるビジネスと受け取る企業もあるものと思われる(リスク共有の裏返し)。各ステークホルダーが固有に負担するべきリスクと固有に期待しうる利益(たとえば一定の成功報酬)とを、リスク共有の取決めにおいて適切に合意しうるかが、この方式の成否にかかわる一つの要点となる。プロジェクト参加者に適切なインセンティブを与える措置が、別途必要となろう。

### (3) プラント輸出における問題性

　なお、國際市場における大規模建設プロジェクトについては、發注者の裁量權、知識、経験、判斷力にきわめてバラツキがある。途上國の發注者と多數のプロジェクト關与者の間で、必要とされる情報の透明性やリスク共有をはかれるかについては、今日もなお懐疑的な意見がみられるのである[62]。

## Ⅴ. それぞれの国のパートナリングの可能性

　近時は、諸外國におけるパートナリングの展開を眺めつつ、各國が獨自のパートナリングの可能性を探る動きもある。Win/Lose の關係をWin/Win の關係に轉換しようとするパートナリングの手法は、契約の對立的構図から信賴・協調的構図に重点を移す、考え方の轉換を促すものであるから[63](對立的契約觀から提携的契約觀へ)、一定の普遍性を備えているが、同時に、各國の事情を踏まえた修正もありうるであろう。そこにおいて決め手となる

---

61) 海外建設協會、前揭注(7)45 頁。

62) Skeggs, supranote13, at471;茂木仁志「パートナリングにおける問題点と對策」OCAJI2004-4-5(2004)24 頁。

63) 海外建設協會、前揭注(7)6 頁。村田達志＝古阪秀三＝金多隆「建築プロジェクトマネジメントにおける主体間の關係性に關する國際比較研究」日本建築學會計畫系論文集562 号(2002 年)237頁、古屋邦彦「21 世紀プロジェクトへの一考察」國際商事法務27 卷8 号(1999)873 頁も參照。

いくつかの点を指摘しておきたい。

(1) まず、各國の從來の建設請負におけるリスク分配は、發注者・受注者間において、リスクをオール・オア・ナッシングに分配する基準を求める傾向が強かったが、このパートナリングによる企業間提携の考え方は、それとはまったく異質な發想であり、リスクと利益の共有の關係を實現しようとするものである。その鍵となるのは、情報の共有と透明性にある。これをどのように實現するかは、各國においてかなりの工夫を要する[64]。

(2) パートナリングは、プロジェクトの推進において、紛爭の發生を抑え、所期の成果をあげる仕組み、また、種々の問題をプロジェクト参加者の内部で解決する仕組みとしてはすぐれており、對立なく工事が進めばその大きな成果が期待できる。しかし、いったん法的紛爭が生じた場合の規律の方法としては、まだ、未確定な部分が多いように思われる。現實のビジネスはその受注、施工、リスク管理にわたってきわめて急速な進化を遂げているのであり、プロジェクトの複雑化、建設サービスの多様化を反映した契約理論の活用が求められるであろう。この点は、すでにパートナリングを導入した諸國においても同様であるが、今後、先例が積み重ねられ、學説による理論整備が進むことが必要である。

(3) また、パートナリングの發想は、發注者、元請、下請工事業者、資材提供者の關係を再構成する刺激となるものである。元請、下請工事業者等は、發注者との關係においてその地位を高め、共通するプロジェクトの對等のパートナーとしての地位を得ることにつながるものと思われる。この可能性は同時に、下請の技量の向上を要求するものとなり、また、從來の下請制度の見直しが必要となろう。

(4) さらに、より根本的には、組織による事業の遂行に關する二つ大きな理念の對立が控えていることに注目しなければならない。すなわち、競爭は自由経済社會の基本原則であり、そこから最善の成果が生まれるという伝統的な考え方と、よい成果を

---

64) パートナリングと系列との大きな相違として、後者の場合は、情報やリスク管理が總合工事業者に偏っているという指摘もある。金多ほか、前掲注(18)227 頁。

えるためには發注者と受注者が敵對するべきではなく、協働の關係こそが最善の結果をもたらすという考え方の對立である(發注方式の点では、前者は最低価格を基準とする競爭入札を、後者は多元的評価によるパートナリング方式をとりやすい65))。過當な競爭を避けつつ、癒着に陥らない協調が必要となるのであり66)、この競爭と協調のジレンマをどのように克服するかが課題となろう。また、パートナリングによる受注は、公共工事において、納税者との關係において問題を生ぜしめるおそれがあるであろう。

(5) パートナリングは、保險契約にとっても新たな問題を提起する。建設請負に参加する個々の当事者が負うべきリスクが不明確になるおそれがあるからである。

(6) なお、パートナリング方式がプラント輸出に必要な考え方であることは指摘したとおりであるが、國内工事にとっても必要な手法かは、なお檢討が必要であろう。


　例えば、日本では、建設請負は基本的にランプサム方式で、最終的な完成物によって請負の成果を判斷するという考え方であるように見える。また、發注者・受注者の關係についても各國において種々の狀況があったようにも思われる67)。さらに、民間の建設工事ではこれまでも、信頼できる建設會社をまず選擇し、価格等の條件は交渉の中で決め、施工プロセスにおいても話し合いで問題を解決するのが一般的であったことも事實である(これは、受注生産型の取引である建設市場が物の賣買市場とは異なることを示している68))。このような多様な事情から、日本ではパートナリングがなじみやすい土壌がすでに存在するという理解を導くべきか、そもそもパートナリング方式は日本には必要がないという判斷を行うべきかについて、今後見極めが必要となっている。


　＊延基榮先生のご健康を祝し、ご業績に敬意を表し、この論文を獻呈します。

---

65) 盛武＝芦田、前揭注(48)170 頁。
66) 岩下繁昭「イギリスの公共建設分野におけるパートナリング」建設業しんこう25 巻5 号(2000 年) 22 頁。
67) 日本では建設關係の法的紛爭がそれほど多くないように見受けられる。しかし、このことは紛爭の原因となる利害對立が少ないことを意味するものではなく、むしろ、利害の對立について爭うこと自体を抑制する狀況が存在すると見る可能性もあろう。
68) 盛武＝芦田、前揭注(48)171 頁。

## 參考文獻 (References)

社団法人海外建設協會『海外に學ぶ建設業のパートナリングの實際』(鹿島出版會、2007年)。

松崎和久(編著)『戰略提携 アライアンス』(學文社、2006年)。

安田洋史『競爭環境における戰略的提携』(NTT出版、2006年)。

茂木仁志「パートナリングにおける問題点と對策」OCAJI 2004-4-5(2004) 24頁。

石井眞一『企業間提携の戰略と組織』(中央経濟社、2003年)。

德田昭夫『グローバル企業の戰略的提携』(ミネルヴァ書房、2000年)。

Alan Ledger, An Agenda for Collaborative Working Arrangement: The Role of Partnering and Alliance in the U.K., 58-JUL Disp. Resol. J. 37, 42(2007).

Clive T. Cain, Profitable Partnering for Lean Construction 61(2004).

Gerald S. Clay/Ann L. MacNaughton/John F. Farnan Jr., Creating Long-Term Success through Expanded "Partnering", 59-APR Disp. Resol. J. 42 (2004).

Richard Honey/Justin Mort, Partnering Contracts for UK Building Projects: Practical Considerations, Const. L.J. 2004, 20(7), 361.

Sally Roe/Jane Jenkins, Partnering and Alliancing in Construction Projects 13 (2003).

Chris Skeggs, Project Partnering in the International Construction Industry, [2003] I.C.L.R. 469.

Sir John Egan, Accelerating Change: A Report by the Strategic Forum for Construction (2002).

Philip Nunn/Ian Cocking, The Tang Report: Catalyst for Change in the Hong Kong Construction Industry, [2001]ICLR 617.

John Bennett and Sarah Jayes / Reding Construction Forum, The Seven Pillars of Partnering 54 (1998).

J. Benett/S. Jayes(Center for Strategic Studies in Construction), Trusting the Team: The Best Practice Guide to Partnering in Construction(1995).

John Bennett/Sarah Jayes, Trusting the Team: The Best Practice Guide to Partnering in Construction(1995).

# Toward the Developement of the Study for the Sports Law and Establishment of the Sports Right in Asia

アジアにおけるスポーツ法学研究の発展とスポーツ権の確立をめざして

SADAO MORIKAWA(森川貞夫)*

*The purpose of this paper is a preliminary discussion of the order to establish the Asian charter of Sports for All. Its main contents include the following,*

1. *Especially with respect to Asian sprts culture,*
2. *On cooperation and cooperation in East Asia Sports,*
3. *The nature of subject formation and central organization that promotes.*

*I hope sincerely that it is realized in the near future with the power of Prof. Dr. Kee-Young Yeun..*

**Key word:** Asian Charter of Physical Education and Sports, Sports for All, Sports Right, Asian Sports Culture

### ▪ はじめに ▪

　私が最初にProfessor　KeeyoungYeun　出會ったのは先生が早稲田大學法學部に留學された時であった。もう10　數年前のことになる。当時は私も早稲田大學教育學部で非常勤講師をしていた關係もあり、毎週水曜日の早稲田大學での講義の合間を縫って先生に連絡したことを覺えている。先生は早稲田大學近くのマンションで生活をされていたと思うが、その後、韓國でのエンターテイメント・スポーツ法學會の設立以來、いくたびかのセミナーなどでたびたびお會いした。その時以來の先生の印象はとても精力的であり、みんなの先頭に立って學會活動を牽引していくリーダー

---

\* The former President of the Asian Sporrts Law Association and Japan Sports Law Association

シップに驚き、とても感嘆したものである。このような先生との出會いをきっかけにして私と先生
との關係は、共にアジアスポーツ法學會の設立に協力してきた「同志」でもある。

　さて、本論は、私がアジアスポーツ法學會並びに日本スポーツ法學會會長として2009年に韓國
エンターテイメント・スポーツ法學會創立10　周年記念2009　スポーツ法國際學術大會に招待さ
れた際の私の「アジア・スポーツ法學會の今後のあり方について(提案)」を今日の時点でもう一度提
案したい。なぜならこの課題はアジアにおけるスポーツ法學研究とアジアにおける「スポーツ權」の
確立にとって今なお重要な課題と思われるからである。さらに加えるなら、延教授が同じく2009
年9　月に東京で開催されたアジア・スポーツ法學會國際學術大會において「韓國におけるスポーツ
法の比較研究の課題」を發表されたが、その内容に大きな刺激を受け、今なお鮮明に印象に殘って
おり、その提案がまさに「世界化、國際化の流れの中で〈アジア連合〉　または〈アジア経濟連合〉
などのアジア機構」の創設という、壯大なヴィジョンを伴うものであったからである。


# Ⅰ. 今、なぜ、「アジア・スポーツ憲章
## (あるいはアジア・スポーツ・フォア・オール憲章)」か。


　周知のように現在、東アジアにおける「平和と安全保障」の問題は、絶えず緊張關係に
ある。その理由は、今日、日本と韓國・中國との關係は芳しいものではないこと、さらに
は北朝鮮の挑發的な對外政策によって引き起こされたものであろう。前者の主たる理由
は、日本政府および國民の歴史認識に起因するものであり、後者は、南北朝鮮という、分
斷國家に規定された現在の北朝鮮の政治体制から生まれたものであろう。

　以上のような意味で、今、アジアの平和にとっても、世界の平和にとってももっとも大
事なことは朝鮮半島をめぐる緊張の緩和であり、危機的状況の回避であり、日本と韓國・
中國との國際關係の改善という問題であろう。ところで、今日の危機を考える時、93～94
年当時の危機との決定的な違いは、問題が單に米朝關係の動向に左右されるのではなく、
すでに米國を加えた韓國、中國、ロシア、日本、それに北朝鮮の「6者協議体制」の枠組み
が存在しており、この「6者協議体制」の枠組みに再び重要な役割を果たさせることではない
かと思われる。そのために私たちはスポーツを通じてどのような貢獻ができるかということ

が問われているのではないか。

　したがって、私たちスポーツ關係者にとっての最大の關心事は、スポーツが「恒久平和、互惠、友好の維持に貢獻し、國際問題解決のための好ましい環境をつくる」(ユネスコ・「体育・スポーツ國際憲章」、1978年)ことにどのような貢獻をなすかということではないかと思われる。もちろん、このユネスコ・「体育・スポーツ國際憲章」の理念は、同時にオリンピック精神にも合致するものである(オリンピック憲章「根本原則」)。

　しかし、殘念ながらこのようなスポーツが持っている國際平和への潛在的な可能性への認識は、一般的にはまだまだ低いように思われる。確かに、スポーツそのものが國際平和を直接的に創り出す力よりは、現實の國際政治の力・作用の方が影響力は大きいし、スポーツだけで國際平和が作り出せるものではない。しかし、あえてここで強調したいことはスポーツによる「國際問題解決のための好ましい環境づくり」ということである。その生きた経驗が13 年前の2002 年日韓共催ワールド・カップ・サッカーであり、その後の若者を中心とした日韓の交流の深まりであった。2002年のワールドカップ共催直後の、日韓兩國の新聞社によるアンケート結果における日本と韓國の友好關係の改善にもかかわらず、殘念ながらその後の歷史的経過はすでにふれやように現在の状況は芳しいものではない。

　加えて、周知のように、日本と韓國の間には第二次世界大戰以前からの日本による朝鮮植民地支配、1945年以後においてもさまざまな問題があった。最近では歷史教科書問題、從軍慰安婦問題はじめ多くの、未解決の問題がある。しかし、こうした困難にもかかわらず、國民、とくに若い世代を中心にして新しい日韓關係を構築していこうという、流れ・動きが弱いながらも形成されつつある。これまでの歷史的経過では2003 年の冬、日本の青森で行われた冬季アジア大會での南北朝鮮チームの參加によって展開された南北朝鮮選手団への熱烈な応援もまたお互いの國の友好と連帶、さらに統一の希望と期待の大きさを示すものであったが、これは当時、日本人の心にもその感動が熱く伝わってきたものである。このような経驗は "World Table Tennis Championship" and "World Youth Soccer Championship" in 1991, North and South Korean athletes participated as a single team をはじめとして "2002 Busan Summer Asian Games" など通しても持續しておこなわれてきたことで

もある。

　まさにスポーツを通じての友好と連帯、平和への熱い期待そのものであった。こうした
ひとつ一つのつみかさねを通して眞の友好・平和、國際理解が進むものと私は固く信じて
いる。加えて多くの平和を望む世界各國と世界中の「戰爭反對、平和」を期待する壓倒的な
市民の聲ではないかと思うのであるが、いかがであろうか。

　その意味で2018年、韓國・平昌で開催される冬季オリンピック大會は絶好の機會では
ないかと思われる。この機會を通じてさらに一層、國際理解、友好、國際平和が進むこと
を期待し、私たちもそのための努力を大いにしたいと心から願っている。


## Ⅱ. アジア・スポーツ憲章の制定をめざして

　かって私は「國際化時代の体育・スポーツ」を特集した雑誌の中で日本のスポーツ組織
の「國際化の指標」を論じたことがある(『体育科教育』1996 年11 月号)。この時は確かに日本
体育學會を中心にこれまでの体育・スポーツ研究の反省から今後のあり方について書いた
のであるが、その視点は、國際化の指標を考えながら、第一に、學會(あるいはそこでの研
究)　の機能や水準が普遍的なものとして海外においても認められ、評価され、受け入れら
れ、理解されること、第二に、國籍・民族・文化を異にする世界の國々との体育・スポー
ツを中心とする學術交流を可能にし、活發化するための制度やルールをもっていること、
第三に、異なる文化や民族をもっている外國人を「開かれた意識と對等な地位」をもって、
受け入れ、認めるということではないかと考えたのである。果たして東アジア全体でこれら
の視点が有効であるかどうか、いかがなものであろうか。

　もちろんこの指標は國際化一般を考えてのことであったが、とくに東アジアを中心に考
えるならば、第三の視点はかなり重要であろう。それを前提にした上でいうならば、自然科
學・人文社會科學系を問わず、日々の私たちの研究の成果・實績が東アジアの人々からも
認められ、評価され、受け入れられ、理解されるものであるのかが第一に問われなければな
らない。これまでの歐米中心の研究が、そのまま東アジアのスポーツの振興や發展に無條

件的に役立つのかどうか、役立つとしてもそのための東アジア各國の行政・制度や人々の生活様式・慣習等々の違い、さらにこうした法的・経濟的・社會的・文化的差異や條件とどのように折合がつけられるのかなどが問題になるはずである。

　15年ほど前の日本体育學會創立50　周年を記念する學會大會(1999年)國際シンポジゥムでは、私は國際交流員會委員長という立場から、「21世紀東アジアの体育・スポーツ科學：スポーツ・フォア・オールの實現に向けて」というテーマを設けた。これは当然ながら、1975年にヨーロッパ評議會が「ヨーロッパ・スポーツ・フォア・オール憲章」を制定(1992年に改訂)し、スポーツが「基本的人權」の一つであると認めて現在にいたっていることを意識しながら、東アジアでの「スポーツ・フォア・オール憲章」はヨーロッパのそれとはかなりちがったものになるのではないかということを予測してテーマを設定した。なぜなら東アジアでは当時も今も民族對立・國家對立が存續し、軍事的・政治的に對立している國・地域があり、さらに發展途上といわれる國々が多く、経濟的には植民地時代が長く續いた地域・國に顯著に見られるように一人当りの國民總生産(GNP)が三桁と極端に低い國もあれば日本・韓國・中國、台湾のようにかなり發展した國もあり、國別あるいは國内外の貧富の差は激しく、さらに近年、東南アジア地域を襲った通貨・金融危機は今なお深刻な経済不安を強いており、そのために東アジア各國は失業や物価高騰など政情不安につながる諸問題をかなり抱えていたからである。したがって多くの東アジアの人々にはスポーツどころではないという意識があるのもやむを得ない。また客觀的にも貧困なスポーツ状況であるいうのも事實である。したがって東アジア各國の政府あるいはスポーツ關係団体・機關のスポーツへの對応は、さまざまな違いを見せているはずである。

　こうした状況の中であっても日本・韓國・中國が存在するこの東アジア地域においてスポーツが人間生活にとって欠かすことのできない基本的人權の一つであることには変わりはなく、また21　世紀の國際社會における東アジアの連帶・協力關係を構築するためにも、スポーツ・フォア・オールを進めることはとっても大切なことではないかというのがこのシンポジゥムを設定した理由であった。だがこのように断言できるのかどうか、あるいはこのような課題意識でいいのかどうかもふくめて東アジアのそれぞれの國の學會をふくめたさま

ざまな議論をしていくことが、今日の時点でもより大事なことではないかと考えている。

## Ⅲ. アジア・スポーツ憲章制定のための予備的討論

すでにふれたが、1975 年に「ヨロッパ・スポーツ・フォア・オール憲章」が制定され、さらに1992年に新・「ヨロッパ・スポーツ憲章」が採擇され。また國際的な機關であるユネスコでは1978年第20回總會において「體育・スポーツ國際憲章」が採擇された。そのことの意義と日本の狀況については2008年10月ソウルで開催された第7回KASELInternational Conference on Sport Law in 2008 において私は「基本的權利としてのスポーツ權の擁護と國民スポーツの振興～日本における現狀とその問題点～」の中でかなりくわしく發表したのでここでは省略したい。

ここ10數年、私は韓國だけでなく中國、シンガポールを訪ね、またヨーロッパではデンマーク、ノルウエー、イタリア、ドイツ、フランス、ポルトガル、スペイン、イギリスなどを訪ねながら、果たして東アジアでは「スポーツ憲章」制定はいかにして可能であろうか、自問自答してきた。ところが最初にふれたが、2009年9月、東京で開催されたアジア・スポーツ法學會國際學術大會2009での開會初日のシンポジウムにおける延會長の「韓國におけるスポーツ法の比較研究の課題」は刺激的な發表であった。この發表を聽きながら私は「スポーツ・フォア・オール」は当然のことだが、東アジアにおける競技力の向上をふくむ總体としてのスポーツ振興と發展のための方策、その方向性を指し示す羅針盤としての「アジア・スポーツ憲章」の制定が目指されるべきだと確信した。それほどに延教授の發表は刺激的であり、強烈なインパクトがあった。

繰り返しになるが、とりあえずは以下の事柄を盛り込みたいと願っている。

### 1. アジア的スポーツ文化に關して

盛り込むべき「憲章」の内容では先ず第一に、東アジアにはヨーロッパには無い多くの武

術・格闘技—例えばテコンドウ、太極拳、柔道、棒術などをはじめとするさまざまな運動文化や身体養生法、健康・身体訓練法がある。したがって東アジアにおける多種多様な文化・民族を包含する東アジア獨特のスポーツ文化とスポーツ觀・身体觀を承認・尊重することが重要ではないかと思われる。

### 2. 東アジア・スポーツにおける協力・協同について

また東アジア各國の経濟的・社會的状況はヨーロッパ以上に異なり、また國家的發展段階もさまざまである。したがって東アジアに住むすべての人々の生活と文化を豊かにするためのスポーツへの貢獻は、その方法・内容だけではなくスポーツの組織の仕方や普及方法においても一様ではなく、互いの経驗交流と情報の共有等、今後さらに努力して協力・協同することが重要であろう。

### 3. 推進組織・主体の形成について

アジアにはEU(ヨーロッパ連合)のような政府機關も非政府機關もまだ存在していない。しかしスポーツの世界ではアジア・オリンピック評議會(Olympic Council of Asia, OCA)があり、またアシアニア・スポーツ・フォア・オール委員會(Asiania Sport for All Association)、そして何よりも私たちのアジア・スポーツ法學會がある。

したがって東アジアにおける「相互互惠・平和友好」の關係を推進し、東アジア地域の協力・協同關係の母体となる「東アジア共同体(East Asian Community)」あるいは「東アジア連合(East Asian Union)」の設立のためにスポーツ界が率先して貢獻していくことが期待される。そのための第一歩として東アジア・スポーツ憲章の制定を實現したいものである。

### おわりに

最後に、繰り返しになるが、2018年韓國・平昌での冬季オリンピック大會開催は、ス

キー、スケートなどの冬季競技種目の普及・發展ばかりでなく、スポーツを通じての「國際理解・友好・國際平和」を推進するための絶好の機會である。とりあえずは韓國・中國・日本が協力しあいながら東北アジアにおけるスポーツを通じての友好・連帶を強化し、スポーツ法學の研究交流を實のあるものにしていく具体的な作業(ワークショップ)が必要ではないかと強く思う。

　当面はアジアスポーツ法學會が關係組織によびかけながら「アジア・スポーツ憲章」の內容づくりを進めるためのプロジェクト・チームを結成し、具体的な作業に取り組むことが重要であり、その大きな支えに延教授を中心にした韓國エンターテイメント・スポーツ法學會という組織が重要な位置を占めているのではないかと私は確信する。尊敬する延教授の還暦という慶事を記念しつつ、延教授のご健康と、以上に書いたような「大事」を實現・推進してくださることを心から祈念してこの小論を終わりにしたい。

## 参考文獻 (References)

Don Anthony(compiled), MAN OF SPORT, MAN OF PEACE, Sports Editions L.T.D. 1991

IOC, OlympicCharter, 2001

UNESCO, International Charter of Physical Education and Sports, 1978

Morikawa, S., 『スポーツ社会学(Sociology of Sports)』, Aoki Syoten, 1980

Sadao Morikawa, "Sports and Human Right", Sport Sociology, Aoki Publishing House, 1980.

Bruce Kidd and Peter Donelly, "Human Rights", IRSS,Vol.35,No.2, 2000.

International Charter of Physical Education and Sports, UNESCO, 1978(revised in 1992)

"White Paper on Sports－Discovery of a new Sports value－", Sasagawa Sports Foundation(SSF), 2006.

# School Education and Sports
# – Revision of Japanese Student Baseball Charter

学校教育とスポーツ－日本学生野球憲章の改正

MICHITARO URAKAWA(浦川道太郎)*

*In a word, baseball is undoubtedly the most popular sport to the people of Japan. Nevertheless, during its evolution baseball has undergone many ups and downs. This paper reviews the history thatbaseball has undergone and introduces the background and the main contents of the latest revisions tothe Revised Charter of the Japanese Student Baseball.*

*It is known that baseball migrated from America to Japan around 1871, when an English teacher, Horace Wilson, began teaching at the University of Tokyo (formerly known as the Tokyo Opening School). Yet, it was not until 1903 that baseball actually gained public attention when a game between Waseda and Keio Universitieswas held, and further when the national middle school championship baseball tournament (currently, national secondary school baseball championship tournament: Gosien of summer) began in 1915. From that time, the public could not get enough of it and so began "Baseball madness age."*

*People's visceral passion for baseball at times ragedout of control, which frequently led to various negativeside-effects such as fights between the fans, violence during games, bribery of officials, accounting fraud of entrance fee revenue, stealing star players from other teams etc. As such, criticism arose against the sport until finally remedial measures were instituted. At the same time, as the wave of the 20thcentury socialism expanded, it was deemed necessary to adopt various rules in order to regulate the social issues around the sport in order to pre-empt future problems. As*

---

\* Professor of Waseda University, Arbitrator of the Japan Center for Settlement of Traffic Accident Dispute, President of Japan Sports Law Association.

*part of this movement, the School Baseball Control Order was finally enacted in 1932. Furthermore, during the start of World War II, school baseball was banned entirely.*

*Following the war, baseball games resumed as did its earlier harmful side effects. Accordingly, schools began to voluntarily regulate baseball by adopting school baseball guidelines. At last, the Ministry of Education revealed the School Baseball Control Order. However, since the guidelines were only a temporary backup measure, the Student Baseball League adopted the Japan Student Baseball Charter (Old Charter) in 1950.*

*Nonetheless, because the Japanese Student Baseball Charter centered around baseball as an amateur sport, it did not address issues related to professional baseball. It is widely known that baseball was included as an Olympic sport with its current open qualifications for baseball players. As the privilege of student star players had been taken for granted, the former Japanese Student Baseball Charter could not but be amended. Responding to the social demand, the so-called New Chapter was enacted in February 2010, and implemented on April 1, 2010.*

*The New Chapter can be characterized as follows: basic principles of student baseball were clarified it becamepart of education; exchange between student baseball and professional baseball was allowed within certain limits; donation and financial support for student baseball was permitted; and mass media could be linked under some restrictions, so long as students are not used for commercial purposes.*

*Accordingly, the New Chapter has an important meaning in that it guarantees as well as activates baseball as a sound sport in the field of education.*

Key word: Sports, School Education, Baseball, Student Baseball Charter, Baseball madness age, Amateurism, Professional baseball, The New Chapter

## Ⅰ. はじめに

日本における最も人氣があるスポーツは野球(Baseball)である。

Baseball は、1871 年にアメリカ人英語教師ホーレス・ウィルソン(HoraceWilson)が東京大學の前身である東京開成學校予科で教えたことが始めといわれ、その後第一高等中學校(後の旧制第一高等學校)の學生でありベースボール部員であった中馬庚(ちゅうまん・かなえ)により野球と譯され、旧制の中等學校、高等學校、大學の課外(部)活動である學生野球として急速に全國的に廣まっていった。

このことからも明らかにように、日本における野球は、學校教育の中で育まれ、國民的スポーツといわれるまでに發展してきたものである。したがって、學校のスポーツ活動について考えるとき、野球との關係を無視することができず、また、野球と學校教育の關係を辿ることは、日本における學校スポーツの在り方を論じることにもなる[1]。

學校スポーツと切り離せない野球では、近年、高等學校、大學における部活動としての野球を監理する公益財団法人・日本學生野球協會(以下「學生野球協會」という。)が學生野球の組織・活動・運用の基準として定めた日本學生野球憲章(以下「學生野球憲章」という。) の見直し、全面的な改正を實施した。この全面改正は、學生野球を現在のスポーツを取り巻く社會環境に適合化させる目的をもつものであるが、同時に、學生野球を學校教育の一環として再確認するものでもあった。

本稿では、學生野球憲章の改正作業の一端に携わった者の立場から、學生野球憲章制定の経緯を辿り、學生野球憲章改正がなぜ必要になったのか、また、改正憲章がどのよう

---

1) 野球が學校スポーツにとって大きな地位を占めているといっても、野球が學校における他のスポーツ活動の模範・典型というわけではない。むしろ野球は、日本のスポーツ界では特殊な組織形態を持ち、特別なルールで運営されているともいえる。すなわち、學校スポーツである學生野球の全國組織は、後述する日本學生野球協會の監理下にあり、學生野球協會は他の多くのスポーツ分野を統括している日本体育協會には加盟していない。また、學生野球は、プロ野球と明確に一線を畫する姿勢を維持しており、ゴルフやテニスのように學生スポーツでもプロ化が進んでいるものや、サッカーのようにプロ選手と學生選手を含むアマチュアとが一体として活動しているものと相違している。したがって、學生野球は、競技者人數と地域・全國大會を大規模に運営していることにより(2011 年の高校野球加盟校は硬式・軟式を合計すると4, 567 校、競技者數177, 908人である。なお高校サッカーの加盟校は4, 174 校、150, 655 人である。高校の學校數が5, 109 校であるので、野球は約90％の高校で實施されている。なお大學野球部で全日本大學野球連盟に加盟しているものは381　校、23, 420 人であり、全國780 校の約50％が地域の競技會(リーグ)に参加している)、他の學校スポーツと比較して學校教育の中で大きな影響力を持っているといえる。

な内容を持っているかを明らかにすることで、日本における學校教育と課外(部)活動として
のスポーツの關係について檢討することにしたい。


## II. 学生野球憲章制定と改正

### 1. 學生野球の展開と野球統制令

野球(Baseball)　は、前述したように、發祥國のアメリカから日本の學校に伝えられたス
ポーツであるが、俳人正岡子規が學生時代に熱中したように[2]、すぐに多くの旧制中學、高
校、大學に廣まった。

1903年に早稲田大學と慶應義塾大學との間の早慶戦が開始され、また1915年に全國中
等學校優勝野球大會(現在の全國高校野球選手権大會[夏の甲子園])が始まると、野球は學
生のみならず大衆に熱狂的に受け入れられ、「野球狂時代」と呼ばれる社會現象が生じるこ
とになる[3]。

しかしながら、熱狂はときに行き過ぎを伴い、応援団間の諍い、試合での騒擾、商業化
によるチーム關係者に對する金錢の提供、入場料收入の不正處理、選手の引き抜きと選手
に對する授業料免除・生活費補助(いわゆる特待生問題)等々を惹き起した。

野球の弊害に關しては、内務官僚であり大日本体育協會副會長を務めた武田千代三郎
は、『學生運動取締論』を著し、「野球ハ近時頗シキ人氣ヲ博シ、野球ニ非ラザレバ運動ニ
非ラザルヤノ觀ヲ呈シ、今ヤ大小ノ學校悉ク野球熱ニ冒サレザルナク」と述べ、「私立學校
ニ於ケル野球団中往々ニシテ、爲ス所毫モ職業団ト異ナル所ナク學業ヲ廢シテ海外ニ巡遊
シ、東奔西走殆ンド虚日ナキガ如キ見ルハ、學校教育ノ本旨ニ背クノ甚ダシキモノト謂ハ
ザルヲ得ズ。」[4]等々と強く批判し、學生競技の取締りの必要性を唱えた。また同様の主張
も多くの識者から行われた。

---

2) 正岡子規の俳句に「まり投げて見たき廣場や春の草」(『寒山落木』1890 年)がある。
3) 學生野球の發展に關しては、中村哲也『學生野球憲章とはなにか』(青弓社、2010 年)に詳しい。本稿執筆に当たっても、同書を参考にした。
4) 武田千代三郎『學生運動取締論』28 頁以下(大阪市立高等商業學校校友會、1925 年)。

　この動きに對応して、文部省も、一方において、學生間に廣まってきた社會主義思想に對する思想善導策としてスポーツを奬勵する意図と、他方において、弊害も目立ち始めた學生野球を規制する意図から、野球の社會的ルール作成に乘り出す。そして、學校關係者を含めた野球統制臨時委員會の議を経て、1932 年に訓令4 号「野球ノ統制並施行ニ關スル件」(以下「野球統制令」という。)を發令・施行する5)。

　野球統制令は、前文、小學校・中學校・大學・高校別のルール、入場料、褒章、応援、附則から構成されているが、中學校の全國大會の開催や大學野球連盟の設置を文部省の承認事項とし、中學・高校・大學の試合日を土曜・日曜・休業日に限定し、さらに留年選手の出場禁止やクラブチームへの參加禁止まで細かく定めている。

　この野球統制令に對しては、施行後に新聞界や野球關係者から官僚統制に對する批判も多く出された6)。しかし、その後、戰時体制に入る中で、野球統制令による規制は緩和されることはなく、むしろ統制令を用いて「敵性スポーツ」たる野球に對する壓迫が次第に強まり、1941 年には中等學校野球大會が中止となり、また1943 年には東京六大學野球連盟に文部省から解散通達が出されて、學生野球は完全に活動停止の狀態になり、戰前期における學生野球は終焉を迎えるのである。

## 2. 戰後における學生野球憲章の制定

### (1) 學生野球の復活と野球統制令の廢止

　太平洋戰爭により學生野球で活躍した多くの學徒も失われたが、1945年8月の敗戰後、學生野球は急速に復活する。大學野球は、敗戰3 カ月後の1945年10月には明治神宮球場で東京六大學ＯＢによる試合で戰後の活動を開始し、翌年には東京六大學・東都・關西六大學の大學連盟を再結成してリーグ戰を再開し、1947年には上記3 連盟が全國大學野球連盟(後に全日本大學野球連盟に發展)を結成する。また、中等學校野球では、1946年に全國中

---

5) 中村・前掲書(3)41 頁。加賀秀雄「わが國における1932 年の學生野球の統制について」北大教育學部紀要51 号(1988 年)1 頁以下。
6) 戰前から戰後にかけて學生野球を一貫して支持し、商業化・興行化に反對しながらも、政府による統制に對して抵抗をした者として野球殿堂入りをした早稲田大學出身の飛田穂洲( とびた・すいしゅう)がいる。

等學校野球連盟(後の全日本高等學校野球連盟〔高野連〕)が結成されて、朝日新聞社との共催で全國中等學校優勝野球大會を再開し、翌47　年には毎日新聞社との共催で選拔中等學校野球大會を再開した[7]。

　このように學生野球は順調に再生し、戰前の繁榮期の狀況を回復していったが、娯樂が少なかった戰爭直後の社會狀況の中で「野球狂時代」も再來し[8]、野球統制令以前にあった弊害も生じ始めた。

　これに對して、學生野球の指導者たちは、一方で、學生野球を健全に發展させることを意図し、他方で、戰前の政府による野球統制を回避することを目的にして[9]、新たな學生野球界の組織的統一と自治的なルール作りを模索する。この努力の成果として全國の旧制中學・專門學校・高校・大學の野球部長また校長及び先輩から選ばれた委員により1946年12月に學校野球団体を統括する日本學生野球協會(現在の學生野球協會の前身)が結成され、學生野球基準要綱(以下「基準要綱」という。)が制定される[10]。そして、これを受けて、文部省は、翌年の1947年5月に文部省訓令6号により野球統制令を廢止し、政府による野球統制の時代が終わることになった。

## (2) 學生野球憲章の制定とその内容

　ところで、基準要綱は簡條書きの応急のものであったため、學生野球協會は、3年間の運用の中で正しさが實証されたとして、1949年に、評議員會の決議により形式的に整備され

---

7) 戰前は中等學校野球は春・夏の甲子園大會ともに朝日新聞社、毎日新聞社の主催であったが、戰後に再開されてからは中等學校野球連盟（高等學校野球連盟）が主催者となり、新聞社と共催の形で現在まで續いている（一時期は新聞社は後援の形をとったこともある）。これは學生野球団体が大會を自治的に運營することが望ましいとする理念と、資金力と運營能力の点で新聞社の支援を必要としている現實との妥協の姿といえる。

8) 日本のプロ野球は、1920年に合資會社日本運動協會が設立された時に始まり、1936年に日本職業野球連盟が設立されてリーグ戰形式の公式戰が開始され、次第に人氣を得ていったが、戰前期には學生野球に對する世間の評価の方が高かった。しかし戰後の1946　年ににプロ野球公式戰が再開されると、有力選手の活躍もあり、また新聞社、鐵道會社、映畫會社等の企業が宣伝媒体として球団を保有したこともあって、急速に人氣を高めていった(1948年にはプロ野球の再編があり、現在のセントラル・リーグとパシフィック・リーグの2　リーグ制になる)。したがって、戰後における野球への世間の關心は、學生野球から次第にプロ野球を主体としたものに変化していったといえる。

9) 戰後においても野球統制令は存續し、文部省は統制令を戰後の狀況に適合させることで維持することを望んだ。これに對して、學生野球界は、強く反發し、學生野球団体の自治的なルールを制定することを指向し、結局、文部省も學生野球界の要望を受入れ、自治的ルールが制定されるならば野球統制令を廢止することに同意した。

10) 中村哲也「日本學生野球協會の成立と『學生野球基準要綱』の制定」一橋大學スポーツ研究26　号25　頁以下(2007　年)。

た學生野球憲章を制定することにした。そして起草を委任された委員會は外岡茂十郎(とのおか・もじゅうろう)[11] を中心として作業を進め、日本學生野球憲章は、最終的には1950年1月22日の學生野球協會評議員會總會の決定により基準要綱の改正として成立することになった[12]。この現在の憲章の原点である改正前の學生野球憲章(以下「旧憲章」という。)は、第2 代學生野球協會會長である天野貞祐(あまの・ていゆう)が起草した前文[13] および總則、大學野球のルール、高校野球のルール、附則から成るものであり、學生野球の商業化・興行化を規制した野球統制令の方針を継受し、基準要綱の考え方を維持しつつ、官僚統制的な色彩を拂拭する概要以下の内容を持つものである:

　① 野球大會を主催する団体の役員を關係學校の責任者及び野球に知識経驗ある者に限定すること(4 條1 項)。

　② 入場料の徴收を學生野球協會の承認がない限り大會等の運營費などの経費に当てる範囲に限ること(7、18 條)。

　③ 選手は學校長が身体・學業・人物について適当と認めた者に限ること(9 條)。

　④ 選手はプロ選手との試合をし、またプロ選手のコーチを受けることができないこと(10條)。

　⑤ 選手は自校を背景とするクラブチームを除き、他のクラブチームの試合に出場しないこと(11條)。

　⑥ 選手として名義の如何を問わず他より學費、生活費等を受けることができないこと(13條)。

---

11) 學生野球憲章制定の中心になった外岡茂十郎は、早稲田大學法學部の家族法の教授であり、飛田穂洲の學生野球に對する考えに共鳴し、1942年から22年間早稲田大學野球部長を務め、大學野球の發展に寄与し、1982 年に野球殿堂入りをした。

12) 中村・前揭書(3)143 頁以下。

13) 天野貞祐は、戰前は京都帝國大學教授であり、戰後は學生野球協會の初代會長安部磯雄の後を受けて第2代會長に就任し、その後、吉田茂首相の下で文部大臣に就任したカント哲學を研究した哲學者である。鈴村裕輔「天野貞祐と野球」ベースボーロジー5 号117 頁以下(2004年)参照。なお、天野の起草した學生野球憲章前文は若干の修正を受けて、現在の學生野球憲章の前文にも採用されている。天野起草の前文では、「われわれの野球は日本學生野球として日本人たることと學生たることの自覺を基礎とする。日本人たることを忘れたり、學生の持場を逸脱したりしてはわれらの野球は成り立ちえない……」となっていたが、その後、「日本人たること」および「日本人たることを忘れたり、學生の持場を逸脱したりしては」の部分が削除され、それに即して若干の修正が施されている。この変更には、高野連が1991年に全國高校体育連盟(高体連)に先驅けて朝鮮人學校に門戸開放したことに表れているように、同世代の學生に廣く野球への参加を促す姿勢を見ることができる。

⑦　選手はコーチ、審判等を行うに当り当然必要な経費以外の金品等を受けることができないこと(14條)。

⑧　本憲章の執行の權限が組織された學生野球協會にあり(2　條)、學生野球協會は學生野球の精神に反した選手、野球部に對して審査室の議を経て警告、謹慎、出場禁止又は除名の處置ができること(20條)。

さらに、このほか次の点も規定された:

⑨　大學野球については春秋各３カ月間のシーズン制を採用し、リーグ戦は常置団体が主催するものとし、また、高校野球の全國大會は高野連の主催するものに限定すること。また、地方大會や對抗試合も關係上部団体等の承認を得て行うこと(3、17條)。

これを見ても分かるように、旧憲章の特色は、第１に、選手資格に學業が擧げられ(③)、また、大學野球についてシーズン制を導入し、リーグ・大會開催を大學野球連盟と高野連の管理下に置く(⑨)など、學校中心・教育重視の姿勢が示されていることである。第２に、入場料の徵收・使途を規制し(②)、主催団体の役員を原則的に學校の責任者や野球知識ある者に限る(①)など、商業化・興行化に歯止めをかけたことである。第３に、プロ選手との試合、プロ選手の指導、クラブチームの試合への出場の禁止(④)、野球に關する謝礼の禁止(⑦)、選手としての學費・生活費援助の禁止(⑥)など、プロとの間に嚴格な垣根を設けて「アマチュアリズム」の徹底を図ったことである。また、第4に、學生野球協會に本憲章の執行權限があり、憲章違反に對して制裁する權限が協會に歸屬することを明らかにして(⑧)、官僚統制を排除した學生野球の自治を明確にしたことも特色である。

## 3. 學生野球憲章の改正

上述したように、旧憲章の制定により、學生野球は、戦前の政府による野球統制から完全に解放され、自治權を獲得するとともに、「アマチュアリズム」を標榜してプロとの間の嚴しい垣根を設けた。これにより、學生野球協會が中心になって學生野球を自治的に運営し、問題事例はあったものの、プロ野球球団による選手爭奪からも學生野球の主体性を維持することができた[14]。

　しかしながら他のスポーツ領域においてプロ・アマの垣根が次第に取り拂われ、選手資格がオープン化された形でオリンピック種目に野球が採用される時代となり、プロとの交流を完全に遮斷した旧憲章に疑問が生じ、また、憲章違反に對する學生野球協會審査室の嚴格な處分に關する手續的保障が十分ではなく、協會及びその傘下の大學野球連盟や高野連の「獨善」的態度に批判も生じてきた。

　このような學生野球を取り巻く社會環境の変化の中で、特待生問題を契機にして、學生野球憲章の改正が浮上してくるのである。

### (1) 特待生問題と學生野球憲章改正

### 1) 高校野球選手の特待生問題

　2007 年に發生した特待生問題は、プロ野球球団が將來の入団を條件に大學選手に裏金を提供していたことが發覺したことに端を發して、当該選手の出身校である高校が中學時代のスポーツの實績に応じて授業料を免除する特典を30人を超える野球部員(特待生)にも与えていたことが明らかになったものである。これは、「選手又は部員は、いかなる名義によるものであっても、他から選手又は部員であることを理由として支給され又は貸与されるものと認められる學費、生活費その他の金品を受けることができない」とする學生野球憲章13　條1　項(上記2(2)⑥参照)に明白に違反する行爲である。しかし、この事件が本問題だけに限局せず學生野球全体を搖るがす大問題に發展したのは、特待生制度が上述の學校のみならず全國的に行われており、學生野球協會もその實態を把握していながら放置しており[15]、學生野球以外では學生の能力により學校から特典を得ることはむしろ常識化していて、特待生を嚴禁する學生野球憲章が時代遅れなのではないかとの疑念を生じさせたからである。

---

14) 第3代高野連會長の佐伯達夫は、プロ野球のスカウトが高校選手に現金を渡してプロ球団への強引な勸誘をしたのに對して、1956年に「佐伯通達」を出し、「高校野球は、決してプロ選手を養成するのが目的ではありません。野球を通じて將來日本のために役立つ立派な人間を作る以外には、なにもない」と述べ、學生野球の教育的意義を強く打ち出し、プロ野球の介入に強い拒否感を示した。

15) 高野連が2007 年5 月に實施した調査でも、特待生を選手登録させていた高校は377 校、選手數7, 920 人であり、登録學校の9％が學生野球憲章に抵触する特待生制度を設けていた。

この問題に對して、高野連は、「高校野球特待生問題有識者會議」を設置して特待生制度の在り方・基準づくりを行い、一定の條件の下に野球特待生制度を認めることにしたが16)、學生野球協會も、特待生問題で學生野球憲章13條と現實との間の隔たりが明らかになったために、學生野球憲章全體を見直す作業に着手することになった。

### 2) 學生野球憲章改正作業の経緯

學生野球協會は、2008年5月に學生野球憲章檢討委員會(以下「檢討委員會」という。)17)を設置して憲章の改正作業に着手した。檢討委員會は關係者から⑤回にわたり意見を聽取した後に、2008年12月から2010年3月まで21回の小委員會を開催して憲章の改正案と付屬規則である審査室の設置、運營に關する規則等を檢討・起草したが、全面改正された學生野球憲章(以下、旧憲章と對照して「新憲章」という。)は、2010年2月に制定、同年4月1日に施行された18)。

## Ⅲ. 学生野球憲章改正の考え方と改正点

### 1. 學生野球憲章改正の基本的な考え方

學生野球憲章を改正するに當たり、檢討委員會が立脚した基本的な考え方は、學生の教育を受ける權利を前提とする教育の一環として學生野球を捉えるとともに、旧憲章の訓示的色彩を拂拭することにあり、この考え方は具体的には次のような形で表現された。

---

16) 高野連有識者會議は、特待生制度を下記の條件で認める答申をし、現在もこの基準で特待生制度は運用されている。1) ①〜④の特待生制度の内容を各學校が予め公開するすること。①能力により入學金、授業料等の免除の特典を受ける特待生制度の存在、②特待生の人數、③特待生採用の基準として學業が一般性と同水準であり、品行方正であること、④中學校長の推薦書があり採用手順を履行すること。2)特待生の人數は各學年5 名以下とすることが望ましい、3)怪我等により特待生の條件を滿たさなくなっても學業継續の措置を講じること、4)國外からの特待生に對して日本語學習の便宜を与えること、など。

17) 委員會は、石井紫郎(元東京大學法學部長)が委員長になり、辻村哲夫(近大姫路大學教育學部長)、望月浩一郎(弁護士)、野村徹(前早稲田大學野球部長)、西岡宏堂(元膳所高校野球部長)、田和一浩(日本學生野球協會理事)、大谷哲夫(駒澤大學總長)、田名部和裕(日本高等學校野球連盟理事)及び筆者の9 名により構成された。

18) 新憲章である日本學生野球憲章は、日本學生野球協會のホームページ(http://www.student-baseball.or.jp/charter_rule/index.html)にその全文が掲載されている。

### (1) 學生野球の基本原理の明確化

改めて言うまでもないことであるが、學生野球の根本的な在り方を定める憲章におい
て、その基本原理・原則を明確にしておくことは必要であり、當然である。

旧憲章は、前文において學生野球の理念を述べているが、憲章の目的としては「學生野
球の健全な發達を図る」(1條)とだけ規定し、いずれも抽象的な內容であった。

新憲章は、學生野球に獨自の教育的な意味を認める旧憲章の思想を受け継ぐと述べる
とともに[19]、より具体的に學生野球が教育の一環であり、學生の人間育成に役立つもので
あり、そのために當然に遵守すべき行動原理[20] と事柄を定めるものとして憲章が存在する
ことを明らかにしている(前文、2條)。

### (2) 教育の一環としての學生野球

新憲章は、教育の一環としての學生野球を基本原理としているが、すべての學生に學
生野球を行う機會が保障されていることを明らかにして(4條)、學生野球が學生全員のもの
であり、一般學生と野球部員は同質・同等であって、その間に區別・差別があってはなら
ないことを示している[21]。

また、野球部員と一般學生との間に相違があってはならないことから、部員は學生とし
て教育を受ける權利が保障されており(5條)、學校教育と野球部活動とは兩立できるもので
なければならず(10條)、學校と指導者は部員に教育課程を履修することを保障しなければな
らない(11條)とも定めている。

---

19) 新憲章の前文は旧憲章の前文を全文引用して「全く正しい思想を表明する」と評価している。

20) 新憲章2 條は、學生野球がスポーツであると同時に教育の一環であることを明確にするために、スポーツの基本理念を示
すオリンピック憲章を踏まえて學生野球の基本原理を示している。

21) 高校・大學の學生で野球部への入部を希望する者があれば、入部の機會は保障され、合理的な理由なく排除してはならず、
また女子學生が學生野球に参加したいと希望する場合にも配慮をすることが求められる。なお、女子學生がマネージャーと
して高校野球に参加し、ベンチ入りすることは既に認められており、大學野球では選手として試合参加も認められ、東京六
大學野球で女子選手が公式試合に出場したこともある。高校野球では、体力差から生じる危険防止のため、選手登録は
現在はできない。なお、女子だけの學生野球(全國高等學校女子硬式野球連盟、全日本大學女子野球連盟)は別に存在
している。

### (3) プロ野球との關係

新・旧憲章間で大きな変化があったのは、この部分である。すなわち、旧憲章は、學生野球とプロ野球との間に大きな障壁を設けて相互交流を原則的に禁止していた(旧憲章10條、前記Ⅱ. 2(2)④)。これに對して、新憲章は、學生野球協會の承認を前提として、一定の條件の下で、學生野球団体と加盟校はプロ野球と練習・試合・講習會・シンポジウムなどの交流することができると定めた(15條)。また、元プロ野球選手や元プロ關係者が學生野球資格[22] を回復して學生野球界に復歸し、コーチ・監督などの指導者として活動できることを明確にした(16條)[23]。

このように、新憲章は、學生野球とプロ野球の交流を促進する立場を明らかにしているが、同時に、選手獲得のためのプロ野球側の金品提供等による學生野球の汚染を防止する規定も設けている。これは學生野球として決して讓ることができない一線であり、加盟校、野球部、部員(親權者・代理人を含む)、指導者に對して、プロ野球球団と選手契約または雇用契約などの締結を條件として金品および経済的利益を受けることを嚴禁している(20條 2項、23條 3項 4項、24條 2項 3項)。

### (4) 學生野球に對する寄附・援助

學生野球が外部から干渉を受けず獨立して運營するためには、外部からの寄附や援助を規制しなければならないが、円滑に活動するためには、必要な資金等を外部から獲得しなければならない。このため、新憲章は學生野球団体、加盟校、野球部、部員、指導者の各々について寄附や援助を受けられる條件を細かく定めている。學生野球団体は、學生野球の發展のために、また加盟校・野球部は、學校長・野球部長の管理下で野球部の運營の

---

22) 新憲章は、アマチュアという概念が明確ではないため、その語を避けて、「學生野球構成員資格(學生野球資格)」という語を用いて「學生野球の部員、クラブチーム参加者、指導者、審判員、學生野球団体の役員となるための資格」と定義して、プロ野球關係者と區別する用語としている。

23) 旧憲章の下でも元プロ野球選手・關係者が學生野球界に復歸する道は存在していたが、それには嚴しい條件が付されていた。新憲章制定後は、學生野球とプロ野球の相互交流を図る意味で、元プロ野球選手等が學生野球資格を回復して學生野球界に復歸する道を擴大しており、現行の「學生野球資格の回復に關する規則」では一定の研修を受けることで元プロ野球選手が學生野球資格を回復することができるとされ、多くの元プロ野球選手が學生野球界に復歸してきている。

ために寄附・援助を受けることができるが、收支を明確にすることが求められ、學生野球
団体は必要な場合には加盟校・野球部に對して收支に關して報告を求めることができると
規定している(19-21 條)[24]。

### (5) 野球に關して部員、指導者が受けることができる援助對価の明確化

學生野球は原則的に経濟的利益を伴わないものであり、それがプロ野球と相違する点
である。しかし學校が野球部を強化しようとすれば、技能優秀な學生に一定の援助を約束
して入學を勸誘することも必要であり、また學生が優秀な野球能力を活かすためにより良
い條件を提供する學校を選択することを否定することはできない。

このような要請の中で特待生問題は生じたのであるが、新憲章は、部員が野球に關し
て加盟校から援助を受ける條件について、奬學金制度に基づくもの、大學野球連盟・高野
連の定める基準に基づく入學金・學費の一部ないし全部の免除に限ることを定めており、
高野連が特待生問題について委員會を設置して定めたルールを踏襲している(23條1項2
項)。

學生野球が盛んになるにしたがって、加盟校の中には、實績のある指導者を招いて野球
部の強化に乗り出すところもあり、元プロ野球選手も指導者に採用されてきている。しか
し、このような指導者が勝利至上主義の下で對価を得て勝利を請け負うようなことがあれ
ば、教育の一環である學生野球の精神と相違することになる。したがって、新憲章は、指
導者に對しても当該學校の一般教職員の給与に準じた社會的相当性の範囲を超える給与・
報酬を得てはならないとして、野球指導を理由とする特別待遇を禁止している(24條1項)。

### (6) マスメディアとの關係

旧憲章制定の時代と大きく変化したものの一つは、スポーツとマスメディアの關係であ

---

24) 高校野球の春・夏の甲子園へは全國から代表校が集まるが、応援団を含めて、その遠征のために多額の費用がかかる。
　　このため代表校になった學校は寄附金を集めるが、この管理・運用がときに不明朗になることがあった。このためもあって、
　　新憲章は、寄附・援助について細かい規定を設ける必要があった。

る。テレビを含むマスメディアの發展により、それが報道する學生野球に對する關心は、戰前および戰爭直後の野球狂時代と比較しても、さらに幅廣い市民層に及んでいる[25]。したがって、學生野球とマスメディアとの關係についても新憲章は規定を置いており、部員を含む學生野球關係者は報道番組に協力することは認められるが、それ以外の目的の場合には學生野球団体の承認が必要であると定めて、不適切な商業活動等に學生野球が利用されない防止策を講じている(26條)。なお、學生野球団体は、試合・大會の報道をマスメディアに認めているが、學生野球団体による報道の承認については、野球關係者は名稱・氏名・肖像・映像等を使用する許諾を団体に与えている旨の規定を置いて、學生野球団体のマスメディアに對する協力がスムーズに實施されるように図っている(27條)。

### (7) 制裁に關する手續的保障

前述したように(Ⅱ. 2(2)⑧)、旧憲章は、政府による野球統制を否定し、憲章を執行する權限が學生野球協會にあり、憲章違反をした監督・部長などの學生野球關係者、部員[26]に對しては學生野球協會が審査室の議を経て一定の制裁ができる旨を定めて學生野球の自治を確立した。この學生野球協會の執行部から獨立した外部委員を含む審査室による憲章違反に對する處置は、學生野球の適切な運営を行ううえで成果を擧げたが、對象者に對する手續保障の面で不十分な点があった。このため、新憲章は、制裁の對象者をより明確に定め、また、制裁の種類を整理して、處分に對する不服申立手續きを整備した。このことにより審査室の行った注意や處分の決定に異議がある者は、學生野球協會に不服申立が可能であり、最終的には日本スポーツ仲裁機構(JSAA)に對して取消しの仲裁を申し立てることができることになった[27]。

---

25) 高校野球の春・夏の甲子園大會は、テレビで全試合が放送されており、大學野球でも人氣ある選手が現れると野球報道の加熱が生じている。

26) 學生野球の本旨に違反し、憲章に抵触する部員の行爲に對する制裁は、大學の野球部員に對しては行われているが、高校生に關しては、教育的配慮から、野球部の對外試合禁止や指導者に對する注意・處分で代替して、部員個人に對する制裁は行っていない。

27) 日本スポーツ仲裁機構に仲裁を付託するには、申立人である競技者と相手方であるスポーツ団体との間の合意が予めなければならない(スポーツ仲裁規則2條1項)。この点について、學生野球協會は申立人からの仲裁申立てに對して自動応諾する旨を明らかにしている。

## IV. おわりに

　日本における學生野球は、戰前・戰後を通じて、學校の場で野球競技を實施するという意味だけではなく、教育重視、教育の一環という立場を堅持している。

　この教育の一環としての野球という意味づけは、戰前には教育の場にとって不純な要素である商業化・興行化を排斥する中で、政府による野球統制にまで至った。そして、そこにおける教育は、野球による人格陶冶・形成という精神的な要素が強調され、戰時體制への移行過程で次第に米國起源の要素を排除する國粹主義的な精神主義が野球に押しつけられるようになっていった。

　學生野球は敗戰後に急速に再興され、新たに學生野球協會が設立され、協會の自治の中で野球憲章が制定されて、野球の國家統制は排除された。しかし、野球による優れた人格形成という精神主義的な意味での教育重視の視點は多分に殘されていたといえよう。

　これに對して、特待生問題を契機に改正された新憲章では、野球の教育的側面として、フェアプレー・連帯の精神を養い、友情を培うという精神的な要素は從來から繼承されているものの、むしろ野球部に屬する學生の教育を受ける權利を保障し、野球活動と教育の兩立を図る方向から、教育重視、教育の一環たる性質が強調されている。これは上からの「學生野球」という精神主義的な押しつけに代わって、學生たる野球部員のスポーツ權の保障という側面から教育の一環という考え方が再定義されて提唱されたものであり、2011年に制定・施行されたスポーツ基本法の趣旨にも合致するものである。

　日本における學生野球は、エリート主義を排して、廣く學生に門戸を解放する中で發展し、現在の高校野球で約4000校、16万人の加盟校・競技者の參加を得ているように、多くの學校と學生から強い支持を受けている。したがって、野球が今後も學校教育の大きな基盤の中で受け入れられていくためには、學生野球に參加するこれらの學生に對して、野球をプレーするよろこびとともに、健全な常識と教養を身につけた市民として成長することを教育の場で制度的に保障しなければならない。今回の學生の教育を受ける權利を基本に据える野球憲章の改正は、この点で重要な意義を持つものといえよう。

（早稻田大學教授うらかわ・みちたろう）

## 參考文獻 (References)

正岡子規の俳句に「まり投げて見たき廣場や春の草」(『寒山落木』1890年)

學生野球の發展に關しては、中村哲也『學生野球憲章とはなにか』(青弓社、2010年)

武田千代三郎『學生運動取締論』28 頁以下(大阪市立高等商業學校校友會、1925年)

加賀秀雄「わが國における1932 年の學生野球の統制について」北大教育學部紀要51号(1988年)

中村哲也「日本學生野球協會の成立と 『學生野球基準要綱』の制定」一橋大學スポーツ研究26 号
　　25 頁以下(2007年)

鈴村裕輔「天野貞祐と野球」ベースボーロジー5 号117 頁以下(2004年)

# A Study on the Sport Rights and the Safety in Playing Sports

スポーツの権利と安全についての試論的考察

－刑事過失認定における危険分配を中心に－

YONG-TAEK YOON (尹龍澤)* ・ YUSUKE ONDA (恩田祐將)**

*The Basic Act on Sport was enacted in June 2011. This Act is the first comprehensive revision of its predecessor in 50 years since the Sports Promotion Act was promulgated in 1961. The Act focuses not only on people who play sports but also on those who watch top-level athletic competitions and professional sports games, as well as those who support sports activities, such as instructors and volunteers. Its purpose is to create an environment where citizens can enjoy sports throughout their lives.*

*In order to achieve this purpose, it states, "Living a happy and fulfilled life through sport is the right of the people " and refers to the Safety in Playing Sport.*

*We discussed briefly about the Safety in Playing Sport and the Sport Rights in this paper, because the Safety in Playing Sport is one of the important contents of the Sport Rights. Yoon considered the Sport Right from the point of view of public law and Onda considered the Safety in Playing Sport from the point of view of criminal negligence.*

*The Safety in Playing Sport is a broad concept which is involved with various areas of law. In this paper, because of limitation of time and resource, we dealt with this concept only in relation to criminal justice, but this should be examined and pursued from multiple viewpoints. We hope our study shall help this discussion and contribute to the Safety in Playing Sport in our future society.*

**Key word:** Basic Act on Sport, Safety in Playing Sport, Sport Right, criminal negligence

---

 * 創価大學法科大學院研究科長・教授、韓國・全北大學校招聘教授、博士(法學)、弁護士、行政法專攻
** 創価大學法學部助教、博士(法學)、刑事法學專攻。

# Ⅰ. 序説

　現代社會に生きる多くの人が、スポーツに親しみ、あるいは何らかの關心を有しているといえる。趣味や娛樂、親睦、健康增進などの目的で、スポーツを樂しんでいる者、記録や勝敗を競い合う競技としてスポーツを行う(プロ・アマを問わず)者、さらにそれの觀戰に情熱を燃やす者など、まさにその程度に差はあっても、ほとんどすべての國民が何らかの形でスポーツを樂しんでいる。最近では、2020年夏のオリンピックの東京招致をめぐって、多くの廣告宣伝活動が行われ、招致活動の動向に關する報道が頻繁になされている。このような狀況に鑑みれば、スポーツは、現代社會に生きる多くの人にとって、有意義であり不可欠なものであるといっても過言ではない。

　ところで、かつてスポーツは、私的活動として國家による法的干渉を受けなかった。このことを千葉正士博士は、宗教や道德、家庭などと同樣に、「法はスポーツに入らずと言われる原則が働いている」として、國家法によるスポーツに對する尊重・遠慮によるものであったと指摘している[1]。しかし、現在では、スポーツの有する公益性がますます注目され、スポーツを行う人々にスポーツへの參加(あるいは不參加)を保障すべきであると考えられるようになった[2]。そして、スポーツの權利[3]、すなわち「スポーツ權」に關する議論も活發に行われ、ついに、日本においても、2011 年にスポーツ基本法(平成23 年法律第78 号)が制定されたことで、スポーツ權が實定法上、初めて認められるに至った。すなわち、スポーツ基本法の前文には、「スポーツを通じて幸福で豊かな生活を營むことは、全ての人々の權利」であることが定められ、また、同法2條1項には、「スポーツは、これを通じて幸福で豊かな生活を營むことが人々の權利であることに……」と定められたのである。

　もちろん、スポーツは、多くの人々にとって有意義である反面、參加者の生命・身體に對する侵害の危險性を內包していることも、また事實である。スポーツ基本法が制定されたことによって、スポーツ權の法的根據が確立されたことは評価できるものの、今後は、ス

---

1) 千葉正士『スポーツ法學序説』信山社(2001年)40 頁以下。
2) 渡邉融『現代社會とスポーツ』放送大學教育振興會(2001年)177 頁參照。
3) 日本において、スポーツ權が法的觀点から本格的に論ぜられるようになったのは、永井憲一教授が1972年に著した「權利としての体育・スポーツ——學校教育の健康教育化のために」『体育科教育1972年12月号』に端を發している。

ポーツ權の具體的な内容についてさらなる分析檢討を加える必要があるが、その際、權利としての「スポーツの安全」を保障するための作業が必要不可欠となる。

　事實、スポーツ基本法自體にも、その前文二段、2條4項、5條1項、12　條1項、14條、21　條に、スポーツの安全に關する規定が設けられており、スポーツ權の理解にあたっては、スポーツ活動の自由の保障と同時に、スポーツの「安全の確保」が最も重要視されなければならない。スポーツの安全を確保するためには、スポーツに關する様々な條件整備が必要とされる。たとえば、安全確保のための各種規定、基準等の整備、各種スポーツ施設における安全對策のための物的設置、社會制度としての保險制度など様々な側面が擧げられる。

　しかし、本稿においては、これらの課題を網羅的に取り扱うのではなく、スポーツ權の法的性質とその課題についての一般的な考察をしたうえで、とくに刑事過失認定論の觀点からスポーツの安全について考察することにする。筆者たちの考察の方法と目的は、スポーツ權について、「スポーツの安全」という側面からアプローチし、スポーツ基本法の安全に關する規定について檢討を加え、それを刑事過失認定における危險分配との關係で考慮することにより、スポーツを安全に實施するために關与者が負担すべき注意義務の内容を明らかにするための一つの示唆を得ようとするものである。

　本稿は、スポーツ法を公法學の觀点から研究している尹と刑事法の觀点から研究している恩田による共同研究であり、主に前半部を尹が、後半部を恩田が執筆したうえで、最終的に二人で調整した。ただ、日本においては、スポーツ權についてさえ未だ見解が一致しているわけではなく、スポーツ基本法も制定されて日が淺い上に、「スポーツの安全」という大きな課題を扱うには筆者の専門は余りにも限られている。本稿では、「スポーツの安全性」の極めて一部である「刑事過失認定における危險分配」について若干の考察を加えただけのものであり、まさに過渡的かつ細部的な試論に過ぎないことを斷っておきたい。

## Ⅱ. スポーツ權

### 1. スポーツ權についての學說

　日本のスポーツ基本法は、第177回通常國會において成立し、2011年6月24日に公布、同年8月24日施行された。スポーツ基本法の前文において「スポーツを通じて幸福で豊かな生活を營むことは、全ての人々の權利」であるとされ、また、同法2條1項には、「スポーツは、これを通じて幸福で豊かな生活を營むことが人々の權利であることに鑑み、國民が生涯にわたりあらゆる場所において、自主的かつ自律的にその適性及び健康狀態に應じて行うことができるようにすることを旨として、推進されなければならない。」と規定している。このことにより、スポーツ權の法的根據が確立されたことになる。

　これまで、スポーツ權の根據規定を日本國憲法の各條文から導きだそうと活發な議論が展開されてきた。伝統的なものとしては、スポーツ權の根據を「教育を受ける權利」(26條)や「健康で文化的な生活をする權利」(25條)に求める見解、あるいは「國民の幸福追求權」(13條)からスポーツ活動の自由權を、「健康で文化的な生活をする權利」から國家にスポーツの條件整備を求める社會權をそれぞれ導きだす見解がある。また、スポーツ權の性質について、スポーツを通じ幸福を追求することは個人の人格的生存に不可欠であることから、憲法13　條の幸福追求權をスポーツの次元においても認めるものであると解する見解[4]、あるいは、包括的權利としての幸福追求權は、自己決定權を包括的に含むものと解することができるが、自己決定權の認められる事項とその範囲については疑問を呈しながらも、その一事項としてスポーツを擧げる見解などがある[5]。

　しかし、このような既存の人權を定めた憲法の條文に依據して「スポーツ權」の性質を基礎づけようとすることに對しては、スポーツ權のもつ獨自の發展の可能性を制限し、さらには人類が幾多の闘爭の中で勝ち取った典型的近代的な人權の保障を弱化させることに陥りかねないとの指摘もある。スポーツ基本法が制定された今日にあっても、スポーツ權については、殘念ながら、「さまざまな學說が展開されてきたにもかかわらず、スポーツ權は、

---

4) 齋藤健司「スポーツ基本法の制定と今後の課題」スポーツ法學會年報第19 号(2012年)8頁。
5) 野村俊彦、中村睦男、高橋和之、高見勝利『憲法Ⅰ第4版』有斐閣(2006年)266-8267頁。

學說および判例によって、規範内容が確定し、法的權利性を有する『新しい人權』であるとは未だに認められていない」[6]狀況が根本的に變化したとは言えないのが現狀である。

## 2. スポーツ權と憲法改正

憲法改正が何時どのような方法で行われるかについては樣々な議論があり、現時点では全く不透明であるが、理念的にはいつの日にか憲法改正は行われるであろうから、スポーツ權を新しい人權として憲法に盛り込むことのメリットとデメリットについても、考察しておく必要がある。まず憲法規定にスポーツ權を加えることのメリットとしては、①法体系の中で最も高い位置にある憲法典にスポーツの振興を位置づけられる、②憲法が硬性であるため、スポーツ振興が立法府の多數派の動向に左右されることなくしっかりと根據づけられる、③立法府や行政府に影響を与えることができる、④市民を導くことができるなどが擧げられるであろう。

ところが、憲法にスポーツ條項を盛り込むために「スポーツ權」を具体化しようとした途端、大きな障害が立ちはだかる。なぜなら、「そもそもスポーツとは何か」というスポーツの定義自体が曖昧で、必ずしも一致をみていないからである。スポーツの種類が多樣な上、スポーツを享受する者の中にも、参加者(プレーヤー)、進行役、指導者、裁定者、ファン、その他の關係者がいるため、スポーツへの關与の仕方で主張する權利の内容が異なってくる。参加者(プレーヤー)も、高度な能力を有するアスリートから一般市民の愛好者まで千差万別である[7]。そのうえ、そもそも憲法を改正してスポーツ條項を憲法に盛り込む際のデメリットとしては、①法的効果がさほど期待できない、②時期尚早、③憲法改正のコストと便益がつり合わない、などが指摘されている。

---

6) 渡邉融『現代社會とスポーツ』放送大學教育振興會(2001 年)177 頁参照。日本において、スポーツ權が法的觀点から本格的に論ぜられるようになったのは、永井憲一教授が1972 年に著した「權利としての体育・スポーツ——學校教育の健康教育化のために」『体育科教育1972 年12 月号』に端を発している。「新しい人權」として承認されるための基準として、芦部信喜博士は、①個人の人格的生存に不可欠か、②誰でも行えるか、③他人の基本權を侵害しないか、などを擧げられるが、「スポーツ權」はスポーツの特性からみて、これらの基準を滿たしていると考えることはさほど困難ではないと思われる。

7) 千葉正士「スポーツ法學の現狀と課題」日本スポーツ法學會設立記念研究集會資料(1992年)5 頁以下参照。千葉博士は、スポーツにおける法的人間像を大別して二つの理念型に區別される。これについては、後述するものとする。

### 3. スポーツ權と基本法

　ところで、日本においては、1947　年に制定された教育基本法を嚆矢として、これまでに40　數本の基本法という名称の法律が制定された。スポーツ基本法もその一つである。もちろん、「基本法」と称していても、その形式的効力においては、いずれも他の法律と同一であり、日本における法の存在形式として「法律」と別途に「基本法」が存在するわけではない。しかし、基本法が對象としている分野では少なくとも、その基本法を實施するために制定された法律は、その目的・趣旨・内容が基本法のそれに沿うように定め解釋されることが要請されることになる。その結果、日本においては、事實上、憲法と法律の間に、もう一つの法の存在形式として「基本法」が認められているような現象を生じている。スポーツ權についても、このスポーツ基本法という受け皿の中で運用されることによって具体的な姿となってくるといえるであろう。スポーツ權という「新しい人權」は、現時点では、憲法規定との直接的な關係を通じて考察するよりも、まずは憲法と法律との"間"の「基本法」との關係を通じて考察することの方が相應しいように思われる。

　「基本法」という仕組みは、憲法上の人權を行政の施策または私人間の關係において具体化するための"橋渡し役"を目的とするものである。このたび架けられたスポーツ基本法という橋の上を様々な事象が往來することによって、両者の關係が明らかとなってくるであろうし、そのような作業の積み重ねの上に、今日までの様々な議論を止揚した「スポーツ權」の具体的な内容と性質が定まるのではなかろうか。


## Ⅲ. スポーツ権とスポーツの安全

### 1. スポーツ基本法における安全に關する規定

　スポーツ權が憲法上の權利であれ、基本法上の權利であれ、少なくとも、その内容の中心をなすものの一つは、「スポーツの安全」であることは明らかである。事實、スポーツ基本法も、以下のとおり、前文二段、2條4項、5條1項、12條1項、14條、21條に、スポー

ツの安全に關する規定を設けている。

前文二段スポーツを通じて幸福で豊かな生活を營むことは、全ての人々の權利であり、全ての國民がその自發性の下に、各々の關心、適性等に応じて、安全かつ公正な環境の下で日常的にスポーツに親しみ、スポーツを樂しみ、又はスポーツを支える活動に參畫することのできる機會が確保されなければならない。

2條4項スポーツは、スポーツを行う者の心身の健康の保持增進及び安全の確保が図られるよう推進されなければならない。

5條1項スポーツ団体は、スポーツの普及及び競技水準の向上に果たすべき重要な役割に鑑み、基本理念にのっとり、スポーツを行う者の權利利益の保護、心身の健康の保持增進及び安全の確保に配慮しつつ、スポーツの推進に主体的に取り組むよう努めるものとする。

12條1項國及び地方公共団体は、國民が身近にスポーツに親しむことができるようにするとともに、競技水準の向上を図ることができるよう、スポーツ施設(スポーツの設備を含む。以下同じ。) の整備、利用者の需要に応じたスポーツ施設の運用の改善、スポーツ施設への指導者等の配置その他の必要な施策を講ずるよう努めなければならない。

14條國及び地方公共団体は、スポーツ事故その他スポーツによって生じる外傷、障害等の防止及びこれらの輕減に資するため、指導者等の研修、スポーツ施設の整備、スポーツにおける心身の健康の保持增進及び安全の確保に關する知識(スポーツ用具の適切な使用に係る知識を含む。)の普及その他の必要な措置を講ずるよう努めなければならない。

21條國及び地方公共団体は、國民がその興味又は關心に応じて身近にスポーツに親しむことができるよう、住民が主体的に運営するスポーツ団体(以下「地域スポーツクラブ」という。) が行う地域におけるスポーツの振興のための事業への支援、住民が安全かつ効果的にスポーツを行うための指導者等の配置、住民が快適にスポーツを行い相互に交流を深めることができるスポーツ施設の整備その他の必要な施策を講ずるよう努めなければならない。

## 2. 權利としてのスポーツの安全

　スポーツ基本法には、以上六つの「スポーツの安全」に關する規定が存在している。とくに、前文二段では、スポーツ權を實現するうえで、參加者個々の關心、適性に応じて環境を整備し、スポーツの安全を確保することが必要不可欠であることを確認したものと解することができる。法律の構造的にいうと、前文は具体的な規範を定めるものではなく、その法律の趣旨、目的、基本原則などを強調したものであり、各本條を解釋するうえでの基準となる。スポーツ基本法の前文にスポーツ權を實現するうえで不可欠なものとして「安全」が明記され、さらに２條４項では、スポーツの基本理念の一つとして、安全の確保が図られるべきことが定められたことは、スポーツの安全を權利として保障すべきことを明確にしたものとして評価することができる。

　このような理解を前提とすれば、スポーツ權の内容として、從來から議論されてきたスポーツ活動の自由を守る自由權的な側面、スポーツの條件整備を要求する社會權的側面に加えて、スポーツにおける安全の確保という側面も含まれると解すべきである[8]。スポーツ權に關する規定は、「生命・身体の危險からスポーツを行う者の安全を保護すること、すなわち『スポーツの安全』を權利として保障」[9]　するものであるといえるであろう。

## 3. 刑事法學からみたスポーツ

　前述したように、スポーツは、有意義である反面、その參加者の生命・身体に對する侵害の危險性を内在している。この点については、刑法學において從來から注目されていた[10]。たとえば、各種格鬪技において相手を攻擊する行爲は、暴行罪や傷害罪の構成要件

---

8) スポーツ權は、基本的には自由權的側面と、スポーツの條件整備を國に要求するという社會的權的側面に二分して考察するのが通常であり、その観点からはスポーツの安全を社會的側面に含めることも可能である。しかし、私見では、スポーツを單なる競技としてではなく文化として捉えるべきであり、そのためには何よりもスポーツの安全確保のための配慮が重要となるのであるから、社會權的側面とは別個の獨立したものと理解すべきであると考えている。

9) 齋藤健司「スポーツに關する權利とスポーツ基本法の基本理念」日本スポーツ法學會編『詳解スポーツ基本法』成文堂(2011年)20 頁。

10) 藤木英雄『過失犯の理論』有信堂(1969年) 36 頁、Vgl.MelanieBerkl, DerSportunfallimLichtedesStrafrecht, 2007, S.25ff., ところが、スポーツ事故が發生した場合、實際に行爲者の刑事責任が問われることは希有である。スポーツ事故に關する刑事判例の少なさの背景については、須之内克彦「スポーツ事故に對する法的處理の現狀」『中山研一先生古稀

に該当し、さらにその相手が死亡した場合には、傷害致死罪や過失致死罪の構成要件に該当することは、刑法學上一般的な理解である。

　しかし、格闘技において一定のルールに従って相手を攻撃する行爲は暴行罪の、相手を死傷させた場合には傷害罪や傷害致死罪の構成要件に該当するが、刑法35　條を適用して、正当業務行爲による違法性阻却を論ずることができる。同様の理解に基づく問題状況として医師による治療行爲があげられる。医師による手術等の治療行爲も、傷害罪の構成要件に該当するが、刑法35條によって違法性が阻却される。このような思考方法の根據は、前者においてはスポーツに名を借り致死傷の故意をもった積極的加害行爲を、後者においては、医療行爲に名を借りた積極的加害行爲や医師側における專斷的治療行爲を排除するという点に求められる。

　前述したように、スポーツの關与者はアスリートから愛好者までおり、それぞれのスポーツの態様もまた千差万別である。千葉博士は、スポーツの多様性に着目し、スポーツの場における法的人間像を大別して以下の二つの理念型に分類される。すなわち、第一に、スポーツにより健康を維持・増進し、あるいは人間的交流を樂しむ人間であり、市民法が前提とする平均人の範囲に屬する者、第二に、スポーツの場で、自己・仲間や相手方に身体的・心理的危害が生ずることを当然のこととして受け止め、他者に優越し、目的を達成するために、危険を冒しても高度の技術を修得しようと指導を受け、鍛錬する人間であり、場合によっては死に至る可能性さえ予想して、たとえそのような事態が生じても、自分で責任を取ろうとする者である[11]。このように、様々な態様が存在するスポーツを刑法上一つの事象として捉え、スポーツ事故が發生した場合にそれを一概に處理しようとすると、被害者の承諾、危険引受けなどの觀点から理論的な障害が生ずる[12]。

---

　　祝賀論文集第4 卷現代刑法の諸相』成文堂(1997年)137 頁以下参照。なお、東京地判昭41・86・822判タ194号175
　　頁、大阪地判昭62・54・521判時1238号160頁、鹿兒島地名瀬支判平19・89・813LEX/DB28135478等では被告
　　人の刑事責任を認めており、千葉地判平7・812・513判時1565号144頁では被害者が引き受けていた危険の現實化及
　　び社會的相当性を根據に違法性阻却を認めている。

11)　千葉・前掲論文注7)5頁以下。ドイツにおいても、刑法學の觀点からスポーツを類型化して檢討しようとする見解が有力で
　　ある。Vgl. Dieter Döolling, Die Behandlung der Köorperverletzung im Sport im System der Strafrechtlichen
　　Sozialkontrolle, ZStW, Bd. 96, 1984, S.38f., Albin Eser, Zur strafrechtlichen Verantwortlichkeit des Sportlers
　　usw., JZ 1978, 368f., Hans-Heinrich Jescheck /Thomas Weigend, Lehrbuch des Strafrecht, Allgemeainer Teil,
　　5. Aufl., 1996, S. 588f., Heinz Zipf, Einwilligung und Risikoüjubernahme im Strafrecht, 1970, S.89ff.

　千葉博士のいう第二の理念型にあたるスポーツの参加者は、競技への参加にあたり、当該競技において通常予想され許容された動作に起因する法益侵害が發生したとしても、その危險を引き受けているものと解することができる[13)]。この場合、被害者の包括的承諾に基づき、刑法35　條の問題として處理することができる。しかし、このような思考方法を用いるためには、競技の性質に加え、包括的承諾の有無、個々の行爲の正當性、参加者の年齡・性別などの觀點から、個別具体的な判斷が必要であることに注意しなければならない。各種格鬪技やその他のスポーツは、その競技の性質上危險が高度に伴うものであっても、プロレベルのもの、レクリエーションや健康增進を目的とするもの、兒童・生徒が心身の育成を目的として行うものなど、樣々な態樣が存在する。したがって、刑法35　條を適用して違法性を阻却するためには、競技の性質に加え、包括的承諾の有無、個々の行爲の正當性、参加者の年齡・性別などの觀點から、行爲無價値性を減少・減失させる事情の有無を個別具体的に判斷しなければならない[14)]。

　これに對して、第一の理念型にあたるスポーツの参加者は、レクリエーションや健康增進などを目的としてスポーツに参加しており、危險性の認識を當初はもってスポーツに参加したとしても、それはスポーツへの参加意思であり、法益侵害に對しては認識にとどまるか、それすら打ち消されていると考えられる。この場合、スポーツに隨伴する危險の現實化としての具体的な結果に對する承諾を与えているわけではないため、被害者の包括的承諾を根據に35　條を適用して、正當業務行爲による違法性阻却を論ずることはできない[15)]。

---

12)　この点については、すでに別稿において論じているので、本稿では再論しない。恩田祐將「危險引受けにおける承諾型と非承諾型の區別」通信教育部論集第13号(2010年)67頁以下、同「刑法における危險引受けと過失認定」創価法學42巻1・82号合併号(2012年)47　頁以下参照。

13)　このような問題狀況を「承諾型の危險引受け」と呼ぶことができる。恩田・前掲「危險引受けにおける承諾型と非承諾型の區別」注11)73　頁参照。

14)　大分地判昭60・55・513判タ562号150　頁は(本件は、民事事件であるが、その思考方法は刑事過失認定においても斟酌することができるであろう)、小學5年の女子兒童が体育授業におけるサッカー競技中、他の生徒が蹴ったボールが左目にあたって失明した事案につき、「…危險が損するからといって、ボールを蹴り返すことを禁ずれば、サッカーゲームは成り立たない」として注意義務違反を否定した。また、前掲・大阪地判昭62・54・521は、深夜の路上における空手練習中、興奮のあまり相手方に對して一方的に毆打・足蹴りなどの暴行を加え死亡せしめた事案につき、「單に練習中であったというだけでは足りず、その危險性に鑑みて、練習の方法、程度が、社會的に相當」である必要があるとして傷害致死罪の成立を認めた。

15)　このような問題狀況を「非承諾型(狹義)の危險引受け」と呼ぶことができる。

## IV. スポーツの安全と危険分配

### 1. 刑事過失論にみる注意義務

刑事過失の中核的要素は、客観的注意義務に違反して結果を惹起したことにあり、その注意義務の内容は、結果回避のための措置義務であると解する[16]。

刑法における危険引き受け(狭義)の問題状況において法益侵害が発生した場合の行爲者の過失認定にあたり、それぞれの關与者の危険制御能力における優越關係という観点から、その問題状況を、①行爲者優越型、②被害者優越型、③注意義務同等型の3つに類型化することができる[17]。このことにより、關与者の注意義務の存否に關する判断を明確に行うことができる。その根底には、危険行爲に参加する各人が自己の立場で負担すべき注意義務を負うことにより、結果回避に努めるべきとする危険分配の思想が存在する。

このような理解を前提とすれば、第1の理念型のスポーツにおいて法益侵害が発生した場合の行爲者の過失認定に際して、刑法における危険引受けの思考方法を適用することは有益であるといえるであろう。

### (1) 行爲者優越型

行爲者が当該スポーツに關する優越した知識を有する地位にあり、被害者が素人である場合である。たとえばレクリエーションを目的としたスポーツの主催者・インストラクターなどの指導者的地位にある者などの業務従事者が、参加者との契約に基づきスポーツ活動を開催する場合を考えることができる。ここでいう「業務」とは、正当業務行爲における業務と同様に、営利的なものに限らず、社會生活において反復・継續して行われる行爲をいう[18]。

スポーツ事故における業務上過失致死罪の成否の判断は、①加害者が業務従事者であ

---

16) なお、客観的注意義務の内容をめぐって結果予見義務説と結果回避義務説の對立がある。この点については、恩田・8前掲論文「刑法における危険引き受けと過失認定」注12)55-56 頁参照。

17) 恩田・5前掲論文「刑法における危険引き受けと過失認定」注12)59 頁以下。

18) 最判昭33・84・818 刑集12巻6号1090 頁では、「反覆継續してなすときは、たといその目的が娛樂のためであつても、なおこれを刑法211 條にいわゆる業務と認むべきものといわねばならない。」旨、判示した。

り、業務の遂行中であることを前提として、②加害者に結果回避義務の前提としての抽象的予見可能性のある状態のもとで、③加害者が注意義務を遵守していたかどうかを檢討し、④さらに業務上過失行爲と死傷の結果との間の因果關係の存否を檢討することにより、行うことができると思われる。

　たとえば、夜間潛水講習死亡事件では、指導者的立場であるインストラクターが、受講生らのそばにいてその動靜を注視すべき注意義務に違反し、不用意に移動を開始して受講生らを見失うに至った点に被告人の注意義務違反の存在を認めている[19]。また、スノシューによる雪上散策ツアーのガイドであった二名の被告人が業務上の注意を怠り、雪崩の危險性のある場所で休憩したため、ツアー参加者二名が雪崩に巻き込まれて死傷した事案について、自然環境下において予測できずに事故が發生したとしても、雪崩の發生及びそれによる死傷の結果の予見可能性及びその義務が具体的に肯定される狀況下で業務上負っていたツアー参加者の死傷の結果を回避すべき注意義務に違反したとして、業務上過失致死傷罪の成立を認めている[20]。

　業務從事者には、業務に含まれる危險を回避するための「特別の注意義務」がその能力にかかわらず課せられているので、これに違反して被害者に死傷等の結果の發生を惹起した場合には、業務上過失致死罪の成立が認められることになる。行爲者が、当該スポーツについての優越した知識を有し、さらに行爲者が当該スポーツを業務として行っている場合や、指導者的立場にある場合などの行爲者に對する特別な監督責任が認められる場合には、行爲者は参加者に對して常に注意を拂い、参加者が安全に当該スポーツを終えることができるよう配慮すべき義務を負うと解する。


## (2) 被害者優越型

　被害者が当該スポーツに關する優越した知識を有する地位にあり、行爲者が素人である場合である。たとえば、ダートトライアル(Dirt　Trial)同乘!者死亡事件では、走行経験が

---

19)　最決平4・512・817　刑集46巻9号683頁。
20)　札幌地小樽支判平12・53・521判時1727号172頁。

淺く運轉技術が未熟でコース狀況も十分に把握していなかった被告人が、7年程度の競技經驗を有する被害者の「指導のために同乘Iしたい」という求めに應じて、自己の運轉する車兩に同乘Jさせ、スピード超過と運轉技術の未熟さが相俟って、コース横の防護柵の丸太に車兩を衝突・轉倒させ、被害者を死亡させた事案について、千葉地裁は、被告人の走行は違法性が阻却されるとした[21]。

本件では、被害者の危險引受けと行爲の社會的相當性の二つの事情を根據に違法性阻却を論じている。しかし、危險引受けという被害者の態度がどのような理論構成によって違法性阻却事由たりうるのか、また、危險引受けと社會的相當性がいかなる關係にあり、兩者がいかにして相互的に作用するのかという点が不明確である。判例は、違法性阻却を論じているが、刑事過失認定の問題として處理すべきであったと思われる。

被害者優越型においては、被害者が結果回避義務の大部分を負擔するのであって、行爲者は小部分を負擔するにすぎない。したがって、他の參加者がその分擔すべき注意義務を遵守することを信賴して、自己の立場で分擔すべき注意義務を遵守している限り、たとえ結果が發生したとしても、行爲者の注意義務違反は否定されることになる。なお、たとえ被害者がプロの資格と十分な經驗を有していたとしても、行爲者は「事故の發生を未然に防止するための措置をとるべき業務上の注意義務を負う」とした高裁判例があることに注意する必要がある[22]。これは、客の側がプロであったとしても、当該スポーツに業務として携わっていた場合には、第一次的に行爲者に注意義務が發生するということを示すものであり、その基本的態度は評価。

### (3) 注意義務同等型

当該スポーツに關する知識が被害者と行爲者とも同等の場合である。この場合、被害者と行爲者は同等に注意義務を負擔する。注意義務同等型のスポーツにおいて法益侵害が發生した場合、被害者側の事情よりも、基本的には行爲者側の注意義務違反を問題とし、

---

21) 千葉地判平7・812・513判時1565号144頁。
22) 福岡高那覇支判平10・54・59高刑速平10号124頁。

過失の有無を檢討しなければならない。その判斷において行爲者が自己の分担すべき注意義務を遵守していたと認められる場合には、行爲者の過失は否定される。

　しかし、行爲者優越型と同樣の注意義務を注意義務同等型の相手方に課すことは困難である。實際にそのような場合に刑事責任を問われるのは例外的である[23]。行爲者の注意義務違反の有無を判斷し、行爲者が注意義務を遵守していたにもかかわらず、被害者に分担すべき注意義務を逸脱するような行爲の有無、避けようのない事情の有無等を判斷することが必要である。行爲者の注意義務違反が認められない場合には、行爲者は不可罰とされるべきである。したがって、トラブルが發生した場合の措置や對處方法を事前に打ち合わせ、それに從っていたか否か、被害者側に危險を誘發するような行爲の有無、さらには突發的な自然條件の變化の有無など、個別具體的な判斷を要し、行爲者側に重大な過失のない限り、基本的に不可罰とすべきであろう[24]。

　注意義務同等型における相手方の注意義務の負担は、比較的緩やかに解するべきであるように思われる。業務從事者等の特別な監督責任を有する者とそれ以外の者とでは注意義務の負担は異なる。さらにスポーツの社會的價値を認め、それを考慮すれば結果が發生したからといって、直ちに刑事責任を問う必要はなく、過失認定は比較的緩やかであって差し支えないであろう。

　以上のような觀點から、スポーツ事故が發生した場合における行爲者の過失認定を行うことにより、それぞれの關与者が負担する注意義務の内容を明らかにすることができる。さらにそれは、スポーツの安全を確保するうえで、關与者が負担しなければならない義務や配慮すべき事柄を認識し、安全の確保に努めるうえでも、有益であると思われる。

## 2. 安全確保のために講ずべき措置

　注意義務の負担に關する檢討を前提とすれば、注意義務の大部分を負担するのは、業務としてスポーツを行うスポーツ団体、指導者などであるといえる。したがって、ここで

---

23）中田誠『ダイビングの事故・法的問題と責任』杏林書院(2001年)、138頁。
24）前揭・大阪地判昭62・84・821 は、前述の事情により行爲者に過失ではなく、故意の傷害致死罪の成立を認めている。

は、スポーツ基本法５条１項の規定に着目し、スポーツ団体が安全の確保のために配慮すべき義務について、基本法と刑事過失認定の両觀点から檢討を加えたい。

スポーツ基本法５条１項は、スポーツ団体に對して、安全の確保に配慮してスポーツを推進することに努めるよう要請している。スポーツ事業を行うスポーツ団体は、当該スポーツの安全確保のために、あらゆる配慮をすべき義務を負擔することは、刑事・民事を問わす当然の理解である。５条１項の規定は、安全確保に關する努力義務を定めたものであるが、基本法において、スポーツ団体の負擔すべき安全確保に關する義務を實定法上確認したものである。

しかし、５条１項は、当該スポーツに關する規則、基準、施設等の條件整備に努めるべきことを單に定めたものであると解すべきでない。條件整備に努めることは当然のことであり、それに加えて当該スポーツにおける事故の發生を未然に防ぐための措置を積極的に講ずべきことを認めたものであると解すべきである。このことは、スポーツ基本法の趣旨を定めた前文や、安全の確保をスポーツの基本理念の一つとして定めた２条４項などの規定に照らしてみても明らかであろう。

具体的には、スポーツ団体が、当該スポーツにおいて發生した事故に關する情報、判例等の收集・分析・檢証を積極的に行うことを擧げることができる。たとえば商品スポーツにおいては、その振興のために「安全性」が強調されがちである。しかし、その「安全性」というのは、スポーツ団体が率先して事故等の原因や、それを未然に防ぐための措置を檢証し、それを当該スポーツ事業の從事者、參加者等のあらゆる關与者に周知徹底し、それらの關与者が一体となって事故防止に努めてこそ担保されるものである[25]。このような措置を講ずることを定めた５条１項の規定は、スポーツの關与者が安全確保のために負擔すべき義務示すものであるといえる。そして、それは刑事過失認定において注意義務の存否の判断をするうえでも、參考にすることができる。さらに、刑事過失認定における判斷プロ

---

25) たとえばスクーバダイビング(Scubadiving)の民間指導団体SSIJAPAN では、インストラクターなどのダイビングを指導・先導するダイブリーダー向けの機關紙において、ダイビング事故を檢証し、防止策を提示し、安全確保のための注意喚起を積極的に行っている。栗山禎尚「ダイビング事故のケーススタディ５－８多發したダイビング事故の檢証から學ぶべきこと」divebusinessinternational2013Vol.2SSI ジャパン(2013年)13 頁以下。

セスは、スポーツ事故を防止するために關与者が負担すべき義務の内容を明らかにするものであり、逆說的ではあるが、スポーツ事故を防止し、スポーツの安全を確保するために講ずべき措置の方向性に關する一つの示唆を得るうえでも有益であろう。

## Ⅴ. むすびにかえて

　スポーツ權の理解にあたっては、その内容の一つとしてスポーツの「安全の確保」が最も重視されなければならない。スポーツの安全を保障するための作業の一端として、本稿では、スポーツ權の法的性質とその課題について一般的な考察を行ったうで、刑事過失認定という觀点から檢討を加えた。その檢討にあたっては、スポーツの關与者がスポーツの安全の確保のために配慮すべき義務を明らかにすることを重視した。このことにより、スポーツを安全に實施するために、とくにスポーツ団体や指導者が負担すべき注意義務を明らかにするための方法論のサンプルを示すことが多少なりともできたように思われる。

　國、地方自治体、スポーツ団体が率先して事故を防止し、スポーツの安全の確保のための努力を續けてこそ、眞のスポーツの振興、そして大衆文化としての確固たる基盤の確立に繋がるのではないであろうか。

　ともあれ、スポーツ基本法が制定されて日の淺い日本であるが、スポーツ基本法が制定されたいまだからこそ、スポーツ權や、權利としてのスポーツの安全の確保に關する研究、議論が積極的に行われる必要があり、それらを現實のスポーツの現場へ反映させていく作業が今後の課題として求められるべきであろう。

## 參考文獻 (References)

尹龍澤『スポーツ權の確立を―憲法改正への位置づけと基本法制定に關する一考察』公明'09年6月
　(2009年)

尹龍澤「アジアスポーツ法學の現狀と方途」日本スポーツ法學會年報第17号(2010年)

恩田祐將「危險引受けにおける承諾型と非承諾型の區別」通信教育部論集第13号(2010年)

恩田祐將「刑法における危險引受けと過失認定」創価法學42卷1・2号合併号(2012年)

栗山禎尚 「ダイビング事故のケーススタディ――多發したダイビング事故の檢証から學ぶべきこと」
　dive business international 2013Vol.2 SSIジャパン(2013年)

齋藤健司「スポーツ基本法の制定と今後の課題」スポーツ法學會年報第19号(2012年)

齋藤健司 「スポーツに關する權利とスポーツ基本法の基本理念」 日本スポーツ法學會編 『詳解ス
　ポーツ基本法』成文堂(2011年)

須之內克彦 「スポーツ事故に對する法的處理の現狀」『中山研一先生古稀祝賀論文集第4卷現代刑
　法の諸相』成文堂(1997年)

野村俊彦、中村睦男、高橋和之、高見勝利『憲法Ⅰ第4版』有斐閣(2006年)

千葉正士「スポーツ法學の現狀と課題」日本スポーツ法學會設立記念研究集會資料(1992年)

中田誠『ダイビングの事故・法的問題と責任』杏林書院(2001年)

藤木英雄『過失犯の理論』有信堂(1969年)

渡邉融『現代社會とスポーツ』放送大學教育振興會(2001年)

AlbinEser, ZurstrafrechtlichenVerantwortlichkeit des Sportlersusw., JZ 1978.

Dieter Dölling, Die BehandlungderKörperverletzungim Sport im System derStrafrechtlichenSozialkontrolle,
　ZStW, Bd. 96, 1984.

Hans-Heinrich Jescheck /Thomas Weigend, Lehrbuch des Strafrecht, AllgemaeinerTeil, 5. Aufl., 1996.

HeinzZipf, Einwilligung und RisikoübernahmeimStrafrecht, 1970, S. 89ff.

Melanie Berkl, DerSportunfallimLichte des Strafrecht, 2007.

# Necessity and Way of Legislation of "Act on Baduk (Korean Checkers) Promotion"

−Centering on the Act on Baduk (Korean Checkers) Promotion proposed by Congressman Inje Lee, etc.−

## 「바둑진흥에 관한 법률」의 제정 필요성과 입법방향*
−이인제 의원 대표발의 바둑진흥법안을 중심으로−

YONG-SUP KIM(金容燮)**

*This paper studies necessity and direction of legislation of an act for promotion of Baduk (Korean checkers). In particular, the study is centered on the draft of the Act on Baduk (Korean Checkers) Promotion proposed by Congressman Inje Lee, etc. to the National Assembly in August 2013.*

*Baduk, one of Korean traditional games, is a kind of mind sports containing the mental value system inherent in Korean people. Tradition of such Baduk culture to next generations, enjoyment of future generations, and enjoyment of young and old alike at home and in work places may contribute to unity of communities.*

*However, Baduk has been in a legal dead zone till now, because it has both cultural and athletic elements and has not been placed under any one of categories.*

*Necessity of legislation of an act for promoting Baduk can be*

* 이 글은 김용섭, "바둑문화 진흥을 위한 특별법 제정의 필요성과 입법방향", 행정법연구 제22호, 2008. 12. 201-223면; 김용섭, 바둑문화의 진흥을 위한 법정책적 과제, 스포츠와 법 제10권 제3호, 2007, 11-40면에서 기술한 일부 내용을 기초로 하면서 2013년 8월 국회에 제출된 이인제 의원 대표발의 바둑진흥법안에 관하여 검토하여 2013. 9. 25. 이인제 의원실 주관의 공청회에서 발표한 논문이다. 이 자리를 빌어 한국스포츠엔터테인먼트법학회의 창립과 발전에 큰 공헌을 하신 大東 연기영 회장님의 화갑을 진심으로 축하드리고, 앞으로 연회장님의 지론인 건강(Health), 행복(Happiness), 치유(Healing)의 3H의 삶이 지속되기를 기원합니다.

** Professor of Law, Dr. jur.(University of Mannheim, Germany), Chunbuk National University School of Law, 전북대 법학전문대학원 교수, 변호사

*found in the fact that it is a constitutional request and a national obligation as well. Baduk not only provides leisure for the public, but also has the effect of protecting the old from dementia and other mental diseases. In addition, Baduk has affirmative functions in the education of the young such as elevation of emotional activities, improvement of personalities, cultivation of logical thinking and problem solving ability, etc. Accordingly, like promotion of Taekwondo, Korean wrestling, traditional martial arts, etc., Baduk is also requested to be promoted under an independently legislated law.*

*When an act for promoting Baduk is legislated, it is considered a desirable way not to simply amend the Act on Culture and Arts Promotion or the Act on National Sports Promotion but to legislate an independent act on Baduk promotion.*

*The draft of the Act on Baduk Promotion proposed by Congressman Inje Lee, etc. consists of a total of 17 articles and appendices. In general, its contents are desirable and acceptable. But, some of its provisions are required to be corrected or complemented for passing the National Assembly. This paper has studied and analyzed them.*

*In future, when an act for promoting Baduk is legislated, it will serve as a good momentum for accelerating setup of the public certification system for Baduk directors, legal incorporation of the Korea Baduk Association, administrative and financial supports for concerned organizations and facilities, international exchanges and advances, etc. and realizing another jump of the Korean Baduk and spreading the Korean Baduk as Korean cultural goods throughout the world.*

**Key word:** Baduk (Korean Checkers), Korea Baduk Association, Act on Baduk Promotion, professional Baduk player, Baduk and law

# Ⅰ. 머리말

바둑은 우리의 전통문화의 일종으로 고유한 정신 가치 체계를 갖고 있는 두뇌스 포츠의 한 분야이다. 이와 같은 바둑문화를 차세대에 전승하여 미래세대 역시 바둑문화를 향유하고 가족단위 또는 직장단위에서 나이와 세대를 넘어 노소동락(老少同樂)하면서 사회통합에 기여할 수 있게 된다.

바둑은 2인의 경기자가 흑돌과 백돌을 가려 가로와 세로 각각 19줄을 일정한 간격으로 그어 361개의 점으로 이루어진 바둑판위의 빈자리에 흑돌을 가진 자가 두기 시작하여 서로 번갈아 가면서 한 점씩 놓아 정해진 규칙에 따라 반상의 집을 많이 차지한 측이 승리하는 경기의 일종이다.[1] 이와 같은 바둑의 정의에 의하면 바둑은 누가 집이나 땅(地)을 많이 차지하는가에 따라 승부를 가르는 영토게임이라고 할 수 있다.[2]

그동안 바둑이 스포츠[3]에 해당하는가를 둘러싸고 논란이 있어 왔으나, 크게 2가지의 입장으로 나뉘고 있다. 먼저 바둑을 신체활동과 관련하여 전형적인 스포츠에 속한다고 하기보다는 전략적 게임 내지 두뇌스포츠로 분류하여 물리적 운동이 중심이 되는 전통적인 스포츠와 일정한 거리를 유지하려는 견해[4]가 있고, 반면에 현대의 스포츠는 신체의 대근육운동에 국한시킬 것이 아니라 인간의 물리적 움직임이 중심이 된 통합적 활동에 포커스를 맞추는 개념이므로 두뇌활동도 다른 신체운동과 마찬가지로 스포츠에 포함시킬 수 있다는 견해[5]가 있다. 가령 사격과 같은 스포츠의 경우에도 실제로 신체적 움직임은 손의 움직임에 한정된 반면에 바둑의 경우에 손으로 두지만 두뇌 등 신체에 미치는 영향이 적지 않다는 점에서 스포츠의 특성을 지니고 있다.

바둑은 스포츠와 기예적 성질을 아울러 갖고 있으면서 창조적·전략적 사고를 필요로 하는 마인드스포츠[6]의 일종이라고 할 수 있다. 이와 같은 바둑은 일반 사회인의

---

1) 한국기원 바둑규칙 제1조에서 "바둑은 두 사람이 백과 흑의 바둑돌로 규칙에 따라 바둑판의 교차점에 교대로 착수하여 쌍방이 차지한 집이 많고 적음으로 승패를 가리는 경기이다"라고 정의하고 있다.

2) 문용직, 바둑의 발견, 도서출판 부키, 2005, 369면.

3) 스포츠의 개념적 특성을 보면 첫째로, 스포츠는 신체적 활동인 "운동(Bewegung)과 모터적 활동(motorische Aktivität)"이 결정적인 기준으로 작용한다. 둘째로, 스포츠는 자기목적(Selbstzweck)과 비생산성을 특징으로 한다. 셋째로, 경쟁과 성과를 내기 위한 노력(Wettkampf- u. Leistungsstreben)이 중요한 기준이 된다. 넷째로, 규칙과 조직형태(Regelung und Organisationsformen)가 있을 것을 요한다.

4) 가령 박주한, 바둑의 스포츠논쟁, 한국체육철학회지, 제10권 제2호, 2002.12, 91면 이하; 권오륜, 황미숙, 이호철, 윤희철, 바둑이 체육 혹은 스포츠가 될 수 있는가?, 한국체육학회지, 제44권 제5호, 2005, 89면 이하

5) 정수현, 바둑, 올림픽으로 가는 길 가능한가, 한국기원, 한화갑의원실, 정범구의원실 (공편), 2001,6면

6) 2008. 10. 3부터 10. 18. 까지 중국 북경에서 바둑과 더불어 브릿지, 체스, 체커, 중국장기 등 5개 종

여가생활을 보장함은 물론 노인들의 여가활동 및 치매 예방등의 정신적 효과를 가져 올 수 있고 청소년의 정서활동이나 성격개선 및 논리적 사고와 문제해결능력의 함양 등 교육적 측면에서도 긍정적 기능을 하고 있다. 이와 같이 바둑은 일상적인 여가활 동으로 국민들의 취미활동의 일환으로 행하여 왔다.

그러나 바둑은 그동안 문화와 체육의 두 가지 요소를 모두 갖고 있음에도 어느 범주에도 속하지 않아 법적으로는 서자취급을 받아 왔다고 볼 수 있다. 다시말해 문 화예술진흥법의 적용도, 국민체육진흥법의 적용도 받지 못하고 있던 것이 바로 바둑 이었다. 지금껏 바둑의 진흥을 도모하는 법률이 없는 상태에서 프로기사를 중심으로 한 한국기원의 내부적 규율로 전문 프로기사양성시스템을 운영하며 세계적으로 위상 을 높여온 것이다. 이와 같은 프로기사의 양성과정에 있어서 정부는 한국기원에 대하 여 재정적 지원은 없었다고 할 수 있다.[7]

바둑진흥에 관한 법률을 제정할 경우 우선은 스포츠와 다른 독자적 문화의 관점 에서 접근하려는 시도와 바둑을 스포츠의 일종으로 파악하여 스포츠법제의 관점에서 제도설계를 하는 방안이 모색될 수 있다. 이 문제는 바둑의 정체성과도 관련되는 바, 바둑진흥에 관한 법률을 제정함에 있어서는 바둑을 전적으로 스포츠로 보는 것에는 한계가 있으므로 문화적 측면과 체육적 측면을 모두 고려하면서 동시에 추구하여야 할 것으로 본다.

여기서는 2013. 8. 27. 국회에 의원입법으로 제출된 이인제 의원 대표발의의 바둑 진흥법안을 검토하기로 한다. 먼저 바둑진흥에 관한 법률의 제정 필요성(Ⅱ)을 고찰 하고, 본 연구의 핵심적 내용인 바둑진흥에 관한 법률의 입법방향(Ⅲ)과 이인제 의원 대표발의의 바둑진흥법안에 대한 검토(Ⅳ)를 하며, 간략히 결론(Ⅳ)의 맺는 순서로 논 의를 진행하기로 한다.

---

목에 걸쳐 제1회 월드 마인드스포츠대회가 개최되었는 바, 바둑은 마인드 스포츠에 속한다고 할 수 있다.

7) 바둑은 그동안 한국 특유의 실전적 역량이 축적되어 일본을 제치고 세계적 강국으로 자리매김 해 왔으나, 중국의 강세에 눌려 한국바둑의 위기 상황을 맞이하고 있으므로 이번의 바둑진흥법 제정을 계기로 한국의 바둑의 제2의 전성기를 맞이할 필요가 있다.

# II. 「바둑진흥에 관한 법률」의 제정 필요성

## 1. 바둑진흥에 대한 국가의 의무

우리 헌법은 문화와 관련하여 전문에서 "유구한 역사와 전통"을 강조하고 있으며, 제9조에서 "국가는 전통문화의 계승·발전과 민족문화의 창달에 노력하여야 한다"고 규정하고 있고, 대통령의 취임선서를 규정한 제69조에서 "민족문화의 창달에 노력한다"고 규정하고 있어 우리 헌법은 문화국가의 원리를 천명하고 있다. 이와 같이 전통문화에 속하는 바둑문화의 계승과 발전을 위하여 자율적 조직인 한국기원에 맡겨두는 것만으로 그 소임을 다하는 것이 아니라 국가는 태권도나 씨름 및 전통무예를 위하여 별도의 법률을 제정하여 진흥을 도모한 경우처럼 적극적으로 바둑진흥법을 제정하여 바둑을 진흥할 수 있다. 이러한 관점에서 바둑진흥법은 규제법이 아닌 조장법 내지 지원법적 성격을 지닌다. 따라서 바둑에 관하여 어떠한 지원정책을 실현해 나갈 것인가는 국회의 입법정책의 자유에 속한다.

## 2. 바둑의 활성화 필요성 : 바둑의 긍정적 기능

오늘날의 바둑은 대중화된 생활문화의 일종이라고 할 수 있다. 바둑은 일상적인 삶의 바쁨속에서 한가하게 시름을 잊는 신선놀음과 같은 성격의 놀이이며 도와 예를 추구하는 고품격 문화의 일종으로 자리매김하여왔다. 통상 바둑은 수담(手談)으로 명명되듯이 커뮤니케이션의 수단이 되고 있으며, 세상사의 복잡함과 시름 나아가 삶의 고통을 잊게 하는 역할을 하기도 한다.[8]

바둑을 통하여 청소년은 두뇌를 구조적으로 계발하여 사고력·정보처리능력을 배양하고 교육적으로도 인성과 정서를 함양할 수 있고, 추리력, 판단력, 기억력, 수리력, 창의력, 집중력, 논리적 사고력을 배양하기 때문에 교육적으로도 바람직한 놀이에 속

---

8) 삼국지에 관우가 바둑을 두는 장면이 나오는데, 화타가 관우의 독화살 맞은 팔을 수술할 때, 뼈를 깎는 수술임에도 불구하고 관우는 태연히 마량과 술을 마시며 바둑을 둠으로써 고통을 잊어버리고 무사히 수술을 마쳤다.

한다.9) 이처럼 바둑은 청소년의 건전한 성장과 인성교육에 도움이 되고, 일반 사회인은 여가 선용과 건전한 문화생활을 영위하게 되며, 노인들은 취미활동은 물론 치매를 예방하는 등의 효과를 얻을 수 있다. 바둑은 삶의 질이 중요시되는 오늘날 여가활동의 일종으로 불건전한 오락이나 게임에 빠지는 다른 중독성 놀이나 게임에 비하여 긍정적 기능을 한다.

이러한 바둑의 긍정적 기능에 주목하여 해외에서는 바둑인구의 저변이 확대되어가고 있고, 우리나라는 해외에서 바둑강국으로 인정받음으로써 국제적 위상을 제고하고 있으나 국내에서는 바둑에 대한 국민적 관심이 낮아짐에 따라 지속적으로 바둑인구가 감소되고 있는 바, 세계적으로 저변이 확대되고 있는 바둑의 지속적인 발전과 우리나라의 국제적 위상강화를 위하여 국가적 차원의 적극적인 바둑 진흥정책을 추진할 필요가 있으며, 이를 통하여 바둑의 세계화에 이바지 할 수 있다.10)

### 3. 태권도, 씨름 및 전통무예의 진흥처럼 바둑진흥의 법제화 필요

바둑은 태권도, 씨름 그리고 전통무예와 같이 우리의 전통문화의 일종이면서 국제경쟁력이 있는 분야이므로 바둑진흥을 위한 중장기 계획을 국가가 수립하도록 의무화하고, 한국기원을 태권도의 국기원과 같이 법률에서 법정단체로 하여 순수한 민법상의 법인과는 달리 이사장 등의 임원을 정부의 승인하에 임명하고 국가의 지원을 받도록 하는 특수법인으로 하여 한국바둑의 위상을 제고하고, 바둑전문기사의 국제교류 및 해외파견프로그램을 활성화 하는 등의 행정적·재정적 지원시스템을 갖추도록 하려면 바둑진흥에 관한 법률을 제정하여 대처하는 것이 효과적이다.11)

---

9) 정수현, 바둑, 올림픽으로 가는 길 가능한가, 한국기원, 한화갑 의원실, 정범구 의원실(공편), 2001, 1면, 8면.
10) 이인제의원 대표발의 법률안 제안이유
11) 한국의 프로바둑은 한국기원이 중심이 되어, 정부의 행정적·재정적 지원없이 고군분투하면서 프로기사를 양성하여 프로바둑의 세계제패의 위업을 달성하여 왔으나, 우리나라의 새로운 대표적 문화상품으로 체계적으로 육성하여 바둑지도자와 바둑전문기사 등 공인자격증 제도를 마련하는 등 제반 여건을 조성하여 태권도 사범이 해외에 진출한 것처럼 적극적으로 바둑문화를 해외에 전파하여 해외시장을 개척할 필요가 있다.

따라서, 한국 프로바둑의 지속적인 발전을 도모하고 바둑의 저변확대와 이를 통한 청소년의 게임에 의존하는 현상을 극복하고 노인의 치매 예방등 다양한 긍정적 기능에 비추어 바둑과 비견되는 태권도의 진흥을 위해 2007. 12. 21. 태권도진흥 및 태권도 공원조성 등에 관한 법률(이하 "태권도진흥법"이라 한다)이 제정되어 2008. 6. 22.부터 시행되고 있고[12], 전통무예 진흥을 위해 2008. 3. 28. 전통무예진흥법이 제정되어 2009. 3. 29.부터 시행중이며, 씨름과 관련하여 2012. 1. 17. 씨름진흥법이 제정되어 같은해 4. 18.부터 시행되고 있다.

바둑과 태권도가 공히 한국의 전통문화로서 세계속에서 그 역할과 위상을 지니는 유사성도 있을 뿐만 아니라, 태권도진흥법에 관한 규율 중 태권도 공원의 조성등에 대한 사항을 제외하고 전통무예진흥법 및 씨름진흥법, 국민체육진흥법을 참고하면서 바둑진흥에 관한 법률을 제정하여 시행할 필요가 있다.

그러기 위해서는 바둑 진흥을 위한 법률을 제정하여 한국기원을 특수법인화하고 정부의 지원을 받도록 하여 프로 바둑과 더불어 바둑의 세계화를 위한 토대를 형성하는 것이 급선무라고 할 것이다. 아울러 프로기사의 급증에 따른 한국기원의 재정적 위기 및 중국의 독주에 따른 한국 프로바둑의 위기를 극복하고, 한국바둑의 세계화의 요청에 부응하기 위하여, 바둑진흥을 위한 법률의 제정이 필요한 실정이다.

## Ⅲ. 「바둑진흥에 관한 법률」의 입법방향

### 1. 기본적 방향

바둑을 문화현상으로 본다면 문화예술진흥법의 적용을 받도록 할 필요가 있다. 그러나, 문화예술진흥법 제2조 제1항 제1호에서 "문화예술"이란 문학, 미술(응용미술을 포함한다), 음악, 무용, 연극, 영화, 연예(演藝), 국악, 사진, 건축, 어문(語文) 및 출판

---

12) 태권도진흥법 제1조(목적)에서 "이 법은 우리 민족 고유의 무도인 태권도를 진흥하고 전세계 태권도인들의 성지인 태권도 공원을 조성하여 국민의 심신단련과 자긍심을 고취시키고 나아가 태권도를 세계적인 무도 및 스포츠로 발전시켜 국위선양에 이바지함을 목적으로 한다"고 규정하고 있다.

을 말한다고 규정하고 있어, 바둑이 문화예술진흥법의 적용을 받는 "문화예술"에 포함되지 않고 있다.[13]

대한바둑협회는 2009년 대한체육회의 정가맹단체로 인정받았으며,[14] 스포츠 토토에 바둑종목을 추가하는 시도를 2011-2012년 추진하였으나 불발에 그친 바도 있듯이 바둑 전체를 곧바로 국민체육진흥법이나 체육시설의 설치·이용에 관한 법률, 스포츠산업진흥법의 규율을 받도록 하기에는 적절하지 않은 측면이 있다.

이러한 바둑의 독특한 특성 때문에 현행법률 체계상 바둑은 문화예술진흥법에서도 규율하지 않고 있을 뿐만 아니라, 국민체육진흥법이나 스포츠산업진흥법에서도 규율하고 있지 않는 법률적 사각지대에 위치하고 있다고 할 것이다. 그렇기 때문에 독자적인 영역으로 바둑에 대하여 따로 별도의 바둑진흥에 관한 법률을 제정하는 것이 올바른 입법정책적 방향이라고 할 것이다.[15]


## 2. 바둑지도자와 바둑전문기사에 관한 규율

바둑전문기사를 프로기사와 아마추어기사로 분류할 필요가 있다. 한국기원의 프로 및 아마추어 규정에서 프로기사와 아마추어에 관한 정의 규정을 두고 있는 바, 동 규정 제3조에서 "프로기사란 본원의 입단대회를 통과하거나 본원이사회의 허가를 득한 자를 말한다."고 규정하고 있고, 동 규정 제4조에서 "아마추어는 바둑을 애호하는 자로서 전조(프로기사를 지칭) 이외의 자를 말한다."고 규정하고 있다.[16]

---

13) 아울러 문화산업진흥기본법 제2조 제1호에서 규정하고 있는 문화산업에도 바둑을 포함시키지 않고 있는 실정이다. 아울러 2007년부터 바둑과 관련하여 문화체육관광부의 예술국에서 체육국으로 업무가 이관된 점도 고려할 필요가 있다.

14) 대한바둑협회는 2012년 기준 국민체육진흥기금에서 경기단체 운영비와 경기력향상지원비로 11억 2,061만원을 지원받은 바 있다.

15) 이와 관련하여 스포츠에 있어서 전문체육과 생활체육으로 구분이 가능하듯이 프로바둑과 아마추어바둑의 규율법제상의 차이가 있는 바, 양자를 아우를 필요가 있다. 아마추어바둑 없이 프로 바둑이 발전할 수 없고, 프로바둑의 발전의 성과 하에 아마추어 바둑이 발전할 수밖에 없다는 점을 인식할 필요가 있다. 양자가 서로 배척하는 관계가 아니라 상호보완하면서 발전해 나가는 관계로 인식하는 것이 중요하다.

16) 프로기사는 개인사정에 의하여 아마추어 기사로 전향할 수 있는데 반하여 아마추어 기사가 프로기

현재 바둑지도자 자격과 관련하여 대학교의 바둑학과의 졸업생 등에게 민간자격증을 부여하고 있으나, 바둑진흥에 관한 법률을 제정하게 될 경우 바둑지도자의 자격도 단순한 민간자격이 아닌 공인된 국가자격으로 할 필요가 있다. 그러기 위해서는 바둑진흥에 관한 법률에 바둑지도자에 관한 규정을 신설하는 것이 필요하다. 바둑전문기사에 관하여도 현재는 한국기원의 정관에 따라 규정을 두고 있으며 국가의 공인된 자격은 아니다.[17] 따라서 하나의 전문직업인으로서 프로기사가 되려는 자의 자격요건 등에 관하여 법률로서 규정할 필요가 있다. 아울러 바둑지도자나 바둑전문기사에 관하여 결격사유를 규정하거나 자격취소나 징계절차 등에 관한 사항은 대통령령에서 규율하기보다는 법률에 근거규정을 마련하는 것이 필요하다.[18]

우리 헌법 제15조에서는 "모든 국민은 직업선택의 자유를 가진다."라고 규정하고 있어 직업선택의 자유를 명문화하고 있다. 헌법 제15조에서의 직업선택의 자유는 좁은 의미인 직업선택 내지 직업결정의 자유에 국한되지 않고, 직업수행의 자유 내지 영업의 자유, 전직의 자유를 포함하는 의미로 이해하는 것이 일반적이다.[19]

자격제도는 직업선택의 자유를 제한하는 형식이며, 보다 자세히 말하면 주관적 사유에 의한 직업선택의 자유를 제한하는 것이다. 즉 본래 기본권주체인 국민 개개인의 노력에 따라 능력이 갖춰지면 차별을 받지 않고 자유로이 직업을 선택할 수 있는 것이 원칙이나, 프로기사와 같이 일정한 자격을 보유한 자 이외에는 영업이나 해당분야에 취업을 금지하는 경우 자격을 얻지 못한 자는 해당 직업에 종사할 수 없다. 이

---

사로 전향하고자 할 때에는 한국기원에서 실시하는 소정의 입단대회를 거쳐 등록하고 승인을 받아야 한다고 되어 있다. 동규정 제6조에서 프로기사는 초단으로부터 시작하여 9단을 초과하지 못하며, 아마추어 기사의 단수는 초단으로부터 시작하여 7단을 초과하지 못한다고 규정되어 있다. 인터넷 바둑으로 인하여 아마추어 바둑의 경우에도 현실적 필요성을 감안하여 9단까지 인정할 필요성이 있다고 할 것이다.

17) 한국기원의 프로기사 양성 및 지원시스템은 그동안 큰 문제없이 이루어져 왔다. 한국기원의 재원이 한정된 가운데 프로기사의 수는 매년 꾸준히 증가하는 추세이기 때문에 이러한 시스템 속에서 대회상금을 획득하는 톱클래스의 몇몇 프로기사를 제외한 다수의 프로기사들에게는 한국기원 소속기사로서 얼마 안되는 단수당인 연구수당과 대국료만이 지급될 뿐이어서 이들의 생존권이 위협받는 처지에 놓여 있어 그 프로기사인 바둑전문기사를 위한 재정적 지원대책이 필요하다고 할 것이다.

18) 김용섭, 생활체육지도자 자격제도의 문제점과 개선방안, 중앙법학, 제8집 제4호, 2006, 140면.

19) 김철수, 헌법학개론, 제17전정판, 2005, 589면.

와 같이 자격제도는 국민의 생명과 건강을 다루는 직업의 경우는 물론이고 전문적 지식과 기술을 가져야만 직업을 원활히 행사할 수 있다고 판단되는 직업에 대해 실시되는 제도이므로, 이와 같은 자격제도는 헌법상 보장된 직업선택 내지 수행의 자유를 의회가 제정한 법률로 전면적으로 금지시켜 놓은 다음 일정한 자격을 갖춘 자에 한하여 직업의 자유를 회복시켜 주는 것에 해당한다. 따라서 법률에 바둑지도자와 바둑전문기사의 자격의 근거를 마련하는 것이 필요하다.

공인자격을 받은 경우에 한하여 기원이나 바둑교실 등을 개설할 수 있도록 하거나 학교 등에 바둑교과목을 신설하고 그 배치를 의무화하는 것이 필요하다. 한편 바둑지도사의 자격제도를 도입하고 체육시설의 설치·이용에 관한 법률에서 규정하고 있는 신고체육시설업에 바둑교실이나 기원을 포함시킬 수 있도록 제도개선을 도모할 필요가 있다.

이와 관련하여 바둑전문기사제도의 인력배출 시스템을 점검해 봐야 한다. 현재는 프로기사 선발제도가 매우 엄격하고 공신력이 있는데 반해, 바둑을 가르치는 지도사의 선발은 다소 허술하게 되어 있다. 대통령령에 상세한 바둑지도자에 관한 규정을 마련하고 결격사유에 대하여도 규정하여 공인된 바둑지도자의 배출시스템을 갖추어 나갈 필요가 있다.[20]

## 3. 정부의 지원과 국·공유재산의 대부·사용 등

보조금 내지 자금지원은 국가의 개인(기업 또는 소비자)에 대하여 특정의 공익에 놓여진 목적을 촉진하기 위하여 행하여지는 금전지원이다. 보조금은 크게 직접적으로 수령자에게 지원을 내용으로 급부보조금과 세금감면 등 간접적인 형태로 행해지는 감면보조금으로 구분할 수 있다. 급부보조금과 관련하여 소비적 보조금, 융자등 재정지원, 국, 공유재산 무상대부와 양여 등으로 구분이 가능하다.[21] 국, 공유재산 무

---

20) 일본의 경우에는 재단법인 일본기원에서 바둑자격과 관련하여 비록 민간자격증이지만, 보급지도원, 공인심판원, 학교위기(바둑)지도원을 두고 있는 점도 감안하여 법률에서 공인자격증을 부여할 수 있도록 규정을 두는 방안을 강구할 필요가 있다.

상대부와 양여 등의 급부보조금과 조세감면 등의 혜택을 부여하는 내용의 감면보조금에 관한 사항은 적어도 법률에 명문의 근거가 필요하다.

바둑진흥을 위한 국가의 지원의 형식은 다양할 수 있다. 지금까지 바둑대회에 대한 지원이 대기업 등 후원사의 스폰서링[22]을 통하여 이루어져 왔으나, 앞으로는 이와 더불어 국가적 차원의 행정적·재정적 지원이 법제화를 통해서 이루어질 필요가 있다. 가령 국가를 대표하여 국제대회에 입상한 우수 기사라든가 이를 양성하는 프로그램과 코치, 나아가 바둑 단체, 각급학교 및 대학에서의 바둑학과에 대한 지원, 공무원 및 직장단체등 바둑동호회 내지 바둑클럽활동에 대한 지원, 각종 바둑대회의 개최에 따른 지원 등을 들 수 있다.

바둑에 관한 보조금의 지원은 직접 바둑전문기사 등에 대하여 지원하기 보다는 바둑문화향상을 도모하기 위한 방식으로 한국기원에 지원되는 것이 바람직하다. 바둑에 관한 보조금의 지원규정도 마련하여야겠지만, 특히 한국기원의 바둑회관의 설립이나 이관과 관련하여 국, 공유재산 무상대부와 사용 등이 가능하도록 바둑진흥에 관한 법률에 이를 명문화 할 필요가 있다.

## 4. 한국기원의 법정법인(특수법인)화

한국기원은 민법상의 재단법인으로서 문화체육관광부 소관 비영리 법인으로 문화체육관광부의 설립허가와 감독을 받도록 되어 있다. 한국기원은 신문, 방송사, 인터넷업체등의 주최하에 각종 프로바둑대회를 주관하고 총운영액의 약 15퍼센트에서 20퍼센트 정도를 공인료로 청구하게 된다. 한국기원은 공인권을 갖고 있으며, 이와 같은 공인권에 기초하여 한국기원 소속 프로기사 및 진행요원을 파견하여 기전의 진행을 도와준다.[23] 한국기원과 프로기사와의 관계는 종속근로관계에 있지 않기 때문

---

21) 김용섭, 스포츠 보조금의 법적 문제, 스포츠와 법 제2권 2001. 222면.
22) 김동훈, 기전운영계약의 기초적 법률관계, 스포츠와 법 제9권, 2006, 187면, 김동훈, 스폰서 계약의 법적고찰, 스포츠와 법, 창간호, 2000, 197면 이하
23) 김동훈, 앞의 논문, 184면.

에 사용자와 근로자의 관계라고 보기 어렵다. 단지 한국기원은 소속 프로기사에게 기전참여 자격부여와 대국료를 지급하는 등 기사들의 이익을 옹호하고, 한국기원 이사회의 결의에 의하여 연구수당 등을 제공함과 아울러 규약상의 제반 의무를 부과하고 이를 이행하지 않을 경우에는 제명 등 제재조치를 취하는 사적 영역에서의 특수한 신분관계에 있다고 할 수 있다. 다시말해 한국기원과 프로기사와의 법률관계는 입단과 동시에 한국기원 정관과 규약상의 권리와 의무를 준수하여야 하는 일종의 공법적 특별권력관계에 준하는 사적인 영역에서의 특수신분관계라고 할 수 있다.24)

한국기원을 특수법인화하고 프로기사인 전문기사의 자격증을 국가 자격증 또는 공인 자격증으로 할 필요가 있다. 아울러 현재 한국기원에 대한 부가가치세법의 적용 문제가 야기되는 바,25) 입법적으로 명확히 하기 위해 한국기원의 활동에 대하여 조세제한특례법에 조세감면조항을 신설할 필요가 있다. 바둑진흥을 위한 국가의 행정적·재정적 지원시스템을 만들기 위해서는 바둑진흥에 대한 국가의 산발적인 지원만으로는 한계가 있으며, 바둑진흥에 관한 법률을 제정하여 한국기원을 특수법인화하고 한국기원이 주축이 되어 바둑인구의 저변확대와 프로바둑을 세계적인 문화상품으로 키워나가는 것이 급선무라고 할 것이다.

한국기원이 현재 민법상 재단법인으로 문화체육관광부의 법인 설립허가를 받아 운영되고 있으나, 각종 활동에 대하여 정부의 지원하에 이를 뒷받침 할 필요성이 있

---

24) 소속기사에 관한 내규 제2조를 살펴보면 "한국기원 소속 전문기사(이하 기사라 함)라 함은 본원(한국기원)에서 실시하는 입단대회에서 입단한 자로서 소정의 절차를 거쳐 본원에 등록된 자를 말한다."고 되어 있고, 제3조에서는 기사의 기량향상과 바둑보급에 대한 노력, 기사로서의 품위와 본원의 명예를 지킬 것 및 본원의 사업목적을 저해하는 행위의 금지를 명시하고 제4조에서는 기사는 본원이 주최·주관·공인·협력하는 각종 대회에 우선적으로 참여할 것과 기사가 본원의 사전 승인을 받지 않고 전항의 기전에 불참할 경우 해당 기사에 대해 출전정지 등의 징계를 할 수 있다고 규정하고 있다.

25) 대법원 1991. 11. 8. 선고 91누 2786 판결. 이 판결에서 재단법인 한국기원이 일반인들을 상대로 바둑급수를 심사하여 인허장을 발급해 준 것은 용역의 공급이고, 각 언론사로부터 위임받은 프로기전 및 아마추어 바둑대회의 주관 및 급수 인허시에 받은 금원은 용역공급의 대가로 보아 부가가치세의 대상이 된다고 본 반면에, 재단법인 한국기원이 문화공보부장관의 허가 아래 기도문화의 발전과 바둑의 보급, 전문기사와 아마기사의 양성등을 목적으로 설립된 비영리 문화단체이고, 각종 바둑대회의 개최나 후원등을 고유의 사업으로 삼고 있음이 명백하므로, 위 법인이 각종 바둑대회를 주관해 준 행위는 부가가치세 면제대상인 비영리 문화행사에 해당한다고 보았다.

다. 따라서 태권도진흥법에서 국기원과 같은 특수법인화 하는 것이 필요하다.[26]

## 5. 한국바둑 국제교류 및 해외확산

한국의 프로바둑이 세계적 강국이고, 한국문화의 해외확산을 위해 바둑의 국제교류와 해외에 바둑을 널리 보급 하는 바둑의 세계화에 진력할 필요가 있다. 한류열기와 더불어 한국의 실전적 바둑에 관심을 갖는 외국인들도 적지 않으므로 이들에게 한국바둑에 관한 활동 및 정보를 폭넓게 제공할 필요성이 있다. 한국바둑을 해외에 널리 전파하기 위해서는 우선 세계적인 바둑행사와 국제교류를 활성화하여 외국인의 관심과 참여를 유도하고 이를 통해 한국바둑을 널리 홍보하는 활동이 필요하다. 효과적인 바둑행사를 위해서는 세계의 바둑팬이 광범위하게 참여할 수 있는 바둑페스티벌, 어린이 바둑캠프, 국제바둑학술대회 등을 고려해 볼 필요가 있다.[27]

우리나라를 세계의 바둑인들이 즐겨 찾는 나라로 만들기 위해서는 한국의 바둑의 역사와 바둑문화자료를 수집하고, 충실한 바둑에 관한 연구자료와 홍보책자 등을 만들 필요가 있으며, 이를 위해서는 특히 정부와 지방자치단체의 행정적·재정적 지원 아래 한국바둑의 총본산이라고 할 수 있는 한국기원이 주축이 되어 바둑진흥에 역점을 둘 필요가 있다.

한국바둑의 세계화를 실현하기 위해서 매년 일정수의 프로기사 중 희망자를 선발한 후 소정의 교육을 거쳐 해외에 파견을 하도록 하는 프로그램을 가동할 필요가 있다.[28]

---

26) 한국기원과는 달리 유사 단체가 법인 등을 설립하여 프로기사를 양성하는 것을 막기 위해서 한국기원과 유사명칭을 사용할 수 없도록 별도의 규정을 마련할 필요가 있다.

27) 타이젬, 국회 바둑정책토론지상중계, 한국바둑, 이대로 좋은가, 2005. 9. 16. 6면.

28) 현재도 한국기원에서 해외프로그램이 있으나 지원 금액이 미미하고, 프로기사의 해외 진출이 활성화 되어 있지 못하고 각 개인이 자구적인 노력을 기울이고 있는 실정이다. 프로기사가 해외에 체류할 경우에 예산이 허락하는 범위내에서 일정기간 체재비 등을 지원해 주는 해외파견제도를 활용하는 방안을 강구할 필요가 있다. 이와 더불어 국내 바둑서적의 영어판을 발행하여 해외에 한국바둑을 알리고 적극 홍보하는 방안을 모색해 나갈 필요가 있다.

# Ⅳ. 이인제 의원 대표발의 바둑진흥법안에 관한 검토

## 1. 바둑진흥법안의 주요내용

2013. 8. 27. 새누리당 이인제 의원 대표발의로 바둑진흥법안(의안번호 1906551호)이 국회에 제출되어 소관 상임위원회인 국회 교육문화체육관광위원회에 회부되었다. 바둑진흥법안(이하 '법안'이라 한다) 은 총 17개 조문과 부칙으로 구성되어 있으며, 주요내용은 다음과 같다.

### 가. 목적규정

법안 제1조에 목적규정을 두면서 "이 법은 바둑의 진흥에 필요한 사항을 정함으로써 국민의 여가선용 기회 확대와 건강한 정신함양 및 바둑의 세계화에 이바지함을 목적으로 한다고 규정하고 있다.

### 나. 바둑진흥기본계획의 수립·시행

법안 제5조에서 문화체육관광부장관은 바둑 진흥의 기본방향, 바둑의 교육·보급에 관한 사항 등이 포함된 바둑진흥기본계획을 수립·시행하도록 규정하고 있다.

### 다. 국가 등의 행정적·재정적 지원

법안 제8조에서 국가 및 지방자치단체는 바둑단체와 바둑시설에 대하여 행정적·재정적 지원을 할 수 있도록 하였다.

### 라. 바둑지도자 양성

법안 제9조에서 문화체육관광부장관은 바둑지도자의 양성과 자질향상을 위하여 필요한 시책을 마련하도록 하였다.

### 마. 자금지원

법안 제10조에서 문화체육관광부장관은 바둑의 연구를 수행하는 관련 연구기관 또는 바둑단체 등에 필요한 자금을 지원하고, 바둑 전문인력을 양성하는 바둑단체에 대하여 필요한 비용의 전부 또는 일부를 지원할 수 있도록 하였다.

### 바. 국제교류 등 바둑의 세계화

법안 제11조에서 문화체육관광부장관은 바둑의 국제교류와 해외확산을 촉진하기 위하여 국제대회 개최 등의 사업을 관련 기관이나 단체에 위탁 또는 대행하게 할 수 있으며, 예산의 범위에서 필요한 경비의 전부 또는 일부를 보조할 수 있도록 하였다.

### 사. 한국기원의 법정법인화

법안 제13조에서 바둑 기술 및 연구개발 등 바둑 진흥을 위한 사업과 활동을 하기 위하여 한국기원을 법정법인으로 설립하도록 하였다.

## 2. 개별적 검토사항

### 가. 바둑지도자의 양성에 관한 사항 검토

#### (1) 법안 제2조 제1호, 제2호 및 제9조

법안 제2조 용어규정에 의하면 1. "바둑지도자"란 바둑의 교육 및 경기를 위하여 일정한 자격이 부여된 사람을 말한다. 2. "바둑전문기사"란 바둑 실력을 검증하는 대회를 통과하여 바둑 전문가 집단의 바둑 경기에 참가할 자격을 부여받은 사람으로서 직업적으로 각종 바둑 활동에 종사하는 사람을 말한다. 고 규정하고 있다.

아울러 법안 제9조에서 바둑지도자의 양성에 관한 다음과 같은 기본적인 규정을 두고 있다.

제9조(바둑지도자의 양성 등) ① 문화체육관광부장관은 바둑 진흥을 위한 바둑지도자의 양성과 자질향상을 위하여 필요한 시책을 마련하여야 한다.

② 바둑지도자의 종류, 등급, 자격기준, 연수, 검정 및 자격부여 등에 필요한 사항은 대통령령으로 정한다.

### (2) 검토사항

바둑지도자의 경우에는 법안 제2조 제1호에서 규정하고 있듯이 "바둑지도자"란 바둑의 교육 및 경기를 위하여 일정한 자격이 부여된 사람을 말한다고 규정할 것이 아니라 그 구체적인 자격요건을 대통령령에 마련하기 때문에 위임의 근거를 두어 대통령령이 정하는 요건을 갖춘 자로 그 요건을 특정하여 규율하는 것이 적절한 용어 정의라고 할 것이다. 바둑전문기사는 한국기원의 정관이 정하는 기준에 적합한 자로 한정하는 것이 적절하다.

즉, 1. "바둑지도자"란 바둑의 교육 및 경기를 위하여 대통령령이 정하는 일정한 자격이 부여된 사람을 말한다. 2. "바둑전문기사"란 한국기원의 정관에 따른 바둑 실력을 검증하는 대회를 통과하여 바둑 전문가 집단의 바둑 경기에 참가할 자격을 부여받은 사람으로서 직업적으로 각종 바둑 활동에 종사하는 사람을 말한다. 는 방향으로 보완할 필요가 있다.

법안에서 바둑지도자와 바둑전문기사에 관한 결격사유에 관한 규정과 자격취소에 관한 규정이 따로 마련되어 있지 않으나, 국민체육진흥법 제11조의 5에서 규정하고 있는 체육지도자의 결격사유에 관한 규정[29]과 동법 제12조에서 규정하고 체육지도자의 자격취소 등에 관한 규정[30]을 바둑진흥법에도 마련할 필요가 있다. 결격사유

---

29) 제11조의5(체육지도자의 결격사유) 다음 각 호의 어느 하나에 해당하는 사람은 체육지도자가 될 수 없다.
　1. 금치산자 또는 한정치산자
　2. 금고 이상의 형을 선고받고 그 집행이 종료되거나 집행을 받지 아니하기로 확정된 후 2년이 경과되지 아니한 사람
　3. 금고 이상의 형의 집행유예를 선고받고 그 유예기간 중에 있는 사람
　4. 제12조제1항에 따라 자격이 취소되거나 같은 조 제3항에 따라 자격검정이 중지 또는 무효로 된 후 3년이 경과되지 아니한 사람
30) 제12조(체육지도자의 자격취소 등) ① 문화체육관광부장관은 체육지도자 자격증을 발급받은 사람이 다음 각 호의 어느 하나에 해당하는 경우에는 그 자격을 취소하여야 한다.

는 바둑지도자나 바둑전문기사가 되기 위해서 필요한 전제요건이며, 이와 더불어 자
격의 취소에 관한 사항을 의회유보의 원칙에 따라 이를 대통령령에 위임하여 규정할
것이 아니라 바둑진흥에 관한 법률에서 직접 규율할 필요가 있다. 태권도법의 경우에
는 체육지도자 자격증을 국민체육진흥법에서 규율하고 있기 때문에 태권도 진흥법에
서 결격사유와 자격취소제도를 별도로 두지 않아도 되겠으나, 바둑지도자나 바둑전
문기사의 경우에는 이를 준용하지 않으므로 바둑진흥에 관한 법률에 이에 관한 사항
을 규정할 필요가 있다.

## 나. 자금지원 등 행정적·재정적 지원

### (1) 법안 제8조 및 제10조

법안 제8조 및 제10조에서 국가 등의 행정적·재정적 지원에 관한 다음의 규정을
두고 있다.

제8조(바둑단체 및 바둑시설의 지원 등) 국가 및 지방자치단체는 바둑 진흥을 위하여 필요
하다고 인정하는 경우 바둑단체와 바둑시설에 대하여 행정적·재정적 지원을 할 수 있다.

제10조(연구활동 등 지원) ① 문화체육관광부장관은 바둑의 연구를 수행하는 관련 연구기
관 또는 바둑단체 등에 대하여 필요한 자금을 지원할 수 있다.
② 문화체육관광부장관은 바둑 전문인력을 양성하는 바둑단체에 대하여 교육 및 훈련에
필요한 비용의 전부 또는 일부를 지원할 수 있다.

---

1. 거짓이나 그 밖의 부정한 방법으로 체육지도자의 자격을 취득한 경우
2. 자격정지 기간 중에 업무를 수행한 경우
3. 체육지도자 자격증을 타인에게 대여한 경우
4. 제11조의5 각 호의 어느 하나에 해당하는 경우
　② 문화체육관광부장관은 체육지도자 자격증을 발급받은 사람이 직무수행 중 부정이나 비위 사
　실이 있는 경우에는 6개월의 범위에서 기간을 정하여 그 자격을 정지할 수 있다.
　③ 자격검정을 받는 사람이 그 검정과정에서 부정행위를 한 때에는 현장에서 그 검정을 중지시
　키거나 무효로 한다.
　④ 제1항에 따라 체육지도자 자격이 취소된 사람은 문화체육관광부령으로 정하는 바에 따라 체
　육지도자 자격증을 문화체육관광부장관에게 반납하여야 한다.
　⑤ 제1항 및 제2항에 따른 행정처분의 세부적인 기준 및 절차는 그 사유와 위반 정도를 고려하
　여 문화체육관광부령으로 정한다.

나아가 법안 제11조 제2항에서 바둑의 국제교류 및 해외확산의 지원과 관련하여 "② 문화체육관광부장관은 바둑의 국제교류와 해외확산을 촉진하기 위하여 국제대회의 개최, 바둑 지도자의 파견, 해외 홍보 등의 사업을 추진할 수 있으며, 이에 필요한 경비의 전부 또는 일부를 보조할 수 있다."고 규정하고 있다.

### (2) 검토사항

법안에서 자금지원 등 국가의 행정적·재정적 지원을 할 수 있는 근거조항을 두고 있는 바, 이 부분과 관련하여 급부보조금을 중심으로 근거조항을 마련하였다는 점에서 의미가 있다.

바둑단체에는 법정법인인 한국기원 뿐만 대한바둑협회가 포함될 수 있는지에 대하여 논란이 있을 수 있다. 대한바둑협회는 기본적으로 대한체육회로부터 자금지원을 받도록 되어 있기 때문에 별도로 지원하는 것이 가능할 수 있다. 향후 한국기원과 대한바둑협회의 상호발전이 모색될 필요가 있다. 나아가 한국기원에 대한 국·공유재산의 대부·사용 등에 관한 규정도 마련할 필요가 있다.

"국가와 지방자치단체는 바둑회관 및 바둑박물관 등의 설립과 운영을 위하여 필요하다고 인정하는 경우에는 「국유재산법」또는 「공유재산 및 물품관리법」에도 불구하고 국유재산이나 공유재산을 제 13조의 규정에 따른 한국기원에 무상으로 대부·사용·수익하게 하거나 매각할 수 있다"는 규정을 마련한다면 한국기원의 바둑회관 건립은 여러 지방자치단체에서 유치할 가능성이 높아 한국기원의 발전과 위상에 있어 탄력을 받을 수 있다.

### 다. 기보에 대한 지식재산권 보호에 관한 사항

#### (1) 법안 제12조, 제2조 제5호, 제5조 제9호, 제13조 제1항 제8호

법안 제12조에서 지식재산권의 보호에 관하여 "문화체육관광부장관은 대국자의 창작물인 기보에 관한 지식재산권 보호시책을 강구하여야 한다."는 규정을 두고 있으며, 법안 제2조 제5호에서 기보의 정의를 하고 있는 바, "기보"란 일정한 양식에 따라

한 판의 바둑을 두어 나간 기록 또는 그 집합을 말한다.고 규정하고 있다. 아울러 법안 제5조 제2항 제9호에서 "9. 기보에 대한 지식재산권의 보호에 관한 사항 문화체육관광부장관이 수립·시행하도록 되어 있는 되어 있는 바둑진흥기본계획의 하나로 규율하고 있고, 법안 제13조 제1항제8호에서 "8. 기보의 지식재산권 보호 관련 사업"을 한국기원의 사업의 하나로 열거하고 있다.

### (2) 검토사항

이와 관련하여 그동안 실무상 기보의 저작권 등에 관하여는 한국기원이 보유하고 있는 것으로 인식하고 있었다.[31] 그러나 기보의 저작권자는 프로기사라고 보아야 한다는 견해도 있으며, 아울러 바둑의 기보는 체스와 마찬가지로 저작물성을 인정할 수 없다는 견해 등 이를 둘러싼 논의가 가닥을 잡은 것은 아니다. 이 부분이 명료하게 마무리 된 후에 법안에 담는 것이 타당하다고 본다. 그러한 관점에서 기보의 저작권적 보호에 관하여 바둑진흥법에 포함시키는 것이 적절한 것인지에 관하여 충분히 검토할 필요가 있다.

기보는 바둑을 두는 대국자의 사상과 감정이 표현된 창작물로 보기 때문에 기보의 저작물성을 인정하는 것이 경희대 이상정 교수의 견해이다.[32] 그러나, 바둑의 기보에 저작물성을 인정할 것인지에 대하여 표현이 대국상대방에 따라 수시로 바뀔 수 있는 우연적 산물이고, 상황적 반응으로 창작적 활동을 보기 어렵다는 반대론도 만만치 않다. 아울러 기보는 공동저작물로서 저작권은 원칙적으로 해당 프로기사에게 있다고 보아야 하는 관점에서 17대 국회에 김기춘 의원이 대표발의한 바 있으나 회기만료로 통과되지 못하였고, 18대 국회[33])에 들어와서 동일한 내용의 저작권법 일부 개정법률안이 발의되었으나 역시 임기만료로 각각 폐기된 바 있다.[34] 따라서 저작권

---

31) 기보의 저작권이 인정된다는 전제에서 한국기원이 보유하고 있다는 논거는 기전에 참가하는 프로기사는 주관자인 한국기원으로부터 소정의 대국료를 받는다. 대국료를 받음으로써 기보의 저작재산권을 양도하였다고 볼 여지가 있지만, 이에 관하여 한국기원의 정관이나 규약에 아무런 규정이 없다.

32) 이상정, 기보와 저작권법, 스포츠와 법 제10권 제3호, 2007, 53면.

33) 이미경 의원 대표발의로 17대 국회 김기춘 의원이 대표발의한 법률안을 다시 제출하였으나 충분한 논의가 필요하다면서 안건 채택을 하지 않고 회기만료로 폐기 되었다..

법[35] 제4조 제1항 제8호의 개정작업이 선행될 필요가 있다.

### 라. 한국기원에 관한 규율

#### (1) 법안 제13조 제1항 및 제6항

법안 제13조 제1항에서는 한국기원의 사업과 활동에 관하여 규율하고 있고, 아울러 제6항에서는 임원에 관한 규정을 두고 있다.

> 제13조(한국기원) ① 바둑 진흥에 관한 다음 각 호의 사업과 활동을 하기 위하여 문화체육관광부장관의 인가를 받아 한국기원을 설립한다.
> 　　1. 바둑 기술 및 연구 개발
> 　　2. 바둑전문기사 자격 인증 대회 개최
> 　　3. 바둑 단급의 심사 및 발급
> 　　4. 바둑 보급과 교육을 위한 각종 사업
> 　　5. 바둑대회의 개최와 주관 또는 후원
> 　　6. 바둑 관련 전문인력의 양성
> 　　7. 바둑의 세계화 및 국제교류 사업
> 　　8. 기보의 지식재산권 보호 관련 사업
> 　　9. 휘장사업
> 　　10. 그 밖에 문화체육관광부장관이 인정하는 사업
> 　　11. 제1호부터 제10호까지의 사업에 부대되는 사업
> ② - ⑤ <생략>
> ⑥ 한국기원은 임원으로서 이사장, 부이사장, 이사 및 감사를 두고, 임원의 정원·임기 및 선출방법 등은 정관으로 정한다.
> ⑦ 한국기원에 관하여 이 법에서 규정한 것을 제외하고는 「민법」중 재단법인에 관한 규정을 준용한다.

#### (2) 검토사항

한국기원의 업무와 관련하여 대한바둑협회와의 관계가 문제될 수 있다. 마치 대

---

34) 이상정 교수는 위 논문에서 저작권법 등을 개정하여 바둑을 두는 과정에서 타인의 기보를 이용하더라도 저작권침해는 아니라는 것을 명시할 필요가 있다는 점을 제안하고 있다.

35) 2013. 7. 16. 개정되어 2013. 10. 17. 시행예정인 저작권법(법률 제11903호) 제4조 제1항 제8호 "8. 지도·도표·설계도·약도·모형 그 밖의 도형저작물"를 ". 지도·도표·설계도·약도·모형·바둑기보 그 밖의 도형저작물"로 개정할 필요가 있다.

한체육회와 국민생활체육협의회처럼 갈등관계로 발전할 수 있으므로, 제1항에 바둑단체에 대한 지원과 협력에 관한 조항을 추가할 필요가 있다. 아울러 태권도진흥법 제19조에서 국기원의 임원에 관한 규정 ⑥ 국기원은 임원으로서 이사장·원장·이사 및 감사를 두고, 임원의 정원·임기 및 선출방법 등은 정관으로 정하며, 이사장은 이사 중에서 선임하되, 문화체육관광부장관의 승인을 받아 취임한다. 다만, 「국가공무원법」 제33조 각 호의 어느 하나에 해당하는 자는 임원이 될 수 없다고 되어 있는 바, 이와 같은 규정과 유사하게 규율할 필요가 있다. 아울러 국민체육진흥법 제33조 (대한체육회)에 관한 규정 제6항에서도 "체육회의 임원중 회장은 정관으로 정하는 바에 따라 선출하되, 문화체육관광부장관의 승인을 받아 취임한다" 고 규정하고 있다. 한국기원이 법정법인화 된 경우에는 이사장은 주무장관의 승인하에 취임하는 것이 통례적인 입법례라고 할 것이다.

따라서 법안의 제13조 제6항을 다음과 같은 규정으로 보완할 필요가 있다.

⑥ 한국기원은 임원으로서 이사장, 부이사장, 이사 및 감사를 두고, 임원의 정원·임기 및 선출방법 등은 정관으로 정하며, 이사장은 이사 중에서 선임하되, 문화체육관광부장관의 승인을 받아 취임한다. 다만, 「국가공무원법」 제33조 각 호의 어느 하나에 해당하는 자는 임원이 될 수 없다.

## 마. 기타 검토사항

### (1) 법률명에 관하여

현재 국회제출법률안의 제명은 "바둑진흥법"으로 되어 있다. "씨름진흥법", "전통무예진흥법"의 제명도 있으므로, 바둑진흥법이라는 제명을 그대로 써도 좋으나, 진흥법의 명칭으로는 "만화진흥에 관한 법률", "음악산업진흥에 관한 법률", "게임산업진흥에 관한 법률", "뉴스통신 진흥에 관한 법률" 등 "○○에 관한 법률"이 많다고 할 것이다. 이는 무엇보다 언어경제적 측면에서 간명하게 '바둑진흥법'이라고 하는 것이 적절하나 법률적 특성을 부각하기 위해서 "바둑진흥에 관한 법률"로 하는 것도 고려할 필요가 있다.

### (2) 목적에 관하여

법안 제1조(목적)에서 "이 법은 바둑의 진흥에 필요한 사항을 정함으로써 국민의 여가선용 기회 확대와 건강한 정신함양 및 바둑의 세계화에 이바지함을 목적으로 한다."고 규정하고 있다.

그러나, 법안 제1조의 목적 조항은 국민체육진흥법 제1조 (목적)에서 "이 법은 국민체육을 진흥하여 국민의 체력을 증진하고, 건전한 정신을 함양하여 명랑한 국민생활을 영위하게 하며, 나아가 체육을 통하여 국위선양에 이바지함을 목적으로 한다"라고 규정하고 있고, 태권도 진흥법 제1조 (목적)에서 "이 법은 우리 민족 고유 무도인 태권도를 진흥하고 전 세계 태권도인들의 성지인 태권도공원을 조성하여 국민의 심신단련과 자긍심을 고취시키고 나아가 태권도를 세계적인 무도 및 스포츠로 발전시켜 국위선양에 이바지함을 목적으로 한다."라고 규정하고 있는 바와 같이, 법안 제1조를 다음과 같이 규정하는 것이 보다 적절하다고 본다.

"제1조(목적) 이 법은 바둑을 진흥하여 국민의 여가선용의 기회를 확대하고 두뇌개발과 건강한 정신을 함양하며 나아가 바둑을 통하여 국위선양에 이바지함을 목적으로 한다."로 정하는 것이 적절하다.

### (3) 관계기관과의 협조에 관하여

법안 제6조에서 다음과 같이 관계기관과의 협조에 관한 규정을 두고 있다.

제6조(관계기관과의 협조) ① 문화체육관광부장관은 기본계획의 수립·시행을 위하여 필요하다고 인정하는 경우 다른 중앙행정기관, 지방자치단체 또는 공공기관 등의 장에게 협조를 요청할 수 있다.
② 제1항에 따른 협조를 요청받은 자는 특별한 사정이 없으면 이에 따라야 한다

그런데, 일반적으로 협조는 상호 협력하여 조화를 이루면서 업무를 처리하는 것을 의미하는데, 제2항의 규정을 둔다고 하더라도 강제성이 있는 내용으로 보여지지

않으므로 제1항과 제2항으로 분리하여 규정할 필요는 없이 태권도진흥법 제6조[36], 씨름진흥법 제6조[37], 국민체육진흥법 제6조[38]와 같이 단일조문으로 하고 그 제명도 "관계기관과의 협조"로 하기보다는 "협조"로 하고 한 개 조문으로 통합하여 다음과 같이 규율하는 것이 간명하다고 할 것이다.

제6조(협조) 진흥기본계획의 수립·시행에 관하여 문화체육관광부장관의 요청이 있을 때에는 지방자치단체, 관계 기관, 법인 또는 단체는 이에 협조하여야 한다.

### (4) 법안 제7조에서는 다음과 같이 바둑의 날에 대하여 규정하고 있다.

제7조(바둑의 날) ① 바둑에 대한 국민의 관심을 제고하고 바둑 보급·전승을 도모하기 위하여 매년 11월 5일을 바둑의 날로 정한다.
② 바둑의 날에 관하여 필요한 사항은 대통령령으로 정한다.

검토하건대, 이와 같은 입법의 유형은 태권도진흥법 제7조[39] 및 씨름진흥법 제7조[40]에서 규정하고 규율방식과 동일하다. 그러나, 이와 같은 입법의 유형으로는 국민체육진흥법 제7조에서 규정하는 바와 같이 바둑의 날과 바둑주간을 함께 설정하고 바둑의 날을 법률에서 특정하지 않고 대통령령에 위임하는 방식이 있다.

국민체육진흥법 제7조(체육의 날과 체육주간) ①국민의 체육의식을 북돋우고 체육을 보급하기 위하여 매년 체육의 날과 체육주간을 설정한다.

---

36) 태권도진흥법 제6조(협조) 진흥기본계획의 수립·시행에 관하여 문화체육관광부장관의 요청이 있을 때에는 지방자치단체, 관계 기관, 법인 또는 단체는 이에 협조하여야 한다.
37) 씨름진흥법 제6조(협조) 진흥기본계획의 수립·시행에 관하여 문화체육관광부장관의 요청이 있을 때에는 지방자치단체, 관계기관, 법인 또는 단체는 이에 협조하여야 한다.
38) 국민체육진흥법 제6조(협조) 제4조에 따른 기본시책과 체육진흥계획의 수립·시행에 관하여 문화체육관광부장관이나 지방자치단체의 장이 요청하면 관계기관과 단체는 이에 협조하여야 한다.
39) 태권도진흥법 제7조(태권도의 날) ① 태권도에 대한 국민의 관심을 제고하고 태권도 보급을 도모하기 위하여 매년 9월 4일을 태권도의 날로 정한다. ② 태권도의 날에 관하여 필요한 사항은 대통령령으로 정한다.
40) 씨름진흥법 제7조(씨름의 날) ①국가는 씨름에 대한 국민의 관심을 제고하고 씨름진흥을 도모하기 위하여 매년 단오(음력 5월 5일)를 씨름의 날로 정한다. ② 그 밖에 씨름의 날에 관하여 필요한 사항은 대통령령으로 정한다.

② 체육의 날과 체육주간 및 그 행사에 필요한 사항은 대통령령으로 정한다.

결국, 국민체육진흥법과 같이 바둑의 날과 바둑주간을 함께 설정하고 체육의 날을 법률에서 특정하기 보다는 대통령령으로 정하는 것이 적절한 측면이 있다. 다만, 11월 5일로 하여, 한국기원의 전신인 한성기원이 설립된 날이며 그동안 기사들 사이에서 그날을 기념해 왔기 때문에 한국기원이 주축이 되어 바둑을 부흥한다는 의미에서 적절하고 바둑인 간에 공감대가 형성되면 그 날로 특정하는 것이 좋고, 그렇지 아니한 경우라면 국민체육진흥법에서 규율하는 바와 같이 바둑의 날과 바둑주간을 대통령령에 위임하여 정하는 것도 하나의 방법이 될 수 있다.[41]

## V. 결론

이상에서는 바둑진흥에 관한 법률 제정의 필요성과 입법방향에 대하여 고찰하면서 이인제 의원 대표발의의 바둑진흥법안에 대하여 다각적으로 검토하였다. 큰 방향에서 이인제 의원 대표발의의 바둑진흥법안에 대하여 전적으로 찬동하며 약간의 미세조정을 거쳐 국회에서 바둑진흥법안을 통과되리라고 본다.

바둑진흥에 관한 법률이 제정된다면 정부가 기본계획을 수립하고 시행하여 바둑문화의 발전을 위한 중장기 정책을 추진할 수 있다. 한국기원을 태권도의 국기원처럼 특수법인화 하여 그 법적 위상을 높이고, 나아가 수익사업을 할 수 있도록 근거조항이 마련되어 한국기원의 재정적 기반을 확충할 수 있고, 보조금의 지원근거 및 국·공유재산에 대한 무상양도를 추가적으로 마련하여 한국기원의 바둑회관의 원활한 확보와 한국기원이 바둑의 총본산으로서의 역할을 수행할 수 있도록 할 필요가 있다 다만, 기보에 대한 저작물성이 해소되지 않은 단계에서 과연 기보의 저작물성을 인정하고 지식재산권의 보호로 나아가는 것이 바둑의 진흥에 기여할 것인지 아니면 바둑

---

41) 국민체육진흥법시행령 제5조 (체육의 날과 체육 주간) ① 법 제7조제1항에 따라 매년 10월 15일을 "체육의 날"로 하고, 매년 4월의 마지막 주간을 "체육 주간"으로 한다.

을 위축시키는 것은 아닌지는 보다 심도있고 면밀한 검토가 필요하다.[42]

새로운 바둑진흥에 관한 법률이 제정되어 국가의 바둑시설과 바둑단체에 대한 행정적·재정적 지원을 통하여 바둑의 활성화와 바둑지도자제도의 공인화와 바둑전문기사의 지위가 향상되고 한국기원에서 경쟁력이 있는 바둑 전문기사가 배출됨과 아울러 공인된 바둑지도자를 양성하게 되어 바둑 인구의 저변확대가 마련되고, 바둑이 새로운 한류 문화상품으로 한국의 바둑을 해외에 적극적으로 전파하게 되기를 기대한다. 바둑의 해외 교류의 확대, 바둑전문기사의 해외 파견이 용이하여 한국 바둑의 국제화 내지 세계화를 실현해 낼 수 있다.

끝으로 한국바둑이 일본과 같은 급격한 바둑쇠퇴를 막고 중국을 다시금 추격하여 세계속의 바둑 최강국으로서의 위상을 높여나가기 위해서는 국가와 지방자치단체의 바둑시설과 단체에 대한 행정적·재정적 지원을 빙자하여 지나친 국가적 개입이 있을 경우에 바둑진흥이 위축될 소지도 있으므로 가급적 프로바둑의 경우에는 한국기원 중심의 자율적 운영 측면을 강조하는 방향으로 정책추진이 실현될 필요가 있다. 이상에서의 필자의 검토한 주장이 국회에 제출된 이인제 의원 대표발의 바둑진흥법안이 조속히 통과되는 데 일조하게 되기를 기대한다.

## 參考文獻 (References)

권오륜 외 3인, 바둑이 체육 혹은 스포츠가 될 수 있는가?, 한국체육학회지 제44권 제5호, 2005.

김동훈, 기전운영계약의 기초적 법률관계, 스포츠와 법 제9권, 2006.

김용섭, 바둑문화의 진흥을 위한 특별법 제정의 필요성과 입법방향, 행정법연구 제22호, 2008.

김용섭, 바둑문화의 진흥을 위한 법정책적 과제, 스포츠와 법 제10권 제3호, 2007.

김용섭, 경륜·경정법의 입법정책적 방향, 스포츠와 법 제7권, 2005.

김용섭, 생활체육지도자 자격제도의 문제점과 개선방안, 중앙법학 제8집 제4호, 2006.

김용섭, 스포츠법의 현황과 전망, 한림법학포럼 제16권, 2005.

김용섭, 스포츠 보조금의 법적 문제, 스포츠와 법 제2권, 2001.

김창규, 문화관련 한국법제의 현황과 과제, 문화법제의 체계화를 중심으로, 법학논총, 제30권 제2

---

42) 이 부분에 대하여는 논란이 있어 법안의 통과가 어려우면 이 부분은 추후에 논의하여 반영여부를 검토하기로 하고, 바둑진흥법을 우선적으로 통과시킬 필요가 있다.

호, 2006.

김철수, 「헌법학 개론」, 박영사, 2005.

남치형, 한국바둑 세계화의 선결과제- 한국바둑의 세계보급상의 문제, 한국바둑의 세계화를 위한 프로기사 행정적 지원논의 세미나, 국회의원 이미경 의원 2008년 정책자료집, 2008. 12. 31

문용직, 「바둑의 발견」, 도서출판 부키, 2005.

박성호, 바둑 기보의 저작물성 판단에 관한 연구, 한국저작권위원회, 2009.

박주환, 바둑의 스포츠논쟁, 한국체육철학회지, 제10권 제2호, 2002.

송윤경, 바둑의 스포츠 종목으로의 전환움직임에 대한 비판, 서울여자대학교 대학원 석사학위논문, 2004.

이상정, 기보와 저작권법, 스포츠와 법, 제10권 제3호, 2007.

장석주, 「인생의 한수를 두다」, 한빛비즈, 2013.

장용근, 헌법상 문화국가원리의 보장, 법학논총 제30권 제2호, 2006.

장재옥, 김용섭, 김은경, 윤석찬, 윤태영, 「스포츠엔터테인먼트법」, 법문사, 2010.

정수현, 바둑 올림픽으로 가는 길 가능한가, 한국기원 한화갑의원실, 정범구 의원실(공편), 2001

조남철/양형모, 「한국바둑의 대부, 조남철 회고록」, 재단법인 한국기원, 2004.

타이젬, 국회 바둑정책토론지상중계, 한국바둑, 이대로 좋은가, 2005.

한상렬, 바둑의 체육전환, 그 후의 행마, 자유공론, 2002.

# Legal Issues about the Disciplinary Action of Sports Club against Athletes

## 스포츠 단체의 선수 징계에 대한 법적 문제

HO-YOUNG SONG(宋鎬煐)*

*The purpose of this study is to examine the legal issues about the disciplinary action which is mainly taken by sports club against athletes.*

*For introduction to these issues, the author leads to some famous cases about disciplinary action of sports club against athletes in Chapter I.*

*Chapter II deals with the legal meaning of the disciplinary action of sports club against athletes. This chapter discusses the applicability and its confines of the principle of association's autonomy. In Chapter III, the author tries to interpret the legal nature of disciplinary action of association. This issue is related to the nature of the articles of association. The author argues here that the nature of the articles of association is to be regarded as a collective agreement, so that incorrect disciplinary action of association is to be placed under the jurisdiction. Chapter IV explores prerequisite, object, process and result of the disciplinary action of sports club against athletes. In this regard these legal principles are emphasized: principle of legal certainty, non-retroactivity, ne bis in idem, proportionality and principle of fault.*

*In Chapter V and finally in Chapter VI, the author proposes for a rational resolution of dispute over disciplinary action between the sports club and athletes an arbitration of KSAC.*

Key word: disciplinary action, association's autonomy, autonomy of statutes, sports association, KSAC(Korea Sports Arbitration Committee)

* Professor of Law, Dr. jur.(Unversity of Osnabrüuck, Germany), Hanyang University School of Law, 한양대학교 법학전문대학원 교수, 법학박사

# I. 머리말: 몇 가지 사례

(가) 스포츠과학 및 체육평의회(ICSSPE)에서 공포한 스포츠 선언에 의하면 스포츠는 "놀이성격의 신체적 운동이나 자기 힘의 한계를 시험하는 신체 활동으로서 다른 사람과 경쟁하는 형태의 신체 활동"으로서, 그러한 신체 활동은 "제도화된 규칙"에 의해서 지배된다. 따라서 스포츠 선수는 자신의 스포츠 활동이 제도화된 규칙에 부합하도록 행동하여야 한다. 스포츠 선수가 준수해야 할 규칙이란 일반적으로 해당 경기의 합리적인 운영을 위한 개별 경기규칙을 의미하지만, 더 나아가 스포츠 선수에게는 경기 외에서도 스포츠 단체가 요구하는 일정한 규칙이나 규정을 준수하여야 할 의무가 주어진다. 그러한 경기에 참여한 선수가 경기규칙에 위반한 경우에는 심판의 판단에 의해서 경기규칙상의 일정한 패널티가 부가된다. 그러나 그러한 패널티는 경기 자체의 승패에 영향을 미치게 되는 불이익에 그칠 뿐, 선수의 활동 자체에 대한 불이익을 주는 것은 아니다. 이에 반해 경기에 참여한 선수가 경기 자체의 운영에 해를 끼칠 만한 불이익한 행동을 하거나 경기 외에서 스포츠 단체에서 선수에게 요구하는 규정을 위반한 경우에는 선수의 일탈 행동에 책임을 묻기 위해서 스포츠 단체 차원에서 선수에게 일정한 징계를 가하게 된다. 그런데 스포츠 단체가 선수에게 내리는 징계는 선수로 하여금 규칙 내지 규정의 준수를 담보하기 위해서 반드시 필요한 제도임에도 불구하고, 스포츠 단체와 선수 사이에 징계 문제를 둘러싸고 갈등과 분쟁이 일게 되는 대표적인 진원지 역할을 하곤 한다. 이에 본 논문은 스포츠 단체가 규칙이나 규정을 위반한 선수에게 내리는 징계가 가지는 법적인 의미와 징계의 행사 요건·절차 및 효과 등에 대해서 법리적으로 살펴본 다음, 그러한 스포츠 단체와 선수 사이의 징계 분쟁을 합리적으로 해결할 수 있는 현실적인 방안에 대해서 생각해보고자 작성된 것이다.

(나) 오늘날 유명 운동선수는 사회적으로 "公人" 또는 "스타"로 인식되고 있어서, 그러한 선수의 일거수일투족은 다른 일반인들에게 많은 영향을 미친다. 특히 규칙과 규정의 준수를 생명으로 삼는 스포츠계에서 유명 선수가 규정을 위반하여 스포츠 단체로부터 징계를 받게 되는 경우에, 그것은 단순히 스포츠 단체와 선수 사이의 개인적인 분쟁거리로 그치는 것이 아니라, 세간의 관심에 의해서 사회문제로까지 비화되기도 한

다. 본고의 본격적인 진행에 앞서 스포츠 단체와 선수 사이의 징계 분쟁이 기사화되어 사회의 반향을 일으킨 몇몇 경우를 간단히 봄으로써, 선수 징계에 관한 분쟁문제에 대하여 관심을 환기시키고자 한다.

### [사례 1] 펜싱 국가대표 남현희 선수 징계 사건

2006년 1월 6일 대한펜싱협회는 이사회를 열어 대표팀 코치의 허락없이 경기력과 무관한 성형수술로 훈련에 성실히 참가하지 않은 남현희에게 대표팀 전체의 기강 확립 차원에서 2년 자격정지의 징계를 내리기로 했다고 밝혔다. 2005년 라이프치히 세계선수권대회 여자플뢰레 단체전 금메달의 주역인 남현희는 이로써 검을 접고 향후 2년간 국내외 모든 대회에 출전할 수 없게 됐다. 이러한 연맹의 징계에 대해서 남현희는 항소를 하였다. 대한펜싱협회는 남현희측이 18일 이의신청서를 제출함에 따라 진상조사위의 조사 결과를 바탕으로 금주내로 상벌위원회를 소집, 징계 수위를 재조정하기로 하였다. 이후 대한펜싱협회는 25일 상벌위원회를 열어 여자 플뢰레 국가대표 남현희의 징계를 당초 선수자격정지 2년에서 국가대표자격정지 6개월로 낮췄다. 협회는 남현희가 소속팀 감독의 지시 아래 경위서를 거짓으로 작성하고, 허위진술로 사태를 확대시킨 책임이 있지만, 그동안 국위를 선양한 공로를 감안, 징계수위를 낮춘다고 밝혔다. 남현희는 "협회의 결정을 겸허히 수용한다"고 말했다.

### [사례 2] 빙상 연맹 도핑 선수 징계 사건

2006년 2월 3일 제87회 전국동계체육대회 쇼트트랙 스피드스케이팅에 출전한 김아무개 선수가 경기 뒤 실시한 도핑검사에서 트리암테렌 양성반응을 보였다. 트리암테렌은 세계반도핑기구(WADA)가 금지약물로 지정한 이뇨제다. 김 선수는 양성반응 뒤 "대회를 앞두고 무릎이 아파 할머니가 복용하던 관절염약을 경기 전닐 밤과 당일 아침에 1봉지씩 2번 복용했다"며 복용 사실을 순순히 시인했다. 김 선수는 중학생 때부터 무릎이 아파 고생을 해온 터였다. 대한체육회와 연맹은 청문회 끝에 선수가 금지약물을 고의로 복용하지 않았고 깊이 반성하는 점을 들어 징계를 '경고'로 결정했다. 선수도 징계에 이의를 제기하지 않았다. 그러나 7개월 뒤 인 지난해 9월 상황이 바뀌었다. 연맹이 갑자기 WADA와 국제빙상경기연맹(ISU)의 방침이라며 김 선수에게 내린 징계(경고)를 없던 일로 하고 자격정지 2년을 부과한 것이다. 이에 김 선수측이 자격정지 2년의 징계가 지나치다며 스포츠중재재판소(CAS)에 항소했다. 이에 대해 2007년 8월 14일 CAS가 내린 판결은 기각이었다. CAS는 "한국에서 벌어진 일이고 한국에도 중재기구가 있으니 거기서 절차를 밟는 것이 온당하다"고 기각사유를 밝혔다.

### [사례 3] 쇼트트랙 국가대표 안현수 아버지 징계 사건

대한빙상경기연맹이 지난 4월 인천공항 입국장에서 연맹부회장을 폭행했던 쇼트트랙 대표팀 안현수(한국체대)의 아버지 안기원(49) 씨에 대해 1년간 빙상연맹주최대회 출입금지처분을 내렸다. 빙상연맹은 18일 "최근 진상조사위원회 활동을 마친 뒤 조사 내용을 토대로 상벌위원회를 열어 안 씨에 대해 1년간 근신처분을 내렸다"고 밝혔다. 이에 따라 빙상연맹은 이미 안 씨에게 이같은 내용을 통보했으며, 안 씨가 1주일 이내에 이의 신청을 하지 않으면 향후 1년간 빙상연맹이 주최하는 국내대회 경기장 출입을 하지 못하게 된다. (중략) 빙상연맹은 "학부모에 대해 특별히 연맹 차원에서 징계를 내릴 수 있는 부분이 적은 게 사실"이라며 "이의 신청이 들어오면 재심을 하게 된다"고 설명했다.

### [사례 4] 축구 대표단 음주 징계 사건

지난 7월 인도네시아에서 열린 아시안컵축구대회 기간 중 숙소 무단이탈과 음주로 물의를 빚은 국가대표 이운재(34·수원)·우성용(34·울산)·김상식(31·성남)·이동국(28·미들즈브러)에게 대표선수 자격정지 1년의 징계가 내려졌다. 그러나 소속팀의 K-리그경기에는 아무런 제재없이 계속 출전할 수 있게 됐다.

대한축구협회는 2일 오전 종로구 신문로 축구회관에서 상벌위원회(위원장이갑진)를 열고 바레인과의 예선 2차전(7월 15일)과 인도네시아와의 최종경기(7월 18일)에 앞서 두 차례 음주를 한 이운재에 대해 대표선수 자격정지 1년(내년 11월 1일까지)과 축구협회주최대회(FA컵과 일반 A매치) 출전정지 3년, 올 연말까지 사회봉사 80시간을 명했다. 인도네시아와의 경기를 앞두고 이운재와 한차례 술자리를 함께한 우성용·김상식·이동국에 대해선 대표선수 자격정지 1년과 축구협회주최대회 출전정지 2년, 사회봉사 40

시간에 처했다. (중략)

이 위원장은 K-리그 출전 정지를 징계에 포함시키지 않은 데 대해선 "국가대표로 차출돼있는 선수들 관리는 대표단 책임으로 소속팀과는 관계가 없어 책임한계를 구분한 것"이라고 설명했다. 그러나 상벌위가 4명 선수들에게 사회봉사 명령을 내린 데 대해선 근거를 제시하지 못했다. 축구협회가 선수징계와 관련해 사회봉사 명령을 내린 것은 이번이 처음. 사회봉사 명령은 사법기관이 범죄자에게 무보수로 일정기간 지역사회를 위해 봉사활동을 하도록 하는 것으로, 지난 1972년 영국에서 시작돼 한국에는 1989년 도입된 제도다. 상벌위는 "법적권한은 없지만 물의를 일으킨 선수들에게 개인 명예를 되찾을 수 있는 기회를 부여한다는 취지에서 그런 결정을 내린 것"이라고 밝혔다.

## Ⅱ. 스포츠 단체의 징계권의 의미

사원으로 구성된 사단법인의 경우에 법인의 대내외적 목적 활동의 원활한 수행을 위해서 정관에다가 사원으로 하여금 특정한 행위를 금지하거나 일정한 의무의 준수를 요구하는 규정을 두고, 만약 이를 위반한 경우에 사원에게 일정한 제재를 가하는 경우가 있다. 예컨대 변호사협회가 非違가 있는 회원변호사에 대해서 과태료를 부과하거나, 노동조합이 자신이 속한 노조에 대해서 불법행위를 한 노조원을 제명하는 경우 등이 그것이다. 이처럼 사단법인이 자신의 구성원인 사원에 대하여 일정한 제재를 가할 수 있는 권한을 사단의 懲戒權(Vereinsstrafgewalt)이라고 한다.

이와 같은 사단의 징계권 법리는 스포츠 단체에도 그대로 적용된다. 예컨대 사단법인 대한축구협회는 경기규칙을 위반한 팀에 대해서 일정기간 출전을 금하는 조치를 내리거나, 대회 중에 심판에게 폭력을 행사한 선수나 지도자 또는 임원에 대해서 출전정지나 자격정지 또는 경우에 따라서는 제명 등의 처분을 내릴 수 있다.

스포츠 단체가 소속팀이나 선수에 대해서 이러한 징계권을 행사할 수 있는 근거는 무엇인가? 그것은 스포츠 단체에 대해서도 우리 헌법이 보장하고 있는 결사의 자유가 보장되고(헌법 제21조 제1항), 결사의 자유의 구체적 실현 방법으로 스포츠 단체는 그

조직의 설립이나 구성 및 운영에 있어서 자율적으로 단체의 자체적인 운영규칙을 정할 수 있는 것이다. 즉 스포츠 단체에 있어서도 이른바 社團自治(Vereinsautonomie)의 원칙이 적용되기 때문에, 스포츠 단체는 자체적으로 구성과 운영에 대해서 자율적인 定款을 정할 수 있다. 그러한 정관에 스포츠 단체의 구성원이 되는 소속경기팀이나 선수에 대해서 징계사항을 규정하고 이를 근거로 그 社員에 해당하는 소속경기팀이나 선수에 대해서 징계조치를 할 수 있게 된다. 스포츠 단체가 징계권을 가지는 이유는 일종의 단체의 내부질서를 유지·확립하기 위한 것인데, 징계를 받는 경기팀이나 선수에게는 스포츠 단체가 부과하는 징계에 따라 팀의 존립이나 선수로서의 생명에 치명적인 영향을 주는 경우가 종종 있다. 따라서 스포츠 단체의 경우에도 사단의 자율적인 조직·운영에 관한 기본적인 원리인 社團自治(Vereinsautonomie) 내지 定款自治(Satzungsautonomie)의 이념이 적용될 것임에도 불구하고 스포츠 단체의 징계권이 소속팀이나 선수에 대해서 내려질 수 있는 근거, 뒤집어서 말하자면 징계를 받게 되는 소속팀이나 선수는 왜 스포츠 단체의 징계권에 복종하여야 하는지에 대한 이유에 대해서 좀더 자세하게 살펴볼 필요가 있다. 또한 스포츠 단체의 징계권 행사가 단체의 정관에 기초하고 있더라도 그것이 통상의 적정성을 넘어선 조치인 경우에도 그러한 징계권의 효력은 존중되어야 하는지가 문제된다. 달리 말하자면 비록 경기팀이나 선수의 비위행위에 비해 징계조치가 과도하더라도 그 징계조치가 스포츠 단체가 자율적으로 설정한 정관에 근거하여 이루어진 것이라면 社團自治 내지 定款自治의 원칙에 따라 그러한 징계조치에 대해서 다툴 수 없는가 하는 문제이다. 즉 정관에 기초한 스포츠 단체의 징계 행위는 사단 내부의 자율적인 사항이기 때문에 외부의 기관이 관여할 수 없는 것인지, 나아가 국가기관인 법원의 판단 대상이 될 수 없는 것인지, 아니면 사단 자치에도 불구하고 스포츠 단체의 징계 행위에 대한 적정성 여부에 대해서 법원이 판단할 수 있는지에 관해서 문제된다. 이것은 곧 스포츠 단체가 그 구성원인 경기팀이나 선수에 대하여 행사할 수 있는 징계권의 근거와 행사 요건 및 그 한계에 관한 문제라고 할 수 있다. 이하에서 그러한 문제들에 대해서 세부적으로 살펴본다. 다만, 스포츠 단체의 징계는 그 구성원인 소속팀이나 소속선수에 대해서 내려질 수 있는 것인데, 여기서는 스포츠 단체가 소속선수에 대해서 내리는 징계 문제와 그를 둘러싼 문제점에 대해서 살펴보기로 한다.

## Ⅲ. 스포츠 단체의 징계권의 법적 성질

### 1. 논의의 의미

스포츠 단체가 선수에 대해서 내리는 징계권이 정당화되기 위한 근거를 찾기 위해서는 우선 스포츠 단체의 징계권의 법적 성질이 무엇인지에 대해서 알아보아야 한다. 그것은 또한 징계권 행사의 적정성 여부를 둘러싸고 선수와 스포츠 단체 사이에 분쟁이 발생하였을 때에 법원 등 제3의 기관이 간여하여 판단할 수 있는지와 결부된다. 스포츠 단체도 사단의 실체를 가지고 있으므로, 사단의 징계권의 법적 성질에 대한 논의는 스포츠 단체의 그것에도 그대로 적용된다. 그런데 이에 관한 논의에 대해서는 아직 우리나라에서는 매우 드문 형편이고 판례도 찾아볼 수 없으므로, 독일의 상황을 비추어서 알아보기로 한다.

우선 사단의 징계권은 정관에 근거가 있어야 하며, 그러한 징계권의 내용을 담은 정관의 작성은 일종의 社團自治의 구체화라는 점에 대해서는 이의가 없다. 그런데 그러한 정관 작성을 통한 사단자치를 어떻게 이해하느냐에 관해서는 견해가 갈린다. 이것은 정관의 법적 성질을 어떻게 이해하느냐와도 밀접한 관련이 있다.

### 2. 학설

#### (1) 規範說

사단의 정관을 일종의 규범으로 보는 견해이다. 이 학설에 의하면 사단은 정관 작성을 통하여 자신의 조직에 대한 독자적이고 자발적인 규율을 할 수 있는 권한을 규범적으로 보장받게 되며 그에 따라 사원은 단체에의 자발적인 가입을 통하여 단체의 징계권에 스스로 복종(Unterwerfung)한 것이므로, 사단의 징계권의 행사는 원칙적으로 법원의 사법적 심사대상이 되지 않는다고 한다. 이는 마치 행정법상 특별권력관계와 유사하게 사단과 사원의 관계는 민사상의 특별권력관계로 볼 수 있다는 것이다. 독일의 초기 판결도 이러한 입장을 좇아 법원이 사단 징계에 대하여 사법적 판단을 하게 되면 사단의 자율성을 침해할 수 있다는 이유로 사법 심사에 소극적이었다.

(2) 契約說

계약설은 사단의 정관을 일종의 계약으로 보는 견해이다. 계약설은 규범설에 대해서 정관을 일종의 규범으로 보는 것은 단체의 자의적인 입법권능을 인정하는 셈으로, 그러한 별종의 "규범"에 근거한 사단의 징계 행위는 죄형법정주의에도 위배될 수도 있다고 비판한다. 계약설에 의하면 원시정관은 단체의 설립자들 사이의 다면적인 의사표시에 의해서 성립하는 특수한 계약이고, 정관설정 이후의 사단에 가입하여 사원이 되는 것은, 규범설의 주장처럼 단체의 정관규범에 자신을 복종(Unterwerfung)시킴으로써 단체의 징계권 행사를 승인하는 것이 아니라, 가입행위를 통하여 징계규정을 포함한 사단과의 모든 규정에 관한 합의가 성립하였음을 의미한다. 정관을 일종의 계약으로 본다면, 정관규정에 따른 의무의 위반은 바로 계약 위반의 의미를 가질 뿐이며, 사단의 징계권의 행사도 계약 위반에 따른 효과의 청구와 다르지 않다. 그렇다면 사단의 징계효과는 일종의 契約罰(Vertragsstraf)에 해당하는 것으로 볼 수 있다.

(3) 私見

규범설의 원류는 법인의 본질에 관해서 19세기 말에 實在的 團體人格說을 주장한 기르케(Otto v. Gierke)로 소급되는데, 그 당시에는 단체가 국가로부터 간섭받지 않고 활동할 수 있는 여건이 절실하였기 때문에 社團自治의 이념이 강한 톤으로 주장될 수밖에 없었고 그에 따라 사단의 자체적인 징계권 행사에 대해서도 법원의 개입을 최소화하는 논리의 개발이 필요하였을 것이다. 그래서 사단의 정관을 일종의 자치적인 규범으로 봄으로써, 단체에 대한 국가의 개입을 막으려는 의도가 깔려있었던 것이다. 규범설에 의하면 일견 社團自治라는 이념 도구가 단체에 간섭하려는 공권력을 막아내는 훌륭한 방패의 모습으로 보여질 수 있다. 그러나 그러한 모습은 다른 면에서는 구성원(특히 소수 사원)에게 가해지는 단체의 불합리한 제재를 은폐하는 장막으로 작용할 수도 있음을 주의하여야 한다. 따라서 오늘날에는 사단자치의 의미도 과거와는 다르게 이해될 필요가 있다. 즉 단체의 설립이나 활동이 비교적 자유로운 오늘날에는 社團自治를 과거처럼 단체의 활동에 개입하려는 국가의 공권력에 맞서기 위한 논리로서가 아니라 사단 내의 구성원들 사이의 자율적인 이해관계 조정을 강조하는 의미로 이해하면 족할 것이다. 그러한 시각에서 본다면, 사단의 정관도 단체를 구성하는 사원들 사이에 형성된 일종의 계약으로 봄이 타당하다고 생각된다. 그것은 물론 통상의 쌍무적인 계약(Synallagma)과는 달리, 단체의 설립과 운영을 목적으로 하는 구성원 사이의 다면적인 계약으로 이해하면 될 것이다.

### 3. 小結

위에서 살펴본 바와 같이, 사단의 정관의 법적 성질은 구성원 사이에 합의된 일종의 계약으로 이해될 수 있다. 그렇다면 스포츠 단체가 가지고 있는 정관의 법적 성질도 스포츠 단체에 소속해 있는 경기팀이나 선수들이 맺은 일종의 계약으로 보아야 할 것이다. 물론 스포츠 단체의 설립 단계부터 구성원으로 참여한 경기팀이나 선수들이 정관 작성에 간여하였다면 이들의 계약관계성은 쉽게 인정될 수 있을 것이지만, 정관 작성 후(구체적으로 말하자면 단체 설립 후) 새로이 소속단체에 가입한 경기팀이나 선수들의 계약관계성은 다소 난점이 있을 수 있다. 그러나 그들의 가입 이전에 작성된 정관도 일종의 약관의 일종으로 보아 소속단체의 가입을 통하여 약관(즉 정관)을 준수하기로 합의하였다고 볼 수 있다는 점에서 이들의 계약관계성도 인정된다고 할 수 있다.

스포츠 단체의 정관을 일종의 계약으로 본다면, 그 정관에 근거하여 내려지는 징계는 일종의 계약 위반에 따른 제재(즉 契約罰)에 불과한 것이고, 따라서 스포츠 단체의 선수징계의 문제도 治外法權의 지위에 있는 것이 아니고 엄연히 司法府의 심사대상이 될 수 있는 것이다.

## IV. 스포츠 단체의 징계권 행사의 요건·대상·절차·효과

### 1. 징계권 행사의 要件

스포츠 단체의 징계권이 정당하게 행사되기 위해서는 다음과 같은 요건을 갖추어야 한다.

(1) 懲戒權에 관한 合意

사단의 징계를 일종의 계약벌의 일종으로 본다면, 스포츠 단체의 징계권 행사를 위해서는 단체와 구성원(소속팀 또는 선수) 사이에 계약상의 합의가 전제되어야 한다. 그러한 합의는 스포츠 단체의 구성원이 단체의 설립 당시에 원시정관의 작성에 동의하거나 혹은 이후 설립이 완료된 단체의 가입시에는 입회계약을 통하여 이루어진 것으로 볼 수 있다. 만약 징계규정이 원시정관의 성립 이후에 정관 변경을 통하여 신설된 경우에는 그러한 징계규정의 설치에 반대하는 구성원의 의사는 多數決原則에 의해서 대체된다.

(2) 明確性의 原則

선수에 대한 모든 징계사항은 부속규정을 포함하여 정관에 명확히 기재되어 있어야 한다. 정관상의 기재를 통하여 선수들로 하여금 어떠한 행위가 징계의 대상인지 그리고 그러한 위반행위의 결과로 어떤 징계조치가 내려질 수 있는지에 대하여 명확히 인지할 수 있도록 하여야 한다. 이것은 형법의 죄형법정주의원칙을 연상시키는 대목이지만, 사단의 징계행위는 형법처럼 엄격한 명확성이 요구되는 것은 아니다. 따라서 이를 테면 정관에 "스포츠 정신에 어긋나는 행위", "연맹에 해를 입히는 행위", "협회의 명예를 실추시키는 행위"와 같은 추상적인 징계요건의 기술도 허용된다. 다만 어떠한 행위가 그러한 추상적인 징계요건에 저촉되는지를 정관의 부속규칙에서 규정하거나 해석을 통해서 구체화하는 것은 무방하지만, 반대로 추상적 징계요건을 확대해서 적용하는 것은 허용되지 아니한다.

이 원칙의 적용례를 보면 다음과 같다. 「대한체육회」의 법제상벌위원회 규정 제15조(징계대상) 3호는 "각종 대회 중 발생한 경기장 질서문란행위"는 징계심사의 대상으로 정하고 있다. 이에 따라 대한체육회산하 「사단법인대한축구협회」 상벌규정 제18조에서는 징계의 종류를 정하고 있고 제19조에서는 1항에서 "대회 중 발생한 경기장 질서문란행위" 징계심의 대상으로 규정하고, 그에 대한 구체적 징계적용기준에 대해서는 동상벌규정의 별지 [유형별징계기준]에서 선수의 경우 ①경기장 무단난입에 대해 출전정지 3개월 이상 1년 이하, ② 시설 및 기물파괴에 대해 출전정지 6개월 이상 3년 이하 및 벌금, ③ 폭력조장, 선동 및 오물투척에 대해 출전정지 6개월 이상 3년 이하의 징계를 부과한다는 기준을 정하고 있다.

(3) 遡及適用의 禁止

스포츠 단체의 정관상 징계의 대상과 내용은 사원의 해당행위가 있기 이전에 이미 기재되어 있어야 한다. 즉 선수의 특정행위 이후에 징계사항을 신설하거나 강화하여 소급해서 적용하는 것은 인정되지 아니한다. 다만 여기서 소급적용이 금지되는 것은 이미 완료된 선수의 행위에 대해서 사후에 정관개정을 통하여 징계하는 이른바 眞正遡及效(echte Rükwirkung)의 경우에 한하고, 선수의 행위가 여전히 지속되는 상태에서 정관을 개정하여 징계하는 이른바 不眞正遡及效(unechte Rükwirkung)는 소급적용금지의 원칙에 해당되지 아니한다.

(4) 선수의 歸責事由

스포츠 단체가 징계를 내리기 위해서는 선수에게 歸責事由가 있어야 한다. 징계행위를 계약위반에 따른 契約罰로 이해한다면, 사원의 귀책사유에 따른 위반 행위에 대해서만 징계의 대상이 됨은 당연하다. 즉 선수가 행한 징계대상인 비위행위가 그의 고의 또는 과실로 인하여 행해진 것이어야 한다. 따라서 선수의 고의 또는 과실에 의하지 않은 행위에 대해서는 비록 결과적으로 비위행위가 발생하였다고 하더라도 징계를 내릴 수 없다. 이를 테면 보디빌딩협회가 금지약물검사에서 양성반응을 보인 보디빌더 선수에 대해서는 영구제명이라는 중 징계처분을 내리기로 하였더라도, 만약 경쟁자를 제거시키기 위해서 누군가 몰래 금지약물을 탄 음료수를 선수가 모른채 마셔서 양성반응이 나왔을 경우에는 그 선수의 고의·과실을 인정할 수 없기 때문에 대회의 출전자격은 정지되더라도 도핑결과를 이유로 제명은 될 수 없다. 이에 반해 선수가 관절염약을 복용하였는데, 그 속에 금지약물성분이 있어 이로 인해 도핑 양성반응이 나왔다면, 비록 선수의 고의성은 없더라도 과실은 인정되므로 스포츠 단체는 그 선수에 대해 징계를 내릴 수 있다. 왜냐하면 출전을 앞둔 선수는 자신이 복용하는 약물의 성분에 대해서 의심하고 혹시라도 있을 약물의 양성반응을 미리 회피할 의무가 있다고 할 수 있고, 이러한 의무를 위반한 것에 선수의 귀책사유가 있는 것이다.

(5) 懲戒事項의 適正性

스포츠 단체의 정관에 기재된 징계사항이 법률이나 공서양속에 반하거나 부당한 것이어서는 안 된다. 즉 스포츠 단체의 자율적인 정관에 따른 징계사항이라고 하더라도 그것은 전체 법질서나 공서양속의 테두리내에서 정해져야 한다. 이를 테면 징계권을 행사함에 있어서 동일한 위반행위에 대해서 선수에 따라 징계내용이나 징계수준을 달리하는 것은 선수에 대한 同等待遇의 原則에 반하며, 위반행위에 비해서 과다한 징계조치는 比例性의 原則에 반하는 것으로 허용될 수 없다. 예컨대 선수촌을 무단이탈한 선수들에 대해서 스포츠 단체는 선수마다 차별적으로 징계수준을 적용해서는 안 된다. 또한 경기력에 관계 없는 성형수술을 하여 며칠간 훈련에 불참하게 된 선수에 대해서 "대표팀 전체의 기강확립 차원에서" 2년의 자격정지를 내린 것은 比例性의原則에 반하는 과다한 징계조치로 상식적인 법질서에 부합하지 않는다. 선수에 대한 징계는 그가 위반한 행위에 대해서만 제재하여야지, 그 징계를 통해 다른 선수에게까지 심리적 위압을 가하기 위해 이른바 '시범케이스'식으로 과도한 징계를 하는 것은 징계권의 남용에 해당된다.

## 2. 징계권 행사의 對象

대한체육회 법제상벌위원회 규정에 의하면 다음과 같은 경우에 징계대상이 된다. 즉 ① 비위사실이 있다고 신고되거나 이첩된 경우, ② 위원회가 비위사실이 있다고 믿을만한 상당한 근거가 있고 그 내용이 중대하다고 인정할 경우, ③ 각종 대회 중 발생한 경기장 질서문란행위, ④ 각종 선수보호위원회로부터 징계요구를 이송받은 경우 등이 그것이다.

사단의 징계권은 원칙적으로 사단의 구성원으로서의 지위를 유지하는 사원에게만 행사될 수 있다. 따라서 선수가 스포츠 단체로부터 탈퇴하여 사원지위를 상실한 경우에는 스포츠 단체는 선수로 있었던 당시의 행위를 이유로 탈퇴한 선수에 대한 징계행위를 내릴 수 없다. 또한 선수에 대한 징계절차가 진행하는 동안에 선수가 탈퇴하여 사원 지위를 상실한 경우에도 마찬가지이다. 그러나 사원 지위를 상실한 전직선수에 대해서도 社員權과 관계없는 징계조치(예, 과태료의 부과, 출입금지조치)는 허용된다.

문제는 스포츠 단체가 스포츠 단체 시설의 이용자 또는 스포츠 단체 행사의 참가자 등, 사원이 아닌 제3자에 대해서도 스포츠 단체의 정관에 따라서 일정한 행위위반을 이유로 징계조치를 할 수 있느냐 하는 것이다. 생각건대 스포츠 단체의 사원 아닌 제3

자에 대한 징계행위는 허용되지 아니함이 원칙이지만, 제3자가 스포츠 단체의 정관상 징계규정에 합의한 경우에는 그에 대한 징계조치는 가능하다고 생각한다. 그러한 징계 합의는 시설이용자가 시설이용계약에 동의하거나 행사참가자가 스포츠 단체의 규정을 준수하기로 서약한 때에 있은 것으로 볼 수 있다. 그러한 합의가 없으면 스포츠 단체의 정관상 징계규정을 제3자에 대해서 적용할 수는 없다. 따라서 스포츠 단체의 임원에 대해서 폭행한 선수의 아버지에 대해서까지 스포츠 단체가 징계권을 행사할 수는 없다. 그러한 비위행위에 대해서 스포츠 단체는 민·형사상책임을 물을수는 있지만, 징계의 효력을 미치게 할 수는 없다.

## 3. 징계권 행사의 節次

### (1) 징계 관할 기구

스포츠 단체 내의 어떤 조직이 사원에 대한 징계판정을 관할하는지에 관해서는 일차적으로 정관에 규정된바에 의하여 정해진다. 예컨대 단체에 따라 명칭은 상이하지만, 통상적으로 정관에 선수에 대한 징계를 관할하는 기관으로 「법제상벌위원회」 또는 「상벌위원회」 등을 두는 경우에 그러한 기구가 선수에 대한 징계절차를 담당하게 된다.

만약 정관에 선수징계를 위한 별도의 기구를 규정한바 없는 경우에는 스포츠 단체의 의사결정기관인 社員總會가 징계관할기구가 된다. 또한 스포츠 단체는 정관에서 선수징계에 관해서 단체 외부의 다른 기관이나 제3자가 관할하도록 정할 수도 있다. 따라서 예컨대 스포츠 단체가 선수징계에 관한 사항을 한국스포츠중재위원회에서 판정하도록 정관에서 정할 수 있다.

한편 징계의 공정성을 담보하기 위해서 상벌위원회의위원 중에 징계대상선수의 친족이거나 징계사유와 관계있는 자가 해당 사건의 징계심사, 의결에 관여하여서는 안 된다.

### (2) 징계절차

통상의 징계절차는 해당 선수에 대한 懲戒請求 → 懲戒審議 → 懲戒決定의 순으로 진행된다. 선수의 비위사실에 대해서 상벌위원회에 징계청구가 접수되면 위원회는 징계일정을 정하고 해당 선수에게 징계절차에 출석을 요구하게 된다. 징계심의과정에서 상벌위원회는 해당 선수에게 어떤 행위 때문에 징계절차가 개시되었는지 그리고 그러한 행위가 스포츠 단체의 정관(즉 상벌규정)상 어느 규정에 해당되는 것인지에 관해서 고지해주어야 한다. 그에 따라 해당 선수에게는 심의과정에 참석하여 징계조치에 대한 자신의 입장을 진술하거나 서면제출 등의 방법으로 자신의 행위를 해명 또는 방어할 수 있는 기회가 반드시 주어져야 한다. 징계과정에서 해당 선수에게 그러한 기회가 주어지지 아니하고 내려진 징계결정은 효력이 없다. 상벌위원회가 심사하여 결정한 징계처분은 해당 선수에게 통보되고, 징계심사 결과에 이의가 있을 때에는 재심사를 요구할 수 있고 재심사 요구가 없을 때에는 상벌위원회가 내린 징계에 대해서 통상 스포츠 단체의 이사회에서 의결함으로써 징계의 효력이 발생하게 된다. 만약 해당 선수가 재심사를 요구하였을 경우에는 징계에 대한 재심은 통상적으로 스포츠 단체의 이사회가 심의·의결하게 된다. 만약 이사회의 징계재심에 대해서도 이의가 있을 때에는 해당 선수는 대한체육회에 이의신청을 할 수 있고, 대한체육회 법제상벌위원회는 이의신청을 받은 날로부터 30일(1회에 한하여 30일 연장 가능) 이내에 이의 신청에 대한 심사를 하여 그 결정 내용을 선수에게 통보하여야 한다(대한체육회법제상벌위원회규정 제23조 4항).

## 4. 징계권 행사의 效果

이상의 징계요건과 징계절차에 따라 스포츠 단체는 해당 선수에 대하여 징계권을 행사할 수 있다. 징계의 종류나 내용은 단체의 정관에 정한바에 따르게 된다. 대한체육회 법제상벌위원회 규정에 의하면 중징계로 資格停止, 出戰停止, 除名을, 경징계로 警告와 勤愼으로 구분한다. 그러한 징계 종류 외에도 스포츠 단체는 罰金, 免職, 減俸 등의 징계를 할 수도 있다. 그러나 징계의 종류로 반인격적인 것(예, 體罰)이나 국가형벌권에 의해서만 가능한것(예, 拘禁) 등은 인정될 수 없음은 물론이다. 또한 징계의 종류는 스포츠 단체의 정관 또는 징계 관련 규정에 반드시 명시되어야 하며, 단체는 명시된 징계 종류에 한해서 징계처분결정을 할 수 있다. 따라서 예컨대 상벌위원회는 아무리 그 취지가 좋다고 하더라도 상벌규정에 명시되어 있지 않은 「社會奉仕命令」 등의 징계를 내리지는 못한다.

선수의 비위행위가 스포츠 단체에게는 징계사유에 해당하고 동시에 형법상 범죄성 립요건에 해당할 경우에, 사단이 해당 사원에 대해서 취하는 징계조치와 국가에 의한 형벌부과는 그 적용원리를 달리하는 것이므로(전자는 私的인 契約罰이고 후자는 公的인 刑罰), 이른바 二重處罰禁止의 原則에 해당하지 않는다.

스포츠 단체의 징계절차는 사단의 자체적인 계약벌의 집행과정일 뿐이므로, 국가의 정식재판과는 그 성질을 달리한다. 따라서 스포츠 단체의 징계절차에 비록 징계위원 중의 일부로 법관이 참여한다고 하더라도, 이를 이유로 스포츠 단체가 해당 선수로 하여금 정식재판을 제기할 수 없도록 할 경우에는 헌법과 법률이 정한 법관에 의한 재판을 받을 권리(헌법 27조 1항)를 침해하는 것이므로 허용될 수 없다.

## V. 스포츠 단체와 선수 사이의 징계권 분쟁의 해결 방안

사단이 소속사원에 대하여 내린 징계처분에 대해서 해당 사원이 징계의 정당성이나 적정성에 불복하는 경우가 있다. 그러한 경우에 사단은 조직 내에서 재심절차를 두거나 상급단체에 이의 절차를 두고 있지만, 재심이나 이의절차에서도 불복할 경우에는 결국 법원의 판결을 통하여 분쟁을 해결할 수밖에 없다. 과거 독일에는 사단의 징계권 행사에 대해서 법원이 심사할 수 있는지에 대해서 다투어지기도 하였다. 독일의 초기 판례는 사단자치의 이념을 강조하여 사단징계권의 문제에 개입하는 것을 꺼려하는 입장을 취하였지만, 오늘날에는 법원이 사단징계에 관한 모든 사실적 및 법률적 판단을 할 수 있다는 적극적인 입장이다. 우리나라의 판례도 여객운송조합의 조합원의 제명처분에 대해 조합의 자치에도 불구하고 징계처분에 대해서 법원이 적극적으로 판단할 수 있다는 입장을 취하고 있다. 그러한 점에 비추어 보면 스포츠 단체와 선수 사이의 발생하는 징계권 분쟁도 종국적으로는 법원을 통하여 해결될 것이지만, 현재 우리나라에서는 그러한 스포츠 단체의 징계권 분쟁에 관한 법원의 판결을 찾아보기 힘들다. 그러나 현장에서는 선수징계가 많이 이루어지고 있다. 그럼에도 불구하고 법원을 통한 징계분쟁 사례가 보이지 않는다는 것은 그만큼 스포츠 단체의 징계가 적절하고 합리적으로 내려지는 까닭에서일까? 이미 서두에서 제시한 몇몇 사례에서도 스포츠 단체의 징계권의 운용에 여러 문제점들이 내포되어 있음을 알 수 있었을 것이다. 그럼에도 불구하고 우리나라의 스포츠 징계판결을 찾기 힘든 이유는 스포츠 단체와 선수 사이의 징계분쟁에 대해서 구태여 법원의 소송으로 가지 않고서 자체적으로 이를 해결하려는 스포츠계의 독특한 위계질서문화에서 기인하는 것으로 추측된다. 지금까지 선수가 자신이 속한 스포츠 단체를 상대로 소송을 제기한다는 것은 현실적으로 선수로서의 생명이 박탈될 수 있다는 것을 각오하지 않는 한, 좀처럼 하기 힘들었다. 그래서 지금까지 선수들은 부당한 징계에 대해서 비록 억울하더라도 선수로서의 생명을 유지하기 위해서 이를 수용하고 감내하는 것이 하나의 미덕처럼 받아들였다. 그러나 앞으로는 운동선수 및 보호자의 권리의식이 강화되고 운동선수의 사회적 대우가 개선되고 스포츠 산업의 경제적인 가치가 보다 높아지는한, 선수들은 과거와 같은 위계질서문화에 순종적일 수는 없을 것이며, 그에 따라 선수징계의 분쟁은 보다 늘어날 가능성이 크다. 그렇다고 선수가 징계에 불복한다고 해서 곧바로 일반 법원에 징계문제를 해결해줄 것을 호소하는 것은 그리 바람직하지는 않다. 왜냐하면 다른 이익단체의 구조와는 달리, 스포츠 단체와 선수 사이에는 독특한 지도·유대관계가 형성되어 있으며 선수들 사이에는 팀웍이 매우 중요하므로, 스포츠 단체와 선수 사이의 갈등문제는 흑백을 가리는 문제로 결론지을 것이 아니라, 가급적 동화적인 방법으로 해결하는 것이 바람직하기 때문이다. 그러한 점에서 한편으로는 스포츠계의 상황에 대해서도 잘 알고 다른 한편으로는 법리적 체계에 대해서도 전문적인 식견을 가진 한국스포츠중재위원회가 스포츠 단체와 선수와의 징계분쟁을 합리적으로 해결할 수 있는 기관으로 중요한 역할을 담당할 수 있다고 생각한다.

## VI. 맺음말: 약간의 제언

스포츠 단체는 헌법상 보장된 결사의 자유와 사단 자치의 원칙에 따라 자율적인 정관을 제정할 수 있으며, 그 정관 또는 부속규정에서 소속선수에 관한 징계규정을 둘 수 있다. 그러한 징계규정에서 징계사항이나 징계대상 및 징계종류 등이 명확히 기재되어 있어야 한다.

그러한 내용들이 불확실한 상태에서 내려진 징계조치는 스포츠 단체와 선수와의 사이에 분쟁을 일으키는 주된 원인이 된다. 따라서 스포츠 단체는 향후의 분쟁을 막기 위한 예방적 차원에서라도 불확실하게 규정된 징계 관련 규정들을 보완하고 정비하여야 할 것이다.

또한 비록 징계규정이 잘 갖추어져 있다고 하더라도, 징계라는 제도 자체가 타인의 인권이나 기본권을 제한하는 것이므로 법리적으로 아주 조심스럽게 다루어야 하는 문제이다. 따라서 징계의 심의나 결정과정에서도 법리적인 문제를 세밀히 검토할 수 있는 법률전문가가 참여하여 징계절차에서 선수의 권익에 위해를 주는 것은 없는지 가려주는 것이 반드시 필요하다. 그럼으로써, 예컨대 '시범케이스'식의 과도한 징계권의 행사로부터 선수를 보호할 수 있을 것이고 그러한 문제점을 미리 막는 것이 결국은 스포츠 단체의 위상을 보전하는 현명한 길이라고 생각한다.

마지막으로 스포츠 단체는 스포츠중재위원회를 적극 활용할 필요가 있다. 스포츠 단체는 자체적으로 상벌위원회를 두어 징계문제를 처리할 수도 있지만, 정관에 징계판정기관을 한국스포츠중재위원회로 위탁하도록 규정하는 것도 스포츠 단체로서는 골치 아픈 징계판정으로 인한 조직 내의 갈등이나 사회적 여파의 부담을 떨칠 수 있는 좋은 방법일 것이라고 생각된다. 또한 스포츠 단체가 자체적으로 내린 징계처분에 대해 불복할 경우에도 현재는 대한체육회의 법제상벌위원회에서 이의 신청을 하도록 되어있는데, 이 경우에도 대한체육회는 한국스포츠중재위원회에 이의 신청의 심사를 위탁할 수 있도록 하는 것이 바람직하다. 왜냐하면 한국스포츠중재위원회는 스포츠계의 현실적인 사정과 법조계의 법리적 식견을 모두 갖추고 있기 때문에 합리적인 판단을 할 수 있는 중립적인 기관으로 평가할 수 있기 때문이다.

<br>

## ▪ 일러두기 ▪

며칠 전 기념논문집간행위원회로부터 이메일을 받았다. 내용인즉, 연기영 선생님께서 회갑을 맞이하시게 되어 스포츠엔터테인먼트법 분야의 글을 모아 화갑기념논문집을 봉정할 계획이라는 것이다. 매우 당황스러운 상황이었다. 이유는 연 선생님이 벌써 회갑을 맞이하셨다는 사실도 믿기지 않을뿐더러, 연 선생님과의 인연을 생각하면 당연히 글을 드려야 하지만, 필자의 여러 사정이 새로운 글을 작성하기에는 매우 어려웠기 때문이다. 그래도 연 선생님께 최소한의 도리라도 하고 싶은 마음에 간행위원회로부터 양해를 받아 필자가 예전에 발표하였던 논문을 출처를 밝히고 화갑기념논문집에 투고하기로 하였다.

연 선생님과 필자의 인연은 1996년으로 거슬러 올라간다. 당시 필자는 독일 오스나브뤼대학의 비교법 연구소에서 유학 중이었었는데, 연 선생님께서 필자의 지도교수이신 폰바아선생님을 만나러 연구소를 방문한 것이다. 그때 연 선생님께서 필자에게 하신 말씀이 지금도 생생한데, 앞으로 스포츠법이 유망하므로 장차 스포츠법학회를 창립하실 계획이라는 것이었다. 그 당시만 하더라도 필자는 연 선생님을 아주 독특한 분야에 관심을 가지시는 분 정도로 생각하였었는데, 정말이지 연 선생님은 혜안을 가지고서 우리나라에 스포츠법을 처음 소개하면서 스포츠법을 엄연한 학문적 분야로까지 반석에 올리신 지대한 공헌을 하셨다. 이후 필자는 연 선생님께서 창립하신 스포츠법학회에서 연구이사로 활동하면서 이어나갔다.

연 선생님과의 인연을 생각하면 응당 새로운 글로 축하드려야 하지만, 선생님께서 창간하신 『스포츠와 법』에 필자가 연구이사로 활동하던 당시 발간되었던 글을 봉헌하면서 연 선생님께 부족한 축하의 마음을 전하고자 한다.

이 글은 한국스포츠엔터테인먼트법학회가 발간한 『스포츠와법』 제11권 제1호(통권 제14호)(2008.2.) 33~52면에 게재된 것과 동일한 논문임을 밝혀둔다.

## 參考文獻 (References)

박종희, 사단의 구성원에 대한 통제권의 법적 기초와 사법심사의 범위–독일의 학설과 판례를 중심으로– 안암법학제 7호(1998), 347-370면.

손석정, 스포츠법학, 서울태근, 2000.

정승재, 스포츠선수의 기본권 보장에 관한 연구, 경희대대학원 박사학위 논문 2004.

AnwaltKommentar BGB, Band 1: Allgemeiner Teil mit EGBGB, Bonn 2005.

Flume, Werner, Allgemeiner Teil des Bügerlichen Rechts, Erster Band, Zweiter Teil: Die juristische Person, Berlin u.a. 1983.

Larenz/Wolf, Allgemeiner Teil des Bügerlichen Rechts, 9. Aufl., Müchen 2004.

Look, Frank van, Vereinsstrafen als Vertragsstrafen, Berlin 1999.

Meyer-Cording, Die Vereinsstrafe, Tüingen 1957.

Reichert, Bernhard, Handbuch Vereins- und Verbandsrecht, 10. Aufl., Müchen u.a. 2005.

Schmidt, Karsten, Gesellschaftsrecht, 4. Aufl., Kön u.a. 2002.

Soergel, Kommentar zum Bügerlichen Gesetzbuch, Band 1, Stuttgart u.a. 2000.

# Contributors

Annie CLEMENT

**1-10, American and Korean Law and Sport: Then and Now,**
Annie CLEMENT, Ph.D., J. D., retired May 2013; University of New Mexico, 2008-2013; Saint Leo University, 2006-2008; Barry University, 2003-2006; Florida State University, 1998-2003; Cleveland State University, 1976-2003, Associate Dean, College of Education, 1976-1984; Bowling Green State University (Ohio), 1969-1976; The Ohio State University, 1967-1969; The University of Iowa, 1962-1966; and Hibbing Public Schools, Hibbing, MN, 1959-1962.

Education: BS and MA, University of Minnesota; Ph.D., University of Iowa; J.D., Cleveland State University; attended Cambridge University and The University of Oslo, Norway.

Professional: Author of three texts, Law in Sport (1 through 4 editions); Teaching Physical Activity; Legal Responsibility in Aquatics. President, National Association for Sport and Physical Education; Who's Who in Aquatics; Fellow, and numerous awards, American Bar Association.

Over one hundred publications; over one hundred and fifty speaking engagements including ones in Korea, Russia, France and England.

Erwin DEUTSCH

**11-23, Controlled Clinical Trials with Doping-substances, in German Sports Law**
Prof. Erwin DEUTSCH, Germany, educated at the University of Heidelberg (Dr. jur.) and Columbia University School of Law (M.C.L.), 1956-1957 Federal Ministry of Justice (Bonn), 1957-1960 assistant at the Law Faculty, University of Munich; 1961 appointed full professor at the University of Kiel, since 1963 full professor at the University of Göttingen and Director of the Institutesof Foreign and Comparative Law and Medical and Pharmaceutical Law. Since 1992 permanent guest professor at the University of Halle.1970-1994 Judge at the Court of Appeals in Celle. Awarded doctor iurishonoriscausa by the National University of Pusan, Korea (1989), the University of Izmir, Turkey (2004) and the University of Halle, Germany (2004) Doctor medicinaehonoriscausa awarded by the Medical Faculty of the University of Köln, Germany(1994) and the Medical University of Hannover (1998).

Prof. Deutschwas a member of the World Medical Assemblies Conference that adopted the Revised Declaration of Helsinki concerning biomedical experimentation in 1957 (Tokyo) and 1989 (Hong Kong).

**Daniel J GANDERT**

25–42, Advancing Players' Rights

Daniel GANDERT, Chicago, United States, Studies in Government and Sociology at Georgetown University in Washington, D.C. (BA), Studies in Law at Northwestern University School of Law in Chicago (JD), Clinical Assistant Professor at Northwestern University School of Law. Member of Illinois Bar, International Association of Sports Law, Sports Lawyers Association, American Bar Association, and Hispanic National Bar Association. Certified Mediator through Center for Conflict Resolution.

Publications in Sports Law.

**Joonwoo Peter KIM**

25–42, Advancing Players' Rights

Joonwoo Peter Kim, Seoul, South Korea, Studies in Economics and Operations Research at Columbia University in the City of New York (BA, cum laude), Studies in Law at Northwestern University School of Law in Chicago (JD). Participation in conference on Sports Law and Marketing. Affiliation with Sports Law Society, MacArthur Justice Center, and Asian/Pacific Law Student Association.

**Anna Di GIANDOMENICO**

43–69, Sports Violence in the Italian Legal System

Prof. Dr. Anna Di GIANDOMENICO, Roseto degli Abruzzi, Italy.

Graduated magna cum laude in Political Sciences, at University of Teramo(Italy)

Phd. in Bioethical and Juridical Sciences at University of Lecce (Italy),

2002–Present Assistant Professor at University of Teramo, Italy,

1996–Present, Member of SIFD (Italian Society of Philosophy of Law)

2009–Present Member of IASL (International Association of Sports Law)

2003–Present teaching Bioethics at Degree Course in Biotechnology of University of Teramo

2006–2009 teaching *Doping: Legal Theory and Case Studies* at Degree Course in Sports Juridical, Economical and Management Sciences of University of Teramo

2009–Present teaching *Legal Theory of Sports Offences* at Degree Course in Tourism and Sport Sciences of University of Teramo

Many publications about Bioethics, especially Law and Biotechnologies, and Sports Law.

HASSIM, J.Z.

**71-91, The Malaysian Sports Law: Governance and Direction**

Hassim, J.Z. The Malaysian Sports Law: Governance And Direction.

Dr. Jady @ Zaidi HASSIM, Kuala Lumpur, Malaysia.

Studies in Law at International Islamic University Malaysia (IIUM) (LL.B (Hons.), M.C.L.), and Ph.D (Sports Law) from the National University Malaysia (UKM).

2007 -Present,Senior Lecturer at UKM, Malaysia; Mediator of the Malaysian Mediation Centre (MMC), Malaysia BAR Council and Founding Committee ofMalaysia Footballer Association, Malaysia (PFAM), Professional Footballers Union (FIFPro Asia/Oceania), Melbourne Australia.Prior to joining Academia, he was an Assistant Director of Sports Department, IIUM, Technical Executive for Malaysian Universities Sports Council (1998- 2002) – Malaysian Taekwondo Association (MTA) and members of the Asia Council of Arbitration for Sports (Seoul, Korea). He is the author of An Introduction to Sports Law in Malaysia: Legal Guidelines for Sportspersons and Sports Administrators Malaysia: LexisNexis. His doctoral thesis explored the legal status of professional footballers and role of player associations with particular attention paid to Football Association of Malaysia (FAM).

Chen-Huang LIN

**93-105, Discourage the Courage? A Comment on the Mu-Yen Chu Case of CAS**

Prof. Chen-Huang LIN, New Taipei City, Republic of China, Studies in Law at National Taiwan University in Taipei(LLB, LLM),

1999-2010, Adjunct lecturer of *Department of Recreation and Leisure Industry Management at National Taiwan Sport University*

2011-*Present, Adjunct assistant professor of Graduate Institute of* International Sport Affairs at National Taiwan Sport University,

2013-Present, Commissioner of Unfair Labor Practices Decision Commission of Council of Labor Affairs,

2008-Present, President of the *Committee of Sports and Entertainment Law of Taipei Bar Association,*

2007-Present, Committeeman of Statutes Committee of Chinese Taipei Olympic Committee,

2003-2009, Director of Taipei Bar Association,

1990-Present, Advocate at the Taipei Bar Association.

**Matthew J. MITTEN**

**107–125, The Sports Broadcasting Act of 1961 and its Effects on Competitive Balance in the National Football League**

Matthew J. MITTEN is a Professor of Law and the Director of the National Sports Law Institute and the LL.M. in Sports Law program for foreign lawyers at Marquette University Law School.

He teaches Amateur Sports Law, Professional Sports Law, Sports Sponsorship Legal and Business Issues, and Torts.A leading sports law scholar, Matt has authored *Sports Law in the United States* (Wolters Kluwer 2011) and numerous law review and medical journal articles about a wide variety of topics.He co-authored *Sports Law and Regulation: Cases, Materials, and Problems* (Wolters Kluwer 2013) and *Sports Law: Governance and Regulation* (Wolters Kluwer 2013).He is a member of the Court of Arbitration for Sport (Lausanne, Switzerland) and the editorial board for *The International Sports Law Journal*, and serves on the Sports Lawyers Association's Board of Directors.He formerly chaired the National Collegiate Athletic Association's Committee on Competitive Safeguards and Medical Aspects of Sports, and previously served on the inaugural Board of Directors of the Forum for the Scholarly Study of Intercollegiate Athletics.He regularly teaches U.S. Sports Law at the University of Melbourne Law School and has spoken at more than 100 sports law conferences throughout the U.S. and in Australia, Canada, China, England, Korea, and Turkey.

**Aaron HERNANDEZ**

**107–125, The Sports Broadcasting Act of 1961 and its Effects on Competitive Balance in the National Football League**

Aaron is a member of the National Collegiate Athletic Association (NCAA) Enforcement Staff in Indianapolis, Indiana.He is responsible for processing numerous secondary/level III infractions cases self-reported by NCAA institutions. Heis also responsible for providing case support to NCAA investigators conducting inquiries involving major NCAA violations, which can include: monitoring, data intake, drafting memos, and a host of other support functions dealing with highly confidentialinformation.

Aaron graduated from Marquette University Law School in May of 2013, earning his Juris Doctor, where he alsoearned a certificate in sports law from the National Sports Law Institute (NSLI). Immediately following graduation, he was successfully admitted to the State Bar of Wisconsin and is a licensed attorney. During his three years at Marquette, Aaron served as a sports law research assistant for both Associate Dean Matthew Parlow and the Director of the NSLI Matthew Mitten. Aaron's work with Professor Mitten included revising his seminal sports law textbook manuscripts for the third edition and conducting research focused on college athletics. Aaron has previously worked for the National Association for Stock Car Auto Racing (NASCAR) Legal Department, Marquette University Athletics Compliance,and the Sun Bowl Association.

A native of El Paso, TX, Aaron received his Bachelor's in Business Administration in Finance from the Mendoza College of Business at the University of Notre Dame in 2010,where he was the Drum Major for the Band of the Fighting Irish.

James A.R.
NAFZIGER

**127–142, The Legal Regime against Doping in Major League Baseball**

James A.R. NAFZIGER is the Thomas B. Stoel Professor of Law and Director of International Programs at Willamette University College of Law. After receiving B.A. and M.A. degrees from the University of Wisconsin and a J.D. from Harvard Law School, Professor Nafziger was Henry Luce Fellow and later Administrative Director of the American Society of International Law. He is a former Fulbright lecturer at the National Autonomous University of Mexico and the National and Otgontenger Universities in Mongolia.

As a Scholar–in–Residence at the Rockefeller Foundation's Study Center in Bellagio, Italy, he completed the first book specifically on international sports law. Professor Nafziger, who has authored or edited two other books and many published articles on international and comparative sports law, serves as Honorary President of the International Association of Sports Law, from which he received that organization's first prize for outstanding contributions to the development of sports law.

He is a recipient of the Burlington Northern Foundation Award for "Excellence in Teaching and Scholarly Activity" and the University President's Award for Excellence in Scholarship, in both cases the first such award given to a member of his law faculty. In 2005 he served as the codirector of The Hague Academy of International Law Centre for Studies and Research. Professor Nafziger currently serves as Secretary of the American Society of International Law, Honorary Vice President of the International Law Association (American Branch), and Chief Administrative Officer of the American Society of Comparative Law. He has chaired the Art Law, International Law, International Legal Exchange, Immigration Law, and Conflict of Laws sections of the Association of American Law Schools.

Dimitrios P.
PANAGIOTOPOULOS

**143–175, The Greek Constitution Concerning Sport and Sports Federation**

Dimitrios P. Panagiotopoulos is a Professor at the University of Athens, Attorney at Law, President of the International Association of Sports Law (IASL) and Vice–Rector of the University of Central Greece 2010–2013

The author has many academic and professional positions as professor, advocate, attorney at–Law in Supreme Court and Council of State, Member of the Athens Bar Association, Legal Consultant of many Legal persons and Sports Federations and Organizations. He is Director of the Law Firm —Panagiotopoulos and Partners‖ that undertakes law cases of Sports Law and cases in the fields of Commercial Law, Civil law, Contracts, & Torts, Product Liability Law, Labour Law, Comparative Law, Finance and Administrative Law. Also, he is a Special Expert in Sports Law in the European Union and member of Sports law committees of Ministry of Culture, as well as member of the Legal Council of the Union of Anonym Society Companies since 2002. Furthermore, the author was a member of the Committee of the European Presidency (2003–2004), responsible of sports legislation and the establishment of the Sports Law Code.

He has participated in the Organization of many Scientific Conferences – Congresses– Seminars – Symposiums, covering the Sports Science and Sports Law. He is a member of many Greek and foreign scientific societies and President of the Hellenic Center for Research on Sports Law (EKEAD) and he has the author and editor of several scientific books and monographies and has published over 200 scientific studies in Greek and

International scientific journals, with many reports of other Greek and foreign scientists. His last, recently published book, has the title of: Sports Law : Lex Sportiva & Lex Olympica (2011). He has been President of the International Association of Sports Law (IASL) since 2009 ("http://www.iasl.org" www.iasl.org). In addition to these, he was also and a Founder member and Secretary General from 1992 until 2008. He is the editor of IASL's international journal "International Sports Law Review Pandektis" and of the Greek journal "Lex Sportiva". He has also been an invited lecturer on subjects concerning Sports Law and Lex Sportiva, in many universities and sports Law Centers, such as in all IASL Sports Law Congress and other International Congress and Seminars in European Countries, Asia, Africa, South and North America (USA).

The author's work has been warmly commented upon by many personalities of the political and scientific world and the daily press in Greece and abroad.

He received several awards and honours:The Distinguished Service to Humankind Award (2010) in the arena of Sports law from the International Biographical Institute of Cambridge and the "Person of the Year in Law" Award (2009) from the American Biographical Institute (INC). In 2005 he received a great scientific distinction, the International Award «Aisimnitis", from the Faculty of the University of Johannesburg. In 2004 he received an Honorary Plaque from the Cyprus Association of Physical Education and Sports Science. A few years earlier, in 1996, he received a Honorary Plague from the Greek Federation of Australia. Finally, also received a Gold Medal by the Greek Sports Press Association for his writing work in sports, in 1987 and 1992.

Contact: Veranzerou str. 4, 10677 Athens GR
E–mail: panagiod@otenet.gr, dpanagio@iasl.org, info@panagiotopouloslaw.gr

**Marios
PAPALOUKAS**

**177–193, Challenges to the Authority of CAS**
**195–204, "De Novo" Hearing and Appealability before the CAS**
Marios PAPALOUKAS is an associate professor of sports law at the University of Peloponnese, Sparta, Greece, Dept. of Sports Management.

He is an Attorney at Law at the Highest Court of Greece specialising in Sports Law, Contracts, Commercial Law, Arbitration and ADR and also the founder of the «*M. Papaloukas & Associates*» Law Firm. He holds a Phd degree («*Legal Aspects of Doping*») and a Master of Laws (LLM) degree. He is a member of the Board of Directors of the National Anti–Doping Committee of Greece and has served as a member of various Sports Lawmaking Committees. Since 1993 he lectured in different Universities sports law courses at an under–graduate as well as at a post–graduate (masters) level. He is the author of a few sports law related articles and a number of books the latest of which is titled «*CAS: The Court of Arbitration for Sport*».

Igor V. PONKIN

### 205-217, Sports as a Sphere of Show-business

Lawyer, doctor of science (Law), full professor of chair of the legal support of the state and municipal services of the faculty "International Institute of Public Administration and Management" of the Russian Presidential Academy of National Economy and Public Administration (Moscow, Russia), State Professor, expert of Consortium of Sports Law Specialists (Moscow, Russia).

At 2000 graduated from the Russian Presidential Academy of Public Administration (Moscow, Russia) (Jurist).

At 2001 -PhD (Law) -at Presidential Academy of Public Administration.

At October 2004 -doctor of science (Law) (highest scientific degree in Russia) -at Presidential Academy of Public Administration.

Since September 2007-full professor ofRussian Presidential Academy of Public Administration (Since September 2011 -Russian Presidential Academy of National Economy and Public Administration).

At May 2013 -State Professor.

E-mail: i.moscou@gmail.com

Alena I. PONKINA

### 205-217, Sports as a Sphere of Show-business

Lawyer, PhD (Law), expert of Consortium of Sports Law Specialists(Moscow, Russia), lecturer of Sports Law Chair of the Kutafin Moscow State Law Academy.

At 2010 she graduated swith honors from Law Faculty of the Russian University of Friendship of Peoples (bachelor's degree).

At 2012 graduated with honors degree from the Law Faculty of the Russian University of People's Friendship (Master degree).

At June 2013 successfully presented and defended her thesis to PhD (Law) on the topic "Public administration and self-government in the field of sport" at the faculty "International Institute of Public Administration and Management" of the Russian Presidential Academy of National Economy and Public Administration (Moscow, Russia).

E-mail: i@lenta.ru

Karl-Heinz
SCHNEIDER

### 219-227, Current Aspects of International and European Sports Policyand European Sports Law

Ministerialrat Karl-Heinz SCHNEIDER

Head of Division for EU and international sport matters at the Federal Ministry of the Interior

Born on 16 March 1952

Married to Dr. med. Hildegard Schneider

One daughter (Laura Alexandra), 18

| 1974 – 1985 | Law studies in Marburg, Mainz, Dijon, Geneva and Strasbourg. |
| | *Diplôe Supéieur de Droit Comparéat* the International Faculty of Comparative Law at Strasbourg University (Diploma of Advanced Studies in Comparative Law). |
| | 1983 Advanced studies of administrative law at the Academy of Administrative Sciences, Speyer. |
| | 1985 Second state examination in law in Mainz (qualification for the judge's office) |
| 1985 – 1986 | Research assistant at the Johannes Gutenberg University in Mainz, at the Chair of Prof. Dr. jur. E. Klein, European law and international law. |
| 1986 – 1989 | Personal assistant to the President of the Council of European Municipalities and Regions and mayor of Mainz, Dr. jur. J. Hofmann. |
| 1989 – 1991 | Desk officer at the Federal Ministry of Intra-German Relations |
| 1991 | Desk officer at the Federal Ministry of the Interior (Division for European law). |
| 1992 – 1996 | Desk officer for press relations at the Federal Ministry of the Interior |
| 1996 | Head of Division in the Directorate-General for civil service law |
| | Head of Division for EU and international sport matters |
| Since 1999 | Several publications, Lectures and seminars in sports law. |
| | Teaching assignment at the Johannes Gutenberg University in Mainz, since 2010, Department 02, Social sciences, media and sports (Sports Politics and sports Law). |

**Olga SHEVCHENKO**

**229-234, Russian Legal Policy of Intellectual Property in Sports Competition**

Ph.D., Assistant Professor, Department of Labor Law and Social Security Law, Moscow State Law University,

General Secretary of the International Association of Sports Law, Executive secretary of the Sports Law Commission of the Russian Association of Lawyers

Legal Consultant to Ministry of Sports of Russia, Sports Federations

Member of the Players Status Committee Russian Football Union

Member of the Legal Commission with the Russian Olympic Committee

Member of the Union Internationale des Avocats

**Jae-Seon SO**
(蘇在先)

**235-254, Korean Product Liability Law**

So Jae-Seon is Professor in the Law School at KyungHee University of Korea. He received his Ph.D in Munich University of Germany in 1992.

He has filled chief of the Institute of legal studies KyungHee University between 2009 and 2012. He is also a vice-president of Korea Civil Law Association and Korea comparative jurisprudence Association. He has written on Korean, German and Chinese Civil Law, especially has studied Korean and German general provisions of the Civil Code, law for protection of tenant, Tort law and Chinese the law of contract, published 27books, including Law School (co-author, Chenglim, 2007), Exposition of Chinese the law of contract (Chenglim, 2008), general provisions of the Civil Code (KyungHee, 2006) etc. And published 155 journal articles.

**Jung-Eun SONG**
(宋娫殷)

### 235-254, Korean Product Liability Law

From 2003 to 2013, SongJungeun has studied at Beijing Language and Culture University and Renmin University in Beijing, China. She began her master's study at Renmin University's law school in 2009. After completing her master's program, she began the law doctoral program at Renmin University and is currently working to finish her thesis.

Since 2007 until now, SongJungeun has been a researcher at the Research Center of Civil and Commercial Jurisprudence of Renmin University. Her main areas of research are Korean and Chinese tort laws and product liability.

Songjungeun has published six papers, three of which have been published in books with other authors. More than 10 papers have been translated.

**Klaus VIEWEG**

### 255-273, 'Techno-Doping' - Legal Issues Concerning a Nebulous and Controversial Phenomenon

Professor Dr. jur. Klaus VIEWEG, Erlangen, Germany,

Director of the Institute of Law and Technology (Institut für Recht und Technik), Chair for Civil Law, Law of Information Technology, Law of Technology and Business with the German and International Sports Law Research Unit at the Law School of Friedrich-Alexander University Erlangen-Nuremberg, Germany

**CV :**

- Law and Sports Studies at the Universities of Bielefeld and Muenster, Germany
- Dissertation and post-doctoral professorship qualification in the areas of civil law, commercial and company law, national and international business law, civil procedural law in Muenster, Germany
- Professor at the Faculty of Economics of the Catholic University of Eichstaett in Ingolstadt, Germany
- Since 1991 Director of the Institute of Law and Technology, Chair for Civil Law, Law of Information Technology, Law of Technology and Business
- 1999-2001 Dean of the Law Faculty, Friedrich-Alexander University Erlangen-Nuremberg
- Since 1992 Board member of the International Association of Sports Law (IASL)
- Since 1997 Vice President of the German Sports Law Association (formerly: Konstanzer Arbeitskreises für Sportrecht - Verein für deutsches und internationales Sportrecht)
- Since 2005 Member of the Acatech German Academy of Sciences of Technology
- Since 2008 Member of the German Court of Arbitration for Sports (DIS)
- Since 2013 Member of the Court of Arbitration of the German Football League (DFL) and the German Football Association (DFB) '

**Main areas of research**: National, European and international facets of Law of Associations and Federations, Sports Law, Tort Law, Property Law, Law of Technology and Business

**Publications**: Selected publications can be found under www.irut.de/Forschung/Veroeffentlichungen.

**Alexandru-Virgil VOICU**

275–291, Arguments for Promoting the Right to Practice Sportsas a Fundamental Right

293–315 Proposals for Improving the Process of Litigation and Mediation of Sports in the "Common Law" and "Lex Sportiva" of the Romanian Law System

Professor Dr. Alexandru-Virgil VOICU, Cluj-Napoca, Romania, Studies in Physical Education and Sports at Babes-Bolyai University in Cluj Napoca and in Bucharest (1972–BA), Studies in Law at Babes-Bolyai University in Cluj-Napoca (1985–BA; 1999– Doctor in Law); Studies in Business Administration at Babes-Bolyai University in Cluj-Napoca (2008–MA). Emeritus coach in weightlifting (Romania 2005)

Professor at Babes-Bolyai University in Cluj-Napoca, Romania Sapientia University in Cluj-Napoca Advocate&Mediator.

Member of "The Advisory Board of the International Sports Law Journal (ISJL) for Romania"; Member of the International Association of Sports Law (IASL) – Member of the IASL Board of Directors Member of the Romanian Sport Science Council; Member of the Romanian National Disciplinary Commission (the Sports Referee Court); Member of the Romanian Olympic and Sports Committee; President of the Juridical Commission of the Romanian Olympic and Sports Committee.

Many publications about sports law, sport management, family law.

E-mail: alexvirgilweisz@gmail.com

Current workplace: Babes-Bolyai University, Cluj-Napoca, Romania Sapientia University, Cluj-Napoca, Romania; Advocate and Mediator Office Doctor Voicu Alexandru-Virgil, Mediator

**John WOLOHAN**

317–335, Sports Image Rights in the United States

Attorney John WOLOHAN (jwolohan@syr.edu) is a professor of Sports Law in the David B. Falk College of Sport and Human Dynamics at Syracuse University. Professor Wolohan is one of the lead editors of the book "Law for Recreation and Sport Managers" by Cotten and Wolohan, as well as being the author of the "Sports Law Report" a monthly article that appears in Athletic Business.Professor Wolohan has also published numerous articles and book chapters in the areas of athlete's rights, intellectual property and drug testing in sport in such Journals as the *Marquette Sports Law Journal, Seton Hall Journal of Sports Law, Villanova Sports & Entertainment Law Journal, University of Missouri– Kansas City Law Review, Educational Law Reporter, International Sports Law Journal, Journal of the Legal Aspects of Sport and the Journal of Sport Management.*

Professor Wolohan, who is a member of the Massachusetts Bar Associations, received his B.A. from the University of Massachusetts – Amherst, and his J.D. from Western New England University, School of Law.

Hui-Ying XIANG

**337-349, Lex Sportiva from Legal Pluralism Perspective**

Prof. Hui-Ying Xiang, Shanghai, China, Studies in education at Hunan Normal University. And then Studies in Sports medicine at Shanghai Sports University. 2003-present work at Shanghai University of Political Science and Law. 2010-present as Secretary General of Shanghai University of Political Science and Law Sports Law Center, member of Chinese Sports Law Association, has published 18 papers in Sports Law.

Kong-Ting YEH

**351-358, A New Trend of Sports Law: The Impacts of 2012 Sport Industry Promotion Law on Taiwan**

Dr. Kong-Ting YEH wasborn on 9 July 1961. In 1997, he gained his sport management doctoral degree from the University of Northern Colorado. His major is sport economics, event management, and sport industry analysis. He teaches all the degrees from doctoral, master, and undergraduate programs.

He also publishes various articles and books in the field of sport management. He is the Professor and Dean, College of Management, National Taiwan Sport University, Taiwan from 2008 until now. In additions, up to today, he is the Honorable President of Taiwan Society for Sport Management, Secretary General of Asian Association for Sport Management, and an Education Committee Member of International Association of Sport Laws.

Kee-Young YEUN

**359-373, The Future Development of Asian Sports Law**
**375-401, The Development of International Sports Arbitration Bodies and Challenges of Legislative Policy for Reestablishment of Sports Arbitration Agency in Korea**

Prof. Dr. Kee-Young YEUN, Seoul, South Korea, Studies in Law and Buddhism at Dongguk University in Seoul(LLB, LLM), Dr. jur.(Göttingen), 1985-Present Professor at Dongguk University in Seoul, Korea, 1999-2002 President of the Korean Association of Sports & Entertainment Law, 1997-2003 Dean of College of Law, Dongguk University, 2001-2005 President of the Korean Association of Buddhist Professors, 2006-present Mediator of the Seoul High Court, Chairman of the 2006 World Religious Leaders' Conference in Seoul, 2003-present Arbilrator of the Korea Commercial Arbitration Board(KCAB), 2006-2010 Borad Member & Arbitrator of Korea Sports Arbitration Committee(KSAC), 2008-present Vice President of Internaional Association of Sports Law(IASA), 2005-2007 Founder and President Asia Sports Law A.(ASLA), Many publications about civil law, product liability, sports law, legal philosophy and Buddhism.

**Wolfgang HEINRICH**

403-419, Die Europäische Union und neuere Entwicklungen im Internationalen Privatrecht (IPR)

Notar a.D. und Rechtsanwalt in Frankfurt am Main

Feldscheidenstraße 45 in. 60435 Frankfurt am Main / Germany

Telefon: 001 49 69 95 42 19 0

Fax: 001 49 69 95 42 19 20

e-Mail: mail@helnrichttm.ae

| | |
|---|---|
| 8.10.1940 | born in Mainz-Gonsenheim as son of Franz Heinrich(Railroad Company) and his wife Frieda Heinrich. born Fröb, Roman Catholic |
| 1947-1960 | primary school in Mainz-Gonsenheim. gymnasium (secondary school) in Mainz (first Schloß gymnasium, then Gutenberggymnasium) |
| Sept. 1974 | admission to the Frankfurt Court of Appeal |
| Oct. 1992 to | president of German-Korean Juridical Association e.V. |
| April. 2005 | Honorary President of German-Korean Juridical Association e.V. |
| since Oct. 2006 | |

**Yi Li
(李 怡)**

421-427, How Sports Law to Support the Combination of Physical Education Policy

Date of Birth: January 10,1979

Email: liyi956@126.com

Postal Add: Changping District FuXue Road No. 27. China University of Political science and Law. Physical Education Department. Beijing, 102249, China

EDUCATION and WORK Experience

09/1995 -7 /1999 Beijing Sport University, Bachelor degree of Education
                 Major: Athletic Training

09/2000 -7/2002  China University of Political Science and Law,
                 Bachelor degree of Law (2nd degree)
                 Major: Law

09/2002 - 3/2006 Beijing Sport University, Master degree of Education(earned in March 2006)
                 Major: Physical Education and Athletic Training

7/1999 - Now     Teacher @ Physical Education Department, China University of Political
                 Science and Law ; and Member of Sport law Research
                 Centre, China University ofPolitical Science and Law

**Jian-Chuan MA**
**(馬建川)**

**429-446, Negative Competition and its Governance**

Prof. Jian-Chuan MA(马建川), xi an, China,, graduated from northwest university of political science and law ,1983-Present Professor at China university of political science and law, 2001-Present the dean of the management of public services department of China university of politics and law, 2005-Present, researcher at the sports law research center of China university of politics and law, 2000 to now director of administrative society of China, 2010-Present director of the Beijing sports law, many publications aboutPublic administration, government reform, sports management and law.

**Zhong-Qiu TAN**
**(谭仲秋)**

**447-460, Research about Online Football Gambling Crimes**

Prof.Zhong-Qiu TAN, Professor at Chengdu Sport University, in P.R.C. China. Graduated from Southwest University of Politics and Law, part-time lawyers, Director of China Sports Law Association, the main lecture on "Economic Law", "legal basis", "Sports Law" and other courses.

**Si-Yuan TIAN**
**(田思源)**

**461-484, On the Sports Law of the People's Republic of China Amended**

Professor Tian is currently the director of the Sports Law Research Center at Qinghua University's Law School in Beijing, China. From 1986 to 2003, he taught as a professor at Jilin University Law School in Changchun, China. Professor Tian also studied abroad at the research institute in Kobe University in Japan from 1997 to 2002. Since 2003 to the present, Professor Tian has been teaching at Qinghua University Law School. He also currently serves as a law expert for China's Law Research Center. As well as a researcher at Renmin University's Administrative Law Research Center. In addition, he is the director of the Chinese Sports Law Research Group and Beijing's Sports Law Department, the Olympic Sports Law Research Center, and the Beijing Sports Law Association. Professor Tian's research focuses on sports law, administrative law and military law.

Yu-Mei WANG
（王玉梅）

**485-497, On Determination of Infringement in the Competitive Sports Field**

Prof. Yu-Mei WANG, Beijing, China. Juris Doctor of China University of Political Science and Law.

2001-2002 Visiting Scholar of University of Paris 1, France, Master's degree.

Proferssor at China University of Political Science and Law. Director of Sports Law Association of China Law Society. Representative of the 12th, 13th and 14th Beijing Municipal People's Congress. Vice-chairman of the 9th Chinese People's Political Consultative Conference of Haidian District, Beijing. Several publications about civil law, commercial law and economic law. Many important research projects of legislation.

Xue-Feng YAN
（闫旭峰）

**499-509, Study on Legal Problems Relative to Doping Search**

Prof. Xue-Feng YAN, Beijing sport University, China. Graduate Student Supervisor, the President of Teaching Institute of Ideological and Political Theory Courses, Member of the University Academic Degree Committee, a Standing Director of Chinese Society of Law (Sports Law Branch), a Member of Chinese Sport Society (in Sports Sociology Branch), a Member of Committee Hearings by Anti-doping Commission, Vice Director of Sportsmanship and Lianzheng Risk Research Center of China.

Li-Xin YANG
（楊立新）

**511-538, Research on Respective Torts**

Li-Xin YANG, born in 1952, Professor of Law School and Director of Research Center for Civil and Commercial Jurisprudence of Renmin University of China. He also acts as Vice Chairman of China Civil Law Society, Chairman of Beijing Law Association for Consumer Rights and Interests Protection and Director-General of Academy for East-Asian Tort Law. He graduated from the 1st Senior Judge Class organized by Law School of Renmin University of China. He used to be the Deputy Chief Justice of Intermediate People's Court of Tonghua, Jilin Province Chief Judge of Trial Court of the Civil Law Division of the Supreme People's Court of P. R. China and Chief Procurator of the Civil and Administrative Department of the Supreme People's Procuratorate of P. R. China. His field of research covers the general principles of civil law, property right law, tort liability law, law of obligation and contract, personality right law, family law, law of consumer protection. He was involved in the legislative work of over 10 laws of China, including the Contract Law, Property Right Law, Tort Liability Law, Law on the Protection of Consumer Rights and Interests. He worked as the key member on the legislative team for Tort Liability Law. He is also the author of a number of well-known books and textbooks, such as Tort Liability Law, The General Principle of Civil Law, Personality Right Law, and Law for Medical Malpractice. He haspublished over 400 papers on journals in China, including Social Sciences in China, Chinese Journal of Law and China Legal Science. Many books and papers have been translated into English, Japanese, Korean and Italian and published overseas.

Osamu KASAI
（笠井修）

**539–568, The Idea of Partnering and the New Development of Construction Contracts**
Prof. Dr. Osamu KASAI, Tokyo, Japan, Studies in Law at Chuo University (LLM) and Hitotsubashi University (Doctor of Laws), 1986–1995 Associate Professor at Teikyo University, 1995–2002, Professor at Seijo University, 2002–2004 Professor at Tsukuba University, 2004–Present Professor at Chuo Law School in Tokyo, Japan. 1993–1995 Research Fellow of Alexander von Humboldt Foundation, 1999–2000 Visiting Scholar of Cornell Law School, 2006–Present Board Member of the Japan Sports Law Association, 2009–Present Board Member of the Japan Association for Consumer Law. Many publications about contract law, construction law, international transaction, and sports law.

Sadao MORIKAWA
（森川貞夫）

**569–576, Toward the Developement of the Study for the Sports Law and Establishment of the Sports Right in Asia**
Prof. Sadao MORIKAWA, Tokyo, JAPAN. Studied in Sociology of Sports at Tokyo University of Education in Tokyo, 1972–2010 Professor at Nippon Sport Science University in Tokyo, 1999–2001 Chairman of Japan Society of Sport Sociology, 2008–2010Chairman of Japan Sports Law Association, 2003–Present Board Member of the Social Education Society in Japan.

Michitaro
URAKAWA
（浦川道太郎）

**577–592, School Education and Sports – Revision of Japanese Student Baseball Charter**
Prof. Dr.h.c.(Göttingen) Michitaro URAKAWA, Tokyo, Japan, Studies in Lawat Waseda University in Tokyo(LLB, LLM),1977–1980 Lecturer, 1980–1985 Associate Professor and 1985–Present Professor at Waseda University, 1977–1979 Scholar of Alexander von Humboldt-Stiftung, 1996–1998 Director of Public Relations Section at Waseda University, 1998–2002 Director of Waseda University Library, 2004–2005 Dean of Waseda Law School, 1997–2007 Member of Social Policy Council(國民生活審議會), 2001–2005 Examination Committee Member of National Bar Examination, 2007–Present Arbitrator of the Japan Center for Settlement of Traffic Accident Dispute, 2010–Present President of Japan Sports Law Asossiation.

Yong-Taek YOON
（尹龍澤）

**593–609, A Study on the Sport Rights and the Safety in Playing Sports**
Pro. Dr. Yong-Taek YOON, Tokyo, Japan, Studies in Law at Soka University (LLB,LLM,SJD), 1982–1986 Research Assistant, 1986–1989 Lecture, 1989–1996 Associate Professor, 1996–Present Professor at Soka University in Tokyo, Japan. 2010–Present Dean of Soka Law School, 1998. Visiting Scholar of Wuhan University in China. 2010–Present Visiting Professor at Chunbuk National University in Korea.

Yusuke ONDA
（恩田祐將）

**593-609, A Study on the Sport Rights and the Safety in Playing Sports**
Dr. Yusuke ONDA, Tokyo, Japan, Studies in Criminal Law at Soka University (LLM, Doctor of Laws), 2013-Assistant Professor at Soka University in Tokyo.

Yong-Sup KIM
（金容燮）

**611-636, Necessity and Way of Legislation of "Act on Baduk (Korean Checkers) Promotion"**
Prof. Dr. Yong-Sup KIM, Seoul, South Korea, Studies in Law at Seoul National University and Kyunghee University in Seoul(LLM, LLB), Dr. jur.(Mannheim), 1990-1996 Director, Ministry of Legislation 1996-2001 Professor at Kyunghee University 2002-2005 Attorney at law, Law firm Aram in Seoul. 2002-2003 President, Theory and Practice of Administrative Law Academy 2004-Present, Vice President of the Korean Association of Sport & Entertainment Law, 2005-Present Professor, Chonbuk National University School of Law, 2007-2009 Chief, Law Research Institute of Chonbuk National university, 2007-Present, Member of Editorial Staff of Human Right and justice, Korean Bar association

Ho-Young SONG
（宋鎬煐）

**637-654, Legal Issues about the Disciplinary Action of Sports Club against Athletes**
Prof. Dr. Ho-Young SONG, Seoul, South Korea, received his Bachelor of Law and Master of Law from Kyungpook National University in Korea and his Dr. iur. from the Universität Osnabrüuck in Germany. As a law professor from 1999 to 2007 he worked at Kwangwoon University, College of Law and since 2007 he is working at Hanyang University, School of Law in Seoul Korea.
Professor Song was a publication director at the Korean Association of Civil Law, a planning director at the Korean Association of Sports & Entertainment Law and a finance director at the Korean Association of Comparative Private.
He is at present Visiting Scholar at Maurer School of Law, Indiana University, USA.